THE LANGUAGE OF REAL ESTATE

SEVENTH EDITION

JOHN W. REILLY, DREI

WITH MARIE S. SPODEK, DREI, CDEI, CNE®, CONTRIBUTING EDITOR

Dearborn™

A Kaplan Real Estate Education Company

This publication is designed to provide accurate and authoritative information in regard to the subject matter covered. It is sold with the understanding that the publisher is not engaged in rendering legal, accounting, or other professional advice. If legal advice or other expert assistance is required, the services of a competent professional should be sought.

President: Dr. Andrew Temte
Chief Learning Officer: Dr. Tim Smaby
Executive Director, Real Estate Education: Melissa Kleeman-Moy
Development Editor: Adam Bissen

THE LANGUAGE OF REAL ESTATE SEVENTH EDITION
©2013 Kaplan, Inc.
Published by DF Institute, Inc., d/b/a Dearborn Real Estate Education
332 Front St. S., Suite 501
La Crosse, WI 54601

Printed in the United States of America

ISBN: 978-1-4277-1480-0 / 1-4277-1480-0
PPN: 1961-0107

CONTENTS

The Language of Real Estate is the result of many years of difficult and thorough work in researching the answers to everyday problems in real estate. Numerous books and articles on real estate taxes, condominiums, appraisal, finance, law, contracts, and the like are good source materials for the real estate broker or salesperson, but their volume requires one to maintain an extensive and expensive real estate library. This book is designed to eliminate that problem. *The Language of Real Estate* is more than a dictionary; it is a totally functional real estate reference book—a comprehensive, encyclopedic, single-volume, instant-answer book to just about any problem or question concerning real estate principles and practice in the United States.

The real estate industry has undergone considerable change since this book was first published in 1977. This seventh edition creation reflects those changes. Numerous new terms have been added to the book, bringing the total number of entries to nearly 3,000. Definitions that appeared in the first six editions have been revised, and in many cases expanded, to provide the reader the most current and precise answers possible. Accompanying each word is a basic definition, several applications, and cross-references to aid in understanding related items.

The Language of Real Estate also contains several helpful special features:

■ A complete subject classification of terms to assist those who are concentrating their studies in specific areas

■ A list of real estate organizations, including Web sites and descriptions

■ A list of designations and certifications that not only provides the meanings of dozens of designations but also references granting organizations on the organizations list so the reader can find out more

■ A list of federal laws, acts, and regulations, which includes detailed descriptions along with Web references for further research

■ Construction diagrams with terms labeled in English and Spanish to help readers visualize difficult ideas in construction

Note: All Spanish in the book is in generic Spanish dialect, for wide applicability.

What started over 30 years ago as a basic 40-page glossary has evolved into the comprehensive real estate reference book you are now reading. The book is designed to quickly resolve the many questions about real estate often posed to me as a real estate attorney, broker, instructor, and lecturer in real estate law and practice. Many people have helped along the way, and to them I extend a warm "Mahalo."

I want to first thank Marie Spodek, DREI, who thoroughly researched and revised the seventh edition of this book. Marie and I have been active members of The Real Estate Educators Association (REEA) for many years.

Special thanks to Jacqueline L. S. Earle, a Honolulu attorney and REALTOR®, who contributed a considerable amount of time, energy, and talent in the process of putting together the original version of the book.

I also wish to acknowledge the time and effort spent in reviewing the original manuscript by two exceptional real estate attorneys in the State of Hawaii: Thomas A. Bodden and Jeffrey S. Grad. A thank you also goes to Alan N. Tonnon of Bellevue, Washington.

For their special assistance and patience in typing the original manuscript, I thank Yvonne Gates, Karen Hara, Irene Honjo, and Aileen Nishimura.

Special gratitude goes to Peter A. Clarke and Paul Cramer of the San Francisco firm of Clarke and Cramer, Inc., for their expertise in developing the industrial and commercial real estate terms in the first edition.

For their contributions to earlier editions, I thank Annette Abdill, Abdill Real Estate School; James A. Ansalmi, CCIM, Academy Real Estate School; Patricia Banta, Collin County Community College; Doris S. Barrell, CRB, CRS, GRI, JLB Realty, LLC; Stuart Bernstein, Best School of Real Estate; Kenneth A. Bigelow, GRI, IFA, Real Estate Education Company; Roger Bomar, Missouri Real Estate School; Maurice A. Boren, National Institute of Real Estate; Fred Brodsky, Brodsky School of Real Estate; Hugh Burdick, BOAI School of Real Estate; Leona Busby, Long & Foster Institute of Real Estate; Rose Mary Chambers, First School of Real Estate; Judy L. Clarke, Mohave Community College; Richard J. Clemmer, Sr., D&D School of Real Estate; Robert J. Connole, PhD, Connole-Morton Real Estate School; Gerald Cortesi, Harper Community College; Nancy K. Currey, Currey Management Institute; Ralph De Martino, GRI, Paducah Community College; Rex R. Denham, Northwestern School of Real Estate; Jeni Durant, Spencer School of Real Estate; Kenneth Edwards, GRI, Community College instructor and author; Linda J. Fields, Professional Institute for Real Estate Training; Thomas D. Fisher, M.Ed., CRB, GRI, Southern Ohio College; Richard Garnitz,

Montgomery College; Joe Giacoma, Jr., Neosho County Kansas Community College; Dolores C. Gick, Montgomery College; Tom Gillett, The Tom Gillette Company, Inc.; Ignacio Gonzalez, Mendocino Community College; Norma Good, Malone College; Linda H. Hamm, The Columbia Academy of Real Estate, Inc.; George R. Harrison, MSA; Vernon Hoven, Vern Hoven Tax Seminars; Kennard P. Howell, MAI, SRA; Steve Hummel, MBA, GRI, Ohio University—Chillicothe; Leon E. Hustad, CRB, CRS, GRI, Las Vegas School of Real Estate; Craig Larabee, Larabee School of Real Estate; Debbie Levitz, Fort Myers Association of REALTORS® Real Estate School; Duane A. Lyman, A. J. Educational Services, Inc.; Bill Martin, Martin School of Real Estate; Anthony J. Martinez, IFAS, National Association of Independent Fee Appraisers; John D. Mayfield, Jr., The Southeast Real Estate Prep School; David N. McAlvey, Hoosier-State Real Estate Education; Bill W. McCoy, III, Dearborn Real Estate Institute; John Medvig, Colorado Real Estate Institute; Tim Meline, Iowa Realty; John Michaels, Oakton Community College; Susan G. Moseley, Moseley Flint Schools of Real Estate; Diantha Muzingo, DREI, Professional Real Estate Education; Patricia S. Norberg, Real Estate Exam Center; D. D. "Del" Nordstrom, PRO/ED; Edward P. Norris, Norris School of Real Estate; Roger Turcotte, CBR, DREI, GRI, Roger Turcotte & Co.; Mike Rieder, GRI, CRS, Gold Coast School of Real Estate II, Inc.; Gerard A. Rivello, G.A.R. School of Real Estate; Dale E. Roach, DREI, Career Training; George R. Safire, Alpha College of Real Estate; Laura L. Selvy, Century 21 Continental Real Estate Academy; Ben Simon, Berks Real Estate Institute; Joshua L. Simon, Attorncy-at-Law; Kathryn "Tootie" Smith, Smith Real Estate School; Dawn M. Svenningsen, Dabbs Academy of Real Estate, Inc.; Randall S. van Reken, Southern Nevada School of Real Estate; John P. Wiedemer, University of Houston; and Timothy M. Wyman, The Professional School of Business.

I also express gratitude to John D. Ballou, Moraine Valley Community College; W. Dean Davis, William Rainey Harper Junior College; Barney Fletcher, Barney Fletcher Schools; Andrew M. Gray, NIRE Schools of Real Estate; William R. Gray, Arizona School of Real Estate; Melvyn Lissner, New Jersey Realty Institute; Lucy Schissler, Jones Real Estate Colleges, Inc.; John L. Schlapman, Wauwatosa Realty Company; Joseph E. Spalding, J. E. Spalding Real Estate; and Ridgely P. Ware, Rutgers University, for their contributions to the previous editions. Note: All professional and school designations are current as of the time of the review.

For their contributions to this seventh edition, I thank the following real estate educators:

Dianna W. Brouthers, DREI, College of Real Estate, Inc.

James Hobbs, licensed real estate broker, Lima, Ohio

Marie S. Spodek, DREI, Professional Real Estate Solutions

It is indeed a rare occasion when an author can work with a publisher that is so well-versed in the subject. Dearborn Real Estate Education retains a team of experts in all phases of real estate publication. They made my writing job a relatively simple one. It was a pleasure working with the many members of their team.

Lastly, a very special word of appreciation goes to my wife, Patty, for all her support and encouragement throughout all stages of the book's production these past 30 years, as well as her role in the production of our three children and four grandsons.

The author and the publisher welcome any comments, criticisms, or suggestions from readers that will help future revisions.

John W. Reilly

Accounting
(*see also* Taxation)

account payable
account receivable
accrual method
accrued
accrued depreciation
acquisition cost
asset
balance sheet
book value
capitalize
cash method
credit
debit
depreciation allowance
disbursement
double entry
income statement
liability
modified accelerated cost recovery
   system (MARCS)
net worth
profit and loss statement
pro forma statement
quick assets
write-off

Agency
(*see also* Brokerage)

agency
agency coupled with an interest
agent
attorney-in-fact
broker

Code of Ethics
commingling
designated agent
dual agency (limited agency)
durable power of attorney
equal dignities rule
ethics
facilitator
fiduciary
full disclosure
general agent
gratuitous agent
implied agency
imputed notice
informed consent
inspection
limited power of attorney
limited referral agent
ministerial acts
ostensible agency
partially disclosed principal
power of attorney
principal
ratification
real estate agent
respondeat superior
scope of authority
special agent
subagent
transaction broker
trustee
undisclosed agency

Appraisal

abnormal sale
abstraction
acceleration principle
accessibility
acquisition appraisal
actual age
adjustments
aesthetic value
age-life depreciation
amenities
appointments
appraisal
Appraisal Foundation, The
appraisal report
appraiser
appraiser independence
   requirements
appreciation
assemblage
assessed valuation
axial growth
band of investment (BOI)
before-and-after method
building residual technique
built-up method
capitalization
capitalization (CAP) rate
cash equivalency
certified appraiser
change
comparables
comparative unit method
concession

conformity
contract rent
contribution
corner influence
cost approach
curable depreciation
curb appeal
deferred maintenance
demand
dcmography
depreciation (appraisal)
depth tables
directional growth
direct sales comparison approach
discounting
economic-base analysis
economic life
economic obsolescence
economic rent
effective age
effective gross income
engineering breakdown method
external obsolescence
fee appraiser
filtering down process
Financial Institutions Reform,
    Recovery, and Enforcement Act
    of 1989 (FIRREA)
forecast
functional obsolescence
going-concern value
goodwill
government forces
gross income multiplier (GIM)
gross rent multiplier (GRM)
highest and best use
homogeneous
income approach
incurable obsolescence
indicated value
infiltration
intrinsic value
Inwood tables
land capacity
land economics
land residual technique

legally permissible
letter report
market conditions
market value
misplaced improvement
modification
multiple regression
narrative report
net operating income (NOI)
nonhomogcnic
observed condition
obsolescence
occupancy rate
operating expense ratio
overimprovement
paired sales analysis
physical deterioration
physical life
plottage value
present value of one dollar
price
principles of appraisal
property residual technique
quantity survey
recapture rate
reconciliation
regression
reproduction cost
residual process
reversionary factor
reversionary value
review appraiser
scarcity
seller's market
situs
special-purpose property
split-rate
square-foot method
state-certified appraiser
subjective value
substitution
summation approach
superadequacy
supply and demand
thin market
Title XI

unbalanced improvement
underimprovement
unearned increment
uniformity
Uniform Residential Appraisal
    Report (URAR)
*Uniform Standards of Professional
    Appraisal Practice (USPAP)*
unit-in-place method
unit valuc
use value
utility value
value
value added
yield capitalization

Banking

accommodation party
cashier's check
certified check
check
clearing account
demand note
discount rate
endorsement
holder in due course
letter of credit
line of credit
maker
negotiable instrument
notice of dishonor
payee
postdated check
setoff
underwriting
without recourse

Brokerage
(*see also* Agency, Listing)

advance fee
advertising
asking price
auction
bird dog
blind ad

blue book
boiler room
Board of REALTORS®
branch office
broker
brokerage
broker-dealer
broker-in-charge
broker price opinion (BPO)
business opportunity
buyer's broker
buyer's market
caravan
client trust account
cold call
cold canvass
commission
consultant
cooperating broker
counseling
courtesy to brokers
customer
deferred commission
DINK (dual income, no kids)
discount broker
draw
employee
empty nester
exposure
false advertising
farm area
fees for service
floor duty
for sale by owner
franchise
generation X
guaranteed sale program (GSP)
independent contractor
industrial broker
in-house sale
limited service broker
lockbox
lottery
middleman
National Do Not Call Registry
one hundred percent commission

open house
participating broker
personal assistant
principal broker (PB)
prospect
puffing
qualified buyer
range of value
ready, willing, and able
rebate
referral
referral agency
relocation company
residual
sales associate
sales kit
salesperson(s)
selling broker
shopping
signs
site office
splitting fees
staging
Standards of Practice
submittal notice
trade-in
trade usage
trust fund account
turnover
unethical
workers' compensation law
yuppie

**Building Terms (*see also*
Construction, Development,
Subdivision)**
absorber
abutment
accessory building
anchor bolt
apartment building
arcade
asbestos
ash dump
attic
backfill

balcony
baluster
band or box sill
baseboard
basement
base shoe
base top molding
batten
bay
bay window
beam
bearing wall
bedrock
berm
blacktop
board foot
bracing
bridging
British thermal unit (Btu)
building height
building paper
bus duct
cantilever
casing
catwalk
caulking
chimney
chimney cap
chimney flashing
chimney pot
cinder fill
clapboard
cleanout door
clear span
collar beam
combed (striated) plywood
conduit
cornice
corridor
curtilage
damper
dampproofing
demising wall
doorstop
double-corner stud
double-load corridor

double plate
double-window header
downspout
drain tile
duct
eave
eave trough
exterior insulating and finishing system (EIFS)
facade
felt joint cover
finish flooring
flashing
floor joists
floor load
flue
foot-candle
footing
Formica®
foundation wall
freestanding building
frieze board
girder
head casing
hearth
HVAC
indirect lighting
insulation
insulation disclosure
jalousie
jamb
joist
lath
leeward
lintel
louver
low-E glass
luminous ceiling
mantel
master switch
miter
mudsill
mullion
muntin
nosing
open wall systems

oriented strandboard (OSB)
overhang
parapet
pilaster
plate
radon
rafter
retaining wall
ridgeboard
roof boards
roofing felt
roofing shingles
shake shingle
shear wall
shoe molding
siding
sill
stringer
subflooring
tongue and groove
tread
trim
truss
under-floor ducts
veneer
vent
wainscoting
wallboard
wall sheathing
wall stud
waste line
window jamb trim
window sash
x-bracing

Closing

abstracter
adjustments
apportionment
arrears
back-to-back escrow
closing (settlement)
closing agent
closing costs
closing statement

collection account
credit
double entry
double escrow
dry closing
escrow
escrow instructions
good-faith estimate (GFE)
good funds
holding escrow
HUD-1 form
impound account
outside of closing
perfect escrow
preclosing
prepaid expenses
prepaid items
proceeds-of-loan escrow
prorate
Real Estate Settlement Procedures Act (RESPA)
relation-back doctrine
settlement
Uniform Settlement Statement
walk-through

Commercial Investment Property

absorption rate
air park
break-even point
build-to-suit
bulk sales transfer
cash flow
cash-flow statement
commercial property
continuous operation clause
convenience store
covenant not to compete
discount department store
discounted cash flow
downside risk
downstroke
flea market
gross area
gross income

income property
institutional property
internal rate of return
land poor
leverage
maintenance
merchants' association
negative cash flow
neighborhood shopping center
net after taxes
net income
net yield
nut
office building
overall rate
pyramiding
rate of return
regional shopping center
resort property
reverse leverage
second-generation
   leasing
shopping center
vacancy factor
yield

Condominium

air space
appurtenant
association of unit owners
bylaws
common areas
common elements
common expenses
common interest
common profits
common wall
condo
condominium map
condominium owners' association
condominium ownership
conversion
cooperative ownership
declaration
highrise

homeowners' association (HOA)
horizontal property acts
house rules
limited common elements
maintenance fee
master deed
mixed use
proprietary lease
proxy
quadrominium
unit

Construction
(*see also* **Building Terms**)

absorption bed
adaptability
addition
A-frame construction
architectural drawings
architecture
artesian well
as-built drawings
bid
blueprint
brownstone
building line
building permit
building standards
bungalow
carport
certificate of completion (CC)
cesspool
chalet
change order
cistern
closed-wall construction
compaction
concrete basement floor
contractor
cost-plus contract
crawlspace
cushion
deck
disposal field
dormer
drainage

dry rot
drywall construction
duplex
dwelling
efficiency unit or apartment
effluence
escarpment
factory-built construction
fastrack construction
fire sprinkler system
fire stop
fire wall
fire yard
flat
floor area ratio
floor plan
frost line
gable
gambrel roof
garden apartment
gazebo
general contractor
granny flats
habitable room
height, building
highrise
International Code Council (ICC)
kiln
kitchenette
knockdown
lanai
leaching cesspool
live load
load
lobby
loft
lowrise
mall
mansard roof
manufactured housing
marina
mezzanine
midrise
module
mold
motel

mudroom
multiple dwelling
on-frame modular
on-site improvement
panelized construction
parquet floor
particleboard
pavilion
payment bond
penthouse
performance bond
pier
pitch
plaster finish
porte cochere
precuts
proceed order
progress payments
punch list
quadraplex (quad)
retainage
rooming house
row house
R-value
sanitary sewer system
semidetached dwelling
septic tank
shoring
single-family residence
single-load corridor
skylight
slab
solar heating
spec home
specifications
split-level
staging
staging area
stick-built on-site
structural alterations
structural defects
structural density
structure
stucco
stud
studio

subcontractor
sump
take off
termite shield
topping-off
town house
tract house
triplex
Uniform Building Code (UBC)
utility room
vestibule
villa
voucher system
walk-up
wall-to-wall carpeting
warehouse
weep hole
wet column
working drawings

Contracts

acceptance
accord and satisfaction
actual damages
addendum
additional deposit
adhesion contract
agreement of sale
aleatory contract
antenuptial agreement
anticipatory breach
arm's-length transaction
"as is"
assignment
backup offer
benefit-of-bargain rule
bilateral contract
boilerplate
breach of contract
buy-back agreement
capacity of parties
competent party
conditional sales contract
consequential damages
consideration

constructive fraud
consummate
contingency
contract
contract for deed
contract of sale
cooling-off period
counteroffer
counterpart
covenants and conditions
damages
date
default
deposit
disaffirm
discharge of contract
disclaimer
disclosure
disclosure statement
down payment
dual contract
dummy
duress
early occupancy
earnest money
election of remedies
electronic signature
equitable conversion
escape clause
executed contract
executory contract
exhibit
extension
first papers
forbearance
force majeure
forfeiture
forum shopping clause
fraud
good consideration
grace period
hold-harmless clause
home inspection
illiterate
implied contract
incorporation by reference

innocent misrepresentation
instrument
ironclad agreement
latent defects
liquidated damages
love and affection
mark
measure of damages
meeting of the minds
menace
minor
misrepresentation
mistake
modification
mutual agreement
mutuality of consent
natural affection
netting out
nominee
nondisclosure
notice
occupancy agreement
offer
offer and acceptance
offeror
on or before
option
oral contract
party to be charged
plain language law
privity
proposition
qualified acceptance
receipt
reformation
release
rescind
rescission
reservation money
risk of loss
roof inspection clause
sale by the acre
short-form document
signature
special conditions
specific performance

statute of frauds
straw man
"subject to" clause
tender
termite inspection
third party
"time is of the essence"
trading on the equity
unconscionability
undue influence
unenforceable contract
Uniform Vendor and Purchaser
  Risk Act
unilateral contract
unjust enrichment
unreasonably withheld consent
upgrades
upset date
valuable consideration
void
voidable
waiver
warranty
witness
X

Conveyance

alienation
assignment of lease
conveyance
counterpart
description
documentary tax stamps
document
exception
execute
federal revenue stamp
government patent
grant
initials
livery of seisin
locus sigilli
master form instrument
mesne conveyance
misnomer

mortmain
patent
revenue stamp
right, title, and interest
rule against perpetuities
sealed and delivered
subscribe
successors and assigns
testimonium clause
transfer tax (conveyance fee)
undersigned
Uniform Land Transactions Act
  (ULTA)

Corporation

annual meeting
annual report
articles of incorporation
association
board of directors
buy-sell agreement
close corporation
collapsible corporation
corporate resolution
corporation
DBA
double taxation
eleemosynary corporation
fictitious company name
fiscal year
foreign corporation
holding company
incorporate
name, reservation of
nonprofit corporations
personal property
S corporation
seal
Section 1244 corporation
spin-off
thin capitalization
ultra vires
unincorporated association

Death

admeasurement of dower
administrator
augmented estate
codicil
collateral heirs
curtesy
decedent
descent
devise
dower
elective share
escheat
executor
heir
heirs and assigns
holographic will
inheritance tax
intestate
jointure
legatee
lineal
nuncupative will
personal representative
per stirpes
probate
testator
widow's quarantine
will
worthier title doctrine

Deed

bargain and sale deed
cession deed
correction deed
covenant
covenants running with the land
deed
deed in trust
deed poll
deed restrictions
delivery
estoppel by deed
gift deed
grant deed

grantee
grantor
habendum clause
indenture deed
legacy
limited warranty deed
nominal consideration
premises
quitclaim deed
reddendum clause
reservation
restrictive covenant
sheriff's deed
special warranty deed
support deed
tax certificate
tax deed
unrecorded deed
warranty deed
wild deed

Development (see also Construction, Subdivision)

affordable housing
air park
bedroom community
business park
bed-and-breakfast
carrying charges
cluster development
commercial acre
common area maintenance (CAM)
community shopping center
completion bond
compliance inspection
contract documents
corridor development
culvert
curb line
cut and fill
developer
development impact fee
development loan
development rights
elevation sheet
entrepreneur

environmental impact statement (EIS)
feasibility study
front-ending
front money
ground area
guest-car ratio
Homeowners' Warranty Program (HOW)
housing for the elderly
housing starts
hundred percent location
impact fees
increment
indirect costs
joint venture
landlease communities
letter of intent
master lease
mobile-home park
model home
modular construction
NHP Foundation (NHPF)
net usable acre
off-site costs
off-street parking
open space
outparcel
pad
pedestrian traffic count
percolation test
plans and specifications
plaza
preliminary costs
presale
project
redevelopment agency
rendering
residence property
Rule of Five
schematics
sight-line
signage
soft money
speculator
starts

subsidy
subsidy rent
sweetheart contract
track record
transfer of development rights
 (TDR)
turnkey project
utilities
venture capital

Discrimination
accessibility
administrative law judge
affirmative marketing program
acquired immunodeficiency syndrome (AIDS)
Americans with Disabilities Act
 (ADA)
ancestor
blockbusting
Civil Rights Act of 1866
conciliation agreement
disability
discrimination
Equal Credit Opportunity Act
 (ECOA)
ethnic group
familial status
federal fair housing law
ghetto
handicap
minority
open housing
panic peddling
protected class
redlining
steering

Easement
adverse use
ancient lights doctrine
avigation easement
building-related illness (BRI)
declaration of restrictions
dominant estate (tenement)

easement
easement by necessity
easement by prescription
easement in gross
eave drip
electromagnetic fields (EMFs)
equitable servitude
implied easement
landlocked
line-of-sight easement
meth labs
National Environmental Protection
 Act (NEPA)
negative easement
party driveway
party wall
reciprocal easements
right-of-way (R/W)
run with the land
scenic easement
servient estate
solar easement
subsurface easement
visual rights

Environmental
abatement
asbestos
asbestos-containing materials
brownfields
Comprehensive Environmental
 Response, Compensation, and
 Liability Act (CERCLA)
de minimus settlement
Endangered Species Act
environmental audit
Environmental Protection Agency
 (EPA)
environmental regulations
environmental risk
formaldehyde
hazardous substance
hazardous waste
indoor air quality
lead poisoning

mitigation
Phase I audit
radon
remediation
sick building syndrome (SBS)
Superfund
underground storage tanks (USTs)
wetlands

Estate (*see also* Title)
adjunction
autre vie
conventional estate
curtesy
dower
estate
estate at will
estate of inheritance
executory interest
fee simple
fee simple defeasible
fee tail
freehold
freeholder
future interest
hereditament
homestead
inchoate
incorporeal rights
land, tenements, and hereditaments
less-than-freehold estate
life estate
life tenant
merger
messuage
possibility of reverter
profit a prendre
pur autre vie
qualified fee
quantum
quarter-section
reentry
remainder estate
remainderman
reversion

right of reentry
right-to-use
seisin
servitude
tenement
tenure
usufructuary right
vested interest

Federal Government

Agricultural Foreign Investment
     Disclosure Act (AFIDA)
Bank Insurance Fund (BIF)
Bureau of Land Management
     (BLM)
Clayton Antitrust Act
Department of Housing and Urban
     Development (HUD)
Drug Enforcement Act
Environmental Protection Agency
     (EPA)
Farm Credit System
Federal Home Loan Banks (FHLB)
Federal Housing Administration
     (FHA)
Federal Reserve System (the
     "Fed")
Federal Savings and Loan Insur-
     ance Corporation (FSLIC)
Federal Trade Commission (FTC)
Foreign Investment in Real Prop-
     erty Tax Act (FIRPTA)
Freddie Mac
General Services Administration
     (GSA)
Home Mortgage Disclosure Act
Lead-Based Paint Hazard Reduc-
     tion Act (LBPHRA)
National Environmental Protection
     Act (NEPA)
Office of Equal Employment
     Opportunity Commission
     (EEOC)
Office of the Comptroller of the
     Currency (OCC)

Resolution Trust Corporation
     (RTC)
Section 8 Program
Section 203(b)
Small Business Administration
     (SBA)
soil bank
standard metropolitan statistical
     area (SMSA)

Financing

A, B, C, D paper
ADC loan
add-back
adjustable-rate loan
advance
affordability index
allotment
amortization
amortization schedule
annual debt service
annual percentage rate (APR)
annuity
arranger of credit
assumption of mortgage
balloon payment
Bank Insurance Fund (BIF)
basis point
basket provision
belly-up
bond
bonus clause
bridge loan
building and loan association
bullet loan
buydown
CAP rate
carryback financing
carve out
certificate of claim
certificate of eligibility
certificate of reasonable value
collateral
collection report
commercial bank

commitment
Community Reinvestment Act
compensating balance
computerized loan origination
     (CLO)
construction loan
contract for deed
conventional loan
co-obligor
creative financing
creditor
credit rating
credit report
credit scoring
credit union
curtail schedule
customer trust fund (CTF)
debenture
debt coverage ratio
debt financing
debtor
debt service
debt-to-equity ratio
direct endorsement
discount
discount points
discount rate
discretionary funds
disintermediation
effective yield
elasticity
Ellwood technique
end loan
equity buildup
equity participation
equity sharing loan
face value
Fair Credit Reporting Act (FCRA)
Fannie Mae
Farmers Home Administration
     (FmHA)
Federal Deposit Insurance Corpora-
     tion (FDIC)
Federal Home Loan Banks (FHLB)
Federal Housing Administration
     (FHA)

inverse condemnation
irrigation districts
just compensation
land grant
larger parcel
letter of patent
local improvement district
occupancy permit
Office of Thrift Supervision (OTC)
ordinances
partial taking
police power
seizure
severance damages
slum clearance
special benefit
subsidized housing
taking
wipeout
zone condemnation

Industrial Property
bumper
drill track
incubator space
industrial park
loading dock
main line
miniwarehouse
piggyback
point of switch
spur track
truck well
up-ramp

Insurance
actual cash value
actuary
all-risks policy
binder
builder's risk insurance
bureau rate
business interruption insurance
business life insurance
certificate of insurance

coinsurance
commercial leasehold insurance
Comprehensive Loss Underwriting
    Exchange (CLUE)
errors and omissions (E&O)
    insurance
face value
fire insurance
flood insurance
Flood Insurance Rate Map (FIRM)
hazard insurance
homeowners' insurance policy
inflation guard
insurable interest
insurance
key man insurance
loss payee
mortgage insurance
Mutual Mortgage Insurance Fund
National Flood Insurance Program
    (NFIP)
owner's policy
premium
private mortgage insurance (PMI)
reinsurance
reissue rate
rider
short rate
tsunami damage
underwriter

**Interest (*see also*
Financing, Mortgage)**
add-back
add-on interest
amortization
arbitrage
block interest
cap
compound interest
constant
discount rate
effective interest rate
interest
lawful interest
legal rate of interest

nominal interest rate
prepaid interest
prevailing rate
prime rate
rediscount rate
Regulation Q
Rule of 72
simple interest
variable interest rate

Land
access
acre (AC)
acre foot
aeolian soil
agreed boundaries
air rights
alluvion
area
beach
bottomland
boundaries
contour map
farmland
filled land
flag lot
floodplain
flood-prone area
foreshore land
fructus naturales
improved land
land
lateral and subjacent support
light and air
littoral land
lot split
marginal land
mineral rights
parcel
public land
quadrangle
range
raw land
real estate
real property

realty
reclamation
shoreline
site
spite fence
subjacent support
tidewater land
topography
tract
unimproved property
wasteland
waterfront property
wetlands
yard

Land Description (Surveying)

angle
azimuth
base line
bearing
benchmark
bounds
call
chain
closure
compass points
connection line
corner stakes
correction lines
degree
description
fractional section
front foot
geodetic survey system
government survey method
grid system
guide meridians
half-section
hectare
high-water mark
land description
landmark
legal description
line stakes
lot, block, and subdivision

maps and plats
meander line
measurement tables
meridian
metes and bounds
mile
monument
more or less
plat map
plot plan
point of beginning (POB)
principal meridian
range line
rod
second
section(s)
spot survey
square
staking
standard parallel
survey
tax map
tier
township
U.S. Geological Survey (USGS)

Leasing

AAA tenant
abandonment
additional space option
anchor tenant
attornment
attraction principle
back-to-back lease
base period
base rent
building lease
cancellation clause
chain store
concession
concurrent lease
construction allowance
constructive eviction
consumer price index (CPI)
cost-of-living index

demise
dispossess proceedings
distraint
effective rate
estover
eviction
exculpatory clause
expansion option
expense stop
first refusal, right of
fixturing period
flat lease
graduated rental lease
gross lease
ground lease
habitable
holdover tenant
implied warranty of habitability
index lease
key money
key tenant
landlord
lease
leased fee
leasehold
lease option
lease purchase agreement
lessee
lessor
let
life-care facility
loss factor
master lease
military clause
minimum rent
mitigation of damages
month-to-month tenancy
most favored tenant clause
net lease
noncompetition clause
normal wear and tear
notice to quit
offer to lease
offset statement
oil and gas lease
option to renew

overage
overriding royalty
owelty
partial eviction
percentage lease
periodic tenancy
permissive waste
prime tenant
quiet enjoyment
reappraisal lease
recapture clause
recreational lease
relocation clause
renegotiation of lease
renewal option
rent
rentable area
rental agent (leasing agent)
rental agreement
rent control
rent escalation
rent-up
retaliatory eviction
right of first refusal
riparian lease
royalty
sale of leased property
sandwich lease
satellite tenant
security deposit
self-help
shell lease
sky lease
space plan
step-up lease
sublease
summary possession
surcharge
surrender
tax participation clause
tax stop clause
tenant
tenant alternative costs
tenant contributions
tenant mix
tenant union

triple-net lease
undertenant
unfinished office space
Uniform Residential Landlord and
    Tenant Act (URLTA)
unlawful detainer action
usable area
vacate
veto clause
waste
wear and tear
work letter
year-to-year tenancy

Legal Terms
(*see also* **Contracts**)
abandonment
abatement
absolute
abstract of judgment
acknowledgment
act of God
actual notice
adjudicated
administrative regulations
affidavit
affirmation
aggrieved
amicus curiae
antitrust laws
apostille
appeal
arbitration
attachment
attestation
attorney fees
attractive nuisance
bankruptcy
benchmark
beneficiary
blue laws
burden of proof
business day
by operation of law
cause of action
caveat emptor

cease and desist order
certified copy
certify
certiorari
change of name
commissioner
common law
compensatory damages
complainant
confession of judgment
confirmation of sale
conservator
constructive
court
coverture
cram down
decree
de facto
default judgment
defendant
deponent
deposition
disclosure statement
discovery
domicile
ejectment
enabling legislation
enjoin
entitlement
equity
estoppel
et al.
et ux.
et vir.
execution
expert witness
family
felony
force and effect of law
forum
garnishment
group boycott
guardian
hearing
holiday
incompetent

indemnification
injunction
interlocutory decree
interpleader
interstate
joint and several liability
judgment
judgment-proof
judicial precedent
jurat
jurisdiction
laches
law
legal age
legal name
levy
liability
limitations of actions
lis pendens (Lis/P)
majority
malfeasance
mandamus
mediation
misdemeanor
name, change of
natural person
notary public
nuisance
null and void
oath
operation of law
parol evidence rule
parties
penalty
person
petition
plaintiff
practice of law
preemption
presumption
prevailing party
price-fixing
prima facie evidence
pro forma
promulgate
punitive damages

quantum meruit
quash
quasi
quorum
reasonable time
receiver
referee
regulation
replevin
residence
restraint of trade
restraint on alienation
resulting trust
revocation
right of contribution
sequestration order
service of process
shall
should
small claims court
spendthrift trust
statute
statute of limitations
subpoena
subpoena duces tecum
subrogation
summons
surety
tie-in contract
tolling
tort
treble damages
trespass
trustee in bankruptcy
unfair and deceptive practices
uniform and model acts
valid
venue
verify
vicarious liability
violation
writ of execution

Licensing
administrative regulations

associate broker
Association of Real Estate License
    Law Officials (ARELLO)
auctioneer
broker-in-charge
continuing education
examination, licensing
forfeiture
inactive license
irrevocable consent
license
licensee
license laws
moral character
moral turpitude
notice of consent
pocket license card
real estate commission/department
reciprocity
recovery fund
single licensing
suspension
vocation

Lien
abstract of judgment
agricultural lien
commencement of work
encumbrance
equitable lien
floating lien
general lien
involuntary lien
judgment lien
lien
materialman
mechanic's lien
mortgage lien
notice of completion
notice of lien
notice of nonresponsibility
special lien
tax lien
vendor's lien

Listing

able
asking price
authorization to sell
cash-out
contingency listing
exclusive agency
exclusive listing
exclusive right to sell
extender clause
implied listing
listing
listor
multiple listing
negotiation
net listing
"no deal/no commission" clause
office exclusive
open listing
option listing
override
pocket listing
procuring cause
termination of listing

Mortgage/Deed of Trust (see also Interest, Lien, Financing)

acceleration clause
additional charge mortgage
adverse financial change condition
alienation clause
all-inclusive deed of trust
allonge
alternative mortgage instrument
anaconda mortgage
annual mortgagor statement
assignment of rents
beneficiary statement
biweekly payment loan
blanket mortgage
blended rate
budget mortgage
call provision
call report
certificate of no defense

closed-end mortgage
closed mortgage
collateralized mortgage
cosigner
credit bid
cross-defaulting clause
debt relief
deed in lieu of foreclosure
deed of reconveyance
deed of trust
defeasance clause
deficiency judgment
deflated mortgage
direct reduction mortgage
dry mortgage
due date
due-on-sale clause
effective rate
entitlement
equity mortgage
equity of redemption
escalator clause
first mortgage
flexible-payment mortgage
FLIP
foreclosure
full reconveyance
funding fee
gift letter
graduated-payment mortgage (GPM)
growing equity mortgage (GEM)
guaranty
hard-money mortgage
hypothecate
installment note
intermediate theory
judicial foreclosure
junior mortgage
law day
leasehold mortgage
level-payment mortgage
lien statement
lien-theory states
lifting clause
lock-in clause

marginal release
maturity
mortgage
mortgage banker
mortgage broker
mortgagee
mortgage lien
mortgage network
mortgage spreading agreement
mortgaging out
mortgagor
nondisturbance
nonjudicial foreclosure
nonrecourse loan
note
notice of default
novation
obligation bond
obligor
offering sheet
open-end mortgage
open mortgage
"or more" clause
outstanding balance
package mortgage
paragraph 17
parity clause
partial reconveyance
partial-release clause
participation mortgage
payoff
PITI
placement fee
pledged account mortgage
power of sale
prepayment penalty
prepayment privilege
primary mortgage market
promissory note
public sale
purchase-money mortgage (PMM)
real estate mortgage trust (REMT)
recognition clause
reconveyance
recourse note
redemption, equitable right of

redemption period
reduction certificate
reinstatement
release clause
renegotiable rate mortgage (RRM)
reserve fund
reverse annuity mortgage (RAM)
satisfaction of mortgage
second mortgage
shared appreciation
short sale
silent second
Soldiers and Sailors Civil Relief
    Act (SSCRA)
straight note
"subject to" mortgage
subordination agreement
subordination clause
subprime loan
substitution of collateral
surmortgage
term mortgage
title-theory states
unsecured
upset price
upside down
variable-payment plan
workout plan
wraparound mortgage

Ownership

absentee owner
abutting owner
air rights
alien
allodial system
bundle of rights
community property
concurrent ownership
condo
contribution, right of
cooperative ownership
corporeal property
cotenancy
disseisin

divided interest
entity, legal
feudal system
general partner
general partnership
home ownership
interest in property
interval ownership
inter vivos trust
joint tenancy
land trust
leased fee
leasehold
limited liability company (LLC)
limited partnership
living trust
master limited partnership
owner occupant
ownership, form of
partition
partnership
passive investor
possession
prescription
principal residence
property
proprietorship
real estate investment trust (REIT)
real estate owned (REO)
right of survivorship
separate property
severalty
sole proprietorship
survivorship, right of
syndication
tacking
tenancy at sufferance
tenancy at will
tenancy by the entirety (entireties)
tenancy for life
tenancy for years
tenancy in common
tenancy in partnership
tenancy in severalty
time-share ownership plan
time-sharing

trust
trust beneficiary
undivided interest
Uniform Simultaneous Death Act
unity (joint tenancy)

Personal Property

asset
bailment
bequeath
bill of sale
capital
chattel
chattel mortgage
emblement
financing statement
fructus industriales
inventory
personal property
security agreement
severance
termination statement
trade fixture
Uniform Commercial Code (UCC)

Property Management
(*see also* Leasing)

budget
fidelity bond
fixed expenses
management agreement
management survey
net spendable income
off-site management
on-site management
operating budget
operating expenses
per-unit cost method
positive cash flow
property management
rent roll
reserve for replacements
resident manager

declining-balance method
deductions
deferred-payment method
deferred taxes
delayed exchange
demolition loss
depletion
depreciable life
depreciable real property
    (accounting)
depreciation (tax)
depreciation recapture
donor
double taxation
enrolled agent
equalization board
estate tax, federal
exchange
excise tax
farm assets
federal revenue stamp
federal tax lien
fixing-up expenses
gain
gift causa mortis
gift tax
grievance period
historic structure
holding period
improvements
imputed interest
income averaging
income tax
individual retirement account
installment sale
intermediary
Internal Revenue Code of 1986
    (IRC)
investment interest
involuntary conversion
Keogh plan
landscaping
leasehold improvements
levy
like-kind property
limited liability company (LLC)

limited partnership
marginal tax rate
marital deduction
mill
modified accelerated cost recovery
    system (MACRS)
multiple-asset exchange
notice of assessment
open space taxation law
ordinary and necessary business
    expense
ordinary gain
organizational expenses,
    partnership
passive loss
property tax
qualified intermediary
recapture
recognition
rehabilitate (rehab)
related parties
relinquished property
repairs
replacement property
reporting requirements
residence, sale of
rollover
safe harbor rule
sale-leaseback
sales-assessment ratio
salvage value
Savings Incentive Match Plan for
    Employees (SIMPLE)
short-term capital gain
silent partner
simplified employee plan (SEP)
special assessment
Starker exchange
stepped-up basis
straight-line method
subchapter S corporation
substantial improvement
sum-of-the-years'-digits (SOYD)
    method
tax abatement
tax base

tax bracket
tax certificate
tax clearance
tax credit
tax deed
tax-deferred exchange
tax-free exchange
tax lien
tax map
tax preference
tax rate
tax roll
tax sale
tax search
tax shelter
trading up
transfer tax (conveyance fee)
undistributed taxable income
unearned income
up-leg
useful life
use tax
vacation home
wasting asset
withholding

Title (*see also* Estates)

accession
accretion
adverse possession
after-acquired
annexation
appurtenance
avulsion
bare title
claim of right
clearing title
clear title
cloud on title
color of title
continuation
diluvion
encroachment
encumbrance
equitable title

erosion
escheat
fixture
free and clear title
gap in title
hostile possession
lost-grant doctrine
marketable title
muniment of title
naked title
open and notorious possession
perfecting title
quiet title action
record owner
record title
root title
slander of title
title
title paramount
unencumbered property
unmarketable title

Title Evidence
(*see also* Recording)

abstracter's certificate
abstract of title
affidavit of title
American Land Title Association
   (ALTA)
bring-down search
cadastral map
certificate of title
chain of title
closing protection letter
deraign
evidence of title
extended coverage
flyspecking
forgery
hiatus
hidden risk
idem sonans
insurable title
late date order
letter report
off-record title defect

opinion of title
owner's duplicate certificate
plant
preliminary report
purchaser's policy
registered land
starter
tax and lien search
tax search
title insurance
title report
title search
Torrens system
transfer certificate of title (TCT)

Water

correlative water right
diffused surface waters
groundwater
mutual water company
navigable waters
overflow right
potable water
prior appropriation
reliction
riparian rights
surface water
water
watercourse
watershed
water table

Zoning
(*see also* Government)

acreage zoning
airport zoning
area regulations
blighted area
buffer zone
building codes
building permit
building restrictions
cemetery lots
central business district
cluster zoning

Coastal Zone Management Act
conditional-use zoning
conservation
density
density zoning
downzoning
dwelling unit
exclusionary zoning
floating zone
general plan
grandfather clause
heavy industry
hotel
inclusionary zoning
inner city
land bank
land-use intensity
land-use map
light industry
livability space ratio
master plan
minimum lot area
moratorium
municipal ordinance
new town
nonconforming use
parking ratio
planning commission
preservation district
pyramid zoning
rural
rurban
satellite city
setback
special-use permit
spot zoning
upzoning
urban enterprise zone
urban renewal
urban sprawl
variance
zero lot line
zoning
zoning estoppel

AAA tenant   A well-known business tenant with an exceptionally high credit rating, or one whose national or local name lends prestige to a shopping center or office project.

A, B, C, D paper   Categorization of borrowers and loans in order of desirability; an A borrower is rated the highest and is eligible for the lowest interest rates; B is lower, with C and D the lowest. (*See* **credit scoring**.)

abandonment   The act of voluntarily surrendering or relinquishing possession of real property without vesting this interest in any other person. An overt act is usually needed to prove abandonment, such as an owner's failure to pay real estate taxes. Each case of possible abandonment must be evaluated to determine whether the property has indeed been legally abandoned. Mere nonuse of the property is insufficient evidence that the possessor will not reclaim the property. For example, the owner of an easement footpath across a neighboring property might demonstrate the intent to abandon the easement by erecting a fence between the two properties. When a condemning authority abandons an easement, the fee owner (condemnee) regains exclusive ownership of the parcel.

  Abandonment can be distinguished from "surrender," which requires some form of agreement (as between lessor and lessee), and from "forfeiture," which occurs against the owner's wishes. Abandonment of use takes place when an owner terminates a permitted right of nonconforming use under the current zoning ordinance. (*See* **forfeiture, surrender**.)

  A tenant who vacates leased property, no longer intending to perform under the terms of the lease, is abandoning the property. The landlord then regains full possession and control, but the lessee remains liable for rent until the lease expires. If the landlord accepts the abandonment (agrees to terminate the tenancy), it is recognized as a surrender, and the tenant is not obligated to pay future rents under the terms of the lease.

  The Uniform Residential Landlord and Tenant Act, adopted by many states, provides that the landlord must make "reasonable efforts" to relet abandoned property at a fair rental. (*See* **Uniform Residential Landlord and Tenant Act [URLTA]**.)

  In states that recognize homestead rights, a claimant may abandon a homestead by filing a declaration of abandonment in the public record. Merely leaving such premises will not officially constitute an abandonment of a person's homestead rights. (*See* **homestead**.)

  An abandonment may have income tax consequences. The taxpayer-owner who abandons real estate may be able to treat the abandonment as a "sale" for which the taxpayer received no payment (other than relief from any mortgages or liens). In this case, the taxpayer may claim a loss to the extent of the adjusted basis in the property.

  Most states have laws covering the rights and obligations of the government and various parties in cases of unclaimed or abandoned personal property. Landlords of miniwarehouses, for example, should carefully examine the possible liabilities involved in disposing of unclaimed property at the termination of a rental. (*See* **escheat**.)

abatement   A reduction or decrease in amount, degree, intensity, or worth. For example, a lessee usually is entitled to an abatement of rent during the time the premises are made uninhabitable by fire, flood, or other acts of God. Also, there may be an abatement of rent if the landlord fails to give the tenant possession at the beginning of the agreed-upon lease term.

A

When a defect is discovered in a seller's title and the seller refuses to correct it before closing, the buyer can seek specific performance of the contract with an abatement from the purchase price because of the defect. For example, a buyer enters into a contract to purchase a $100,000 house. Before closing, a title search reveals that the sellers have not paid $5,000 in property taxes. The sellers refuse to pay the taxes and decide not to sell the property. The buyer could deposit $95,000 into court and force a sale of the property in an action for specific performance. The sellers would then pay the state the $5,000 in unpaid taxes to obtain clear title to the property.

Tax abatement occurs when there is tax reduction or cessation of an initial assessed valuation, such as an error in the tax assessment.

A summary abatement is the court-ordered destruction of premises that are considered unsafe or partially destroyed.

If a property owner is maintaining a nuisance, such as a chemical plant emitting harmful fumes, an abutting owner may bring an action to abate the nuisance.

An asbestos abatement plan outlines the method to handle the control of asbestos found in a property. Abatement methods include removal by specially licensed asbestos abatement contractors; encapsulation of the asbestos-containing materials (ACMs) so that the fibers may not easily be released; enclosure by covering the ACMs with a protective wrap or jacket; or sealing off an area that contains the asbestos, such as a crawlspace.

able   Refers to financial ability in the phrase "ready, willing, and able buyer," used to determine whether a broker is entitled to a commission. It does not mean that the buyer must have all the cash for the purchase but that the buyer must be able to qualify for and arrange the necessary financing within the time specified in the purchase agreement. (*See* **contingency**, **procuring cause**.)

abnormal sale   A real estate sale that is unusual for the marketplace. The appraiser must consider the merit of such real estate as a reliable comparable; for example, whether the sellers sold the property to their children at less than market value. (*See* **direct sales comparison approach**.)

absentee owner   A property owner who does not reside on the property and who often relies on a property manager to manage the investment.

Federal tax laws deal with the ownership of depreciable real property when the owner is absent most of the year but occupies the property on vacations or at other times for part of the year. These changes are aimed at reducing the tax depreciation advantages when an absentee owner uses the property as a second home. Consult experienced counsel for specific details. (*See* **real property securities registration**, **vacation home**.)

Many states now require the sellers of property to give the buyer a property condition report. This presents a problem for absentee owners. As an alternative, the absentee owner may want to give the buyer a report from a professional property inspector. In some states, the absentee owner is exempt from having to provide the report.

absolute   Unrestricted and without conditions or limitations, as in a fee simple absolute estate, an absolute conveyance, or absolute liability (strict liability).

absorber   A coated panel in a solar heat collector that absorbs the solar radiation, which is then transmitted through the cover plate by absorber fluid passages and converted to heat energy.

absorption bed   A shallow trench that contains a distribution pipe to pass effluent from the septic tank so that it is absorbed into the soil.

absorption rate   An estimate of the rate at which a particular classification of space—such as new office space, new housing, or new condominium units—will be sold or occupied each year. A prediction of this rate is often involved in a feasibility study or an appraisal in connection with a request for financing. (*See* **appraisal**, **feasibility study**.)

abstracter   One who prepares an abstract of title. Also spelled *abstractor*. (*See* **abstract of title**.)

abstracter's certificate   A warranty by an abstracter that an abstract contains all matters of public record affecting title to a specific tract of land. (*See* **abstract of title**.)

abstraction   An appraisal method whereby the appraiser estimates the land value of any improved property by deducting, or abstracting, the value of any site improvements from the overall sales price of the property. The amount remaining is the estimated sales price, or indicated value, of the land. Also called the *allocation* or *extraction method*. (*See* **appraisal**.)

abstract of judgment   Document used to effectuate a judgment lien. Must be filed in any county where the judgment debtor has real estate. (*See* **attachment, general lien, judgment lien, lis pendens [Lis/P]**.)

abstract of title   A full summary of all consecutive grants, conveyances, wills, records, and judicial proceedings affecting title to a specific parcel of real estate, together with a statement of all recorded liens and encumbrances affecting the property and their present status. The person preparing the abstract of title, called an *abstracter*, searches the title as recorded or registered with the county recorder, county registrar, circuit court, and/or other official sources. The abstractor summarizes the various instruments affecting the property and arranges them in the chronological order of recording, starting with the original grant of title.

The abstract includes a list of public records searched and not searched in preparation of the report. In summarizing a deed in the chain of title, the abstracter might note the recorder's book and page number, the date of the deed, the recording date, the names of the grantor and grantee, a brief description of the property, the type of deed, and any conditions or restrictions contained in the deed.

The abstract of title does not guarantee or ensure the validity of the title of the property. Rather, it is a condensed history that merely discloses those items about the property that are of public record; thus, it does not reveal such things as encroachments and forgeries. Therefore, abstracters are usually liable only for damages caused by their own negligence in searching the public records. (*See* **certificate of title, chain of title, preliminary report, title insurance, title report**.)

abutment   A specific part of a wall or pier on which an object presses, such as the supports at either end of a bridge.

abutting owner   An owner whose land adjoins a public road or any contiguous property. The major problems between abutting owners occur regarding encroachments, party walls, access, light and air easements, and lateral support. Abutter's rights include the right to see and be seen from the street. (*See* **access, lateral and subjacent support**.)

accelerated cost recovery system (ACRS)   A simplified depreciation system originally created under the Economic Recovery Tax Act of 1981 to replace the old "ADS class life" system. Costs can be written off over a predetermined amount of time depending on the class or property. ACRS applied to most equipment placed in service between 1980 and before 1987. (*See* **accelerated depreciation, depreciation [tax], salvage value, useful life**.)

The Tax Reform Act of 1986 contained several changes to the ACRS rules. The changes are generally effective for property placed in service after December 31, 1986. (*See* **modified accelerated cost recovery system [MACRS], Tax Reform Act of 1986**.)

accelerated depreciation   For tax purposes, a method of calculating the cost write-off (depreciation) of certain personal property and improvements to real property at a faster rate than would be achieved by using the straight-line method of depreciation. The property must be used in a trade or business or held for the production of income. This method assumes that an asset deteriorates more rapidly in its early years. (*See* **depreciation [tax]**.)

A

For a description of the basic techniques, *see* **declining-balance method, sum-of-the-years'-digits (SOYD) method.**

For property previously placed in service, the original period and method of depreciation or cost recovery will remain in effect for as long as the same owner keeps the property in service for an eligible use. Thus, some taxpayers will compute depreciation separately for property placed in service before 1981, ACRS property placed in service between 1981 and 1986, and property placed in service after 1986. (*See* **accelerated cost recovery system [ACRS], modified accelerated cost recovery system [MACRS], straight-line method.**)

acceleration clause   A provision in a mortgage, trust deed, promissory note, or contract for deed (agreement of sale) that, upon the occurrence of a specified event, gives the lender (payee, obligee, or mortgagee) the right to call all sums due and payable in advance of the fixed payment date. This event might be default on an installment payment, destruction (waste) of the premises, placement of an encumbrance on the property, or its sale or assignment. Usually the payee has the option to accelerate the note upon default of payment of any installment of interest or principal when due, provided he or she gives adequate notice and specifies a time within which the defaulting party may cure the default. The payee may also accelerate for other breaches of provisions in the contract, such as failure to pay taxes and assessments or to keep the property insured or in repair. A lender may also exercise acceleration when it is discovered that the borrower (mortgagor) does not hold good title to the mortgaged property, contrary to prior claims at the time the mortgage was created, or upon condemnation of all or part of the premises.

The provision for acceleration does not exist unless it is expressly set forth in the mortgage or contract-for-deed document. The acceleration provisions stated in the mortgage should be consistent with those stated in the promissory note. An acceleration clause is also called a **due-on-sale clause** or **alienation clause** when it provides for acceleration upon the sale of the property. A court might hold an acceleration clause to be unenforceable if it is deemed an unreasonable restraint or restriction on alienation.

The seller under a contract for deed usually inserts an acceleration clause in order to declare the entire balance due and payable when the buyer fails to cure a default. Without this clause, the seller would have to sue the buyer as each installment payment became due and unpaid. (*See* **due-on-sale clause, mortgage, prepayment privilege.**)

acceleration principle   An event that has greater impact on demand or prices than can be traced directly to that event alone. The catalyst that attracts trade, business, and/or industry to a given location.

acceptance

1. The expression of intent of a person receiving an offer (offeree, such as the seller in a real estate transaction) to be bound by the terms of the offer. Acceptance must be communicated to the person making the offer (offeror, such as a buyer). The communication need not be in writing—it may be a mere nod of the head—but if the offer is in writing and pertains to real property, the acceptance also must be in writing to be enforceable.

A buyer may revoke an offer at any time before receiving notice of the seller's acceptance, even if the buyer has stated a willingness to keep the offer open for a certain time. Thus, the sales contract should include a statement that requires the exact time of the acceptance and that acceptance should be communicated to the buyer or offeror as soon as practicable. Communication is particularly significant because the buyer might effectively revoke the offer to purchase after the seller has accepted the offer but before the acceptance has been effectively communicated to the buyer.

Also, the acceptance must be made within the time limit stated in the offer. If no time limit is stated, then the acceptance is valid if made within a reasonable time of the offer, which differs in each case and custom within the community. To avoid the confusion that might be caused by the communication rule, some offers specify that the acceptance is not effective unless a signed copy is received by the offeror or broker within a certain time.

If the offer prescribes a specific method of acceptance, such as facsimile or electronic record, then the acceptance is not effective unless that method is used. For instance, acceptance of a mailed offer becomes an effective and binding contract when deposited in the mails. (The law presumes that the buyer appointed the post office as the agent to receive notification of acceptance.) Where the acceptance is communicated in an unusual manner (such as placing it in a newspaper ad), then the contract is not effective until and unless the acceptance is received by the buyer within a reasonable time. (*See* **Uniform Electronic Transaction Act [UETA].**)

An owner who listed property with a broker is under no obligation to accept an offer from a buyer at the listing price. The listing is an employment agreement, not an offer to sell. Therefore, it creates no power of acceptance in the buyer. The owner may, however, owe money damages to the broker.

Although silence is usually not sufficient indication of intent to accept, sometimes it may be. For example, where a broker has handled many sales for a developer at a 4 percent commission and the developer offers another property that the broker sells, the broker may be held to have agreed to another 4 percent rate, even though a more reasonable rate in the community might be 7 percent.

2. Voluntary and unconditional acceptance of a deed by the grantee is essential to a valid delivery of the deed—a grantee who does not want title to the property need not take it. Acceptance is often presumed by the courts when beneficial to the grantee (called *constructive acceptance*), as in cases of a beneficial conveyance to a person incapable of consenting, such as a deed to a minor or an incompetent person. The acceptance can be presumed by the grantee retaining the deed, taking possession, recording the deed, paying the sales price, encumbering the title, or any other act of ownership.

For example, a court probably would not presume acceptance when the grantor grants his $100,000 farm—heavily encumbered with $600,000 in debt and full of building code violations—to a grantee, who dies without ever being aware the property was deeded to him. If, however, the property were free and clear of debt and code violations, the court probably would presume acceptance by the unaware decedent, and the property would thus pass to his estate, provided there was a valid delivery. (*See* **deed, contract, delivery, listing, offer and acceptance.**)

access   A means by which property is approached or a method of entrance into or upon a property. Access is also a general or specific right of ingress and egress to a particular property. A property owner usually has the right to have access to and from the property to a public street or highway abutting thereon, including the right to the unrestricted flow of light and air from the street to the property. The term *access* also refers to the right of a riparian owner to pass to and from the waters upon which the property borders.

Many state laws maintain that a residential tenant may not unreasonably withhold consent from the landlord to enter the dwelling unit in order to inspect the premises; make necessary or agreed repairs; supply services as agreed; show the dwelling unit to prospective purchasers, mortgagees, or tenants; or demand rent. However, the landlord may not abuse this right of access or use it to harass the tenant and should enter only after giving the tenant reasonable notice or in cases of emergency or when impracticable to do so.

A

Condominium rules create easements and other rights for owners to gain access to their units across common elements. (*See* **abutting owner, landlocked, Uniform Residential Landlord and Tenant Act [URLTA].**)

accessibility
1. The relative ease of entry to a site and its location with respect to different transportation facilities is an important factor in evaluating the suitability of a site for a particular use.
2. The ability of a person with a handicap or disability to more easily and independently approach and use facilities. Actions can include changing door widths, increasing wheelchair radius, installing grab bars, audible and visual signals, and the like. (*See* **federal fair housing law; Americans with Disabilities Act [ADA].**)

accession   (*accesión*)   The acquisition of title to additional land or to improvements as a result of the annexation of fixtures or as a result of alluvial deposits along the banks of streams by accretion. For example, if Ben Brown builds a fence on his neighbor's property without an agreement permitting Brown to remove it, ownership of the fence accedes to the neighbor, unless the neighbor requires that it be removed. (*See* **accretion, alluvion, annexation, fixture, improvements.**)

accessory building   (*edificación complementaria*)   A building used for a purpose other than that of the principal building on the same lot. For example, a garage, pump house, or storage shed would be considered an accessory building if erected on the same parcel of land as the property's main building.

accommodating party   A person or entity who agrees to take title to a property in connection with a Section 1031 tax exchange. Also called the intermediary. (*See* **delayed exchange.**)

accommodation party   A party who signs a negotiable instrument (such as a promissory note) as maker, acceptor, or endorser, without receiving any consideration, to accommodate another party and enhance the creditworthiness of the paper by lending his name as further security. For example, a brother who co-signs a bank note with his sister so that she can borrow money to buy a house would be an accommodation party to the lending contract. (*See* **consideration, guarantor, negotiable instrument.**)

accord and satisfaction   The settlement of an obligation. An accord is an agreement by a creditor to accept something different from or less than what the creditor feels entitled to. When the creditor accepts the consideration offered by the debtor for the accord, the acceptance constitutes a satisfaction and the obligation of the debtor is extinguished.

For these rules to apply, it is essential that the obligation be in dispute (that is, an unliquidated debt). For example, if Gary Green clearly owes Bob Brown $100 and Green sends a $75 check marked "payment in full," Brown still has a claim against Green for the $25 balance. If, however, the amount owed is disputed and Green offers a $75 check as payment in full, then the act of cashing the check would be an accord and satisfaction, and the obligation would be extinguished. (*See* **novation.**)

accounting   The fiduciary duty of an agent to maintain and preserve the property and money of the principal. The agent must keep accurate records of funds and documents received. (*See* **agent, fiduciary, principal.**)

account payable   A liability (debt) representing an amount owed to a creditor, usually arising from the purchase of merchandise, supplies, or services. It is not necessarily due immediately.

account receivable   A claim against a debtor, usually arising from sales or services rendered to the debtor. The opposite of an account payable, an account receivable is not necessarily due or past due at any specific time.

Accredited Land Consultant (ALC)   A professional designation conferred by the REALTORS® Land Institute (RLI). (*See* Appendix B.)

Accredited Management Organization (AMO)   A professional designation conferred upon management organizations meeting the standards set by the Institute of Real Estate Management (IREM). (*See* Appendix B.)

Accredited Resident Manager (ARM)   A professional designation conferred by the Institute of Real Estate Management (IREM). (*See* Appendix B.)

Accredited Rural Appraiser (ARA)   A professional designation conferred by the American Society of Farm and Rural Appraisers. (*See* Appendix B.)

accretion   The gradual and imperceptible addition of land by alluvial deposits of soil through natural causes, such as shoreline movement caused by streams or rivers. This added land upon a bank or stream, navigable or not, becomes the property of the riparian or littoral owner, and it also becomes subject to any existing mortgages. Conversely, the owner can lose title to land that is gradually washed away through erosion. (*See* **alluvion**, **erosion**, **littoral land**, **riparian rights**.)

accrual method   An accounting method of reporting income and expenses in which expenses incurred and income earned for a given period are reported whether or not the expenses were paid or income was received. The *right* to receive, not the actual receipt, determines the inclusion of the amount in gross income. Similarly, expenses are deducted when the taxpayer's liability becomes fixed and definite, not when the taxpayer actually pays the expense. Generally, the accrual method is available to businesses and is not for use by individuals.

For a description of the other accounting method for reporting income and expenses, *see* **cash method**.

accrued   Accumulated over a period of time, such as accrued depreciation, accrued interest, or accrued expenses. Accrued expenses, such as real property taxes, have been incurred but are not yet payable. In a closing statement, accrued expenses are credited to the purchaser, who will pay these expenses at a later date for the benefit of the seller.

accrued depreciation   (*depreciación acumulada*)
1. In accounting, a bookkeeping account that shows the total amount of depreciation taken on an asset since it was acquired; also called **accumulated depreciation**. (*See* **depreciation [tax]**.)
2. For appraisal purposes, the difference between the cost to reproduce the property (as of the appraisal date) and the property's current value as judged by its "competitive condition." In this context, accrued depreciation is often called *diminished utility*. (*See* **book value**, **depreciation [appraisal]**.)

accumulated depreciation   *See* **accrued depreciation**.

acknowledgment   A formal declaration made before a duly authorized officer, usually a notary public, by a person who has signed a document; also, the document itself. An acknowledgment is designed to prevent forged and fraudulently induced documents from taking effect. The officer confirms that the signing is the voluntary act and genuine signature of a person who is known to the officer or who provides adequate identification. Though typical, it is not necessary that the person sign in the presence of the officer. The officer is liable for damages caused by the negligent failure to identify the person correctly—for instance, if forgery occurs because the officer accepted verification by telephone.

In most states, a document will not be accepted for recording unless it is acknowledged. A *foreign acknowledgment* (one that has taken place outside of the state in which it is to be recorded) is generally valid if it is valid where made. The signature of the foreign officer is sufficient evidence that the acknowledgment is taken in accordance with the laws of the place where made and of the authority of the officer to take the acknowledgment, thus entitling the acknowledged document to be recorded and, where appropriate, to be read into evidence in any judicial proceeding without further proof of its authenticity. However, for documents signed outside the United States, many states require that the acknowledgment be made by an official at a U.S. Consulate Office.

If any material is crossed out, erased, or changed in the document, the officer should initial these changes if so approved by the parties. Otherwise, the document may not be acceptable for recordation. Because of modern methods of reproducing documents, it is generally recommended that signatures be made in black ink. (*See* **affidavit**, **apostille**, **attestation**, **notary public**, **recording**.)

There are different types of acknowledgment forms for corporations, partnerships, trustees, and attorneys-in-fact. A typical acknowledgment for an individual's signature is shown here.

STATE OF: SS:

COUNTY OF:

On this _____ day of _____, 20___,
before me personally appeared _____,
to me known to be the person(s) described in and who executed
the foregoing instrument and acknowledged to me that _____
executed the same as ____ free act and deed.

_____

Notary Public

(NOTARY SEAL)

My Commission Expires: _____

---

acquired immunodeficiency syndrome (AIDS)   A serious disease of the immune system. Persons with acquired immunodeficiency syndrome are protected under most federal and state discrimination laws. Many states have amended their licensing laws to provide that the fact that someone has AIDS is not deemed a material fact and therefore does not form the basis for a claim that a broker concealed a material fact. Also protected are persons with AIDS-related complex (ARC) or human immunodeficiency virus infection (HIV).

acquisition appraisal   The appraisal for market value of a property to be acquired for a public use by governmental condemnation or negotiation. The purpose of the appraisal is to estimate market value so the government can set the amount of just compensation to be offered the property owner. (*See* **appraisal**, **condemnation**, **market value**.)

acquisition cost   The amount of money or other valuable consideration expended to obtain title to property. Includes, in addition to the purchase price, such items as closing costs, appraisal fees, and title insurance. (*See* **basis**, **consideration**, **title**.)

acre (AC) (*acre*)   A measure of land area equal to 43,560 square feet or 208.71 feet by 208.71 feet. Equivalent to 4,840 square yards, 4,047 square meters, 160 square rods, or 0.4047 hectare. A square mile contains 640 acres (25.6 hectares). (*See* **measurement tables**, **more or less**.)

acreage zoning   Zoning intended to reduce residential density by requiring large building lots. Also called *large-lot zoning* or *snob zoning*. (*See* **density**, **density zoning**, **zoning**.)

A

acre foot A volume of water, sand, or minerals equal to an area of one acre with a depth of one foot (43,560 cubic feet); used in measuring irrigation water. If a liquid, it equals 325,850 gallons.

ACRS *See* **accelerated cost recovery system (ACRS)**.

act of God (*caso fortuito, fuerza mayor*) An act of nature beyond human control, such as a tidal wave, flood, hurricane, volcanic eruption, or earthquake. Many contracts include a *force majeure* clause, which temporarily or permanently relieves the parties of performance of a contract where an act of God has destroyed or damaged the subject matter or prevented performance. Under the name *destroyed or materially damaged clause*, this provision relieves the parties to a real estate sales contract from performance when an act of God has damaged the property's improvements before the transfer of title. (*See* **force majeure**.)

actual age The chronological age of a building; the opposite of its effective age, as indicated by the building's condition and utility. For example, a building with an actual age of 15 years might have an effective age of 20 years because of deferred maintenance. (*See* **effective age**.)

actual cash value An insurance term for the monetary worth of an improvement. Actual cash value is calculated by subtracting the value of the physical wear and tear of a property from its replacement cost.

actual damages Those damages that a court of law will recognize and that are a direct result of a wrong. In contrast, special or punitive damages are imposed by courts as a deterrent and as a punishment. (*See* **damages**.)

actual notice Express information or fact; that which is known; actual knowledge. Constructive notice, on the other hand, is knowledge that is implied by law—that which the law charges one with knowing.

A person having either actual or constructive notice of a third party's prior rights to a property normally takes the property subject to that third party's rights. One cannot claim the benefits of the recording law if taking title to property with actual notice of a previously executed but unrecorded instrument. There is also a type of notice called *inquiry notice*, where circumstances, appearances, or rumors are such that one has a duty to inquire further in order to determine whether property ownership exists with a person other than the one claiming that ownership. (*See* **constructive notice**, **inquiry notice**, **legal notice**, **notice**, **recording**.)

actual eviction The process of physically removing a tenant after the court issues a judgment decree for possession in favor of the owner and the tenant does not voluntarily leave. It is sometimes called *ejectment* or *repossession*. (*See* **eviction**.)

actuary A person usually associated with an insurance company or savings and loan association, and skilled in calculating the value of life interests, pension plans, and annuities. (*See* **annuity**, **life estate**.)

ADA *See* **Americans with Disabilities Act (ADA)**.

adaptability The ability at a later date to easily change the physical designs in residential or commercial units to accommodate needs for those encountering mobility limitations. For example, the installation of reinforcements in bathroom walls allows quick and easy installation of grab bars later.

ADC loan A type of loan that covers the acquisition, development, and construction of a development project.

add-back For a loan that defers payment of a portion of interest due, the deferred amount added to the balloon payment due at the end of the loan. (*See* **balloon payment**, **negative amortization**.)

A

addendum   Additional material attached to and made part of a document. If there is space insufficient to write all the details of a transaction on the sales contract form, the parties will attach an addendum or supplement to the document. The sales contract should incorporate the addendum by referring to it as part of the agreement. The addendum should refer to the sales contract and be dated and signed or initialed by all the parties. (*See* **rider**.)

addition   Any construction that increases a building's size or significantly adds to it. For example, construction of a second floor on top of a one-level structure is an addition.

additional charge mortgage   A mortgage-type instrument used to secure an additional advance of money from the holder of the mortgage to the mortgagor after the original loan transaction. Used to avoid any question as to whether the two debts are related. (*See* **advance**, **anaconda mortgage**.)

additional deposit   The additional earnest money given by the buyer to the seller or to escrow under a purchase agreement. The additional deposit is usually tendered within a short period of time after acceptance of the offer. For example, the buyer might deposit $1,000 with her offer to purchase the seller's $150,000 condominium unit and agree to pay an additional deposit of $4,000 within five working days after the seller's acceptance. If the buyer breaches the contract, the seller may elect to keep all deposit money, including the additional deposit, as damages.

   If the buyer is late in making the additional deposit payment, the seller may be able to terminate the contract if a court holds that failure to make timely payment is a material breach. One way for the seller to ensure this result is to make the seller's acceptance conditioned upon timely payment of the additional deposit. (*See* **breach of contract**, **deposit**, **earnest money**.)

additional space option   A right within a lease giving a tenant the option to expand the tenant's leased space during the lease term as required and on terms specified in the lease.

add-on interest   Interest charged on the entire principal amount for the specified term, regardless of any repayments of principal. The borrower is paying interest on the full principal sum for the entire loan period (and not on the declining balance), even though the principal is being reduced each month. Also called **block interest**. (*See* **interest**.)

   For example, a $10,000 loan with add-on interest at 12 percent payable over three years would require equal annual interest payments of $1,200 until completely paid, regardless of the unpaid principal amount. As a rule, to determine the effective rate of interest (true annual interest), double the stated add-on interest rate. Thus, in the example, the true annual interest on the $10,000 loan would be almost 24 percent.

adhesion contract   A contract that is one-sided, favoring the party who drafted the document. In fact, an adhesion contract can be so one-sided that doubt arises as to its being a voluntary and uncoerced agreement because it implies a serious inequality of bargaining power. Courts will not enforce provisions in adhesion contracts that are unfair and oppressive to the party who did not prepare the contract. Also called a *take-it-or-leave-it contract*.

   Contracts with a lot of fine print, such as franchise agreements, mortgages, and leases, are sometimes challenged as adhesion contracts on the basis that the nondrafting party did not have a chance to bargain on the various provisions of the agreement.

   An insurance contract (property, title, life) also is sometimes challenged as being an adhesion contract. Courts have held that any ambiguity is to be construed in favor of the insured, and any exclusion from coverage must be clearly and conspicuously stated. Courts will also apply the doctrine of unconscionability. (*See* **boilerplate**, **plain language law**, **unconscionability**.)

adjudicated   Something that has been finally decided by a court or governmental agency.

adjunction   (*adjunción*)   The process of annexing one parcel of land to a larger parcel.

adjustable-rate loan   A broad term for a loan (mortgage or deed of trust) with rates and terms that can change. The Federal Housing Finance Agency (FHFA), which oversees Fannie Mae and Freddie Mac, the Comptroller of the Currency, which regulates national banks, and the Office of Thrift Supervision, which governs federal savings and loan associations, have issued guidelines allowing the issuance of real estate loans having provisions to increase or decrease the rate of interest at certain time intervals (e.g., every six months) within a certain range (e.g., 1 percent).

   The adjustable-rate loan has become commonplace, with allowable ranges as to time intervals, percentage of increase or decrease and total increases or decreases likely to change as market conditions change. (*See* **biweekly payment loan, cap**.)

   The adjustable-rate loan has created its own glossary of terms, such as the following:

Current index: The current value of a recognized index as calculated and published nationally or regionally. The current index value changes periodically and is used in calculating the new note rate as of each rate adjustment date.

Fully indexed note rate: The index value at the time of application plus the gross margin stated in the note.

Gross margin: An amount, expressed as percentage points, added to the current index value on the rate adjustment date to establish the new note rate. The gross margin is stated in the loan document.

Initial rate: The below-market rate charged for the first adjustment period to attract borrowers (the "teaser rate").

Initial rate discount: The index value at the time of loan application plus the gross margin minus the initial note rate.

Life of loan cap: A ceiling that the note rate cannot exceed over the life of the loan.

Note rate: The rate that determines the amount of annual interest charged to the borrower. The note rate is also called the *accrual rate*, *contract rate*, or *coupon rate*.

Payment adjustment date: The date on which the borrower's monthly principal and interest payment may change.

Payment cap: A limit on the amount of increase in the borrower's monthly principal and interest at the payment adjustment date. This takes effect if the principal and interest increase called for by the interest rate increase exceeds the payment cap percentage. This limitation is often at the borrower's option and may result in negative amortization.

Payment rate: The rate at which the borrower repays the loan. This rate reflects buydowns or payment caps.

Periodic interest rate cap: A limit on the increase or decrease in the note rate at each rate adjustment, thereby limiting the borrower's payment increase or decrease at the time of adjustment.

Rate adjustment date: The date on which the borrower's note rate may change.

Subsidy buydown: Funds provided, usually by the builder or the seller, to sweeten a selling price by temporarily reducing the borrower's monthly principal and interest payment.

adjustable-rate mortgage (ARM)   (*hipoteca con tasa ajustable*)   *See* **adjustable-rate loan**.

adjusted basis   The original cost basis of a property reduced by certain deductions and increased by certain improvement costs. The original basis determined at the time of acquisition is reduced by the amount of allowable depreciation or depletion allowances taken by the taxpayer, and by the amount of any uncompensated property losses suffered by the taxpayer. It is then increased by the

A

cost of capital improvements plus certain carrying costs and assessments. The amount of gain or loss recognized by the taxpayer upon sale of the property is determined by subtracting the adjusted basis on the date of sale from the adjusted sales price. (*See* **basis, book value, capital gain, capital loss, depreciation [tax]**.)

adjustment interval   The frequency with which the interest rate and the monthly payment amount can be reset in an adjustable-rate mortgage loan. (See **adjustable-rate loan**.)

adjustments

1. In appraisal, the increases or decreases to the sales price of a comparable property to arrive at an indicated value for the property being appraised. Adjustments may be made for several reasons. The first adjustment is for seller concessions or conditions of sale; then for financing terms. Another is for time of sale if there has been a change in market conditions since the comparable sale. Adjustments are then made for location and dissimilarities between the physical characteristics of the subject and the comparable property. The indicated value is increased or decreased for each difference or dissimilarity. (*See* **appraisal, comparables, direct sales comparison approach**.)
2. In real estate closings, the credits and debits of a settlement statement, such as real property tax, insurance, and rent prorations. (*See* **closing [settlement]**.)

adjustment sheet   *See* **closing statement**.

admeasurement of dower   The determination and apportionment of shares. In the administration of an estate, the admeasurement of dower is an heir's judicial remedy when the widow has been assigned more than she was entitled to under her dower right. In valuing the widow's dower interest, standard annuity tables of mortality are used to ascertain the actuarial value of her future life interest, which is then applied to her proportionate share of the estate. (*See* **dower**.)

administrative law judge   In the United States, the administrative law judge (ALJ) is the presiding officer who conducts administrative hearings at which the parties present evidence. Usually, the ALJ can administer oaths and affirmations, issue subpoenas, rule on evidence presented, take depositions, regulate the course of the hearing, and make or recommend decisions. The ALJ's authority is essentially one of making recommendations.

administrative regulations   Regulations having the force and effect of law, issued by an administrative agency. The state's real estate commission often adopts regulations to complement the licensing law.

administrator

1. A person appointed by the court to settle the estate of a person who has died intestate (leaving no will). Sometimes called the *personal representative*. (*See* **executor, personal representative**.)
2. One who regulates securities.

ADS   *See* **Tax Reform Act of 1986**.

ad valorem   Latin for "according to valuation," usually referring to a type of tax or assessment. Real property tax is an ad valorem tax based on the assessed valuation of the property. Each property bears a tax burden proportionate to its value, as opposed to a specific tax per unit based on quantity, such as a tax per gallon of gasoline or package of cigarettes.

advance   To give consideration before it is due. Money is advanced by one party (such as a mortgagee or vendor) to cover carrying charges (such as taxes and insurance) on the property that were not properly paid by the other party in default. These amounts are credited to the account of the advancing party. For example, a second mortgagee might advance delinquent first-mortgage payments of the borrower in order to prevent a foreclosure of the secured property.

An important issue for lenders is whether a recorded mortgage securing future advances takes priority over a subsequent mortgage recorded before the date of the advance but subsequent to the recording of the first mortgage. Other advances include additional funds disbursed under an open-end mortgage or advances made by a construction lender to a developer-borrower. (*See* **additional charge mortgage**, **draw**.)

advance fee   A fee paid before any services are rendered. For example, a broker may obtain a nonrefundable fee from the seller in advance to cover the advertising of properties or businesses for sale while giving no guarantee that a buyer will be found. Brokers must keep accurate records of expenditures.

adverse financial change condition   A condition in a loan commitment entitling the lender to cancel the commitment if the borrower's financial circumstances suffer a materially adverse change, typically loss of job.

adverse possession   (*prescripción adquisitiva*)   The acquiring of title to real property owned by someone else by means of open, notorious, hostile, and continuous possession for a statutory period of time. The main purpose of adverse possession statutes is to ensure the fullest and most productive use of privately owned land. The burden to prove title is on the possessors, who must show that four conditions were met: (1) They have been in possession under a claim of right. (2) They were in actual, open, and notorious possession of the premises so as to constitute reasonable notice to the record owner. (3) Possession was both exclusive and hostile to the title of the owner (that is, without the owner's permission and evidencing an intention to maintain the claim of ownership against all who may contest it). (4) Possession was uninterrupted and continuous for at least the prescriptive period stipulated by state law. In this regard, successive occupation of the premises by persons who are successors in interest (that is, by privity of contract or descent) can be added together to meet the continuous-use requirement. For example, a father adversely occupies a certain parcel of land for four years. Upon his death, his son succeeds to his interest and "tacks on" to his father's four-year prior possession. Two words can serve as memory aids: *POACH* (possession is *o*pen, *a*ctual, *c*ontinuous, and *h*ostile); *CANOE* (possession is *c*ontinuous, *a*ctual, *n*otorious, *o*pen, and *e*xclusive).

The statutory period does not run against any individual under a legal disability (insanity) or until the individual has a legal cause of action to oust the possessor. For example, an adverse possessor could acquire title against a life tenant but not against the remainderman, who has no right to possession until the prior life estate is terminated.

Persons who claim title to property by adverse possession do not have readily marketable title until they obtain and record a judicial decree "quieting" the title or obtain a quitclaim deed from the ousted owner. When all requirements have been met, the owner's title is extinguished and a new title is created in favor of the adverse possessor. The effective date of the new title, as far as the original owner is concerned, is the first adverse entry. Thus, suits by the former owner based on trespass, profits, or rents during the adverse period are barred.

Most states do not require the claimant to have paid taxes on the property for any certain period of time (although in some states, a claimant's paying taxes may shorten the prescriptive period). However, a court might consider that failure to pay taxes is evidence that the claimant really did not claim ownership of the property.

The courts do not usually allow a claim of adverse possession if owner and claimant have a close family relationship, such as father and son or husband and wife, because in these cases, hostile claims are too difficult to prove. Cotenants normally cannot claim adverse possession against each other without an actual and clear ejectment of one cotenant by another.

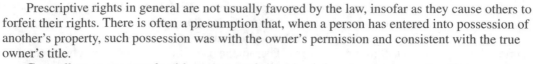

Prescriptive rights in general are not usually favored by the law, insofar as they cause others to forfeit their rights. There is often a presumption that, when a person has entered into possession of another's property, such possession was with the owner's permission and consistent with the true owner's title.

Generally, one cannot take title to state or federal lands by adverse possession. However, the federal Color of Title Act provides that a claimant who has met all four tests of adverse possession on public land may receive a patent to such land, provided that the land does not exceed 160 acres and that all taxes are paid. The United States, however, reserves the right to all coal and mineral rights to the property. In addition, title to Torrens-registered property usually cannot be taken by adverse possession. (*See* **color of title**, **open and notorious possession**, **prescription**, **quiet title action**, **trespass**.)

adverse use   The prescriptive acquisition of the right to a limited use of another's land; for example, a pathway easement across another's property. To acquire an easement by adverse use, the claimant must generally satisfy the same requirements as those for adverse possession, including the prescriptive period. Whereas most easements cannot be lost by mere nonuse, an easement created by adverse use can be terminated by nonuse for the prescriptive period of adverse possession. (*See* **easement by prescription**, **lost-grant doctrine**.)

advertising   The public promotion of one's products and services. In real estate, advertising is governed by various rules and regulations established by federal, state, local, and private authorities. Many of the same advertising rules apply when property is advertised on Web sites over the Internet.

A broker needs a client's written authorization to advertise a property, and in any offering the price quoted may not be other than that agreed on with the owner as the offering price. Many state license laws prohibit brokers from using blind ads—that is, advertisements placed on behalf of the seller that do not include the name of the licensed real estate broker. Salespeople may not advertise in their name alone. (*See* **blind ad**, **false advertising**.)

Three areas are key in terms of advertising real estate:

Condominiums and subdivisions: Many state condominium, time-sharing, and subdivision laws control advertising relating to condominium and subdivision sales. These laws require that ads contain no false or misleading statements and that no part of any material contained in a public report or public offering statement be used for advertising purposes unless the report is used in its entirety. In addition, some state agencies insist on reviewing all such ads before publication; other states have passed strict disclosure laws that apply to real estate advertising. In many states, a developer's right to advertise new projects may be restricted until certain state registration requirements have been met.

Discrimination: Federal regulations prohibit housing advertisements that discriminate on the basis of race, color, religion, sex, handicap/disability, familial status, or national origin. Some state and municipal regulations also include marital status, age, sexual preference, or source of income.

Truth in lending: Federal truth-in-lending law requires certain types of disclosure information if the ad includes specific financing terms or credit terms. (*See* **Truth in Lending Act**.)

aeolian soil   A type of soil that has been formed from windblown solid materials, such as sand dunes and volcanic ash deposits. Also, soil transported by the wind.

aesthetic value   In appraisal of residential property, an intangible benefit of property that is exceptionally attractive or pleasing, as opposed to purely utilitarian. Protecting the aesthetic value of features such as a hillside site overlooking the ocean, for example, by implementing a zoning ordinance, is a permissible exercise of the government's police power.

aesthetic zoning   *See* **zoning**.

affiant   Person making an affidavit.

affidavit   A sworn statement written down and made under oath before a notary public or other official authorized by law to administer an oath. The term literally means "has pledged one's faith." The affiant (person making the oath, sometimes called the "deponent") must swear before the notary that the facts contained in the affidavit are true and correct. An affidavit is a complete instrument within itself, whereas an acknowledgment is always part of, or an appendage to, another instrument. An affidavit is sworn to, but an acknowledgment is not.

   The purpose of an affidavit is to help establish or prove a fact, such as identity, age, residence, marital status, and occupancy of property.

   An example of a simple affidavit format is shown below. (*See* **affirmation, jurat, notary public**.)

STATE OF: SS:

COUNTY OF:

_____ being duly sworn, deposes and says

that (he) (she) is the _____ of _____,

the applicant named in the foregoing application, and that the statements made in the application are true and correct

to the best of (his) (her) knowledge and belief.

_____
                    (signature)
Subscribed and sworn to before me this
_____ day of _____, 20_____
Notary Public
My Commission Expires: _____

---

affidavit of title (affidavit of ownership)   A written statement made under oath by the seller or the grantor and acknowledged before a notary public in which the grantor (1) identifies herself and indicates marital status; (2) certifies that since the examination of title on the date of the contract there are no judgments, bankruptcies, or divorces against him or her, no unrecorded deeds or contracts, no repairs or improvements that have not been paid for, and no known defects in the title; and (3) certifies that the grantor is in possession of the premises. Customarily used in several states. (*See* **continuation**.)

affiliate licensee   The licensee who practices real estate under the guidance of a broker. Depending on state law, affiliate licensees may hold a license as a salesperson or a broker. Because the agency relationship is between the broker and the consumer, affiliate licensees may receive compensation for their real estate activities only from their employing broker, not directly from a consumer. (*See* **associate broker, broker, brokerage**.)

affirmation   A declaration as to the truth of a statement. An affirmation is used in lieu of an oath, especially when the affiant or deponent objects to taking an oath for personal or religious reasons. (*See* **affidavit**.)

A

affirmative marketing program   A voluntary proactive program designed by the U. S. Department of Housing and Urban Development (HUD) to inform all buyers, including those "least likely to apply," of homes for sale without discrimination and to provide real estate licensees with procedures and educational materials to assist in compliance with the law. Affirmative marketing requires no specific goals or quotas.

Local associations of REALTORS® can meet with HUD to discuss the National Fair Housing Partnership Resolution to ensure equal opportunity in housing for all. This approach emphasizes flexibility for local participation and community action programs. (*See* **discrimination**, **federal fair housing law**.)

affordability index   A standard established by the National Association of REALTORS® to gauge the financial ability of consumers to buy a home. On the index, 100 means that a family earning the national median income has exactly enough money to qualify for a mortgage on a median-priced home. Some economists maintain that every one-point increase in the home mortgage interest rate results in 300,000 fewer home sales.

affordable housing   Housing for individuals or families whose income is a certain percentage of or below the median for the area as determined by HUD and adjusted for family size. Affordable housing projects are usually developed in conjunction with governmental assistance and/or as a condition of a development agreement with the appropriate government authority.

The intent of affordable housing projects is to recognize the acute shortage of housing and to provide housing for persons otherwise unable to afford it. An affordable housing unit may be subject to certain conditions, restrictions, and requirements in respect of resale and occupancy requirements.

AFIDA   *See* **Agricultural Foreign Investment Disclosure Act (AFIDA)**.

A-frame construction   A type of residential construction in which the exterior design of the building resembles the letter *A*.

after-acquired   Acquired after a certain event takes place. An after-acquired title is obtained by a grantor of property *after* the grantor has attempted to convey good title. Upon the grantor's obtaining good title, it will automatically pass by operation of law to the grantee. For example, Smith conveyed his farm to Jones on January 1, 2004, by warranty deed. However, Smith did not have valid title on January 1 because he held title to the property under a forged deed. On March 5, 2005, Smith did receive good title under a properly executed deed, so Jones automatically acquired good title on March 5.

Note that an after-acquired title will not pass to a grantee under a quitclaim deed, because such an instrument only purports to transfer the grantor's current interest in the land, if any. (*See* **quitclaim deed**.)

Fixtures that are bought, paid for, and installed by the property owner-mortgagor are subject to the lien of the mortgage. In addition, many mortgages provide that all fixtures found on the property *after* the mortgage has been made are subject to the mortgage. The Uniform Commercial Code (UCC) has established guidelines to settle conflicting claims between mortgagees and chattel security claimants involving prior rights to after-acquired property, such as appliances bought on time and installed on the mortgaged premises. Under the UCC, a debtor can grant a superior security interest in such after-acquired property to a chattel mortgagee. (*See* **fixture**.)

after-tax income   In accounting, the amount left after deducting income tax liability from taxable income. The cash flow from an investment after deducting applicable taxes; also called *after-tax cash flow (ATCF)*.

age, effective   (*edad de vigencia*)   *See* **effective age**.

age-life depreciation   An appraisal method of computing depreciation based on the condition of a property and its economic life. Under this method, the estimated effective age (based on condition) is added to the estimated remaining economic life of the property. The effective age is then divided by that sum to indicate the total percentage of depreciation. Example: A house has an effective age of ten years and a remaining economic life of 40 years; thus, the depreciation is 20 percent (ten divided by 50).

agency   A relationship created when one person, the *principal*, delegates to another, the *agent*, the right to act on his behalf in business transactions and to exercise some degree of discretion while so acting. An agency gives rise to a fiduciary or statutory relationship and imposes on the agent, as the representative of the principal, certain duties, obligations, and high standards of good faith and loyalty.

A vast body of common and statutory law controls the rights and duties of principal and agent. In addition to this general law of agency, which applies to all business transactions, state real estate licensing laws directly affect the agency relationship among real estate licensees, their clients, and the public. Even though agency law is separate from contract law, the two frequently come together in interpreting relationships between real estate agents and their principals.

Note that the payment of consideration need not be involved in an agency relationship. One may gratuitously undertake to act as an agent and will be held to the standards of agency upon assumption of those duties. (*See* **consideration**.)

An agency may be a *general agency*, as when a principal gives a property manager the power to manage a real estate project on behalf of the principal on a continuing basis, or it may be a *special agency*, such as the standard listing contract wherein the broker is employed only to find a ready, willing, and able buyer and is neither authorized to sell the property nor to bind the principal to any contract for the sale of the property.

The creation of the agency relationship may be implied from the acts of the parties and does not depend on the existence of a written contract. For example, some states recognize an agency relationship between buyers and the agent with whom they are working, even without a written agreement. Once the agency relationship is created, certain rights and obligations attach to it, making the broker liable for any breaches of duty.

In the typical real estate transaction, the broker who represents the seller is called the *listing agent* (which includes the associate licensees working for the broker); the broker who works with the buyer is called the *selling agent* (or *cooperating broker* or *co-broker*) and is either the agent of the buyer or, less likely, the subagent of the seller. In some cases, the listing agent is the only broker involved. If the broker also represents the buyer, then the broker may become a *dual agent* or *limited agent*. In some states, this relationship defaults to *transaction brokerage*.

The real estate licensee is generally subject to two distinct areas of liability for breach of fiduciary duties to the principal: (1) The principal can bring civil action against the licensee-agent for money damages. (2) The state licensing authority can bring disciplinary proceedings for violation of its regulations. The state is very protective of the consumer in this area, for the principal is legally bound to the acts and representations of the agent done within the scope of authority.

Under common-law principles, the agent owes the principal personal performance, loyalty, obedience, disclosure of material facts (such as a proposed new school, highway relocation, or new zoning ordinance that would tend to increase the property value over the agreed-on listing price), reasonable care not to exceed the authority granted to the agent or not to misrepresent material facts to the principal or to third parties, proper accounting of all monies, and placement of the principal's interests above those of the persons dealing with the principal. Note that an agent has expanded authority in an emergency, including the right to disobey instructions when it is clearly in the best interests of the principal to do so.

Without the principal's authorization, an agent cannot disclose to a third party confidential information or information that hurts the principal's bargaining position. For example, the fact that the seller is forced to sell due to job loss, poor health, pending divorce, or that the seller will actually accept less than the listing price cannot be disclosed without authorization.

In most states, confidential information learned during the course of the agency cannot be used at a later date against the principal, even after the transaction is closed. This includes financial information used in negotiations involving subsequently listed properties.

Agents are required by law to provide their principals with all material and pertinent facts, but race, national origin, color, handicap/disability, religion, familial status, and sex are not material facts and should not be disclosed even at the principal's request.

Frequently, an agent may secure an offer to purchase from a buyer who agrees to list the buyer's own home with the same agent. A prudent broker will disclose this fact to the seller when submitting the offer; otherwise, the broker may be accused of receiving undisclosed profits.

Various state license laws require additional duties of the agent in a principal/agent relationship. For instance, an agent must disclose in writing any interest the agent may have in the property, such as when one of the salespeople or a relative or related corporation submits offers to purchase the listed property; for example, an agent must disclose that his wife was submitting an offer using her birth name. An agent may not act for both the seller and the buyer without their written consent, nor may the agent commingle the principal's money or other property with his own. A broker may not advertise property without the specific authorization of the owner. A broker must present all offers to his or her principal.

Most states have adopted agency disclosure laws requiring the licensee to disclose early in the transaction whom the licensee represents and to verify this disclosure in writing. States have also created new terms and definitions of working with consumers, such as "limited agent," "designated agent," "transaction coordinator," and "facilitator."

In dealing with third persons (for whom they are not the agent), agents must be honest and must exercise care and diligence because they are liable for any material misrepresentations or negligent acts made by the broker. Principals may also be vicariously liable to a third person for all acts that agents perform within the scope of their employment. Some states have statutorily removed liability back to the consumer (abrogated vicarious liability).

An agency may be terminated between a principal and an agent at any time, except if the agency is coupled with an interest. However, if the agency is terminated before the stated expiration date, there might be a claim for money damages. An agency is terminated by the death or incapacity of either party (notice of death is not necessary), destruction or condemnation of the property, expiration of the terms of the agency, mutual agreement, renunciation by the agent or revocation by the principal, bankruptcy of the principal (because the title of the property is transferred to a receiver), or completion of the agency. (*See* **agency by ratification, agency coupled with an interest, broker, buyer's broker, dual agency [limited agency], implied agency, listing, ostensible agency, respondeat superior, revocation, scope of authority, subagent, termination of listing, undisclosed agency**.)

agency by ratification   An agency created "after the fact" by a principal expressly or impliedly affirming the conduct of a party claiming to act as her agent. There must be some proof that the principal was aware of the act or acts and either accepted the benefits or elected to be bound by the agent's conduct. (*See* **agency**.)

agency coupled with an interest   An agency relationship in which the agent acquires an estate or interest in the subject of the agency (the property). Such an agency cannot be revoked by the principal, nor is it terminated upon the death of the principal. For example, a broker may supply the financing for a condominium development, provided the developer agrees to give the broker an exclusive listing to sell the furnished condominium units. The developer would not be able to revoke the listing after the broker had provided the financing. (*See* **agency**.)

agent   One authorized to represent and to act on behalf of another person (called the *principal*). Unlike an employee, who merely works for a principal, an agent works in the place of a principal. The main difference between an agent and an employee is that agent may bind the principal by contract, if within the scope of authority, whereas an employee may not unless given express authorization.

A real estate broker is the agent of the client (seller or buyer) to whom she owes a fiduciary or statutory obligation. A salesperson, on the other hand, is the agent of his broker and does not have a direct personal contractual relationship with either the seller or the buyer. This fact is relevant when a salesperson decides to change firms and becomes upset when the broker won't let the salesperson take his listings.

Note that minors cannot appoint an agent to execute their contracts, but an adult may designate a minor to act as an agent. (*See* **agency, broker, buyer's broker, dual agency [limited agency], fiduciary, general agent, independent contractor, scope of authority, special agent, subagent**.)

aggrieved   Having suffered loss or injury from infringement or denial of rights. The term also refers to an injured party or a person who has lost some personal or property rights or has had a prejudicial obligation or burden imposed on her.

agreed boundaries   A doctrine affecting rights of ownership to boundaries. Where there is uncertainty as to the location of the true boundary line between adjoining parcels of land, the landowners can mutually agree and establish a boundary line. If the parties act in conformity with the agreed boundary, then the doctrine of agreed boundaries holds that line to be the legal boundary between the properties.

agreement of sale   Terms that transfer ownership from one owner to another. In real estate, the agreement of sale (purchase agreement) includes agreements about price, timing, and interests.

In a few states, an agreement of sale refers to a land contract or contract for deed. (*See* **contract for deed, contract of sale, land contract**.)

Agricultural Foreign Investment Disclosure Act (AFIDA)   A 1978 federal law requiring foreign persons who have an interest in U.S. agricultural land of more than one acre to file disclosure information with the secretary of agriculture.

agricultural lien   A statutory lien advanced to a farmer to secure money or supplies for raising a crop. The lien attaches only to the crop, not to the land. (*See* **lien**.)

AIDS   *See* **acquired immunodeficiency syndrome (AIDS)**.

AIREA   *See* **American Institute of Real Estate Appraisers**.

air park   A tract of land that adjoins or is part of an airport and is improved with commercial, industrial, and office space.

airport zoning   Regulations that aim to eliminate potential hazards to aircraft (including electronic interference) by governing land uses, building height, and natural growth in the areas surrounding an airport. (*See* **zoning**.)

air rights   (*derechos aéreos*)   Rights to the use of the open space or vertical plane above a property. Ownership of land includes the right to all air above the property. Until the advent of the airplane, this right was unlimited, but now the courts permit reasonable interference with one's air rights, such as is necessary for aircraft, so long as the owner's right to use and occupy the land is not lessened. Thus, low-flying aircraft might be unreasonably trespassing, and their owners would be liable for any

A

damages. Governments and airport authorities often purchase air rights adjacent to an airport, called an *avigation easement*, to provide glide patterns for air traffic. (*See* **avigation easement, trespass**.)

The air itself is not real property; airspace, however, is real property when described in three dimensions with reference to a specific parcel of land, as in a condominium unit. (*See* **real property**.)

A Maryland case has decided that separate owners of the land and the air rights may be separately assessed for tax purposes. Air rights may be sold or leased and buildings constructed thereon, as was done with the Pan Am Building constructed above Grand Central Station in New York City.

Air rights may also be transferred by way of easements, such as those used in constructing elevated highways or in acquiring scenic easements or easements of light and air. Because of the scarcity of land, many developers are examining the possibilities for developing properties in the airspace above prime properties owned by schools, churches, railways, and cemeteries. (*See* **easement**.)

air space
1. Any area between two surfaces, such as the space between two panes of glass for effective insulation
2. In condominium ownership, what is actually owned by the unit owner (in addition to tenancy in common for the common areas). Generally, this includes wall-to-wall and floor-to-floor.

ALC   *See* **Accredited Land Consultant (ALC)**.

ALDA   *See* **American Land Development Association (ALDA)**.

aleatory contract   A contract that depends on a contingency or uncertain event, such as a fire insurance contract or a lottery agreement. (*See* **contract**.)

alien   A person born outside the jurisdiction of the United States who has not been naturalized under the Constitution and U.S. laws and is not a citizen of the United States. In most states, aliens are allowed to acquire and hold an interest in land, although some states do limit the ability of businesses and nonresident aliens to purchase and hold property. Some of the forms of restraint are limitations on the amount of holdings, restricted use for agricultural or industrial purposes, and identification requirements.

Under the Foreign Investment Real Property Tax Act (FIRPTA), the buyer of real property from a nonresident alien must withhold up to 10 percent of the sales price and direct that money to the U.S. Treasury to be used to offset any tax liability of the alien. (*See* **Agricultural Foreign Investment Disclosure Act [AFIDA], Foreign Investment in Real Property Tax Act [FIRPTA]**.)

alienation   (*enajenación*)   The act of transferring ownership, title, or an interest or estate in real property from one person to another. Property is usually sold or conveyed by voluntary alienation, as with a deed or an assignment of lease. Involuntary alienation takes place when property is sold against the owner's will, as in a foreclosure sale or a tax sale. Unreasonable restraints on alienation may be held void. (*See* **deed, due-on-sale clause, foreclosure, restraint on alienation, title**.)

alienation clause   (*cláusula de enajenación*)   A provision sometimes found in a promissory note or mortgage that provides that the balance of the secured debt becomes immediately due and payable at the option of the mortgagee upon the alienation of the property by the mortgagor. Alienation is usually broadly defined to include any transfer of ownership, title, or an interest or estate in real property, including a sale by way of a contract for deed. Also called a **due-on-sale clause**. (*See* **acceleration clause, assignment, due-on-sale clause**.)

aliquot   A fractional section ownership used in U.S. public land states. The aliquot specifies the specific parcel within the section, township, and range. Aliquot descriptions are popular in Alaska.

all-inclusive deed of trust   A purchase-money deed of trust subordinate to, but still including, the original encumbrance or encumbrances. It is similar to a wraparound mortgage, except that a deed of trust is used rather than a mortgage. (*See* **wraparound mortgage.**)

allocation method   (*método de asignación*)   *See* **abstraction**.

allodial system   (*sistema alodial*)   An estate holding the potential of existing indefinitely, with free and full ownership of rights in land by individuals, which is the basis of real property law in the United States. By contrast, under the feudal system, ownership of land was vested in the king or sovereign who then allotted select land to his noblemen, chiefs, and others. Such allotments were revocable and represented only the right to use the land. (*See* **real property**.)

allonge   A piece of paper annexed to a promissory note for the purpose of writing endorsements; sometimes used when notes are assigned to an investor.

allotment   The funds allocated for the purchase of mortgages within a specified time by a permanent investor with whom a mortgage loan originator has a relationship but not a specific contract in the form of a commitment. The allotment may state the investor's requirements as to processing, loan terms, and/or underwriting standards. (*See* **secondary mortgage market**.)

all-risks policy   Previously, a term used to describe a homeowner's insurance policy. The policy never covered *all* risks, and the industry now uses the term *Special Form.* The HO-3 homeowners' policy is a special form coverage on the dwelling and named peril on the contents.

alluvion   The material that constitutes the increase of soil on a shore or riverbank, added by the process of accretion. Also called *alluvium* or *alluvial deposits*, it is the fine material, such as sand or mud, carried by water and deposited on land. The words **alluvion** and **accretion** are sometimes mistakenly used synonymously. (*See* **accretion**, **erosion**.)

alluvium   *See* **alluvion**.

ALTA   *See* **American Land Title Association (ALTA)** in Appendix A.

alternative depreciation system (ADS)   *See* **Tax Reform Act of 1986**.

alternative mortgage instrument   A type of mortgage that differs from the standard fixed mortgage in the interest, repayment terms, or the periodic payments. Some examples are the variable-rate mortgage, graduated-payment mortgage, renegotiable-rate mortgage, the adjustable-rate loan, the pledged account mortgage, the reverse annuity mortgage, and the shared appreciation mortgage.

ambient air   Any unconfined portion of the atmosphere; the outside air. Federal clean air laws set standards for ambient air.

amenities   Features, both tangible and intangible, that enhance and add to the value or desirability of real estate. In a condominium community, for example, common amenities include a swimming pool, clubhouse, and a good view. (*See* **intrinsic value**, **value**.)

American Institute of Real Estate Appraisers (AIREA)   *See* Appendix A.

American Land Development Association (ALDA)   *See* Appendix A.

American Land Title Association (ALTA)   *See* Appendix A.

American National Standards Institute (ANSI)   *See* Appendix A.

American Society for Industrial Security   *See* Appendix A.

American Society of Appraisers (ASA)   *See* Appendix A.

American Society of Farm Managers and Rural Appraisers   *See* Appendix A.

American Society of Home Inspectors (ASHI)   *See* Appendix A.

A

American Society of Real Estate Counselors (ASREC)   *See* Appendix A.

Americans with Disabilities Act (ADA)   (*Ley sobre los estadounidenses incapacitados*)   A federal law, effective in 1992, designed to eliminate discrimination against individuals with disabilities by mandating equal access to jobs, public accommodations, government services, public transportation, and telecommunications.

ADA prohibits discrimination due to a disability in the full and equal enjoyment of goods and services provided by a place of "public accommodation," including hotels, shopping centers, and professional offices, and applies to private entities that own, lease, or operate virtually all commercial facilities. Exempted are private clubs and religious organizations.

ADA prohibits employers from discriminating against qualified individuals with disabilities (for example, a physical or mental impairment that substantially limits one or more major life activities). This proscription also includes persons thought to have an impairment, such as disfiguration due to an accident. Employers of a minimum number of employees must make reasonable accommodations to the job or work environment so as to enable a qualified person with a disability to perform the functions of that employment position. Examples include schedule modifications, special equipment, reserved accessible parking spaces, and access to rest rooms.

Specific requirements include removal of architectural and communication barriers (if such removal is "readily achievable") in existing privately owned places of public accommodation.

Legal remedies include private civil action to obtain corrective action in providing auxiliary aids or facility alteration. ADA encourages the use of alternative dispute resolution including settlement, mediation, and arbitration. Courts may assess a civil penalty against an entity found to be in noncompliance with the act. Fines are assessed in an amount not exceeding $55,000 for a first violation and in an amount not exceeding $110,000 for any subsequent violation.

Real estate brokers, salespersons, and appraisers need to evaluate the possible application of ADA to their practice. In particular, brokers and salespersons should alert their commercial real estate and investor clients to the existence of ADA, to the need to have leases reviewed by knowledgeable counsel, and to the advisability of having offices inspected by a knowledgeable architect to ascertain whether they are ADA-compliant. Because of the potential liability to fee appraisers under ADA, real estate appraisers may need to insert a limiting condition in their appraisal reports. (*See* **disability**.)

amicus curiae   Latin for "friend of the court." Amici curiae who are not parties to a lawsuit but are interested in the outcome may be permitted to file legal briefs (called *amicus curiae briefs*) with the court.

AMO   *See* **Accredited Management Organization (AMO).**

amortization   (*amortización*)   Self-liquidating (literally, "killing-off"). The gradual repayment or retiring of a debt by means of systematic payments of principal and/or interest over a set period, so that a zero balance remains at the end of the period. The principal is thus directly reduced or amortized over the life of the loan (hence the term *direct reduction loan*).

Before the many realty foreclosures during the 1930s depression, most mortgages were straight loans payable at interest only for five years, with the entire principal due at maturity. Savings and loan associations were the leaders in introducing amortized loans for residences. The standards set by the Federal Housing Administration were also influential in switching to the long-term amortized loan.

Most pre-1980 mortgages are fully amortized (i.e., self-liquidating) and are paid in equal monthly installments, which include interest and amortization of principal. The interest is set at a predetermined percentage rate and is charged only on the unpaid balance. As the payments are made, the amount allocated to interest decreases while that applied to reduction of principal increases.

Example: Mr. Shaw obtains a new mortgage of $100,000, amortized over a 30-year period at 4 percent interest. Based on amortization tables, the monthly mortgage payment is $4,77.42. If Shaw continues to make this monthly payment for 30 years, at the end of that period, the mortgage will have been repaid in full, including interest. At the beginning of the loan period, the monthly payment will go primarily to the payment of interest, with only a small amount going toward the principal. The first monthly payment on his $100,000 loan includes $333.33 of interest and $144.08 of principal. As the principal amount is reduced, the interest is calculated on a progressively lower amount, the monthly payment of interest decreases, and the balance credited toward principal increases. After 228 monthly payments (19 years), the loan balance has been reduced to $50,915. The interest payment will be only $170.74, while the principal payment will have increased to $306.68. At the end of 30 years, Shaw will have paid a total of $171,869.51 to pay back his original $100,000 loan.

An *extended-term amortized loan*, or *balloon mortgage*, is often used in contracts for deed and in commercial and industrial real estate loans with very stable and secure tenants. The amortized payments are based on a payment schedule that is longer than the actual term of the loan. (*See* **balloon payment.**)

Due to the effects of inflation and deregulation, most lenders in the 1980s used alternative mortgage instruments to avoid getting locked into fixed-rate amortized loans for long periods. (*See* **alternative mortgage instrument, negative amortization.**)

amortization schedule   A table showing the amounts of principal and interest due at regular intervals and the unpaid balance of the loan after each payment is made. An example of a 9 percent amortization table used for a second mortgage is shown here. (*See* **constant.**)

Monthly Amortized Payments (P&I)
Term (Years)

Amount	5	10	15	20	25	30	35
$90,000	$1,657.49	$911.21	$665.75	$545.38	$475.05	$429.67	$398.50
$100,000	$1,841.65	$1,012.45	$739.69	$605.98	$527.84	$477.42	$442.77
$110,000	$2,025.82	$1,113.70	$813.66	$666.58	$580.62	$525.16	$487.05

anaconda mortgage   A mortgage containing a clause, sometimes called a *dragnet clause* or *Mother Hubbard clause*, stating that the mortgage secures all debts of the mortgagor that shall at any time be due and owing to the mortgagee. Because the mortgagee could acquire all mortgagor debts at substantial discounts and then enforce them by threat of foreclosure, the courts regard such clauses with disfavor. The unsuspecting debtor becomes "enwrapped in the folds of indebtedness"—thus the name *anaconda*.

Most courts require some relationship between the two debts as well as some specific reference in the second loan agreement to the earlier anaconda clause. Also, if the second debt is secured by its own collateral, the anaconda clause usually will not apply. (*See* **additional charge mortgage, mortgage.**)

ancestor   A person from whom one lineally descends (such as a father or grandmother) and from whom land is lawfully inherited. Under some state discrimination laws, it is unlawful to discriminate on the grounds of a person's ancestry. Under the federal fair housing law, it is unlawful to discriminate on the basis of a person's national origin. (*See* **collateral heirs, descent.**)

anchor bolt   A bolt that secures the sill of the house to the foundation wall.

A

anchor tenant   A major department or chain store strategically located at a shopping center so as to give maximum exposure to smaller, satellite stores. An anchor tenant is called a *magnet store* or a *traffic generator*. In the typical strip shopping center, two anchor stores, such as a supermarket and a large drugstore, are located at opposite ends of a mall, with smaller stores in between. This helps to generate maximum sales volume in the entire shopping center. This strategy is important to the lessor because most commercial lease rents are based on a percentage of gross sales.

In recent years, the Federal Trade Commission has sought to limit the powers of the anchor tenant in controlling the selection of satellite tenants and their merchandise. (*See* **percentage lease**, **shopping center**.)

ancient lights doctrine   This legal principle of early English common law prevented an adjoining owner from construction that would block off the light admitted into a neighbor's window. This ancient lights principle has not been accepted by modern U.S. courts, although the courts are starting to refer to it as they develop new laws regarding solar easements.

angle   A measure of rotation around a point, generally used in surveys to show the relationship of one line to another. Usually, angles are measured in a clockwise direction and in degrees—360 degrees to a full circle or one full rotation back to the point of beginning. Each degree is broken down into 60 minutes, and each minute into 60 seconds. For example, the direction of a line may be written as North 42° 20' 15" *easterly*. This line would be located using north as the line of reference and measuring an angle 40 degrees, 20 minutes, and 15 seconds clockwise from north to east.

Reference lines can be north or south. Angles can be east or west of the reference line. (*See* **azimuth, degree**.)

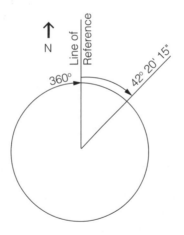

annexation   An addition to property by the act of joining or uniting one thing to another, as in attaching personal property to real property and thereby creating a fixture. For example, a sink becomes a fixture when it is annexed to the plumbing outlet. (*See* **fixture**.)

annual constant   *See* **constant**.

annual debt service   The amount of money required on an annual basis for payment of interest and principal on all security interests on the real property (for example, mortgages, deeds of trust, and contracts for deed); also called *debt service coverage*.

Note that many real estate lenders are more concerned with the ratio between net operating income and annual debt service than they are with the loan-to-value ratio. (*See* **amortization, constant, loan-to-value [LTV] ratio, qualification**.)

annual exclusion for gift tax   An amount of gift income that the donor may exclude from gift taxation. In 2012, each person is entitled to an annual gift tax exclusion of $13,000 per donee. Thus, a mother could make six $13,000 gifts to six different children in one year (a total of $78,000), no part of which would be subject to the gift tax. She could repeat the process every year. Her husband could give an additional $13,000 per donee per year. (*See* **gift tax**.)

annual meeting   A yearly meeting of shareholders of a corporation or members of an association held for the purpose of permitting them to vote on the election of directors and various other matters of corporate or association business. Absent shareholders may vote by proxy.

A condominium association or cooperative society usually has an annual meeting in addition to special meetings throughout the year. (*See* **proxy**.)

annual mortgagor statement   A report by the lender or servicing agent to the mortgagor detailing what taxes and interest were paid during the year and how much principal balance remains.

annual percentage rate (APR)   An expression of the relationship of the total finance charge to the total amount to be financed as required under the federal Truth in Lending Act. Tables available from any Federal Reserve banks may be used to compute the rate, which must be calculated to the nearest one-eighth of 1 percent. Use of the APR permits a standard expression of credit costs, which facilitates easy comparison of lenders. (The act permits use of the abbreviation *APR*.) (*See* **interest**, **Truth in Lending Act**.)

annual report   A statement of the financial status and progress of a corporation during its previous fiscal year, usually containing a balance sheet, operating statement and auditor's report. It is presented to the corporate stockholders before the annual stockholders' meeting. If a security is registered with the Securities and Exchange Commission (SEC), an SEC annual report must be filed.

annuity   A sum of money received by the annuitant at fixed intervals as one of a series of periodic payments. Real property is sometimes traded or exchanged for a private annuity. The distinguishing characteristic of an annuity transaction is that the annuitant has an interest only in the payments themselves, not in any principal fund or source from which they may be derived. The buyer pays for the property by guaranteeing a monthly income to the seller for the seller's remaining life. The payments are determined by reference to standard annuity tables. Properly structured, a private annuity transaction involving the transfer of realty to another member of an annuitant's family can produce savings in estate, income, and gift taxes.

The proper use of annuity tables, such as the Inwood tables, provides a factor to be multiplied by the desired yearly income to estimate the present worth of an investment (what amount the investor should pay to acquire the property).

antenuptial agreement   A contract entered into by two people contemplating marriage for the purpose of settling the property rights of both in advance, also called a *prenuptial* ("*prenup*"). It is advisable for each person to have his own legal counsel to negotiate such a contract. The enforceability of an antenuptial (or prenuptial) agreement may depend on the completeness of disclosure and the existence of independent counsel for each party. (*See* **jointure**.)

antiassignment clause   *See* **assignment**.

antichurning provisions   *See* **churning**.

anticipatory breach   A declaration of intention not to perform made by a buyer or a seller through words or acts prior to closing. At that time, the other party, not being in default, is entitled to enforce the contract in court without first having to offer or tender performance. (*See* **contract**, **contract of sale**, **tender**.)

antideficiency legislation   *See* **deficiency judgment**.

A

antidiscrimination laws   *See* **discrimination, federal fair housing law.**

antifraud provisions   The provisions in federal and state securities laws that make it unlawful for any person, in connection with the offer, sale, or purchase of any security, to directly or indirectly employ any device, scheme, or artifice to defraud; to make any untrue statement of a material fact or to omit a material fact, which omission makes a statement misleading; or to engage in any act, practice, or course of business that operates or would operate as a fraud or deceit upon any person.

 The federal antifraud provisions are covered under Rule 10-B5 of the Securities Exchange Act of 1934 and come into play when there is minimal contact with interstate commerce in the offer of the security, such as when the U.S. mail is used. Note that, even though the offer of a security may be exempt from the registration requirement under the private offering exemption, the intrastate offering exemption, or the Regulation A exemption of the federal laws, the offer is still subject to the anti-fraud provisions of the Securities Exchange Act of 1934 and the licensing requirements.

 Purchasers of securities who are injured by any violation of the antifraud provision may sue for rescission of the contract and recover the amount paid for the security plus interest from the date the security was purchased. (*See* **intrastate exemption, private offering, Regulation A, rescission, Rule 10-B5, security.**)

antitrust laws   (*leyes antimonopolios*)   State and federal laws designed to maintain and preserve business competition.

 Antitrust situations include price-fixing, certain types of boycotts, allocation of customers or markets, restrictions on competition in shopping center leases, and certain restraints placed on franchisees by franchisors. Also challenged are certain "tie-in" arrangements, as when a developer conditions a sale by insisting that the buyer promise to list the property with the developer if the buyer wishes to resell, or when a property manager attempts to force a client's commitment to list with the manager in the event of sale.

 Certain real estate brokerage activities have come under public scrutiny by the Federal Trade Commission and the Department of Justice. These activities include the fixing of general commission rates by local boards or groups of brokers and the exclusion of brokers from membership in local boards or in multiple-listing arrangements due to unreasonable membership requirements. As a result of court cases, local real estate boards no longer directly or indirectly influence fixed commission rates or commission splits between cooperating brokers. Moreover, in some states, clients must be specifically informed that the commission rates are negotiable between client and broker. (*See* **Clayton Antitrust Act, Sherman Antitrust Act.**)

apartment building   A building having separate units for permanent tenants who rent or lease them. The owner of the building provides common facilities, such as lights, heat, elevator, and garbage disposal services, and maintains common entrances and hallways.

apostille   A certificate issued by an authority appointed for such purpose by a foreign nation. The apostille takes the place of diplomatic or consular acknowledgment of a document pursuant to the Hague "Convention Abolishing the Requirement for the Legislation for Foreign Public Documents." (*See* **acknowledgment.**)

appeal   (*apelación*)
1. The process under law of taking a case decision to a higher court to seek review, reversal, or retrial of the case. The party making the appeal is the *appellant*; the other party is the *appellee*.
2. The legal process by which a property owner may challenge a property tax assessment. In most states, the opportunity to do so is very strictly limited.

appointments   Furnishings, fixtures, or equipment found in a home, office, or other building. These items may either enhance or detract from the intrinsic value of the property.

apportionment
1. The division or partition of property into proportionate (though not necessarily equal) parts. For example, tenants in common might seek partition of a property.
2. The pro rata division of real estate carrying charges between buyer and seller at closing. (*See* **carrying charges, prorate**.)

appraisal   *(avalúo)*   The process of developing and communicating an opinion about a property's value. An appraisal is usually required when real property is sold, financed, condemned, taxed, insured, or partitioned. Note that an appraisal is an estimate, not a determination, of value. An appraisal may be in the form of a lengthy written report, a completed preprinted form, a simple letter, or even an oral report.

Three approaches are used to estimate market value of a property: the direct sales comparison approach, the cost approach, and the income approach.

The *direct sales comparison approach* is a comparative analysis of recent sales prices of similar properties, after adjusting for seller concessions, time, financing, and any differences in the properties. This approach, formerly called the *market-data approach*, is used most frequently by real estate brokers in the valuation of residences and is the approach usually preferred in court.

The *cost approach* is an estimated value based on the reproduction or replacement cost of the improvements, less depreciation, plus the value of the land (land value being usually determined by the direct sales comparison approach). The cost approach is most useful in appraising new or proposed construction, as well as service properties such as churches and post offices. (*See* **depreciation [appraisal]**.)

The *income approach* is an estimated value based on the capitalization of net operating income from a property at an acceptable market rate. Often referred to as the *income capitalization approach*, it is most useful in appraising investment properties such as apartment buildings, office buildings, and shopping centers.

In most appraisals, the appraiser reconciles (correlates) the indication of value by each of the three approaches. The appraiser considers the definition of value, the purpose of the appraisal, the type of property and the adequacy of the compiled data to determine the relative weight (if any) to be given to each approach in reaching a final estimate of value. Moreover, in that each method is based on data obtained from the market, the three approaches serve as checks on each other.

When an independent appraisal is necessary, most lending institutions require the services of a state-licensed or state-certified appraiser and that the appraisals conform to the *Uniform Standards of Professional Appraisal Practice*. (*See* **appraiser, before-and-after method, concession, cost approach, direct sales comparison approach, engineering breakdown method, income approach**.)

Appraisal Foundation, The   *See* Appendix A.

Appraisal Institute   *See* Appendix A.

Appraisal Institute of Canada   *See* Appendix A.

appraisal report   A report that contains the definition of value to be applied; the estimate and effective date of the valuation; the appraiser's signature and certifications, along with any limiting conditions; description of the property and rights being appraised; general and specific data; sufficient justification to support the value estimate; consideration of each of the three approaches; and the reconciliation. It is common for the report to include such supporting documentation as maps, floor plans, and photos.

appraiser (*valuador, tasador*)   One who estimates value. Not only must appraisers possess the necessary qualifications, ability, education, and experience to conduct an appraisal of real or personal property, they must be state-certified or state-licensed to appraise property that involves a federally insured or regulated agency.

    Appraisers may be independent contractors or employed by the government, lending institutions, or trust companies. An appraiser's fees are typically based on time and expenses; fees are never based on a percentage of the appraised value.

    While mathematics is a helpful tool in making an appraisal, the final opinion of value is based primarily on the experience and training of the particular appraiser.

appraiser independence requirements (AIR)   Established standards that provide protections for mortgage investors, homebuyers, and the housing market by ensuring that appraisals are conducted without pressure from lenders and real estate agents to manipulate property values. Required by Subtitle F of the Dodd-Frank Act, the standards were developed by Fannie Mae, the Federal Housing Finance Agency (FHFA), Freddie Mac, and key industry participants to replace the Home Valuation Code of Conduct (HVCC). The standards apply to all loans of one-to-four unit properties, except for loans that are insured or guaranteed by a federal agency, such as FHA and VA loans. At a minimum, the appraiser must be licensed or certified by the state in which the property is located. Lenders may order appraisals directly from an individual appraiser and not go through an appraisal management company.

appreciation   A temporary or permanent increase in the worth or value of property due to economic causes; the opposite of depreciation.

appropriation
1. The act of selecting or setting apart land for a particular public use or purpose, such as a public park or school; also called *dedication*. (*See* **dedication**.)
2. The taking of a *public thing* for a *private use* (the opposite of condemnation), as in the taking of water from a natural stream for private use, which in some states is sufficient to establish a prior right against other owners to the continued use of that water. (*See* **eminent domain**.)
3. Legislatively designating funds for a public project.

appropriative water right   *See* **correlative water right**.

appurtenance   That, which belongs to something, but not for all time; all those rights, privileges, and improvements that belong to and pass with the transfer of property but are not necessarily a part of the actual property. Appurtenances to real property pass with the real property to which they are appurtenant unless a contrary intention is manifested. A deed normally describes the property granted and then states, "together with all appurtenances." Typical appurtenances are rights-of-way, easements, water rights, condominium parking stalls, and property improvements. (*See* **run with the land**.)

appurtenant   Belonging to; adjunctive; appended; or annexed to. For example, the garage is appurtenant to the house, and the common interest in the common elements of a condominium is appurtenant to each apartment. Appurtenant items run with the land when the property is transferred. (*See* **limited common elements**.)

ARA   *See* **Accredited Rural Appraiser (ARA)**.

arbitrage
1. The spread, or difference, between interest rates; a common item in all-inclusive or wrap-around mortgage financing. Example: Joe Smith sells his parcel to Mary Jones for $10,000 by way of a purchase-money mortgage at 12 percent. Mary Jones then sells the parcel to

Susan Brown under a wraparound mortgage at 12.5 percent. Mary Jones uses the monthly payments to pay her debt to Mr. Smith, and the 0.5 percent arbitrage is considered income to Mary Jones. (*See* **wraparound mortgage**.)

2. The simultaneous purchase and sale of mortgages or mortgage-backed securities in different markets to profit from price differentials. (*See* **secondary mortgage market**.)

arbitration   (*arbitraje*)   The nonjudicial submission of a controversy to selected third parties for their determination in a manner provided by agreement or by law. Disputes between listing REALTORS® and cooperating REALTORS® are often settled by arbitration, with both parties agreeing to comply with the final decision of the arbitrator.

Many disputes are settled according to detailed rules established by the American Arbitration Association. (*See* Appendix A.) The prime feature of a binding arbitration is that it is fast and final, as well as the fact that the findings remain "private." (*See* **mediation**.)

arcade   (*galería*)
1. A series of open or closed arches on the same plane.
2. A walkway or passageway with an arched roof, frequently with shops along one or both sides.
3. A passageway open on the street side, usually colonnaded.
4. A colonnaded sidewalk.

architectural drawings   Data prepared or assembled by an architect that form part of a proposal or part of contract documents. The data may include plot plans, floor plans, elevations, or sections; usually, however, they do not include mechanical, electrical, or structural plans or other specialized data furnished by consultants to the architect. (*See* **working drawings**.)

architecture
1. The science and art of structural design.
2. The style in which a building is designed and built.

are   One hundred square meters. (*See* **hectare**.)

area   (*área*)   A parcel of land assumed to be level and at sea level. These assumptions are used to obtain consistent descriptions of land. Thus, the land surface of a ten-acre sloping parcel actually contains more usable square feet than a ten-acre level parcel, although the legal descriptions of both parcels are the same. (*See* **legal description**.)

The area of a house includes through the outside walls to the main flat surface of exterior brick or wood siding and to the least thickness of shakes and shingles. The total living area often includes stairways, porches, utility rooms, common walls, servants' quarters, and garage apartments that are separate units.

area management broker (AMB)   Property managers who work directly for the Federal Housing Administration in the field of subsidized housing. Their principal duties include taking over the property, preparing repair specifications, soliciting repair bids from contractors, coordinating and inspecting repair work, supervising maintenance and security, and submitting financial reports.

area regulations   The part of the zoning and building ordinances that regulates the positioning of improvements on the land, such as setbacks for the rear and sidelines.

ARELLO   *See* **Association of Real Estate License Law Officials (ARELLO)** in Appendix A.

ARM   *See* **Accredited Resident Manager, adjustable-rate loan**.

arm's-length transaction   (*transacción donde se guarda distancia*)   A transaction in which the parties are dealing from equal bargaining positions. Parties are said to deal "at arm's length" when each stands on the strict letter of her rights and conducts the business in a formal manner without

A

trusting the other's fairness or integrity and without being subject to the other's control or dominant influence (as is sometimes the case in transactions between family members). The absence of an arm's-length transaction may give rise to tax consequences when property is transferred at less than fair market value. Whether a transaction was at arm's length is also relevant to the "willing-buyer, willing-seller" concept in the estimation of market value.

arranger of credit   As defined under the federal Truth in Lending Act, a person who regularly arranges for the extension of consumer credit by another person if a finance charge will be imposed, if there are to be more than four installments, and if the person extending the credit is not a creditor. At present, the term does not include a real estate broker who arranges seller financing of a dwelling or real property.

arrears
1. The state of being delinquent in paying a debt.
2. At or after the end of the period for which expenses are due or levied; the opposite of *in advance*. Mortgage interest and real estate taxes are often paid in arrears.

artesian well   A hole dug deeply into the ground so that the internal pressure forces the water to the surface.

articles of agreement for deed   *See* **contract for deed**.

articles of association   *See* **articles of incorporation**.

articles of incorporation   The document that sets forth the purposes, powers, and basic rules of operation for a corporation. Also called articles of association. (*See* **bylaws**, **corporation**.)

asbestos   (*asbesto*)   A mineral fiber found in rocks. Asbestos fibers are fire resistant and not easily destroyed or degraded by natural processes. Asbestos has been used in a wide variety of household products, such as appliances, ceilings, wall and pipe coverings, floor tiles, roofing, and siding materials. The Environmental Protection Agency (EPA) reports that, according to studies of workers and others exposed to asbestos, the fiber has been found to cause lung and stomach cancer. Real estate salespeople, especially those in commercial sales, must reveal to the prospective buyer the known presence of asbestos on the property. Removal or containment of asbestos usually requires the use of specially licensed asbestos abatement contractors. (*See* **abatement**, **asbestos-containing materials [ACMs]**.)

asbestos-containing materials (ACMs)   A combination of asbestos and other materials; ACMs are either nonfriable (sheathed and/or crumbling) or friable, easily crumbled by hand pressure. Friable ACM is generally considered more dangerous because the asbestos particles can be loosened and become airborne.

as-built drawings   Architectural drawings showing the precise method of construction and the location for the installation of equipment and utility lines. As-built drawings are usually prepared by an architect with the cooperation of the general contractor to the project.

ash dump   A container under a fireplace where ashes are temporarily deposited. Ashes can be removed later through a cleanout door.

"as is"   Words in a contract intended to signify that the seller offers the property in its present condition, with no modifications or improvement, and is usually intended to be a disclaimer of warranties or representations. The recent trend in the courts is to favor consumers by preventing sellers from using as-is wording in a contract to shield themselves from possible fraud charges brought on by neglecting to disclose known material defects in the property.

   Even though an as-is clause may give some protection to the seller from unknown defects, the clause is inoperative when the seller actively misrepresents the condition of the property. It does not shield the seller who fails to disclose a readily observable defect, basically saying, "You take it as you see it." The idea is that the buyer takes the visible condition into account when making an offer and setting the purchase price. Therefore, if a buyer should be expected to discover a defect upon a reasonable inspection, the buyer will be charged with notice; otherwise, the broker and/or seller have the affirmative duty to inform the buyer of the defect, preferably in writing.

Sellers can protect themselves by being specific in the contract, for example, about recurring plumbing problems, a cracked foundation, leaky roof, den built without a building permit, all in as-is condition. If, for example, the roof defect was not obvious and the buyer did not know of this material defect but the seller did know, then a general as-is clause is probably worthless.

Many contracts contain standard language that must be evaluated in light of an as-is clause. For example, the seller may still be required to provide a pest control report even though the property is sold as is. In such a case, the seller may want to affirmatively delete the standard termite clause. Also, "as is" does not normally cover title or encroachment matters unless specifically noted.

Even where an as-is clause can protect a seller, many courts hold that a broker cannot use the as-is clause to avoid liability for misrepresentation because the broker is not a party to the contract in which the as-is clause is contained.

In appraisals, "as is" is an indication that the value estimate is made with the property in its current condition, which may not be the highest and best use or may not include needed repairs. (*See* **caveat emptor**, **highest and best use**.)

asking price   (*precio demandado*)   The listed price of a parcel of real estate—the price at which it is offered to the public by the seller or the broker. An asking price differs from a firm price in that it implies some degree of flexibility in negotiation. For this reason, some sellers object to their listing broker using the phrase "asking price" in advertising the property.

assemblage   The combining of two or more adjoining lots into one large tract. This is usually done to increase the value of the individual lots because a larger building capable of producing a larger net return may be erected on the larger parcel. The resulting added value is called *plottage value*. The developer often makes use of option contracts to tie up the right to purchase the desired adjacent parcels. Care must be taken through exact surveys to avoid the creation of gaps or strips between the acquired parcels through faulty legal descriptions. (*See* **plottage value**.)

assessed valuation   The value of real property established for the purpose of computing real property taxes. In general, property is valued or assessed for tax purposes by county and township assessors. The land is usually appraised separately from the building, and the building value is usually determined from a manual or set of rules covering unit cost prices and rates of depreciation, although some states require assessments to be a certain percentage of true or market value (assessment ratio). State laws may provide for property to be reassessed periodically. Each taxing district has its own methods for constantly updating assessments, although most use a combination of building permit records, on-site inspections, and conveyance tax records. Generally, property owners claiming that errors were made in determining the assessed value of their property may present their objections to the local boards of appeal or boards of equalization. (*See* **property tax**, **tax rate**.)

assessment   (*tasación*)
  1. An official valuation of real property for tax purposes based on appraisals by local government officials; the term is synonymous with *assessed value*. Sales prices of comparable land are used to estimate land values, whereas building values are based on an amount representing the improvement's replacement cost less depreciation.
  2. The allocation of the proportionate individual share of a common expense, as when the owners of condominium or cooperative units are assessed for their proportionate share of unusual

A

maintenance expenses for the buildings that benefit the project as a whole and are not funded through regular maintenance charges.

3. A specific levy for a definite purpose, such as adding curbs or sewers in a neighborhood. (*See* **impact fees**, **special assessment**.)
4. An official determination of the just compensation to be paid a property owner for the taking of his or her property for a public purpose (condemnation).
5. An additional capital contribution of corporate shareholders or members of a partnership or association to cover a capital expenditure.

assessment rolls   Public records of the assessed values of all lands and buildings within a specific area. Thus, owners can compare their property's assessed valuation with that of similar properties and appeal if they feel their property was overassessed.

assessment-roll spread   *See* **special assessment**.

assessor   A public official who appraises property for tax purposes. The official determines only the assessed value, not the tax rate.

asset   Something of value owned by a person; a useful item of property. Assets are either financial (cash or bonds), tangible or intangible, or physical (real or personal property). Accountants analyze financial balance sheets made up of assets and liabilities to determine net worth, which is the difference between the two. (*See* **property**, **quick assets**, **wasting asset**.)

asset depreciation range system (ADR)   The part of the Internal Revenue Service regulations covering guidelines and standards for determining the period over which to depreciate an asset. The ADR gives the taxpayer a choice of depreciating the property over a shorter or longer life than the guideline period. (*See* **accelerated cost recovery system [ACRS]**, **modified accelerated cost recovery system [MARCS]**, **declining balance method**, **straight-line-method**.)

assignment   The transfer of the right, title, and interest in the property of one person (the assignor) to another (the assignee). There are assignments of, among other things, mortgages, sales contracts, contracts for deed, leases, and options.

Most contracts consist of rights and duties that, unless they are personal, can normally be delegated or assigned. For example, a listing contract creating an agency relationship is personal in nature and, therefore, the listing broker cannot assign the contract to another broker without the principal's consent. On the other hand, the duty to pay rent is not personal and normally can be assigned. Unless restricted by the contract language, real estate contracts are usually assignable. Some sellers specifically prohibit the assignment of the sales contract; they do not want the buyers "trading on the equity," especially when there is a long closing period.

In any assignment, the assignee becomes primarily liable, and the assignor remains secondarily liable as surety, unless there is a novation agreement relieving the assignor from liability. The assignee acquires the same title, right, and interest in the particular contract that the assignor had.

An attempted assignment of a mortgage lien without the promissory note transfers nothing to the assignee, but the assignment of the note without the mortgage gives the assignee the right to the security. If an assignment of a mortgage or trust deed (deed of trust) is recorded, constructive notice is given to all persons as to that assignment. The mortgagor must then pay the assignee and is unprotected if payments are inadvertently made to the assignor (the original mortgagee).

Many contracts for deed provide that buyers may not assign their interest in the contract without the prior written approval of the seller, although an assignment in violation of this provision is nevertheless valid between the assignor and assignee. When the seller wants an antiassignment clause, the prudent buyer should require in the sales contract that the contract for deed contain language to the effect that the seller's consent to a proposed assignment shall not be unreasonably withheld.

Mortgagees frequently use nonassignment clauses in mortgages to limit assignment of the obligation—this may be a factor in determining whether the seller should use a land contract or a purchase-money mortgage. A prohibition against assignment of a contract does not prevent the assignment of a claim for damages caused by a breach of the contract, nor does it prevent assignment of the right to receive money payments due (or that will become due) under the contract. The prohibition is for the benefit of the vendor (seller, lender), who can waive it expressly or by conduct (such as by accepting payments direct from the assignee).

When purchasing property subject to existing leases, the purchaser should obtain a written assignment of the seller's interest in those leases in recordable form.

With most leases, the tenant may sublet or assign the lease without the landlord's approval unless otherwise provided in the written rental agreement. The important distinction between an assignment and a sublease, from the landlord's viewpoint, is that the landlord cannot directly sue the sublessee, whereas it is possible to sue the assignee. (*See* **assignment of lease**, **estoppel**, **novation**, **option**, **sublease**.)

assignment of lease　　The transfer of all title, right, and interest that a lessee possesses in certain real property. The document used to convey a leasehold estate is called an *assignment of lease* rather than a deed.

The assignee of a lease is liable on the basis of the assignee's holding the land, legally known as *privity of estate*. The assignor is liable on the basis of privity of contract with the landlord.

If a lease has an assignment clause requiring the consent of the landlord, the landlord may not unreasonably or arbitrarily withhold consent. An assignment of a lease in violation of an antiassignment restriction is not void but is voidable at the lessor's discretion. Such an assignment is good between assignor and assignee. The issue that it is invalid on the basis of a lack of lessor's approval can be raised only by the lessor.

A lender may condition the loan for the leased premises on obtaining assignment of leases as collateral. The assignment may even permit the lessor to collect the rental payments.

assignment of rents　　An agreement between a property owner and a mortgagee by which the mortgagee receives, as security, the right to collect rents from the mortgagor's tenants, although the mortgagor continues to have the sole obligation to the tenants under the lease. (*See* **foreclosure**.)

associate broker　　A real estate license classification used in some states to describe a person who has qualified as a real estate broker but still works for and is supervised by another broker; also called a **broker-salesperson(s)**, **broker-associate**, or **affiliate broker**.

associate licensee　　Another name for a licensed real estate salesperson, also known as affiliate licensee. (*See* **salesperson[s]**.)

association　　(*asociación*)　　A group of people gathered together for a business purpose, sometimes treated as a corporation under tax law. If a partnership or limited partnership agreement is poorly drafted, the Internal Revenue Service (IRS) may attempt to treat the partnership as an association taxable as a corporation. The IRS uses the following test: If the organization has more corporate than noncorporate characteristics, it will be taxable as a corporation, with the resulting unfavorable tax features. The four major corporate characteristics generally are continuity of life, centralization of management, limited liability, and transferability of interest. (*See* **condominium owners' association**, **limited liability company [LLC]**, **unincorporated association**.)

Association of Real Estate License Law Officials (ARELLO)　　*See* Appendix A.

association of unit owners　　All unit owners of a condominium acting as a group for the administration of the project, in accordance with the declaration and bylaws. The association of unit owners may be incorporated or unincorporated. (*See* **condominium owners' association**.)

A

assumed business name   *See* **fictitious company name**.

assumption of mortgage   (*adquisición de hipoteca*)   The acts of acquiring title to property that has an existing mortgage and agreeing to be personally liable for the terms and conditions of the mortgage, including payments. In effect, the buyer (grantee) becomes the principal guarantor on the mortgage note and is primarily liable for the amount of any deficiency judgment resulting from a default and foreclosure on the property. The original mortgagor (grantor) is still liable as surety on the note if the grantee defaults. The personal liability of the purchaser to pay the mortgage debt is usually created by an assumption clause in the deed (or assignment of lease if a leasehold mortgage is involved). Normally, a deed need be signed only by the grantor, but where there is an assumption clause, both buyer and seller sign the deed so that the buyer becomes personally bound to the assumption. Because of continued liability, the seller usually asks a higher price for the property if the buyer is to assume a mortgage—the seller is, in effect, trading on the low interest rate of the existing mortgage. The lender is, in effect, a third-party beneficiary of the assumption agreement.

When the seller is taking back a second mortgage, the contract should state whether any adjustments in the assumed loan balance should be applied to the down payment or to the second-mortgage amount.

There is little reason for a lender to relieve the original seller from liability on the assumed note, so most lenders prefer to have both the buyer and the seller remain liable on the note. In certain cases, however, the lender will relieve the seller from continuing liability by way of a novation. Note that if the mortgagee changes any of the mortgage terms with the new owner, the original mortgagor may be released of all liability on the note. The lender normally charges an assumption fee. When interest rates are escalating, few lenders approve the assumption unless they can renegotiate the terms of the loan, raising the interest rate, and/or charging a fee. Some courts have sustained the right of the lender to require payment of an assumption fee and loan interest modification as consideration for its waiver of the acceleration clause in a mortgage. (*See* **acceleration clause**, **due-on-sale clause**, **novation**, **"subject to" mortgage**, **subrogation**.)

at-risk rules   Special rules set up by the IRS to restrict leverage opportunity by limiting the taxpayer's deductible losses to the amount the taxpayer has "at risk." A taxpayer is generally considered at risk to the extent of cash contributed and amounts borrowed for which the taxpayer is liable for payment from personal assets (recourse debt).

The act extends the at-risk rules to real estate investment losses incurred on property placed in service after December 31, 1986, subject to certain exceptions. The most important exception provides that nonrecourse debt secured by real estate used in the business activity is treated as an amount at risk, so long as the loan is made by a party who is regularly and actively engaged in real estate lending. This is true even if the loan is made by a related party, provided that the terms of the loan are commercially reasonable and substantially the same as could be obtained from an unrelated lender. Except in unusual circumstances, seller financing of real property of any type generally will not be considered at risk.

After a taxpayer's cumulative total deductions in connection with a property exceed the amount for which the taxpayer is at risk, the taxpayer can take no further deductions on the property until the amount for which the taxpayer is at risk is increased. Losses that are disallowed for a taxable year under the at-risk rule are carried forward indefinitely and are allowed as deductions in a succeeding tax year to the extent that the taxpayer increases the amount at risk in the activity giving rise to the losses. (*See* **nonrecourse loan**.)

atrium   Usually the main areas of a structure with a ceiling of a translucent material that allows sunlight into the interior quarters.

attachment   (*embargo*)   The legal process of seizing the real or personal property of a defendant in a lawsuit by levy or judicial order, and holding it in court custody as security for satisfaction of a judgment. The lien is thus created by operation of law, not by private agreement. The plaintiff may recover such property in any action upon a contract, express or implied.

Real property is attached by recording a copy of the writ of attachment in the public record. The attachment thus creates a lien against the property before entry of a judgment so that the plaintiff is assured there will be property left to satisfy the judgment. The lien can be enforced by issuance of an execution after a judgment for the plaintiff.

An attachment may arise from an action for payment of money upon an unsecured contract. The property may not be sold or encumbered free of the attachment without satisfaction or release of the attachment, or without the posting of a cash bond equal to plaintiff's claim plus costs. An attachment is not available when a party brings an action to collect payment of a secured obligation (mortgage). (*See* **lis pendens [Lis/P]**.)

attestation   The act of witnessing a person's signing of an instrument by a subscribing witness.

attic   Accessible space located between the top of a ceiling and the underside of a roof. Inaccessible spaces are considered structural cavities.

attorney fees   Monies an attorney charges for legal services. Unless provided for by statute or in a contract, attorney fees usually cannot be recovered by an aggrieved party. Therefore, it is important to insert a clause in all contracts (especially promissory notes) to the effect that, in the event of litigation arising from the contract, the prevailing party shall be entitled to reimbursement of all attorney fees and costs.

attorney-in-fact   (*apoderado, mandatario*)   A competent and disinterested person authorized by another person to act in her place. In real estate conveyance transactions, an attorney-in-fact, who has a fiduciary relationship with the principal, should be so authorized by way of a written, notarized, and recordable instrument called a *power of attorney*. The attorney-in-fact need not be an attorney-at-law, although people often give a power of attorney to their lawyers.

An attorney-in-fact may have a general or specific power; however, even one with general powers may not act in any way contrary to the principal's interests (for instance, selling the principal's property for inadequate consideration) or act in his own interests (for example, conveying the principal's land to himself). The listing broker should think carefully about possible conflicts of interest before accepting a power of attorney from the client and should also consider having separate written instructions detailing exactly what actions, and/or on what terms, the broker is authorized to act.

An attorney-in-fact appointed by a minor is not competent to convey title to real property owned by the minor.

A husband cannot be his wife's attorney-in-fact for purposes of releasing her dower rights. (*See* **agent, power of attorney**.)

attornment   The act of a tenant formally agreeing to become the tenant of a successor landlord; as in attorning to a mortgagee who has foreclosed on the leased premises. Attornment establishes a new tenancy, with the mortgagee being the landlord, and acts as a defense against the defaulting mortgagor's claim for rent.

In a long-term lease situation, an attornment agreement is typically entered into by a sublessee with a fee owner of the land and a mortgagee holding a mortgage on the fee or on the master leasehold estate. The sublessee seeks to protect his estate from destruction by reason of the premature termination of the master leasehold or from loss by reason of the foreclosure of the mortgage when the sublessor defaults. The attornment agreement provides that, in the event of termination or foreclosure, the sublease will continue, just as though the owner or the mortgagee were the lessor in

A

a lease with the sublessee for a term equal to the unexpired term of the sublease, and upon the same terms and provisions. (*See* **nondisturbance**.)

attraction principle   The pulling force of a commercial business center due to one or more of various merchandising factors. A shopping center, made up of many diverse businesses, holds cumulative attraction for consumers.

attractive nuisance   A doctrine of tort law stating that persons who maintain on their property a condition that is both dangerous and conceivably inviting to children owes a duty to exercise reasonable care to protect children from the danger. Thus, an owner who maintains a swimming pool or unmarked open pit, or discards a refrigerator or freezer may be liable for injuries to trespassing children. Construction sites should be adequately secured to prevent inquisitive children from being injured.

auction   (*subasta*)   A form of selling land or personal property whereby oral offers are taken and the property is sold to the highest bidder. Some states require auctioneers selling real estate to carry a special license. Real estate auctions are generally used in mortgage foreclosure sales, tax sales, and with hard-to-sell properties. If the auction is "without reserve," the auctioneer cannot withdraw goods or bid on them personally or through an agent.

  In the secondary mortgage market, Fannie Mae uses an auction-type purchasing procedure termed *free market system auction* to buy mortgages from approved lenders. In recent years, auctions have become an alternative method of marketing real estate, especially by lenders or developers attempting to sell multiple properties quickly. (*See* **bid**.)

auctioneer   (*martillador*)   A person licensed or authorized to sell real or personal property at public auction. Some states require the auctioneer to be licensed both as an auctioneer and as a real estate broker to sell real property.

augmented estate   A concept to calculate which of the decedent's assets are subject to the surviving spouse's right of election ("forced share"), regardless of whether the deceased spouse dies testate or intestate. The augmented estate includes certain lifetime transfers of property by the decedent during marriage to donees other than the surviving spouse. The addition of these lifetime transfers supports the policy of preventing the decedent from deliberately disinheriting the surviving spouse. (*See* **dower**.)

authorization to sell   A listing contract whereby an agent is employed by a seller to procure a buyer for the property. It usually does not give the agent the authority to enter into a binding contract of sale; such unusual authority typically requires a special authorization, as in a limited power of attorney. (*See* **listing**.)

autre vie   *See* **pur autre vie**.

avenue   A fully improved through-roadway, serving local or minor collector traffic, that is landscaped and planted with trees.

avigation easement   An easement acquired through purchase or condemnation to permit aircraft approaching an airport to fly at low elevations above private property. This effectively prevents the landowners near airports from building above a set height or requires the trimming of trees. (*See* **air rights**.)

avulsion   (*avulsión*)   The loss of land as a result of its being washed away by a sudden or violent action of nature. A riparian owner generally does not lose title to land lost by avulsion—the boundary lines stay the same no matter how much soil is lost, and the former owner can reclaim the lost land. In contrast, the riparian owner loses title to land washed away by erosion, which is the gradual and imperceptible washing away of soil. (*See* **erosion**, **riparian rights**.)

axial growth   City growth that occurs outward along main transportation routes. This pattern is usually star-shaped.

azimuth   The direction of a boundary line in relation to a north-south line or meridian, or the angle between a north-south line and the boundary line measured from the north point in the northern hemisphere and the south point in the southern hemisphere. Every line has two azimuths, depending on the direction one looks down the line. This, the azimuth of line A → B is 240°, but the azimuth of line B → A is 60°.

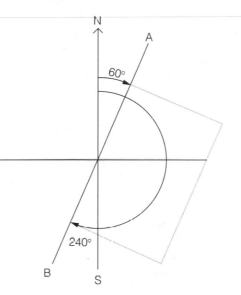

B

backfill   The earth or selected material such as aggregate, used for one of three purposes: to fill in around foundation walls after they are completed, to fill other excavated voids, or to compact soil.

back-to-back escrow   An escrow set up to handle the concurrent sale of one property and the purchase of another property by the same party. To obtain the $20,000 cash down payment needed to purchase a new three-bedroom home, John Lark must close the sale of his present two-bedroom home. John may set up a back-to-back escrow with an escrow company, which will close the sale of his old home and then apply the necessary proceeds to close the purchase of his new home. (*See* **double escrow, escrow**.)

back-to-back lease   An agreement made by a landlord as a concession to a prospective tenant, in which the landlord agrees to take over the tenant's existing lease in return for the tenant's agreement to lease space in the landlord's commercial building (office building, industrial park). (*See* **concession**.)

B

backup offer   An offer to buy submitted to a seller with the understanding that the seller has already accepted a prior offer; a secondary offer. Sometimes the seller accepts the backup offer contingent on the failure of the sales transaction on the part of the first purchaser within a specified period of time. The seller must be careful in how she proceeds, however, when the time for buyer's performance under the first contract has expired. Rather than just immediately treat the contract as terminated and arrange to convey the property to the backup buyer, the seller should make sure that the seller has fully performed, or made a full and adequate tender of such performance, to the first purchaser. Otherwise, the seller may be contractually bound to convey the same property to two different buyers. The best practice is to obtain a release from the first purchaser. (*See* **tender**.)

   The real estate agent should be cautious about encouraging the seller-client to breach any existing contract in order to accept a better second offer. The agent might be sued by the first buyer for the tort of intentional interference with contract.

   Buyers should consider reserving the right to withdraw from the accepted backup offer at any time prior to notice that the seller has canceled the first contract. This gives the buyer some flexibility in continuing to look for other properties.

bailment   The delivery of personal property from the bailor to the bailee with the agreement, express or implied, that the property will be returned or property accounted for when the special purpose of the bailment is accomplished, such as leaving a car with a parking attendant. Property stored in a miniwarehouse may be subject to the special rules of bailment law.

balance sheet   An itemized financial statement setting forth personal or corporate assets, liabilities, and net worth (the difference between assets and liabilities) as of a specified date. It is a quick cross-section analysis of the business. Most lending institutions require an applicant for real estate financing to submit a balance sheet, usually on a form attached to the loan application. Some lenders also require a profit and loss statement showing income and expenses. Some states have enacted false statement acts to penalize the falsification of statements used in the loan process. (*See* **profit and loss statement**.)

balcony   (*balcón*)   A platform enclosed by a railing or parapet, which projects from the wall of a building for the private use of tenants or for exterior access to the upper floors. When a balcony is roofed and enclosed and has operating windows, it is considered part of the room it serves. (*See* **lanai**.)

balloon payment   (*pago mayor*)   A final payment that is substantially larger than the previous installment payments and repays the debt in full; the remaining balance that is due at the maturity of a note or obligation. Balloon payments are frequently used in second mortgages (to keep installments low when paying first and second mortgages concurrently) and in similar situations where the monthly payment does not fully amortize the principal balance over the life of the obligation. A note or obligation that provides for a lump-sum payment at the end of the term is sometimes called a *partially amortized loan*.

   For example, Mr. Clay sells his condominium studio apartment for $150,000, with a down payment of $15,000 and a balance of $135,000 by way of a contract for deed at 10 percent interest, payable at $809.39 per month (amortized on a 30-year schedule), with the balance due in full at the end of five years. If the buyer makes the full five years of payments, at the end of that time, the buyer will have paid off only $9,376.40 of principal, leaving a balance of $125,623.60 to be paid in the final balloon payment. If the buyer elects to pay off the contract in a shorter period of time, the balloon payment will be correspondingly higher. A loan progress chart can be used to determine what portion of a fully amortized loan remains to be paid at any given moment in time and the amount of the balloon payment. When federal truth-in-lending provisions apply, the amount of a balloon payment must be clearly stated in the contract.

baluster   One of a string of small poles used to support the handrail of a stairway.

band of investment (BOI)   An appraisal method used in evaluating income property to build the interest rate portion of the appropriate capitalization rate to apply to the subject property; the sum of the mortgage and equity positions of the buyer. This technique is popular in estimating an appropriate discount (risk) rate. Equity investors seek to obtain the best financing deal in order to maximize the advantage of leverage.

The band of investment for a particular property is derived from a synthesis of mortgage and equity rates that market data reveal to be applicable to comparable properties. The appropriate "CAP rate" is the sum of the mortgage requirement rate (a constant representing the interest on and recapture of the mortgage component of the total value of the property) and the equity rate (the anticipated cash flow to the equity investment, as indicated by comparable sales). Thus, each portion of a property's interest or ownership is multiplied by the rate of return required to attract money into that type of ownership position.

For example, assume that an investor wishes to purchase a hotel. As her broker, you have investigated similar recent sales and found that mortgage money is available for two-thirds of the property value at 9.25 percent interest for a term of 25 years. The mortgage requirement rate (constant) is 10.28 percent. The remaining one-third of the value of the property must be paid by your investor in cash, and she can expect an equity rate of 11 percent. The overall CAP rate, then, is derived as follows:

	Percent of Value	Rate	Product
Mortgage	66.67	0.1028	6.85
Equity	33.33	0.11	3.67
CAP rate (weighted average)			10.52

(*See* **capitalization [CAP] rate, constant, income approach, internal rate of return**.)

band or box sill   The two horizontal members that connect the pier to the floor joist in pier and beam foundations. The boards are joined to create a right angle, and the joist is placed perpendicular to the upright angle. This perpendicular placement provides the foundation with the necessary rigidity.

Bank Insurance Fund (BIF)   The name of a fund of the Federal Deposit Insurance Corporation (FDIC), which received premiums for deposit insurance coverage from commercial banks and savings banks. BIF was abolished by the Federal Deposit Insurance Act of 2005, which created a single Deposit Insurance Fund. (*See* **Deposit Insurance Fund [DIF], Federal Deposit Insurance Act of 2005** [in Appendix D], **Federal Deposit Insurance Corporation [FDIC]**.)

bankruptcy   (*quiebra, bancarrota*)   A condition of financial insolvency in which a person's liabilities exceed assets and the person is unable to pay current debts. Bankruptcy may be voluntary, as when debtors petition the court on their own accord; or it may be involuntary, as when a creditor forces payment of a debt of $1,000 or more, which the debtor cannot pay.

When a person enters into federal bankruptcy proceedings, all assets become vested in a court-appointed trustee or receiver, who liquidates these assets to pay claims held against the debtor by the debtor's general creditors. Bankruptcy discharges the debtor from further liability on all debts then owed, except for such exempted debts as tax claims, alimony, and support payments, liability for malicious injury and fraud, and debts not scheduled. Usually, a bankruptcy is reported by most credit agencies for a period of ten years.

B

A creditor of the bankrupt, whose claim is secured by a mortgage on real property, is normally entitled to the proceeds of the mortgaged property before any distribution of the bankrupt's assets to general creditors. As a rule, the discharge in bankruptcy affects a debtor's personal obligations but does not destroy liens against the debtor's property. Fraudulent conveyances, however, are void, and transfer of the insolvent debtor's property to a creditor within prescribed periods (such as 90 days) of filing the bankruptcy petition may be voided by the trustee in bankruptcy because it enables a preferred creditor to get a greater percentage of the debt over other creditors. One fundamental policy of bankruptcy is to ensure equality of distribution among creditors.

The bankruptcy of either party to a real estate agency agreement (listing) terminates the agency because title to the property passes to the trustee in bankruptcy. A discharge in bankruptcy does not generally relieve a real estate licensee from the penalties resulting from payment out of the state licensing agency's real estate recovery fund to defrauded consumers.

A broker representing the debtor in the sale of property in a bankruptcy case should note three points: (1) The broker must be a disinterested person. (2) Court approval for the employment of a broker is required. (3) Once the sale is completed, the bankruptcy court must approve the commission, not to exceed a reasonable amount.

Bankruptcy of a lessee or a vendee is usually a stated ground for default under a lease or contract for deed. Many leases and contracts for deed contain bankruptcy default clauses that provide the owner-landlord with the right of termination if the buyer-tenant goes bankrupt. Under the Federal Bankruptcy Act, however, forfeiture and termination clauses conditioned on insolvency or bankruptcy may be unenforceable.

The bankruptcy of a mortgagor or a trustor to a trust deed note affects foreclosure proceedings if the bankruptcy is initiated before the foreclosure proceedings have begun. In such cases, title to the property passes to the trustee in bankruptcy, and the referee (usually the judge) of the bankruptcy court must authorize the foreclosure proceedings. Filing of the petition in bankruptcy acts as an automatic stay of the foreclosure proceedings in state court.

Other types of bankruptcy actions are designed to reorganize and save a debtor's business operation. These actions have the debtor's "rehabilitation" as their prime goal. It does not affect secured debts—that is, those secured by liens (mortgage loans, real estate taxes)—although it does suspend any pending foreclosure proceedings. A court-appointed referee is responsible for setting up the reorganization of the operation. The debtor is allowed to retain possession of the property while arranging a plan for payment. Although such proceedings deal only with unsecured property, the court can order a suspension of all actions by a mortgagee and thus prevent foreclosure. (*See* **cram down**.)

Bankruptcy Abuse Prevention and Consumer Protection Act of 2005 (BAPCPA)   Also known as the *New Bankruptcy Law*, the law requires debtors to pass a means test to determine whether they can have their medical bills, credit card debt, car loans, and other debts liquidated through Chapter 7 or whether they must enter a repayment plan through Chapter 13. Additionally, debtors are required to complete an approved credit counseling course within 180 days before filing a petition.

bare title   *See* **naked title**.

bargain and sale deed   A deed, formerly in the form of a contract between buyer and seller, reciting a consideration and conveying all of the grantor's interest in the property to the grantee. A bargain and sale deed usually does not include warranties as to the title of the property conveyed; however, the grantor asserts by implication that he has possession of, a claim to, or an interest in the property conveyed. The courts usually hold that the grantor promises only that the grantor has done nothing to cause a defect in title and is thus not liable for unknown defects. Trustees, fiduciaries, executors, and officers of the court often convey the real property under their control by way of a bargain and sale deed, sometimes with a covenant against the grantor's acts. (*See* **covenant, quitclaim deed, warranty deed**.)

bargain money   *See* **earnest money**.

bargain sale   A sale of property for less than its fair market value. The Internal Revenue Service may treat such a sale as a part-gift and part-sale transaction. (*See* **gift tax**.)

baseboard   A board running around the bottom of the wall perpendicular to the floor. Sometimes called *wains*, a baseboard covers the gap coating between the floor and the wall, protects the wall from scuffs, and provides a decorative accent.

base line
1. One of a set of imaginary lines running east and west used by surveyors for reference in locating and describing land under the government survey method of property description. (*See* **government survey method**.)
2. A topographic centerline of a survey, as for the route of a freeway.

basement   (*sótano*)   A space of full-story height that is below the first floor, wholly or partly below the exterior grade, generally not used primarily for living accommodations. The FHA does not permit the basement area to be included in the finished gross living area at the grade level. (*See* **concrete basement floor**.)

base period   A time interval or starting point used for calculating certain business and economic data, frequently found in escalation clauses. The determination of the base period has great significance in commercial leases, where it is used to establish the cutoff year preceding rent escalations. The parties usually arrive at a complex formula for determining the base index, which is adopted as 100, from which stem future rent increases to match increases in operating expenses, utilities, services, and property taxes.

For example, if 2013 were used in a lease as the base year, it would be given an index of 100; if costs increased 8 percent during 2014 in relation to 2013 costs, then the 2014 index would be 108 and lease rents would be raised if so specified in the lease document.

base rent   The minimum rental stipulated under a percentage lease. The first year is called the *base year*. The second and each succeeding year is called a *comparison year*. (*See* **percentage lease**.)

base shoe   Molding used at the junction of the baseboard and the floor; also called a *carpet strip*.

base top molding   A thin strip placed on top of the baseboard and perpendicular to the wall to cover gaps between the wall and the baseboard and give the molding a finished appearance.

base year   *See* **base rent**.

basis   The dollar amount that the Internal Revenue Service attributes to an asset for purposes of determining annual depreciation or cost recovery, and gain or loss on the sale of the asset. All property has a basis that, once determined, is of fundamental importance in tax aspects on the sale of the asset. If property was acquired by purchase, the owner's basis is the cost of the property plus the value of any capital expenditures for improvements to the property, reduced by any cost recovery depreciation actually taken or allowable. The basis is also reduced by any untaxed gain "carried over" to the new property in cases where the new property is a replacement of a former residence sold under the two-year rollover rules of Section 1034 or is acquired through a like-kind exchange or through an involuntary conversion. This new basis is called the property's *adjusted basis*.

If property was acquired by a lifetime gift, the basis is the donor's basis at the time of the gift plus the value of any capital expenditures for improvements made to the property by the donee plus any gift tax paid by the donor, reduced by any depreciation allowable or actually taken by the donee. In certain cases in which the transaction is part gift and part sale, the maximum basis is the fair market value of the property on the date of the transfer plus any capital expenditures by the new owner for improvements to the property, minus any depreciation allowable or actually taken by the new owner.

If the property was acquired by inheritance, the heir (or heirs) will assume, as the basis for determining gain, the "stepped-up" basis of the property—that is, generally the fair market value of the property as of the date of death (the federal estate tax value of the asset in the decedent's estate) or the alternative valuation date, if elected, six months later.

If the property was acquired in a totally or partially tax-deferred exchange, the basis of the new property received in the exchange is determined by reference to the basis of the old property exchanged. Frequently, however, tax-deferred exchanges become partially taxable because of the receipt of cash or other unlike property in addition to the property of a like kind. If cash or other property is received, the gain on the exchange is taxable to the extent of such cash or other property. Thus, when a gain is partly recognized, the basis of the property received is the basis of the property exchanged, reduced by other property or cash received and increased by the amount of taxable gain. (*See* **capital gain**.)

A personal residence is not depreciable for tax purposes because it is neither "property used in a trade or business" nor "property held for the production of income," as required under the Internal Revenue Code. The original basis of residential property may be adjusted upward in the amount of any capital expenditures made for improvements to the residence; thus, the taxpayer should maintain accurate records and receipts of substantial household improvements. When a property is sold, the amount of gain or loss is determined by comparing the adjusted basis on the date of sale with the net proceeds of the sale.

An important aspect is the allocation of basis. A taxpayer who purchases depreciable real estate must allocate the basis between the land, which is not depreciable, and the improvements, which are depreciable. A taxpayer often uses the same allocation as that determined by the state tax assessor, although this is neither required nor binding upon the taxpayer. The taxpayer must also allocate the basis between the building and the fixtures and furniture in the building for separate calculation of depreciation, gain, or loss. When substantial improvements are made to the property, their cost must be added to the taxpayer's depreciable basis.

Due to the importance of basis, the various adjustments to it and the tax consequences arising from the various adjustments, real estate investors should seek competent advice on a real estate investment from a tax advisor, a tax attorney, or an experienced commercial-investment broker. (*See* **accelerated depreciation**, **adjusted basis**, **capital expenditure**, **depreciable real property [accounting]**, **easement**, **residence**, **stepped-up basis**.)

basis point   A unit of measure; $\frac{1}{100}$ of 1 percent. Used to describe the amount of change in the market price of bonds and many debt instruments, including mortgages. For example, 50 basis points is the difference between a 13 percent and a 13½ percent loan.

basket provision   A provision contained in the regulatory acts governing the investments of insurance companies, savings and loan associations, and mutual savings banks that allows for a certain small percentage of total assets to be placed in investments not otherwise permitted by the regulatory acts. A loan made under this provision, such as a high-yield second mortgage, or wraparound mortgage, would be called a *basket (bucket) money loan*. These acceptable miscellaneous transactions are collected into a separate basket, so to speak.

batten   Narrow strips of wood or metal used to cover joints on either the interior or the exterior; used for decorative effect.

bay   An unfinished area or space between a row of columns and the bearing wall typically found in industrial and warehouse facilities. Usually, the smallest area into which a building floor can be partitioned.

bay window   A window that forms a bay in a room, projects outward from the wall, and is supported by its own foundation.

beach   Land on the margin of a sea, a lake, or a river. If the tide ebbs and flows over the land, such land is called *tideland*; land not subject to tidal action is called *shoreland*.

beam   A structural member that transversely supports a load.

bearing   A surveying term for a horizontal angle measured from 0° to 90°, fixing the direction of a course or distance in relation to true north or south.

bearing wall   (*muro de carga*)   A main or supporting wall referred to as a *load-bearing wall*, usually supporting a roof above. In a condominium, all bearing walls are common elements, and nonbearing walls, such as certain partitions, are owned by the apartment owners.

bed-and-breakfast   A portion of a single-family home that is rented on a short-term basis, typically in resort areas. In addition to lodging, breakfast is sometimes provided in the owner's home. Local ordinances should be checked to see whether such homestay use is permitted.

bedrock   The solid rock underlying soils and other surficial formations.

bedroom community   A section of the community that serves as a residential area for an adjoining or nearby metropolitan area. Also known as a *dormitory town*.

before-and-after method   An appraisal method employed in determining just compensation for land that has been partially taken by condemnation; also known as the *federal rule*. The value of the property taken is the difference between the value of the entire property before the partial taking and the value of the remainder property. Under the before-and-after method, the amount of compensation in the condemnation award due for the property acquired is the difference between the value of the whole property before the taking and the value of the remainder after the taking, calculated as the total value *before*, *less* the total value of the remainder, *equals* the total compensation, which includes payment for the land taken and severance damages.

Sometimes the taking results in an increase in the value of the remaining property, in which case this "special benefits" value would reduce the condemnation award in the federal system. In most states, special benefits may offset severance damages only—not the part taken. (*See* **condemnation, just compensation, severance damages**.)

The before-and-after method is also used in modernization cases; that is, an appraiser may take the value of property before and after remodeling to determine whether the value increased more than modernization costs.

belly-up   Slang for a failed real estate project or a failed business.

benchmark   (*punto de referencia*)
1. The standard or base from which specific estimates are made.

A permanent reference mark (PRM) (see illustration following) affixed to a durable object, such as an iron post or brass marker embedded in a sidewalk, used to establish elevations and altitudes above sea level over a surveyed area; also used in tidal observation.

The elevations are based on the official datum, and each benchmark has its own recognized official elevation. Thus, a surveyor can start at any benchmark to set the elevation measurements. Where there is no datum for an area, surveyors use the base elevations set by the U.S. Geological Survey. (*See* **datum, geodetic survey system, monument**.)

2. A major court decision that serves as the precedent or guideline for future decisions.

beneficial interests   *See* **bundle of rights**.

beneficiary   (*beneficiario, fideicomisario*)   A person who receives benefits from the gifts or acts of another, as in the case of one designated to receive the proceeds from a will, insurance policy, or trust; the real owner, as opposed to the trustee, who holds only legal title. With a trust, the trustee holds the legal title, but the beneficiary enjoys the benefits of ownership. (*See* **deed in trust**.)

beneficiary statement   A statement of the unpaid balance of a loan and the condition of the indebtedness, as it relates to a deed of trust transaction. (*See* **reduction certificate**.)

benefit-of-bargain rule   A rule of damages in which a buyer who has been defrauded can recover the difference between the actual value of the property and the value of the property as represented to him or her, as opposed to merely recovering the out-of-pocket loss. (*See* **damages**.)

benefits   The betterment gained from a public improvement for which private property has been taken in an eminent domain proceeding. Benefits may be general, which enhance generally all property in the area, or *special*, in which only the subject property (or a very limited number of properties) is enhanced. (*See* **condemnation**.)

bequeath   To leave personal property to another by will, as a bequest. To leave real property by will is to devise. In modern terminology *bequeath* is frequently used to convey a gift by will, whether it be real or personal property. (*See* **legacy**.)

bequest   *See* **bequeath**.

berm   A ledge or shoulder, as along the edge of a paved road.

betterment   An improvement to real property, such as a sidewalk or road, which substantially increases the property's value. The measure of value is not in the improvement's actual cost, but rather in the enhanced value added to the property. It does not result from an acquisition of new property, nor is it a mere restoration of the property; it is a capital expenditure as compared with repairs or replacements. (*See* **special benefit**.)

biannual   Occurring twice a year, or semiannually. For example, real property tax payments may be due biannually, in November and May of each year.

bid   (*licitación*)
1. An offer to purchase property for a specified amount, such as at an auction, foreclosure, or probate sale. Often the owner of property put up for auction will put in a protective bid to

prevent the property from being sold at a sacrifice price. A mortgagee may bid in at a fore-closure auction up to the amount of the outstanding loan. (*See* **auction, upset price.**)

2. Formal procedure of submission, by a list of contract bidders, of sealed proposals to perform certain work at a cost specified in the proposal, usually within a set period of time. Intended to ensure the client and the contractors of an objective and competitive method of fulfilling job requirements at lowest cost.

biennial   Occurring every two years. Some states require biennial renewal of real estate licenses.

bikeways   Paths specially designed for bicycle traffic.

bilateral contract   A contract in which each party promises to perform an act in exchange for the other party's promise to perform.

The usual real estate sales contract is an example of a bilateral contract in which the buyer and the seller exchange reciprocal promises respectively to buy and sell the property. If one party refuses to honor a promise and the other party is ready to perform, the nonperforming party is said to be *in default*. Neither party is liable to the other until there is first a performance, or tender of perfor-mance, by the nondefaulting party. Thus, when the buyer refuses to pay the purchase price, the seller usually must tender the deed into escrow to show readiness to perform. In some cases, however, tender is not necessary.

Depending on its wording, a listing form may be considered a bilateral contract, with the broker agreeing to use best efforts to locate a ready, willing, and able purchaser for the property, and the seller promising to pay the broker a commission if the broker produces such a buyer or if the prop-erty is sold. Once signed by the broker and the seller, such a listing contract becomes binding on both. (*See* **option, tender, unilateral contract.**)

bill of sale   A written agreement by which one person sells, assigns, or transfers to another a right to, or interest in, personal property. A bill of sale is sometimes used by the seller of real estate to evidence the transfer of personal property, such as when the owner of a store sells the building and includes the store equipment and trade fixtures. The transfer of the personal property can be effected by mention in the deed or, as is more common, by a separate bill-of-sale document. A bill of sale may be with or without warranties covering defects or unpaid liens of the property.

A bill of sale is normally used when the purchaser is an investor and, for tax reasons (faster depreciation write-off), wants a separate accounting for the personal property involved, especially if the property is valued at an amount greater than the standard price for similar property. The broker in a transaction involving personal property should see that an accurate inventory is taken of the items included in the bill of sale.

binder

1. An agreement formed by the receipt of an earnest money deposit for the purchase of real property as evidence of the purchaser's good faith and intention to complete the transaction. The agreement is used to bind the parties until a more formal contract can be prepared and executed. Receipt of the binder money, or deposit, is usually evidenced in the sales contract. (*See* **earnest money.**)

2. A written instrument giving immediate fire and extended insurance coverage until a regu-lar insurance policy can be issued, sometimes obtained pending the closing of a real estate transaction.

3. A temporary contract of title insurance in which the insurer agrees to issue a specified policy within a certain period of time. Excluded from coverage are any defects, liens, or encum-brances affecting the title and intervening between the date of the binder and the date of the conveyance to the proposed insured.

Because a preliminary report does not constitute a commitment to insure the title, it may sometimes be advisable to obtain a binder or commitment from the title insurer stating its willingness to insure the title, particularly in complex transactions with multiple simultaneous closings.

bird dog

1. A salesperson whose sole job is to "flush out" new listings. Upon obtaining a lead, the bird-dog salesperson turns everything over to a broker or to a more experienced salesperson to handle the transaction.
2. Any person capable of furnishing leads, such as postal carrier, mover, barber, or beautician.

biweekly payment loan   A loan that calls for 26 half-month payments a year, resulting in an earlier loan retirement date and lower total interest costs than with a typical fully amortized loan with regular monthly payments.

blacktop   Asphalt paving used in streets and driveways.

blanket mortgage   A mortgage secured by several properties or a number of lots. A blanket mortgage is often used to secure construction financing for proposed subdivisions or condominium development projects. The developer normally seeks to have a "partial release" clause inserted in the mortgage in order to obtain a release from the blanket mortgage for each lot as it is sold, according to a specified release schedule. For example, if a developer obtains a $500,000 mortgage to cover the development of 50 lots, he might be required to pay off $12,500 of principal to get each lot released from under the blanket mortgage. Sometimes, land developers have a "special recognition" clause put in the blanket mortgage whereby the lender agrees to recognize the rights of each individual parcel owner, even if the developer defaults and there is a foreclosure. Occasionally, the federal government secures a blanket lien against all properties owned by persons who have defaulted on their income taxes. (*See* **partial-release clause**.)

A blanket mortgage may also be used when a purchaser buys a house plus an adjacent vacant lot and finances the purchase with a single mortgage that covers both properties. It may also be used where the equity in one property is insufficient to meet the lender's requirements.

blended rate   An interest rate of a newly refinanced loan that is higher than the existing rate but lower than the current market rate; often used with a wraparound mortgage.

blighted area   A declining area, usually in the inner city, in which real property values are seriously affected by detrimental influences, such as encroaching inharmonious property use mixture or rapidly depreciating buildings, with no immediate prospect of improvement. (*See* **urban renewal**.)

blind ad   An advertisement that does not include the name and address of the person placing the ad, only a phone number or post office box address. State license laws generally prohibit licensed brokers from using blind ads. (*See* **advertising**.)

blind pool   A securities offering of interests in unspecified and yet-to-be-determined properties; a nonspecified property offering in which an investor usually relies on the general partner's ability to locate and put together suitable investments. Some states, such as New York, prohibit blind pool offerings; that is, they permit the offering of securities in only existing, selected properties or specific properties proposed for development. Other states permit blind pool offerings that meet prescribed requirements. (*See* **real property securities registration**.)

BLM   *See* **Bureau of Land Management (BLM)**.

block   (*manzana*)   *See* **lot, block, and subdivision**.

blockbusting   (*rompe cuadras*)   An illegal and discriminatory practice whereby one person induces another to enter into a real estate transaction from which the first person may benefit financially by inferring that a change may occur in the neighborhood with respect to race, sex, religion, color, handicap/disability, familial status, or ancestry of the occupants, a change possibly resulting in the lowering of the property values, a decline in the quality of schools, or an increase in the crime rate. Blockbusting generally violates both state and federal fair housing antidiscrimination laws.

The practice of blockbusting, also called **panic peddling**, includes subtle as well as obvious forms of racial inducements, so that the inference may be unlawful even if race is not explicitly mentioned. For example, the uninvited solicitations of real estate listings in a racially transitional neighborhood are prohibited representations if it can be shown that the solicitations are made for profit; are intended to induce the sale of a dwelling; and that under the circumstances, the solicitations would convey to a reasonable person the idea that members of a particular race are or may be entering the neighborhood. (*See* **discrimination**, **federal fair housing law**, **panic peddling**.)

block interest   *See* **add-on interest**.

blue book   One of any number of handy reference books that list new and used values and frequently contain amortization and balloon payment tables.

blue laws   Laws handed down from colonial days restricting the transaction of business on Sundays and certain religious holidays. The name is derived from the original practice of printing these laws on blue paper.

blueprint   A working plan used on a construction job by tradespeople; an architectural drafting or drawing that is transferred to chemically treated paper by exposure to strong light, causing the paper to turn blue and thus reproducing the drawing in white. (*See* **as-built drawings**.)

blue-sky laws   State securities laws designed to protect the public from fraudulent practices in the promotion and sale of securities ("promising the sky"); for example, through limited partnerships, syndications, and bonds. Blue-sky laws normally require that securities be registered with the securities commissioner in the state where the offers are being made and that the issuer disclose (usually in a prospectus) all pertinent facts about the investment to prospective purchasers.

Unlike federal securities laws, some state laws also impose qualitative standards upon issuers of securities and require that each offering be "fair, just, and equitable." This requirement may be applied to limit the amount of commissions or other compensation paid, the nature of the investment, or other related matters. (*See* **security**.)

board
1. A local organization of the state association of REALTORS®, which belongs to the National Association of REALTORS®. (*See* **National Association of REALTORS® [NAR]**.)
2. Sometimes refers to the state real estate commission.
3. Sometimes references the board of directors of a condominium or cooperative community

board foot   A measure of lumber one-foot square by one-inch thick; 144 cubic inches = 1' × 1' × 1".

board of directors   The governing body of a corporation authorized to carry on and control the business affairs of the company, the members of which are elected periodically by shareholders. Unless required in the bylaws, the directors usually need not be shareholders of the corporation. State law establishes the minimum number allowed, as well as how many must be residents of the state.

A director who acts as a broker in negotiating the sale or purchase of corporate property cannot accept a commission for services without express authorization from the board of directors to act as a broker and receive a commission.

A condominium owners' association is generally administered by a board of directors. Among other duties, the board is charged by law with seeing that adequate insurance is obtained if so required by the bylaws. Failure to do so would subject individual directors to personal liability. (*See* **articles of incorporation**, **condominium owners' association**, **corporate resolution**, **corporation**.)

board of equalization   *See* **equalization board**.

Board of REALTORS®   A local organization of licensed real estate brokers and salespersons, termed REALTORS® and REALTOR-ASSOCIATES®, belonging to the National Association of REALTORS® and the state association of REALTORS®. There are more than 1,800 local boards of REALTORS® in the United States, although some may be called associations.

boilerplate   The standard, fixed language in a contract, such as that found in most mortgages, contracts of sale, contracts for deed, leases, and CC&Rs (covenants, conditions, and restrictions). Where such language is too one-sided, the contract might be challenged as an adhesion contract. When a form contract or lease is used, any uncertain or ambiguous terms are construed against the party who furnished the form. (*See* **adhesion contract**, **contract**, **incorporation by reference**, **plain language law**.)

boiler room   A questionable promotional technique whereby multiple "cold pitch" phone calls are made by land sales companies to the public to create leads for the sale of real estate, usually vacant land or property located in another area or state. These telephone solicitors are usually required to have real estate licenses.

BOMA International   *See* **Building Owners and Managers Association (BOMA) International**.

bona fide purchaser (BFP)   A party who acquires property in good faith and for a valuable consideration without knowledge, actual or constructive, of the prior rights or equities of third parties. Usually, BFPs are protected under the state recording acts against the rights of third parties with a prior unrecorded interest in the same property. (*See* **constructive notice**, **good faith**, **innocent purchaser for value**, **possession**, **recording**.)

bond   (*bono*)
1. A written promise that generally accompanies a mortgage and is the primary evidence of the debt obligation secured by the mortgage; may also refer to a completion bond or a performance bond. (*See* **performance bond**.)
2. A debt instrument; an obligation to pay; a security issued by a corporation by means of which the corporation borrows money. Such a bond may be secured (mortgage) or unsecured (debenture).
3. An interest-bearing certificate issued by a government as a means of financing real estate projects and community improvements such as schools and parks. General obligation bonds are designated to be repaid out of property taxes. (*See* **debenture**, **promissory note**.)

bond for deed   *See* **contract for deed**.

bonus clause   A prepayment clause in an installment contract, deed of trust, mortgage, or note providing for a special payment to be made to the lender in the event of full or partial payment before the scheduled due date. (*See* **prepayment**.)

bonus depreciation   *See* **first-year depreciation**.

book value   (*valor en libros*)   The amount at which an asset is carried on the financial books of a person, partnership, association, or corporation.

   Book value is the capitalized cost of an asset less depreciation taken for accounting purposes, based on the method used for the computation of depreciation over the recovery period of the asset. It is the adjusted basis of an asset and usually differs from appraised or market value. Book value serves as the basis of computing profits or losses derived from a sale. The book value of a property can be readily determined by adding the depreciated value of the improvement to the allocated value of the land. (*See* **basis**, **value**.)

boot   Money or other property that is not like-kind, which is given to make up any difference in value or equity between exchanged properties. Boot may be in the form of cash; notes; gems; or the market value of an asset such as a mortgage, land contract, personal property, goodwill, or a service or a patent offered in an exchange. The taxable gain in a like-kind exchange is recognized immediately to the extent of boot, whereas other gain from the exchange may be deferred until subsequent transfer.

     Where liabilities (mortgages, deeds of trust) are assumed by both parties to an exchange of property, the amounts of the liabilities are netted to determine a net boot. An excess amount of liability assumed by one party to the exchange is boot to the other party. This is true whether the party to whom the property is transferred assumes the liability or merely takes the property subject to the liability. (*See* **basis**, **exchange**.)

bottomland   Lowlands located in a valley or dale or near a river or creek. Also, land that is often underwater, such as tideland or a floodplain.

boulevard   A major street with or without a median strip, generally shorter than a highway and usually serving through traffic on a continuous route.

boundaries   The perimeters or the limits of a parcel of land as fixed by legal description. Boundary disputes are controversies between adjoining owners as to the proper location of the dividing line between the properties. Some abutting owners enter into a boundary agreement in which they stipulate that a certain dividing line, such as a fence, serves as the true boundary of the properties.

     A frequent dispute arises where the branches of a tree located on one owner's property extend over the boundary line onto a neighbor's property, thereby invading the neighbor's air rights. In some states, the neighbor can cut the branches up to the boundary line or seek court action for money damages and an abatement of the nuisance. To lessen the risks of boundary disputes, prudent buyers require the seller to stake or survey the property. (*See* **agreed boundaries**.)

bounds   A reference to direction, based on terminal points and angles. In a metes-and-bounds legal description, metes represents the measurement of length and bounds confines the length to a given area. (*See* **metes and bounds**.)

box sill   *See* **band or box sill**.

bracing   Framing lumber nailed at an angle in order to provide rigidity.

branch office   (*sucursal*)   Any secondary place of business apart from the principal or main office from which real estate business is conducted. Generally, each branch office must have a broker-in-charge, or branch manager, who is responsible for the operations of the branch. In some states, this manager need only be a salesperson. Most states require each branch office to be registered and issued a special license.

breach of contract   (*violación de contrato*)   Violation of any of the terms or conditions of a contract without legal excuse; default; nonperformance. The nonbreaching party can usually seek one of three alternative remedies upon a material breach of the contract: rescission of the contract, action for money damages, or an action for specific performance. (*See* **anticipatory breach**, **damages**, **election of remedies**, **rescission**, **specific performance**.)

breakdown method   *See* **depreciation (appraisal)**.

break-even point   (*punto de equilibrio*)   In residential or commercial property, the figure at which rental income is equal to all required expenses and debt service. It is the point at which gross income is equal to fixed costs plus all variable costs incurred in developing that income. Use of the break-even analysis is important to calculation of the profitability of a building. In large commercial projects, the standby financing commitments usually require that the project be leased up to its break-even point before a permanent lender will fund a takeout mortgage.

B

bridge loan

1. Short-term loan to cover the period between the termination of one loan, such as an interim construction loan, and the beginning of another loan, such as a permanent takeout loan; the loan between the acquisition of a property and its improvement or development to make it qualify for a permanent loan. A bridge loan is sometimes used to provide funds for the costs incurred in converting an apartment house into a condominium. (*See* **gap financing, swing loan**.)

2. A residential financing arrangement in which the buyer of a new home borrows money and gives a second mortgage on the buyer's unsold home to fund the acquisition of a new home. This loan is useful where the seller of the new home will not accept an offer "subject to the sale of the buyer's home" or where the buyer needs to raise the down payment by a certain date or else lose the new home.

bridging
Small wood or metal pieces placed diagonally between floor joists. Bridgings disperse weight on the floor over adjacent joists, thus increasing the floor's load capacity.

bring-down search
A continuation of a title search to verify that no liens have been filed against the property between the time of the original search and the recording of the deed or mortgage; also called a **take-down search** or a **continuation**. In many states, the buyer customarily pays the fee for this continuation. (*See* **title search**.)

British thermal unit (Btu)
A unit of measure of heat, used in rating the capacity of air-conditioning and heating equipment (radiators, boilers). One Btu represents the amount of heat required to raise the temperature of one pound of water one degree Fahrenheit at approximately 39.2°F.

broker   (*corredor*)
One who acts as an intermediary between parties to a transaction. A real estate broker is a properly licensed party (individual, corporation, or partnership) who, for a valuable consideration or promise of consideration, serves as a special agent to others to facilitate the sale or lease of real property.

A real estate broker is an independent businessperson who sets the office policies. A broker hires employees and affiliate licensees (either salesperson or broker), determines their compensation, and supervises their activities. The broker is free to accept or reject agency relationships with principals.

Brokers represent their principals and accept the fiduciary and/or statutory responsibilities of exercising care, skill, and integrity in carrying out their instructions. Generally, a broker's duties are confined to advertising property and to finding a person ready, willing, and able to deal on the terms stipulated by and acceptable to the principal. However, legal restrictions are imposed on brokers by legislative action, and federal, state, and local fair housing laws place new social obligations on them. Brokers cannot legally refuse, due to race, religion, sex, or national origin, to show, sell, rent, or otherwise negotiate regarding property listed with them. The broker must submit all offers to the principal.

State real estate license laws determine the requirements to qualify as a real estate broker. Generally, the applicant must pass a written examination, meet educational requirements, evidence good character, and pay the required fees.

A broker is permitted by law to hire others to assist the brokerage in representing its clients. Some brokers continue to sell actively, some are sales managers, and others are primarily administrative brokers doing little or no listing and selling.

The broker is the primary agent in any agency relationship with buyer or seller. This is true even though the salespeople, who are agents of the broker, have most of the direct contact with the buyer or the seller client. (*See* **agency, associate broker, buyer's broker, commission, cooperating broker, examination, fiduciary, independent contractor, license laws, listing, principal broker [PB], salesperson[s]**.)

brokerage   (*corretaje*)   The aspect of the real estate business that is concerned with bringing together the parties and completing a real estate transaction involving exchanges, rentals, and trade-ins of property, as well as sales. Typically, but not always, the brokerage is compensated for this service by a commission often based on the percentage of the gross sales price taken from the seller's equity. This commission is paid directly to the broker (or brokerage company), who then may compensate the selling affiliate licensee according to a prearranged schedule. (*See* **commission**.)

brokerage commission   *See* **commission**.

broker associate   *See* **associate broker**.

broker-dealer   One licensed to buy and sell securities. The National Association of Securities Dealers issues a broker-dealer license for general securities or a direct participation program license limited to real estate securities. (*See* **agent**, **real property securities registration**, **security**.)

broker-in-charge   In many states, a broker designated by the principal broker of a real estate brokerage company and registered with the state real estate license commission as the person directly in charge of, and responsible to, the principal broker for the real estate operations conducted at a branch office. (*See* **branch office**.)

broker price opinion (BPO)   A broker's written opinion of the value of a particular property, often in the form of a competitive market analysis. Depending on state law, the broker may charge a separate fee for a BPO, provided it is not used in connection with originating a federally related loan and is not labeled as an appraisal. BPOs are often requested by relocation companies and lenders involved in "short sales" of distressed properties.

broker-salesperson   *See* **associate broker**.

brownfields   Industrial properties in which the expansion, redevelopment, or reuse may be complicated by the presence or potential presence of a hazardous substance, pollutant, or contaminant. The EPA's brownfields and land revitalization programs recognize that cleaning up and reinvesting in these properties protects the environment, reduces blight, and takes development pressures off green spaces and working lands. The brownfields programs provide funds to assess and clean up brownfields while providing jobs and increasing the value of adjacent residential properties. (*See* **Small Business Liability Relief and Brownfields Revitalization Act** [in Appendix D].)

brownstone
  1. A row house constructed with reddish-brown sandstone, typically with little street frontage. Usually refers to a structure constructed during the 19th century and found in older large cities.
  2. A dark-colored red sandstone, often used as a facing for row houses.

Btu   *See* **British thermal unit (Btu)**.

budget   A balance sheet or statement of estimated receipts and expenditures. The cash operating budget details the positive and negative cash flows of a property from month to month. It usually does not contain depreciation, bad-debt losses, and other noncash items. The capital improvements budget outlines a fiscal program for making capital repairs, replacements or additions to a property over a stated period of time. A budget is no more reliable than the person who prepares it.

budget mortgage   A mortgage with payments set up to cover more than interest and principal reductions. In addition to monthly amortized principal and interest payments, the monthly payments may include an amount equal to 1/12 of the year's property taxes, a pro rata share of the fire insurance premium (together known as *PITI*), and any other similar charges that if not paid, could result in a foreclosure. A budget mortgage with all-inclusive payments facilitates the payment by the purchaser of such expenses and protects the mortgagee in case the purchaser cannot make these payments

B

when they become due as one large, lump-sum payment. Use of the budget mortgage is especially common in conventional residential mortgage loans and in VA and FHA loans. (*See* **mortgage lien**.)

buffer zone   In zoning, a strip of land separating one land use from another. Sometimes a developer of a large residential subdivision leaves certain land undeveloped as a buffer against adjoining land that might be incompatibly zoned, such as an industrial park.

builder's risk insurance   Fire, liability, and extended-coverage insurance written to cover the special risks of a building under construction. Coverage increases automatically as the building progresses and terminates upon its completion. Such a policy should be replaced by permanent insurance when the building is ready for occupancy. Premiums may be based on the estimated "completed value" or based on a "full reporting clause" in which the builder periodically reports the increases in value as construction progresses.

building and loan association   An incorporated mutual organization that invests its members' funds in residential mortgages and repays the interest earned to its member depositors in periodic dividends. (*See* **savings and loan association [S&L]**.)

building codes   (*reglamentos de construcción*)   Rules set up by local, state, or municipal governments to regulate building and construction standards often based on national standards. Building codes are designed to provide minimum standards to safeguard the health, safety, and welfare of the public by regulating and controlling the design, construction, quality, use and occupancy, location, and maintenance of all buildings and structures. The establishment of building codes is a valid exercise of the state's police power, and thus codes are valid restrictions on an owner's use of his or her property. Codes are enforced by the issuing of building permits and certificates of occupancy and by inspections, with fines being imposed on violators. (*See* **building permit**, **Uniform Building Code [UBC]**, **zoning**.)

building height   The total height measured from the ground floor to the top of the outer surface of the roof. Typically, local zoning ordinances regulate the maximum height, sometimes restricting or reducing heights based on the proximity of a structure to setback lines.

building lease   A long-term lease of raw land under which the tenant agrees to pay a set ground rent and further agrees to construct and maintain specified improvement of the premises. (*See* **ground lease**.)

building line   A setback line; a line beyond which one may not build any improvement. Building line restrictions may be created by designating them on a recorded subdivision plat or by inserting a restriction in the subdivider's deed. Establishing building lines ensures a degree of uniformity in the appearance of buildings and creates a right to unobstructed light, air, and view.

Building Owners and Managers International (BOMI)   *See* Appendix A.

building paper   Fiber-reinforced, waterproof paper treated with bitumen, a natural asphalt from coal, petroleum, or some other water-resistant compound. Building paper is placed between siding and wall sheathing, around door and window frames, and in other areas to insulate the house and keep out moisture.

building permit   (*permiso de edificación*)   A written governmental permission for the construction of a new building or other improvement, the demolition or substantial repair of an existing structure, or the installation of factory-built housing. The proposed construction must conform to local zoning and building codes and usually must be inspected and approved upon completion. In most cases, a building permit must be obtained before the start of a project, which provides a convenient way for local authorities to monitor compliance with the zoning code.

A prudent developer should include in the purchase agreement for a proposed development site not only a condition that the developer obtain a building permit but that it is obtained by a stipulated deadline. Otherwise, the developer could unreasonably delay seeking the permit while keeping the seller's property off the market.

Any owner contemplating an addition and/or change to property should first check with the appropriate county or municipal building department to avoid any building code violations, which will generally render a seller's title unmarketable. Failure to disclose such violations may constitute a material misrepresentation, entitling the buyer to rescind the transaction and obtain the return of his or her money. (*See* **certificate of occupancy**, **zoning**.)

building-related illness (BRI)   A clinically diagnosed condition caused by toxic substances or pathogens that persist when an occupant leaves the building. Symptoms can include hypersensitivity, pneumonitis, asthma, and certain allergic reactions. One such example is Legionnaires' disease, caused by a known bacterium, which is sometimes found in air conditioner cooling towers, getting into the ventilation ductwork. In the 1970s, a major hotel was closed for several years after several deaths occurred.

building residual technique   (*técnica de remanente de construcción*)   An appraisal term for a method of determining the contribution of an improvement to the present value of the entire property. Normally used in appraising income property. Also used to determine whether the value of a building after renovation is greater than the renovation costs.

When the value of land is known, the appraiser deducts from the net income produced by the property the amount of net income that must be attributed to the land to justify its value. Example: If the land value is $10,000 and the going rate of interest is 12 percent, then the land itself must return 12 percent of its value, or $1,200 per year, if it is to justify its purchase price. The balance or residue of the net income represents that income attributable to or earned by the building. The residual is then capitalized at a rate that provides a market-acceptable return on the building and recapture of the wasting asset (building) to arrive at the indicated value of the building. Land value is added to arrive at the value of the property as a whole. (*See* **income approach**.)

building restrictions   (*limitaciones de construcción*)   Limitations on the size or types of improvements established by zoning acts or by private restrictions inserted in a deed or ground lease. Violations of building restrictions may render the title unmarketable. (*See* **marketable title**, **restriction**.)

building standards   The specific elements of construction the owner/developer chooses to use throughout a building. The building standard offered an office tenant, for example, would relate to the type of partitions, doors, ceiling tile, light fixtures, carpet, draperies, and so forth.

build-to-suit   An understanding or contract in which a lessor agrees to develop a property or finish certain space to the specifications of a lessee in return for a lease commitment on the part of the prospective tenant. The cost of work done, or a portion thereof, is usually amortized in the form of additional rental payments. Possession is given upon completion. (*See* **turnkey project**.)

built-ins   Certain stationary equipment—such as some kitchen appliances, bookcases, desks, shelving, cabinets, and furniture—permanently affixed to real property and understood to be included when the property is sold. A built-in may also refer to a garage that is under the same roof as the main building it serves. (*See* **fixture**.)

built-up method   An appraisal method of determining the discount, or interest, rate used in selection of the appropriate capitalization rate. The four basic components of the discount rate are the safe rate, burden of management, nonliquidity, and risk for the specific type of property being appraised. Sometimes referred to as the *summation method of rate selection*. (*See* **discount rate**, **income approach**.)

B

bulk sales transfer   Any transfer in bulk (and not a transfer in the ordinary course of the seller's business) of a major part of the materials, inventory, or supplies of an enterprise. The Uniform Commercial Code (UCC) regulates bulk transfers to deal with such commercial frauds as a merchant selling out stock, pocketing the proceeds, and leaving creditors unpaid. The UCC requires the buyer of the goods to demand that the seller provide a schedule of all the property and a list of all creditors and that the buyer give notice to creditors of the pending sale. Failure to comply with the UCC means that the transfer or sale is ineffective in respect to the claims of any creditor of the seller. Bulk transfers usually become relevant upon the liquidation or sale of a business.

Under state law, a bulk sale must be reported by the seller to the state tax authorities, and the purchaser must withhold payment until the seller's tax clearance is received. If the tax clearance is not made, the purchaser may become liable for any unpaid taxes that are a lien against the items sold. (*See* **Uniform Commercial Code [UCC]**.)

bulk zoning   *See* **zoning**.

bullet loan   A short-term, interest-only loan with a balloon payment, often with no right to prepay or, if prepayment is allowed, a substantial prepayment penalty.

bumper   A device of wood, rubber, or other material used around a loading dock to cushion the impact of parking trucks.

bundle of rights   An ownership concept describing all the legal rights that attach to the ownership of real property, including the right to sell, lease, encumber, use, enjoy, exclude, and devise by will. These rights also include the rights of use, occupancy, cultivation and exploration, and the rights to license, dedicate, give away, share, mortgage and trade, or exchange. When purchasing real estate, the buyer actually buys the rights previously held by the seller, except those that are reserved or limited in the sale. These rights are called *beneficial interests associated with real property interests*.

bungalow   A small one- or one-and-a-half-story house.

burden of proof   The obligation to prove the truth or falsity of a fact, in either a trial or an administrative hearing. In a discrimination complaint, the burden of proof is on the complainant.

Bureau of Land Management (BLM)   *See* Appendix A.

bureau rate   A standard rate for hazard insurance, and for title insurance in some states, established by a rating bureau for all companies writing policies in a specific area.

bus duct   Electrical conductors that group together multiple circuits used to provide service along a given line in an industrial plant.

business brokerage   *See* **business opportunity**.

business chance brokerage   *See* **business opportunity**.

business day   (*día hábil*)   A day of the week, except Saturdays, Sundays, and holidays; a normal working day. Because of accepted custom and practice, the term *business day* is preferable to the term *banking day* or *working day*.

Some laws require notice within five business days; for example, notice to quit for tenant's failure to pay rent; other laws refer to calendar days. A dispute can arise if a contract fails to state whether the notice be within business days or calendar days, although the usual interpretation is that it is calendar days unless specified otherwise. (*See* **date**, **holiday**.)

business energy property tax credit   A tax credit as incentive for businesses to invest in or purchase solar water heat, solar space heat, solar thermal electric, solar thermal process heat, photovoltaics, geothermal electric, fuel cells, solar hybrid lighting, direct-use geothermal, or microturbines. The Energy Policy Act of 2005 expands the credit to fuel cells and microturbines installed in 2006 and 2007 and to hybrid solar lighting systems installed on or after January 1, 2006. The tax credits range from 10 to 30 percent.

business interruption insurance   Insurance that covers losses incurred as a result of a business owner's inability to conduct business during the repair of a building following a fire or other insured hazard.

business life insurance   Life insurance purchased by a business enterprise on the life of a member of the firm. It is often bought by partnerships to protect the surviving partners against loss caused by the death of a partner, or by a corporation to reimburse it for loss caused by the death of a key employee. Also referred to as **key employee insurance**.

business name   *See* **DBA**, **fictitious company name**.

business opportunity   Any type of business that is for sale (also called *business chance brokerage* or simply *business brokerage*). The sale or lease of the business and goodwill of an existing business, enterprise, or opportunity, including a sale of all or substantially all of the assets or stock of a corporation, or assets of a partnership or sole proprietorship.

   Generally, if real property is an asset of the business, a real estate broker's license is required to sell the business. Because a broker may not be aware of many of the special problems involved in selling a business, however, the advice of an experienced business counselor or attorney may be appropriate. Both seller and buyer should be aware of the application of the bulk transfer laws on the sale of the business. They should also be aware that, under the Uniform Commercial Code, any contract involving the sale of goods of $500 or more must be in writing to be enforceable. (*See* **bulk sales transfer**, **goodwill**.)

business park   A development or subdivision designed for office-warehouse or like use. Also known as an *office park*, it is an outgrowth of industrial parks.

buy-back agreement   A provision in a sales contract that provides that the seller (and, in some cases, the broker) will buy back the property within a specified period, usually for the original selling price, upon the happening of a certain event, such as the purchaser being transferred from the area.

buydown   A financing technique used to reduce the monthly payment for the home-buying borrower during the initial years. Under some buydown plans, a residential developer, a builder, or the seller will make subsidy payments (in the form of points) to the lender that "buy down," or lower, the effective interest rate paid by the homebuyer, thus reducing monthly payments for their buyers for a set period of time, while reducing their own profit.

   The amount of the interest supplement may remain fixed for the entire buydown period, or it may be graduated, with the amount of the subsidy declining each year. Buydowns are costly: for example, with certain lenders, a three-year buydown might carry 2.7 points for each one-percentage-point drop of interest.

buyer's broker   A broker who represents the buyer in a statutory or fiduciary capacity. Some buyer's brokers practice single agency, in which they represent either buyers or sellers, but never both in the same transaction. Some buyers' brokers represent only buyers and refer prospective sellers to other brokers—these brokers are called *exclusive buyer brokers*. The broker is paid by the buyer, or through the seller or listing broker at closing, provided all parties consent.

   With the widespread acceptance of buyer representation, there is a good probability that the listing firm will also have a buyer-client interested in one of its listings. Many companies develop office policy based on whether to continue representing both clients under a consensual dual agency or to practice single agency by referring one of the parties to another brokerage. (*See* **agent**, **designated agent**, **fiduciary**.)

buyer's market

1. An economic situation in which the supply of properties available for sale exceeds the demand. As a result, sellers are often forced to lower their prices and sometimes assist in the financing (with purchase-money mortgages) in order to attract buyers.
2. A decline in prices resulting from an oversupply.

buy-sell agreement

1. An agreement among partners or shareholders to the effect that one party will sell and another party will buy a business interest at a stated price upon the occurrence of a stated event. This form of buy-sell agreement is popularly used in closely held corporations and partnerships to cover the possibility of death or disability of a key participant. Life insurance is commonly used to ensure that funds will be available to effect the buyout.
2. An agreement entered into by an interim and a permanent lender for the sale and assignment of a mortgage to the permanent lender when a building has been completed. Often the mortgagor is a party to this agreement on the theory that the mortgagor would have a contractual right to insist that the permanent lender buy the mortgage.

bylaws   The regulations, rules, or laws adopted by a condominium owners' association or corporation for the condominium's management and operation. Bylaws cover such matters as the manner and selection of the board of directors and the duties and obligations of the corporation members. These self-imposed rules are a form of private law. Whereas a corporate resolution applies to a single act of the corporation, a bylaw is a continuing rule to be applied on all future occasions. Condominium bylaws are initially established by the developer and then are subject to change when the owners' association takes over. The bylaws may be amended as noted in the original condominium declaration. (*See* **corporate resolution**.)

by operation of law   Refers to the effect and power of the law acting upon property; property rights determined by some positive rule or amendment, by which someone may acquire or lose rights without any act on his part. For example, a wife may acquire a one-third life interest in her husband's real property through operation of the law of dower.

cadastral map   (*plano catastral*)   A map, used in connection with title recording, indicating legal boundaries and ownership of real property. A *cadastral program* refers to a complete inventory of land in an area by ownership, description, and values as used in the tax assessment process.

CAI   *See* **Community Associations Institute (CAI)**.

caissons   The foundation supports for a building.

call   A reference, made in the surveying or platting of a parcel of land, to a course, distance, or monument when a boundary is being described or "run."

call provision

1. A clause in a mortgage or trust deed that gives the mortgagee or beneficiary the right to accelerate payment of the mortgage debt in full on a certain date or upon the happening of specified conditions. (*See* **due-on-sale clause**.)

2. The borrower's ability to redeem, or call in, a bond.
3. An option to buy real estate. (An option to sell is called a *put.*) (*See* **option**.)

call report   A report on mortgage delinquencies.

cancellation clause   (*cláusula resolutoria*)

1. A clause that may be included in a commercial or industrial lease granting the lessor or the lessee the right to terminate the lease term upon the happening of certain stated events or occurrences by the payment from one party to the other of definite amounts of money as consideration. Such consideration usually tends to cover expenses or damages of the party whose rights are being canceled, such as unamortized costs of special improvements, broker-age fees, and possible loss of rental before the property is rerented.

    If the tenant cancels, the consideration fee paid to the landlord and any unamortized cost of improvements is a deductible income tax expense in the year of cancellation.

    If the landlord cancels, the cancellation fee paid to the tenant is a capital expenditure of the landlord and is amortized over the remaining term of the canceled lease. The cancellation pay-ment to the tenant is akin to a sale and, if the lease is of land that is nondepreciable property, it is a capital asset and the tenant is entitled to report the cancellation fee as a capital gain in the year of receipt.

2. A provision in a residential lease whereby the landlord can cancel the lease upon the sale of the fee simple property; otherwise, the new owner would have to take title subject to the lease.

3. A clause making a sales contract effective only upon cancellation of an earlier contract. Before accepting a "backup offer," the seller should insert a clause to the effect that accep-tance is subject to the written cancellation of the prior accepted contract. (*See* **backup offer**.)

CAN-SPAM Act   A federal law enacted in 2003 setting national standards for commercial e-mails and applies to any business use that uses e-mail in its marketing campaigns. CAN-SPAM requires that the subject line clearly and truthfully communicates the content of the message. The "to" and "from" information must be correct, and there must be a way for consumers to "opt out" from receiving fu-ture messages. Additionally, the company must respond within ten days, and all commercial e-mails must include a postal address.

cantilever   A projecting beam or overhanging portion of a structure supported at one end only, such as a bay window or balcony.

cap   A ceiling or limit on the adjustments made in the payments, interest rate, or balance of an adjust-able-rate loan. (*See* **adjustable-rate loan**.)

capacity of parties   The legal ability of people or organizations to enter into a valid contract. A per-son entering into a contract will have full, limited, or no capacity to contract.

    Full capacity to contract: The unlimited ability of a person to enter into a contract that is legally binding. Most adults, including those who are illiterate, have full capacity to contract and are said to be *competent parties*. (*See* **contract**.)

    Limited capacity to contract: The ability of a person to enter into a contract that is legally binding upon that person only under certain circumstances. For example, minors have limited ability to contract, which means that the contract of a minor is valid only if the minor does not disaffirm a contract entered into during minority or shortly after reaching majority. Contracts made by minors to obtain such necessities as food, clothing, and shelter, however, are not void-able by the minor and will be enforced against the minor. (*See* **minor**.)

No capacity to contract: The inability of a person to enter into a valid contract under any circumstances. Such inability can arise when a person has been adjudicated insane or is an officer of a corporation who is not authorized to execute a contract on behalf of the corporation. Lack of capacity would also cover acts of a corporation beyond the powers as defined in the articles of incorporation. (*See* **corporate resolution, incompetent, trustee, ultra vires**.)

capital   That money and/or property comprising the wealth owned or used by a person or business enterprise; the accumulated wealth of a person or business.

capital assets   All property except that held by a taxpayer primarily for sale to customers in the ordinary course of one's trade or business. Capital assets include such property as the taxpayer's personal residence, land held for investment, stocks, securities, and machinery or equipment used in business.

capital expenditure   The cost of a capital improvement that extends the life of the asset. In depreciable property, a capital expenditure usually must be amortized over the life of the property or that portion of the property to which the improvement belongs. The expense is not currently tax deductible, as are repairs. (*See* **basis, capital gain, repairs**.)

capital gain   (*ganancia de capital*)   The taxable profit derived from the sale of a capital asset. The capital gain is the difference between the sales price and the basis of the property, after making appropriate adjustments for closing costs, capital improvements, and allowable depreciation.

   A capital gain is considered a long-term gain if the asset is owned for more than 12 months and a short-term gain if the asset is owned for exactly 12 months or less. Short-term gains are treated as ordinary income for tax purposes but taxes on long-term gains can range from 5 percent to 28 percent.

   With all the recent changes in the tax code, it is necessary to understand at which rate sales are taxed. This depends on income from other sources, how long the asset was held, and what type of asset it is. Record keeping is essential.

capital improvement   Any structure erected as a permanent improvement to real property; any improvement made to extend the useful life of a property, or to add to the value of the property. For example, the replacement of a roof is considered a capital improvement, whereas the repair of screen doors is not. Other typical capital improvements are boiler replacement, a paved driveway, landscaping, and extensive remodeling. (*See* **capital expenditure**.)

capitalization   (*capitalización*)
1. A mathematical process for converting net income into an indication of value, commonly used in the income approach to value. The net income of the property is divided by an appropriate (capitalization) rate of return to give the indicated value. (*See* **appraisal, capitalization [CAP] rate, income approach**.)
2. The par value of the stock of a corporation plus the face amount of outstanding bonds and loans. (*See* **thin capitalization**.)

capitalization (CAP) rate   (*tasa de capitalización*)   The percentage selected for use in the income approach to valuation of improved property. The CAP rate is designed to reflect the recapture of the original investment over the economic life of the improvement to give investors an acceptable rate of return (yield) on their original investments and to provide for the return of the invested equity. In other words, if the property includes a depreciating building, the CAP rate provides for the return of invested capital in the building by the end of the economic life (the recapture rate that allows for the building's future depreciation) and the return on the investment in the land and the building (similar to yield).

Example: If a building has a 50-year economic life, then the recapture rate is set at 2 percent per year. If the rate of return on the investment is 8 percent and the recapture rate is 2 percent, then the overall capitalization rate applicable to the building is 10 percent.

An appropriate CAP rate is influenced by the conditions under which the particular investment is being operated, as well as the availability of funds, prevailing interest rates, and risk. If the property earns $100,000 per year and the cap rate is 9 percent, then determining what the property is worth to the investor is as follows: $100,000 ÷ 0.09 = $1,111,111. Only an experienced appraiser can select the appropriate CAP rate—a mere 1 percent difference in the suggested CAP rate could make a 12½ percent difference in the value estimate.

The CAP rate measures the risk involved in an investment; thus, the higher the risk, the higher the CAP rate; the lower the risk, the lower the CAP rate. (*See* **band of investment [BOI]**, **income approach**, **internal rate of return**.)

capitalize
1. To provide cash; to fund.
2. An accounting procedure whereby a company records an expense as a capital asset on its books instead of charging it to expenses for the year. This is normally done with capital expenditures, such as the cost of a new roof. (*See* **capital expenditure**, **capital improvement**.)

capitalized-income approach   *See* **income approach**.

capital loss   (*pérdida de capital*)   A loss derived from the sale of a capital asset, securities (such as stocks), or bonds. If the taxpayers' capital losses exceed their capital gains, the excess can be used to reduce taxable income such as wages, up to annual limit of $3,000, or $1,500 if they are married filing separately. If their net capital loss is more than their yearly limit, the excess can be carried over to the next taxable year until the loss has been fully deducted.

Capital losses are not recognized on the sale of a taxpayer's personal residence. (*See* **basis**.)

CAP rate   *See* **capitalization [CAP] rate**.

caravan   A slang term used in some parts of the country for a group inspection tour of listed properties by a broker's sales staff.

carpet strip   *See* **base shoe**.

carport   A roofed space having at least one side open to the weather. A carport is often made by extending the house roof to one side and is primarily designed or used for motor vehicles. This term is usually related to small one- and two-family dwellings. In multifamily properties, a garage may have one or more sides open to the weather.

carryback financing   Financing in which the seller takes back a note for part of the purchase price and is secured by a junior mortgage (a second or third mortgage), wraparound mortgage, or contract for deed.

carrying charges
1. The regular costs of maintaining a property, such as taxes, insurance, utilities, and accrued interest. These costs are often apportioned between buyer and seller at the closing of a real estate transaction. (*See* **closing [settlement]**.)
2. Costs incurred in owning property up to the time the development of the property is completed. Normal carrying charges include a developer's costs for payments of property taxes and interest on the land acquisition and construction loans during the time the property is under development. Also called *front money*.

   If a developer has a proposed development pending and has little or no income to absorb tax deductions, the developer will want to capitalize the carrying charges. The rule is that the developer can capitalize annual taxes, mortgage interest, and other true carrying charges over a ten-year period if the property is unimproved or unproductive. The election to capitalize is made annually when preparing a tax return. After the project is completed, the developer *must* deduct the expenses. (*See* **front money**.)

C

carryover clause   *See* **extender clause**.

carve out   Refers to commercial loans wherein the lender "carves out" certain specific personal liabilities in an otherwise nonrecourse loan. Rather than allow the borrower a blanket exemption from personal liability, the lender takes exception for a default caused by such failures as those involving an environmental issue, fraud, misapplication of funds, bankruptcy, or allowing an uncontested involuntary filing of bankruptcy.

case law   *See* **common law**.

Case-Shiller Index   Created by Fiserv and published monthly by Standard & Poor's, the Case-Shiller Index includes several analyses of the average change in home prices in 20 individual and 2 composite retail markets. It is calculated using data from repeat sales of single-family homes. Sales are analyzed to eliminate possible distorting factors, such as non-arm's-length (i.e., no family members) sales, substantial changes to the property, when the property type has been changed, and suspected faulty data. Often referred to as *S&P/Case-Shiller Home Price Indices*.

cash equivalency   An adjustment made to a comparable property sale that was financed in a manner not typical of the marketplace. The adjusted sales price should reflect the price that would have been paid, assuming typical financing were used. Thus, a sale with the seller carrying back a no-interest loan would be adjusted downward based on cash equivalency principles.

cash flow   The spendable income from an investment after deducting from gross income all operating and fixed expenses, including principal and interest. The amount of cash derived over a certain measured period of time from operation of income-producing property after debt services and operating expenses, but before depreciation and income taxes. "Net after-tax" cash flow, or cash available for distribution, includes an allowance for income tax attributable to the income. Pre-tax cash flow is sometimes called *cash throw-off*.

  Cash flow is different from "net profit." To arrive at net profit, the owner will make a deduction for depreciation but will not deduct for loan amortization.

  Two benefits of investing in improved, income-producing real property are the tax shelter provided during ownership and the anticipated appreciation in the property value that may be realized upon its sale. Thus, an investment can turn out to be profitable even if there is monthly negative cash flow. Under the 1986 Tax Reform Act, real estate tax shelters were severely limited. (*See* **internal rate of return**, **negative cash flow**, **tax shelter**.)

cash-flow statement   A yearly financial report showing the bottom-line return after taxes. The property manager is often responsible for preparing a cash-flow analysis so that the property owner can evaluate the return on the investment in the property.

cashier's check   A bill of exchange (check) drawn by a bank (usually signed by its cashier) upon itself as drawer and payable upon demand, like a promissory note executed by the bank. A cashier's check is preferred to an ordinary personal check, and it (or a certified check) is usually required of the purchaser of property by the contract terms to close a transaction.

  A cashier's check, however, is still subject to a stop-payment order of the maker. The certified check is subject to a stop-payment order only if the maker obtains the bank certification, not when the payee has the maker's check certified in the maker's bank. (*See* **certified check**.)

cash method   An accounting method of reporting income in the taxable year in which the income is actually or constructively received and reporting expenses when actually paid out. Income is constructively received when it is credited, set apart, or otherwise made available to the taxpayer without substantial limitations or restrictions so that the taxpayer could have received it on request. The cash method is sometimes called the *cash receipts and disbursements method*. It contrasts with the accrual method of accounting. The cash basis is the usual method for real estate brokerage firms and other service businesses. (*See* **accrual method**.)

C

cash on cash   The before-tax cash flow divided by the capital invested in the property; a method to determine how efficiently capital invested in the property is used.

cash-out   In a listing, an indication that the seller desires to receive the complete sales price in cash, rather than accept less by taking back a purchase-money mortgage or selling under a contract for deed. In other words, no carryback financing is acceptable. It could mean "cash to mortgage" where the buyer pays the seller's equity in cash and assumes or takes subject to the existing mortgage.

cash receipts and disbursements method   *See* **cash method**.

casing   (*marco*)   A frame, as of a window or door.

catwalk   A narrow footing on a bridge or along a girder of a large building. A catwalk may also be a walkway strung from one girder to another or placed over uncovered attic joists.

caulking   A flexible putty-like substance used to fill gaps at fixed joints on a building to reduce the passage of air and moisture, as in making building windows watertight.

cause of action   Facts or circumstances that give rise to a right to file a lawsuit.

caution money   *See* **earnest money**.

caveat emptor   (*caveat emptor*)   Latin for "let the buyer beware." Buyers should inspect the goods or realty before purchase because they buy "as is" and at their own risk.

   The modern judicial trend is to soften the effect of this ancient doctrine. Today, the seller has more of an affirmative duty to disclose any and all factors that might influence the buyer's decision to purchase. For residential properties of one to four units, many states now require that sellers deliver to the buyer a written disclosure about certain conditions about the property. Buyers should not rely on the seller's disclosure as either a warranty or a guarantee. Buyers have not only a right but also a responsibility to "discover" issues about the property that are important to them. In other words, the written seller's disclosure places the burden on the seller to disclose and on the buyer to discover.

   Although some sellers may "forget" to make certain disclosures, buyers should also remember that sellers cannot disclose that of which they are not aware. Licensees must still disclose those issues of which they have knowledge because the courts have generally held that a prospective purchaser, as a member of the public, can rely on the statements made by a licensed salesperson or broker.

   The doctrine of caveat emptor has been substantially altered with respect to residential leases. In the past, a landlord would lease residential premises "as is" with no obligation to make them habitable or to make repairs. In several states, this doctrine has been replaced in residential leases by an implied warranty of habitability, whereby the landlord has an obligation to make the premises fit before the tenant moves in and to continue to keep the premises fit during the lease. (*See* **"as is,"** **implied warranty of habitability**.)

CBD   *See* **central business district (CBD)**.

CC&Rs   (*CC&Rs*)   *See* **covenants, conditions, and restrictions (CC&Rs); declaration of restrictions; restriction**.

C

cease and desist order   An order from a government authority directing a person violating the law to refrain from continuing to do so. For example, many state agencies can issue a cease and desist order against a respondent found to have committed a discriminatory act, or against a seller of condominiums or subdivisions in violation of applicable regulations.

cemetery lots   A special land-use designation created when the landowner or cemetery authority dedicates property exclusively to cemetery use. In many states, cemetery owners are exempt from paying real property taxes.

The subdivision laws usually are not applicable to the sale of cemetery lots. Cemetery lot salespeople do not generally need a real estate license, but often they are required to have a special cemetery salesperson's license. The purchaser of a cemetery lot often acquires only an easement or license right of burial—not a fee simple title to the lot. Joint tenant owners each have a vested right of interment.

With the current scarcity of developable land, some developers look to the development of the airspace above cemeteries. The modern trend of cemeteries is toward the lawn cemetery with no upright tombstones and an open park appearance.

central business district (CBD)   A city's downtown area where the main business, governmental, recreational, professional, and service activities of the community are concentrated.

CERCLA   *See* **Comprehensive Environmental Response, Compensation, and Liability Act (CERCLA)**.

certificate of claim   A contingent promise to reimburse an FHA-insured mortgagee for certain costs incurred during foreclosure of an insured mortgage, provided that the proceeds from the sale of the property are enough to cover the costs.

certificate of completion (CC)   A document generally issued by an architect or an engineer after inspection of a property attesting that the construction has been completed in compliance with plans and specifications. Final payment under the construction contract is then due and payable. Also known as a *certificate of occupancy* or *completion order*. (*See* **certificate of occupancy [CO]**.)

certificate of eligibility   A certificate issued by a Department of Veterans Affairs regional office to veterans who qualify for a VA loan.

The Veteran Housing Act permits regional administrators to restore a veteran's entitlement to loan-guarantee benefits after his or her property purchased with an existing VA-guaranteed loan has been disposed of and (1) this loan has been paid in full; (2) the administrator is released from liability under the guarantee; or (3) any loss suffered by the administrator has been repaid in full. It is no longer required that property ownership be transferred for a compelling reason.

Veterans are now allowed a one-time-only allowance for the veteran to regain entitlement by paying off the loan without having to dispose of the property.

The act also authorizes regional administrators to restore a veteran/seller's entitlement to loan-guarantee benefits and release the veteran from liability to the VA when another veteran has agreed to assume the outstanding balance on the veteran/seller's existing VA-guaranteed loan and consented to the use of his entitlement to the same extent that the veteran/transferor had used the original entitlement. This is not a release from the lender, however. The veteran/transferee and the property must otherwise meet the requirements of the law. Reinstatement of eligibility is never automatic but must always be applied for, preferably at the time of the sale of property purchased with an existing VA-guaranteed loan. (*See* **Veterans Affairs [VA] loan**.)

certificate of insurance   A certificate in which an insurance company verifies that a particular policy insuring certain parties is in effect for given amounts and coverage. This certificate is often issued when a commercial lease requires the lessee to maintain certain specified insurance coverage. (*See* **private mortgage insurance [PMI]**.)

certificate of no defense

1. A legal instrument executed by a mortgagor setting forth the exact unpaid balance of a mortgage, the current rate of interest and the date to which interest has been paid. It further states that the mortgagor has no defenses or offsets against the mortgagee at the time of the execution of the certificate. Once the mortgagor has executed a certificate of no defense, the mortgagor cannot thereafter claim that he or she did not owe the amount indicated in the certificate.

   Also called an *estoppel certificate*, a certificate of no defense is most frequently used when the mortgagee is selling the mortgage to a third party and the purchaser wants to be assured of the amount and terms of the mortgage and that the mortgagor acknowledges the full amount of the debt. Most mortgage documents contain a clause obligating the mortgagor to execute a certificate of no defense upon written notice from the mortgagee. (*See* **reduction certificate**.)

2. In a landlord-tenant situation, a certificate of no defense is a statement by the tenant setting forth the amount of rent payable and the term of the lease and acknowledging that the tenant claims no defenses or offsets against the landlord. A certificate of no defense is sometimes required when the landlord is selling the property or is assigning the lease. This is also called an **offset statement** or *estoppel letter*.

certificate of occupancy (CO)   A certificate issued by a governmental authority indicating that a building is ready and fit for occupancy and that there are no building code violations.

Some condominium developers insert language into the sales contract to the effect that upon notification that the units are ready for occupancy, the buyer must accept the unit despite any construction defects that may exist, although acceptance will not bar the buyer from obtaining redress for such defects. Once the building has been certified for occupancy, the developer can then close the individual sales, transfer title to the buyers and, most important, begin to pay off the construction loan and eliminate the interest payments.

certificate of reasonable value (CRV)   (*certificado de valor razonable*)   A certificate issued by the Department of Veterans Affairs setting forth a property's current market value estimate, based on a VA-approved appraisal. The CRV places a ceiling on the amount of a VA-guaranteed loan allowed for a particular property. If the purchase price exceeds the CRV, then the veteran may pay the excess in cash because secondary financing is somewhat restricted under VA regulations. The VA reserves the right to verify the source of cash funds. (*See* **Veterans Affairs [VA] loan**.)

certificate of title   (*certificado de título*)   A statement of opinion prepared by a title company, a licensed abstracter, or an attorney on the status of a title to a parcel of real property, based on an examination of specified public records. This certificate of title should not be confused with the certificate of title issued to a titleholder of land registered under the Torrens system, or with a title insurance policy.

A certificate of title does not guarantee title, but it does certify the condition of title as of the date the certificate is issued, on the basis of an examination of the public records maintained by the recorder of deeds, the county clerk, the county treasurer, the city clerk and collector, and clerks of various courts of record. The certificate also may include records involving taxes, special assessments, ordinances, zoning, and building codes.

A certificate of title does not offer protection against "off-the-record" matters such as undisclosed liens, rights of parties in possession, and matters of survey and location. Nor does it protect against "hidden defects" in the records themselves, such as fraud, forgery, lack of competency, or lack of delivery. A title insurance policy, not a certificate of title, protects against certain off-the-record and hidden defects risks.

An owner's certificate of title normally will not be issued for less than the sales price of the property. A mortgagee's certificate is usually issued for the amount of the loan being certified. A new certificate must be issued with any change in ownership. Liability is usually limited to the party requesting the title evidence, such as a mortgagee, owner, or vendee.

The preparer of the certificate of title is liable only for negligence in preparing the report and this liability is usually limited to the extent of personal assets or the assets of the local abstracting company that employs the preparer.

In many states, the sellers provide a certificate of title at their own expense, certifying the condition of the title as of the closing date. A buyer who desires title insurance would pay the difference between the cost of the certificate of title and the cost of the title insurance policy. (*See* **abstract of title, hidden risk, title insurance, Torrens system, transfer certificate of title [TCT]**.)

certified appraiser   A person who has met minimum education and examination requirements and has been certified (licensed) by the appropriate state agency to value real property in that state. Only certified appraisers can appraise certain types of real property that involve federally related loans. (*See* **Financial Institutions Reform, Recovery, and Enforcement Act [FIRREA]**.)

certified check   A check that the issuer (usually a bank) guarantees to be good, and against which a stop payment directive is ineffective if the payee obtains the certification.

Payment by certified check immediately discharges the buyer's duty of performance under a contract. Payment by personal check, however, constitutes conditional performance and does not discharge the buyer's obligation until the check clears (that is, is paid by the depositor's bank).

Certified checks are normally required by escrow companies from purchasers who use out-of-state banks—a reason many brokers have their clients set up a local checking account and transfer funds for the closing of a purchase. Many escrow companies now require all parties to make their closing payment by way of a certified check before escrow will record the conveyance documents. Some brokers require prospective buyers to use a certified check for an earnest money deposit. (*See* **cashier's check**)

Certified Commercial Investment Member (CCIM)   *See* Appendix B.

certified copy   A copy of a document (such as a deed, marriage, or birth certificate) signed by the person having possession of the original and declaring it to be a true copy.

Certified Property Manager (CPM)   *See* Appendix B.

certify   (*certificar*)   To testify in writing; to confirm; to guarantee in writing, as in a certified check; to endorse, as with a proper seal.

certiorari   A review by a higher court of a case or proceeding conducted by an inferior court, officer, board, or tribunal to certify the record of such proceeding. A means of obtaining a judicial review.

cession deed   A form of deed used to transfer the street rights of an abutting owner to a government agency. Subdividers who dedicate their streets to the municipality would use a cession deed. (*See* **dedication**.)

cesspool   (*fosa séptica*)   An underground porous pit used to catch and temporarily contain sewage and other liquid refuse, where it decomposes and is absorbed into the soil. Purchasers should check with the local building department to discover whether there are requirements to upgrade to a septic system. (*See* **effluence, leaching cesspool, septic tank**.)

chain
1. An engineer's chain is a series of 100 wire links, each of which is one foot in length.
2. A surveyor's chain is a series of wire links, each of which is 7.92 inches long. The total length of the chain is four rods, or 66 feet. Ten square chains of land are equal to one acre. The chain unit is a method of measurement used in the U.S. Public Land Surveys.

chain of title   (*cadena de título*)   The recorded history of matters that affect the title to a specific parcel of real property, such as ownership, encumbrances, and liens, usually beginning with the original recorded source of the title. The chain of title shows the successive changes of ownership, each one linked to the next so that a "chain" is formed.

Ownership of a particular property frequently passes through many hands subsequent to the original grant. If any link is broken in a property's chain of title, then the current "owner" does not have valid title to the property. For example, if a forged deed were somewhere in the chain, then no subsequent grantee would have acquired legal title to the property.

An abstracter searches and notes the chain of title (also called *running the chain of title*) in an examination of the title at the office of the county recorder or clerk, tracing the title from the original grant up to the present ownership. In the United States, chains of title in colonial states frequently date back to a grant from the king of England. In those states admitted to the Union after the formation of the United States, the deeds of conveyance in chains of title generally stem from the patent issued by the U.S. government. In a few states, such as Louisiana and Texas, chains of title generally date back to a point before acquisition of the land by the federal government.

To be within the unbroken chain of title, the instrument must be discoverable or traceable through linking conveyances from the present owner through successive owners to a common grantor. If not, a "gap" exists in the chain, creating a "cloud" on the title. In these cases, it is usually necessary to establish ownership by a court action called a *suit to quiet title*.

All documents recorded in the chain of title are said to give *constructive notice* of the document and its contents. However, if a document is not recorded in the chain of title, so that even a diligent search using the grantor-grantee index will not reveal its presence, then there is no constructive notice given of the existence of the unrecorded document. A deed not properly recorded is said to be a *wild deed* and is not valid against a subsequent recorded deed to a good-faith purchaser.

In practice, abstracters rarely search back more than 60 years. Some states have adopted a marketable title act that extinguishes certain interests and cures certain title defects that arose before the "root of title" was recorded. The root of title is the most recent conveyance (deed, court decree) that furnishes a basis for title marketability and has been of record for 40 years or more.

Other chain of title problems arise when a person acquires title using one name and then conveys the property under another name. In such cases, the grantor should indicate the name by which she acquired title; for example, "Sally Hines, who acquired title as Sally Fromm." Because of the importance of the chain of title, it is necessary that the parties' names be consistent and spelled out properly in all documents. (*See* **grantor-grantee index**, **recording**, **title search**, **wild deed**.)

chain store   Any one of a number of retail stores under common ownership and central management, selling standard merchandise and operating under a uniform policy. Often, a major chain store is an anchor tenant in a shopping center. (*See* **anchor tenant**.)

chalet   An A-frame housing construction style originated in the Swiss Alps and found mainly in mountainous regions, especially ski resort areas. Its design features large, overhanging eaves that offer protection from heavy winter snowfall.

change   (*cambio*)   An appraisal principle recognizing that economic and social forces are constantly at work. The appraiser must view real property and its environment as if in transition, taking note of trends that may affect the property in the future.

change of name   *See* **name, change of**.

change order   An order to a contractor from the owner, architect, or engineer on a construction project authorizing changes or modifications to the original work as shown in the contract drawings, plans, or specifications. A standard AIA form is normally used. A change order usually changes the original contract price.

    Condominium developers generally require purchasers of apartment units under construction to submit change orders and pay for special changes to the original apartment package, such as custom carpeting or appliances.

chattel   An item of tangible personal property. The word *chattel* evolved from the word *cattle*, one of the early important possessions. *Chattels real* are annexed to real estate, whereas *chattels personal* are movable. A lease is an example of a chattel real.

    Chattels are transferred by means of a bill of sale. The Uniform Commercial Code regulates the transfer of chattels and the use of chattels as security for debts. (*See* **financing statement**.)

chattel mortgage   A mortgage secured by personal property. Under the Uniform Commercial Code, chattel mortgages have been replaced by security agreements. (*See* **security agreement**.)

check (*cheque*)   A negotiable instrument signed by a maker or drawer authorizing a bank to pay money to the payee or bearer. (*See* **cashier's check, certified check, postdated check**.)

chimney (*chimenea*)   A stack of brick or other masonry extending above the surface of the roof that carries the smoke to the outside. The smoke is carried inside the chimney through the flue.

chimney cap   Ornamental stone or concrete edging around the top of the chimney stack that helps protect the masonry from the elements and improves the draft in the chimney.

chimney flashing   A strip of material, usually metal, placed over the junction of the chimney and the roof to make the joint watertight. Flashings are used wherever the slope of the roof is broken up by a vertical structure.

chimney pot   A fireclay or terra-cotta pipe projecting from the top of the chimney stack. The chimney pot is decorative and also increases the draft of the chimney.

Chinese American Real Estate Professional Association (CAREPA)   *See* Appendix A.

churning   The practice of transferring property to gain some advantage. The Internal Revenue Code contains various "antichurning" provisions to discourage certain tax avoidance transfers. These antichurning restrictions affect property transferred to or from a related party and transfers of certain leased property.

cinder fill   A layer of cinders placed between the ground and the basement floor or between the ground and the foundation walls to aid in water drainage.

circle   A roadway having a circular form with only one access point to the adjoining street.

cistern (*cisterna, aljibe*)   An artificial reservoir or tank, often underground, for the storing of rainwater collected from a roof.

Civil Rights Act of 1866   A federal act that prohibits *all* racial discrimination, affirmed in 1968, in *Jones v. Alfred H. Mayer Company*. Therefore, although the Civil Rights Act of 1968 exempts certain homeowners and groups, the 1866 *prohibits all racial discrimination without exception. Where race is involved, no exceptions apply.* Importantly, Jones affirmed that racial discrimination is prohibited in the sale or rental of privately held property. Enforcement of 1866 is through federal courts, not HUD.

Civil Rights Act of 1968   *See* **federal fair housing law**.

claim of right   The occupancy of property by one having no legal right to title but nevertheless claiming such a right. It is an adverse possessor's claim to a fee simple title, either under some apparent color of title or by mere naked claim. Example: A father gives his daughter the family farm, and she works the farm for 25 years until the father dies. No deed was ever prepared as is required under the statute of frauds. Most courts would hold that although an oral grant itself is invalid, when accompanied by an actual entry and possession for the statutory period of time, it will ripen into title by adverse possession because of her claim of right.

There is a definite split of court decisions where the occupant places a fence two feet onto a neighbor's property thinking it is really the occupant's property. Some courts hold that there can be no adverse possession if the occupant believes he already owns the property, thus not asserting any hostile claim of right. (*See* **adverse possession**.)

C

clapboard   Siding of narrow boards thicker at one edge and used as an exterior finish for frame houses.

Clayton Antitrust Act   Federal statute passed in 1914, to clarify and supplement the Sherman Antitrust Act of 1890. Clayton defined varied types of illegal business practices that helped to form monopolies, and it prohibited exclusive sales contracts, local price cutting to freeze out competitors, certain rebates, and certain corporate acquisitions of stock and interlocking directorates. (*See* **antitrust laws**, **Sherman Antitrust Act**.)

cleanout door   An exterior door located at the base of the chimney for convenient removal of ashes put through the ash dump.

clearing account   A bank account used for the temporary deposit of funds until the funds can be transferred into a permanent account.

clearing title   The process of examining all recorded and unrecorded instruments affecting a particular property and taking any necessary action to remove or otherwise cure the title of any defects or clouds in order that the title may become a good, marketable title. (*See* **marketable title**, **title search**.)

clear span   The condition within a building wherein a given floor area is free of posts, support columns, or shear walls.

clear title   Title to property that is free from liens, defects, or other encumbrances, except those the buyer has agreed to accept, such as a mortgage to be assumed or a restriction of record; established title; title without clouds. (*See* **cloud on title**, **marketable title**.)

client   (*cliente*)   The person who employs an agent to perform a service for a fee; also called a **principal**. The client is owed the duty of care and diligence, fiduciary duties in common-law states and statutory duties where the common law has been abrogated. Depending on the transaction, a broker may represent a seller, a buyer, a landlord or a tenant. (*See* **agent**, **customer**.)

client trust account   A separate bank account set up by a broker to keep a client's monies segregated from the broker's general funds; also called a *trust account*. In general, each broker is required by state law to deposit funds, which are not to be immediately released to escrow, into a trust fund account with a bank or recognized depository within a certain time after receipt. The broker is the trustee of the client trust account, and all funds deposited in the account must be available for withdrawal upon demand. A single client trust account can usually serve all the broker's clients, provided that detailed records are maintained and made subject to inspection by the proper state licensing agency. The principal broker in an agency is responsible for all trust monies and, although the broker will usually authorize a salesperson in writing to deposit client monies, the broker is ultimately responsible for the account. These accounts may or may not earn interest, according to state regulations, and if interest is earned, the state will specify who may benefit from interest earned. The broker may suggest the use of an interest-bearing account when substantial funds are involved—there should be a clear understanding of who will benefit from the interest (usually the buyer, not the seller or the broker).

A main reason for requiring a broker to maintain a client trust account separate from the general account is to protect these monies from possibly being "frozen" during legal actions against the

C

broker, such as creditor attachments or probate of a deceased broker's estate. In addition, because the account is custodial in nature, the Federal Deposit Insurance Corporation personally insures each client's funds up to $250,000 if each account is specifically designated as custodial and the name and interest of each owner in the deposit is disclosed on the depositor's records. This insurance will not apply if the broker commingles personal or business funds with clients' funds.

In addition to a client trust account for use with earnest money deposits, it is good practice for a broker to set up a management trust account when acting as property manager for several income rental properties. It is not necessary to open a separate trust account for each transaction; rather, a simple ledger system is sufficient. (*See* **commingling, customer trust fund [CTF]**.)

close corporation   *See* **corporation**.

closed-door discount store   *See* **discount department store**.

closed-end mortgage   A mortgage that prohibits the mortgagor from using the property as security for further loans; it contains a "no further encumbrance" provision.

closed mortgage   A "lock-in" mortgage; one that cannot be prepaid during a specified period of time or until maturity.

closed-wall construction   Wall components completely finished at the factory that arrive at the building site complete with factory-installed electrical and plumbing systems.

closing (settlement)   (*cierre*)   The consummation of a real estate transaction, when the seller delivers title to the buyer in exchange for payment by the buyer of the purchase price. Closing in some areas may not occur until the documents are recorded; however, under general rules of real estate law, transfer of title takes place upon delivery of the deed to the grantee. In many states, there is no joint meeting of buyer and seller; each performs separately.

In real estate practice, several informal meanings are given the word *closing*. For example, the phrase *closing a sale* is often used to describe the process of getting the buyer and the seller to agree to and sign the purchase agreement; the term *legal closing* refers to the moment that title and money are exchanged; and *financial closing* refers to the actual disbursements of monies, as directed in the closing or settlement statements. A person who says, "I'm going to the closing this afternoon," is usually referring to the act of going to the attorney's office, broker's office, mortgagee's office, or escrow company to finalize the transaction (sign the final documents, such as a mortgage, deed, or assignment of lease).

The broker usually estimates the date of closing when the purchase agreement is drawn up. Thirty to forty-five days is a normal period, giving the buyer enough time to inspect the property, examine the title, and arrange financing, while permitting the seller to prepare the conveyance documents and clear any problems with the title. If the purchase agreement calls for a contract for deed, the processing time is usually shorter.

Licensed escrow companies, lenders, banks, attorneys, brokers, or the parties themselves may conduct closings. Although the procedures usually are not controlled by statute, certain aspects of the closing may be regulated by laws such as the federal Real Estate Settlement Procedures Act (RESPA).

Prorations of expenses shared by buyer and seller (usually for such operating items as real property taxes and ground lease rent) are normally computed as of the closing date unless a different date (such as the date of occupancy) is specifically stated in the purchase agreement. The term *closing date* in this instance refers to the legal closing date—the date on which documents transferring title from the seller to the buyer are delivered and recorded. (*See* **escrow**.)

Internal Revenue Service rules require settlement agents to report details of the closing to the IRS using Form 1099-B. Sales or exchanges of residences with four or fewer units must be reported.

closing agent A neutral third party responsible for assembling documents for the transfer of real property. A closing agent may also be a person or firm that conducts the transaction, such as a real estate broker, a lender, a title insurance company, and/or an attorney. (*See* **closing [settlement]**.)

closing costs Expenses of the sale (or loan refinancing) that must be paid in addition to the purchase price (in the case of the buyer's expenses) or be deducted from the proceeds of the sale (in the case of the seller's expenses). Some closing costs result from legal requirements; others are a matter of local custom and practice. To avoid disputes, the contract should clearly define which party will pay for what "closing cost" items. Typical expenses that might be incurred by the seller and the buyer in an ordinary transaction are listed below.

Seller's Expenses	Buyer's Expenses
Cost of clearing title	New loan or assumption fees
Certificate of title	Prepaid interest/new loan
Abstract, continuation, title insurance (when required by the sales contract)	Deed and mortgage recording fees
	Escrow fee (share with seller)
	Title insurance, if desired
Attorney fees for drafting deed or assignment of lease, bill of sale	Reimbursement to seller for prepaid taxes
Conveyance tax	Appraisal and inspection fees
Broker's commission	Attorney fees for drafting contract for deed
Escrow fee (share with buyer)	Condominium transfer fee
Interest in arrears/old loan	Well/septic inspection
Lessor's consent to assignment	
Prepayment penalty	
Survey and stacking (If required)	
Pest control inspection	

In addition to these closing costs, which are fixed at a specified amount regardless of the closing date, other variable expenses—items such as real property taxes, prepaid insurance premiums, interest on assumed obligations, rents, and so on—must be prorated between the seller and the buyer. Because these expenses are directly related to property ownership, they are normally prorated as of the date on which title to the property passes, thus making the sellers responsible for expenses for the period that they owned the property, and the buyers responsible for expenses accruing from the date they take title. In some areas, the buyer assumes the expenses as of the closing day.

Under the provisions of the federal RESPA, the lender is required to give the borrower a copy of HUD's settlement cost booklet *Shopping for Your Home Loan* (available at *www.HUD.gov*) and provide a good-faith estimate of closing costs likely to be incurred in financing the property. If the booklet and the estimate are not provided at the time of loan application, they must be mailed within three business days of the completed loan application. The application is not considered complete until the property is identified.

closing protection letter A document issued by the title insurance company to insured lenders and, in some unusual cases, to insured owners. The letter indicates the title insurers' responsibilities for negligence, fraud, and errors that might be made when their agents or approved attorneys handle the closing ("quasi-fidelity coverage").

closing statement (*declaración de cierre*) A detailed cash accounting of a real estate transaction prepared by a broker, escrow officer, attorney, or other person designated to process the mechanics of the sale, showing all cash received, all charges and credits made, and all cash paid out in the transaction. A closing statement may also be called a settlement statement or adjustment sheet—in all federally related loans, the HUD-1 settlement sheet is used. The statement shows how all closing and adjustment costs plus prepaid and unpaid expenses are allocated between the buyer and the seller. In many areas, separate closing statements are prepared for the buyers, showing credits, charges, and the balance due from them at closing; for the sellers, showing credits, charges, and the proceeds they will receive at closing; and for the broker, showing a detailed accounting of all monies received and disbursed in the transaction. (*See* **closing costs**, **prorate**.)

closure   In a metes-and-bounds description, the process of returning to the point of the beginning. Unless the described parcel is thus "closed," the description has no legal status.

cloud on title   Any document, claim, unreleased lien, or encumbrance that may superficially impair or injure the title to a property or cast doubt on the title's validity. Clouds on title are usually revealed by a title search and may be removed from the record by a quitclaim deed or a quiet title proceeding initiated by the property owner. Usually, the owner is prevented from conveying a marketable title while the "cloud" remains, unless it is only for a minor nuisance item.

Typical clouds on title are (1) a recorded contract for deed that has not been removed from the record, but under which the buyer has defaulted; (2) a recorded option that was not exercised, but that still appears on the record; (3) a recorded mortgage paid in full, but with no satisfaction of mortgage recorded; (4) property sold without the wife's release of her dower interest; (5) an heir of a prior owner with a questionable claim to the property; (6) the situation in which one of many heirs has not signed a deed; (7) a lis pendens (pending litigation) having been dropped but not removed from the record; (8) a lessee in default having an option to purchase, which probably will not be enforceable if the lessee breaches the lease; or (9) a prior conveyance with an incomplete legal description. (*See* **quiet title action**.)

CLUE Report   *See* **Comprehensive Loss Underwriting Exchange (CLUE)**.

cluster development   The grouping of housing units on less-than-normal-size home sites, with remaining land used as common areas. For example, rather than build ten units per acre on a ten-acre site, a developer might cluster 20 units per acre and prepare five acres as a common area with facilities for recreation. (*See* **planned unit development [PUD]**.)

cluster zoning   A zoning provision whereby a specific residential or unit density is prescribed for an entire area. The developer is free to concentrate or disperse the density within the area in accordance with flexible site-planning criteria. This differs from traditional zoning ordinances that allocate zoning on a lot-by-lot basis, prescribing the same maximum density for all single-structure lots within the zoning district. (*See* **planned unit development [PUD]**, **zero lot line**.)

Coastal Zone Management Act   A federal law passed in 1972, recognizing the national interest in the effective planning, management, beneficial use, protection, and development of the saltwater and Great Lakes coastal zones. The act calls for states to plan and develop management programs for the land and water resources of their coastal zones.

Code of Ethics   (*código de ética*)   A written system of standards of ethical conduct. Real estate brokerage is a profession, an occupation that requires special skill and advanced training. Because of the nature of the relationship between a broker and a client or other persons in a real estate transaction, a high standard of ethics is needed to ensure that brokers act in the best interests of both their principal and any third parties.

Most professional organizations incorporate a set of self-governing rules that also include the application of penalties for inappropriate behavior or negligence. Although technically only members are held to these standards, increasingly, courts look to the profession's code of ethics.

Members of the National Association of REALTORS® (NAR) subscribe to a code of ethics that is in a constant state of flux. NAR has published the booklet *Interpretation of the Code of Ethics*, applying the code to practical situations. There are also approved Standards of Practice, which interpret some of the articles of the Code of Ethics, which may be cited as additional support for alleged violations of the code. REALTORS® are required to complete ethics training within each four-year cycle. The Code is available in six languages: English, Chinese, Korean, Spanish, Tagalog, and Vietnamese at *www.realtor.org*.

codicil   A supplement or addition to a will that normally does not revoke the entire will. A codicil must be executed with the same formalities as a will and be witnessed by the required number of people. (*See* **will**.)

cognovit note   *See* **confession of judgment**.

coinsurance

1. A common provision in building insurance policies under which the insured agree to maintain insurance on their property in an amount equal to at least 80 percent of the replacement cost. If the property is not insured to that amount and a loss is incurred, the insurance company will make the insured share in the loss on a pro rata basis. Example: If the building is insured for only 60 percent of its value and there is a $10,000 loss, the insurance company will pay only $7,500 (i.e., 60% ÷ 80% [or ⁶⁄₈] = $10,000). Because property values are steadily increasing, it is important for property owners to review their insurance policies from time to time to keep within the 80 percent minimum. In addition, the insured can pay for inflation guard coverage. In any event, liability under any insurance policy is limited to the face amount of the policy. One reason for the 80 percent rule is that generally no more than 80 percent of a building's value is destroyed by fire; a certain part of the structure will usually be available for salvage. Coinsurance requirements generally are included in commercial and industrial hazard policies, and a similar type of coinsurance coverage is found in homeowners' policies.

    A typical clause reads:

    If at the time of loss, the amount of insurance in this policy on the damaged building is less than 80 percent of the full replacement cost of the building immediately prior to the loss, we will pay the larger of the following amounts, but not exceeding the limit of liability under this policy applying to the building:

    (a) the actual cash value of that part of the building damaged; or

    (b) that portion of the cost to repair or replace, without deduction for depreciation, of that part of the building damaged, which the total amount of insurance in this policy on the damaged building bears to 80 percent of the replacement cost of the building.

2. Insurance coverage that is underwritten by several different insurers. (*See* **insurance**.)

cold call   (*llamada en frío*)   An unsolicited inquiry from a real estate office or salesperson to a prospective buyer or seller, a way to introduce the company or salesperson to a prospect. The federal Telephone Solicitation Act prohibits making cold calls after 9:00 pm and before 8:00 am In addition, the new federal do-not call law prohibits making unsolicited calls to consumers who have registered their phone numbers. (*See* **National Do Not Call Registry**, **floor duty**.)

cold canvass   (*búsqueda en frío*)   Obtaining listings by door-to-door solicitation of homeowners. Real estate salespeople usually employ this method when seeking listings in a specific area or when looking for homes of a certain type or with certain features.

collapsible corporation   The prearranged use of a corporation to convert ordinary income into capital gain to avoid corporate taxation—a situation prevented by a set of Internal Revenue Service rules. This concept is most easily understood by looking at a hypothetical situation: Two real estate dealers organize a corporation to develop a condominium. The corporation constructs the building, which substantially increases the value of the land. Before the units are sold, the dealers sell their stock in the corporation to a third party and claim capital gain treatment on the sale of their stock. If an IRS agent were to examine this transaction, the agent probably would apply the collapsible corporation rules if the property had been held for less than three years. The IRS then would claim that the sale of the stock was equivalent to the sale of the development and be similarly taxable—that is, taxable at ordinary income rates. The collapsible corporation rules penalize these stockholders by treating the sale of their stock as ordinary income, which it would have been considered if the corporation itself had sold the development. These rules were important prior to the 1986 Tax Reform Act. Since 1986, a corporation cannot liquidate its assets without recognition of the gain nor can the corporation's shareholders sell their stock without the gain being recognized at the corporate level.

collar beam   A horizontal beam connecting the rafters at the lower end. The collar beam adds rigidity and helps divert the weight of snow on the roof from the exterior walls.

collateral   Something of value given or pledged as security for a debt or obligation. The collateral for a real estate mortgage loan is the hypothecated mortgaged property itself. (*See* **hypothecation**.)

collateral heirs   Heirs descending from the same common ancestor but not from one another. Collateral heirs are not in a direct line of descent—they may be siblings, aunts, uncles, or cousins, but cannot be sons or daughters, who are lineal descendants.

collateralized mortgage   A loan secured by collateral in addition to real estate, as with a pledged savings account. Collateralization is taking an existing mortgage and using it as security or collateral for a loan (without having to discount it).

collateralized mortgage obligation (CMO)   A mortgage-backed security that represents claims to specific cash flows from large pools of home mortgages. The CMO investor owns a bond collateralized by a pool of mortgages. The issuer of the bond then segments the cash flows in a manner that allows payoff of the different classes of bonds in a sequential manner. Thus, investors are offered a choice of maturities that make this kind of mortgage-backed security more attractive to a broader market. The CMOs that consisted of low-credit-quality loans (known as *subprime mortgage loans*) were a major contribution to the financial crisis of 2008. (*See* **Freddie Mac.**)

collection account   An account established by someone to receive periodic payments on a debt or obligation, to make disbursements as requested by the payee, and to make an accounting to both parties. For example, many contracts for deed require the buyer to put payments into a collection account at a bank or escrow company, which in turn pays the real estate taxes, lease rent, maintenance fees, mortgage payments (if any), and insurance payments. An agreement between the parties determines who pays the fees. Collection accounts are also used in wraparound mortgage situations.

collection report   The form used by a loan correspondent (servicer) in reporting collections from mortgagors, including payments in full, repayment of advances, tax and insurance funds for foreclosed mortgages, and any other items remitted as regular installment payments.

color of title   A condition in which a title appears to be good, but because of a certain defect, is in fact invalid (paper title).

For example, the seller conveys a ten-acre farm to the buyer by deed. The buyer enters into possession unaware that the seller held title under a forged deed. Thus, the buyer does not have valid title to the property. By occupying the premises for a prescribed period of time, the buyer can acquire legal title to the entire ten-acre parcel by means of adverse possession under color of title, even though he physically occupied only part of the ten acres, because the adverse claimant under color of title need only possess a portion of the premises described in the ineffective conveyance to acquire title to the whole parcel. If no deed were involved and the buyer adversely occupied just part of the ten acres, after the prescribed period, the buyer would acquire title only to the acreage actually occupied (or fenced or cultivated). In addition, a claimant not under color of title has a stronger burden of proof on each of the required elements for adverse possession.

In some states, a possessor of property under color of title must be in good faith in order to acquire title by adverse possession. That is, the possessor must believe the deed is really valid even though it is actually defective (i.e., the possessor cannot be a squatter). Thus, the defect in the deed must not be so obvious that a reasonable person would know the deed was not valid. (*See* **adverse possession**.)

combed (striated) plywood　Common building material in modern homes, particularly for interior finish. The exposed surface is combed in parallel grooves.

combination trust　*See* **real estate mortgage trust (REMT)**.

commencement of work　The noticeable beginning of an improvement on real estate as determined under local law. This exact time has significance relative to the effective date of a mechanic's lien (and thus the priority against other liens such as mortgages), as well as protecting a builder against changes in the zoning rules. (*See* **mechanic's lien**, **zoning estoppel**.)

commercial acre　That portion of an acre of newly subdivided land remaining after dedication for streets, sidewalks, parks and so on; that portion on which the developer is free to build.

commercial bank　A financial institution designed to act as a safe depository and lender for many commercial activities (usually short-term loans). Commercial banks rely heavily on demand deposits—checking accounts—for their basic supply of loanable funds, although they also receive capital from savings accounts, loans from other banks, short-term loan interest, and the equity invested by their owners.

Commercial Investment Real Estate Institute　*See* Appendix A.

commercial leasehold insurance　Insurance to cover the payment of rent in the event the insured (tenant) cannot pay it; sometimes required by a commercial lender in a shopping center development as a prerequisite to issuing a leasehold mortgage.

commercial property　(*propiedad comercial*)　A classification of real estate that includes income-producing property such as office buildings, gasoline stations, restaurants, shopping centers, hotels and motels, parking lots, and stores. Commercial property usually must be zoned for business purposes.

commingling　To mingle or mix; for example, to deposit client funds in the broker's personal or general account. Licensees found guilty of commingling funds may generally have their license suspended or revoked by the state licensing agency. Some commingling situations are rather obvious; others are more involved, such as a broker acting as property manager who takes a fee out of the tenant's security deposit.

Commingling may occur when a broker fails to deposit trust funds into escrow, a client trust, or earnest money account at a bank or recognized depository within the time frame mandated by rule or regulation.

Commingling does not occur when the broker keeps a minimum amount of the broker's own money in the client trust account in order to keep the account open. The amount is often regulated by rule or regulation. In many states (but not all), it is permissible to hold an uncashed check until acceptance of an offer when directed to do so by the buyer (offeror); however, before the seller accepts the offer, the broker must specifically disclose the fact that the check is being held in an uncashed form.

C

As a matter of policy, not cashing checks until an offer is accepted may prevent problems for the broker. Often a buyer submits an offer with a personal check as an earnest money deposit. If the broker deposits the check in the client's trust account and the offer is rejected, then the broker may be in a position of having to refund the earnest money deposit before the broker knows whether the buyer's check has cleared. If the broker delays in returning the earnest money deposit, the buyer will be irritated and their business relationship ruined. Yet, if the broker returns the deposit and the check bounces, the broker is out the money.

A more serious offense than commingling is conversion, which is the actual misappropriation of client monies. (*See* **conversion**.)

commission   The compensation paid to a real estate broker (usually by the seller) for services rendered in connection with the sale or exchange of real property. To collect a commission, the broker must be licensed in the state, have a written employment agreement (listing) with the seller, and sell the property and/or execute a valid contract of sale for the property.

The commission is typically stated as a percentage of the gross sales price, a flat fee, or even an hourly rate, and the exact rate is subject to negotiation; any attempt by a group of brokers to fix brokerage rates would be a violation of antitrust laws.

Many listing contracts now provide a statement to the effect that "commission rates are negotiable and are not fixed by law." Some state laws require a written employment agreement (listing) before the broker can recover a commission. Some state laws require a disclosure in the listing agreement to the effect that commissions are negotiable.

Often a broker will share the commission with another broker who has cooperated in the transaction. To share a commission with a salesperson associated with another broker, a broker must process the money through the salesperson's employing broker, except in the case of deferred commissions earned under a prior broker. A salesperson cannot accept payment directly from a consumer, only through the employing broker.

Once the seller accepts the offer from a ready, willing, and able buyer, the seller is technically liable to the broker for the full commission, regardless of whether the buyer completes the purchase. However, in a case where the broker knew or should have known that the buyer was not financially able to complete the purchase, the courts tend to prevent a broker from seeking a full commission from the seller. Of course, if the offer is made subject to a condition, the broker cannot collect a commission until the condition is satisfied. Also, if a property is listed and is later taken under condemnation or sold at a foreclosure sale, the broker usually receives no commission, because the broker did not negotiate the sale.

A broker who has produced a ready, willing, and able buyer on the listing terms is generally still entitled to commission if the transaction is not consummated for any of the following reasons:
- The owners (sellers) change their mind and refuse to sell.
- The buyer defaults and refuses to buy. Some state courts now refuse to enforce the commission agreement where the buyer defaults through no fault of the seller.
- The owner's spouse refuses to sign the contract or deed.
- Defects in the owner's title have not been corrected.
- The owner commits fraud with respect to the transaction.
- The owner is unable to deliver possession within a reasonable time.
- The owner insists on terms not in the listing, such as the right to restrict the use of the property.
- The owner and the buyer agree to cancel the signed contract to purchase.

Most license laws prohibit a broker from sharing a commission with someone who is not licensed as a salesperson or broker. Commission here has been construed to include such things as certain items of personal property (a broker giving a new TV to "a friend" for providing a valuable lead) and other premiums (vacations and so on), as well as finder's fees and actual percentages of the commission.

Payment of the commission is not the determining factor in an agency relationship, which can be created whether the seller pays the fee, the buyer pays the fee, each pays, or neither pays. Still, prudent brokers should discuss and document whom they represent and who is paying for their service to avoid any misunderstandings that the broker must have represented the person who eventually paid the broker's commission.

The courts have held that real estate brokers or salespeople buying property through their own brokerage firm for personal use must still be taxed on the commission they would have received for the sale, even though it is reflected as a discount (or a "contra") against the purchase price. Commission income, whether received by an employee or independent contractor, is considered "personal service" or "earned" income.

Once the broker has received the commission, it is usually divided according to a prearranged formula between the brokerage agency ("the house") and the salespeople involved in the transaction. Because commission splits vary considerably from company to company, salespeople must have a clear understanding (preferably in writing) with their employing broker as to how they are to be paid, when, and at what percentage of the gross commission earned. Some offices are 100 percent offices in which the affiliated licensee receives the entire commission and pays back a monthly fee to cover office expenses.

Leasing commissions are usually based on graduated percentages over the entire lease term. The broker usually receives no monetary compensation for time and expenses involved with showings that do not lead to sales.

(*See* **antitrust laws, deferred commission, draw, finder's fee, listing, one hundred percent commission, procuring cause**.)

commissioner
1. A member of a state real estate commission.
2. A person appointed by a court of equity in a partition proceeding to advise the court as to the best method of partitioning a property among cotenants.
3. A person appointed by a court to supervise a mortgage foreclosure sale. (*See* **partition, real estate commission/department**.)

commitment   A pledge or promise to do a certain act, such as the promise of a lending institution to loan a certain amount of money at a specified rate of interest to a qualified buyer, provided the loan is made by a certain date. Unlike a contract for sale, a party such as a lender bound by a commitment cannot be forced judicially to specifically perform; however, an aggrieved party may seek money damages upon refusal to loan on the commitment.

A conventional loan commitment may be either firm or conditional. The borrower applies directly to the lender, usually on a standard form application. After analyzing the applicant's purpose and financial ability to repay the loan, the lender writes the borrower a commitment letter. This commitment letter is, in effect, a detailed offer to loan money according to specific terms. If the borrower accepts the commitment and satisfies any conditions the lender may have made, such as providing satisfactory appraisal and credit reports, the lending institution prepares the proper mortgage documentation. When the mortgage papers have been executed and the title approved, the lending institution will release the mortgage proceeds to be applied for the purposes for which the loan was made, such as refinancing.

For FHA loans, a conditional commitment is an agreement to loan a definite amount of money on a particular property subject to FHA approval of a presently unknown borrower whose credit and eligibility will have to be checked. A firm FHA commitment is an agreement to insure a loan in a certain amount on a specific property to a designated borrower. A conditional loan commitment fee is usually refunded from the closing costs when the loan is actually made. FHA conditional commitments are good for six months and may be renewed for another six months upon payment of an additional fee.

In large developments, developers often pay for or "purchase" a commitment for permanent takeout financing. (*See* **buydown, standby fee**.)

Commitment also refers to an agreement by a title insurance company to issue a policy in favor of a proposed insured upon acquisition of a specific property. Unlike a binder, however, it is not a contract for temporary insurance. The commitment is for a short period of time and identifies the type of policy to be issued, the estate or interest of the insured, vesting of title, legal description of the property being covered, and any exceptions to coverage.

common area maintenance (CAM)   Fees charged directly to tenants by owners for upkeep of common areas. In shopping centers, for example, tenants are charged for landscaping, snow removal, and utilities in the common areas.

common areas   Land or improvements in a condominium development designated for the use and benefit of all residents, property owners, and tenants. Common areas frequently include such amenities as corridor or hall areas and elevators, and parks, playgrounds, and barbecue areas, which are sometimes called *greenbelts*. In shopping centers, the common areas are parking lots, malls, and traffic lanes.

common elements   Parts of a property necessary or convenient to the existence, maintenance, and safety of a condominium, or are normally in common use by all of the condominium residents. All condominium owners have an undivided ownership interest in the common elements. Maintenance of the common elements is paid for by the condominium owners' association, and each owner must pay a monthly maintenance assessment prorated according to his or her individual common interest. Typical common elements are elevators, load-bearing walls, floors, roofs, hallways, swimming pools, and so on. (*See* **common areas, common expenses, common interest, common profits, limited common elements**.)

common expenses   The operating expenses of condominium common elements, together with all other sums designated as common expenses by or pursuant to the condominium declaration or bylaws.

common interest   The percentage of undivided ownership in the common elements belonging to each condominium apartment, as established in the condominium declaration. The applicable percentage is usually computed as the ratio of the square footage of a particular apartment to the total square footage of all the apartment units, or as the ratio of the apartment's purchase price to the total sales price of all the apartment units. The ratio is expressed as a percentage, such as 1.47 percent or 0.0147. The percentage of common interest determines an owner's interest in the common elements, the amount an owner will be assessed for maintenance and operation of the common properties, the real estate tax levied against an individual unit, and the number of votes an owner has in the condominium owners' association. (*See* **common elements**.)

common law   That body of law based on usage, general acceptance, and custom, as manifested in decrees and judgments of the courts; judge-made law ("case law") as opposed to codified or statutory law (or civil law as found in a few states like Louisiana). This manner of jurisprudence originated in England and was later incorporated into the U.S. legal system by either statute or custom.

common profits
1. In a condominium, the balance of all income, rents, profits, and revenues from the common elements remaining after the deduction of the common expenses.
2. The profits derived from the operations of a partnership or corporation.

common wall   A wall separating two living units in a condominium project. Most developers declare the common walls between two apartments to be common elements, and thus traditional party-wall rules do not apply. (*See* **party wall**.)

Community Associations Institute (CAI)   *See* Appendix A.

community property   A system of property ownership based on the theory that each spouse has an equal interest in the property acquired by the efforts of either spouse during marriage. This system stemmed from Germanic tribes and, through Spain, came to the Spanish colonies of North and South America. The system was unknown under English common law. States that maintain a community property system include California, Arizona, Idaho, Louisiana, Nevada, New Mexico, Texas, and Washington.

In community property states, there are two classifications of property—separate property and community property. Separate property is property that either the husband or the wife owned at the time of marriage or that one spouse acquired during marriage by inheritance, will, or gift. Separate property is entirely free from all interest or claim on the part of the other spouse. All other property is community property and is automatically owned equally by each spouse regardless of whose name record title is held under.

The signatures of both spouses are required to appear on a listing contract or any instruments of conveyance if community property is involved. In determining the proper tenancy for a buyer to take title, expert tax advice should be obtained.

Spouses may transfer their own separate property, and the other need not sign the deed. However, as a matter of practice, title insurance companies and others prefer the signature of both spouses to eliminate any question as to whether the property is actually separate property or community property. Prudent licensees recognize the need for obtaining, among other things, the signature of both parties on an instrument of conveyance, or on any other instrument that might affect the title to real property. It is wise to indicate on the instrument whether the grantor is a single person, in order to communicate immediately to anyone seeing the instrument that there was no community property interest in the grantor.

Community states do not recognize dower, curtesy, and survivorship rights. Upon the death of one spouse, half the property passes to the decedent's heirs and the surviving spouse retains his half-share in the community property. (*See* **dower**, **curtesy**.)

Community Reinvestment Act   A federal act that requires lenders to meet the credit needs of the communities in which they do business by expanding credit to low- and moderate-income people.

community shopping center   A shopping center of approximately 150,000 square feet and 20 to 70 retail spaces classified between the smaller neighborhood center and the larger regional center and supported by more than 5,000 families. (*See* **shopping center**.)

compaction   Matted down or compressed extra soil added to a lot to fill in the low areas or raise the level of the parcel.

comparables   Recently sold or leased properties that are similar to a particular property being evaluated and are used to indicate a value for the subject property. "Comps" need not be identical to the subject in physical characteristics or location, but the highest and best use, land-to-building ratio, terms of the sale, and the market conditions should be similar, or relatively easy to adjust for comparison.

C

In addition to adjustments for financing, time, and conditions of sale, adjustments may be necessary for differences in location and all features that are recognized by the market as having value.

In general terms, the more recent the sale and the fewer the dissimilarities, the better the comparable. Comps must also fit the definition of value to be applied. Distressed properties are not arm's length. Sales of distressed properties generally do not fit the definition of market value. The appraiser must carefully select only those comparables that actually fit the definition of value being used. (*See* **direct sales comparison approach.**)

comparative unit method   A method used to determine the reproduction cost in which all components of a building are added together on a unit basis, such as cost per square foot. Some components are framing, exterior finish, and floor and roof construction. (*See* **reproduction cost.**)

comparison method   *See* **direct sales comparison approach.**

compass points   The 32 positions marked on a compass to indicate directions, usually used when recording a metes-and-bounds description or other legal description.

compensating balance   Funds deposited by a borrower with a lending institution as a means of inducing the lender to make a loan or extend a line of credit to the borrower. Usually applies to commercial loans, not to mortgage loans.

compensation   *See* **commission, consideration, just compensation.**

compensatory damages   The damages awarded to the plaintiff by a court, intended to cover the actual injury or economic loss. This award does not include punitive damages or damages for grossly negligent behavior. (*See* **actual damages, consequential damages, damages, punitive damages.**)

competent party   A party to a contract who possesses the legal capacity to enter into a binding contract. (*See* **capacity of parties.**)

competitive market analysis (CMA)   (*análisis del mercado comparativo o compe-titivo*)   A tool used by brokers and salespeople to assist consumers in determining a property's sale price. It is not an appraisal. The CMA consists of information about three types of properties similar to the subject property: prices of those sold, on the market, and expired. The "solds" indicate what other buyers were willing to pay for a property similar to the subject property and are the base for the official appraisal. The "expireds" indicate the value other buyers have not been willing to pay for a property similar to the subject property. A seller's agent should guide the seller into setting the list price in "competition" with those properties currently on the market. A CMA done by the buyer's agent can reassure the buyers that their offer is fair and in line with what others have paid. (*See* **direct sales comparison approach.**)

complainant   A person who makes a complaint or instigates legal action against another (the respondent).

completion bond   A surety bond posted by a landowner or a developer to guarantee that a proposed development completes according to specifications, free and clear of all mechanics' liens. A completion bond is distinct and separate from a performance bond, which is given to an owner by a party to a contract (normally the contractor or subcontractor) to ensure performance of the contract, provided the party is paid.

With a completion bond, the landowner or developer may have no underlying contract to perform. Most county subdivision ordinances require the subdivider to post a cash completion bond as a condition to the county's granting approval of a proposed subdivision. Some lenders require an owner to provide a completion bond in addition to a performance bond from the contractor, thus assuring the lender that the development (which is the security for the loan) will be completed whether or not the owner pays the contractor. The bond is drawn in the amount of the total construction cost and is exercisable only if the developer cannot complete the project. If this happens, the lender can use the bond proceeds to complete and then sell the building to recover the interim loan funds. (*See* **payment bond, performance bond, surety**.)

completion order   *See* **certificate of completion (CC), certificate of occupancy (CO).**

compliance inspection

1. Inspection by a public official of a structure to ensure that it meets all building codes and specifications.
2. Inspection of a construction site or structure by either a lending institution (for conventional mortgage loan) or a government representative (for an FHA or VA loan) to ensure that it complies with all relevant requirements before a mortgage is made or before advances are made under a construction loan. (*See* **inspection**.)

component depreciation   Once used as a tax-saving method of depreciating the components of a building separately (in contrast to composite or unitary depreciation, where the entire asset depreciates at the same rate). Component depreciation is advantageous in that it provides considerably faster depreciation deduction on those structural elements that have a much shorter life than the building as a whole. The shorter-lived the component and the higher its cost in relation to the building as a whole, the greater the potential tax savings. For example, the useful life of a building may be 40 years, but certain of its component parts have shorter lives, such as air-conditioning—10 years; elevator—15 years; wiring—15 years; plumbing—15 years; roof—15 years.

As a result of the Economic Recovery Tax Act of 1981, component depreciation generally is not usable for any property placed in service after 1980. (*See* **accelerated cost recovery system [ACRS], useful life**.)

compound interest   (*interés compuesto*)   Interest computed on the principal sum *plus* accrued interest. At the beginning of the new interest period, all interest is added to the principal, forming a new principal figure on which interest is then calculated. This process repeats itself each interest period—interest compounding daily, monthly, semiannually, or annually. Thus, on a $1,000 savings account at 5 percent interest compounded annually, for the first year the amount of interest is $50. In the second year, the new principal balance is $1,050, thus making the second-year interest $52.50.

Some states specifically prohibit (as usurious) actions to recover compound interest on loans, so that contracts charging interest on interest cannot have the extra interest enforced. However, after simple interest has become due, interest upon it may be contracted for and collected under a new special agreement. (*See* **interest**.)

Comprehensive Environmental Response, Compensation, and Liability Act (CERCLA)   A federal law, enacted in 1980 and reauthorized by the Superfund Amendments and Reauthorization Act of 1986 (SARA), which imposes on owners, lenders, occupants, and operators liability for correcting environmental problems discovered on a property. *Superfund*, as the statutes are known collectively, establishes a fund to clean hazardous waste sites and respond to spills and releases on property. Generally, Superfund establishes a means for identifying parties liable for cleaning operations as well as providing for reimbursement by those parties deemed to be ultimately responsible for cleanup costs.

Associated with the CERCLA and SARA provisions is the Resource Conservation and Recovery Act of 1976 (RCRA), drafted with the "cradle-to-grave" approach to the regulation of the licensing and notification requirements, for those who generate, store, treat, or dispose of hazardous waste. Under RCRA, treatment, storage, and disposal of hazardous wastes require a permit from the Environmental Protection Agency (EPA). The EPA is the administrative agency charged with enforcing

C

CERCLA, SARA, and RCRA. In addition, many states have enacted their own Superfund statutes dealing with hazardous waste cleanup, and each has a governmental agency to enforce the statutes.

CERCLA imposes liability for a release of hazardous waste resulting in the government or a private party incurring response costs. A *release* is very broadly defined as any spilling, leaking, pumping, pouring, emitting, emptying, discharging, injecting, escaping, leaking, dumping, or dispersing into the environment, including even a passive release such as the burying of barrels containing hazardous substances. The buyer may be liable even for a release that occurred prior. There are severe civil and criminal penalties for failure to file a timely report of a spill.

Under CERCLA, liability is based on strict liability, not on fairness or fault. Under Superfund, "potentially responsible parties" includes current owners and operators of a hazardous substance facility, past owners and operators of a hazardous substance facility at the time of disposal and persons who transport or arrange for treatment or disposal of hazardous substances at the facility.

Those who consider selling, buying, leasing, or managing real estate should evaluate the impact of Superfund on their potential liability. If the site is likely to contain hazardous substances, the real estate agent should routinely recommend the use of environmental experts to examine the property for potential problems. One way to limit liability is to demonstrate that, prior to purchase, the buyer conducted "all appropriate inquiry" through a due diligence inspection of the property. Experts hired to conduct a Phase I audit of the property investigate the site, public records, and surrounding properties. Action to correct or to remove hazardous substances is referred to as *remediation*.

Lenders on commercial properties are concerned that the security for their loan may be substantially impaired if the property is found to contain hazardous substances, so they frequently insist on at least a Phase I audit prior to making a loan. Lenders are also concerned that they could be a potentially responsible party under CERCLA if they take back a property in foreclosure or participate in management of the secured property. Therefore, lenders require extensive documentation on environmental issues. (*See* **de minimus settlement**, **Phase I audit**.)

Comprehensive Loss Underwriting Exchange (CLUE)   A database of consumer insurance claims generated by LexisNexis® Risk Solutions and utilized by participating insurance companies when underwriting or rating a new insurance policy. Under the Fair and Accurate Credit Transaction Act (FACT Act), owners (sellers) have the right to access and challenge the accuracy of claim information, type of loss and amounts paid, and the description of the property covered. The information is stored for five years.

Because insurance companies have found a correlation between consumers' prior loss history and their future insurance loss potential, most insurance companies will use this information to make decisions about issuing policies and pricing premiums. Buyers may discover that their own claims history may make it difficult to obtain affordable homeowners' insurance. (*See* **Fair Credit Reporting Act [FCRA]**.)

computerized loan origination (CLO)   A computer network tied into a major lender that allows agents across the country to initiate mortgage loan applications in their own offices. Real estate brokers, insurance agents, lawyers, and others who may earn a loan origination fee may undertake such loan origination. HUD has approved the procedure as being in compliance with RESPA so long as (1) full disclosure is made of the fee, (2) multiple lenders are displayed on the computer screen to give the borrower some basis for comparison, and (3) the fee is charged as a dollar amount rather than a percentage of the loan.

concentric circle theory   An economic theory of city growth stating that, if there are no barriers, cities tend to expand in concentric circles from their point of origin. The model city consists of five zones: the central business district, a zone of transition, a zone of independent working people's homes, a region of better residences, and a group of commuter zones.

C

concession

1. Discount given to prospective tenants by landlords to induce them to sign a lease. Concessions are negotiable points in a lease, resolved in favor of the prospective tenant and utilized in both residential and commercial leases. Concessions impact the owner, and a purchaser of any income-producing property should check all existing leases to see whether there are any lease concessions that would reduce the amount of rent receivable in the future. Examples of concessions include free cable TV, one month's free rent per year for the term of the lease, an allowance for renovating or customizing the space, or even the owner's assumption of the prospective tenants' lease in another property. If so, the value of these concessions should be computed to reduce the amount of contract rent specified. An estoppel certificate should also be obtained from the tenant. Some state laws require concessions to be noted on a lease by special wording.
2. A lease of a portion of premises to conduct a business on property controlled by someone else, such as a refreshment stand at a recreational center.
3. A franchise right granted by a governmental agency to conduct a business.
4. In appraising, unusual terms given by a seller that may warrant the buyer paying a higher contract price for a property than would be the case if the seller did not give the special terms.

conciliation agreement   A settlement or compromise agreement. Under the Federal Fair Housing Act, the Department of Housing and Urban Development (HUD) tries to reach a conciliation agreement with the respondent charged with a discriminatory practice. The conciliation agreement must protect the complainant and the public. If an agreement is signed, then HUD takes no further action. The agreement may require the respondent to do affirmative acts such as selling or renting to the complainant, or to refrain in the future from committing discriminatory acts. If HUD discovers that the conciliation agreement is being breached, HUD can recommend that the attorney general file suit.

concrete basement floor   Generally constructed of concrete reinforced with steel bars within the concrete. The basement floor along with the foundation walls and the piers provide the support for the structure. Concrete is used because it is moistureproof and inexpensive.

concurrent lease   A lease that overlaps the term of an existing shorter-term lease in which the new lessee takes subject to the rights of the first lessee. In effect, the new lessee takes control of the property in the place of the lessor and is entitled to the rents until the first lease expires, at which time the new lessee is entitled to exclusive possession. The concurrent lease may cover all or part of the same premises as the earlier lease.

concurrent ownership   Ownership by two or more persons at the same time, such as joint tenants, tenants by the entirety, tenants in common, or community property owners.

condemnation   A judicial or administrative proceeding to exercise the power of eminent domain; the action of the government (federal, state, local, improvement district) to take private property for public use. The agency taking the property is the condemnor, and the person whose property is being taken is the condemnee. In the taking of private property for public use, a fee simple estate or any lesser right, such as an easement, may be acquired. A common example of condemnation is the taking of an owner's access to a street entrance when the county builds a highway or dedicates the area for county use.

    The right of eminent domain is limited by the Fifth Amendment to the U.S. Constitution, which states: "No person shall be deprived of life, liberty, or property without due process of law; nor shall private property be taken for public use without just compensation." Private property may be taken without the consent of the owner, whose defenses may be that the land was not taken for a sufficient

C

public use or, as is more frequently the case, that just compensation was not paid. The modern trend of the courts is to define the term *public use* broadly to include not only public facilities such as streets, railroads, schools, and parks, but also property that would provide intangible public benefits, such as scenic easements. In fact, in 2005, in *Kelo v. New London*, the Supreme Court ruled that local governments can condemn private property for private economic development when the municipality decides that such development will benefit the public, even if the property is not blighted and the success of the new project is not guaranteed.

The actual appraised value of the property at the date of the appraisal is generally the measure of valuation used to determine the amount of "just compensation." Certain items are *not* considered in determining the value of condemned property, such as loss of goodwill, relocation expenses, inconvenience, and the value of improvements added to the property after the date of the taking. This exclusion is especially harmful to operating businesses whose real estate value is much lower than the value of the business as an ongoing concern.

After a property has been condemned, all preexisting liens and encumbrances are extinguished, and their claims must be asserted against the condemnation award. Typically, the condemnee receives the condemnation award when final judgment is rendered. If listed property is condemned, the listing broker typically is not entitled to a commission, because the broker did not negotiate the sale.

Under a lease, tenants may be entitled to their share of the condemnation award to compensate them for the loss of their leasehold estates. To avoid this, many lessors insert a condemnation clause into the lease, which provides that the lease will be canceled upon condemnation, with all proceeds going to the lessor.

Condemnation also refers to the decision by the appropriate public agency that a property is no longer fit and must therefore be closed or destroyed.

When property is condemned, or sold under a threat of condemnation, the owner may defer any profit realized by treating the disposition as an involuntary conversion. The owner must replace the converted property with property similar in use within three taxable years following the end of the tax year in which the conversion occurs. Any excess of the condemnation proceeds over the cost of the new property is then taxable. (*See* **acquisition appraisal**, **before-and-after method**, **eminent domain**, **excess condemnation**, **inverse condemnation**, **involuntary conversion**, **just compensation**, **police power**, **severance damages**, **special benefit**.)

conditional sales contract   A contract in which the seller retains title to the item sold, but the item is given to the purchasers so long as they are not in default on any of the conditions of the contract; sometimes called an *executory contract*. Under this kind of contract, the seller has a security interest in the property, and the buyer has an equitable interest.

Usually, personal property (such as an air conditioner, a hot tub, or an appliance) is the subject of a conditional sales contract. When real property is the subject of the contract, the contract is called a *contract for deed*. Upon the buyer's full performance of the conditions of the conditional sales contract, the seller must transfer legal title to the buyer. The conditional sales contract creating a security interest in a fixture or in an article that will become a fixture has been replaced under the Uniform Commercial Code by an instrument known as a *security agreement*. (*See* **contract for deed**, **security agreement**.)

conditional-use zoning   A special land use tentatively approved by a zoning ordinance, which ordinarily requires compliance with stated standards. Such zoning might permit the use of a hospital in a residential zone but limit the types of functions the hospital can perform. Also called *special-use zoning*.

conditions   *See* **covenants and conditions**.

condo   A common reference to a condominium unit or development; refers to either a particular unit or the entire building. (*See* **condominium ownership**.)

condominium   (*condominio*)   *See* **condominium ownership**.

condominium conversion   *See* **conversion**.

condominium declaration   *See* **declaration**.

condominium map   The detailed site plan of a condo project containing the layout, location, unit numbers, and dimensions of the condominium units. The condominium map is generally certified by an architect, land surveyor, or engineer and filed for record at the same time as the condominium declaration. Also called *condominium plan*.

condominium owners' association   (*asociación de propietarios de condominios*)   An association of the owners of condominium units, often in an unincorporated association form, and with the main purpose of controlling, regulating, and maintaining the common elements in the condominium. The voting power of owners in an association is usually measured by the percentage of undivided interest each holds in the condominium. Through the bylaws, the association's board of directors is authorized to regulate and administer the affairs of the condominium, especially in regard to maintenance and repair of the common elements. The association has the authority to assess and collect sufficient money to maintain the common areas and to ensure the financial stability of the condominium. When a unit owner is in default of the monthly charges or special assessments, the association may place a lien against that owner's apartment, which can be foreclosed to satisfy the debt.

The condominium owners' association can elect to be treated as a tax-exempt organization, in which case the association is not taxed on membership dues, fees, and assessments if certain income and expenditure tests are met: at least 60 percent of the association's gross income comes from membership dues, fees, or assessments; at least 90 percent of its expenditures is used to acquire, manage, maintain, or improve association properties; and substantially all the units or lots owned by members are used as residences (although they need not be owner-occupied).

The association is still taxed as a corporation on investment income and income from trade or business (for example, rental income or fees from third parties for use of the association's facilities).

condominium ownership   An estate in real property consisting of an individual interest in a unit (residential, commercial, or industrial) and an undivided common interest in the common areas in the condo project such as the land, parking areas, elevators, stairways, exterior structure, and so on. Each condominium unit is a statutory entity that may be mortgaged, taxed, sold, or otherwise transferred in ownership, separately and independently of all other units in the condo project. Units are separately assessed and taxed based on the combined value of the individual living unit and the proportionate ownership of the common areas. The unit also can be separately foreclosed upon in case of default on the mortgage note or other lienable payments.

In effect, the condominium permits ownership of a specific horizontal layer of airspace as opposed to the traditional view of vertical property ownership from the center of the earth to the sky. Typically, the unit, the percentage of common interest, and the limited common elements are appurtenant to each other and cannot be sold or transferred separately.

Condominium ownership is popular in many urban and resort areas due to general scarcity of desirable and usable land and to tax and other advantages of fee ownership versus apartment rentals. In addition to residential condominiums, many office and professional buildings, industrial plants, medical clinics, warehouses, recreational developments, and combined apartment and office buildings use the condominium form of ownership. Condominium owners have exclusive ownership of their individual unit but nevertheless must comply with the requirements of the declaration, bylaws, and house rules set up for the protection and comfort of all the condominium owners.

Under individual state laws, the developer/owner of a condominium must execute and record a master deed together with a condominium declaration accompanied by a true copy of the bylaws, a condominium map, floor plans, and elevations. The establishment of a condominium is not an ir-revocable step—state statutes may permit the removal of a building from condominium ownership with the consent of all or most owners and lienholders. The unit owner's voting power is typically based on a percentage of common interest (note that in a cooperative, each owner has one equal vote regardless of the unit size).

Resale of a condominium may be subject to the right of first refusal of other owners. Generally speaking, however, resales are not as restricted as in the cooperative form of common ownership.

Condominium units tend to sell at prices below those of single-family homes. However, the life-cycle cost of a condominium (mortgage, utilities, maintenance, and condominium fees) may be equal to or, in some cases, even greater than other forms of housing. (*See* **common expenses**, **common interest**, **common wall**, **conversion**, **cooperative ownership**, **declaration**, **empty nester**, **horizontal property acts**, **insurance**, **interstate land sales**, **property tax**.)

condominium plan   *See* **condominium map**.

conduit   A metal pipe in which electrical wiring is installed.

confession of judgment   The act of a debtor in permitting judgment to be entered against him or her by a written statement to that effect without the necessity for the creditor to institute any legal pro-ceedings. Leases and judgment notes generally include a judgment clause (also called a *cognovit*) by which a tenant or debtor authorizes an attorney to make a confession of judgment against her in case of default. This allows the creditor to get a speedy judgment by simply having an attorney file an af-fidavit to the effect that a default has taken place. A confession of judgment may also generally give a lender a judgment lien against all real and personal property (usually within a certain jurisdiction) owned by the debtor. Some state laws prohibit residential lessees and others from executing confes-sion of judgment clauses before they are in default in payment of rent or other debts.

confirmation of sale   A court approval of the sale of property by an executor, administrator, guard-ian, conservator, or commissioner in a foreclosure sale. In most cases, the amount of the broker's commission must also be approved by the court. (*See* **probate**.)

confirmatory deed   *See* **correction deed**.

conforming loan   A standardized conventional loan, written on uniform documents, that meets the purchase requirements of Fannie Mae and Freddie Mac. (*See* **Fannie Mae**, **Freddie Mac**, **jumbo loan**.)

conformity
1. An appraisal principle of value based on the concept that the more a property or its compo-nents are in harmony with the surrounding properties or components, the greater the con-tributory value.
2. The concept that maximum value is realized when the four agents of production (labor, capi-tal, management, and land) are in economic balance.

connection line   A line used in surveying land that connects a surveyor's monument with a perma-nent reference mark. (*See* **survey**.)

consequential damages
1. A money award made by a court to compensate an injured party from a breach of contract for all losses that a reasonable person could have foreseen at the time the contract was made.

2. That damage arising from the acts of public bodies or adjacent owners to a given parcel of land that impairs the value of that parcel without actually condemning its use in whole or in part. For example, in an inverse condemnation proceeding, consequential damages might be awarded when land is used for a public sewage treatment plant, and private land located downwind of the plant suffers a loss in value due to noxious odors.

conservation   A practice by federal, state, and local governments and private landowners of protecting and preserving the natural and scenic resources in order to ensure the highest long-term benefits for all residents. Also, a specific land-use designation in land-use and zoning laws restricting the property to noncommercial uses. (*See* **Environmental Protection Agency [EPA]**.)

conservator   A guardian, protector, preserver, or receiver appointed by a court to administer the person and property of another (usually an incapable adult) and to ensure that the property is properly managed. A conservator may not need a real estate license to sell the protected real estate, although the sale does require court approval.

consideration   An act or the promise thereof, which is offered by one party to induce another to enter into a contract; that which is given in exchange for something from another; also the promise to refrain from doing a certain act, like filing a justifiable lawsuit (the forbearance of a right). Consideration, which distinguishes a contractual obligation from a gift, is usually something of value, such as the purchase price in money; it may be personal services or exchanged property. It is the price bargained for and paid for a promise, or it may be a return promise.

The actual consideration that supports the contract is the mutual exchange of promises by buyers and sellers legally to obligate themselves to do something they were not legally required to do before; that is, the sellers agree to sell a property for a certain price, and the buyers agree to pay that price to buy the described property. Thus, the mere promise to pay money is sufficient consideration, so an earnest money deposit is not necessary for purposes of creating a binding contract. As a rule, the following apply:

■ There should be a recital of consideration in a deed as presumptive evidence that something of value was given for the transfer of the realty. Although most contracts must be supported by a "valuable" consideration, a "good" consideration (love and affection) is sufficient to support a gift deed. Except when a fiduciary executes a deed, the actual consideration need not be stated but may be proved by any other legal evidence.

■ In practice, the price paid for property is calculated by checking the deed to find the transfer tax paid (if applicable) and computing the taxable consideration.

■ Unless the consideration is obviously a nominal one, a real estate licensee may be disciplined for being a party to naming a false consideration. (*See* **dual contract**, **nominal consideration**.)

■ An option must be supported by actual consideration.

■ In a lease, the periodic payment of rent over the rental term constitutes consideration for the use and occupancy of the premises.

■ There must be present consideration to support a contract. For example, Betty rescues Charley from a burning house. Charley then promises in writing to convey his farm to Betty in gratitude for her rescue efforts. Charley's promise is not supported by present consideration and, if Charley should change his mind, Betty could not have the promise specifically enforced. Likewise, a mortgage is not valid when given to secure a preexisting debt without any new consideration, such as an extension of time, as an inducement for the execution of the mortgage.

■ Courts will not usually inquire into the adequacy of consideration to support a contract. However, a court will deny an action for specific performance if the parties were not

C

in an equal bargaining position and if the party bringing the action had not paid a fair and sufficient consideration. Example: If the market value of the property in question is $200,000 (at the time the contract is made), and a buyer (who did not disclose that he was a licensed broker) seeks specific performance of a purchase contract in which the purchase price agreed on is $20,000, a court would probably deny the action.

The question of adequacy of consideration also arises in cases involving an alleged fraudulent conveyance under the Uniform Fraudulent Conveyance Act. That is, suppose a seller conveys a property a few months before filing for bankruptcy. The trustee in bankruptcy will be able to set aside the conveyance as fraudulent if the price was inadequate. In certain cases, inadequacy of consideration is asserted as evidence of undue influence and as evidence that the buyer was not a "bona fide purchaser" for value under the recording laws. (*See* **deposit**, **love and affection**, **nominal consideration**, **recital of consideration**, **valuable consideration**.)

consolidate   To unite, combine, or incorporate by reference, as in combining two mortgages on one property into a single loan; to combine two or more parcels of land (the reverse of the subdivision process); or to join a land sales registration with an earlier registration, especially when the property is developed and sold in succeeding phases or increments. A developer owning a 100-acre parcel may subdivide 50 acres into 100 half-acre lots and register that as a subdivision with the appropriate state and federal agencies. Later, when developing the remaining 50 acres, the owner can consolidate this new registration with the 50-acre subdivision registered earlier and sell both increments under the same registration. Both state and federal (HUD) regulations permit consolidated registration of subdivided lands.

constant
1. A percentage applied directly to the face value of a debt. It develops into the annual amount of money necessary to pay a specified net rate of interest on the reducing balance and to liquidate the principal debt in a specified time period; a method for determining rate and term *on an annual basis*.
2. The annual payment required per dollar of mortgage money, including both interest and amortized principal. The mortgage constant varies with each change in interest rate and each change in the amortization term. (*See* **amortization**.)

construction allowance   Money or other financial inducement provided to a lessee by the lessor to cover the cost, in whole or in part, of preparing a structure for the lessee's occupancy. This allowance could cover costs for partitions, wiring, lighting, and standard carpeting. Also called *tenant improvements*.

construction loan   A short-term or interim loan to cover the construction costs of a building or development project, with loan proceeds advanced periodically in the form of installment payments as the work progresses (called *draws*). In this manner, the outstanding loan balance matches the value of the collateral as it grows. Interest on the borrowed money is not normally charged until the incremental construction draws are advanced. Upon completion of the project, one or more long-term permanent loans, such as those end loans taken out by the buyers of individual condominium units, will take out (pay off) the construction loan. The loan-to-value ratio for these loans is usually 75 percent of the appraised value. Primary sources of construction loans are commercial banks and savings and loan associations. (*See* **interim financing**, **subordination agreement**, **takeout financing**.)

constructive   An inference created by the law, as in constructive eviction or constructive notice.

constructive eviction   Conduct by the landlord that so materially disturbs or impairs a tenant's enjoyment of the leased premises that the tenant is effectively forced to move out and terminate the lease without liability for further rent. This concept is a product of modern property law, which now tends to place more emphasis on the quality of possession or habitability under a lease. Constructive eviction might occur when a landlord cuts off the electricity or fails to provide heating, makes extensive alterations to the premises or attempts to lease the property to others, or fails to provide elevator service in a highrise building. There can be no constructive eviction without the tenant's vacating the premises within a reasonable time of the landlord's act.

The tenant's duty to pay rent is not terminated if the tenant remains in possession. The tenant can sue to recover possession or bring an action for damages based on breach of the covenant for quiet enjoyment. (*See* **eviction**.)

constructive fraud   Breach of a legal or equitable duty that the law declares fraudulent because of its tendency to deceive others, despite no showing of dishonesty or intent to deceive. A broker may be charged with constructive fraud for failing to disclose a known material fact when the broker had a duty to speak—for example, if a listing broker failed to disclose a *known* major foundation problem not readily observable upon an ordinary inspection.

constructive notice   Notice of certain facts that may be discovered by due diligence or inquiry into a public record; a legal presumption that a person is responsible for knowing these facts. The proper recording of a document gives constructive notice to the world of the document's existence and contents. Possession of property also imparts constructive notice of the rights of the party in possession. Examples of rights of parties in possession are rights under an unrecorded deed, contract for deed, lease-option, and rights of adverse possession. Constructive notice is also referred to as *legal notice* and is in contrast to actual notice, which is express or direct knowledge acquired in the course of a transaction. (*See* **actual notice, chain of title, inquiry notice, recording**.)

constructive receipt   A theory of tax law to the effect that the unrestricted right to receive money is the same as the actual receipt of that money. For example, for tax purposes, receipt of a demand promissory note is the same as money received. Thus, if a person has the right and ability to receive payment, which includes profit or income, that profit is taxed when the right to receive it arises, regardless of when payment is actually accepted.

consultant   One who gives advice in a specific area, such as a financial adviser. A real estate consultant who performs services similar to a real estate broker would have to be licensed under state law. (*See* **counseling**.)

Consumer Credit Protection Act   *See* **Truth in Lending Act**.

Consumer Financial Protection Bureau (CFPB)   A consumer protection agency created by the Dodd-Frank Act that is primarily responsible with rule-making, supervision, and enforcement for federal consumer financial protection laws, including combining certain disclosures that consumers receive under the Truth in Lending Act, Regulation Z and Regulation X of the Real Estate Settlement Procedures Act. It is an independent unit within the Federal Reserve.

consumer price index (CPI)   A statistical measure of changes in consumer goods prices prepared by the Bureau of Labor Statistics (BLS) of the federal Department of Labor. As of August 2009, the BLS reduced the reporting to three expenditure categories: food, energy, and all items less food and energy.

Two different CPI categories are published: the CPI for all urban consumers (CPI-U) and the CPI for urban wage earners and clerical workers (CPI-W). The base index set by the government for 1982–1984 is 100. In August 2011, the CPI-U was 230.379 and the CPI-W was 227.056. The CPI is often used as a standard in making rent adjustments in commercial leases. (*See* **base year, cost-of-living index**.)

consummate   To bring to completion. A sale of real property is generally consummated upon the closing of the transaction, usually evidenced by delivery of the deed and funds and recording of the conveyance documents. (*See* **closing [settlement]**.)

consummate dower   *See* **dower**.

contiguous   In proximity to; adjoining or abutting; near, coterminous (having the same boundaries). Many state subdivision laws define a subdivision to include any land consisting of two or more lots, contiguous or not, offered as part of a common promotional plan of advertising and sale. Condominium property does not have to be contiguous either (as when it includes a parking lot across the street), but it must be in the same vicinity. Contiguous owners must yield, to a reasonable degree, their privacy to the general welfare of the community. For example, reasonable inconvenience may be suffered by owners whose properties are contiguous to commercial enterprises and railroads.

   Often a partial release clause in a mortgage may require that a partial release be given only on a parcel that is contiguous to a parcel previously released. The term *contiguous* should be precisely defined so the release clause will not be challenged on grounds of uncertainty and vagueness.

contingency   A provision in a contract that requires the completion of a certain act or the happening of a particular event before that contract is binding. Often a buyer will submit an offer to purchase contingent on obtaining financing or rezoning. In such a case, the seller should be sure that the contingency is specifically detailed and unambiguous and that there is a definite cutoff date; otherwise, the buyer could tie up the seller's property indefinitely while attempting to get financing or rezoning. Parties may waive any contingency clause that was inserted for their benefit. For example, the buyer could force the seller to sell the property even though the buyer was not able to obtain the zoning—the original contingency in the contract for sale. Contingency implies a promise to use one's efforts to bring it about.

   If a contingency is worded too loosely, such as "contingent on my deciding whether it is a good deal or not," then the entire contract is considered "illusory" and unenforceable by either party due to lack of "mutuality of obligation." If the sale is contingent on a "satisfactory" inspection or attorney's review of lease, the courts will try to impose standards of good faith and reasonability so a party cannot back out just because of a change in that party's plans.

   A contingent sale is different from an option. In an option, the optionee has absolute discretion whether to exercise the option. In a contingency, the buyer must buy upon the occurrence or nonoccurrence of a specified event, such as loan qualification.

   The financing contingency is not only the most frequently used contingency, it is also the most controversial. Even a well-written contingency statement can cause problems. For instance, assume that a financing contingency stated that the offer was contingent upon buyer obtaining a first mortgage loan commitment for $167,500 with interest not to exceed 5 percent per annum and for a term of not less than 30 years, and monthly payments for principal and interest not to exceed $800.18 plus $\frac{1}{12}$ the estimated annual real property taxes and $\frac{1}{12}$ the annual insurance premium. Buyers agreed to use good faith and due diligence in obtaining such a loan. Buyers qualified for the loan but refused to take it because the lender added an interest rate escalation clause. Even though a court might allow some deviation in the financing commitment, the inclusion of an escalation clause is a material deviation of the terms of the offer to purchase and thus the buyer would not be in breach of the contract for refusing to complete the purchase; the buyer is entitled to a return of the deposit money. However, a buyer who did qualify for financing on the terms stated in an offer but who later gets divorced or otherwise changes circumstances so as to not be qualified at the time of closing may have difficulty defending a lawsuit for enforcement of the purchase contract. Sometimes, a cautious seller might add a clause to the effect that "the execution of any loan documents by the buyer shall be deemed to be an acceptance of such loan and a waiver of this contingency." (*See* **special conditions**.)

contingency listing   A type of listing used in a multiple listing service that has unusual or special conditions; sometimes designated by the letter *C* placed in front of the MLS number. Contingencies may include shorter-than-normal listing duration, an unusual structure, or a short sale.

continuation   An update of a title search, which is "run to date." In a typical transaction, the title company issues a preliminary title report soon after a sales contract or an offer to purchase is signed or escrow is opened. At the closing date, the title company is usually asked to continue the search down to the time of recording the final documents by checking the public record to be sure no intervening rights in the property have arisen. The final title report will then show title in the grantee. The buyer usually pays for the continuation. (*See* **bring-down search, title search.**)

C

continuing education   A requirement in most states that real estate and appraiser licensees complete a specified number of educational offerings as a prerequisite to license renewal or reinstatement.

continuous operation clause   A shopping center lease provision requiring that key tenants keep their stores in operation during their lease terms. This clause is for the benefit of both the landlord and the other tenants.

contour map   A topographic map showing the lay of the land of an area by means of a series of lines that connect points of equal elevation at set intervals depending on the scale used.

contract (*contrato*)   A legally enforceable agreement between competent parties who agree to perform or refrain from performing certain acts for a consideration. In essence, a contract is an enforceable promise.

    In real estate, there are many different types of contracts, including contracts for sale, options, mortgages, leases, contracts for deed, escrow agreements, and loan commitments. Each of these contracts must meet the minimum requirements as described in the following paragraphs.

Competent parties: There must be at least two bona fide parties to any contract. Thus, Juan cannot agree to deed property to himself. He could, however, convey property to himself and to Martina as tenants in common. Both parties must possess at least limited capacity to contract. In this respect, minors cannot deed property they own because they lack the capacity to convey property; such a deed would be voidable by the minor (in some states, it is automatically void). A minor, however, does possess the limited capacity to enter into a valid contract to purchase property from an adult; such a contract would be enforceable by the minor against the adult, but would be voidable by the minor if he chose not to complete the purchase during his minority. A fiduciary and a corporation must have the proper authority to enter into a contract. Depending on the terms of the contract, when a party to the contract dies, the heirs and assigns of the deceased may be bound to the contract. (*See* **capacity of parties, deed, minor.**)

Writing: Unless otherwise required by law, oral contracts can be just as valid as written contracts. Generally, however, real estate contracts—except those for leases of one year or less—must be in writing to be enforceable. All essential terms of the contract must be complete and certain so that the entire agreement is set forth in writing and nothing material is left to be agreed on in the future. Until the contract is signed, everything is negotiable. The contract is no longer negotiable once the contract is signed. In order to modify the contract terms, the parties must offer and accept new consideration. (*See* **statute of frauds.**)

Description: If the contract involves real property, then the property must be accurately described so that the parties can identify the subject matter of the contract. A deed, mortgage, or assignment of lease should contain a complete legal description. Most contracts for sale usually contain a good description of the property (address, size, and tax map number) but not a full legal description. (*See* **legal description.**)

C

Meeting of the minds: There must be a valid offer and an unqualified acceptance of that offer, so that the seller understands the terms of the buyer's offer and the buyer understands the method of purchase of the identified property. (*See* **offer and acceptance**.)

Consideration: The contract must be supported by consideration; that is, both parties must be required to do something they were not previously obligated to do. Most contracts require a valuable consideration, such as a promise to pay money. A gift deed, however, is valid if it recites a good, rather than valuable, consideration, such as "for love and affection." (*See* **consideration**, **option**.)

Legal purpose: To be enforceable, a contract must contemplate a legitimate purpose. Thus, a contract to lease a building for an illegal gambling casino is not enforceable nor is a listing contract to pay a commission to an unlicensed person. A *usurious contract* is not fully enforceable.

Signature: To be bound by a contract, a party must have signed it. In the usual real estate transaction, both buyer and seller sign the contract for sale.

It is any ambiguity in a contract, the courts will construe the contract most strictly against the party who prepared it. For example, because the broker prepares the listing contract, it is construed very strictly against the broker. Thus, if there were any doubt whether the listing was an exclusive agency or an exclusive right to sell, the courts would construe it to be an exclusive agency.

It is not necessary for one formal document to represent the contract of the contracting parties, though it may be preferable in order to eliminate any dispute as to whether a contract was formed. Sometimes, the essentials of a contract (the offer and acceptance) arise from separate correspondence between the parties, so one formal contract is never actually signed. All parties must agree, however, on all essential terms in the contract and should not leave anything to subsequent agreement. If this happens, the "contract" may be construed as preliminary negotiations rather than as a true contract.

Some contracts may be discharged due to impossibility of performance. For example, if the promisor of a personal service contract dies, ordinarily the contract is discharged. Thus, a contract with a renowned architect to design a special building would probably be discharged if the architect died. However, if the work and/or services may be performed by others, such as with a plumbing contract, the obligation will survive the death and bind the promisor's estate. Normally, contracts pertaining to real estate are binding on the heirs and assigns of the deceased. The court sometimes discharges a contract if it feels the terms would be impossible for a reasonable person or organization to perform.

The essential element in every contract is that both parties clearly understand what their agreement is. Poorly drafted documents, especially those containing extensive legal language, are subject to various interpretations and often lead to litigation. In most instances, the parties involved in a real estate transaction would be best advised to engage the services of an experienced real estate attorney to draft a contract that accurately reflects the true intentions of the parties. Note that a broker who drafts legal contracts may be deemed guilty of the unauthorized practice of law. (*See* **adhesion contract**, **boilerplate**, **contract for sale**, **deed**, **executed contract**, **implied contract**, **investment contract**, **lease**, **plain language law**, **practice of law**, **statute of frauds**.)

contract documents In terms of real estate development, the agreement between two parties together with all supporting elements that assist in defining, amending, or modifying the agreement and its attendant conditions (drawings, specifications, change orders, addenda). The term is used in standard form documents used by the American Institute of Architects (AIA), such as those between the owner, architect, and general contractor.

contract for deed   (*contrato por escritura*)   An agreement between the seller (vendor) and the buyer (vendee) for the purchase of real property in which the payment of all or a portion of the selling price is deferred. The purchase price may be paid in installments (of either principal and interest or interest only) over the period of the contract, with the balance due at maturity. When the buyer completes the required payments, the seller must deliver good legal title to the buyer by way of a deed or assignment of lease (if the property is leasehold property). Under the terms of the contract for deed, the buyer is given possession of the property and equitable title to the property, while the seller holds legal title and continues to be primarily liable for payment of any underlying mortgage. The features of the buyer's equitable title and obligation to purchase distinguish a contract for deed from a lease-option.

The contract for deed document must meet the requirements for any contract and will also contain a lengthy statement of the rights and obligations of the parties, similar to those under a mortgage, including use of premises, risk of loss, maintenance of premises, payment of taxes and insurance, and remedies in case of default. Specific rights, such as acceleration or the right to prepay without penalty must be expressly written into the agreement. The contract is usually signed by both parties, acknowledged, and recorded.

The contract for deed is used extensively in many areas, where it may be called a *land contract, agreement of sale, installment contract, articles of agreement, conditional sales contract, bond for deed, selling under contract*, or *real estate contract*. They are useful in a tight money market where if it is difficult to qualify prospective buyers for conventional financing, the contract for deed is frequently the best method to sell or purchase a property. Others who benefit are first-time buyers or immigrants, who might have difficulty qualifying for a bank loan at the time of entering into the contract for deed, but whose incomes will increase before maturity of the agreement, enabling them to refinance and pay off the contract for deed.

Sellers may prefer to sell on a contract for deed because it can create an installment sale, which enables them to defer payment of a portion of tax. In addition, if the buyer defaults, the sellers can sue for strict foreclosure, something they cannot do with a mortgage. However, a seller who chooses this remedy is rescinding the contract and cannot seek a deficiency judgment for the unpaid balance. (*See* **contract price, forfeiture, installment sale.**)

Some contracts for deed provide that sellers and/or buyers can convert a contract into a conventional security transaction. For example, upon payment of 40 percent of the purchase price, the seller may be required to deliver a deed and take back a purchase-money mortgage from the buyer for the balance of the purchase price.

Use of a contract for deed is not without some disadvantages. From the buyer's viewpoint:

■ Because the seller need not deliver good marketable title until the final payment, the buyer must, at the risk of default, continue to make payments even when there may be a doubt whether the seller will be able to perform when all payments are made. Some attorneys include a clause that "the property is to be conveyed free and clear of all encumbrances except (those specified herein) and to remain free and clear except for the above-stated encumbrances." The seller is then discouraged from placing further mortgages and encumbrances on the property during the period of the contract for deed.

■ The buyer may have difficulty getting the seller to deed the property upon satisfaction. By withholding a large enough final payment, the buyer often can persuade a seller to pay the costs of drafting the deed. In addition, at the time of final payment, the seller

C

might be suffering a legal disability or be missing, bankrupt, or dead, and the property might be tied up in probate.

■ The buyer might be restricted from assigning her interest in the contract for deed by covenants against assignment.

■ Liens that arise against the seller could cloud the title.

■ Unless a collection account is used, problems could arise if the seller does not apply the buyer's payments to the underlying mortgage.

From the seller's viewpoint:

■ If the buyer defaults, the process of clearing record title may be time-consuming and costly, especially if the buyer is under a legal disability, is bankrupt, is a nonresident, or has created encumbrances in favor of persons who might have to be joined in any quiet title action.

■ The seller's interest in the contract for deed is less salable than a mortgagee's interest would have been had the seller sold under a purchase-money mortgage.

■ By its very nature, the contract for deed is a contract, and all contracts are subject to differing interpretations with the possibility of disputes and litigation. (*See* **collection account, holding escrow, land contract, vendor**.)

contract of sale   (*contrato de compraventa*)   A contract for the purchase and sale of real property in which the buyer agrees to purchase for a certain price and the seller agrees to convey title by way of a deed or an assignment of lease (for leasehold property). In addition to binding the parties to the purchase and sale of the property during the period of time required to close the transaction, the contract frequently serves as the initial directions to the closing agent or escrow company to process the mechanics of the transaction. The parties must agree in the contract on all of the pertinent closing details, such as who pays the various expenses of the sale, who bears the risk of loss, the date of occupancy, and the proration date. In essence, the contract of sale is an executory contract to convey property, serving as the vehicle to get to the deed, which finally conveys title. Once the sales contract is signed, the remainder of the transaction is primarily mechanical.

Some of the many names for this contract are *sales contract, purchase agreement, deposit receipt, offer and acceptance, agreement of sale, offer to lease*, or *purchase and sale agreement*.

To be enforceable, the contract of sale must be in writing, be signed by both parties, contain the buyer's and seller's names, contain an adequate description of the property (a full legal description is advisable, however, in the sale of unimproved land), state the sales price, and have a legitimate purpose. The spouse of a married seller should also sign the contract so that the spouse will be bound to release all marital rights (if applicable) when the deed is delivered. For example, if a wife fails to sign, the contract is nonetheless valid and enforceable against her husband; however, she must be willing to join in the deed to release her dower and/or homestead rights.

Most contracts of sale are not recorded unless the parties anticipate a particularly long period of time to close the transaction. However, a contract for deed should be recorded to protect the buyer because it may be years before the buyer pays off the contract and obtains legal title to the property.

If the buyer defaults and does not purchase the property, the seller can keep the deposit as liquidated damages, sue the buyer for money damages, or sue the buyer to complete the purchase under the terms of the agreement. This last remedy of specific performance is possible only in the rare case that money damages cannot adequately compensate the seller for the loss. If the seller defaults, the buyer can rescind the agreement and obtain the return of the deposit money or sue the seller for specific performance to have the court compel the seller to sell the property on the agreed terms.

A broker typically uses a standard, preprinted contract of sale form. Under most state laws, a broker who does not charge a separate fee for completing this form is not engaging in the unauthorized practice of law. As long as this service is rendered incidentally to representing the client in the purchase or sale of the property, such service is permissible. (*See* **conditional sales contract**, **contract**, **contract for deed**, **equitable conversion**, **executory contract**, **inventory**, **specific performance**, **vendor**.)

contractor   One who contracts or covenants, with either a public body or a private party, to construct works or erect buildings at a certain price. A contractor is ordinarily understood to be the person who undertakes to supply labor and materials for specific improvements under a contract with an owner or principal. A general contractor is one whose business operations require the use of more than two unrelated building trades or crafts whose work the contractor superintends or does in whole or in part; the term *general contractor* does not include an individual who does all work personally without employees or other "specialty contractors." A contractor may contract a complete job as the prime contractor or may contract with a general contractor to do part of a job as subcontractor. (*See* **general contractor**, **subcontractor**.)

contract price   A tax term used in computation of gain realized from an installment sale. The contract price represents a property's selling price, minus any mortgages assumed or taken subject to by the buyer, plus the excess (if any) of any such liens collected in addition to the seller's adjusted basis at the time of sale. In essence, the contract price is the seller's equity in the property.

One of the advantages of the contract for deed for the seller is that it permits the "contract price" to be the same as the selling price and thus defer taxes much better than if the buyer assumed or took subject to the mortgage. Example: A taxpayer sells property for $100,000, basis of $70,000 and the gain is $30,000; the down payment is $20,000 with an assumption of an existing $60,000 first mortgage and a purchase-money second mortgage of $20,000. Although the selling price is $100,000, the contract price is only $40,000. Thus, of the total amount the seller is to receive ($40,000), the gain ($30,000) represents 75 percent. Therefore, 75 percent of the down payment and each principal payment on the purchase-money mortgage is gain, and only the remaining 25 percent is considered nontaxable return of basis.

Alternatively, if the property is sold on a contract for deed, the entire $100,000 selling price would also be the contract price. Therefore, only 30 percent of the down payment would be gain. The remaining gain consists of 30 percent of principal payments received under the contract for deed, which would be taxable only as those principal payments are received. (*See* **installment sale**.)

contract rent   The rental income as stipulated by the parties in a lease. Appraisers often contrast this with market rent, which is the amount of rent obtainable if the property were vacant and available on the open market.

contribution   (*contribución*)   An appraisal principle in which the worth of an improvement is what it adds to the entire property's market value, regardless of the actual cost of the improvement. A remodeled basement may not contribute its entire cost to the value of the property, whereas a new bedroom usually will increase a house's value by more than its installation cost.

contribution, right of   *See* **right of contribution**.

controlled access highway   *See* **limited access highway**.

controlled business arrangements   As defined under the Real Estate Settlement Procedures Act (RESPA), an arrangement or combination in which an individual or a firm has more than a 1 percent interest in a company to which the individual or firm regularly refers business. Such arrangement is permitted, provided that written disclosure of the affiliation is made, an estimated charge for the service is provided, consumers are free to obtain the services elsewhere, and referral fees are not exchanged among the affiliated companies.

convenience store   A retail store that sells items (food, liquors, sundries) usually bought randomly and impulsively at the most convenient place available.

conventional estate   An estate purposely created by the parties to a transaction; differs from an estate created by operation of law, such as a life estate created under dower laws.

C

conventional loan   A loan made with real estate as security and not involving government participation in the form of insuring (FHA) or guaranteeing (VA) the loan. The mortgagee can be an institutional lender or a private party. The loan is conventional in the sense that it conforms to accepted standards and that the lender looks solely to the credit of the borrower and the security of the property to ensure payment of the debt. Conventional loans include those loans insured by private mortgage insurance companies.

  Because the lender is not subject to the more stringent government regulations of the FHA and VA, conventional loans are frequently more flexible with respect to terms and interest rates, although they sometimes reflect a higher interest rate and larger down payment requirements due to the higher risk involved. In some cases, lenders can offer zero-down-payment mortgages to low-income persons with excellent credit ratings. Conventional loans are subject to institutional regulation, which may be statutory (federal, state) or self-created.

conversion

1. The process of transforming an income-producing property, such as a rental apartment building or hotel, into condominium apartments for sale to separate owners. The building is often renovated, the existing leases are allowed to lapse or are terminated, and the project is registered with the proper state agency and the title brought under the condominium act. The process requires considerable expertise in each of the following stages: cost and market analysis, purchase, initial remodeling, appraisal, interim and long-term financing, tenant relocation, and sales. State law often requires the developer to give existing tenants a long period in which to relocate if they elect not to purchase their unit. Due to increased construction costs, many developers are exploring condominium conversion as the answer to housing shortages. Yet, because of tenant displacement problems, many communities have placed restrictions (and even moratoriums) on condominium conversions. (*See* **condominium ownership**.)

2. The appropriation of property belonging to another. The conversion may be illegal (as when a broker misappropriates client funds), or it may be legal (as when the government condemns property under the right of eminent domain). (*See* **commingling, involuntary conversion**.)

3. The process of converting from one use to another for tax purposes, for example, changing a personal residence into a rental property.

conveyance   (*traspaso*)   The transfer of title or an interest in real property by means of a written instrument such as a deed or an assignment of lease. Note that a decree of divorce or a property settlement agreement involving real property does not in itself act as an effective conveyance. The Uniform Land Transactions Act proposes a simplified method of transferring title to real property.

conveyance tax   *See* **transfer tax (conveyance fee)**.

co-obligor   One sharing in an obligation with another, such as a cosigner of a promissory note.

cooling-off period   A kind of grace period provided by law or by contract in which a party to a contract can legally back out of the contract; a right of rescission. The federal Truth in Lending Act specifies a cooling-off period in refinancing transactions involving a borrower's personal residence. The federal Interstate Land Sales Full Disclosure Act has a cooling-off period of seven calendar days. Many states have their own statutory cooling-off periods for condominium, time-share, and subdivision sales. Contrary to some popular belief, however, there is no automatic right to rescind a real estate purchase contract unless so specified by statute or by contract. (*See* **rescission**.)

cooperating broker   A broker who assists another broker (usually the "listor") in the sale of real property. Usually, the cooperating broker is the (selling) broker who found the buyer who offers to buy a piece of property listed with another (listing) broker. The cooperating broker has no contractual relationship with the seller and therefore must look solely to the listing broker for a commission. Cooperating brokers should be aware that cooperation does not necessarily mean compensation; they should always verify the compensation offered by the listing broker.

    Negotiations concerning property listed exclusively with one broker should be carried on with the listing broker, not with the owner (except with the consent of the listing broker).

C

cooperative ownership   Ownership of an apartment unit in which the apartment owner has purchased shares in the corporation (or partnership or trust) that holds title to the entire apartment building. The cooperative owner is, in essence, a shareholder in a corporation whose principal asset is a building. In return for stock in the corporation, the owner receives a proprietary lease granting occupancy of a specific unit in the building. The owner thus occupies under a lease but does not own the unit, and the owner's interest is treated as personal property. Each unit owner must pay a pro rata share of the corporation's expenses, which includes any mortgage charges, real estate taxes, maintenance, payroll, and so on. The owners can deduct for tax purposes their individual share of the taxes and interest charges (provided 80 percent of a cooperative's income is derived from tenant/owner rentals). Note that the stock certificate usually is freely assignable; however, the proprietary lease typically has severe restrictions on its assignability.

    Voting power in a co-op is usually one vote per unit. The co-op corporation may take out or assume a single mortgage on the entire building. Co-op buyers may have more difficulty in obtaining financing to purchase because they are buying personal, not real property.

    Upon resale, the co-op tenant normally must obtain the co-op's board of directors' approval of the proposed purchaser or lessee. For example, boards have objected to rock musicians, movie stars, or even ex-presidents, and they may do so, as long as the objection is not based on any protected class under state and federal fair housing laws.

    In a co-op, when an owner (tenant/shareholder) defaults on mortgage or tax payments, the other shareholders must cure the default or risk having the entire project sold for taxes or foreclosed under the blanket mortgage. This contingent liability is one major drawback of co-op ownership. To protect against this risk, many co-ops assess a monthly charge to set up a prepayment reserve fund to cover real property taxes.

    When preparing a sales contract involving a co-op, the following language may be used to describe the property: "Ten shares of stock in Paige Apartments, Inc., entitling owner to proprietary use of Apartment 67 and parking stall #3, and co-use of common elements." (*See* **proprietary lease**.)

co-ownership   *See* **cotenancy**.

core space   *See* **rentable area, usable area**.

corner influence   The effect on value of location or proximity to the intersection of two streets. Commercial corner lots are generally worth more than inside lots.

corner stakes   Used by a surveyor in running a survey by metes and bounds. The stakes are set at every change of direction.

cornice   A decorative horizontal projection or molding at the top of the exterior walls under the eaves that aids water drainage. Any molded projection at the top of an interior or exterior wall, in the enclosure at the roof eaves or at the rake of the roof.

corporate resolution   A summary of a specific action taken by the board of directors of a corporation normally recorded by the corporate secretary in the corporation's minute book.

C

Lenders often request a certificate of resolution to verify that the corporate board has authorized the borrowing of money or the opening of an account. This is called a *borrowing resolution* and usually uses language similar to the following: "Upon motion duly made, seconded, and unanimously passed, the following resolution was adopted on the 5th day of October, 2012. Resolved that the Corporation hereby authorizes the borrowing of $250,000 from the Bank of Paradise to purchase a grocery store."

When a corporation is the seller of real property, the purchaser should request a resolution from the seller's board of directors authorizing the sale and designating an authorized officer to sign the conveyance instrument. As a rule, if the corporation is selling most of its assets, a resolution of the shareholders to authorize the sale is also required. (*See* **corporation**.)

corporation   (*corporación*)   A legal entity created under state law, consisting of an association of one or more individuals but regarded under the law as having an existence and personality separate from such individuals. The main characteristics of a corporation are its perpetual existence (that is, the corporation exists indefinitely and only ceases to exist if and when it is properly dissolved through legal proceedings), centralized management in the board of directors, liability of a shareholder limited to the amount of his or her investment, and free transferability of corporate shares.

A corporation has independent capacity to contract and to hold title to real property consistent with the powers given it in its articles of incorporation. Contracts into which the corporation has not been empowered to enter (*ultra vires*, or "beyond its powers") may not be valid. Therefore, it is important to ascertain whether the corporation is empowered to enter into the contract and whether the person signing on behalf of the corporation is so authorized. This information is verified by requesting a copy of the board of directors' certificate of resolution authorizing the contract and from the person signing it. Normally, board approval is sufficient to authorize a sale of corporate property, but when the sale constitutes most of the corporate assets, shareholder approval may be required.

When a new corporation is buying real property, it is important to verify that the articles have been filed and the corporation has in fact been legally formed; otherwise, the deed is invalid for lack of grantee.

A corporation (except an S corporation) is taxed at special corporate income tax rates, and the stockholders must pay an added tax on dividends or other profits received from the corporation.

A closely held corporation is one owned by relatively few people, all or most of whom are directly involved in the conduct of the business, with very little stock held by outside investors.

Corporations are subject to regulation in the state of their incorporation and in the states where they do business. (*See* **association**, **board of directors**, **corporate resolution**, **double taxation**, **foreign corporation**, **limited liability company [LLC]**, **S corporation**, **ultra vires**.)

corporeal property   Tangible real or personal property such as buildings, fixtures, and fences. Incorporeal property includes intangibles such as rents, easements, and goodwill.

correction deed   Any type of deed used to correct a prior erroneous deed, as when the grantor's name has been misspelled or when some minor mistake of fact has been made. For example, a correction deed is used to amend an inaccurate description of a parcel discovered when a property is resurveyed. Though exempt from the conveyance tax, the correction deed is subject to the appropriate recording fee. Grantors can be forced to execute a correction deed if they gave a covenant of further assurance in the original deed. An appropriate marginal note is made to the original deed. Also called a *deed of confirmation*, a *reformation deed*, or a *confirmatory deed*.

correction lines   Provisions in the government survey method made to compensate for the curvature of the earth's surface. Every fourth township line (at 24-mile intervals) serves as a correction line on which the intervals between the north and south range lines are measured and corrected to a full six miles. (*See* **government survey method.**)

correlation   *See* **reconciliation**.

correlative water right   A modern law exercised in some states that holds that a riparian owner who has rights in a common water source is entitled to take only a reasonable amount of the total water supply for the beneficial use of the land (such as irrigation). Under the appropriative water right favored in some states, the owner has the exclusive right to take all the water for specific beneficial uses.

corridor   A passageway or hallway that provides a common way of travel to an exit. A dead-end corridor provides only one direction of travel to an exit.

corridor development   The growth of businesses or plants along major arteries connecting two large industrial or commercial centers some distance from each other.

cosigner   An additional person signing a contract or a note who is equally obligated to perform along with the principal party to the contract. A lender may require a barely qualified borrower to obtain a cosigner who will be required to take over payments if the borrower defaults. (*See* **co-obligor.**)

cost approach   (*cálculo de costos*)   An approach to the valuation of property based on the improvement's reproduction cost or replacement cost. The cost approach is also called the *summation approach*, in that it involves adding together the building and land values, each computed separately. The primary steps are (1) to estimate the land value, (2) to estimate the replacement cost of the building new, (3) to deduct all accrued depreciation from the replacement cost, and (4) to add the estimated land value to the depreciated replacement cost.

   To estimate land value, the land is presumed to be vacant and ready for development. The appraiser bases value on comparisons of sales of comparable land. Although land does not depreciate, its current use and external factors affect its value.

   To estimate reproduction cost, the comparative cost method is often used based on current market costs to construct buildings that are identical in design, type, size, and quality of construction. Accrued depreciation due to physical deterioration, functional obsolescence, and external obsolescence is deducted from this reproduction cost. Finally, the estimated land value is added to the depreciated cost of the building. Because most people will not pay more for a property than it would cost to acquire a similar site and erect a similar structure on it, the current replacement cost of the building plus the value of the land tends to set the upper limit of a property's value. (*See* **appraisal, comparables, reproduction cost, summation approach.**)

cost-of-living index   An index number indicating the relative change in the cost of living between a selected period of time (using a factor of 100) and another period of time. Escalator clauses in commercial leases often refer to an increase in maintenance expenses to match the increase in the cost of living or an increase in the U.S. Department of Labor's consumer price index (which uses a 1982 reference base of 100). (*See* **base period, consumer price index [CPI].**)

cost-plus contract   A construction agreement in which the owner pays the cost of all labor and materials plus a certain additional amount based on a set percentage of the cost, representing profit and contractor's overhead. This type of contract contrasts with a fixed-price contract.

cost recovery   A form of deduction applicable to real and personal property used in a trade or business or held for the production of income. The Economic Recovery Tax Act of 1981 adopted this method in place of depreciation and applies to new and used real or personal property "placed in service" by the taxpayer after 1980. Unlike depreciation, cost recovery does not depend on the "use-

C

ful life" or the "salvage value" of property. Rather, the entire cost (of the depreciable portion) of property may be deducted over an arbitrary period of time.

The Tax Reform Act lengthened the cost recovery periods for certain depreciable assets, including real estate. The cost recovery period for residential rental property increased to 27.5 years and for nonresidential real property to 39 years. The act also adopts a mid-month convention: property is treated as having been "placed in service" in the middle of the month, no matter what day it was actually placed in service. (*See* **accelerated cost recovery system [ACRS], depreciable real property [accounting], depreciation [tax].**)

cost recovery method   *See* **deferred-payment method.**

cotenancy   A form of concurrent property ownership in which two or more persons own an undivided interest in the same property. When title to one parcel of real estate is vested in (or owned by) two or more persons or other entities, such persons or entities are said to be *co-owners* of the property. There are several forms of co-ownership, each one having unique legal characteristics. The forms of co-ownership most commonly recognized by the various states are tenancy in common, joint tenancy, tenancy by the entirety, community property, condominium and cooperative ownership, and partnership property. (*See* **community property, condominium ownership, cooperative ownership, grantee, joint tenancy, partnership, right of contribution, tenancy by the entirety [entireties], tenancy in common, undivided interest.**)

Council of Real Estate Brokerage Managers   *See* Appendix A.

Council of Residential Specialists   *See* Appendix A.

counseling   A specialty within the real estate industry that involves providing skilled, independent advice and professional guidance on a variety of real estate problems. A counselor attempts to provide the client with direction in choosing from among alternative courses of action.

Counselor of Real Estate (CRE)   A professional designation conferred by the Counselors of Real Estate. *See* Appendix B.

counteroffer   (*contraoferta*)   A new offer made in response to an offer received from an offeror. A counteroffer has the effect of rejecting the original offer, which cannot thereafter be accepted unless revived by the offeror's repeating it.

Once the buyer submits an offer to buy for the seller's acceptance, if the seller makes any change to the offer—no matter how slight—such change constitutes a counteroffer, and terminates the original offer and bars its subsequent acceptance. Thus, if the seller changes the suggested closing date from 10:00 AM November 10, 2013, to 11:00 AM November 10, 2013, initials the change, and signs the sales contract, the seller has made a counteroffer. The roles of the parties then reverse. There is no obligation on the buyer to either accept or reject the counteroffer. To create a valid contract, the buyer must accept the terms of the counteroffer within a certain period of time. Note that a simple inquiry as to whether the offeror would be willing to change the terms of an offer is not sufficient to constitute a rejection of the offer or a counteroffer.

A common practice has been for the seller to make a change to the buyers' sales contract, initial and date the change, and transmit it to the buyers for acceptance. If the buyers then wanted to make a change to the altered contract, they in effect would be making a counter-counteroffer.

It is poor practice to rely on a contract that has many initialed changes, because it is difficult to determine at what point a valid contract actually exists. The parties should execute a written counteroffer. If a buyer wishes to make a counteroffer in response to the seller's counteroffer form, the buyer should probably begin the process anew by completing a new sales contract offer.

Because it is important to be able to determine the chronology of events, each change should be time-dated. In addition, the broker must give a copy of the changes to the signing party at the time such changes are made, not afterward. (*See* **meeting of the minds**, **offer and acceptance**.)

counterpart (*contraparte*)   A duplicate or copy of a document. Sometimes used in preparing conveyance documents when there are multiple parties and time is inadequate for sending a single document to parties located throughout the country for signatures. In such a case, a copy of the document can be sent to each signing party, and then all the executed copies can be recorded as one document. Normally counterparts will be treated as a single document although not created simultaneously.

county   A governmental division of a state. It is usually the largest administrative division within a state.

court
1. A short roadway partially or wholly enclosed by buildings, giving the impression of a small open square.
2. An open area enclosed on two or more sides by walls or buildings.
3. An official session for the administration of justice—a court of law. The federal court system consists of the U.S. Supreme Court, which is the highest court in the land; the courts of appeals and circuit courts—the intermediate courts; and the district courts—the lower courts. The United States also has specialized courts, such as the U.S. Tax Court, Patents Court, Bankruptcy Court, Court of Claims, and Customs Court.

    State court systems vary, but their fundamental concepts are basically the same as the federal system. Generally, there is a high court, called the *supreme court*; intermediate courts, labeled *appellate courts*; and lower courts, called *district courts*, *county courts*, *lower claims courts*, or *small-claims courts*. There are also special courts to handle traffic violations, probate, and land matters (such as the Torrens system).

courtesy to brokers   The practice of sharing commissions between listing and cooperating brokers. For example, in the sale of a large condominium project, the listing real estate broker may work for the developer. If a prospective buyer is a client of another broker, the listing broker may extend "courtesy" to the buyer's broker (called the *selling broker*), and share part of the commission with the other broker. It is not uncommon for developers who control their own brokerage company to decide not to extend courtesy to "outside" brokers unless there are marketing difficulties in selling the project.

court of equity   *See* **equity**.

covenant   An agreement or promise between two or more parties in which they pledge to perform (or not perform) specified acts on a property; or a written agreement that specifies certain uses or nonuses of the property. Covenants are found in real estate documents such as leases, mortgages, contracts for deed, and deeds. Damages may be claimed for breach of a covenant.

Covenants found in warranty deeds (general and special) are promises made by the grantor, binding both the grantor and the grantor's heirs and assigns, warranting that the title is of a certain character and that if the title should be found to be not of that character, the grantor or the grantor's heirs will compensate the grantee for any loss suffered. In many areas, covenants are implied by use of certain language in a deed, such as "convey and warrant," "warrant generally," or "warrant specially." Some typical covenants found in warranty deeds follow:

Covenant against grantor's acts: This covenant is used in special warranty deeds in which the grantor is a fiduciary, such as an executor, trustee, or guardian. In effect, the covenant states that the grantor has not done or suffered anything to encumber the property, but that she makes no

C

warranties concerning the title before taking title. This covenant does not "run with the land" (it does not benefit future grantees).

Covenant of seisin: The grantor guarantees that, at the time of the conveyance, he owns and is in possession of the property and has the good right to sell it. This covenant relates to the time of transfer and is broken, if at all, at the time of delivery of the deed. The covenant is not broken if there is a lien on the land, but it is broken if the title is held by a third person or if the grantor does not have the extent of the estate he purports to convey. For instance, the covenant of seisin is breached where the grantor warrants that he "is seized of" a fee simple estate, yet possesses only a life estate.

Covenant against encumbrances: This covenant warrants that the property is clear of any and all encumbrances not specifically excepted in the deed. Therefore, it is important to state all encumbrances as exceptions in the deed. Otherwise, if any encumbrance exists against the property and is not excepted in the deed, the grantees can recover their expense in paying off the encumbrance, such as unpaid taxes. Like the covenant of seisin, this covenant limits any recovery to the price paid and is broken, if at all, at the time of delivery of the deed. It covers all encumbrances, including those known and unknown to both grantor and grantee. A covenant against encumbrances is not breached, however, when there are open and visible physical encumbrances, such as an easement for power lines or an irrigation ditch.

Covenant of quiet enjoyment: The grantor warrants that the grantee and the heirs and assigns of the grantee will have the right to a property free of interference from the acts or claims of third parties. The innocent grantees are thus protected from title disputes arising between the grantor and a former claimant. The covenant of quiet enjoyment is breached only by an eviction, actual or constructive, by reason of a title superior to that of the grantor.

Covenant of warranty of title: This covenant assures the grantee that the grantor will bear the expense of defending the grantee's title to the property if any person asserts a rightful claim to the property. If the covenant is broken due to some third person having a better title, then the grantee may sue for damages up to the value of the property at the time of sale. It usually reads, "That the grantor will forever warrant the title to said premises."

Covenant of further assurance: This covenant obligates the grantor to perform any acts necessary to perfect the title in the grantee. It is also used to force a grantor to execute a correction deed when there has been some error in the original deed. The covenant is breached when the grantor refuses to pay the proper expenses and charges for obtaining the necessary documents, such as failure to record a satisfaction of mortgage where required or failure to obtain a quitclaim deed releasing an unrecorded interest in property or a dower interest. This covenant is usually enforced in an action for specific performance rather than in a suit for damages. Also called the *covenant of further assistance*. (*See* **covenants and conditions**, **deed**, **special warranty deed**, **warranty deed**.)

covenant not to compete Agreement given by a seller of a business not to compete against the purchaser in an agreed area for a specified time. This protects the purchaser of the business against the seller opening a competing business and regaining all former customers. It also allows the purchaser to amortize and write off the payment for the covenant over the life of the covenant. Real estate brokers have included similar agreements in employment contracts.

However, the courts generally do not favor such covenants. Noncompete clauses are closely scrutinized for possible violation of antitrust laws and as unreasonable restraints on doing business or employment.

covenants and conditions   *Covenants* are unconditional promises contained in contracts, the breach of which entitles a person to damages. *Conditions*, on the other hand, are contingencies, qualifications, or occurrences upon which an estate or property right (like a fee simple) would be gained or lost. Covenants are indicated by words such as *promise, undertake, agree*; conditions are indicated by words such as *if, when, unless,* and *provided.* Because both are limitations only and do not create obligations, failure of the condition to occur will not entitle either party to damages against the other party.

Conditions may be either precedent or subsequent. A *condition precedent* must happen or be performed before a right or estate is gained; a *condition subsequent* causes a right to be lost or an estate to be terminated upon its occurrence.

For example, a lease may contain covenants to repair, or pay taxes, assessments, or rent. If the tenant breaches a covenant, the landlord may sue the tenant for damages. If the lease contains a certain condition and the tenant breaches the condition, then the leasehold interest terminates. Thus, a commercial lease often contains a condition in a defeasance clause that the tenant will forfeit the lease upon the tenant's being declared bankrupt or upon illegal use of the premises.

Promises may be both conditions and covenants. For example, the concurrent conditions found in contracts for sale are also covenants. The delivery of the deed by the seller and the payment of the purchase price by the buyer are concurrent conditions; also, they are covenants. Thus, the buyer could sue the defaulting seller for damages only after the buyer met the condition of tendering performance (by placing the purchase money into escrow). (*See* **contingency, covenant**.)

covenants, conditions, and restrictions (CC&Rs)   Private restrictions on the use of real property; in some states, simply called *restrictions*, that must be enforced by homeowners' associations, not municipalities. CC&Rs are also the rights and obligations of owners of condominium units, townhouses, PUDs, and similar associations. (*See* **restriction**.)

covenants running with the land   Covenants that become part of the property rights and benefit or bind successive owners of the property. For the burden of a covenant to run with the land, the covenant must have been created in writing by a promise between a grantor and a grantee of the property, it must "touch and concern" the land, it must have been the intention of the original parties that the covenant run with the land, and subsequent grantees must have notice of the existence of the covenant. An example of a restrictive covenant may be a prohibition contained in a deed against erecting a pigpen on the property. Such restrictions are enforced privately, not by municipalities, and may not violate current laws. (*See* **restrictive covenant**.)

coverture   A common-law term for a woman's legal status during marriage.

CPI   *See* **consumer price index (CPI)**.

CPM   **Certified Property Manager (CPM)**. *See* Appendix B.

cramdown   A provision that permits a bankruptcy reorganization plan in certain situations even without the consent of all classes of creditors. (*See* **bankruptcy**).

crawlspace
1. The space between the first floor and the ground surface, often found in houses with no basement.
2. The space between the ceiling of the top floor and the roof, often taking the place of an attic.

CRE   Counselor of Real Estate. *See* Appendix B.

creative financing   A generic term used to describe a wide variety of innovative financing techniques used to finance a property. (*See* **alternative mortgage instrument**.)

C

credit   (*crédito*)
1. Obligations that are due or are to become due to a person.
2. In closing statements, that which is due and payable to either the buyer or the seller—the opposite of a charge or debit. The credit appears in the right-hand column of the accounting statement.

credit bid   The amount a lender can bid in a foreclosure sale of one of its secured properties representing amounts owed under the defaulted promissory note.

creditor   The person to whom a debtor owes a debt or an obligation; a lender.

credit rating   A rating given to a person or company to establish creditworthiness based on present financial condition, experience, and past credit history.

credit report   A report listing present and past debts, detailing the borrower's ability to make timely payments, and including information found from public records, such as tax liens and judgments. This information is maintained and issued by credit reporting agencies, such as Dun & Bradstreet, TransUnion, Equifax, and Experian.

credit scoring   A financial snapshot of a borrower's credit history and current usage of credit at a given point in time determined by a mathematical formula based on information maintained by credit bureaus and other sources. Sample scores range from 400 to 900, and the lower the number, the greater the risk of default. Based on the credit score, number of late mortgage payments, and/or bankruptcies, a letter grade is often assigned to the loan. The lower the letter grade, the more risk to the lender who will charge the borrower a higher rate of interest.

credit union   A cooperative nonprofit organization in which members (labor unions, clubs, churches, REALTORS®) place money in savings accounts, usually at higher interest rates than at other savings institutions. Credit unions pay no income tax. They usually make only short-term installment loans but may occasionally make loans secured by a lien on real property—typically second mortgages. Credit unions are a good source for home improvement loans as well as home loans themselves.

Under the Federal Credit Union Act, credit unions have authority to make 30-year real estate loans to members to finance their principal residences. Credit unions can also make loans for FHA/VA loans at interest rates comparable to the market value. The National Credit Union Share Insurance Fund insures deposits in federally chartered credit unions and state-chartered ones that apply and qualify up to $250,000 per depositor. The National Credit Union Administration (NCUA), an independent agency of the federal government that regulates and supervises the activities of federal credit unions, administers the fund.

cross-defaulting clause   A provision in many junior mortgages stipulating that a default in one mortgage also triggers a default in the mortgage in which the clause appears.

cross-easement   *See* **party wall**.

CRV   *See* **certificate of reasonable value (CRV)**.

cul-de-sac   A street that is open at one end only and usually has a circular turnaround at the other end; a blind alley. The use of cul-de-sacs has become popular in residential subdivisions in place of the traditional grid pattern with numerous intersections. (*See* **planned unit development [PUD]**.)

culvert   A drain or sewer built under a road, protecting it by carrying runoff or sewage under rather than directly over it.

cumulative attraction   *See* **attraction principle**.

curable depreciation   Depreciation that can be corrected at a reasonable and economically feasible cost.

C

curb appeal   The impression gained, whether good or bad, of a property when it is first seen, usually from the street while driving by.

curb line   The line between the vehicular and pedestrian rights of way on a road.

curtail schedule   *See* **amortization schedule**.

curtesy   The interest, recognized in some states, of a husband in property owned by his wife at the time of her death. During her life, the husband has no curtesy interest whatsoever in his wife's property and thus does not need to sign off his curtesy rights (as a wife would her dower rights) on any conveyance document executed by the wife. Upon his wife's death, a husband may have a vested life interest in one-third of the wife's real estate, depending on state law. The husband is usually not entitled to curtesy if he is guilty of desertion or neglect. (*See* **dower**.)

curtilage   The enclosed ground space surrounding a dwelling, such as the lawn or a patio.

curvilinear   Having boundaries of curved lines. Usually refers to the use by subdivision developers of curves in street and lot layouts, as opposed to the older grid patterns. This type of design pattern is more aesthetically pleasing, offers more privacy, and results in fewer traffic accidents.

cushion   An amount of money computed into a contractor's bid for a project to protect the contractor against possible unforeseen occurrences, such as delays in governmental approvals, poor weather, and bidding mistakes.

custody
1. The care and keeping of something.
2. Responsibility for a property, as when a mortgagee turns foreclosed property over to the Department of Veterans Affairs (if it was a VA loan). This specialized VA term may or may not include the right of possession of the property.

customer   The unrepresented third party in an agency relationship. For example, the listing broker's client is the seller. The broker can "work with" the unrepresented buyer as a customer. On the other hand, if the broker represents a buyer, the broker can "work with" an unrepresented seller as customer. Most state laws require that real estate licensees who work with customers exercise reasonable skill and care, disclose material and relevant facts about the property, disclose from whom the licensee will receive compensation, and follow any other duties required of the licensee in law or regulations. (*See* **client**.)

customer trust fund (CTF)   An impound account maintained for the purpose of setting up a reserve to pay certain periodic obligations such as real property taxes, insurance premiums, lease rent, and maintenance fees. Many lenders require the borrower/owner of a condominium apartment or other residence to maintain such funds to ensure that the carrying charges are paid on time. (*See* **impound account**.)

cut and fill   The excavation of part of an area and use of the excavated material for embankments or fill areas on or near the property.

cyclical movement   In economics, shifts in the business cycle of the national economy from prosperity through recession, depression, recovery, and back to prosperity.

D

damages   The compensation recoverable in a lawsuit by a complainant who sustained an injury, to person or property, through the act or default of another. Determining the appropriate measure (amount) of damages for specific types of injuries is complex. In cases of fraud, courts often use the benefit-of-bargain rule, awarding as damages the cash difference between the actual value of the property and the value of the property as fraudulently represented to the buyer. In some cases, the courts apply the "out-of-pocket" rule, awarding as damages the difference, if any, between the actual value of what the plaintiff (the person seeking damages) paid (i.e., the consideration) plus any amounts expended in reliance on the fraudulent party and the actual value of what was received.

Often the seller in a real estate contract retains the buyer's deposit money as damages when the buyer decides not to perform the contract to purchase the property. Sometimes the parties agree when signing their contract that a defaulting party will pay a certain amount to liquidate or settle any damages. Damages recoverable by an owner for a lessee's breach of contract to lease would be the excess (if any) of the agreed or contract rent, over and above the rental price the owner would be forced to accept in reletting the premises in a pressure situation. The burden of proving damages is always on the plaintiff. (*See* **actual damages**, **benefit-of-bargain rule**, **consequential damages**, **liquidated damages**, **mitigation of damages**, **severance damages**.)

damper   An adjustable valve at the top of a fireplace that regulates the flow of heated gases into the chimney.

dampproofing   A layer of plastic, lead, asphalt, or other water-resistant materials placed between the interior and exterior walls to exclude moisture.

date   (*fecha*)   Usually the exact day a legal document is signed. Certain documents, such as deeds or long-term leases, often contain several dates evidencing different events, such as the day the parties signed the document, the day the document was acknowledged, the day it was recorded, and/or the day an action begins or ends (e.g., option).

A date is not essential for the validity of most real estate contracts. Having a date is useful for proving a deed was delivered on the date specified, determining priority between unrecorded deeds, establishing time limits for performance (such as "seller has 48 hours to accept from the date of this offer") and proving whether the statute of limitations has run.

If the parties to a purchase agreement intend the closing to take place on a certain date (with no extensions of time), they should specify the date and expressly declare that "time is of the essence."

In a contract for deed, the date may be important in determining which party is liable for a casualty loss, personal injuries to a guest, or liability for a special assessment.

Avoid confusion by being quite specific about terms; i.e., "the seller pays up *to and including* March 28." A period running "to" a certain date does not include that date unless the words *to* and *including* are used. Instead of "to 12:00 am," which can create doubt as to whether it is midnight or noon, use 11:30 am or 11:30 pm. Rather than saying "a 90-day period," state a specific termination date to avoid arguments over whether it is calendar days or 30-day months and whether first and last days are counted.

The date of the appraisal, also called *valuation date*, is the date the value estimate applies ("date of value"), not necessarily the date the report is written ("date of report").

datum (*nivel de referencia*)   A level surface to which heights and depths are referred; the datum plane. The datum may be an assumed point (such as a monument), or it may be tidal in nature (that is, mean sea level). (*See* **benchmark**.)

days of grace   *See* **grace period**.

days on the market   The time period between listing a property and either getting it under contract or removing it from the market.

DBA   "Doing business as"; used to identify a trade name or a fictitious business name. (*See* **fictitious company name**.)

DBH   Diameter breast-high: the diameter of a tree at 4½ feet from the ground.

dead-end street (*calle sin salida*)   A street with only one entrance; sometimes leading into a cul-de-sac.

dealer   An Internal Revenue Service designation for a person who regularly buys and sells real property. A person is classified as a dealer with respect to the property if, at the time of a property's sale, the person held the property "primarily" for sale to customers in the ordinary course of business. Courts have interpreted "primarily" to mean principally or of first importance. A dealer must pay tax at ordinary income rates on any gains from the sale of property but may also take ordinary deductions for losses. In addition, dealer property may not be depreciated and does not qualify for tax-deferred treatment in an IRC Section 1031 exchange or for IRC Section 453, installment reporting of gains. (*See* **exchange**, **like-kind property**.)

Determination of dealer status is made on a case-by-case basis. One may be a dealer for some properties and an investor to others, depending on the facts of each case. Anyone who deals extensively must maintain detailed records of each transaction to prove status as an investor, not as a dealer. Some IRS tests for determining dealer status are the purpose for purchasing the property, the length of time the property was held, the number of sales activities of the owner, the existence of other income and other businesses and the extent of improvements made on the property by the taxpayer. If the owner subdivides and develops the property, it is likely the owner is a dealer; there are exceptions, however, especially with one-time subdividers.

Some real estate investors who actively manage their properties consider switching from investor to dealer status to avoid the passive income limitation on loss deductions. If an investor does not "materially participate" in the investment, then losses can be used only to offset income from other passive investments. Passive losses cannot be used to offset earned income, interest, or dividends.

debenture   A type of long-term note or bond given as evidence of debt. Unlike a mortgage note, a debenture is not secured by a specific property. Usually, the issuer executes an indenture or agreement with a trustee such as a bank. The indenture states the amount, interest rate, maturity, and special features of the bond issue, such as its ability to be accelerated or converted. To avoid restriction of future borrowing power, many issuers use subordinated debentures—that is, loans that may be subordinated to other company loans in the terms provided for in the debenture. Sinking fund debentures require a certain amount to be escrowed annually so there will be funds available for redemption.

Fannie Mae issues debentures to finance the acquisition of mortgages in the secondary mortgage market. If a borrower defaults on an FHA loan, the government gives interest-bearing debentures to the mortgagee after the title is transferred to the FHA. (*See* **Federal Housing Administration [FHA]**.)

debit (*debe*)   A charge on an accounting statement or balance sheet (appearing in the left column); the opposite of a credit. Used in bookkeeping and in preparing the closing statement in a real estate transaction.

debt coverage ratio   The ratio of annual net income to annual debt service. For example, a lender may require that a qualified corporate borrower have net income of 1.5 times the debt service of the loan being approved.

debt financing   The payment, in whole or in part, for a capital investment with borrowed monies, as opposed to investing one's own funds. Usually, in real estate, the property itself serves as the security for the debt.

D

debtor   (*deudor*)   One who owes money; a borrower, a maker of a note; a mortgagor.

debt relief   The forgiveness of a legal obligation to pay money. Although the Mortgage Debt Relief Act of 2007 provided tax relief, after December 31, 2013, when the lender decides to forgive the payment of all or a portion of a promissory note, as in a "short sale" situation, the Internal Revenue Service requires that the lender file a Form 1099. The seller/borrower will owe taxes on the amount of forgiven debt, which is considered ordinary income.

debt service   The amount of money needed to meet the periodic payments of principal and interest on a loan or debt that is being amortized. If the periodic payments are constant, in equal amounts, then a portion will pay off accrued interest with the remainder reducing principal. (*See* **amortization**, **constant**.)

debt-to-equity ratio   The relationship between the total loan owed the lender and the invested capital of the owner; also known as the *leverage ratio*.

decedent   A dead person, especially one who has died recently.

deck   An open, flat flooring area, that may cover a roof or surround a hot tub or swimming pool; similar to a patio or porch.

declarant   The original person or developer creating the condominium, PUD, or town-house community, who records the appropriate documents, including the CC&Rs. (*See* **condominium**, **declaration**.)

declaration   The legal document that the developer of a condominium must generally file and record in order to create a condominium under state law. The declaration usually consists of a precise description of the land on which the project is located; whether it is fee or leased; a description of the apartments, common elements, and limited common elements; a statement indicating the use of the building or buildings and apartments, including restrictive uses; and a statement of other detailed legal requirements, such as service of process and provision for amendment of the declaration. The declaration must generally be recorded, together with a true copy of the bylaws governing the operation of the project and a condominium map showing the floor plan, elevations and so forth. The developer usually must also record a master deed or lease. (*See* **condominium ownership**.)

declaration of homestead   *See* homestead.

declaration of restrictions   A statement of all the covenants, conditions, and restrictions (CC&Rs) that affect a parcel of land. When recording the subdivision plat, restrictions may be noted on the map or plan or, if numerous, on a separate document called a declaration. The restrictions usually aim for uniformity by requiring all lot owners to comply with certain building standards and conform to certain restrictions. For example, the CC&Rs may require lot owners to construct homes valued over a certain amount or to obtain prior design approval from a designated architectural control committee. Once recorded, these restrictions in the declaration run with the land and bind all future lot owners unless terminated by a lapse of a specified time or by agreement of all benefited parties. An owner can enforce the restrictions against any other owner who violates any of the restrictions.

The following are typical provisions of a declaration of restrictions:

■ "Each building or other structure shall be constructed, erected, and maintained in strict accordance with the approved plans and specifications."

- "No building shall be located on any lot nearer than 35 feet to the street lot line, nearer than 30 feet to the rear lot line, or nearer than 10 feet to the side lot lines."
- "No building or structure shall be more than 25 feet in height as measured from the highest natural grade at any point on the perimeter of the foundation of the structure to the highest point of the roof."
- "No animals, livestock, or poultry of any kind shall be raised, bred, or kept on any land in the subdivision except by special permit issued by the board of directors. However, a reasonable number of dogs, cats, or other common household pets may be kept without the necessity of obtaining such permit."

Restrictions may not violate public law, such as referencing race or religion. They should be carefully drafted to avoid ambiguity. For example, if trailers are prohibited, does that prohibition also exclude mobile homes? Does the word *structure* include a swimming pool or fence? What is a home business? (*See* **covenants, conditions, and restrictions [CC&Rs]; restrictions**.)

declining-balance method   An accounting method of depreciation for income-tax purposes designed to provide larger-than-straight-line deductions in the early years of a property's life and applicable to property placed in service before 1981.

The declining-balance method of calculation is applied in the IRS percentage tables for determining ACRS depreciation deductions applicable to personal property. The 3-, 5-, 7-, and 10-year classes use the 200 percent declining-balance method, switching to straight-line at the appropriate time, and the 15- and 20-year classes use the 150 percent declining-balance method, also switching to straight-line. (*See* **accelerated cost recovery system [ACRS]**.)

decree   (*decreto*)   A court order or judgment. (*See* **interlocutory decree**.)

dedication   The transfer of privately owned land to the public without consideration, with the intent that the land will be accepted and used for public purposes. A landowner may dedicate the entire fee simple interest or an easement such as a public right-of-way across the landowner's property.

There are two types of dedication: statutory and common law. A statutory dedication is accomplished by recording a subdivision map approved by local officials and expressly indicating on the map those areas dedicated to the public, such as parks and streets.

A common-law dedication is a matter of contract and thus requires an offer, evidenced by an intention and an unequivocal act of dedication on the part of the owner and acceptance on the part of the public. The dedication may be *express* (as when a developer or subdivider deeds roads to the county) or *implied* (as when the owner has acquiesced to the public use of the owner's property, usually for the prescriptive period). (*See* **cession deed**.)

For example, to prevent the public from claiming a dedication, the Rockefeller Center closes off its streets and sidewalks for one day out of the year. This shows that the public's right to use the property is a mere license and that Rockefeller Center is definitely not dedicating its property to the public. Some owners also imbed into their sidewalk a metal plaque stating, "Private Property, Permission to Use Revocable." Signs that say "No Trespassing" may be insufficient for purposes of preventing the public from claiming a dedication.

The fee interest acquired by dedication is similar to a qualified fee. For example, upon abandonment of the dedicated public use, the fee goes to the owner under a possibility of reverter, while the government may not divert the property to a new use.

Dedication of property such as streets and open spaces is sometimes made a prerequisite to governmental approval of a proposed development. In some cases, the developer can pay a fee rather than dedicate land. (*See* **transfer of development rights [TDR]**.)

deductions   Ordinary and necessary expenses paid in a taxable year, which reduce the amount of taxable income and therefore tax liability. Common examples are deductions for mortgage interest and real property taxes for individuals, and automobile and office expenses for businesses.

deed   (*escritura*)   A written instrument by which a property owner as "grantor" conveys and transfers to a "grantee" an ownership interest in real property. Types of deeds differ by the type of covenant made by the grantor and include warranty deeds (most commonly used), grant deeds, bargain and sale deeds, quitclaim deeds, gift deeds, guardian's deeds, executor's deeds, personal representative's deeds (probate), sheriff's deeds, commissioner's deeds (foreclosure), and deeds in trust. Title to leasehold property is transferred by way of an "assignment of lease" document rather than a deed. (*See* **freehold, leasehold**.)

    To be valid as between grantor and grantee, a deed must contain the following elements:

Grantor: The deed must name a grantor who is of age and of sound mind. A mistake in the spelling of the grantor's name or signature will not invalidate the deed if the grantor's identity is otherwise clear. If there are multiple grantors, each must be named as a grantor in the deed to convey each grantor's interest, or each may convey separately in separate deeds. (*See* **grantor**.)

Grantee: There must be an actual grantee. A deed delivered to a corporation before its coming into legal existence (by filing its articles of incorporation) is void for lack of a grantee, as is a deed delivered to the estate of a dead grantee. A deed delivered to a minor or incompetent is valid. A deed to a fictitious person is void, but a deed to a person using a fictitious name is valid. It is good practice to include the status of the parties—such as married, minor, trustee, or personal representative. A grantor cannot be the sole grantee, but the grantor could convey the deed jointly to the grantor and another person or to the grantor's corporation.

    A deed is not a valid conveyance until the grantee's name is inserted in it by the grantor personally, by someone at the grantor's request and in the grantor's presence, or by the grantor's agent duly authorized in writing.

Consideration: A deed should recite some consideration, although in most instances it need not be the actual consideration. Most deeds recite a nominal consideration, such as "for $10 and other good and valuable consideration." Deeds granted by fiduciaries, however, must state the actual consideration, and in all cases the contract of sale states the actual consideration. (*See* **consideration**.)

Words of conveyance: Words of conveyance, such as "I hereby grant and convey," distinguish the deed from a mortgage instrument. (*See* **mortgage**.)

Legal description: There must be a legal description of the land conveyed, by metes and bounds; by lot, block, and subdivision; or by a government survey. In a condominium deed, the unit designation and post office address are generally sufficient because the full legal description is already recited in the recorded declaration. If the deed attempts to convey more property than the seller actually owns (through an incorrect legal description), the deed is not void but is usually valid for that portion of the description actually owned by the grantor.

Signature: The grantor must sign the deed. If the grantee is assuming an existing mortgage or is agreeing to abide by a restrictive provision in the deed, then the grantee is also required to sign. In some states, the signature must be witnessed and/or notarized. A date of execution is not essential but is customary and tends to establish the date of delivery.

Delivery: Delivery is the final act of the grantor, signifying an intention that the deed will take effect. A deed must be delivered and accepted during the lifetime of both the grantor and the grantee to be valid; title passes and the deed is no longer an operative instrument, and its loss or destruction does not affect the grantee's title. However, when transferring property registered under the Torrens system, registration of the deed and not the act of delivery conveys title.

The destruction of a deed normally has no effect on the deed, because it is simply evidence of the title, not the title itself. Therefore, title cannot be reinvested in the grantor by the grantee's destroying the deed even with the intent to restore the grantor's original title. (*See* **delivery**.)

Though not essential for validity, a deed is normally recorded to protect the grantee against claims of any third party. For valid recordation, a deed must be properly recorded in the chain of title. (*See* **acceptance**, **bargain and sale deed**, **cession deed**, **delivery**, **chain of title**, **correction deed**, **covenant**, **gift deed**, **grantee**, **indenture deed**, **merger**, **quitclaim deed**, **recording**, **warranty deed**.)

deed in lieu of foreclosure   A deed to a lender given by an owner conveying mortgaged property in which the mortgage is in default. It is an alternative to a foreclosure action. Its main disadvantage to a lender is that the deed does not wipe out junior liens, as a foreclosure action would. Also called a *voluntary deed*. (*See* **foreclosure**.)

deed in trust   A form of deed by which real estate is conveyed to a trustee, usually to establish a land trust. Under the terms of such an instrument, full powers to sell, to contract to sell, to mortgage, and to subdivide are granted to the trustee. The trustee's use of these powers, however, is controlled by the beneficiary under the provisions of the trust agreement. Deeds in trust are used in those states that recognize land trusts.

deed of confirmation   *See* **correction deed**.

deed of reconveyance   A document used to transfer legal title from the trustee back to the borrower (trustor) after a debt secured by a deed of trust has been paid to the lender (beneficiary). Also called a *release deed*. (*See* **deed of trust**.)

deed of trust   A legal document in which title to property is transferred to a third-party trustee as security for an obligation owed by the trustor (borrower) to the beneficiary (lender). Also called a *trust deed*. A deed of trust is similar to a mortgage—the main difference is that it involves three parties. When a borrower repays the note secured by a deed of trust, the trustee must reconvey title back to the borrower by way of a deed of reconveyance, which is also called a *release deed*. (*See* **mortgage**.)

In some states (such as California), a judicial foreclosure proceeding is avoided when the trustee can sell the property under a power of sale after allowing the trustor a legally prescribed period of time to reinstate the delinquent loan. In some states, the borrower-trustor is given a short period of time (such as three months) in which to pay back the amount due plus a named reinstatement fee and reinstate the loan. Thus, the trustee cannot accelerate the entire note immediately upon the trustor's default but must wait the statutory period.

Lenders in many states prefer to make residential property loans under a trust deed for several reasons: (1) In states that permit it, a trustee may be given the power to sell property after default without going through the time-consuming judicial foreclosure process. (2) The statute of limitations may bar an action on the note in a mortgage transaction; however, this is not so with a deed of trust containing a power of sale, because the trustee technically has legal title and thus can sell the property at any time after default to pay off the debt. (3) Deeds of trust can be used to secure more than one note. (4) A lender who wishes to remain anonymous need not be named in the deed of trust. (5) Usually, there is no statutory right of redemption after the sale under the power of sale.

One disadvantage to naming a noninstitutional trustee under a deed of trust is that problems sometimes arise in locating such a trustee to obtain a reconveyance after the debt has been paid. Preferably, a corporate trustee is named in the document.

The deed of trust is an alternative to the mortgage document as a security device. In some states, a deed of trust may still be legally enforceable even though there is no promissory note; this is not true of a mortgage.

deed poll   A deed signed by only the grantor. In early practice, such a deed had a clean-shaven edge, whereas an indenture deed, signed by both grantor and grantee, had a wavy or indented edge and could be proven by matching up the edges of both copies. The deed poll (like a lease) binds the grantee upon acceptance to any covenants of the grantee contained in such deed, even though the deed is not signed by the grantee. (*See* **indenture deed**.)

D

deed restrictions   (*limitaciones en la escritura*)   Provisions placed in deeds to control future uses of the property. (*See* **qualified fee**, **restriction**, **restrictive covenant**.)

de facto   Latin for "in fact," as opposed to *de jure*, meaning "by right." A de facto corporation may be acting as a business entity yet have failed to file the technical papers needed under state law to form a valid corporation.

default   The nonperformance of a duty or obligation that is part of a contract. A default is normally a breach of contract, and the nondefaulting party can seek legal remedies to recover any loss. Defaults in long-term leases or contracts for deed include nonpayment of money when due, failure to renew insurance policies, failure to pay real estate taxes, damage to the property, and so forth.

Note that a buyer's good-faith inability to obtain financing under a contingency provision of a purchase agreement is not considered a default (the performance of the contract depends on the buyer's getting the property financed), and in this case, the seller generally must return the buyer's deposit.

Junior mortgages usually contain a clause authorizing the holder of the junior mortgage to advance money to cure any default of the mortgagor under a prior mortgage. Were the first mortgage to remain in default and the lender to foreclose, it would have the effect of wiping out the junior mortgage. (*See* **cross-defaulting clause**, **junior mortgage**, **notice of default**.)

default judgment   A court order in favor of the plaintiff resulting from the defendant's failure to answer a complaint or appear in court to defend the action.

defeasance clause   A clause used in leases and mortgages to defeat or cancel a certain right upon the happening of a specified condition. A defeasance clause typically found in mortgages provides that if the borrower repays the debt when due (by the "law day"), then the words of grant are void and the mortgage is thereby canceled, divesting the mortgagee of title and reinvesting title in the mortgagor. Automatic defeasance was important under the common law and in title theory states where title is transferred under a mortgage. To clear the lien of a paid mortgage or trust deed from the public records, the borrower must first obtain and then record a satisfaction, reconveyance, or release deed.

A document that the parties call a *deed* or *sale-leaseback* might be treated by the courts as actually being a mortgage if it contains a defeasance clause permitting reconveyance back to the grantor upon full satisfaction of a debt.

defeasible fee simple   *See* **fee simple defeasible**.

defect of record   Any encumbrance on a title that is made a part of the public record. Recorded defects include judgments, deeds of trust, mortgages, other liens, and easements. (*See* **clear title**.)

defendant   The person being sued by the plaintiff in a lawsuit; the person charged with the wrong and from whom recovery is sought.

deferred commission   A commission that has been earned but not yet fully paid; also called a **residual**. For example, in a real estate sale, a broker earns a commission when the buyer signs and the seller accepts the purchase agreement. But, by prior arrangement between seller and broker, the commission may possibly be paid in part upon the down payment, and in full—the residual—upon closing which, with a new project under construction, could be as much as 18 months away.

Salespeople may not ordinarily receive compensation from anyone other than their present employing broker. In the case of deferred commissions from a previous employer, however, the salesperson may usually receive such commissions direct from the former employing broker. A cash-basis taxpayer/salesperson would not have to pay income tax on earnings until actually receiving those earnings.

Often commissions are deferred when insufficient cash has been received by the seller in an installment sale. For example, in the sale of a condominium to be constructed, the broker may receive part of the commission from the down payment and the remainder when the project is completed and the buyer pays in full and receives title.

deferred maintenance   Physical deterioration or loss in value of a building resulting from postponed maintenance to the building. This type of deterioration, sometimes called *curable physical depreciation*, is normally curable by making the necessary repairs and improvements.

A prospective purchaser of a building in which there is a significant amount of deferred maintenance should be especially careful to factor the estimated repair and replacement costs into an investment analysis of the property.

deferred-payment method   An accounting method of reporting taxable income on a deferred basis; also called the *cost-recovery method* or the *return-of-capital method*. Under the deferred-payment method, no gain is taxed to the seller until payments received from the buyer exceed the basis of the property and the cost of sale. This method can be used only in those cases in which the seller receives part of the sales price in the year of the sale, but the balance of the payment is not evidenced by a promissory note having a fair market value. (*See* **installment sale**.)

deferred taxes   The lawful delay of paying income taxes under specified provisions of the Internal Revenue Code, as in a tax-free exchange or installment sale. (*See* **exchange**.)

deficiency judgment   A judgment against a borrower, endorser, or guarantor for the balance of a debt owed when the security for a loan is insufficient to satisfy the debt. A deficiency occurs when the foreclosure sale of a property produces less than the amount needed to pay the costs and expenses of the action and to satisfy the obligation secured by the foreclosed mortgage. The deficiency is entered as a personal judgment against the original mortgagor and operates as a lien on the judgment debtor's assets. It is enforceable and collectible in the same manner as any judgment at law. If this judgment proves uncollectible, the lender is probably entitled to claim a bad-debt deduction on the lender's income taxes. In the case of a corporate mortgage, this would be a bad business debt and may fully offset against ordinary income.

In states where mortgages generally carry a power of sale, creditors must bring a separate action to obtain a deficiency judgment because the jurisdiction of a court is not invoked. If parties agree that the lender can look only to the collateral (the mortgaged property) in the event of a default, they include language to the effect that "this note is without recourse," which has the effect of preventing a deficiency judgment. In California and other states, the mortgagee cannot recover a deficiency judgment on a purchase-money mortgage; these states have enacted so-called antideficiency legislation.

A purchaser who assumes the seller's existing mortgage thereby becomes personally liable (along with the seller) for any deficiency. However, when purchasers buy property "subject to" an existing mortgage, they cannot be held personally liable for any deficiency; thus, upon default, the purchaser's liability would extend only to the loss of the property. (*See* **bankruptcy**, **dry mortgage**, **foreclosure**, **judgment lien**, **nonrecourse loan**, **power of sale**.)

deflated mortgage   A mortgage in which the parties agree to reduce the amount of the principal debt and increase the interest rate. In this way, the seller receives the same amount of dollars, but the buyer obtains a greater interest deduction.

degree   A surveying term meaning ¹⁄₃₆₀ of a full rotation about a point in a plane. (*See* **angle**.)

delayed exchange   An attempt to qualify a real estate transaction as an IRC Section 1031 exchange where "exchange" of the properties is not simultaneous. As a result of a limited number of federal court rulings (the *Starker* cases), some tax practitioners set up elaborate procedures to put the sales proceeds in a trust to be used to purchase properties in the future. Present regulations establish a deadline of 45 days for the purchase and 180 days for the closing of the second property in the exchange (or April 15, unless the filing deadline is extended, whichever comes first). The entity holding the funds in trust and the title to the property is called the *exchange accommodator or intermediary*. (*See* **exchange**.)

delinquent   The past-due status of a financial obligation such as a promissory note.

delivery   The legal act of transferring ownership. Documents such as deeds and mortgages must be delivered and accepted before becoming valid. Legal delivery refers to the intention of the grantor, not the act of manually transferring the document. The grantor must intend that the deed be currently operative and effective to transfer title to the grantee and intend that the grantee become the legal owner. Additionally, the grantor must be competent at the time of signing and acknowledging the deed, and also at the time of its delivery.

  For example, a grantor may voluntarily hand over a deed to a grantee only for review by the grantee's attorney. This would not be a valid delivery, because the grantor did not intend to relinquish all control over the deed.

  If the requisite intention is present, valid delivery of the deed is consummated even though the grantee's right to possession and enjoyment of the property may be deferred to a future date—delivery need not be physical or direct.

  For example, when the deed is given to a third person by the grantor with instructions to give it to the grantee upon satisfaction of a condition that is certain to occur, delivery is effective and the third person holds the deed as agent for the grantee. Specifically, when Juan gives a deed to an escrow agent with instructions to deliver it to Sunita "when I die," with no other conditions being imposed on the delivery, then it is a valid delivery and effectively transfers title to Sunita with possession and enjoyment delayed until Juan's death. But if Juan had instructed the agent to give the deed to Sunita "in case I die," then there would be no valid delivery—Juan did not intend a present transfer of title.

  When the grantor makes a constructive delivery to a third person, the grantor must relinquish all control over the deed—otherwise there is no effective delivery. There is no valid delivery upon an unauthorized delivery by an escrow agent before full performance of the stated escrow conditions. Once there is a valid delivery and acceptance, the act of the grantee in surrendering the property or the deed will not put title back in the original grantor. To accomplish this, the grantee must execute a new deed back to the original grantor.

  Although a deed does not generally have to be recorded to be valid, some states provide that the settlement agent may not close a transaction and disburse the proceeds of sale until the deed (or assignment of lease or contract for deed, if applicable) is recorded. Thus, the transaction is finally closed *after* the time title technically has passed to the buyer. Title to Torrens property is transferred only upon registration of the deed on the certificate of title with the registrar of titles and the issuance of a transfer certificate of title to the new owner, not upon delivery of the deed.

  A deed is presumed to have been delivered if the deed is found in the possession of the grantee or if the deed is recorded. Conversely, a deed still in the possession of the grantor is presumed not to have been delivered, although these presumptions may be rebutted. This issue sometimes arises when the grantor intends immediate transfer of title yet does not want the transfer made public at the time of transfer. The grantor thus will request that the grantee delay recordation until after the grantor's death.

Historically, title to real property was transferred by *livery of seisin*, the act of giving possession of the property to the grantee. This act was sometimes symbolized by the grantor's standing on the property and handing the grantee a twig or a handful of earth. Sometimes, a witness recorded the act on a document. Today, the transferring of possession is represented by delivery of the document reflecting the grantor's intent to transfer title to the property. (*See* **acceptance**, **deed**, **escrow**.)

delta
1. A land survey term used in metes-and-bounds descriptions for the angle between two intersecting lines, shown by the Greek letter Δ.
2. A symbol used as a variable in yield capitalization formula that represents an expected percentage change in property value over a holding period.

demand (*demanda*)
1. A letter from a creditor requesting payment of the amount due, as in a loan or lease.
2. The desire for economic goods that can be bought at a certain price, in a given market, at a particular time; what the marketplace will demand. Effective demand is the desire to buy coupled with the ability to pay. Demand is an essential element of highest and best use and value.

demand note   A promissory note that permits the holder, upon notice, to call in the loan at any time. In comparison, a term note is not payable until the time specified.

de minimus   Refers to the minimum level. For example, under the federal regulations, transactions of less than $250,000 do not require an appraisal by state-licensed or state-certified appraisers.

de minimis PUD   *See* **planned unit development (PUD)**.

de minimus settlement   An arrangement between the Environmental Protection Agency and a person who is potentially liable under the Superfund law regarding hazardous substances. The EPA will consider limiting the amount a landowner has to contribute to the cost of hazardous waste cleanup if the landowner acquired the property without knowing or having reason to know of the disposal of hazardous substances. (*See* **Comprehensive Environmental Response, Compensation, and Liability Act [CERCLA], due diligence**.)

demise
1. A conveyance of an estate or interest in real property to someone for a certain number of years, for life or at will—most commonly for years, as in a lease. A lease often refers to the "demised premises." The use of the word *demise* often implies a covenant of quiet enjoyment by which the lessor undertakes to guarantee that the lessee will not be disturbed in the lessee's use of the premises by superior claims of others. Do not confuse with *devise*.
2. A synonym for the term *let* in a lease.
3. A synonym for *death*.

demising wall   A partition or dividing wall found in a building housing two or more tenants, separating the area leased by one party from that leased by others.

demography (*demografía*)   The statistical study of human populations, especially in reference to size, density, and distribution. Demographic information is useful in evaluating commercial locations or shopping center sites.

demolition clause   A clause in a lease that gives the lessor the right to cancel the lease upon proper notice in the event that the lessor chooses to demolish the building. The clause is usually required only by owners of older buildings who want to leave their option open for new construction at some indefinite future date.

demolition loss   A loss in value due to physical destruction of the premises. If an owner purchases the property with the intent of demolishing the existing building, the demolition loss is not an ordinary loss but a cost that must be allocated to the basis of the land. In addition, the cost of demolishing a certified historic structure cannot be deducted—such costs must be treated as additional land cost.

demonstration home   *See* **model home**.

density   When used in connection with zoning requirements, the number of building units per acre or the number of occupants or families per unit of land area (acre, square mile); usually the ratio of land area to improvement area. (*See* **floor area ratio**, **land-use intensity**, **zoning**.)

density zoning   A type of zoning ordinance generally associated with a subdivision, restricting the average maximum number of houses per acre that may be built within a particular subdivision. For example, if a subdivision were zoned at a 15,000-square-foot-lot minimum, the developer could build only 2.5 houses per acre. On the other hand, if the area is density zoned at an average maximum 2.5 houses per acre, the developer is free to achieve an open, clustered effect by slightly reducing the individual lot sizes. Regardless of lot size or the number of units clustered, the subdivider is in compliance with the ordinance as long as the average number of units in the development remains at or below the maximum density. This average is called *gross density*.

Developers often try to work closely with zoning officials to develop ordinances and standards most beneficial to living comfort and aesthetic values.

Department of Housing and Urban Development (HUD)   (*Departamento de la Vivienda y del Desarrollo Urbano*)   *See* **HUD**, Appendix A.

depletion   A reduction in size or quantity. The exhaustion of an asset, such as gas, oil, mineral oil, or timber. Depletion may be deducted in certain mineral programs and thereby provides attractive tax-shelter benefits.

deponent   Person making an affidavit.

deposit   (*depósito*)   Money offered by a prospective buyer as an indication of good faith in entering into a contract to purchase; also known as earnest money; security for the buyer's performance of a contract. An earnest money deposit is not necessary to create a valid purchase contract because the mutual promises of the parties to buy and to sell are sufficient consideration to enforce the contract. If the buyer completes the purchase, the deposit money is applied toward the purchase price. If the buyer defaults, the contract may provide that the seller can retain the deposit money as liquidated damages. Contracts also often require the seller to split the deposit money with the broker, up to an amount not exceeding the broker's commission (per the terms of the listing or the contract of sale). If the seller defaults, the deposit should be returned in full to the buyer.

For protection, sellers often require a deposit large enough to cover the broker's commission, the cost of the title search, and the loss of time and opportunity to sell elsewhere. The amount is totally negotiable between the seller and the buyer. Some buyers use a large deposit as a negotiating tool to strengthen their offers. If the seller requires too substantial a deposit, however, a defaulting buyer might seek a return of part of it, claiming that the deposit did not accurately serve as liquidated damages, but rather as a forfeiture or penalty. Some states set standards; if the deposit exceeds that amount, the seller has the burden of proving that the deposit was, in fact, reasonable and not a penalty.

A deposit involving a large amount of money is often placed in an interest-bearing account for the buyer's benefit.

Disputes about deposit ownership sometimes occur. Although the money never belongs to the broker, the broker may receive some of the deposit if the buyer defaults, and then the seller retains the deposit as liquidated damages. In many states, the deposit money must be placed in a neutral escrow account and cannot be withdrawn until the transaction is consummated, or with the written agreement of the buyer and the seller.

If the sellers authorize the broker to accept deposit money on their behalf, the deposit money belongs to the sellers when the broker accepts it. If the broker absconds with the deposit money, and the sellers had authorized the broker to accept the deposit, the sellers would suffer the loss. On the other hand, if the sellers have not authorized the broker to accept the deposit money, the broker is acting as the buyer's agent in handling the money until such time as the sellers accept the buyer's offer to purchase. Thus the *buyer* would suffer the loss if the broker were to steal the money. Such authorization is specifically contained in many exclusive-right-to-sell listing contracts. (*See* **additional deposit, earnest money, election of remedies, liquidated damages, security deposit**.)

deposition   The formal testimony made by a witness or a party to a lawsuit (the deponent) before the trial. Any party may take the testimony of any other person in a deposition by using an oral examination or written questions (called *interrogatories*) for the purpose of discovery (ascertaining evidence) or use as evidence, for preserving testimony in the legal action, or both.

Depositors Insurance Fund (DIF)   A private, industry-sponsored insurance fund created by the Federal Deposit Insurance Reform Act of 2005 that merged the Bank Insurance Fund (BIF) and the Savings Association Insurance Fund (SAIF). The DIF insures all deposits above the FDIC limits and since March 31, 2006, the DIF is funded by insurance payments made by the banks. The Dodd-Frank Act requires a minimum designated reserve ratio (DRR) of 1.35 percent of estimated insured deposits, requires that the FDIC determine how to restore the fund's balance if it falls below 1.35 percent, and provides dividends to the industry if the fund balance exceeds 1.5 percent. The DIF insures all deposits over FDIC limits.

Insured deposit coverage is a maximum of $250,000 for each depositor. (*See* **Federal Deposit Insurance Corporation [FDIC], Savings Association Insurance Fund [SAIF], credit union, savings banks**.)

Depository Institutions Deregulation and Monetary Control Act (1980)   Federal legislation that ended major deregulation of federally chartered commercial banks and savings and loan institutions phasing out caps on the rates that banks could pay on savings and time deposits. The act deregulated the mortgage market by making more home loans available by abolishing state usury caps that had limited the interest rates that banks could charge for primary mortgage loans. The act authorized savings and loans to make consumer loans, including auto loans and credit card loans, up to 20 percent of total assets and permitted. It also raised the deposit insurance of U.S. banks and credit unions from $40,000 to $100,000.

depreciable life   The time period over which cost recovery of an asset is to be allocated. For tax returns, depreciable life may be shorter or longer than estimated service life. (*See* **cost recovery, depreciation [tax]**.)

depreciable real property (accounting)   Property subject to wear and tear that is used in a trade or business or held for the production of income. Consequently, land and the taxpayer's personal residence are not depreciable. If the taxpayer uses part of his residence for business purposes, a pro rata depreciation deduction can be taken for that allocated use. However, the tax law imposes stringent requirements on the business deduction.

Depreciation rules for real property changed dramatically under the 1986 Tax Reform Act. Cost recovery periods are lengthened, and accelerated cost recovery methods are no longer available.

It is not essential that the property actually produce income; it is usually sufficient that the property is held with the *expectation* of producing income or making a profit. However, if a property is determined to be for "hobby" purposes, the depreciation will be limited. Only improvements to real property can be depreciated, such as buildings, sidewalks, and fences. Although depreciation deductions have been replaced with "cost recovery," this latter deduction is still limited to depreciable property, and the depreciable portion thereof. (*See* **cost recovery**, **depreciation [tax]**, **vacation home**.)

depreciation allowance   The accounting charge made to allow for the fact that the asset may become economically obsolete before its physical deterioration. The purpose is to write off the original cost by distributing it over the estimated useful life of the asset. It appears in both the profit and loss statement and the balance sheet. (*See* **cost recovery**, **depreciation [tax]**.)

depreciation (appraisal)   (*depreciación*)   In the cost approach, a loss in value due to any cause; any condition that adversely affects the value of an improvement. For appraisal purposes, depreciation is divided into three classes according to its cause: physical deterioration, functional obsolescence, and external obsolescence. The most common method of measuring depreciation in the past was the straight-line or age-life method, but today many appraisers use the breakdown method, where they break down the depreciation into all three classes, with each class measured separately, whether such depreciation is curable or incurable.

Physical deterioration of an improvement is indicated by decay or disintegration, cracks, wear and tear, settling of foundations, structural defects, actions of the elements, any loss of physical soundness, and termite damage.

Functional obsolescence (inside property lines) is indicated by obsolete boilers, ancient plumbing, unnecessarily high ceilings, out-of-date lighting fixtures, and outmoded architecture. A superadequacy, such as a swimming pool that contributes less to the property value than cost, may also be considered functional obsolescence.

External obsolescence (outside property lines) is indicated by population decreases, incongruous uses of property, legislative action (city, state and national), changes in a neighborhood, and invasion of other conditions that lower the value of the property being appraised. Obsolescence that affects the entire area is said to comprise a change in the market.

Accrued depreciation, also called *past depreciation*, is depreciation existing as of the date of appraisal. In contrast, *future depreciation* is an estimation of the loss in value that is likely to occur in the future.

Because of depreciation factors, it is unlikely that any two properties will be valued exactly alike. Assume, for example, that two buildings were constructed at the same time, using similar materials. After two years, the properties would have different values due to the independent effect of depreciation forces on the separate buildings; for example, one building may now have termites. (*See* **age-life depreciation**, **appraisal**, **cost approach**, **curable depreciation**, **observed condition**.)

depreciation recapture   An Internal Revenue Service provision making excess depreciation taken on real property subject to income tax upon sale of the property; gains due to recapture of depreciation deductions are taxable at 25 percent.

depreciation (tax)   An expense deduction taken for an investment in depreciable property to allow for the recovery of the cost of the investment. Depreciation can occur even when the market value of a property increases. (Non-income-producing property, such as a personal residence, cannot be depreciated.)

The annual amount of the depreciation deduction results from an arbitrary apportionment of the investment in the building systematically spread over its useful life. Thus, tax depreciation is a statutory concept that occurs even though the property itself may have actually appreciated in value. Land is not depreciable (although the cost of landscaping may be depreciated in certain cases). Therefore, there must be an allocation of basis between the land and the building. Most taxpayers use the allocation as set by the state tax assessor.

If the taxpayer does not take depreciation, the Internal Revenue Service will compute the allowable straight-line depreciation for the taxpayer and apply it to reduce the basis upon the sale of the property. The taxpayer who is entitled to take the depreciation deduction is the one who suffers the economic loss due to the decrease in value. Usually this is the owner, though bare legal title alone is not sufficient. For example, a life tenant is entitled to the deduction as if she were the absolute owner of the property. When the life tenant dies, the depreciation deduction, if any, passes to the remainderman. (*See* **accelerated cost recovery system [ACRS]**, **accelerated depreciation**, **basis**, **component depreciation**, **cost recovery**, **depreciable real property [accounting]**, **recapture**, **useful life**.)

depth influence   *See* **depth tables**.

depth tables   Tables of percentage used by some assessors to provide a uniform system of measuring the additional value of lots, for which value accrues because of added depth, with the extra depth valued according to the added utility that it creates (called *depth influence*). Depth tables are used by tax assessors seeking to achieve uniformity in assessment practices. One of the earliest depth tables established was the "4-3-2-1 rule," which provided that the front quarter of the lot holds 40 percent of the value; the second, 30 percent; the third, 20 percent; and the fourth, 10 percent. This rule has been expanded to provide percentages for each few feet of the lot. Many appraisers consider general preprinted depth tables to be unreliable because they do not reflect the specific time and market conditions that affect the subject property.

deraign   To prove ownership of land; to trace title.

dereliction   The gradual receding of water that leaves dry land. (*See* **accretion**, **reliction**.)

descent   (*sucesión*)   The acquisition of an estate by inheritance when an heir succeeds to the property by operation of law. Descent literally means the hereditary succession of an heir to the property of an ancestor who dies intestate.

Rights under laws of descent vary from state to state. The law of the state in which the property is located will not only prescribe the persons to inherit the property but also provide the respective shares each is to receive. When a person dies leaving a spouse and one child, the spouse and child usually take the entire estate between them—some states dividing it equally and some allowing only one-third to the surviving spouse. If, however, a spouse and two or more children survive, it is customary for the spouse to take one-third and the children to divide the remaining two-thirds equally among them. If a spouse but no children or descendants of the children exist, some state laws give the spouse one-half of the estate and the other half is divided equally among collateral heirs such as parents, brothers, and sisters of the decedent; in some states, however, the surviving spouse takes all.

All states make provisions for legally adopted children, who are usually considered heirs of the adopting parents. They are not considered heirs of ancestors of the adopting parents.

In most states, illegitimate children inherit from the mother, but not from the father unless he has admitted parentage in writing or parentage has been established legally. Of course, if he legally adopts such a child, that child inherits as an adopted child. State law should be consulted. (*See* **curtesy**, **dower**, **elective share**, **intestate**, **probate**.)

description   The portion of a conveyance document that defines the property being transferred. To be valid, documents such as deeds, assignments of leases, certain leases, and mortgages must contain a full legal description of the property to be conveyed. Usually a contract for the sale of real property need only contain a description sufficient to identify the property, such as street address and/or tax map key number.

In a deed, the description is normally divided into two parts: the general and the specific. The general description usually identifies the parcel in question by location, name, or reference to previous known owners. It leads into the specific description with the phrase "more particularly described as follows," or by reference to public maps, plats, or other recorded information.

The specific description exactly defines the limits of the property involved. These limits may be defined by one (or any combination) of three basic methods of real estate description: metes and bounds, government (rectangular) survey, and subdivision plat.

Great care must be exercised to avoid ambiguities. For example, the "next contiguous 40 acres" is ambiguous because an acre can have any shape; the "south one-half of the farm" is adequate if the lot is rectangular but not if it is irregular in shape.

Some contracts for large, bulk real estate sales include what are known as *Mother Hubbard clauses*. These clauses state that the description includes all property owned by the seller at the location or, if appropriate, all real estate owned by the seller in that particular area. (*See* **government survey method**, **legal description**, **metes and bounds**, **plat map**.)

designated agent   In some states, where allowed by law, a designated agent is classified under state law as the agent for either the buyer or the seller to the exclusion of all other agents in the brokerage; another salesperson in the firm could be designated the agent of the other party without thereby creating a dual agency for the individual agents. Designated agency is a solution to the potential conflict of interest that arises during an in-house transaction. (*See* **dual agency [limited agency]**.)

designated broker   *See* **principal broker [PB]**.

destroyed or materially damaged clause   *See* **act of God**.

determinable fee   *See* **fee simple determinable**.

developer   (*desarrollador*)   One who attempts to put land to its most profitable use through the construction of improvements, such as commercial condominiums or subdivision projects. The developer organizes and supervises the entire project, usually from the acquisition of land all the way through construction and final sales, and sometimes continuing with the maintenance of the project. Although the developer's financial rewards are sometimes substantial, the risks are also high. All aspects of development are becoming so specialized and highly technical that developers frequently retain consultants, such as construction and finance experts, to assist them throughout the various stages of development. (*See* **entrepreneur**.)

development impact fee   An amount of money charged to a developer by a local governmental body to cover the costs of providing essential services to the proposed project, such as fire and police protection and road maintenance.

development loan   A loan to cover the costs of improving property; an interim loan. In a typical case, a subdivider acquiring land seeks financing to cover the costs of both on-site and off-site improvements (site preparation, roads, sewer, water, and drainage) to bring the individual lots up to a standard so they can be profitably marketed. Often the development loan specifies a schedule of partial releases to permit individual lots to be sold free and clear of the loan lien. Development loans on large subdivisions are often structured in phases to match the incremental development of the project.

development rights   The rights a landowner sells to another to develop and improve the property. In some areas, where residential units are built on land to be leased at economic or market levels, development rights are the premium paid by the developer for the privilege of improving the property and bringing the future seller and the landowner together to create the leasehold estate. Sometimes, only the development rights themselves are sold, and, after the improvements are built and sold, the purchasers lease the land directly from the landowner. Often, the developer purchases a master lease in conjunction with the development rights and then subleases the improved lots to the ultimate purchasers. Development rights may be sold by the developer to a subdeveloper provided the landowner consents to such assignment. (*See* **transfer of development rights [TDR].**)

devise   (*legado*)   A transfer of real property under a will. The donor is the *devisor*, and the recipient is the *devisee*. When there is no will, the real property *descends* to the heirs. In some states, a deed is not required to transfer property by devise because the will acts as the instrument of conveyance upon the donor's death. (*See* **bequeath, descent.**)

diffused surface waters   Waters coming from rain, snow, or underground springs and spreading over the surface of the ground.

diluvion   The gradual and imperceptible washing away and resultant loss of soil along a watercourse; opposite of *alluvion*.

diminished utility   *See* **accrued depreciation.**

DINK (dual income, no kids)   Slang for couples with two salaries or two sources of income who have no dependent children; considered excellent prospects for home ownership or other real estate investments. (*See* **yuppie.**)

direct endorsement   Ability of an FHA-approved lender to secure FHA single-family and multifamily mortgage insurance by following FHA guidelines. Under the direct endorsement program, an approved lender who certifies that the mortgage complies with applicable FHA requirements can underwrite many of the FHA's mortgage insurance programs. The lender performs all appraisal duties and analyzes the borrower's credit. Direct endorsement leaves FHA with the risk of loss from default but gives it control through its ability to remove the lender from the program.

directional growth   The direction or location toward which a community appears destined to grow. Mortgage underwriting and appraisal considers directional growth because it plays a role in determining supply and demand, highest and best use, and the present and future value of real estate.

direct participation program licenses   National licenses issued by the nonprofit National Association of Securities Dealers to securities salespeople selling real estate securities (such as resort condominiums with rental pools) and tax shelters in programs providing a direct "pass-through" of tax benefits (limited partnerships and REITs, but not stock in ordinary corporations). The two types of licenses are the Limited Representative License and the Limited Principal's License.

direct reduction mortgage   A mortgage that requires payment of a fixed amount of principal each period (loan recapture). The total payment varies because the interest portion is reduced with each payment. Most likely found in financing between private parties.

   Under the direct reduction payment plan, the mortgagor easily calculates how much has been paid on the principal because this amount remains the same each month. What varies is the amount applying to interest. Thus, in the early years of the loan, the combined monthly principal and interest payments are larger than in a constant or level mortgage payment plan. (*See* **amortization.**)

D

direct sales comparison approach   A method of appraising or valuing real property based on the principle of substitution (comparison). The appraiser using this method estimates the value of property by comparing the prices paid for similar properties and concludes the value accordingly. The three main steps in what was formerly called the *market-data approach* are the following:

1. Locate comparable properties (properties with the same "highest and best use") that have sold recently, usually within the past six months, in arm's-length transactions. This excludes certain sales, such as bankruptcy, short sales, or foreclosure sales, sales by the government, sales between relatives, and so on. Adjust the contract sales price to an effective sales price, considering unusual seller concessions and changes in market conditions from the time of sale.

2. Compare these properties with the subject property and make all necessary adjustments in the sales prices for any significant differences in the property, such as age, location, and physical characteristics. Adjustments are necessary even in comparing vacant land, such as hookups for utilities, soil composition, and location. There should be similarities in the number of rooms, bathrooms, bedrooms, size of lot, building age, style, and condition.

3. Reconcile all the comparable information and draw a conclusion of value.

The direct sales comparison approach is the most reliable gauge of the market and is most frequently used in appraising residential property, where the amenities are often difficult to measure. This approach is also a component for use in the other two methods of determining value. In the cost approach, market data are used to determine the depreciation figure, and in the income approach, market data are used to determine the market rent and capitalization rate. The direct sales comparison approach requires an active real estate market for the type of property being appraised. (*See* **appraisal, comparables, concession, contribution, corner influence, progression, regression, supply and demand**.)

disability   (*incapacidad*)   *See* the legal term **handicap**.

disaffirm   To repudiate or revoke a contract. If the contract is voidable, the injured party may elect to disaffirm it.

disbursement   Money paid out, or expended, in an accounting process such as an escrow closing. Disbursements may be entered as a credit on the closing statement (such as when the net proceeds of the sale are disbursed to the seller) or as a debit (as when attorney fees or the title search are paid). Other examples of disbursements are construction loan draws and advances.

discharge of contract   Cancellation or termination of a contract. Some common grounds on which the obligations of a contract may be discharged are mutual cancellation; rescission; performance or nonperformance; accord and satisfaction; illegality; and in certain circumstances, to the extent a court will not enforce the contract, by the statute of limitations, the statute of frauds, and the Bankruptcy Act. There is no discharge in the event of a breach of contract, but there are remedies to the nonbreaching party.

disclaimer   A statement denying legal responsibility, frequently found in the form of the statement, "There are no promises, representations, oral understandings, or agreements except as contained herein." Such a statement, however, would not relieve the maker of any liabilities for fraudulent acts or misrepresentations. Also called an *exoneration clause* or *exculpatory clause*.

A common disclaimer found in a brokers' information fact sheet is as follows: "The information contained on this fact sheet is taken from sources deemed reliable. However, we cannot guarantee the accuracy of such information." Note that this type of disclaimer may be effective to protect one against liability for an innocent misstatement of fact but will not protect one who makes an intentionally false statement.

Courts generally enforce disclaimers strictly against the party drafting the disclaimer. Thus, a disclaimer in a lockbox authorization form that the broker is not liable for loss suffered by theft does not protect a broker negligent in giving out the combination to the lockbox. (*See* **exculpatory clause**.)

disclosure   To reveal, make known. A recognized risk-reduction tool for real estate brokers. (*See* **disclosure statement**.)

disclosure statement
1. An information report required under the federal Truth in Lending Act to be given to consumer borrowers by creditors. State statutes often require disclosure reports in condominium, time-sharing, and subdivision sales. (*See* **Truth in Lending Act**.)
2. Any statement of fact required by law, such as the settlement disclosure required under the federal Real Estate Settlement Procedures Act or the federal lead-based paint disclosures for property built before 1978. State law may require certain disclosures in condominium and subdivision sales, as well as agency disclosure of whom the broker represents.
3. Information conveyed by the seller of the property to the buyer, and now required by many states in the transfer of one-to-four dwelling properties. Seller disclosure places the burden of disclosing property condition on the seller, not the real estate licensee. Buyers should not rely only on the sellers' disclosures because the sellers cannot disclose that of which they are not aware; some of the important information may be missing. For example, an older couple prepares to sell the home in which they have lived for 50 years. They indicate no known plumbing problems. However, the buyers, a family with several young children taking many showers and washing many loads of clothes a day, may encounter plumbing problems. Did the seller lie? No, but the buyers will no doubt have a plumbing problem.

discount   (*rebaja*)   To sell at a reduced value; the difference between face value and cash value. Some companies specialize in buying mortgages and real estate contracts (often referred to as *paper*) at a discount. Often the original lender, wanting to cash out on the loan, will thus sell the mortgage at the current published mortgage discount rate. If the discount rate is 12 percent, for example, the lender could sell a $100,000 mortgage at 88 percent of its worth ($88,000 or 12 percent below par). Discounting any type of loan usually increases its effective yield to the lender and/or interest cost to the buyer. (*See* **buydown**, **end loan**, **origination fee**, **points**, **takeout financing**, **usury**.)

discount broker   A licensed real estate broker who specifically provides brokerage services at lower rates than most brokers do. Some discount brokers limit their services; for example, they do not sit open houses or pay for advertising.

discount department store   A specialized type of shopping center or large single store with emphasis on lower prices. Some discount stores ("closed-door discount stores") are open only to qualifying members.

discounted cash flow   Used in measuring return from a real estate investment, the present value of a future income stream as determined by a given discount rate (using present value tables). This measure weighs dollars received early in the life of an investment more heavily than those received later. Two common methods are the internal rate of return method and the net present value method. Also known as *present value analysis*. (*See* **internal rate of return**, **present value of one dollar**.)

discounting   The appraisal process of mathematically computing the value of a property based on the present worth of anticipated future cash flows or income. (*See* **present value of one dollar**.)

discount points   An added loan fee charged by a lender to increase the yield on a lower-than-market-interest loan and to make the loan more competitive with higher-interest loans. Borrowers often pay discount points upfront in order to gain a long-term, lower interest rate, an advantage for the buyer who plans on keeping the loan for a long period of time, and not so useful for loans held only a few years. Each point is equal to 1 percent of the loan amount. Either the buyer or the seller may pay the points. Points paid for residential real estate can usually be used to reduce taxable income in the year in which they are paid, a benefit to the buyer, even if the seller pays the points. (*See* **basis point, points.**)

D

discount rate
1. An annual competitive rate of return on total invested capital necessary to compensate the investor for the risks inherent in a particular investment.
2. The rate at which the Federal Reserve lends money to its eligible banks. These are short-term loans to fulfill immediate cash needs, not supplement the bank's capital. Thus, the discount rate is not a cost of funds indicator but more of a signal to the banking community. (*See* **Federal Reserve System [the "Fed"], rediscount rate.**)

discovery   The legal process by which lawyers preparing for trial can require witnesses for the other side to produce documents and answer written or oral questions.

discretionary funds   Money available for investment; money in excess of that needed for basic needs.

discrimination   The act of making a distinction against or in favor of a person on the basis of the group or class to which the person belongs; the failure to treat people equally under the law. The Civil Rights Act of 1866 prohibits any discrimination based on race. In 1968, this act was upheld by the U.S. Supreme Court in *Jones v. Alfred H. Mayer Company*, when the court ruled that the 1866 federal law "prohibits all racial discrimination, private and public, in the sale and rental of property."

The federal Fair Housing Act, contained in Title VIII of the Civil Rights Act of 1968, took the 1866 law one step further, making it unlawful to discriminate on the basis of race, color, religion, sex, or national origin when selling or leasing residential property or vacant land for the construction of residential buildings. The Housing and Community Development Act of 1974 prohibits discrimination based on sex. The Fair Housing Amendments Act of 1988 prohibits discrimination based on physical and mental handicaps and familial status and granted HUD the authority to enforce fair housing laws and provided greater fines and penalties for such violations.

The law lists various types of prohibited discriminatory practices in real estate transactions, including related financial practices. Discrimination in financing transactions is further regulated under several federal laws: Equal Credit Opportunity Act, the Community Reinvestment Act of Title VIII of the federal Civil Rights Act, the Community Reinvestment Act, and the Home Mortgage Disclosure Act.

The law and its amendments exempt the following:
- The sale or rental of a single-family home when the home is owned by an individual who does not own more than three such homes at one time, even though the owner is not living in the dwelling at the time of the transaction or was not the most recent occupant. Only one such sale by an individual is exempt within any 24-month period and may not involve a real estate licensee, or discriminatory advertising.
- The rental of rooms or units in an owner-occupied building designed for four or fewer families.
- Dwelling units owned by religious organizations and not operated commercially may be restricted to persons of the same religion if membership in the organization is not restricted on the basis of race, color, sex, or national origin.

■ A private club that, in fact, is not open to the public may restrict the rental or occupancy of lodgings it owns to its members as long as the lodgings are not operated commercially.

■ Dwelling units in qualified elderly housing situations are permitted to exclude children.

The federal Fair Housing Act of 1968 also prohibits blockbusting, steering, and redlining. The act is administered by the secretary of the Department of Housing and Urban Development. An aggrieved person may file a complaint with the secretary or a delegate of the secretary within one year after an alleged discriminatory act occurs. The secretary's efforts to resolve the dispute are limited to conference, conciliation, and persuasion. Several state and municipal fair housing laws have been ruled as "substantially equivalent" to the federal law. All complaints in that state or locality, including those filed with HUD, are referred to and handled by the state agencies.

An aggrieved party may also take the alleged violator to court, either U.S. District Court or a state court if the state's fair housing laws are substantially equivalent. Court actions may also be brought by the U.S. attorney general in cases where accused violators of the federal law are engaged in a pattern of discrimination or practices that raise an issue of general public importance. Complaints brought under the Civil Rights Act of 1866 must be taken directly to a federal court.

Real estate licensees as well as property owners are charged with upholding fair housing laws. Brokers should inform principals of the provisions of the law and terminate the agency with any principal who persists in discrimination. Many state and local governments have enacted their own antidiscrimination laws, which also have an impact on the real estate professional. If there is a discrepancy between the federal and local laws, the more restrictive generally prevails.

Both FHA and VA regulations prohibit the use of discriminatory restrictive covenants by those participating in their respective loan programs. In addition, under the U.S. Supreme Court's decision in *Shelley v. Kraemer*, discriminatory restrictive provisions in deeds are not enforceable.

The Justice Department, HUD, and the National Association of REALTORS® have created affirmative marketing agreements to assure that protected classes have free and open access to housing via comprehensive, voluntary programs. (*See* **Americans with Disabilities Act [ADA]**, **blockbusting**, **federal fair housing law**, **redlining**, **steering**.)

disintermediation   The process of individuals investing their funds directly instead of placing their savings with banks, savings and loan associations, and similar institutions for investment by such institutions. Investors bypass financial institutions when proportionately higher yields are available on secure investments (such as high-grade corporate bonds, money market funds, and government securities) than can be obtained on savings deposits. Disintermediation has a direct influence on the scarcity of mortgage money, in that diverted savings rarely find their way into mortgages.

disparate impact   A legal doctrine used in federal discrimination cases to show a violation even when the defendant's actions have no apparent relationship to a protected class. In a disparate impact case, intent to discriminate is not necessary. The disparate impact doctrine prohibits a neutral restriction that has a statistically greater effect on a protected class than on other classes. Once a plaintiff shows that there is a substantial disparate impact on a protected class, the burden is shifted to the defendant to show that there is a valid nondiscriminatory reason for the statistical imbalance.

For instance, the U.S. Supreme Court has held that aptitude tests that are a prerequisite to employment and that fail substantially more African Americans than whites constitute a disparate impact. A disparate impact analysis might be applied to a condominium association's house rules and their impact in a familial status or handicap case. (*See* **federal fair housing law**.)

disposal field   A drainage area, not close to the water supply, where waste from a septic tank is dispersed. The waste is drained into the ground through tile and gravel.

dispossess proceedings   Legal action to evict someone not in legal possession. (*See* **eviction, summary possession**.)

disseisin   The ouster or wrongful dispossession of someone lawfully possessed of real property (one seized of a freehold).

Distinguished Real Estate Instructor (DREI)   A professional designation awarded by the Real Estate Educators Association (REEA). *See* Appendix B.

distraint   A common-law concept that allows a landlord to seize a tenant's belongings for rents in arrears. Most states now require a court order. Also called *distress for rent due* or *landlord's warrant*. (*See* **abandonment**.)

distressed property   Property that brings an insufficient return to the owner or is in difficulty for other reasons. Sometimes, it is property that must be sold due to pending foreclosure or probate of an insolvent estate.

distress for rent due   *See* **distraint**.

divided interest   An interest in various parts of a whole property, such as the interest of the fee owner, lessee, or mortgagee.

dock-high building   An industrial building in which the floor level of the main floor is constructed at a height sufficient to permit direct loading onto the beds of trucks parked at ground level outside.

doctrine of relation back   *See* **relation-back doctrine**.

document   (*documento*)   A legal instrument such as a conveyancing document (deeds, leases, mortgages), contract (options, exchanges, purchase agreements), or other legal form (wills, bills of sale). (*See* **instrument**.)

documentary tax stamps   *See* **transfer tax (conveyance fee)**.

doing business as   *See* **DBA**.

domicile   From *domus*, Latin for "house." The state where an individual has her true, fixed permanent home and principal business establishment and where that person has the intention of returning whenever absent from it. Once established, a domicile is never lost until there is a concurrence of specific intent to abandon the old domicile, intent to acquire a specific new domicile, and actual physical presence in the new domicile.

   Though a person may have residences in different states and reside at each at different times of the year, it is possible to have only one domicile. Because domicile consists of physical presence plus an intention to make the state one's permanent abode, such factors as local registration of autos, driver's license, voting, paying taxes, membership in local organizations, local bank accounts, and local business interest are all important in establishing the requisite intent. (*See* **dwelling, residence**.)

dominant estate (tenement)   (*dominante, predio dominante*)   The estate that is said to attach to and derive benefit from the servient estate in reference to an easement appurtenant. For example, an easement road passes over an owner's land (the servient estate) to give access to an adjacent parcel (the dominant estate). The dominant estate usually adjoins the servient estate. (*See* **easement, easement in gross**.)

donor   One who gives or makes a gift. The recipient of the gift is the donee. (*See* **gift tax**.)

Do Not Call Registry   *See* **National Do Not Call Registry**.

doorstop   A device attached to the wall or the floor to prevent a door from opening too far and damaging the wall.

dormer   A projection built out from the slope of a roof, used to house windows on the upper floor and to provide additional headroom. Common types of dormers are the gable dormer and the shed dormer.

dormitory town   *See* **bedroom community**.

double-corner stud   Two vertical studs joined at right angles to form the corner of the frame. The double studs are heavier than regular studs and provide greater support.

double entry   In reference to a settlement or closing statement, the practice of entering a dollar amount as both a debit entry and a credit entry. For example, taxes paid in arrears would be prorated and appear as a credit to the buyer and a debit to the seller. Other items, such as deposit money, are single entries on the statement. (*See* **closing statement**.)

double escrow   Two concurrent escrows on the same property, in which the seller attempts to use the buyer's money to acquire title to property X in one escrow to be able to convey title to property X to the buyer in the second escrow. A double escrow is prohibited in some states unless full disclosure has been to both the buyer and the seller that the buyer's funds in the second escrow are being used to complete the seller's purchase in the first escrow, usually at a profit.

   Example: Assume that a seller had a contract in escrow to purchase a certain property for $240,000. The seller then contracts to sell the same property for $250,000, the buyer puts down $10,000 as a deposit, and a second escrow is set up. The seller expects to use the buyer's money to acquire title in the first escrow and simultaneously transfer title to the buyer in the second escrow. When the buyer fails to put the balance of the purchase price in escrow, the seller is forced to default on the original $240,000 contract. The buyer asks for return of the $10,000 deposit, and a court holds that because the seller was unable to place the deed in escrow, the seller was also in default and could not hold the buyer's deposit because, "in a contract for the sale of real estate, the delivery of the deed and the payment of the purchase price are dependent and concurrent conditions. Neither party could place the other in default unless he was able to perform or tender performance." (*See* **back-to-back escrow**, **escrow**.)

double-load corridor   A building design in which apartment units are located on both sides of a corridor, as in many hotels. A single-load corridor has units on only one side.

double plate   Two horizontal boards on top of and connecting the studs. The plate serves as a foundation for the rafters.

double taxation   Two or more taxes paid for the same asset or financial transaction, and often used in reference to income taxes assessed first on the corporate level and second as dividend income on the earnings distributed to the shareholders. Under the corporate form of ownership, as a separate legal taxable entity for income tax purposes, a corporation must pay tax on its earnings. Earnings distributed to the stockholders are also taxed as regular income.

   S corporations, real estate investment trusts (REITs), limited liability companies, mutual funds, and partnerships are pass-through entities that are not subject to corporate taxes, thus effectively avoiding double taxation.

   Double taxation also refers to the situation of paying two separate taxes on the same property, such as the payment of state and federal taxes in more than one state. It may also refer to the situation when federal estate taxes are paid once upon the death of one joint tenant and again upon the death of the surviving joint tenant. (*See* **corporation**, **limited partnership**, **S corporation**.)

double-window header   Two boards laid on the edge that forms the upper portion of a door or window.

dower   The legal right or interest recognized in some states that a wife acquires in the property her husband holds or acquires anytime during their marriage. During the husband's life, the dower is an expectant, or inchoate, interest that does not actually become a legal estate (called *consummate dower*) until the husband's death. The parties must be validly married (note that some states recognize common-law marriages). In those states still recognizing dower, in order for the husband to convey clear title to his own property, it is necessary for the wife to sign a release of her dower.

Dower rights have been eliminated in many states, and in states that have adopted the Uniform Probate Code, dower has been replaced by the surviving spouse's right to an elective share upon the death of one spouse. (*See* **admeasurement of dower, curtesy, elective share, jointure**.)

down payment   (*abono inicial*)   The amount of cash a purchaser will pay at the time of purchase. Even though down payment usually includes the earnest money deposit, the terms are not synonymous. Earnest money is applied toward the total amount of cash down payment due at the closing. (*See* **earnest money**.)

downside risk   The risk that an investor will lose money in a particular venture.

downspout   A vertical pipe made of cement, metal, clay, or plastic that carries rainwater from the eaves through to the ground.

downzoning   A change in zoning from a higher to a lower or more active to less active classification, such as from residential to conservation, or multifamily to single-family use. In these cases, there is no taking under eminent domain and thus no compensation paid to the affected landowner who helplessly sees the property lose value. (*See* **zoning**.)

dragnet clause   *See* **anaconda mortgage**.

drainage   (*drenaje*)   A system of gradually drawing off water and moisture from land, naturally or artificially, by means of pipes and conduits.

draw   (*giro*)   An advancement of money. Draw refers to the periodic advancing of funds under a construction loan agreement. Also, a real estate brokerage company sometimes advances money to its more experienced sales associates to apply either against commissions earned but not paid or against future commissions. Court cases have held that a broker cannot recover the difference between the amount advanced and the commission actually earned when the commission is less than the advance.

DREI   *See* **Distinguished Real Estate Instructor**.

drill track   A segment of rail track that is an intermediary between a main line and the individual industry tracks (spurs) that serve private industrial property.

Drug Enforcement Act   A 1988 federal law establishing the right of federal drug enforcement authorities to seize real property on which illegal drug activity is taking place. To avoid forfeiture of title, owners have the burden either to prove that they had no knowledge their property was used for illegal drug activity or that they had knowledge and made reasonable efforts to stop the illegal use. Real estate licensees acting as property managers for absentee owners should be diligent in notifying owners of illegal drug activity on the managed property. At the same time, the manager should avoid wrongly accusing a tenant of illegal drug activity. Some states have their own seizure and forfeiture rules concerning criminal activities on real property.

dry closing   A closing that is complete except for the final act of disbursing funds and delivering documents. The parties have fulfilled their obligations of signing documents and paying money, leaving it to the escrow agent to complete the closing.

dry mortgage   A mortgage or deed of trust in which the lender looks solely to the real property for recovery of the debt in case of default; that is, there is no personal liability for any deficiency upon foreclosure; a nonrecourse mortgage. (*See* **deficiency judgment**.)

dry rot   Fungus-caused decay in timber that reduces wood to a fine powder.

drywall construction   Any type of interior wall construction not using plaster as finish material. Wood paneling, plywood, plasterboard, gypsum board, or other types of wallboard are usually used for drywall.

D

dual agency (limited agency)   A situation in which an agent (or agency in some states) represents both principals to a transaction. States that allow dual agency generally require that licensees gain consent to the "potential" of dual agency early in the relationship. Written consent by both parties is generally required before an offer is written and submitted.

Some states prohibit dual agency; instead, licensees may only continue to work with both parties as a transaction broker.

Dual agency became an issue in the early 1980s. Previously, under subagency, all licensees represented the seller and were expected to work fairly with the buyer, as customer. Common-law agency principles stress the fiduciary duty of loyalty an agent owes to a principal. Thus, potential conflicts of interest arise if a broker represents both the seller, who wants the highest price, and the buyer, who wants the lowest price.

In many brokerage offices, the office represents the seller when taking the listing, thus obligating every licensee in the office to represent the seller. Similarly, if a licensee represents a buyer, all other licensees in the office now represent the buyer. The dual agency results when the represented buyer wants to pursue an office listing (in-house).

In an attempt to avoid dual agency for in-house transactions, some states now recognize "designated/appointed agency." The broker may designate one licensee to the exclusion of all other licensees to represent the seller, and designate another licensee to the exclusion of all other licensees to represent the buyer. Thus, designated/appointed agency avoids in-house dual agencies except for the situation in which the listing agent is also representing the buyer of that listing.

The fact that a broker is paid by one party does not necessarily make the broker the exclusive agent of that party.

(*See* **agency, designated agency, informed consent, subagent.**)

dual contract   An improper or fraudulent contract to buy property that contains terms and financial conditions that differ from the original or true agreement and falsely represents the parties' true intentions. The fraudulent dual contract may then be submitted to a lending institution in hopes of obtaining a larger loan. This fraudulent practice is sometimes known as *kiting*. An example of such a contract might be one in which the parties show a lower purchase price than was actually agreed on so that the buyer is eligible for a maximum FHA loan or the broker may accept a large earnest money deposit in the form of a check, agreeing never to deposit it, in an attempt to impress the mortgage company with the buyer's financial resources. In addition to notifying the seller about the agreement not to deposit, the broker must take steps to ensure that the mortgagee is not defrauded.

A broker who participates in any way in the preparation of a dual contract may be subject to license suspension or revocation, a fine for misconduct, or civil damages. Also, the broker cannot be a party to the naming of a false consideration.

Some brokers have been accused of using an addendum that commits the seller to provide a sum of money to the buyers at closing for replacing carpeting or repairing fences when, in fact, there is no intention to use this money for the stated purpose. Instead, the buyers assign the funds to the closing agent as all or part of the equity investment in the property being purchased. Such addendum is not shown with the FHA application, because such a kickback effectively lowers the purchase price to the buyers, who are not providing an equity investment out of their own funds. When a federally chartered lender is involved, this type of dual contract practice is a federal criminal offense.

duct   A tube, pipe, or channel for conveying or carrying fluids, cables, wires, or tempered air. Under-floor duct systems are commonly used to provide for telephone and electrical lines.

due date   A date set in a note or contract for payment to be made. If not paid by the contracted due date, the payment is past due. Most contracts specify a grace period during which late payment is acceptable. The last day of the grace period is the delinquency date. (*See* **grace period**.)

due diligence

1. A fair, proper, and due degree of care and activity. An expressed or implied requirement in certain real estate contracts stating that a person use good-faith efforts to perform obligations under a contract. A buyer who makes an offer contingent on obtaining financing must use due diligence in seeking such financing. Under the Superfund law, a buyer who fails to conduct a due diligence inspection of a property later discovered to contain hazardous substances may be liable for full cleanup expenses.

2. A term used in securities law to refer to the duty of the issuer or the broker to ensure that the offering prospectus is accurate and does not misstate or omit material information.

3. A time period in which a buyer is given the opportunity to have experts inspect the property, examine the title, and review the leases to determine whether the property matches the buyers' needs. If the buyers find objectionable conditions, they typically have the right to withdraw from the purchase prior to expiration of the due diligence period.

due-on-sale clause   An acceleration clause found in most mortgage loans, requiring the mortgagor to pay off the mortgage debt when the property is sold, resulting in automatic maturity of the note at the lender's option. This clause effectively eliminates the possibility of the new buyer's assuming the mortgage unless the mortgagee permits the assumption, in which case the mortgagee might increase the interest rate or charge an assumption fee. Also called an **alienation clause**, *nonassumption clause*, *call clause*, or a *right-to-sell clause*, it can be found in contracts for deed and deeds of trust.

   Although such clauses are upheld in a majority of states, some state courts and legislatures have invalidated them on the grounds of unreasonable restraint against alienation, at least without a showing that the transfer will impair the lender's security in the property (the "bankrupt-arsonist buyer").

   Related to the due-on-sale clause is a *due-on-encumbrance clause*, found in a mortgage or a deed of trust, which allows the holder of a mortgage to accelerate the mortgage note if the mortgagor places junior financing on the property. The justification for the clause is that the mortgagee feels that any additional financing reduces the mortgagor's equity in the property and increases the likelihood of default. Some courts have also invalidated such clauses on grounds that they constitute unreasonable restraints on the free marketability of property.

   VA and FHA mortgages issued prior to 1990 do not contain due-on-sale clauses. (*See* **acceleration clause**, **assumption, paragraph 17**.)

dummy   *See* **straw man**.

duplex   A structure that provides housing accommodations for two families and supplies each with separate entrances, kitchens, bedrooms, living rooms, and bathrooms. A two-family dwelling with the units either side by side (in some areas called a *twin*) or one above the other.

   In subdivisions that are restricted to single-family dwellings, some duplex owners argue that a duplex is merely the combining of two separate single-family dwellings with a party wall. To prevent arguments of this type, many subdividers restrict use to "detached single-family dwellings." A duplex apartment is one in which rooms are on two floors.

durable power of attorney   A power-of-attorney instrument containing language to the effect the power of the attorney in fact will continue beyond the physical or mental incapacity of the principal. Like all powers of attorney, it terminates upon death of the principal.

duress   (*coacción*)   Unlawful force or action by one person against another in an attempt to coerce the person to perform some act against her will; the threat of force is called *menace*. Duress is a useful defense against enforcing a contract because there is no genuine meeting of the minds. A contract entered into under duress is not enforceable against the forced party. Courts are reluctant to give much weight to economic duress in which a person maintains he was forced into a contract due to financial pressures. (*See* **undue influence, voidable**.)

Dutch interest   *See* **construction loan**.

dwelling   (*morada*, *vivienda*)   Any building, structure, or part thereof used and occupied for human habitation or intended to be so used, including any appurtenances. Many municipalities have adopted ordinances relating to the repair, closing, and demolition of dwellings unfit for human habitation. (*See* **domicile, residence**.)

dwelling unit   As defined in many zoning codes, a room (or connected rooms), constituting an independent housekeeping unit for a family, and containing a single kitchen, unlike a hotel room. Under the federal Fair Housing Act, the term is used to denote any place that is intended for someone to live, but excludes hotel, motel, and similar accommodations.

early occupancy   Refers to the practice of allowing the buyer to take possession of real property before closing. Such a practice should be carefully evaluated because of the risks of mechanics' liens, inadequate insurance coverage, and "buyer's remorse" with possible lawsuit. In addition, the buyer who moves in is not generally subject to landlord-tenant rules, so if the buyer fails to buy, the seller may have a great deal of difficulty evicting the buyer. The parties should sign a written early-occupancy agreement to cover these risks. (*See* **occupancy agreement, risk of loss**.)

earnest money   (*arras*)   The cash deposit (including initial and additional deposits) paid by the prospective buyer of real property as evidence of good-faith intention to complete the transaction; also called *bargain money, caution money, hand money*, or a **binder**. The amount of earnest money is negotiable between the parties, and its primary purpose is to serve as a source of payment of damages should the buyer default.

Earnest money is *not* essential to make a purchase agreement binding if the buyer's and the seller's exchange of mutual promises of performance (that is, the buyer's promise to purchase and the seller's promise to sell at a specified price and terms) constitutes the consideration for the contract. Thought should be given to placing the money in an interest-bearing account for the buyer's benefit, which can be done by the parties agreeing in writing to place it with a neutral third party such as an escrow company, subject to state law.

The deposit, or earnest money, may be held by the listing broker, the buyers' broker, or a neutral third party at the time the sales contract is signed. The broker's authority to hold this money on behalf of the seller should be specifically set forth in the listing because such authority is not implied in law. The broker may never commingle this money with the broker's own general funds.

Exactly who owns the earnest money once it is put on deposit is uncertain. Until the offer is accepted, the money is the buyer's. The seller is not entitled to it until the transaction is complete. When the transaction is consummated, the earnest money is credited toward the down payment.

Issues arise when either party defaults. But once the seller accepts the offer, the money may be disbursed only with the knowledge and consent of both parties. This uncertain nature of earnest money deposits makes it absolutely necessary that such funds be properly protected pending final decision on how they are to be disbursed. (*See* **additional deposit**, **binder**, **client trust account**, **commingling**, **deposit**, **down payment**.)

earnest money account   *See* **client trust account**.

earnest money contract   *See* **contract of sale**.

easement (*servidumbre*) A nonpossessory (incorporeal) property interest (short of an estate) that one person (the benefited party) has in land owned by another (the burdened party), entitling the holder of the interest to limited use or enjoyment of the other's land. An easement fulfills the needs of one property at the expense of another. Because an easement is an actual interest in land, the statute of frauds applies and an express grant of easement must be in writing, usually in the form of a separate deed or a reservation in a deed. Thus, an easement is an interest in land rather than a mere contractual agreement. Easements are also created by necessity (as in landlocked situations), by implication, or by prescription.

Because the easement is both a benefit to the holder and a burden to the servient property owner, it significantly affects the value of the respective properties and the extent of the easement should be clearly understood. Most easements originate by express grant, so the drafter should clearly express the rights and duties associated with the easement. An easement can be an affirmative easement, such as a right-of-way to cross the property, or a negative easement, such as a restriction on fence height. It can also be created for different periods of time—for a term of months, years or for life.

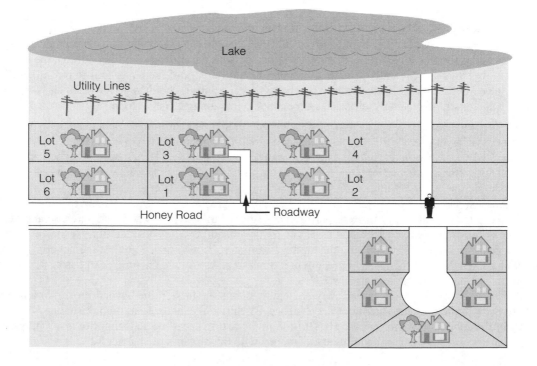

Easements are classified as either appurtenant or in gross. An easement appurtenant is a right in another's land (servient estate) that benefits and attaches to the owner's land (dominant estate). An easement in gross is personal in nature and does not pass with the land because it does not benefit or attach to a dominant estate.

In the figure, the owners of lots 5 and 6 may agree that the owner of 5 will not build a building so high that it cuts off the view of the lake, which the owner of 6 enjoys. This is called a *negative easement*. The right of aircraft to fly below certain altitudes over or near property bordering an airport is called an *avigation easement* (aerial navigation).

Litigation involving easements usually results from the initial failure to adequately define the easement area (the floating easement problem), the uses to which it may be put, or which party has responsibility for repair and upkeep. An easement for access purposes might not be appropriate for later use to lay utility lines to the property. When an easement or right-of-way is located by a grant that does not define its specific width, such width is assumed to be one that is suitable and convenient for ordinary, free passage.

Easements should not be confused with profits or licenses. A *profit* is the right to take the soil, minerals, or products of the land. A *license* is not an interest in land, merely permission to use the land of another for some limited purpose; it can be revoked at any time.

Easements may be terminated in six ways:

1. Merger: When the owner of the dominant estate becomes the owner of the servient estate.
2. Abandonment: Mere nonuse is insufficient cause because there must be clear acts showing intent to abandon, such as the owners of the dominant estate erecting a fence across their easement right-of-way.
3. Release: When the owners of the dominant estate release their interest, usually by means of a quitclaim deed affecting the servient estate.
4. Purpose: When an easement has been created for a particular purpose and that purpose ceases.
5. Operation by law: When the easement is taken by eminent domain or is lost by adverse possession.
6. Overburdening: When the grantee makes use of the easement for an improper purpose.

An easement cannot be terminated due to an inconvenience or hardship experienced because the owner of the servient tenement cannot develop the property without added expense. The owner of the servient tenement cannot relocate the easement simply to suit personal needs—to do so would be, in essence, a private right of eminent domain. (*See* **dominant estate [tenement]**, **easement by necessity**, **easement by prescription**, **easement in gross**, **implied easement**, **license**, **line-of-sight easement**, **party driveway**, **party wall**, **profit**, **scenic easement**, **servient estate**.)

easement appurtenant　　An easement that runs with the land. In the figure, lot 3 has a 30-foot roadway easement across lot 1. This easement is appurtenant to and passes with 3 regardless of whether the owner of 3 expressly transfers the easement when 3, the dominant estate, is sold. It also binds the succeeding owner of 1 whether or not the deed to 1 refers to the easement. Common examples of easements appurtenant are the right to travel over another's property, party walls, and shared driveways. In a condominium, the rights to walk over the parking area, to have utility lines running through the walls, or to have a sewer pipe running beneath the land surface are also examples of easements appurtenant. In the figure, the owners of the lots in the cul-de-sac (dominant tenements) have access to the lake over lots 2 and 4 (servient tenements). (*See* **easement**.)

easement by implied grant　　*See* **easement by necessity**.

E

easement by necessity (*servidumbre por necesidad*)   An easement created by a court of law in cases where justice and necessity dictate it, especially in a classic landlocked situation (*see* lot 3 in the preceding figure). Two essential elements are key to this type of easement: There must have been a common grantor of the dominant and servient estates, and reasonable necessity for the easement, not merely convenience, must be the rationale. For example, if George Brown had owned lots 1–6 (see the figure) and then conveyed lot 3 to Jane Lee without mention of any easement of passage across lot 1, most courts would imply an easement by necessity. This easement is based on the presumed intention of the parties. Because the easement is created by operation of law, the statute of frauds is not applicable and no written agreement is required. Also called an *easement by implied grant*.

easement by prescription (*servidumbre por prescripción*)   A right acquired by an adverse user to use the land of another. As with acquiring title through adverse possession, the use that results in an easement by prescription must be adverse, hostile, open, notorious, and continuous for the statutory period. An easement by prescription cannot usually be acquired on public land or on property registered under Torrens. Unlike easements by express or implied grant, an easement by prescription may be extinguished by nonuse for the prescriptive period without evidence of actual abandonment. (*See* **adverse possession, adverse use, lost-grant doctrine**.)

easement for light and air *See* **light and air**.

easement in gross   The limited right of one person to use another's land (servient estate) when such right is not created for the benefit of any land owned by the owner of the easement. In such a case, there is no dominant estate because the easement attaches personally to the owner, not to the land. The easement in gross is an encumbrance on the servient estate. Common examples of this type of situation are utility easements, power line easements, billboard-site easements, and the like. If there is uncertainty as to whether an easement is appurtenant or in gross, most courts interpret it to be an easement appurtenant.

  An easement in gross is similar to a license, except that an easement in gross is irrevocable for the period of the owner's life. For example, the owner of lot 3 in the preceding figure may give his friend a nonrevocable right to cross over lot 3 and fish in the lake. This right, or easement in gross, terminates upon the death of the friend or upon the conveyance of lot 3 to a new owner, whichever occurs first. The friend may not assign his right to anyone else. A personal easement in gross may not be assigned by the owner to a third party. Commercial easements in gross, however, such as rights given utility companies to install pipelines and power lines, are a more substantial property interest and are assignable.

eave   The overhang of a sloping roof that extends beyond the walls of the house. Also called *roof projection*.

eave drip   The drainage of water from the eaves of a structure onto the land of another. If such drainage continues for the statutory time, a prescriptive easement right could develop.

eave trough   A channel, usually metal pipe, placed at the edge of the eaves to carry rainwater to the downspout.

economic-base analysis   An appraisal term to describe a means of measuring the economic activity of a community that enables it to attract income from outside its borders; the study of the relationship between basic and nonbasic employment patterns as a means of predicting population, income, and other variables having an effect on real estate and land use. This term refers to the ways in which people in a community make their livings.

economic life   (*vida económica*)   The estimated period over which an improved property may be profitably utilized so that it will yield a return over and above the economic rent attributable to the land itself; the period during which an improvement has value in excess of its salvage value. In the case of an older structure or improvement, economic life refers to the remaining period during which the improvements to the real property (not land) are depreciated for tax purposes. The economic lives of such improvements are normally shorter than their actual physical lives. Also called *service life*. (*See* **useful life**.)

economic obsolescence   A specific kind of situation, external to the property, that adversely affects the economics of an area, such as the relocation of a major industry that reduces the value of property. (*See* **external obsolescence**.)

E

economic rent   (*renta económica*)   The rental income (market rent) that real estate can command in an open, competitive market at any given time, as contrasted with contract rent, or the income actually received under a lease agreement. For example, if a new plant is being built, but as yet no new housing is being built, the appraiser should consider this fact because rents will increase under normal supply and demand principles. (*See* **contract rent**.)

effective age   The apparent age of a building (improvement) based on observed condition rather than chronological age. The effective age of improvements to real property at the time of inspection differs from actual age by such variable factors as depreciation, quality of maintenance, and the like. Thus, remodeling can extend the economic life of a structure by reducing or mitigating the impact of actual age, and increase the structure's life expectancy.

effective gross income   The anticipated income resulting from the estimated potential gross income from a rental property less an allowance for vacancy and bad debts.

effective interest rate   The actual rate or yield of a loan, regardless of the amount stated on the debt instrument. (*See* **annual percentage rate [APR]**.)

effective rate
1. The average lease rate of a property per square foot after deducting negotiated concessions such as free rent, construction allowances over and above the cost of building standard items, or the costs of the landlord's assumption of a tenant's existing lease.
2. A payment amount on certain mortgage notes, usually buydown types, that offers lower payment amounts that is calculated with an "effective rate" that is less than the face rate.

effective yield   A calculation of the return on investment that considers the price paid, the time held, and the interest charged. The effective yield on a discounted mortgage loan is greater than the interest charged. Suppose a lender charges four discount points on a $10,000 loan for one year at 10 percent simple interest. Rather than receive $10,000, the borrower receives $9,600 but is obligated to repay $10,000 plus $1,000 in interest. This makes an effective yield of $1,400 ÷ $9,600, or 14.6 percent rather than 10 percent.

efficiency unit or apartment   A small, compact apartment unit sometimes called a *studio apartment*. It consists of a combination living room/bedroom, kitchenette, and bathroom.

effluence   A flowing out; excrement deposited by a soil-absorption waste system that may seep or flow out onto the ground or into a creek, stream, river, or lake, particularly in times of flooding or high groundwater levels.

egress   A way to exit from a property; the opposite of ingress.

E

ejectment   (*acción reivindicatoria*)
   1. A legal action by an owner to regain possession of real property when there is no landlord-tenant relationship between the owner and the occupant.
   2. An action to oust someone who is not legally in possession of real property, such as a trespasser (potential adverse possessor) or a tenant at sufferance whose lease has expired, or in an action by a mortgagee to get possession from a defaulting mortgagor. (*See* **eviction**.)

elasticity   (*elasticidad*)
   1. The ability of the real estate supply to respond to price increases over a short period of time.
   2. An economics term indicating the ability of a product to maintain its level of supply or demand despite changes in its price.

elderly housing   Housing occupied by persons age 62 or older. Under the federal fair housing law, housing for the elderly is not required to accept families with children. However, recent changes in the Housing for the Older Persons Act (HOPA) permit owners of housing directed to the "near elderly" (i.e., 55 and older) to accept a family with children, but they are not obligated to. This near-elderly property must still meet other requirements: at least 80 percent of its occupants must have at least one occupant who is 55 or older.

election of remedies   A remedy for breach of contract that is selected from several alternative courses of action. For example, if the buyer defaults on an agreement to purchase, the seller must elect whether to retain the deposit as liquidated damages, tender the deed and sue for specific performance, or sue for damages. The seller, however, cannot elect to pursue all possible remedies. (*See* **contract of sale**, **damages**, **liquidated damages**, **specific performance**.)

elective share   A minimum share of a deceased spouse's probate estate (one-third, for example), which a surviving spouse may claim in lieu of any amount specified in the deceased spouse's will; usually found in states that have abolished dower and curtesy. For example, a wife omitted from her husband's will may still claim an elective share of his estate. (*See* **descent**.)

electronic signature   A digital format that recognizes a person has authorized a document. It may also be referred to as a *digital signature* and may be encrypted.

electromagnetic fields (EMFs)   Energy fields, either naturally occurring or created, found near power lines, in homes near electrical appliances, and in offices near any equipment that has an electric motor. Although some data suggests otherwise, there is no convincing evidence to classify EMFs as health hazards.

eleemosynary corporation   *See* **nonprofit corporation**.

elevation sheet   Drawings that provide views of the front and the sides of a building as it will appear when completed.

Ellwood technique   An advanced method of appraising mortgaged income property by a capitalization rate based on the ratio of investment represented by debt and by equity.

emblement   A growing crop (called *fructus industriales*), such as grapes or corn, which is produced annually through labor and industry. Emblements are regarded as personal property even before harvest; thus, a tenant has the right to take the annual crop resulting from his labor, even if the harvest does not occur until after tenancy has ended. A landlord cannot lease land to a tenant farmer and then terminate the lease without giving the tenant the right to reenter the land to harvest any crops grown by the tenant. The purchase agreement should clearly and adequately address these issues of re-entering and harvesting if the property is sold prior to harvest by the tenant.

eminent domain   The right of government (both state and federal), public corporations (school districts, sanitation districts), public utilities, and public service corporations (railroads, power companies) to take private property for a necessary public use, with just compensation paid to the owner. Generally, however, the law will not allow compensation for lost profits, inconvenience, loss of goodwill, and the like, although severance damages may be awarded for a loss in value to the remaining property that is not actually condemned. Through eminent domain, the state may acquire land (fee, leasehold, or easement) for streets, parks, public buildings, public rights-of-way, and similar uses. No private property is exempt from this exercise of government power.

If the owner and the government cannot negotiate a satisfactory voluntary acquisition of the property, the government can initiate a condemnation action to take the property. In such cases, an owner's main grounds for complaint would usually be that the intended use is not a sufficient public use or that the valuation given the property in the condemnation proceeding is unjust. Generally speaking, the courts will not permit a taking in fee if an easement will do; an entire piece cannot be taken if only a part is needed.

Whether a taking is for a public purpose is broadly construed. The 2005 Supreme Court decision *Kelo v. City of New London* affirmed the right of government to condemn an urban blighted area to sell it to a private developer for private purposes. However, the court added that states are free to ban the taking of property for such projects.

Eminent domain is an outright acquisition of property with payment of compensation. It is not an uncompensated regulation of the use of property (as in the case of restrictive zoning).

Upon the vesting of title in the government, all preexisting liens and encumbrances are extinguished; anyone affected by this change, such as mortgagees, must look to the award of condemnation money for satisfaction of their claims.

Generally, when an owner's property is taken by eminent domain, recognition of gain realized from the condemnation money can be deferred under IRS 1033. Depending on the property, the qualified replacement property must be identified and/or purchased within two to three years from the end of the year in which the taxable gain is realized. In most cases, for the replacement property to qualify, it must be similar or related in use ("like-kind" property).

A lessee is usually given the right to cancel a lease when a large portion of the leased premises is taken. Long-term leases usually provide for a condemnation award to be apportioned between lessor and lessee, according to the value of the parties' respective estates. (*See* **condemnation, just compensation, police power, severance damages**.)

employee   One who works under the supervision and control of another. For purposes of state licensing law, the real estate salesperson is employed by the broker. For income tax purposes, the salesperson may be treated as an independent contractor. (*See* **independent contractor**.)

empty nester   An older family whose children have grown up and left home.

enabling legislation   A statute creating the power or authority to carry out an activity, as under the provisions of a federal housing program, or to do something not previously authorized; for example, a condominium law creating the unique condominium form of ownership.

encroachment   An unauthorized invasion or intrusion of an improvement or other real property onto another's property, thus reducing the size and value of the invaded property. Common examples of encroachments are the roof of a building that extends over the property line or the front of a building that extends over the building setback line or extends onto a neighbor's property. Most encroachments are the result of carelessness or poor planning rather than bad intent, as in the case of a driveway or fence built without a survey to find the lot line.

Because an undisclosed encroachment could render a title unmarketable, its existence should be noted in the listing, and the contract of sale should be made subject to the existence of the particular encroachment.

An encroachment is a *trespass* if it encroaches on the land and a *nuisance* if it violates the neighbor's airspace, as in the case of overhanging tree branches. The injured party can seek a judicial remedy in ejectment, quiet title, or injunction and damages. A court can order removal of the encroachment. However, if the encroachment is insignificant, the cost of its removal is great and its creation was unintentional, a court may decide to award money damages in lieu of ordering removal.

If there is any doubt as to possible encroachments, purchasers should obtain their own surveys when purchasing property because an accurate land survey will disclose most encroachments. If a survey reveals encroachments not previously disclosed by the seller, the buyer may compel the seller to remove the encroachment (or to reduce the purchase price accordingly) and pay for the survey. In some cases, neighbors will sign an encroachment agreement, granting a license to continue the encroachment of a wall or fence onto a neighbor's property.

Encroachments are not normally revealed in the chain of title and thus are not warranted against in a title insurance policy. Also, most standard title insurance policies do not insure against matters an accurate survey would reveal. An extended-coverage title policy often insures against encroachments. (*See* **extended coverage, nuisance, survey, trespass**.)

encumbrance   Any claim, lien, charge, or liability attached to and binding on real property that may lessen its value or burden, obstruct, or impair the use of a property but not necessarily prevent transfer of title; a right or interest in a property held by one who is not the legal owner of the property. Also spelled *incumbrance*.

There are two general classifications of encumbrances: those that affect the title, such as judgments, mortgages, mechanics' liens, and other liens, which are charges on property used to secure a debt or obligation; and those that affect the physical condition of the property, such as restrictions, encroachments, and easements.

A covenant against encumbrances guarantees that there are no encumbrances against the property except those specifically disclosed. If no encumbrances are disclosed as exceptions in the contract of sale, the buyer may proceed with the purchase on the assumption that none exist.

Encumbrances should be noted on the deed following the property description. (*See* **deed, easement, lien**.)

Endangered Species Act   A federal law originally intended to protect endangered species on federal lands but since expanded to control land used for the protection of certain fish, animal, and plant life. Listings for farm and land for development are likely to be impacted by this act because habitat for many protected species may not be disturbed or modified. Licensees should always advise sellers and buyers to consult with environmental specialists.

end loan   A permanent mortgage used to finance the purchase of a new condominium unit or a lot within a developed subdivision; often called *takeout financing*. The lender who makes the development or interim loan for a construction project might also provide the permanent financing to individual unit buyers to "take out" the developer after the project is completed and sold; hence, the terms *takeout financing* and *end loan*. (*See* **permanent financing**.)

end money   The amount of money held in reserve in case project costs exceed estimates. Called over-and-above money in FHA rental-housing projects. (*See* **front money**.)

endorsement   (*endoso*)
1. A method of transferring title to a negotiable instrument, such as a check or promissory note, by signing the owner's name on the reverse side of such instrument. A blank endorsement guarantees payment to subsequent holders. An endorsement stating that it is without recourse does not guarantee payment to subsequent holders. A special endorsement specifies the person to whom or to whose order the instrument is payable.

2. A notation added to an instrument after its execution that is made to change or clarify the document's contents. In insurance policies, coverage may be restricted or broadened by endorsing the policy. For example, there are more than 100 special endorsements that may be added to the standard title insurance policy. In FHA loans, an endorsement is placed on the note by the FHA to indicate that the loan is insured under the National Housing Act.

   Sometimes spelled *indorsement*. (*See* **direct endorsement**.)

engineering breakdown method   An appraisal method of estimating accrued depreciation that considers separate estimates of each major building component, such as roof, elevators, and air-conditioning. (*See* **appraisal**.)

enjoin   To forbid, or in some cases to command, performance of an act. For example, a property owner may ask the court to enjoin a neighbor to clean up his backyard if it has become an unhealthy nuisance. The courts can issue injunctions against a pattern of discrimination in real estate transactions. Both federal and state agencies generally have injunctive powers against subdividers who sell land in violation of land sales laws. (*See* **injunction**.)

enrolled agent   A tax professional licensed by the federal government to deal with the Internal Revenue Service on behalf of consumers. An enrolled agent has demonstrated competence in the field of taxation and is authorized to represent consumers before all administrative levels of the IRS.

enterprise zone   An area in which business firms receive special tax advantages for locating their businesses in certain depressed neighborhoods. (*See* **urban enterprise zone**.)

entitlement
1. To be owed something under the law.
2. That portion of a VA-guaranteed loan that protects a lender if the veteran defaults. (*See* **certificate of eligibility**, **Veterans Affairs [VA] loan**.)

entity, legal   Any person or artificial being such as a corporation, partnership, proprietorship, or association that can sue or be sued and has the legal capacity to enter into contractual arrangements possibly resulting in debts and other obligations. All buyers, especially investors, should carefully weigh the liabilities and tax considerations in order to choose the appropriate entity for holding title. (*See* **ownership, form of**.)

entrepreneur   One who takes the initiative to organize, start, and manage an enterprise or business, usually assuming a substantial portion of the risks, losses, and profits; a promoter or developer.

environmental audit   An independent inspection of real property to evaluate compliance with applicable federal, state, and local regulations, systems, programs, and policies for all lands, facilities, and operations supervised by the Department of the Interior. (*See* **Comprehensive Environmental Response, Compensation, and Liability Act [CERCLA]**, **due diligence**, **Phase I audit**.)

environmental impact statement (EIS)   (*informe de impacto ambiental*)   A report required by the National Environmental Policy Act (NEPA) of all federal agencies that propose projects that can significantly affect the environment locally and regionally. The EIS is a decision-making tool describing the project's positive and negative effects and listing possible alternatives. Federal agencies file environmental impact statements with the Federal Council on Environmental Quality and obtain the council's approval for all proposed government actions. Government actions have been interpreted to include anything from approval of a federal license or permit to policy determinants, provisos, and proposed legislation. Such impact statements must include the following information:
- A detailed description of the proposed action
- A discussion of the direct and indirect impact on the environment that might result from the action

- Identification of unavoidable adverse environmental effects
- An assessment of any feasible alternatives to the proposed action
- A description of the action's cumulative and long-term effects on the surface of the earth
- Identification of any irreversible commitment of resources that might result from the action

(*See* **National Environmental Protection Act**, **Environmental Protection Agency [EPA]**.)

Environmental Protection Agency (EPA)   A federal agency created in 1970 to protect human health and the environment. The EPA is involved with environmental issues of air and water pollution, solid-waste management, pesticides, radiation, and noise. In these areas, the EPA sets standards, determines how much pollution is tolerable, establishes timetables to bring polluters into line with its standards, and enforces environmental laws. The EPA conducts an extensive environmental research program; provides technical, financial, and managerial help to state, regional, and municipal pollution-control agencies; and allocates funds for sewage-treatment facilities. The original authority of the EPA was broadened by passage of more specific laws from 1970 to 1972: Clean Air Amendments and the Resource Recovery Act; the Federal Water Pollution Control Act, the Federal Environmental Pesticide Control Act, the Noise Control Act, and the Marine Protection Research and Sanctuaries Act; the Safe Drinking Water Act; and the Comprehensive Environmental Response, Compensation, and Liability Act in 1980. (*See* **environmental impact statement [EIS]**, **National Environmental Protection Act [NEPA]**.)

environmental regulations   Standards set by the federal EPA and state departments of health to control air, water, noise pollution, and other environmental conditions, including the cleanup of hazardous substances. (*See* **Environmental Protection Agency [EPA]**, **Comprehensive Environmental Response, Compensation, and Liability Act [CERCLA]**.)

environmental risk   The risk associated with the ownership of real property involving environmental hazards such as contaminated building materials and pollutants, as well as nonhazardous conditions such as wetlands and endangered species. Appraisers often attach an environmental addendum to their appraisal reports to note any observable environmental risks that may reduce property value.

environmental site assessment (ESA)   An investigation by an environmental engineer or other well-qualified specialist to determine whether there are any environmental hazards or concerns that affect the use of a property or impose future financial liability. The ESA assists the seller in making proper disclosures and the buyer in making an informed offer. Lenders often insist on an ESA before committing to any financing.

Equal Credit Opportunity Act (ECOA)   (*Ley de igualdad de oportunidades para obtener crédito*)   Federal legislation, passed in 1974, to extend credit based on the applicant's ability to repay the loan and without regard to the applicant's race, color, religion, national origin, sex, marital status, age, or receipt of income from public assistance programs (food stamps, Social Security), and to ensure good-faith exercise of any right under the Consumer Credit Protection Act. The creditor must state reasons for denial of credit because factors such as income, expenses, debt, and credit history all factor into the final decision.

The act applies to all who regularly extend or arrange for the extension of credit. A real estate licensee is considered a creditor if the licensee routinely assists sellers in determining whether a proposed buyer in a land contract or purchase-money mortgage is creditworthy. Regulation B, which implements the act, contains partial exemptions from procedural provisions for business, securities, and public utilities credit. Although a number of federal and state agencies are charged with ECOA enforcement, the primary agency is the Federal Trade Commission.

Creditors must generally provide applicants with the following written notice: "The Federal Equal Credit Opportunity Act prohibits creditors from discriminating against credit applicants. The federal agency that administers compliance with this law concerning this [insert appropriate description—bank, store, etc.] is [name and address of the appropriate agency]."

Applicants who feel that they were denied credit for discriminatory reasons may file suit. The creditor may be liable for the actual damages; up to $10,000 punitive damages; and if a class action, the lesser of $500,000 or 1 percent of the net worth of the creditor. The court may also award court costs and attorney fees.

equal dignities rule A rule of agency law stipulating that when a contract is required by law to be in writing, the authority of an agent to enter into such a contract on behalf of the principal must also be in writing. For example, a power of attorney for real estate contracts must be in writing because state statutes of fraud generally require that all real estate contracts be in writing and that the agent's authority likewise be in writing. Usually, the power of attorney must also be recorded if the real estate contract (such as a land contract for deed) is expected to be recorded. (*See* **power of attorney**.)

equalization board A state or county reviewing agency with the power to adjust certain inequities in tax assessments. Equalization is the adjustment of the assessed valuation of real property in a particular taxing district to achieve parity with the level of assessment in other districts. Reviewing agencies establish equalization factors to ensure that all property owners in the state pay an equitable and uniform share of the state tax. Inequities could arise when the state bases its taxes on the assessments made by local assessors under local rules. For example, if one county appears to have assessments that are 15 percent lower than the state average assessment, this underassessment may be corrected by applying a 115 percent factor to each assessment in that county. (*See* **property tax**.)

equitable conversion A rule of law created to give the buyer under an executory contract of sale title to the property for certain purposes before the date set for closing. Because a court of equity "regards as done that which ought to be done," the doctrine of equitable conversion holds that immediately upon the making of the contract, the seller holds the legal title for the buyer, who has the beneficial, equitable title.

In essence, the seller's interest (legal title of the real estate) is converted into an interest in personal property (the money to be paid to purchase the property). Conversely, the buyer's interest (purchase money) becomes an interest in real estate. Thus if, at the time of the sales contract's execution, the seller is still in possession of the property (as is the usual case), he holds the property subject to a legal obligation to take care of it for the buyer and must be sure the property does not suffer damage.

The doctrine applies in cases involving the valuation of the seller's interest at death, and also in cases involving risk of loss or destruction of the premises. Example: A seller had agreed to sell her farm for $100,000, but she died before closing. She had willed her personal property to Mike Waters and her real property to Pat Parker. Through the doctrine of equitable conversion, the seller's interest in the farm is treated as personal property, and thus the proceeds from the sale would pass to Waters. (*See* **equitable title, risk of loss**.)

equitable lien A lien arising out of a written contract that shows an intention of the parties to charge some particular property as security for a debt or obligation. A court may decide that an equitable lien exists based on principles of fairness and justice, such as when the parties intended to create a lien but there was a defective execution of a mortgage instrument. Examples of equitable liens include a vendee's lien, which a buyer holds against a property in the amount of the deposit when a seller defaults in the performance of a sales contract, and a vendor's lien, which is the security lien behind a purchase-money loan that is not secured by a mortgage. Occasionally, a lender will make an unsecured loan but have the borrower agree not to convey or encumber the real property owned by the borrower.

equitable servitude   An easement of use enforced in equity that permits restrictive covenants not running with the land to be enforced as though they do run with the land. To enforce such equitable servitudes, it must appear that the restrictive covenants are designed for the benefit of the lot owners in a particular subdivision or tract, that there is a dominant or benefited land, that there is a general scheme or plan of improvement or development for the entire tract, and that the covenants are intended as restrictions on the land conveyed and incident to its ownership, the purchaser accepting the lot subject to that burden. The doctrine of equitable servitude might be asserted by a homeowner against a person attempting to build an apartment building in a tract designed for single-family homes. (*See* **servitude**.)

equitable theory of mortgages   *See* **lien-theory states**.

equitable title   The interest held by a vendee under a purchase contract, contract for deed, or an installment purchase agreement; the equitable right to obtain absolute ownership to property when legal title is held in another's name. This interest is transferable by deed, assignment, subcontract, or mortgage and passes to the vendee's heirs and devisees upon death. Though the vendor retains the bare legal title, the vendee has the right to demand that legal title be transferred upon payment of the full purchase price. In other words, the buyer can sue in equity for specific performance if the seller refuses to sell once a contract of sale is signed and the buyer tenders performance. In such cases, the courts say that the buyer becomes "the owner of the land in equity." The vendee benefits from any increase in value between the date of the purchase agreement and delivery of the deed. The vendee also takes the risk of any adverse circumstances, such as a change in zoning.

   Under a trust deed in some states, the trustee holds the bare legal title, and the trustor has the equitable title. (*See* **contract for deed**.)

equity
1. That interest or value remaining in property after payment of all liens or other charges on the property. An owner's equity in property is normally the monetary interest the owner retains over and above the mortgage indebtedness. The mortgagor's equity in property encumbered with a long-term mortgage increases with each monthly principal mortgage payment and increasing value through appreciation.

    Equity builds up gradually in the early years of the mortgage, as most of the monthly payment is applied to the interest on the loan rather than to the principal. The greater an owner's equity, the less risk for a mortgagee who lends money based on the security of the property. (*See* **appreciation**.)
2. A *court of equity*, under English common law, was a separate court to handle complaints for which there was no adequate remedy in the regular law courts, particularly cases in which money damages would not adequately compensate the aggrieved party. For example, if a seller refused to perform his contract to sell his farm to a buyer, the buyer's only remedy at law would be to sue for money damages. A court of equity, however, could force specific performance of the contract. Most states have merged courts of equity with courts of law, but the distinction between legal and equitable remedies in regard to specific performance and proceedings that do not involve injury is still of importance. Federal bankruptcy courts still operate as courts of equity. (*See* **specific performance**.)

equity buildup   The gradual reduction of outstanding principal due on the mortgage, usually through periodic amortized payments. Such payments build up the difference (equity) between the property value and amount of remaining debt.

equity of redemption   The right of a mortgagor, *before* a foreclosure sale, to reclaim property forfeited due to mortgage default. The mortgagor can redeem the property by paying the full debt plus interest and costs. Any attempt to have the mortgagor waive the equity of redemption is unenforceable and void as being contrary to public policy. Equity of redemption has been held to be an interest in real estate and is thus affected by the ordinary laws and rules concerning conveyances, including the statute of frauds.

Any right to redeem *after* a foreclosure sale must be created by state statute. In those states that permit a power of sale to be inserted in the mortgage document, most foreclosures of property are conducted pursuant to the nonjudicial foreclosure statute. Upon a foreclosure sale, the equity of redemption is terminated. (*See* **foreclosure, power of sale, redemption period, tax deed**.)

E

equity mortgage   A line of credit made against the equity in the borrower's home. The equity is based on a percentage of the appraised value of the home, minus any outstanding mortgage. It is secured by a second open-end mortgage on the home, and not on the creditworthiness of the owner.

equity participation   The arrangement between a potential buyer and an investor in which the investor shares an equity interest in a real property purchase in exchange for assisting with the financing of the acquisition. The investor may provide all or part of the down payment, closing costs, or monthly payment. Investors may be private parties, corporations, mortgage lenders, or even the seller. It is most important to obtain competent tax advice on the proper allocation of tax deductions such as mortgage interest, depreciation, and property tax.

equity sharing loan   A loan in which a resident-owner splits his or her equity or the increase in the value of the home with an investor-owner, who contributes toward the down payment and also to monthly payments and benefits in deducting a share of the tax write-offs. (*See* **shared appreciation**.)

erosion   The gradual loss of soil due to the operation of currents, tides or winds; the opposite of accretion. (*See* **accretion, avulsion**.)

errors and omissions (E&O) insurance   A form of insurance that covers liabilities for errors, mistakes, and negligence in the usual listing and selling activities of a real estate office or escrow company. It does not, however, cover fraudulent behavior or punitive damages or claims based on transactions for the personal account of a real estate agent. Considering the enormous exposure to liability real estate licensees and appraisers have under the broad liability provisions of the law, the importance of E&O insurance is obvious. Errors and omissions insurance policies are typically written on a claims-made basis (i.e., the insured is covered only if the claim is made during the period of the policy).

escalator clause   A contract provision permitting an adjustment of certain payments, not controlled by either part, to move up or down to cover certain contingencies. An escalator clause is designed to protect the lessor's investment position against a reduction in the rate of return over the term of the lease by increasing the yield during periods of inflation. Many fixed-rental net leases, particularly long-term commercial leases, contain a clause in which the parties agree to an adjustment of rent based on set increases in taxes, insurance, maintenance, and other operating costs. Similarly, the rent may be tied into the cost-of-living index to cover increases in the maintenance expenses and raised at stated intervals. (*See* **consumer price index [CPI]**.)

Another use of an escalator clause in a promissory note is to increase the interest rate in the event of late payment or default.

The escalator clause should not be confused with an alienation or due-on-sale clause. Often, a borrower who is selling the mortgaged property "voluntarily" agrees to an increase in the stated interest rate as suggested by the lender rather than have the lender call in the loan under the due-on-sale provision.

Sample language for an escalator clause might read: "At any time from date hereof, and from time to time thereafter, the legal holder of this note may, upon three months' prior written notice, decrease or increase the interest rate of this note then in effect, provided, however, that after receipt of any notice to increase the interest rate, the undersigned may within such three months' period prepay the balance remaining unpaid hereunder without payment of any prepayment charges as are provided in this note."

escape clause

1. A contract provision relieving a party of liability for failure to perform, as where a stated contingency does not occur. If such a clause allows the party to cancel the contract for no reason whatsoever, there really is no enforceable contract, for mutuality of obligation is lacking. (*See* **contingency**.)
2. A clause in a proprietary lease of a tenant-stockholder that permits the tenant to surrender the stock and lease back to the cooperative association and thereby terminate continuing liability for payments due under the lease.

escarpment   A long, steep face of a rock or land.

escheat   The reversion of property to the state or county, as provided by state law, in cases where a decedent dies intestate and there are no heirs capable of inheriting or when the property is abandoned. In some states, bank accounts unused for more than seven years escheat to the government.

escrow   (*depósito en garantía*)   The process, in some parts of the country in which a disinterested third person (a stakeholder) holds money and/or documents until satisfaction of the terms and conditions of the escrow instructions (as prepared by the parties to the escrow) have been achieved. Once these terms have been satisfied, delivery and transfer of the escrowed funds and documents takes place. (Escrow should not be confused with closings.)

A valid escrow is set up when a binding and enforceable contract of sale has been deposited with the escrow holder along with a fully executed deed. The escrow holder acts as a fiduciary and retains documents and entrusted assets until specified conditions are fulfilled. The holder is the special and impartial agent for *both* parties and acts according to the escrow instructions given by both. Depositors have no control over the documents after they are deposited into escrow, so the death or incapacity of one of the parties to the escrow does not terminate the escrow. Upon performance of the decedent's part of the contract, the other party is entitled to have escrow concluded according to the terms of the contract.

Although in some states, a real estate broker is authorized to handle escrow functions, the common practice is to employ the services of a licensed escrow company, title company, or lending institution. An escrow agent does not prepare or review the legal documents—escrow merely takes directions from the parties to the contract and acts on them in a confidential manner. Neither party should rely on the escrow agent to discover defects in the transaction. If an established escrow company is not involved in the transaction, an attorney should be consulted.

Because of the escrow's limited duties of disclosure and the confidentiality of the escrow in general, facts known to the escrow holder are normally not imputed or implied to the other party. Escrow is a limited agent for both parties, but once the conditions to the escrow transaction have been performed, the nature of the dual agency changes—escrow then becomes the agent for the seller for the money and the buyer for the deed. Escrow acts as the "clearinghouse" for the details of the transaction. Escrow cannot be unilaterally revoked, and in the event of disagreement, the escrow can only be amended, changed, or revoked by mutual agreement.

Escrow can be used to close the following types of real estate transactions: sales, mortgages, and exchanges; sales by means of a contract for deed; and leases of real estate. Real estate licensees often are responsible for advising the parties and properly preparing the purchase agreement. The sales contract usually serves as the basis for escrow instructions for both seller and buyer because it contains (or should contain) the agreement of the parties as to who must pay the various expenses, the proration date, and the like. If the contract has been unprofessionally prepared, the escrow company may be delayed or even prevented from closing the transaction.

In closing a real estate transaction, the escrow company may perform such duties as paying liens, computing prorations, ordering title evidence, having new documents prepared, drawing up closing statements, obtaining necessary signatures, recording documents, and receiving and disbursing funds. After payment of their respective closing costs, the buyer is thus assured of receiving a clear title and the seller is assured of receiving the appropriate funds. Typically, escrow fees are split equally between buyer and seller.

An escrow is usually not opened until major contingencies in the contract of sale have been met. Such major contingencies might be the arrangement of new financing or the approval of a loan assumption, building permit, zoning change, or the like. Among the contingencies that can be taken care of after the start of escrow are the appliance check, the termite inspection, and the signing of bylaws or house rules. (*See* **back-to-back escrow, closing [settlement], delivery, double escrow, holding escrow, interest, interpleader, perfect escrow, relation-back doctrine**.)

escrow instructions   In a sales transaction, writing signed by buyer and seller that details the procedures necessary to close a transaction and directs the escrow agent how to proceed. Sometimes the buyer and the seller execute separate instructions and sometimes the contract of sale itself serves as the escrow instructions. A broker who does not join in the escrow agreement could find the seller successfully ordering the escrow company not to pay the broker the listing commission.

estate
1. The degree, quantity, nature, and extent of ownership interest that a person has in real property referring to one's legal interest or rights, not to the physical quantity of land. To be an estate, an interest must be one that is (or may become) possessory and whose ownership is measured in terms of duration. A *freehold estate* (a fee simple or a life estate) is an interest in land for an uncertain duration. All other interests are less than freehold and include leasehold interests, such as an estate for years or an estate at will.

   Not all interests in land are estates. For example, a mortgage is a lien or charge on land, but it is not a part of ownership and thus is not an estate. Also, an easement is an interest in land but not an estate because it cannot vest in possession. Estates that are created by operation of law (such as dower) are known as *legal estates*—as distinguished from conventional estates, or those created by the parties. The word *estate* has its origin in the historic feudal system in which a person's "status" was determined primarily by the extent of that person's land ownership. (*See* **conventional estate; dominant estate [tenement]; ownership, form of**.)
2. The property owned by a decedent that may be subject to probate administration, federal and state tax, and claims by creditors.

estate at will   *See* **tenancy at will**.

estate of inheritance   A freehold estate that can be passed by descent or by will after the owner's death, such as a fee simple absolute. A life estate is not an estate of inheritance.

estate tax, federal   An excise tax imposed by the federal government under the Internal Revenue Code upon the transfer of property from the estate of a deceased to a beneficiary upon, or by reason of, the decedent's death. All property in which the deceased had an interest, *including* jointly held property, life insurance proceeds, and property in which the decedent had retained a life estate, may be subject to federal estate tax. Less than 1 percent of all estates are subject to the federal estate tax. The 2012 act keeps estate, gift, and generation-skipping transfer exemption levels at $5 million (indexed for inflation) but increases the applicable tax rate from 35 percent to 40 percent.

E

Gift taxes and estate taxes are set up under a common rate schedule. Lifetime transfers over the annual gift exclusion and transfers effective at death are cumulated for determining estate tax; however, any gift tax paid is subtracted from any estate tax due. The basis of inherited property is its value at the time of decedent's death or six months later (which is called the *alternate valuation date*), whichever is lower.

Extension on payment of the tax may be granted upon petition showing that the estate would have to sell an asset at a "sacrifice" price. For example, beneficiaries inheriting a family farm or business may be granted an extension to pay the estate tax. Where this extension is granted, the U.S. Treasury has a lien on the property, and lenders may be reluctant to lend money to owners of such real estate. Now, the Treasury may subordinate its lien to that of a bank. In the sale of real property, the preliminary title report will raise the exception of unpaid estate taxes.

Competent legal advice, careful estate planning, the proper choice of form of ownership, and the use of inter vivos trusts can serve to eliminate much of the estate tax burden and the cost of probate administration. (*See* **consideration**, **gift tax**, **inheritance tax**, **probate**, **stepped-up basis**.)

estoppel   A legal doctrine by which a person is prevented from asserting rights or facts that are inconsistent with a previous position or representation made by act, conduct, or silence. For example, a mortgagor who certifies that he has no defense against the mortgagee would be estopped to later assert any defenses against a person who purchased the mortgage in reliance on the mortgagor's certificate of no defense. An estoppel differs from a waiver in that a waiver generally refers to a voluntary surrender or relinquishment of some known right, whereas estoppel creates an inability to assert a defense or right.

If the conduct of one party to an agreement is such that it misleads another, and the first party relies on that conduct, an estoppel is created to prevent the first party from denying the effect of her conduct (called *estoppel in pais*). When a grantor conveys more interest in land than he in fact has, and later acquires the full title, such grantor can be barred by estoppel from denying the grantee's full interest in the land. When a real estate owner allows another person to act as though she is the true owner, and an innocent purchaser buys the land from that other person, the true owner is estopped from asserting ownership.

In boundary cases, a landowner is sometimes estopped to assert that the true boundary line is different from the line previously agreed on by the owner and the neighboring property owner. This is especially true if the neighbor has acted in reliance on the landowner's representations of the location of the line and built a fence or driveway, planted crops, made improvements, or the like.

Sometimes a seller under an oral contract of sale is estopped to assert the statute of frauds as a defense to the buyer's suit for specific performance when the buyer has entered into possession, paid money, or made improvements, and the buyer can demonstrate irreparable injury and hardship if the contract were not enforced.

Equitable estoppel may be asserted by a developer who obtained a building permit but then finds the government has downzoned the parcel or changed the land use. (*See* **nonconforming use**.)

A purchaser of rental property might have the existing tenants execute estoppel statements acknowledging their obligation to pay the proper amount of rent according to the specified terms of their leases. (*See* **certificate of no defense**, **laches**, **reduction certificate**.)

estoppel by deed   A legal doctrine that applies to a person who, without having legal title to a property, deeds the property to another and then subsequently obtains good title to the property. The grantor is then estopped from denying any lack of title at the time of the original conveyance, thus automatically vesting complete legal title in the grantee. Also called *title by estoppel*. (*See* **after-acquired**.)

estoppel certificate   *See* **certificate of no defense**.

estover   A necessity allowed by law, such as the right of a tenant to use whatever timber there may be on leased premises in order to support his or her minimum needs for fuel, repairs, and tools.

et al.   Latin abbreviation for *et alii*, meaning "and others."

ethics   A system of moral principles, rules, and standards of conduct. High ethical standards are more important in real estate than in certain other transactions where the clients may be more familiar with the services performed. Good ethics is concerned with fidelity, integrity, and competency. (*See* **Code of Ethics**.)

ethnic group   A group of people identified by a common heritage of language, culture, customs, race, religion, national origin, language, kinship, and/or cultural similarities. (*See* **discrimination**.)

F

et ux.   Latin abbreviation for *et uxor*, meaning "and wife."

et vir.   Latin for "and husband."

eviction   (*1. evicción; 2. desalojo, desahucio, lanzamiento*)
1. The legal process of removing a tenant from the premises for some breach of the lease.
      In the case of a partial eviction, the tenant is deprived of the use of part of the premises. Upon eviction, the tenant is no longer responsible for paying rent, unless the lease contains a survival clause stating that the tenant's liability for rent survives eviction.
      Typical grounds for the eviction of a tenant by a landlord include nonpayment of rent, unlawful use of the premises violating the use provisions of the lease (such as conducting a business in a rental unit leased strictly for residential purposes), and noncompliance with health and safety codes.
2. The disturbance of a tenant's enjoyment of all or any material part of the leased premises by act of the landlord or by claim of a superior title by a third party.

   (*See* **actual conviction, constructive eviction, ejectment, summary possession**.)

evidence of title   Proof of ownership of property. Common examples of such evidence are a certificate of title, title insurance policy or, with Torrens-registered property, a Torrens certificate of title.
      A person who contracts to sell property must furnish the buyer with a marketable title to the property. Unless the contract provides otherwise, however, the seller is not obliged to furnish the buyer with any prior evidence that the title is good and marketable. Generally, either party (or in some states, both parties) may pay for a lawyer's abstract of title or title insurance policy. This usually depends on local practice and custom as reflected in the contract terms. (*See* **certificate of title, tax and lien search, title insurance**.)

examination, licensing   In *all* states, anyone seeking a real estate license must take a written examination and demonstrate a reasonable knowledge of general real property laws and principles, documents, and state licensing laws. Separate examinations are generally given to salespeople and brokers. Specific requirements vary from state to state, and details and qualifications for each state's exam can be obtained from the appropriate state licensing officials. Licensing examinations are required for state-certified or licensed appraisers.

exception
1. As used in a conveyance of real property, the exclusion from the conveyance of some part of the property granted. The title to that withdrawn part remains in the grantor by virtue of the original title rights. A conveyance by Grant Park to Bob Lee of a ten-acre parcel "excepting therefrom a strip of land ten feet wide running along the northerly boundary" constitutes a legal exception. An exception is to be distinguished from a reservation, the creation on behalf of the grantor of a new right issuing out of the thing granted, such as the reservation

of an easement by the grantor to cross the property or the reservation of a life estate in the conveyed property. (*See* **reservation**.)

2. Liens and encumbrances specifically excluded from coverage under a title insurance policy.
3. Those matters noted in the "subject to" clause of the contract of sale, in which the seller agrees to convey clear and marketable title "subject to the following exceptions."

excess condemnation   The taking of more land than is actually used to meet the public purpose of the condemnation. The excess is sometimes sold at public auction after the project is completed.

E

exchange   A transaction in which all or part of the consideration for the purchase of real property is the transfer of property of "like kind" (i.e., real estate for real estate). The Internal Revenue Code Section 1031 is not a *tax-free exchange* because it only defers the tax, and involves the exchange of property held for investment or the production of income for property of a like kind (which includes improved and unimproved property) until the property is later disposed of in a taxable transaction. The 1031 has become a popular device for deferring capital gains taxes. The underlying philosophy behind an exchange is that income tax should not apply as long as an investment remains intact in the form of real estate. Therefore, the exchange of a personal residence does not qualify for this tax-deferred treatment. These exchanges hinge on meeting certain criteria of date and time, so the assistance of a very knowledgeable person is highly recommended.

A leasehold with 30 or more years remaining under the lease is considered "like" a fee title to improved or unimproved property. One disadvantage to an investor in a tax-free exchange is that the basis in the new property is lower than it would have been had the new property been purchased and the old property been sold in separate transactions. Such a reduced basis thus results in smaller depreciation deductions. It is important that the contract indicate the taxpayer's intention to exchange rather than sell the property.

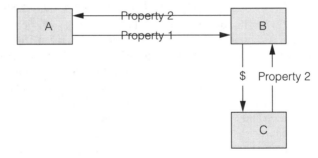

The most frequent types of exchanges are the "three-cornered" exchanges. In one type, the exchanging party (*A*) conveys his property 1 to the purchaser (*B*) in exchange for new property 2, which the purchaser previously obtained pursuant to the exchanging party's directions.

In another type, the exchanging party (*A*) conveys his property 1 to the purchaser (*B*) in exchange for new property 2 received directly from a third-party seller (*C*) in a simultaneous or delayed exchange.

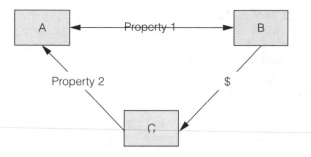

It is rare to find two properties of equal value and equity; therefore, to balance the equities, one party usually also pays some money or assumes a larger amount of underlying debt. If received by the party seeking the tax-free exchange, this money or additional debt from which a person is relieved would be treated as *boot*, and gain will be taxable to the extent of that boot.

Example: Angelo Domni wants to exchange his $500,000 apartment building subject to a $400,000 mortgage lien for Howard Wong's apartment building, valued at $450,000 with a $400,000 mortgage. Domni's equity is $100,000 and Wong's equity is $50,000. Therefore, Wong would have to pay $50,000 in boot to equalize the equities. Or, if the equities were the same but Wong's property had only a $350,000 mortgage (so that Domni was relieved of $400,000 but assumed only $350,000), then Domni would again be considered to have received $50,000 of boot in the form of debt relief.

In many cases, the exchanger needs time to locate the replacement ("up-leg") property. Under special delayed exchange rules, the exchange need not be simultaneous, but the taxpayer must identify the replacement property(s) in writing to the qualified intermediary within 45 days. The replacement property must be purchased by the earlier of these two dates: the 180th day after the date of the sale of the relinquished property or the due date of the taxpayer's income tax return, including any extensions. If either the 45th or the 180th day is a holiday, the taxpayer must close before the date. The replacement property must be located within the United States if the exchanged property is U.S. property. (It is permissible to exchange foreign property for foreign property.)

If any of the exchangers are married, the spouse should release any marital rights in the exchange deed. (*See* **boot, delayed exchange, dower, like-kind property, multiple-asset exchange**.)

excise tax A direct tax, imposed without assessment, and measured according to the amount of services performed, income received, or similar criteria; it is not a tax imposed on property. Examples are license fees, sales tax, and federal estate tax.

exclusionary zoning The zoning of an area in such a way as to exclude minorities and low-income people. For example, the requirement of minimum lot or house size might have a discriminatory effect, whether intentional or not, unless justified on grounds of protecting the general health, safety, and welfare of the community.

exclusive agency A written listing agreement giving a sole agent the right to sell a property for a specified time, but the owner reserves the right to sell the property without owing a commission. The exclusive agent is entitled to a commission if personally selling the property or if it is sold by anyone other than the seller. It is exclusive in the sense the property is listed with only one broker. The multiple listing service must accept exclusive-agency listings submitted by participating brokers. (*See* **exclusive right to sell**.)

E

exclusive listing   (*venta exclusiva*)   A written listing of real property in which the seller agrees to appoint only one broker to sell the property for a specified period of time. The two types of exclusive listings are the exclusive agency and the exclusive right to sell. Generally, exclusive listings must stipulate a definite termination date and may not include a rollover clause. A listing for an indefinite period is frowned on by the courts, is illegal in many states, and is generally poor practice. This is to protect sellers who, unaware that the listing is still in effect after the end of the initial listing period because they failed to give a cancellation notice, may list the property with another broker and thus find themselves liable for the payment of two full commissions. (*See* **extender clause**.)

exclusive right to sell   A written listing agreement appointing a broker the exclusive agent for the sale of property for a specified period of time. The listing broker is entitled to a commission if the owner, the broker or anyone else sells the property. The phrase "right to sell" really means the right to find a buyer; it does not mean that the agent has a power of attorney from the owner to sell the property. Unless the contract clearly states it is an exclusive right or authorization to sell, most courts treat it as being a mere exclusive-agency listing. (*See* **exclusive agency**, **listing**, **termination of listing**.)

exculpatory clause
1. A clause sometimes inserted in a mortgage note in which the lender waives the right to a deficiency judgment.
2. As used in a lease, a clause that intends to clear or relieve the landlord from liability for tenants' personal injury and property damage. It may not, however, protect the landlord from injuries to third parties. Many states frown on exculpatory clauses in leases, requiring the tenant to waive the right to sue. (*See* **disclaimer**.)

execute   The act of making a document legally valid, such as formalizing a contract by signing, or acknowledging and delivering a deed. In some cases, *execution of a document* may refer solely to the act of signing; in other cases, it may refer to complete performance of the document's terms.

executed contract   A contract that has been performed fully.

execution   A judicial process whereby the court directs an officer to levy (seize) the property of a judgment debtor in satisfaction of a judgment lien. State laws usually protect certain properties from execution. (*See* **homestead**, **writ of execution**.)

executor   (*albacea*)   A person appointed by a testator to carry out the directions and requests in a last will and testament, and to dispose of the deceased's property according to the provisions of the will. State probate laws generally refer to this person as a "personal representative of the decedent."

    The executor is entitled to possession and control of the testator's real estate pending determination of heirs, payment of claims, and distribution of the property. Unless the power to sell the decedent's real property is given to the executor in the will, the executor must request court approval before selling the property. The executor does not generally need a real estate license to sell the property but must be authorized to do so by the probate court. When the will authorizes the executor to sell real property, the property may be sold either at public auction or private sale, without prior notice to the court (however, title does not pass until the sale has been confirmed by the court). Usually, the executor must make a final accounting within one year of having been appointed. (*See* **administrator**, **probate**.)

executory contract   A contract in which one or both parties has not yet performed, such as a contract for sale. An *executed contract*, on the other hand, is one in which there is nothing left to be done by either party; it has been completely performed by both parties. The instrument is no longer a contract but rather is evidence of an executed agreement. The distinction is important: For example, the statute of frauds does not generally apply to an executed oral agreement; thus, one who conveys property by deed in accordance with an oral contract of sale cannot later assert the statute of frauds to try to rescind the contract and regain the property. If the contract is executory, however, the seller could not be forced to convey the deed under oral contract.

executory interest   An interest in real property that shifts title from one transferee to another ("to Harry Green and his heirs, but if Alice Gorski marries Mike Cwik, then to Alice Gorski and her heirs") or "springs out" of the grantor in the future ("to Harry Green and his heirs when and if Harry Green marries Carol Kaiser"). A fee simple subject to an executory interest is an estate where, upon the happening of an event designated in the grant, the fee simple is automatically transferred to a third person and not to the original grantor or his or her heirs. For example, Jim Winn grants his farm "to George Zito so long as it is used during the next 20 years to grow wheat and if not so used, then to Ed Schultz and his heirs."

The distinction between an executory interest and a possibility of reverter (when the property reverts to the grantor) is important because the executory interest must generally become possessory within the period allowed under state law. (*See* **future interest**, **possibility of reverter**, **rule against perpetuities**.)

exemplary damage   *See* **punitive damages**.

exhibit   A document or section of a document presented as part of the supporting data for the principal document. For example, a contract of sale may attach a legal description as an exhibit; an inventory of furniture may also be attached as an exhibit. (*See* **addendum**.)

exoneration clause   *See* **disclaimer**.

expansion option   A provision in a lease granting a tenant the option to lease additional adjacent space after a specified period of time.

expense stop   A dollar limit above which the lessee in a commercial lease agrees to pay the operating expenses. This protects the lessor against unexpected increases in operating expenses, such as real property taxes or inflated heating or cooling costs.

expert witness   A person qualified to render testimony by virtue of specialized knowledge and/or experience. For example, an experienced real estate broker may be asked to testify as to the standard of care of brokers in the community; or an appraiser may testify as to the value of property involved in a legal proceeding.

exposure
1. Where and/or how a property is situated in terms of compass direction or its accessibility to air, light, or facilities. Many commercial tenants prefer the south and west sides of business streets because the pedestrian traffic seeks the shady side of the street in warm weather. In addition, merchandise displayed in store windows on this side of the street is less prone to damage by the sun.
2. In marketing terms, a property for sale given visibility in the open market. A property's exposure to the market includes how it is displayed, exhibited, and/or allowed to be seen by qualified buyers.

expropriation   The taking of private land for a public purpose under the government's right of eminent domain, as exercised in a condemnation suit. (*See* **eminent domain**.)

extended coverage
1. A term used widely in fire insurance policies to denote that the policies cover damage by wind, hail, explosion, riot, smoke, and other perils.
2. A title insurance policy that covers risks usually excluded by most standard-coverage policies. The standard policy normally insures the title only as shown by the public records. It

does not cover unrecorded matters that might be discovered by an inspection of the premises. Most lenders require extended-coverage mortgage title insurance policies. Extended coverage indemnifies the insured against such things as mechanics' liens, tax liens, miscellaneous liens, encumbrances, easements, rights of parties in possession, and encroachments, which may not be disclosed by the public records. (*See* **American Land Title Association [ALTA]**, **hidden risk**, **title insurance**.)

extender clause

1. A "carryover" clause (often referred to as a *safety clause* or *protection clause*) in a listing that provides that a broker is still entitled to a commission for a set period of time after the listing has expired if the property is sold to a prospect of the broker introduced to the property during the period of the listing. A sample clause might read like this: "If within 90 days after expiration of the listing agreement, the property is sold to or exchanged with any person who physically inspected the property with the broker or any cooperating broker during the listing period if the broker gave the seller the name of such a person in writing within five days after the stated expiration date of the listing agreement." The owner should disclose any expired listings to any broker seeking a listing. Unless careful disclosure is made of any extender clauses in such expired listings, the owner could be faced with a claim for commissions from both the former broker who showed the buyer the property and the new broker. In many states, the extender clause is revoked once the owner relists the property with another broker.

2. Previously, a condition providing that the listing would continue for a set period of time and then be automatically renewable until the parties agreed to terminate it. Today, the use of such clauses in listing contracts is frowned on by the courts and violates many state license laws.

   (*See* **negotiation**, **override**.)

extension   (*prórroga*)

1. An agreement to continue the period of performance beyond a specified period. For example, under the terms of a sales contract, the seller's broker may have the right to extend the time for closing an additional 30 days.

   In periods of tight money, when buyers with maturing contracts for deed find it difficult to sell or refinance their property before the maturity date, many buyers are willing to pay a premium to extend the agreement and thus avoid a default. However, care should be taken by a mortgagee in extending a debt because, in the case of deed assumptions, an extension may have the effect of changing the original contract so that the guarantors and prior grantees are released from liability.

2. A lease extension is an agreement by which the lease is made effective for an additional period of time beyond its effective date; it is often called a *lease renewal*.

exterior insulating and finish system (EIFS)   A multilayered exterior siding system used on commercial buildings and homes, also called *synthetic stucco*. The value of EIFS is that it is virtually indestructible, so water that penetrates EIFS becomes trapped behind it, causing many instances of mold buildup and water damage to the wood or gypsum board foundation. Both the EIFS industry and the National Association of Home Builders recommend annual inspections to detect intrusions in their early stages should they occur. So far, the lawsuits have been against EIFS installers and manufacturers, not real estate licensees. If EIFS has been used extensively, real estate licensees should avoid making any representations of condition and strongly advise buyers to obtain an EIFS inspection.

external obsolescence (*obsolescencia externa*)   A loss of value (typically incurable) resulting from extraneous factors that exist outside of the property itself; a type of depreciation caused by environmental, social, or economic forces over which an owner has little or no control. If there is a change in zoning, external obsolescence is likely to occur, as in the following examples: to a residence if an industrial plant is built next to it; to a well-maintained house in a deteriorating neighborhood; and to a motel if a new highway is built that results in difficult access to the motel. Other causes might be proximity to nuisances and changes in land use or population. Also called *locational* or *environmental obsolescence*. (*See* **cost approach, depreciation [appraisal], obsolescence, economic obsolescence.**)

extraction method   *See* **abstraction.**

eye appeal   Amenities and positive features of a property, such as an attractive view or a landscaped yard.

facade (*fachada*)   The exposed or front face of a building; often used to describe an exterior that features a unique architectural design or concept.

face value
1. The amount due at the maturity of an instrument; the par value as shown on its face, not the real value or the market value. Mortgage notes are often sold at a discount below their face value.
2. The dollar amount of insurance coverage.

facilitator   A real estate licensee who assists a buyer and a seller in reaching an agreement in a real estate transaction but does not have an agency relationship with that party. Several states have enacted legislation creating statutory duties for a facilitator different from those of a dual agent; sometimes called a *transaction coordinator*, an *intermediary*, or *transaction broker*. (*See* **dual agency [limited agency], finder, middleman.**)

factory-built construction   Any construction product that is built all or in part in the controlled conditions of a factory. Examples range from trusses and prehung doors to completed buildings such as modular and manufactured housing. (*See* **manufactured housing, modular construction, on-frame modular.**)

Fair Credit Reporting Act (FCRA)   A federal law designed to protect the public from the reporting of inaccurate information by credit agencies, including ChoicePoint, which gathers information for the insurance industry. Under the act, individuals have the right to inspect information in their file at the credit bureau, correct any errors, and attach explanatory statements as a supplement to the file. The act also requires that if a seller of real estate refuses to sell to a prospective buyer or a seller or lender refuses to extend the buyer credit because of the buyer's credit report, the seller or lender must disclose to the prospect the identity of the reporting credit agency. In 2005, Congress amended FCRA to require that each agency provide one free credit report per year and to guarantee consumers access to their credit scores at a reasonable fee. Other changes make it easier to prevent identity theft and place limitations on how credit bureaus can use information from credit reports. Most adverse information about a debtor is dropped after seven years (except bankruptcy information, which is held ten years). (*See* **identity theft**, **credit scoring**, **FICO score**, **Comprehensive Loss Underwriting Exchange [CLUE]**.)

Fair Debt Collection Practices Act   A federal law concerned with regulating the activities of debt collectors when collecting consumer debts—that is, debts incurred by a natural person to obtain money, property, insurance, or services primarily for personal, family, or household debts. A debt collector is any person whose business is principally the collection of debts or who (directly or indirectly) regularly collects or attempts to collect debts owed to another person or entity, including property managers and attorneys who attempt to collect debts for their clients. The law provides protection from illegal and unethical debt collection tactics, outlines what information debt collectors can gather, lists specific rules on how they can communicate with consumers at home and at work, and prescribes the types and timing of notices required prior to collecting the debts. As mandated by the Dodd-Frank Act, primary enforcement is now with the Consumer Financial Protection Bureau, along with the FTC and other federal agencies.

Fair Housing Act   (*Ley de Igualdad de Vivienda*)   *See* **federal fair housing law**.

Fair Housing Amendment Act of 1988   An amendment to the federal Fair Housing Act, effective March 12, 1989, that added two more protected classes: those physically and mentally handicapped and those households with children under 18 years of age ("familial status"). *See* **federal fair housing laws**.

Fair Isaac & Company (FICO)   *See* Appendix A.

fair market value (FMV)   An appraisal term for the most probable price in terms of money that a property, if offered for sale for a reasonable period of time in a competitive market, would bring to a seller who is willing but not compelled to sell, from a buyer who is willing but not compelled to buy, both parties being fully informed of all the purposes to which the property is best adapted and ways it is capable of being used. The accepted term today is *market value*. (*See* **market value**.)

false advertising   Advertising that contains blatantly untrue or misleading information. False advertising by a seller constitutes misrepresentation and thus gives the buyer relying on it grounds for canceling a contract to purchase. In certain cases, false advertising may constitute fraud and would be grounds for a court to award a money judgment for any damages suffered. Generally, a real estate licensee found responsible for false advertising is subject to suspension or license revocation. A nonlicensee who makes false representations (for instance, in respect to a subdivision) may be subject to criminal prosecution. (*See* **advertising**, **blind ad**.)

FAMC   *See* **Federal Agricultural Mortgage Corporation (FAMC)**.

familial status   As defined in the Fair Housing Act, a protected class consisting of one or more individuals under age 18 living with a parent or legal guardian or another person given written permission from a parent. Specifically covered are pregnant women, a person in the process of securing legal custody, and foster parents. (*See* **fair housing**.)

family   In the traditional sense, persons related to each other by blood or marriage. In the more modern sense, the term *family* is given a broader interpretation to include certain nontraditional living arrangements. It is important to check definitions under local zoning ordinances to see whether "single-family dwellings" permit unmarried, unrelated groups such as the elderly or disabled to live together. (*See* **related parties**.)

Fannie Mae   An active participant in the secondary mortgage market. Fannie Mae (formerly the Federal National Mortgage Association [FNMA]) is a government-sponsored enterprise (GSE) chartered by Congress that works in the secondary market, buying mortgage loans to ensure that mortgage money is readily available. Fannie Mae is not permitted to originate loans or lend money directly to consumers in the primary mortgage market.

Fannie Mae was established in 1938 to purchase FHA loans from loan originators to provide some liquidity for government-insured loans in a depression-wracked economy when few lending institutions would undertake this type of loan. In 1944, VA loans were added to Fannie Mae's purchase program. In 1968, Congress partitioned Fannie Mae into a continuing government agency known as *Ginnie Mae*, the Government National Mortgage Association (under the Department of HUD), and issued a federal charter to Fannie Mae to operate as a private corporation. As the market recovers from the 2008 housing crisis, Fannie Mae continues to keep funds flowing into the mortgage market, to help distressed homeowners, and to encourage sustainable housing.

Both Fannie Mae and Freddie Mac (FHLMC) limit the size and kind of loans they buy, which must be written in accordance with specific requirements. To simplify these requirements for loan originators, these agencies have brought into the market a new kind of conventional loan, identified as a "conforming loan." (*See* **Freddie Mac**.)

Fannie Mae purchases mortgage loans and mortgage-related assets and securitizes lender-originated mortgage loans into Fannie Mae mortgage-based securities (Fannie Mae MBS). Funds are derived from issuing debt securities in the domestic and international capital markets and other investments to increase the supply of affordable housing. Fannie Mae is regulated primarily by the Federal Housing Finance Agency (FHFA). (*See* **Federal Housing Finance Agency (FHFA)**, **government-sponsored enterprises [GSE]**.)

Farm and Land Institute   *See* Appendix A.

farm area   (*área de cultivo*)   A real estate licensee's term to indicate either a selected geographical area or a group of people from which to solicit real estate business and to which a real estate salesperson devotes special attention and study. A good salesperson learns everything there is to know about a particular geographical area, including all recent comparable sales, and tries to solicit real estate business, especially listings from this community. In a similar manner, licensees seek business from their "people farm."

farm assets   The component assets of a ranch or farm, including farmland; personal residence; other residences and structures used in the business of farming or ranching; vines, trees, pipelines, fences, irrigation systems, and livestock; and unharvested crops sold to the purchaser.

These assets are subject to special treatment for income-tax purposes, as provided for in the Internal Revenue Code and the regulations of the Internal Revenue Service. Therefore, price allocation upon sale, exchange, or lease of the whole ranch or farm property, or some part thereof, is important. (*See* **farmland**.)

Farm Credit Administration (FCA)   *See* Appendix A.

Farm Credit System   A federal program inaugurated under the Federal Farm Loan Act of 1916 and designed to serve the unique financial requirements of farmers, ranchers, producers, and harvesters of agricultural products, rural homeowners, and owners of selected farm-related businesses. The 50 states are divided into 12 Farm Credit Districts, operating independently under the supervision of the Federal Farm Credit Administration. (*See* **federal land bank [FLB]**.)

Farm Credit System Banks (FCSB)   *See* Appendix A.

Farmer Mac   Nickname of the Federal Agricultural Mortgage Corporation. (*See* **Federal Agricultural Mortgage Corporation [FAMC]**.)

Farmers Home Administration (FmHA)   A federal agency under the U.S. Department of Agriculture, originally designed to handle emergency farm financing, to channel credit to farmers and rural residents and communities. FmHA was replaced by the Rural Housing Service (RHS) and was fully terminated in 2006.

farmland   Land used specifically for agricultural purposes in the raising of crops or livestock. Also, land so designated in zoning laws for agricultural purposes. (*See* **farm assets**.)

Farm Service Agency   *See* Appendix A.

fastrack construction   A construction method in which building commences under a negotiated contract before all plans and specifications have been completed. The construction progresses as plans come off the drawing board.

FDIC   *See* **Federal Deposit Insurance Corporation (FDIC)**.

feasibility study   (*estudio de viabilidad*)
1. An analysis of a proposed subject or property with emphasis on the attainable income, probable expenses, and most advantageous use and design. A feasibility study is often used by a developer to entice investors to put up the front money for a proposed development. Such a study is required by some mortgage investors and lending institutions before granting a loan commitment. In addition to being a decision-making tool for the developer and lender, it is also a valuable sales tool. However, it is different from a marketability study, which is more concerned with demand for the contemplated use. (*See* **absorption rate**, **front money**.)
   The purpose of a feasibility study is to estimate the rate of return obtainable for a specific project and to determine whether the proposed project is economically feasible.
2. A survey of an urban area using federal funds to determine whether it is practicable to undertake an urban renewal project within that area.

Federal Agricultural Mortgage Corporation (FAMC)   A federal agency created by the Agricultural Credit Act of 1987 as a separate entity within the Farm Credit System to develop a secondary market in farm real estate loans. Popularly known as Farmer Mac, it is a stockholder-owned, government-sponsored enterprise (GSE) that purchase agricultural loans from originators, issues long-term standby purchase commitments (LTSPCs) for eligible loans, and purchases and guarantees loan-backed securities secured by eligible loans called AgVAntage® bonds through three programs: Farmer Mac I, Farmer Mac II, and Rural Utilities.

Federal Deposit Insurance Corporation (FDIC)   (*Corporación Federal Aseguradora de Depósito*)   An independent agency created by Congress to insure the deposits of all banks entitled to federal deposit insurance. Individual accounts are insured up to $250,000, per depositor, per insured bank, for each account ownership category. FDIC is funded by premiums paid by banks and thrift institutions. (*See* **Federal Deposit Insurance Reform Act**, **Bank Insurance Fund [BIF]**, **Financial Institutions Reform, Recovery, and Enforcement Act [FIRREA]**, **Savings Association Insurance Fund [SAIF]**, **Appendix A**.)

Federal Deposit Insurance Reform Act (FDIRA)   A federal law that increased the deposit insurance to $250,000, indexing the amount to inflation, and merged two deposit insurance funds—Savings Association Insurance Fund (SAIF) and Bank Insurance Fund (BIF), into the Depositor Insurance Fund (DIF). FDIRA also requires that the FDIC issue rebates to the banking industry if the level of the deposit insurance fund rises above 1.5 percent of total insured deposits. (*See* **Federal Deposit Insurance Corporation [FDIC]**.)

Federal Emergency Management Agency (FEMA)   A federal agency responsible for disaster mitigation, preparedness, response and recovery planning. FEMA is part of the U.S. Department of Homeland Security (DHS), and its continuing mission is to lead the effort to prepare the nation for all hazards and effectively manage federal response and recovery efforts following any national incident. FEMA also initiates proactive mitigation activities, trains first responders, and manages the National Flood Insurance Program and the U.S. Fire Administration. (*See* **National Flood Insurance Program [NFIP], Appendix A**.)

federal fair housing law   A federal law enacted in 1968 and subsequently amended, Title VIII of the Civil Rights Act is called the *federal Fair Housing Act*, which declared a national policy of providing fair housing throughout the United States (reference Sections 3601–3631 of Title 42, U.S. Code). Discrimination is illegal when based on race, color, sex, familial status, handicap, religion, or national origin in connection with the sale or rental of most dwellings (including time-sharing units) and any vacant land offered for residential construction or use. The law does not prohibit discrimination in other types of real estate transactions, such as those involving commercial or industrial properties. The law is administered by the Office of Equal Opportunity (OEO) under the direction of the secretary of the Department of Housing and Urban Development (HUD).

As amended in 1972, the law requires the display of equal opportunity posters (11 inches by 14 inches) at real estate brokerage houses, model home sites, mortgage lenders' offices, and other related locations. Failure to display the poster constitutes prima facie evidence of discrimination if a broker who does not display the sign is investigated by HUD on charges of discrimination. The poster must show the equal housing opportunity slogan: Equal Housing Opportunity. It must also carry the equal housing opportunity statement: "We are pledged to the letter and spirit of U.S. policy for the achievement of equal housing opportunity throughout the Nation. We encourage and support an affirmative advertising and marketing program in which there are no barriers to obtaining housing because of race, color, religion, sex, familial status, handicap, or national origin." The equal housing opportunity logo shown here also must be displayed on the poster:

The fair housing law provides protection against the following acts of discrimination, if they are based on race, color, sex, familial status, handicap, religion, or national origin:

■ Refusing to sell or rent to, deal, or negotiate with any person
■ Misrepresenting terms or conditions for buying or renting housing
■ Advertising that housing is available only to persons of a certain race, color, sex, familial status, handicap, religion, or national origin (such as placing Sold signs when the property in fact is not sold)
■ Denying that housing is available for inspection, sale, or rent when it really is available (includes a practice called steering, whereby certain brokers may direct members of certain minority groups away from some of their listings in racially unmixed areas)
■ Blockbusting, a practice whereby a broker hopes to profit through persuading owners to sell or rent housing by telling them that minority groups are moving into the neighborhood; also called **panic peddling**
■ Denying or requiring different terms or conditions for home loans made by commercial lenders such as banks, savings, and loan associations, and insurance companies

- Denying to anyone the use of, or participation in, any real estate service such as broker's organizations, multiple listing services, or other facilities related to the selling or renting of housing

The Fair Housing Act applies to the following:
- Single-family housing owned by private individuals when a broker or other person in the business of selling or renting dwellings is employed (includes use of MLS) and/or discriminatory advertising is used
- Single-family housing not owned by private individuals, such as those owned by development corporations
- Single-family housing owned by a private individual who owns more than three such dwellings or who, in any two-year period, sells more than one dwelling in which the owner was not the most recent resident
- Multifamily dwellings of five or more units
- Multifamily dwellings containing four or fewer units, if the owner does not reside in one of the units

Exceptions: The following situations are exempt from the Fair Housing Act (but covered by the post–Civil War 1866 antidiscrimination civil rights law, if based on race):
- The sale or rental of single-family housing if neither a broker nor discriminatory advertising is used, and no more than one dwelling in which the owner was not the most recent resident is sold during any two-year period
- The rental of rooms or units in owner-occupied multiple dwellings for two to four families, if discriminatory advertising is not used (the "Mrs. Murphy exemption" in which Mrs. Murphy represents the small investor living in one of her own units)
- The sale, rental, or occupancy of dwellings owned and operated by a religious organization for other than commercial purposes to persons of the same religion, if membership in that religion is not restricted on account of race, color, sex, or national origin; the religious organization can give preference to its members (e.g., it could levy a surcharge on nonmembers)
- The restriction of lodgings owned or operated by a private club for other than a commercial purpose to rental or occupancy by its own members

The 1988 amendments to the federal Fair Housing Act bar discrimination based on handicap or familial status of the buyer or the renter or anyone associated with the buyer or the renter. "Handicap" means a physical or mental impairment, including cancer, AIDS, alcoholism, or a speech, visual, or hearing impairment (but not including illegal drug use). The landlord must allow the tenants to make reasonable modifications of existing premises at the tenant's expense. Discrimination also includes the failure to make reasonable accommodation in rules, policies, practices, or services to allow a disabled person an equal opportunity to use or enjoy a dwelling.

The law bars discrimination in the sale and rental of housing based on the presence of children (under 18 years of age) in the family, including pregnancy or a pending adoption. The law still permits reasonable limitations on the number of occupants per unit under state and private regulation (a child under 2 years is not counted as an occupant). Under the Housing for Older Persons Act of 1995 (HOPA), housing for older persons is exempt from the familial status prohibitions if (1) the building is occupied solely by those 62 years of age or older or (2) at least 80 percent of the dwellings are occupied by at least one person 55 years of age or older. (*See* **Housing for Older Persons Act [HOPA].**)

Two remedial avenues, one administrative and one judicial, are available. An aggrieved person may complain directly to a U.S. district court within one year of the alleged discriminatory practice, whether or not a verified complaint has been filed with the secretary of HUD. However, in states with equivalent antidiscrimination judicial rights and remedies, such a suit would have to be brought in the state court. The burden of proof is on the complainant. The court can grant permanent or temporary injunctions, temporary restraining orders, or other appropriate relief and may award actual damages and unlimited punitive damages. The parties can agree to have the case decided by an administrative law judge.

Criminal penalties are provided for those who coerce, intimidate, threaten, or interfere with a person's buying, renting, or selling housing; anyone making a complaint of discrimination; or anyone exercising any rights in connection with this law. Licensees should keep detailed records of all transactions and rentals in order to defend themselves against possible discrimination complaints. Violations are frequently proved through the use of "testers," and the courts have ruled that there is no requirement that the testers actually be bona fide purchasers or renters. (*See* **blockbusting, conciliation agreement, discrimination, familial status, handicap, panic peddling, steering**.)

HUD has identified certain words that should be avoided because they may tend to convey discriminatory intent. Examples are *White, Black, Colored, Catholic, Jew, Protestant, Chinese, Chicano, Irish, restricted, ghetto, disadvantaged, private, membership approval*.

Advertising should never state or imply that the rental of separate units in a dwelling is restricted to persons of only one sex unless the sharing of living areas is involved.

Even directions to the real estate for sale may be discriminatory, such as references to synagogues or "near Martin Luther King memorial," or close to a specific country club or private school that caters to particular racial, religious, or ethnic groups. (*See* **advertising**.)

The selective use of advertising media or content based on ethnic considerations could be considered as violating the intent of the law. An example might be the sole use of an English-language newspaper in an area like Miami, Florida, where there are many Hispanic publications. Although an advertiser cannot be forced to advertise in a minority media, such failure will be a consideration in a discrimination hearing, as would be a policy of using as human models members of only one sex, race, or other group (it is not necessary, however, to have an exact percentage of the various groups in the local population).

Discrimination in federally subsidized housing projects is prohibited under Title VI, Civil Rights Act of 1964, which states, "No person in the United States shall, on the ground of race, color, or national origin, be excluded from participation in, be denied the benefits of, or be subject to discrimination under any program or activity receiving federal financial assistance."

Federal Farm Credit Administration (FFCA) *See* **Farm Credit System**.

Federal Financial Institutions Examinations Council (FFIEC) A council of federal regulatory agency representatives organized to promote uniformity among commercial banks, savings associations, and credit unions. Members include the Federal Reserve System, Office of the Comptroller of the Currency, FDIC, Office of Thrift Supervision, and National Credit Union Administration.

Federal Home Loan Banks (FHLB) A class of federally chartered savings associations set up as 12 regional Federal Home Loan Banks to provide a credit reserve for its members, established in 1932. The banks functioned under the supervision of the Federal Home Loan Bank Board until 1989, when the board was abolished and replaced by the Federal Housing Finance Board.

Federal Home Loan Mortgage Corporation (FHLMC) (*Corporación Federal de Préstamos Hipotecarios para Viviendas*) *See* **Freddie Mac**.

Federal Housing Administration (FHA) A federal agency established in 1934 under the National Housing Act to encourage improvement in housing standards and conditions, to provide an adequate home-financing system through the insurance of housing mortgages and credit, and to exert a stabilizing influence on the mortgage market. FHA was the government's response to a lack of quality housing, excessive foreclosures, and a building industry that collapsed during the Depression.

Important achievements of the FHA program include the general acceptance of the fully amortized loan, standardization of appraisal processes, and better planning and land use by developers. FHA loans have traditionally played an important part in home financing through the use of high loan-to-value ratios combined with a small down payment requirement and are popular with borrowers with less than perfect credit. Until 2008, FHA loans received heavy competition from conventional mortgages, which offered high loan-to-value ratios backed by private mortgage insurance (such as MGIC). FHA mortgage loans are limited by loan amounts.

FHA, which is part of HUD, neither builds homes nor lends money directly. Rather it insures loans on real property, including condominiums, made by approved lending institutions. If the homeowner defaults on the mortgage, the lending institution does not incur any significant losses because FHA has insured the lender against that risk. This is accomplished under a mutual mortgage insurance plan.

Most of the popular FHA programs require the borrower to pay two mortgage insurance premiums (MIPs), one at closing and an annual premium, which is paid monthly. Because the upfront MIP covers the life of the loan, a refund is possible if loan payoff is made early, but it must be requested. However, the annual premium is no longer subject to a refund. By 2010, FHA-insured loans constituted more than 30 percent of all mortgages.

Insurance claims on defaulted loans: In 1987, the FHA altered its policy for payment of its insurance in the event of a loan default. The "claims without conveyance" rule allows the mortgagee to submit a claim for mortgage insurance benefits without granting title to the FHA to the property. The FHA sets an "adjusted market value" for the property in the event of foreclosure. When the lender takes title to the property, it can claim only the difference between the FHA's adjusted market value and the amount of the insured commitment. An additional rule requires the lender to seek a deficiency judgment against the defaulted borrower.

Properties that the FHA takes title to in foreclosure actions generally resell in one of two ways: (1) as is on a bid basis or (2) at a market price as set by the FHA after the property has been rehabilitated. With the increase in foreclosures that resulted from economic declines in several sections of the country, the FHA resorted to auction sales of some of its properties. At these auctions, a potential homebuyer could be prequalified for a loan to assist in bidding successfully.

Interest rates and loan amounts: Prior to 1982, the maximum allowable interest rate for an FHA-insured loan was set by the HUD secretary. Since 1982, the FHA allowed rates to be set at whatever level was agreed on between borrower and lender. However, the practice of requiring a loan discount remains as a negotiable cost of borrowing money and may be paid for by either the buyer or the seller.

The maximum loan amount available on a specific property is based on the purchase price or the FHA-appraised value, whichever is less, and varies from one part of the country to another. The FHA recognizes VA appraisals but not conventional appraisals. FHA requires the real estate sales contract to include a contingency provision (usually in the form of an addendum) that, should the property appraise for less than the sales price, the seller agrees to refund the buyer's good-faith deposit and cancel the contract if the buyer does not wish to complete the transaction.

First and second mortgages cannot exceed the applicable loan-to-value ratio or maximum mortgage limit for that area. Payments on the second mortgage must be collected monthly and must be within the mortgagor's reasonable ability to pay. Also, the second mortgage must permit prepayment without penalty and may not provide for a balloon payment before ten years. The borrower who does not obtain secondary financing must be prepared to pay the difference in cash at closing.

For most programs, the borrower must pay for all prepaid items at closing—usually the escrow requirements for property tax and hazard insurance. Allowable closing costs may no longer be added to the sales price to calculate maximum loan amount. The borrower must provide 3 percent of the sales price to be used toward the down payment and closing costs; the seller is allowed to contribute up to 6 percent of the sales price toward discount points, prepaids, and other allowable closing costs. The borrower must provide evidence of the needed funds before FHA will make its commitment to insure the loan. There is no prohibition against placing secondary financing on the property after the FHA mortgage is closed and FHA has issued FHA mortgage insurance to the lender.

F

Loan fees and discount points: An FHA loan applicant is allowed to pay a loan origination fee of not more than 1 percent of the amount borrowed (or 2½ percent for construction loans when the lender makes inspection and partial disbursements during building construction).

Programs: Title I FHA loans are granted for home improvements, alterations, and repairs. These loans are for relatively low amounts with a repayment term of no longer than 7 years and 32 days.

Title II FHA loans are granted for construction or purchase of a home. They may also be obtained to refinance existing mortgage debt. There are a number of Title II programs, but the most popular are the following:

- Section 203(b): The most widely used program is available for owner-occupants purchasing or refinancing one- to four-family homes; the maximum loan-to-value ratio is 98.75 percent.
- Section 203(v)—Veteran: Qualified veterans may purchase one- to four-family homes as owner-occupants with a loan-to-value ratio that may exceed 97 percent due to a slightly lower down payment (the "required investment") than the standard 203(b) loan requires.
- Section 203(k): A rehab loan for the acquisition and rehabilitation and repair of single-family homes. Providing one loan that consolidates both acquisition and repair costs enables qualified buyers to avoid high interest rates and the short amortization periods of rehab loans.
- Section 234: Condominiums being built or converted are covered under this program, which in most respects is similar to the basic 203(b) program. Purchasers use 203(b) for purchase of an existing condominium unit in an FHA-approved project. To obtain an FHA loan in a condominium, it is necessary that the condominium itself be FHA-approved.
- Section 245: The graduated-payment mortgage permits lower monthly payments in the early years of the mortgage for the purpose of offering easier qualification of homebuyers. Qualification of the borrower's income is based on the first year's monthly payment amounts rather than payments of an amortized loan. The lower initial monthly payments rise sufficiently to allow a set percentage of increase each succeeding year until the monthly payment reaches a level that will fully amortize the remaining balance of the loan. Unpaid interest resulting from the lower early monthly payments is added to the principal balance each year, resulting in "negative amortization." The FHA offers five different payment plans, with Plan III being the most popular.
- Section 251: Adjustable-rate loans (ARMS) are loans in which the interest rate will probably change at some future date. FHA offers two ARM programs: the standard

one-year ARM and the hybrid adjustable-rate programs. The lifetime cap of the FHA adjustable mortgage is no more than 5 percent over the initial start rate, so the FHA ARM can take five years before reaching its maximum rate.

Assumptions: FHA loans may be assumed subject to certain restrictions, such as a due-on-sale clause, which prohibits loan assumptions. A simple assumption allows the loan to be assumed without notification to the FHA. There is no change in the interest rate or underlying conditions of the loan, and the original borrower remains fully liable for repayment in the event of a subsequent default. Further, the original obligor can be reported to national credit bureaus as the delinquent party in the event of a delinquency or a default.

A *formal* assumption requires FHA approval of the new buyer, the loan must be current, the new buyer must meet FHA qualification standards for creditworthiness, and the new buyer must agree to the loan assumption. If these conditions are met, the loan can be assumed with no change in the interest rate or underlying conditions, and the original borrower (the seller) is released from further liability.

FHA has three different rules on loan assumptions, depending on the date of the original loan application. For loans originated before December 1, 1986, the mortgagor can choose between a simple or formal assumption. For loans originated between December 1, 1986, and December 15, 1989, there is a restriction on early assumptions, after which time they can be freely assumed. For owner-occupants, the time is 12 months; for investors, the assumption cannot be made without approval during the first 24 months after execution of the mortgage. After these periods, loans are assumable without prior approval. If the loan is not in default after five years, the seller is automatically released from liability.

For loans originated on or after December 15, 1989, the creditworthiness of the new buyer must be ensured prior to conveyance of title in *all* assumptions. The due-on-sale rules apply to transactions using a contract for deed, lease option, or a wraparound note.

Commitments: A developer or a builder sometimes seeks an FHA commitment to insure the mortgages on a project to be constructed. In such cases, the FHA may give a conditional commitment to insure that is dependent on the structures or houses being satisfactorily completed according to FHA standards as verified by FHA inspection. Some commitments depend on the sale of the building to a purchaser satisfactory to the FHA. (*See* **closing costs**, **commitment**, **conventional loan**, **debenture**, **graduated-payment mortgage [GPM]**, **in-service loan**, **inspection**, **minimum property requirement**, **mutual mortgage insurance fund**, **private mortgage insurance [PMI]**, **Veterans Affairs [VA] loan**.)

Federal Housing Finance Agency (FHFA)   An independent federal agency created in 2008 to provide supervision, regulation, and housing mission oversight of Fannie Mae, Freddie Mac, and the 12 Federal Home Loan Banks.

Federal Housing Finance Board (FHFB)   A board created to oversee mortgage lending by the 12 regional Federal Home Loan Banks. In 2008, it was replaced by the Federal Housing Finance Agency (FHFA). *See* **Federal Housing Finance Agency (FHFA)**.

federal land bank (FLB)   A privately owned cooperative organization administered by the Farm Credit Administration to provide low-cost, long-term loans to farmers and livestock corporations that belong to the Federal Land Bank Association.

federally related transactions   Any sale transaction that ultimately involves a federal agency in either the primary or secondary mortgage market. Under FIRREA, state-certified or state-licensed appraisers must be used for certain loans in federally related transactions.

Federal National Mortgage Association (FNMA)   (*Asociación Nacional Hipotecaria Federal*)   The original name of Fannie Mae. (*See* **Fannie Mae**.)

Federal Reserve System ("the Fed")   (*Sistema de la Reserva Federal*)   The nation's central bank created by the Federal Reserve Act of 1913. Its purpose is to help stabilize the economy through the judicious handling of the money supply and credit available in this country. The system functions through a seven-member Board of Governors (appointed by the President) and 12 Federal Reserve District Banks, each with its own president. The system sets policies and works with the privately owned commercial banks.

Revised in 2005, the Fed's responsibilities include:

- Influencing money and credit conditions in the economy
- Supervising and regulating banks and other important financial institutions
- Maintaining the stability of the financial systems
- Providing certain financial services to the US government, financial institutions, and overseeing the nation's payment systems

The Fed uses four tools to influence and stabilize the economy:

1. Having the authority to create money, the Fed determines the rate of growth in the nation's money supply and attempts to match the increase with the growth in the nation's economy. An oversupply of money creates inflationary pressures; an undersupply can cause recession.
2. The Fed regulates reserve requirements for all depository institutions offering transaction (checking) accounts. Depository institutions must keep a specified percent of their deposits in a noninterest-bearing reserve held by the Fed. This reserve is a cushion and can be used by the Fed for short-term loans to its members.
3. The Fed sets the "discount rate" of interest, which is the rate it charges for loans to its members. The Fed lends money to members only on an emergency basis—that is, when members have a need for cash. The money cannot be used for working capital, so a change in the discount rate serves more as a signal to the banking community than as an indicator of cost of funds.
4. Open market operations can be undertaken. This strategy encompasses the movement of cash into or out of the commercial banks through the buying or selling of government bonds. When the Fed buys bonds, the banks receive an influx of cash used to make more loans and thus lift the economy.

In addition to its important role in stabilizing the economy, the Fed is responsible for supervision of the Truth-in-Lending Act, the Equal Credit Opportunity Act, Home Mortgage Disclosure Act and the Community Reinvestment Act.

The fact that the Fed is empowered to place a 2 percent surcharge on loans to member banks that borrow frequently from it is an illustration of how the agency can regulate lending practices. *See* **Emergency Economic Stabilization Act of 2008 (ESSA), Appendix E**.

federal revenue stamp   A documentary transfer tax that, up until 1968, was levied by the federal government upon the transfer of title to real property and payment was evidenced by red stamps placed on the document. After repeal of this federal tax, many states instituted their own conveyance or transfer taxes. (*See* **transfer tax [conveyance fee]**.)

federal savings and loan association   A savings and loan institution that is federally chartered and privately owned by shareholders (stock savings and loan) or depositors (mutual savings and loan), previously regulated by the Office of Thrift Supervision and now by the Federal Reserve Board. Deposits are insured by the Federal Deposit Insurance Corporation (FDIC). (*See* **savings and loan association [S&L]**.)

Federal Savings and Loan Insurance Corporation (FSLIC)   An institution that performed a function similar to that of the Federal Deposit Insurance Corporation (FDIC) by insuring deposits in federal savings and loan associations. The FSLIC was dissolved by FIRREA in 1989, and its insolvent insurance fund transferred to the new Savings Association Insurance Fund (SAIF) under the management of FDIC.

federal tax lien   A lien that attaches to real property either if the federal estate tax is not paid or the taxpayer has violated the federal income tax or payroll tax laws.

Under the Federal Tax Lien Act of 1966, a junior federal tax lien is not divested by a nonjudicial foreclosure proceeding (under a power of sale) taken under state law unless the federal government consents in writing to the sale or unless written notice of the proposed sale is given, thus providing the federal government an opportunity to collect its lien from the proceeds of the sale. Accordingly, most attorneys obtain a current title report before commencing a nonjudicial foreclosure in order to ascertain that there are no outstanding federal tax liens on the subject property.

A federal tax lien is generally subject to the interest of purchasers and creditors who record their interest before notice of the federal tax lien is recorded. As with other liens, a federal tax lien is subject to liens of real property taxes and special assessments owed to the state or county, whether they are recorded before or after notice of the federal tax lien is recorded.

If the taxpayer becomes insolvent, the federal government follows different and more complex rules, claiming the priority of its lien over previously recorded liens.

Under federal tax law, providing for the priority of federal tax liens is contingent on public indexing of the liens at Internal Revenue Service offices for the area in which the property is located. An index of liens affecting personal property is maintained in the district office for the area in which the taxpayer resides at the time of the filing of the notice of a lien.

A tenant in common could be surprised to find the real property sold or partitioned to satisfy a federal tax lien against a cotenant in common. This potential threat of partition is also a concern to a purchaser in a time-sharing project.

Under federal tax law, where the estate elects special (lower) valuation for estate taxes with respect to a "family farm" or certain real property used in a family business, a special tax lien attaches to that property for ten years or more so that, if the property is sold during that period, the taxes "saved" as a result of that special valuation will be "recaptured." (*See* **recapture**.)

Federal Trade Commission (FTC)   A federal agency created to investigate and eliminate unfair and deceptive trade practices or unfair methods of competition in interstate commerce. Deceptive practices generally include such actions as an affirmative misstatement of fact—an express statement that is false, as well as any false implication that reasonably may be drawn from such a statement. This could encompass a developer's misleading representations of his or her intent to resell property for purchasers. Unfair practices generally include any practice in which the following three elements are present: (1) the practice offends public policy; (2) it is immoral, unethical, oppressive, or unscrupulous; and/or (3) it causes injury to consumers. Unfair practices also include such actions as inducing purchasers to buy through scare tactics or high-pressure gimmicks. The FTC enforces the federal Truth-in-Lending laws, monitors the Equal Credit Opportunity Act, the Fair Credit Reporting Act, and the Home Mortgage Disclosure Act. (*See* **antitrust laws**.)

federal underwriters   Four federal agencies—Fannie Mae, Ginnie Mae, Freddie Mac, and FAMC—are authorized to issue guarantees as credit enhancement for mortgage-backed securities. The guarantees provide the purchaser of a mortgage-backed security with further assurance of the return of principal and interest on a timely basis. Each agency differs in its scope of authority to issue guarantees, the mortgages it can guarantee, and the markets it serves.

fee appraiser   A professional who furnishes appraisal services for a fee, rendering an appraisal of a parcel of real property and typically submitting an appraisal report. Appraisal services include valuation, review, or consultation. (*See* **review appraiser**.)

fees for service   An alternative to traditional brokerage fees. The real estate service charges are "unbundled" and the consumer only pays for services actually used.

fee simple   (*pleno dominio*)   The maximum possible estate one can possess in real property. A fee simple estate is the least limited interest and the most complete and absolute ownership in land; it is of indefinite duration, freely transferable, and inheritable. Fee simple title is sometimes referred to as "the fee." All other estates may be created from it, which means that all other estates must be something less than fee simple (such as life estates or leaseholds). Any limitations that exist on the control and use of the land held in fee do not result from the nature of the estate itself but are founded on public or private controls governing the use of the land (zoning ordinances and building codes or restrictions and conditions). The fee may also be encumbered, either by voluntary (e.g., mortgage) or involuntary (e.g., tax lien) encumbrances. Such encumbrances tend to reduce the value of the fee interest. (*See* **freehold**, **restriction**.)

fee simple defeasible   An estate in land in which the holder has a fee simple title subject to being divested upon the happening of a specified condition; also called a **qualified fee** or a *defeasible fee*. There are two categories of fee defeasible estates—fee simple determinable and fee simple subject to a condition subsequent. The term *fee simple determinable* implies that the duration of the estate can be determined from the deed itself. This is not true of a fee simple subject to a condition subsequent, in which case the estate's duration depends on the grantor's independent choice of whether to terminate the estate.

     A fee simple determinable is an estate in real property that exists "so long as," "while" or "during the period" that a certain prescribed use continues. Such use is described in the grant of conveyance. For example, a conveyance to a university "so long as" the real estate is used for educational purposes would give the university title, provided the granted land is used as prescribed. If, at some future time, the university were to stop using the property for educational purposes, title would revert to the original grantor if living or to the heirs if the grantor is deceased. A fee simple determinable automatically ends when the purpose for which it has been prescribed terminates. Upon the grant of a fee simple determinable, there remains in the grantor a possibility of reverter.

     A fee simple subject to a condition subsequent, on the other hand, is an estate conveyed "provided that," "on the condition that," or "if" it is used for a specific purpose. If it is no longer used for that purpose, it reverts to the original grantor or his heirs. This type of estate is much the same as a fee determinable, except that in a fee determinable conveyance the words are of duration while a fee condition subsequent refers strictly to a specific condition. In addition, unlike a fee determinable, when fee condition subsequent property is no longer used for its prescribed purpose, the original grantor (or heirs) must physically retake possession of the property within a reasonable period of time after the breach (i.e., the grantor must exercise his or her right of reentry). Any transaction involving a fee simple defeasible estate should be referred to an attorney for a professional opinion. (*See* **possibility of reverter**, **right of reentry**.)

fee tail   A freehold estate that has the potential of continuing forever but will necessarily cease if and when the first fee tail tenant's lineal descendants die out. It is an estate in which the right of inheritance is limited to a fixed line of succession, consisting of the direct "issue of the body," or blood relatives. Under common law, words of inheritance and procreation were needed to create a fee tail estate—that is, "Harry Hopes and the heirs of his body." The property is said to be "in entail." This type of estate is opposed to a fee simple estate, which can pass to both collateral and lineal heirs and has been abolished in most states.

F

felony   A serious crime punishable by imprisonment in a state or federal prison. Violation of certain real estate laws are classified as felonies. (*See* **misdemeanor**.)

felt joint cover   A covering of tightly woven wool treated with a bitumen tar derivative that prevents seepage at the joints of plumbing pipes.

feudal system   An ancient system of land ownership. Under old English common law, the government or king held title to all lands. The individual was merely a tenant whose rights of use and occupancy of real property were held at the sufferance of an overlord. In the 17th century, the feudal system evolved into the allodial system of individual ownership. (*See* **allodial system**.)

FHA   *See* **Federal Housing Administration (FHA)**.

FHLMC   *See* **Freddie Mac**.

FIABCI   Abbreviation for the Fédération Internationale de Biens Consuls Immobliérs, the former name for IREF, the International Real Estate Federation.

FICO scores   Mathematical scores developed by the Fair Isaac Company and used by credit bureaus and lenders to evaluate the risk associated in lending money. FICO scores range from 450 to 850; the lower the score, the higher the risk. Each credit bureau—Experian, TransUnion, and Equifax—uses the score differently based on the information that the credit bureau maintains. All three FICO scores affect how much and what loan terms lenders offer a consumer, and as the information changes, the credit scores change. Improving FICO scores can help qualify the consumer for better rates from lenders. FICO is regulated by the Fair Credit Reporting Act (FCRA). (*See* **credit scores**, **Fair Credit Reporting Act [FCRA]**.)

fictitious company name   A business name other than that of the person under whom the business is registered, for example "XYZ Real Estate" or "Greenfields Realty." Also called an **assumed name**. Most state license laws require such brokerage offices operating under an assumed name to be jointly registered under the supervising broker's name and the business's fictitious name, such as "Elmo Schwartz, broker, also known as Bonanza Real Estate Brokers." Most states require the filing of a fictitious name certificate or a trade name registration. (*See* **DBA**.)

fidelity bond   Also known as a *surety bond*, a fidelity bond is purchased by an employer to cover employees who are entrusted with sums of money or are responsible for valuable assets. Such bonded persons are required by the bonding or insurance company to carry out their duties and responsibilities effectively and honestly. Property managers and escrow companies often are required to post a fidelity bond.

fiduciary   A relationship that implies a position of trust and confidence wherein one person is usually entrusted to hold or manage property or money for another. The term *fiduciary* describes the faithful relationship owed by an attorney to a client or by a broker (and salesperson) to a principal. The fiduciary owes complete *allegiance* to the client. The fiduciary owes to a principal the duties of loyalty, obedience, and full disclosure; the duty to use skill, care, and diligence; and the duty to account for all monies. When an agent breaches any of these fiduciary duties, the principal can usually bring civil action for money damages, sue to impress a constructive trust upon any secret profit, or compel the agent to forfeit any compensation.

Because of the close personal relationship between broker (agent) and seller or buyer (principal), the broker often learns certain confidential information about the client and/or financial situation of the principal. In most states, this information cannot be disclosed by a broker, even after the transaction is completed and the fiduciary relationship terminated. One reason it is so difficult to represent both parties in a real estate transaction is the conflict of interest that arises for the broker, who has a duty to keep confidential that information learned from the principal and also a duty to disclose all pertinent information to the principal. (*See* **agency, agent, broker, buyer's broker, dual agency [limited agency], subagent**.)

file To place an original document on public record. Most legal documents are recorded (i.e., kept in the form of a literal copy produced by electrostatic process and microfilm). After recordation, the original is returned to the person noted on the top left portion of the document. Documents relating to registered property (Torrens system) are filed with the registrar of titles, who retains the document. (*See* **recording, registrar [recorder], Torrens system**.)

filled land An area where depositing or dumping dirt, gravel, or rock has raised the grade. The seller, and thus the broker, of such land would, under most circumstances, have a duty to disclose to the buyer the fact that the property is on filled land. Failure to disclose such information would make the seller and the broker liable if an unaware buyer subsequently suffered damages (for example, if the land were to slip or subside during construction) and sought to rescind the transaction upon discovery that the property is on filled land. This disclosure rule does not apply if it is obvious that the entire community is on filled land that has been used for a relatively long time without any adverse effects. (*See* **caveat emptor**.)

filtering down process The process by which housing units formerly occupied by middle- and upper-income families decline in quality and value and become available to lower-income occupants.

finance charge The total of all costs imposed directly or indirectly by the creditor and payable directly or indirectly by the customer, as defined by the federal Truth in Lending Act. (*See* **annual percentage rate [APR], Truth in Lending Act**.)

finance fee A mortgage brokerage fee to cover the expenses incurred in placing a mortgage with a lending institution; a mortgage service charge or origination fee. The finance fee is sometimes stated in points, with each point being equal to 1 percent of the loan amount (for example, 2 percent would become two points). (*See* **origination fee, points**.)

financial institution An intermediary organization that obtains funds through deposits and then lends those funds to earn a return. Some prime financial institutions are savings and loan associations, commercial banks, credit unions, and mutual savings banks.

Financial Institutions Reform, Recovery, and Enforcement Act (FIRREA) (*Ley de Reforma, Recuperación y Ejecución de las Institutiones Financieras*) A comprehensive law passed in 1989 to provide guidelines for the regulation of financial institutions. Referred to as the "savings and loan bailout bill," FIRREA created the Savings Association Insurance Fund (SAIF) and the Bank Insurance Fund (BIF), both of which are administered by the restructured Federal Deposit Insurance Corporation (FDIC). FIRREA also created the now dissolved Resolution Trust Corporation (RTC) to manage the assets of insolvent savings and loan associations. One part of the law created the Appraisal Foundation and requires the use of state-certified or state-licensed appraisers to appraise properties involving a federally insured or federally regulated industry.

financial statement A formal statement of the financial status and net worth of a person or company, setting forth and classifying assets and liabilities as of a specified date. Sometimes the requester of the financial statement may require that it be certified by a recognized certified public accounting firm. The recent trend among mortgage bankers is to require a certified financial statement from every loan applicant.

Under some state subdivision laws, the subdivider must present a current financial statement when registering a proposed subdivision. Financial statements are required by HUD in interstate land sales in accordance with the Interstate Land Sales Full Disclosure Act. Such statements must be certified if the subdivision is over a certain value and number of lots.

F

F

financing   That part of the purchase price for a property exclusive of the down payment and typically secured by mortgages, deeds of trust, contracts for deed, and the like. Typical sources for financing are banks, savings and loan associations, insurance companies, credit unions, mortgage bankers, and private parties. According to the Federal Reserve Board, mortgage credit represents the largest single category of credit outstanding in the United States (that is, after the debt of the federal government).

Normally, several instruments are used in financing real estate. Two of them are a note, which evidences the obligation of the borrower to repay, and the security instrument, which may be a mortgage or deed of trust. In the case of a purchase under a contract for deed, there is no note. The cost to a borrower in obtaining financing varies directly with the availability of lenders seeking investments in real estate. (*See* **contract for deed, deed of trust, mortgage**.)

Since the 1980s, alternative financing devices such as mortgages involving a renegotiable rate, graduated payment, wraparound, flexible loan insurance plan, shared appreciation, buydown, and a greater use of syndication have been utilized in lieu of traditional debt financing. Some sellers have even used the lottery system to help finance the buyer's purchase of their property.

financing gap   The difference between the selling price of a home and the funds available to the potential homebuyer to purchase the home.

financing statement   A brief document (required under the Uniform Commercial Code) filed to "perfect" or establish a creditor's security interest in a chattel or other personal property. In real estate, this protects the creditor's interest in personal property that is used as security for a debt, but that becomes a fixture when it is attached to realty. For example, if Sue Brown buys a sink from the D.S. Count Department Store on a conditional sales contract and then installs the sink in her home, the sink becomes a fixture subject to all existing recorded liens. The store, however, may protect its security interest by immediately recording a copy of the financing statement (Form UCC-1), which would give it a prior secured right to the sink that would be superior to the rights of the home mortgagee in the event that Brown defaults on her home mortgage and the bank forecloses on the realty.

It is the security agreement between debtor and creditor that creates the lien. However, it is the filing of the financing statement that "perfects" the lien (i.e., makes the lien effective against later creditors). While the use of a financing statement is not applicable to real property mortgages, many mortgagees still file a financing statement in those borderline cases where there is uncertainty whether the security is to be treated as personal or real property.

When filed, a financing statement is effective for five years from the date of filing and lapses upon expiration of that period unless it is extended by a continuation statement filed any time within the six-month period preceding the expiration of the five-year period. (*See* **fixture, security agreement, Uniform Commercial Code [UCC]**.)

finder's fee   A fee paid to someone for producing either a buyer to purchase or a seller to list property; also called a *referral fee*. A finder is a person who finds, interests, introduces, or brings together parties in a deal, even though the finder has no part in negotiating the terms of the transaction.

In many states, a broker can split a commission only with another real estate licensee or with a real estate broker from another state who does not participate in any of the negotiations within the state. The question sometimes arises as to whether an owner can pay a finder's fee to an unlicensed person such as a tenant in a building for referring other prospective tenants. In accepting such a fee, the finder runs the serious risk of being classified as a real estate salesperson and found in violation of state license laws for accepting compensation without being licensed.

The federal Real Estate Settlement Procedures Act prohibits kickbacks (i.e., paying a fee or other thing of value in exchange for receiving a referral when the transaction itself involves an original federally related mortgage loan). This provision does not cover payments made for services actually rendered or performed by a finder. (*See* **middleman**.)

finish flooring   The visible interior floor surface, consisting of wood, carpet, tile, vinyl, and so on.

fire insurance   A form of property insurance covering losses due to fire, usually not as comprehensive as a homeowners' insurance policy that includes coverage against other perils, including liability. (*See* **insurance**.)

fire sprinkler system   A fire protection system activated by heat within a given building area, which automatically provides a flow of pressurized water from overhead nozzles when the temperature exceeds a certain predetermined level. To prevent the water-supply pipes from freezing, they are often filled with compressed air to hold the water behind the dry valve; the system is called a *dry system.*

fire stop   Short boards placed horizontally between the studs or the joists that decrease drafts and thus help retard fires.

fire wall   A wall constructed of fire-retardant materials, the purpose of which is to prevent the spread of fire within a building. The fire wall carries a standard rating that designates its ability to constrain fire in terms of hours.

fire yard   An area, the length of one or more sides of a building, which must be kept clear in order to facilitate the passage of fire vehicles, according to certain building codes.

firm commitment   A definite undertaking by a lender to lend a set amount of money at a specified interest rate for a certain term; also, a commitment by the FHA to insure a mortgage on certain property to a specified mortgagor (as opposed to a commitment conditioned on approval of a yet-to-be-determined mortgagor).

   A real estate broker has a duty to see that financial obligations and commitments regarding real estate transactions are in writing and express the exact agreements of the parties, and that copies of such agreements are placed in the hands of all parties involved at the time that the agreements are executed.

firm price   *See* **asking price**.

FIRREA   *See* **Financial Institutions Reform, Recovery, and Enforcement Act (FIRREA)**.

first mortgage   A mortgage on property that is superior in right to any other mortgage. It is not enough that a mortgage is the first to be executed or that the parties call it a first mortgage; absent subordination, it must be recorded first. (*See* **junior mortgage**, **second mortgage**, **subordination agreement**.)

first papers   Reference to the binder or an earnest money agreement; the initial documentation in the transaction.

first refusal, right of   *See* **right of first refusal**.

first-year depreciation   Under IRS Code Section 179, a provision that allows a sole proprietor, partnership, or corporation to full expense tangible property in the year in which it is purchased. The maximum amount available in 2011 was $500,000. Eligible property includes machinery and equipment, furniture and fixtures, and most storage facilities. Ineligible property includes buildings, income-producing properties, and various other real estate holdings.

fiscal year   A business year used for tax, corporate, or accounting purposes, as opposed to a calendar year. For example, a commonly used fiscal year is the 12-month period from July 1 through June 30 of the following year. Individuals and partnerships ordinarily use a calendar year.

five-year forecast   A long-term projection of estimated income and expense for a property based on predictable changes.

fixed expenses   Those recurring expenses that have to be paid regardless of whether the property is occupied—for example, real property taxes, hazard insurance, and debt service. These expenses contrast with operating expenses necessary to maintain the production of income from the operation of a property. (*See* **operating expenses.**)

fixed lease   *See* **gross lease.**

fixed-rate loan   A loan with the same rate of interest for the life of the loan. Until recently, the fixed-rate loan was the predominant real estate loan, but more and more consumers are taking adjustable-rate loans.

fixer-upper   A property needing a lot of repair work, usually sold below market value. (*See* **"as is."**)

fixing-up expenses   Expenses (such as painting and carpet cleaning) incurred in repairing and refurbishing a primary residence in order to facilitate its sale; no longer deductible under current rules for sales of personal residence. (*See* **residence**, **sale of.**)

F

fixture

1. An article (such as a stove, a bookcase, plumbing, track lighting, or tile) that was once personal property but has been so affixed to real estate that it has become real property. Whether an article is a fixture depends on the intention of the parties and may be determined by the manner in which the item is attached, its type and adaptability to the real property, the purpose it serves, and the relationship of the parties. Generally, the test of whether an item is a fixture as a result of its method of attachment depends more on the firmness of its installation than on the damage that might be caused by its removal. The fact that removal leaves a dirty or unpainted spot is irrelevant. Some articles are so closely associated with a structure that they are deemed to be fixtures under the constructive annexation theory (as in the case of house keys, which pass to the buyer upon sale of the property). Also called *easily removable real estate items*.

    If an article is determined to be a fixture, it passes with the property even though it is not mentioned in the deed. When a fixture is wrongfully removed from property, damages are generally measured in terms of the value of the fixture as part of the realty, not the price the fixture would command on the open market after removal.

    An exception to the fixture rule is made for trade or tenant fixtures. A business tenant can normally remove trade fixtures at the termination of the lease because the courts reason that the parties did not intend that the tenant's fixtures would become a permanent part of the building. The trade fixture rule applies only to those articles installed by the tenant, not to those installed by the landlord. If the tenant fails to remove trade fixtures, the landlord takes title to the abandoned property.

    The question of whether an item is a fixture, and thus part of the real estate, arises in several cases: in determining real estate value for tax purposes, in determining whether a real estate sale included the item or items in question, in determining whether the item in question is part of the security given by a mortgagor to a mortgagee, in determining the ownership of the item in question when the lease is terminated, and in determining coverage under a hazard insurance policy that excludes personal property items.

    The question of whether an item is a fixture has become especially important in modern transactions because of the different rules of lien priority for fixtures and nonfixtures set forth by the Uniform Commercial Code.

    A seller must deliver all fixtures unless noted as exceptions in the contract of sale. This applies to unowned fixtures as well. A broker taking a listing should inspect the premises carefully and determine whether any of the apparent fixtures, such as air conditioners or carpeting, are rented or being purchased under a UCC financing statement. The contract of sale should specify who is to own certain doubtful items, such as television antennas, solar devices, security systems, blinds, satellite dishes, and mirrors. (*See* **emblement**, **financing statement**, **personal property**, **trade fixture**.)

2. The permanent parts of a plumbing system, such as toilets and bathtubs.

fixturing period   In a commercial lease situation, the period during which the lessee enters the premises to install improvements in preparation for opening its business.

flag lot   A land parcel having the configuration of an extended flag and pole. The pole represents access to the site, which is usually located to the rear of another lot fronting a main street. A parcel may be subdivided into one or two flag lots, as shown in the following figure.

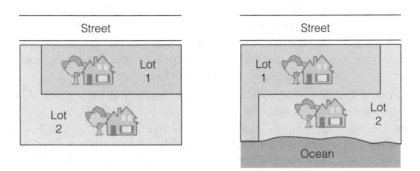

flashing   Sheet metal or other impervious material used in roof and wall construction to protect a building from seepage of water.

flat   An apartment unit or an entire floor of a building used for residential purposes.

flat lease   A lease that requires periodic, equal rental payments to be made throughout the term of the lease. Whether payments are to be made monthly, annually, or otherwise is stipulated in the contract. (*See* **gross lease**.)

flea market   A large building or open grounds, part of which is leased to individuals who use it to sell merchandise. A popular area for a flea market is a drive-in theater or large parking lot.

flexible-payment mortgage   A loan that employs a computerized method of calculating the payments required by a pledged account mortgage. Often, interest rates are initially lower than ordinary mortgages and the initial payments are below those of an amortized mortgage and may result in negative amortization.

   Under the flexible loan insurance payment mortgage, or FLIP, potential buyers can reduce their monthly payments by as much as 20 percent during the initial year of the mortgage and then graduate upward over the next five years. The buyer places the down payment in an interest-bearing savings account as pledged cash collateral. Only the lender can draw on the pledged account, and the monies can be used to supplement the buyer's monthly payment or to apply against principal if the borrower defaults or the property is sold. Private mortgage insurance covers the top 20 percent of the loan, thus reducing the lender's risk. Also called a pledged account mortgage. (*See* **negative amortization**, **variable-payment plan**.)

flip   A transaction in which one party contracts to buy a property with the intention of quickly transferring (flipping) the property over to the ultimate buyer. (*See* **back-to-back escrow**, **trading on the equity**.)

FLIP   Flexible loan insurance payment mortgage. (*See* **flexible-payment mortgage**.)

float
1. A mortgage banking term that refers to the spread of the variable interest rate on a loan; the "pegged rate"—for example, the interest on a development loan might be set at 3 percent above the local prime rate. A float can have a floor or a ceiling, such as, "in no event below 9 percent or above 15 percent"; or it can have no limitation, as in a full float. A typical float clause is this: "Three and three-fourths percent (3¾%) over and floating with Bank of Equity prime, but not less than three and three-fourths percent (3¾%) over Bank of Equity prime at the time of loan closing." (*See* **prime rate**, **variable rate**.)
2. A banking term that refers to a check that has not yet been cleared for collection. Local checks may float for two or three before clearing. This term may also refer to the bank's use of the money before the check's clearing.

floating lien   A lien, such as a mortgage, that attaches to property that is later acquired. To be a floating lien, the mortgage must contain a special clause; otherwise, the security is limited to the property existing at the time of the mortgage. (*See* **anaconda mortgage**.)

floating zone   A land area described in the text of zoning regulations but not placed on the zoning map until a developer applies for rezoning.

flood insurance   Subsidized, federally backed insurance offered through private insurance companies that through an agreement with the Federal Insurance and Mitigation Administration may sell and service federal flood insurance policies. Flood insurance provides coverage for damage from floods, tidal waves, or any rising water. Flood insurance is always a separate policy, never part of a homeowner's policy. Primary and secondary lending institutions regulated by the federal government require flood insurance on any financed property located within certain flood-prone areas as identified by the Federal Emergency Management Agency (FEMA).

The HUD-1 requires a flood certification because every property is located in a flood zone. If the certification indicates that the property is located in a Special Flood Hazard Area (SFHA) (Zones A, V, or AV), then federal banking laws mandate flood insurance. Lenders have options whether to require or not require flood insurance for properties not located in a SFHA. (*See* **flood-prone area**.)

Flood Insurance Rate Map (FIRM)   Official maps showing areas within the 100-year-flood boundary, which are designated *Special Flood Hazard Areas* and further divided into insurance risk zones. The 100-year flood refers to a flood having a 1 percent chance of being equaled or exceeded in any given year, not to a flood that occurs once every 100 years.

floodplain   The flat portions of land located along watercourses and streams, which are subject to overflow and flooding. Building in these areas is usually restricted by governmental controls.

flood-prone area   An area having a 1 percent annual chance of flooding or a likelihood that a flood may occur once every 100 years. (*See* **Flood Insurance Rate Map [FIRM]**.)

floor area ratio   The ratio of floor area to land area (often land on which the building sits). It may be expressed as a percent or decimal and is determined by dividing the total floor area of the building by the lot area. Used in zoning ordinances as a formula to regulate building volume. A restriction on the amount of building per lot area; a density restriction.

floor duty   The frequent practice in real estate brokerage offices of assigning one sales agent the responsibility for handling all telephone calls and office visitors for a specified period of time. The person "on floor" often has the opportunity to meet new clients if the caller does not ask to speak to a particular salesperson ("up call"). This person must be a licensed real estate agent, not a secretary. (*See* **cold call**.)

floor joists　Horizontal boards laid on edge resting on the beams that provide the main support for the floor. The subflooring is nailed directly to the joists. Joists are also found in ceilings.

floor load　(*carga total*)　The pounds of weight per square foot that the floor of a building is capable of supporting, if such weight is evenly distributed.

floor loan　A loan amount that is below the maximum loan approved. That part of the loan that is disbursed when the physical improvements are complete. For example, a lender may agree to make a $2,000,000 permanent loan as follows: $1,200,000 upon closing and the balance of $800,000 on a certain date—provided the premises are 75 percent leased by that date. The $800,000 gap will be funded only if the occupancy level specified is attained within the specified period after the funding of the floor loan. If this occupancy is not obtained, the developer must seek gap financing, which is very expensive because of the high risks involved. (*See* **gap financing**.)

floor plan　The architectural drawings showing the floor layout of a building, including the exact room sizes and their interrelationships. Under many state condominium laws, a developer must file a set of floor plans and elevations of a building together with a verified statement of the architect or engineer showing the layout when the developer records the declaration.

　　An examination of the floor plan is an important consideration in the appraisal valuation process. A poor floor plan or room layout could result in devaluation because of incurable functional obsolescence.

flue　An enclosed passage in a chimney or any duct or pipe through which smoke, hot air, and gases pass upward. Flues are usually made of fireclay or terracotta pipe.

flyspecking　Careful review of a document, especially an abstract of title, to discover any technical defect. Theoretically, careful searches should even disclose flyspecks.

FmHA　*See* **Farmers Home Administration (FmHA)**; now replaced by the **Rural Housing Service (RHS)**.

FNMA　*See* **Fannie Mae**.

folio　*See* **liber**.

foot-candle　A determination of light intensity. One foot-candle is the illumination measured on a surface one foot distant from the source of one candle. Therefore, the light level in an office space may be described as, say, 85 foot-candles.

footing　A concrete support under a foundation, chimney, or column that usually rests on solid ground and is wider than the structure being supported. Footings are designed to distribute the weight of the structure over the ground.

forbearance　The act of refraining from taking legal action despite the fact that payment of a promissory note in a mortgage or deed of trust is in arrears. It is usually granted only when a borrower makes a satisfactory arrangement by which the arrears will be paid at a future date. (*See* **consideration, debt relief, workout**.)

force and effect of law　A phrase referring to the fact that an administrative regulation has the same legal significance as a legislative act. When a state's real estate commission adopts a regulation implementing the licensing law, the regulation has equal validity with the licensing law itself.

forced sale　An involuntary sale resulting from the owner's failure to make payments to outstanding creditors. (*See* **distressed property**.)

force majeure　A term originally used in insurance law for a superior or irresistible force, which cannot be foreseen or controlled (a "vis major"). It refers to a clause found in many construction contracts that is designed to protect the parties when part of the contract cannot be performed or the time of performance must be delayed due to causes beyond the control of the parties that cannot be prevented by the exercise of due care and prudence. For example, a subcontractor might agree to pay $500 per day in damages for each day past December 31 that installation of the plumbing is not complete, except if the delay is caused by acts of God, labor disputes, an inability to obtain materials, fire, and the like. Thus, if a shipping strike were to cause a 30-day delay in the arrival of the plumbing lines, the subcontractor would not have to pay the $500 per day, at least through January 31.

Sometimes a force majeure clause is inserted in a ground lease to protect a tenant who is obligated to complete an improvement by a certain date from a default caused by unavoidable delays in completing the project. (*See* **act of God**.)

forecast   Estimate of the outcome of future occurrences, particularly financial statements of future periods based on such estimates.

F

foreclosure   A legal procedure whereby property used as security for a debt is sold to satisfy the debt in the event of default in payment of the mortgage note or default of other terms in the mortgage document. The foreclosure procedure brings the rights of all parties to a conclusion and passes the title in the mortgage property to either the holder of the mortgage or a third party who may purchase the realty at the foreclosure sale, free of all encumbrances affecting the property subsequent to the mortgage. There are three general types of foreclosure proceedings—judicial foreclosure, nonjudicial foreclosure, and strict foreclosure.

Judicial foreclosure, normally used in those states in which no "power of sale" is included in the mortgage document, provides that upon sufficient public notice the property may be sold by court order. If a mortgagor defaults in making payments or in fulfilling any requirements of the mortgage—such as paying taxes—the mortgagee can enforce his rights. The mortgagee's first action may be to accelerate the due date of all remaining monthly payments. The attorney for the mortgagee can then file a suit to foreclose the lien of the mortgage. Upon presentation of the facts in court, the property is ordered sold by court order. A public sale is advertised and held, and the real estate is sold to the highest bidder.

Some states allow *nonjudicial foreclosure procedures* when a power of sale is contained in a mortgage or trust deed permitting the lender (or the lender's trustee if a deed of trust is used), the right to sell the mortgaged property upon default without being required to spend the time and money involved in a court foreclosure suit. A borrower's redemption time is shortened considerably by the elimination of the statutory redemption period sometimes granted in the judicial process. Notice of default is recorded by the trustee at the county recorder's office within the jurisdiction's designated time period to give notice to the public of the intended auction. Advertisements in public newspapers state the total amount due and the date of the public sale and give publicity to the sale, not to give notice to the defaulting mortgagor. After selling the property, the mortgagee or trustee may be required to file a copy of a notice of sale or affidavit of foreclosure.

Although the judicial and nonjudicial foreclosure procedures are the prevalent practices today, it is still possible in some states for a lender to acquire the mortgaged property by a *strict foreclosure* process. After appropriate notice has been given to the delinquent borrower and the proper papers have been prepared and filed, the court establishes a specific time period during which the balance of the defaulted debt must be paid in full. If full payment is not made, the borrower's equitable and statutory redemption rights are waived, depending on the special circumstances involved in the case, and the court awards full legal title to the lender. There can be no deficiency judgment in strict foreclosure cases.

A few states permit foreclosure by entry and possession. If the mortgagee holds possession for the redemption period, the mortgage debt is deemed paid to the extent of the value of the real property.

In preparing a foreclosure proceeding, a current title report should be obtained because all prior and subsequent mortgage creditors must be joined as parties to the judicial action, and junior federal tax liens are not divested by nonjudicial foreclosure proceedings unless the federal government consents or is given notice of the sale. If the state statute of limitations pertaining to real estate actions has run out, the mortgagee is barred from exercising its power of sale.

Most states allow a defaulted mortgagor a period of time during which the property may be redeemed after the foreclosure sale. During this statutory redemption period (which may be as long as one year), the court may appoint a receiver to take charge of the property, collect rents, or pay operating expenses. If the mortgagor can raise the necessary funds to redeem the property within the statutory period, the redemption money is paid to the court. Because the mortgage debt was paid from the proceeds of sale, the mortgagor can take possession free and clear of the former defaulted mortgage. Historically, the right of redemption is inherited from the old chancery proceedings in which the court sale ended the "equitable right of redemption." In many states, a statutory redemption period is provided by state law to begin after the sale to give the mortgagor an opportunity to regain title to the land. (Note, however, that if the mortgagee accepts any payment on the mortgage debt after default and before right of redemption expires, most courts hold that the mortgagee has waived the right to complete the foreclosure.)

If redemption is not made, or if no redemption period is allowed by state law, then the successful bidder at the sale receives a deed to the real estate, sometimes called a *commissioner's deed*. This is a statutory form of deed that may be executed by a sheriff or master-in-chancery to convey such title as the mortgagor had to the purchaser at the sale. There are no warranties with such a deed; the title passes "as is," but free of the former defaulted mortgage. The purchaser obtains no better title than the mortgagor held.

Excess proceeds, if any, of the foreclosure sale after deducting expenses, are paid to the mortgagor. If the proceeds from the sale are not sufficient to repay the foreclosed debt, further action may be taken against the debtor to recover the deficiency. If the deficiency occurs in a judicial foreclosure, the court can enter a deficiency judgment, which operates as a general lien on the debtor's assets. If a deficiency results from a sale under nonjudicial foreclosure, however, the mortgagee must institute new proceedings to obtain a deficiency judgment.

There are tax consequences upon foreclosure. Under tax laws, defaulting owners are considered to have sold their property for a price equal to the unpaid debt at the time of disposition. Assuming that the mortgage balance exceeds its adjusted basis (reduced by depreciation), the defaulting owner may realize a taxable gain as a result of the foreclosure sale even though no money is received from the sale. The courts have held this rule to apply to defaults of contracts for deed as well as terminations of mortgages and trust deeds. There is also a recapture of any accelerated depreciation.

A borrower who files Chapter 13 bankruptcy can effectively interfere with the foreclosure proceedings. Once bankruptcy is filed, no creditor can take action against the debtor outside of bankruptcy court. Therefore, any foreclosure action is automatically stayed (or delayed) while the bankruptcy is pending. Also, if the foreclosure sale takes place within one year before the filing of bankruptcy, the sale can be voided if the foreclosure sales price is substantially less than the actual fair market value of the secured property.

An alternative to foreclosure is for the mortgagee to accept a deed in lieu of foreclosure from the mortgagor. This is sometimes known as a *friendly foreclosure*, because it is settled by agreement rather than by civil action. The major disadvantage to this type of default settlement is that the mortgagee takes the real estate subject to all junior liens, whereas foreclosure eliminates all such liens and the right to seek a deficiency judgment. (*See* **deed of trust**, **deficiency judgment**, **equity of redemption**, **federal tax lien**, **mortgage**, **power of sale**, **upset price**.)

foreign corporation   Any corporation organized under the laws of another state or country and not organized under a given state's laws but that conducts a portion of its business in that state. All foreign corporations that do business in a state or attempt to take, hold, demise, sell, or convey real estate there must generally qualify to do business and obtain an annual license to do business in the state. (*See* **corporation**.)

Foreign Investment in Real Property Tax Act (FIRPTA)   A federal law designed to subject nonresident aliens and foreign corporations to U.S. income tax upon their gain from the disposition of a U.S. real property interest in (1) real property located in the United States and (2) any domestic corporation that was a "United States real property holding corporation" at any time during the five-year period before disposition of the interest, or during the period the taxpayer held the interest after June 18, 1980, if shorter.

A U.S. real property corporation is a domestic or foreign corporation whose interest in U.S. real property is 50 percent or more of its total assets. The test apparently can be made on any day of the calendar year.

For purposes of computing the tax, a nonresident alien or foreign corporation is treated as being "engaged in a trade or business within the United States," and the gain is treated as "effectively connected" with the U.S. trade or business. Thus, a foreign investor is subject to tax at regular rates. Expenses attributable to the gain may be deducted.

In 2012, the gain of nonresident alien individuals for the sale of an interest in U.S. real property is taxed at 30 percent of certain capital gains during any tax year in which they are present in the United States for 183 days or more, unless a tax treaty provides for a lesser rate of taxation.

The prudent listing broker requires a foreign seller to sign an affidavit if the seller is a resident alien. Otherwise, the broker may be liable for failing to advise the buyer to withhold the required 10 percent. These rules are complicated, and brokers should develop a clear policy on handling listings and sales from foreign sellers. Some states have their own withholding rules on nonresident sellers.

foreshore land   Land that is above sea level only at low tide. Because of the action of the tide, this land alternates between wet and dry. (*See* **shoreline**.)

forfeiture   Loss of the right to something as a result of nonperformance of an obligation or condition. A forfeiture loss usually bears no true relationship to the amount of damages allowed by law, and thus there is strong public policy against enforcing forfeitures. Courts frequently refuse to enforce provisions in contracts that require the defaulting party to forfeit all amounts paid under an installment purchase contract (that is, a contract for deed). Even where forfeitures are recognized by some courts, the right to forfeiture must be specifically provided for in the contract, or else the sole remedy is rescission.

When buyers default on a mortgage or trust deed in which they hold substantial equity, forfeiture may be inequitable. In such cases, upon proper application, the court may prohibit the forfeiture and order the property sold, with the proceeds necessary to pay off the note distributed to the mortgagee and the balance paid to the mortgagor.

Real property may be acquired by forfeiture, such as when a grantor has conveyed real estate subject to a condition subsequent. Should the condition be breached, the grantor can reacquire the property by forfeiture by exercising the right of reentry.

A real estate license may be lost through forfeiture when the licensee fails to pay the appropriate renewal fees or to fulfill any continuing education requirements. (*See* **Drug Enforcement Act**, **foreclosure**, **rescission**.)

forgery   The illegal act of counterfeiting documents or making a false signature, alteration, or falsification. A forged deed is void and ineffective to transfer any title to the grantee, and recording will not make it valid. Even if a later purchaser for value acquires the property with no notice of the prior forged deed, the purchaser does not obtain valid title (i.e., the forged owner [or heirs] would still have legal title). A title insurance policy compensates such a purchaser for a loss from forgery in the chain of title.

formaldehyde   A colorless organic compound readily identifiable and measurable, with a strong, pronounced odor and found in just about every product in modern building materials, especially newly constructed or renovated properties. The EPA classifies formaldehyde as a "probable human carcinogen" and has yet to set allowable standards. Formaldehyde is one of the substances contributing to "sick building syndrome."

form contract   *See* **boilerplate**.

Formica®   A trade name for a plastic material used primarily for countertops but also for wall coverings, as a veneer for plywood panels or as a wallboard where a fire-resistive material is desirable. Similar and competitive materials are produced under other names.

for sale by owner (FSBO)   An unrepresented seller; a situation in which the owner attempts to sell a property without listing with a real estate broker. Many owners cooperate with and compensate a broker representing a buyer. The broker approaching an unrepresented seller should clarify in writing whether the broker represents the owner/seller or the buyer. This is also true when brokers buy directly for their own account. (*See* **cold call**, **courtesy to brokers**.)

forum   A place or jurisdiction where disputes are heard, such as a court, an administrative agency (e.g., a state real estate commission), or a private group (e.g., board of REALTORS® arbitration panel).

forum shopping clause   An agreement clause specifying the state that the parties agree to bring the lawsuits in and designating which state laws will apply. Typical language is as follows: "This contract shall be interpreted and construed under and governed by the laws of the State of *Home State*, and any lawsuit arising out of or because of this contract shall be brought in the state courts. The judgment of the State Supreme Court shall be final and binding on all parties hereto."

Generally, such a clause is upheld if the designated state and state statute(s) bear some relationship to the place of making or place of performing of the original contract.

foundation drain line   A pipe, usually clay, placed next to the foundation footing to aid in water runoff.

foundation wall   The masonry or concrete walls below ground level that serve as the main support for the frame structure. Foundation walls form the side walls of the basement.

four-three-two-one rule (4-3-2-1)   *See* **depth tables**.

fractional interest   A partial interest in real estate representing less than the full bundle of rights (e.g., a subleasehold interest).

fractional ownership   A vacation home ownership found typically in prime resort locations for which buyers receive a deed to the property for a certain number of months per year. The owners share in the equity appreciation and the share can be sold on the open market. Although similar to time-shares, fractional ownerships are linked to a particular home or group of homes, most often expensive homes in vacation destinations.

fractional section   In the government survey method, an irregular-size section usually larger than a quarter-section, perhaps resulting from errors in the survey or partial submersion under water.

franchise   (*franquicia*)

1. A right or privilege conferred by law, such as a state charter authorizing the formation and existence of corporations. The privilege granted to conduct certain service businesses, such as the operation of a taxicab company, is a franchise.

2. The private contractual right to operate a business using a designated trade name and the operating procedures of a parent company (the franchisor), such as McDonald's restaurant. In the financing of income property, a franchise may have value as additional security to a loan. It may also be assigned to the lender.

    Since the early 1970s, firms such as Century 21, ERA, and Realty World operate national franchised brokerages and do not own the individual offices outright; rather, they license their standardized trade names, reputations, operating procedure, and referral services to independently owned and operated brokerages. These referral services take the idea of the multiple listing service one step further, having the capability to refer prospects across town or across the country.

    The major advantages and disadvantages usually cited for real estate franchises are summarized in the following paragraphs.

    Advantages: Market identification through the use of an established trademark and trade name provided through mass advertising techniques. Also, brokers benefit from a referral system by which franchise members trade leads and listings, receive volume discounts (e.g., advertising), have easier recruitment of sales personnel, are provided with management support, and obtain good sales training programs not otherwise available.

    Disadvantages: Fees, whether initial or a royalty override, may be higher than necessary in terms of the benefits derived. There is an original identity loss that cannot be recaptured. Certain bookkeeping requirements are an imposition in the opinion of many brokers. Because of the necessity of group approval for certain activities, specifically those related to marketing, difficulties arise in agreeing on concerted unified actions. Referrals can sometimes lead to tensions between individual franchisees in large market areas. There is reduced ability to choose business associates, particularly when franchisors are more interested in quantity than quality. In some instances, a franchisor may not live up to initial promises. A trade name and trademark may turn out to be a poor substitute for a long-established local name.

    The Federal Trade Commission has adopted a business and franchise rule designed to alleviate "widespread evidence of unfair practices in connection with the sale of franchises" where the franchisee operates under the trade name of a franchisor or where the franchisor has significant control or gives significant assistance to the franchisee. The FTC rule goes far beyond many state laws governing franchises and creates a whole new set of protection for franchisees. The FTC rule was designed to curb abuses by franchisors, while allowing continued development of the franchise system that is growing into a dynamic and mature business activity.

fraud   Any form of deceit, trickery, breach of confidence, or misrepresentation by which one party attempts to gain some unfair or dishonest advantage over another. Unlike negligence, fraud is a deceitful practice or material misstatement of a material fact, known to be false, and done with intent to deceive, or with reckless indifference as to its truth, and relied on by the injured parties to their damage. For example, in response to a buyer's question regarding termites, the seller produces a falsified termite report. Not disclosing known defects or remaining "silent" can be considered fraud; in some cases, silence may not be golden.

It is important to distinguish between fraud in the inducement and fraud in the execution of a contract. If the party knows what he is signing, but the consent to sign is induced by fraud, the contract is voidable. If the party does not actually know what she is signing because of deception as to the nature of such an act, and if the deceived party did not intend to enter into a contract at all, then the contract is void. The voidable contract is binding until rescinded, whereas the void contract has no force or effect whatsoever.

The state statute of limitations for a court action based on fraud is generally computed from the date of the fraud or from the time the defrauded person could discover, or should have discovered, the fraud.

In accordance with the REALTORS® Code of Ethics, it is the duty of a REALTOR® to protect the public against fraud, misrepresentation, or unethical practices in real estate. All state licensing laws provide that a broker's license can be suspended or revoked for fraudulent acts. (*See* **misrepresentation, negligence**.)

Freddie Mac   A federally chartered corporation established as the Federal Home Loan Mortgage Corporation (FHLMC) in 1970 for the purpose of purchasing mortgages in the secondary market. Today, Freddie Mac is operating under a conservatorship that began on September 6, 2008, conducting its business under the direction of the Federal Housing Finance Agency (FHFA). Its statutory mission is to provide liquidity, stability, and affordability to the U.S. housing market by purchasing loans from lenders to replenish their supply of funds so that they can make more mortgage loans to other borrowers.

Freddie Mac's Web site itemizes the LTV ratio requirements for the conforming mortgage loans it will buy, including fixed-rate, ARMs, and 5- or 7-year balloon/reset mortgages. Freddie Mac uses the Loan Prospector, its automated underwriting service. Freddie Mac will also purchase super conforming mortgages—mortgage loans originated using higher maximum loan limits that are permitted in designated high-cost areas. The effect is to lower mortgage financing costs for borrowers located in these areas.

To raise money for the purchase of loans, Freddie Mac may sell its own securities. However, from its beginning, Freddie Mac has been a leader in the use of mortgage-backed securities for its cash. Rather than borrow money through the sale of an issue of bonds, Freddie Mac has converted blocks of mortgage loans into securities, thus passing the interest risk on to the security investor. The vehicle that Freddie Mac uses is the mortgage participation certificate (known as PCs in the financial markets), which represents an undivided interest in a large, geographically diversified group of residential mortgages and is unconditionally guaranteed by Freddie Mac. This is an "agency" type of guarantee, *not* a federal government guarantee.

In 1983, Freddie Mac introduced a variation of the mortgage-backed security called a *collateralized mortgage obligation (CMO)*. The CMO segments the cash flows from the underlying block of mortgage loans into usually four basic classes of bonds with differing maturities. (*See* **collateralized mortgage obligation [CMO], Federal Housing Finance Agency, participation certificate [PC], secondary mortgage market**.)

free and clear title   Title to real property that is absolute and unburdened by any liens, mortgages, clouds, or other encumbrances. (*See* **marketable title**.)

freehold   An estate in real property, the exact termination date of which is unknown (for a described yet indefinite period of time); those estates that have a potentially indefinite duration (fee simple) or a period of years incapable of exact determination (life estate). Freehold estates may be categorized as estates of inheritance, such as fee simple, and lesser estates for life, which extend only for the life of an individual (includes dower and curtesy). Nonfreehold (leasehold) estates can be measured in calendar time. In the old English court system, only an owner of freehold property could bring a real action (as opposed to a personal action for money damages). Thus, only freehold estates were regarded as real property. The two principal elements of a freehold estate are actual ownership of real property and unpredictable duration.

freeholder   One who owns land that he can transfer without anyone's permission; the owner of a free-hold estate. Some state license laws require a license applicant to furnish character references from at least two "freeholders" of the county where the applicant resides.

free market system auction   *See* **auction**.

freestanding building   A building containing one business rather than a row of stores or businesses with a common roof and side walls.

freeway   A divided arterial roadway for through traffic with full control of access and with grade separations at intersections.

friendly foreclosure   *See* **foreclosure**.

frieze board   A horizontal exterior band or molding, often decorated with sculpture, resting directly below the cornice.

frontage   The length of a property abutting a street or body of water—that is, the number of feet that front the street or water. Frontage differs from width, which sometimes decreases or increases as the lot extends back from the street.

frontage street   A street that is parallel and adjacent to a major street providing access to abutting properties but protected from heavy through traffic.

front-ending   Recognition of profit from a transaction before periods during which it is earned or despite significant risks that could result in subsequent losses; also called *front-loading*.

front foot   A measurement of property frontage abutting the street line or waterfront line, with each front foot presumed to extend the depth of the lot. Lots of varying depth but with the same front foot may be compared for valuation purposes by using a depth table. When a lot measurement is given, such as 75 feet by 150 feet, the first figure (75 feet) refers to the front feet. If such a lot were valued at $22,500, it would be worth $300 per front foot. The permissible size of signs often is based on the front footage. (*See* **depth tables**, **special assessment**.)

front-loading   *See* **front-ending**.

front money   A popular expression in the real estate development business that refers to the amount of hard money (cash as opposed to borrowed monies) the developer must have ready in order to purchase the land and to pay attorney fees, loan charges, and other initial expenses before actually developing the project. Front money is sometimes called *start-up costs* or *seed money*. (*See* **end money**.)

frost line   The depth of frost penetration in the soil. The frost line varies throughout the United States, and footings should be placed below this depth to prevent movement of the structure.

fructus industriales   Annual plantings and harvestable crops requiring cultivation and generally classified as personal property. (*See* **emblement**.)

fructus naturales   Uncultivated crops and perennial plantings, such as trees and bushes, generally classified as real property.

FSLIC   *See* **Federal Savings and Loan Insurance Corporation (FSLIC)**.

FTC   *See* **Federal Trade Commission (FTC)**.

full disclosure   A requirement to reveal fully and accurately all material facts, a requirement based on the theory that no fraud is committed if the purchaser has accurate and full information regarding the property to be purchased. A broker is under a legal obligation to disclose in full to a client all known, relevant facts affecting a proposed transaction. Many state subdivision and condominium laws, as well as the federal Interstate Land Sales Full Disclosure Act (concerning subdivisions), require a developer to disclose fully all material facts of a project to each prospective purchaser or lessee through required distribution of a public report. (*See* **disclosure**.)

full reconveyance   Upon payment in full of the debt secured by a deed of trust, reconveyance of the property by the trustee to the person or persons entitled thereto on written request of the grantor and the beneficiary, or upon satisfaction of the obligation secured and written request for reconveyance made by the beneficiary or his assignee. It is acknowledged by the trustee and should be recorded immediately. (*See* **deed of trust**.)

functional obsolescence   A loss in value of an improvement due to functional inadequacies, often caused by age or poor design. For example, functional obsolescence may be attributable to such things as outmoded plumbing or fixtures, inadequate closet space, poor floor plan, excessively high or low ceilings, or antiquated architecture. Thus, a warehouse with nine-foot ceilings would probably suffer a loss in value because a modern forklift could not operate in such a small space. Functional obsolescence may be incurable (as in the case of wide columns) or curable (as in the case of an inadequate electrical system replaceable with new wiring). It is generally incurable when the improvements do not conform to the neighborhood (e.g., a large, expensive home built in a neighborhood of smaller, less expensive structures). Functional obsolescence depends on the changing requirements of the buying public and thus involves features that are unfashionable or unnecessary, such as a kitchen without modern built-in cabinets and sinks. (*See* **depreciation [appraisal]**.)

funding fee   A fee paid to secure certain types of mortgage protection, such as the fee paid to the Department of Veterans Affairs for the VA to guarantee a veteran's loan.

future interest   A right of personal use or ownership not yet acquired.

G

gable   (*gablete*)   The triangular portion of an end wall rising from the level top wall under the inverted V of a sloping roof that aids water drainage. A gable can be made of weatherboard, tile, or masonry and can extend above the rafters.

gain   Profit received upon the sale of an asset. (*See* **capital gain**, **recapture**.)

gambrel roof   A curb roof, having a steep lower slope and a flatter one above, as seen in Dutch colonial architecture.

gap financing   The financing used to make up the difference between the underlying loan (floor loan) and the total amount required. Gap financing usually fills a temporary need until permanent financing is obtained, and thus is sometimes called a *bridge loan* or *swing loan*.

   Gap financing may also be used when permanent takeout financing is difficult to obtain or is too expensive. By obtaining gap financing and waiting, it is possible that more favorable terms may be reached. (*See* **rent-up**.)

gap group   Homebuyers in the moderate-income bracket who need some type of assistance or subsidy to qualify for financing.

gap in title   (*inmatriculación*)   A break in the chain of title, such as when the records do not reflect a transfer to a particular grantor. This could happen if that grantor failed to record the deed. (*See* **chain of title**.)

garden apartment   A type of multiple-unit dwelling providing for a lawn and/or garden area, typically found in a lowrise condominium project.

garnishment   A legal process designed to provide a means for creditors to safeguard their interest in a debtor's personal property that is in the hands of a third party (garnishee). The types of properties that may be garnisheed include goods or effects of the debtor concealed in the hands of third parties, debts owed to the debtor by the garnishee, wages payable by the garnishee as allowed by law and security interests of the debtor in the hands of the garnishee. The procedures usually require the service of a *writ of garnishment* upon the garnishee, who must secure all property of the creditor in order to pay the creditor-plaintiff the amount of judgment the plaintiff has recovered (postjudgment) or may recover (prejudgment). The debtor may obtain release of garnisheed property by filing a bond with the court in the amount sufficient to pay the claim of the creditor, together with costs and interest, and conditioned upon judgment in favor of the creditor.

   If garnishment takes place *after* judgment, then the property is paid over to the creditor. If the debt is disputed, then the garnishee should deposit the property with the court. Generally, the complaint and writ of garnishment are issued pursuant to the creditor's petition for process or by subsequent motion of the creditor requesting the court to insert in the process a direction to the officer serving the garnishment papers to leave a copy with the garnishee and to summon the garnishee to answer certain questions. Because of U.S. Supreme Court decisions requiring notice and a hearing prior to a garnishment of wages or property, a garnishment process that does not adhere to this requirement may be subject to challenge on constitutional grounds.

gazebo   An ornamental garden structure from which a view may be enjoyed, often constructed of light metal or wood.

general agent   One authorized by a principal to perform any and all acts associated with the continued operation of a particular job or a certain business of the principal. The essential feature of a general agency is the continuity of service, such as that provided by a property manager of a large condominium project. Most real estate brokers are treated as special agents when they are given limited authorization to act under a listing agreement but not to make decisions. (*See* **agent**, **special agent**, **universal agent**.)

general contractor   A construction specialist who enters into a formal construction contract with a developer to construct a real estate building or project. Also called the *prime contractor*, this person often negotiates individual contracts with various subcontractors who specialize in particular aspects of the building process, such as plumbing, electricity, air-conditioning, drywall, and the like. If the general contractor fails to pay them, the subcontractors can assert mechanics' liens against the entire project. Owners therefore should not make final payment to the general contractor until assurances are received that all subcontractors have been paid. To become a general contractor, one must usually pass a qualifying examination and obtain a license from the appropriate state regulatory agency. (*See* **contractor**, **holdback**, **mechanic's lien**, **performance bond**.)

general improvement district   A local public entity, such as a water district, created to perform a specific governmental function. It issues bonds and levies general taxes to carry out its functions. (*See* **special assessment**.)

general lien   The right of a creditor to have all the debtor's property, real and personal, sold to satisfy a debt. Unlike a specific lien against certain property, a general lien is directed against the individual debtors and attaches to all of their property. Common examples of general liens are judgment liens and government tax liens arising from unpaid taxes, such as income, gift, estate, inheritance, and franchise taxes. (*See* **lien**.)

general partner   A co-owner of a partnership who is empowered to enter into contracts on behalf of the partnership and be fully liable for all partnership debts. The general partner may be a corporation or an individual. In a limited partnership, the general partner is in charge of managing the partnership, has authority to act unilaterally on behalf of the partnership, is accountable to the limited partners as a fiduciary, and has full liability for the debts and obligations of the partnership. (*See* **partnership**.)

general partnership   A form of business organization in which two or more co-owners carry on a business for profit. All the owners are general partners and share a full liability for the debts and obligations of the partnership. Although advisable, a written agreement is not required. A general partnership is subject to dissolution by reason of the death, withdrawal, bankruptcy, or legal disability of any general partner. (*See* **partnership**.)

general plan   A long-range governmental program to regulate the use and development of property in an orderly fashion; a plan aimed at a well-balanced community growth.

G

In planning a subdivision, a developer might establish a general building scheme, or general plan, in order to achieve a degree of uniformity in the subdivided community. With a general plan, the subdivider will make each conveyance subject to recorded restrictions to keep the general plan in operation. This way, a lot owner can enjoin any other lot owner from violating the general plan. For example, in a subdivision generally planned for residential use only, one lot owner could prevent another one from constructing a restaurant. (*See* **equitable servitude, restriction**.)

generation X   A term used in demographics, the social sciences, and more broadly in popular culture to define persons born in the 1960s and 1970s. Born after baby boomers, Gen X-ers grew up with television and personal computers. Because they are more likely to live in a two-income household, Gen X-ers generally bought homes earlier, shortly after finishing their education. They have often been assisted in their buying by their more affluent parents. They are now buying from the baby boomers.

General Services Administration (GSA)   An independent agency organized in 1949 to manage, lease, and sell buildings belonging to the U.S. government.

geodetic survey system   Refers to the United States Coast and Geodetic Survey System, the skeleton of which consists of a network of benchmarks covering the entire country. Each benchmark is located by its latitude and longitude. The system was initiated to identify tracts of land owned by the federal government, but it has gradually been extended throughout the nation. The term *geodetic* refers to the science of measuring the earth and exactly locating points on its surface. (*See* **government survey method**.)

ghetto   A term that originated in Eastern Europe, used to describe a particular section of a city in which people of a certain race, religion, or nationality reside in heavy concentrations; sometimes used to refer to a densely populated area in which low-income families live in generally run-down housing. Lenders must be careful not to violate federal and state discrimination laws prohibiting redlining by arbitrarily denying loans in these areas. (*See* **redlining**.)

gift causa mortis   An older term for a gift made in contemplation of death, or intended to take effect only in the event of, or upon, death of the donor. For purposes of the federal estate tax for decedents dying before 1982, a gift made within three years of death was considered as a gift made in contemplation of death and, except to the extent of the annual exclusion, was automatically included in the estate of the decedent. For persons dying after 1981, this provision no longer applies, except in the case of a gift of a life insurance policy. (*See* **gift tax**.)

gift deed   A deed in which the consideration is "love and affection." Because the deed is not supported by valuable consideration, the donee (recipient of the gift) may not be able to enforce against the donor certain promises or agreements contained in the deed. A gift deed is valid unless made to defraud creditors. Usually, an attorney-in-fact is not authorized to execute a gift deed.

When a gift deed has been used to transfer real estate, a title report usually shows the possibility of an unpaid gift tax, a cloud that must then be eliminated by a clearance from tax officials. (*See* **deed**, **gift tax**.)

gift letter   A letter provided to a lender or government agency acknowledging that the money being used (often, the down payment) to purchase real property was a gift from a relative and carries no obligation to repay. Some lenders restrict the use of gift letters, depending on the type of loan.

gift tax   A graduated federal tax paid by a donor upon making a gift. For purposes of the gift tax, a gift is defined as the transfer by an individual of any type of property for less than adequate consideration in money or money's worth ("detached and disinterested generosity"). There is an exclusion of $13,000 per donor, per donee (recipient of the gift), per year, which can be deducted by the donor from the taxable value of gifts to each donee. These gifts are not tax-deductible, however.

For example, each year, a mother may give each of her five children a gift of $11,000. Her husband can also give $11,000 to each of their five children.

Tax laws are changing, so for specific information, a knowledgeable tax attorney or account should be consulted.

Federal tax law also contains an annual exclusion for gifts made for the purpose of paying medical expenses or educational expenses (specifically, tuition). Note that payments for room and board do not qualify. (*See* **annual exclusion for gift tax**.)

GI loan   Government-guaranteed loan. (*See* **Veterans Affairs [VA] loan**.)

Ginnie Mae   A wholly owned government corporation within the U.S. Department of Housing and Urban Development (HUD). Ginnie Mae was created in 1968 when the Federal National Mortgage Association (FNMA), now Fannie Mae, was partitioned into two separate corporations. Fannie Mae continues to support the conventional market. Ginnie Mae guarantees the principal and interest payments from mortgage-backed securities (MBS) that are collateralized by cash flows from insured or guaranteed loans obtained through the Federal Housing Administration (FHA), Department of Veterans Affairs Home Loan Program for Veterans (VA), Office of Public and Indian Housing (PIH), and the U.S. Department of Agriculture Rural Development (RD).

By ensuring that payments will be made, Ginnie Mae brings together global capital markets to the U.S. housing markets. Ginnie Mae does not purchase mortgages and it does not buy, sell, or issue MBS, and it cannot issue debt securities or hold an MBS investment portfolio. Ginnie Mae is self-financed through various fees.

Because Ginnie Mae cannot purchase mortgage loans to create pools, it works with loan poolers, usually large financial institutions, who assemble approved pools. Loans acceptable into a Ginnie Mae pool are only those approved by Ginnie Mae and are limited to FHA, VA, and certain FmHA loans. (*See* **guaranteed mortgage certificate [GMS]**, **mortgage-backed security [MBS]**, **tandem plan**.)

girder   A heavy wooden or steel beam supporting the floor joists and providing the main horizontal support for the floor.

GNMA   *See* **Ginnie Mae**.

going-concern value   The value existing in an established business property as compared with the value of selling the real estate and other assets of a concern whose business is not yet established, usually related to the value in use concept, as opposed to the market value concept. The term takes into account the goodwill and earning capacity of a business. Sometimes used in the test of determining solvency or insolvency or in computing value for purposes of corporate merger or issuance of stock.

good consideration A consideration founded on love and affection for kindred by blood or marriage, which may be found in a gift deed. However, a good consideration is not sufficient to support a contract. For example, if a father promises in writing to give his farm to his daughter on her 21st birthday and later changes his mind, the daughter would have no legal basis to sue for breach of contract because she had not given any valuable consideration to support his promise. (*See* **consideration**, **gift deed**.)

good faith Bona fide; an act is done in good faith if it is in fact done honestly, whether negligently or not. The recording laws are designed to protect a good-faith purchaser. Most antidiscrimination laws require a broker to transmit all good-faith offers to lease or buy. Many states add a requirement of good faith for a person to acquire title to someone else's real property by adverse possession.

Sometimes an act done in "bad faith" is punishable as a crime. For instance, if an investor-borrower applies for an owner-occupant loan and lies about his intent to occupy, this type of falsehood is punishable as a misdemeanor under the National Banking Act. (*See* **bona fide**, **recording**.)

good-faith estimate (GFE) A preliminary accounting of expected closing costs. The Real Estate Settlement Procedures Act requires the lender to promptly give loan applicants a good-faith estimate of closing costs within three business days of the completed loan application. The application is not considered complete until the property is actually identified. The purpose of the GFE is to provide enough information for the consumer to shop around for the best loan and terms. The GFE also regulates fees that may or may not change prior to closing. For example, changing lender fees, such as points, origination fees, underwriting, and loan processing fees trigger a new three-day waiting period. A three-day waiting period is also triggered when fees increase more than 10 percent by a lender-selected settlement provider or when the borrower selects the provider from the lender's list. Fees over which the lender has no control, such as those for escrow and title insurance, may increase without triggering a waiting period. (*See* **HUD-1 form**.)

good funds State law requiring assurance by escrow companies of receipt of loan funds (deposit or electronic wiring) prior to closing a transaction, thus eliminating a practice in which lenders obtained several days of float on the loan proceeds.

goodwill An intangible, salable asset arising from the reputation of a business; the expectation of continued public patronage; including other intangible assets like trade name and going-concern value. When a business is sold, the sales price often reflects its goodwill value. Goodwill is not a depreciable asset, although it is a capital asset. Thus, a seller prefers to place a high value on the goodwill (and obtain a capital gain), while a buyer prefers a lower value (because goodwill cannot be depreciated). If goodwill is considered in a market value appraisal, the appraiser should specifically identify it. (*See* **business opportunity**, **condemnation**.)

government forces In appraisal theory, one of four forces affecting real estate value (e.g., government controls and regulations, public services, zoning, and building codes). The other three forces are environmental, economic, and social.

government lot *See* **quarter-section**.

Government National Mortgage Association (GNMA) (*Asociación Gubernamental Hipotecaria Nacional*) *See* **Ginnie Mae**.

government patent The original U.S. land grant that conveyed government-owned land to the people.

government-sponsored enterprises (GSE)   A financial services corporation established and chartered by the U.S. Congress for public policy purposes. Although they carry the implicit backing of the U.S. government, GSE securities are not backed by the full faith and credit of the federal government. Examples include Fannie Mae, Freddie Mac, the Federal Home Loan Bank System, and the Farm Credit System.

government survey method   A system of land description that applies to much of the land in the United States (over 30 states), particularly in the western states; also called the **geodetic** or **rectangular survey system**. It is based on pairs of principal meridians and base lines, with each pair governing the surveys in a designated area. Principal meridians run north and south, and base lines extend east and west. The government survey method was designed to create a checkerboard of identical squares covering a given area. The largest squares measure 24 miles on each side and are called *quadrangles*. Each quadrangle is further divided into 16 squares called *townships*, whose four boundaries each measure six miles. A column of townships extending north-south is called a *range* and is numbered numerically east and west according to its distance from the principal meridian. There are now 36 principal meridians located in different parts of the United States.

Because of the curvature of the earth, the north-south lines, or range lines, converge as they extend northward. To keep them as close to six miles apart as possible and thus preserve the square shape of the township, the lines are laid out for approximately 24 miles and then adjusted so that they are again six miles apart. (*See* **correction lines**.)

A township is six miles square and contains 36 square miles. Townships are numbered north and south from the base line. Each square mile, which is equivalent to 640 acres, is designated as a *section*. Sections within a township are numbered from the northeast corner, following a back-and-forth course, until the last section (36) is reached in the southeast corner. This method of numbering (shown in the accompanying illustration) ensures that any two sections with contiguous numbers also have contiguous boundaries. For purposes of land description, sections are commonly divided into half-sections containing 320 acres, quarter-sections containing 160 acres, and so forth. Land acreage descriptions are then generally made by referring to a particular quarter of a particular township, or tier, either north or south of a particular base line and east or west of a particular meridian.

A section is the smallest subdivision usually surveyed by government surveyors, and at each section corner, there is a marker known as a *survey monument*. A sample government survey description is "the N½ of the NE¼ of the SE¼ of Section 17, Township 14 North, Range 4 West of the 6th Principal Meridian."

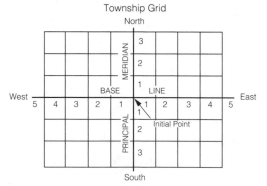

Township Grid

Numbering
of Sections in Township

36	31	32	33	34	35	36	31
1	6	5	4	3	2	1	6
12	7	8	9	10	11	12	7
13	18	17	16	15	14	13	18
24	19	20	21	22	23	24	19
25	30	29	28	27	26	25	30
36	31	32	33	34	35	36	31
1	6	5	4	3	2	1	6

Adjoining Sections

Section 20
5,280 Feet

1,320 20 Chains	1,320 80 Rods	2,640 40 Chains 160 Rods		
W 1/2 of NW 1/4 (80 Acres)	E 1/2 of NW 1/4 (80 Acres)	NE 1/4 (160 Acres)		
NW 1/4 of SW 1/4 (40 Acres)	A NE 1/4 of SW 1/4 (40 Acres)	N 1/2 of NW 1/4 of SE 1/4 (20 Acres) 20 Acres	W 1/2 of NE 1/4 of SE 1/4 20 Acres 1 Furlong	20 Acres
SW 1/4 of SW 1/4 (40 Acres) 80 rods	40 Acres 440 Yards	(10 Acres)(10 Acres) 660 Feet 660 Feet	5 Acres 5 Acres SE 1/4 of SE 1/4 of SE 1/4 10 Acres	5 Acs. 5 Acs.

Note that, generally, the longer the description, the smaller the parcel of land. This method is good for identifying large parcels, but not for pinpointing small lots.

grace period   An agreed-on time after an obligation is past due during which a party can perform without being considered in default. For example, if a mortgage payment is due March 1, but the mortgage contains a ten-day grace period, the mortgagor is not in default so long as payment is made by March 10. Also known as *days of grace*.

With monetary defaults, there is usually no requirement of prior written notice to the debtor. But with nonmonetary defaults such as waste or failure to keep a property insured, the grace period usually begins to run only after written notice is given.

G

grade   The elevation of a hill, road, sidewalk, or slope to the degree that it is inclined from level ground. The slope of an inclined surface of a road or lot is generally expressed as a percentage of the level or horizontal distance; a 5 percent grade rises 5 feet in each 100 feet of level distance. The *grade level* of a lot refers to the general elevation of the land. *Rough grade* is a surface on which topsoil is spread to elevate the lot to a finished grade level.

gradient   (*pendiente, declive*)   The slope or rate of increase or decrease in elevation, of a surface, road, or pipe. Gradient is expressed in inches of rise and fall per horizontal linear foot of ascent or descent.

Graduate, REALTORS® Institute (GRI)   *See* Appendix B.

graduated-payment mortgage (GPM)   (*hipoteca con pagos graduados*)   A mortgage in which the monthly payment for principal and interest increases by a certain percentage each year for a specific number of years and then levels off for the remaining term of the mortgage. There are five different versions of the plan available in the FHA-245 program, which is available only to owner occupants.

The FHA-245 program is especially attractive to persons just starting their careers and anticipating increases in their incomes to obtain a home with initially a lower monthly installment obligation than would be available under a level payment plan. This plan helps borrowers qualify for loans by basing repayment schedules on salary expectations and anticipated home price appreciation. Because FHA underwriting guidelines are based on the first year's monthly requirement for principal and interest amortization, persons using FHA-245 can qualify for larger loan amounts than would ordinarily be available under other forms of financing.

Three features unique to the graduated-payment mortgage are as follows:

- The size of the individual payments is less than it would be under a fixed-payment loan.
- Negative amortization occurs during the initial years.
- The face amount of the note is greater than the funds disbursed at closing.

graduated rental lease   A lease in which the rent payments commence at a fixed, often low, rate but increase at set intervals as the lease term matures. Such increases might be based on a percentage of the increased value of the land based on a periodic appraisal. This gives long-term commercial tenants an opportunity to get started in business without a heavy financial burden during the early years. It may also be preferred by the lessor for tax purposes in order to reduce cash flow in a certain high-tax period. A graduated rental lease is often an excellent device for attracting tenants in a tough market or for a facility that is difficult to lease. Also called a *graded lease*. (*See* **cash flow**, **escalator clause**, **step-up lease**.)

grandfather clause   A common expression used to convey the idea that something that was once permissible continues to be permissible despite changes in the controlling law. For instance, a developer with prior county planning approval to build on 10,000-square-foot minimum-size lots can be granted the right to build on such lots even if the current zoning regulations are amended to require 12,000-square-foot minimum-size lots. The developer is "grandfathered" under the originally approved subdivision plan. This situation is similar to nonconforming use.

Under state legislation regarding real estate prelicensing educational requirements, current licensees may be "grandfathered," or exempted, from such new requirements. (*See* **nonconforming use**.)

granny flats   A slang term to describe accessory apartments in single-family-zoned areas. Also called *in-law apartments*, these separate rental units (for example, above a garage or in an attic or a basement) are illegal under most zoning laws.

grant   The act of conveying or transferring title to real property. Historically, the operative words in a conveyance of real estate are *grant, bargain, sell, warrant, convey*. The grantor delivers the grant, in the form of a deed to the grantee. If a leasehold is involved, an assignment of lease is used to transfer the leasehold title. (*See* **deed**.)

grant deed   A type of deed in which grantors warrant that they have not previously conveyed the estate being granted to another, that they have not encumbered the property except as noted in the deed, and that they will convey to a grantee any title to the property they may later acquire. Grant deeds are very common in California, especially where the buyer also receives a title insurance policy.

grantee   The person who receives from the grantor a conveyance of real property. The grantee must be a person, either natural or otherwise, who exists at the time of the conveyance and is capable of taking title. As a rule, grantors cannot convey title to themselves alone. They may, however, convey title to themselves and others; for example, John Park conveys title to John Park and George Ant as joint tenants.

Some general applications of these principles are as follows:

- If the grantee is dead at the time of delivery of the deed, the deed is void. (Delivery is deemed to have taken place when the executed deed is placed in escrow, not necessarily when it is actually delivered to the grantee.)
- If the grantee is a corporation, an informal club, or a society that did not file its incorporation papers prior to delivery of the deed, the deed is void for lack of a competent grantee.
- A deed conveying an estate to the heirs of a living person is void, in that no person can be an heir during the lifetime of his or her ancestor. (The correct wording would be "to Joe Young and his heirs and assigns . . .")
- When the grantee's name has been omitted, the deed generally is ineffective to convey full title until the name is filled in with the grantor's permission.

When title is transferred to multiple grantees, there are many possible variations of title ownership. For example, if a mother and father buy a home with their daughter and son-in-law, title may be held as follows: "To James Lynch and Carolee Lynch, husband and wife, as joint tenants, an undivided one-third interest and Paul Jones and Mary Jones, husband and wife, as tenants by the entirety, an undivided two-thirds interest of Lot 123. . . ." Thus, upon the death of James Lynch, Carolee will own a one-third undivided interest as tenant in common with Paul and Mary Jones, who continue to own their two-thirds undivided interest as tenants by the entirety. (*See* **deed; ownership, form of.**)

grantor   The person transferring title to, or an interest in, real property. A grantor must be competent to convey; thus, a mentally retarded person cannot convey title to real property. A deed from a minor usually is voidable (not void) and may be disaffirmed before or within a reasonable time after the grantor reaches majority. A corporate grantor must have legal existence, be authorized to hold and convey title to real property, and be represented by a duly authorized officer of the corporation.

Grantors must be clearly identified in a deed. Misspellings do not render a deed inoperative unless the discrepancy is so extensive that a grantor cannot reasonably be identified. Grantors should convey title under the same name in which they acquired title. If the grantor has changed names, the conveyance should reflect the change—for example, "Joan Henry, who acquired title under the name Joan H. Adams . . ."

Both grantor and grantee must be living and cannot be the same person. For example, a husband cannot convey his interest in a joint tenancy to himself as a tenant in common. A conveyance to "Joe Gomez and Fred Jackson, their heirs and assigns" would be valid, however, even if Gomez and Jackson were dead at the time of the conveyance.

G

When title is vested in two or more persons, they must convey their individual separate interest. Usually all co-owners will join in one deed, although separate deeds are perfectly valid to transfer the complete title to the grantee.

Even though one spouse may not be a co-owner of the property, that spouse should join in the deed conveying the other spouse's property in order to release dower, curtesy, and/or homestead rights (if applicable). Therefore, the marital status of the grantor should be inserted in the deed. In fact, the recorder may not accept a deed for recordation unless it contains the marital status and address of the grantor. (*See* **deed**.)

grantor-grantee index   Public record books that are maintained in the official recorder's office, listing all recorded instruments and the liber (book) and page numbers where the complete and exact document can be found in the record books. Separate index books are maintained for grantors and grantees so that a document can be located by searching under either name. These books are indexed by year and are in alphabetical order by grantor in the grantor index and by grantee in the grantee index. They contain the following information: kind of instrument; name of grantor; name of grantee; date of instrument; book, page, and date of recording; and description. Also called *name-indices*.

An example of one method for searching a title using the grantor-grantee indexes follows: Abe Adams owned a farm in 1890. In 1925, Adams conveyed the farm to Bill Benny by deed. In 1950, Benny conveyed the farm to Clarice Carver by deed. In 1960, Carver borrowed $50,000 from the Commercial Bank and gave a mortgage on the property. In 1974, Carver conveyed the farm to Diane Dealer by deed and now Dealer enters into a contract to sell the property to Elbert Edwidge.

The basic title search procedure is that each owner, beginning with the most recent, is traced back through the grantee index to the source of his ownership. Thus, in the above example, the title searcher would start by looking in the grantee index under Dealer's name from the present back to 1974, where he finds the deed to Dealer from Carver. He would then look under Carver's name from 1974 back to 1950, where he finds the deed from Benny to Carver; then under Benny's name back to 1925, where he finds the deed from Adams to Benny; then under Adams's name from 1925 back to 1890. The searcher would then look in the grantor index under Adams's name from 1890 and "search up" to 1925, then under Benny's name from 1925 to 1950, then under Carver's name from 1950 to 1974, then under Dealer's name from 1974 to the present. In this way, the searcher will find the mortgage to the Commercial Bank, which is recorded in 1960 in the grantor's index under Carver's name. (*See* **recording**, **title search**, **wild deed**.)

gratuitous agent   An agent who receives no compensation for services. Real estate agents typically work on a payment basis contingent on selling a property. Even though unpaid, the agent still owes full fiduciary or statutory duties to the principal. This may be true even though a licensed agent may have volunteered to help a friend.

green belts   *See* **common areas**.

GRI   Graduate, REALTORS® Institute. *See* Appendix B.

gridiron   A term used to describe the rectangular street pattern of cities or subdivision developments.

grid system   The state-sponsored survey points to which metes-and-bounds surveys can be referenced. Also called *coordinate system*, it is especially helpful for surveying large parcels of remote area land. (*See* **metes and bounds**.)

grievance period   A specified day or group of days during which the public may register complaints about tax assessments or other problems on the local level.

gross area   The total floor area of a building, measured from the exterior of its walls (excluding uncovered areas such as courtyards or patios). In *commercial* leasing, the gross floor area is the entire square footage within the floor's perimeter, measured to the *inside* finish of the permanent outer building walls or to the glass line in newer buildings, with no allowance made for structural projections and with a required minimum ceiling height of 7½ feet.

gross density   *See* **density zoning**.

gross income   (*ingreso bruto*)   The total income derived from a business, wages, or income-producing property before adjustments or deductions for expenses, depreciation, taxes, and similar allowances—that is, all income, "the top line."

gross income multiplier (GIM)   (*multiplicador de ingreso bruto*)   A numerical factor for estimating the market value of industrial and commercial properties that expresses the relationship of gross income to sales price or value. A ratio to convert annual income into market value, GIM is calculated by dividing price by gross annual income. (*See* **gross rent multiplier [GRM]**.)

gross lease   A lease of property under which the lessee pays a fixed rent and the lessor pays the taxes, insurance, and other charges regularly incurred through ownership; also called a *fixed* or **flat lease**. In a net lease, the lessee pays some or all of the operating expenses. Most residential and commercial office leases are gross leases. Most residential ground leases and commercial and industrial building leases are net leases. (*See* **net lease, triple-net lease**.)

gross rent multiplier (GRM)   (*multiplicador de alquiler bruto*)   A useful rule of thumb for estimating the market value of income-producing residential property. The multiplier is derived by using comparable sales divided by the actual or estimated monthly rentals to arrive at an acceptable average. By multiplying the estimated rent of the property under consideration by the multiplier, one can compute a rough estimate of the property's market value. Only a rough estimate of value is thus produced because the gross rent does not allow for variations in vacancies, uncollectible rents, property taxes, management, and similar unpredictable circumstances. To be most accurate, the estimate should generally be based on unfurnished rentals.

Use of the gross rent multiplier, sometimes called the gross income multiplier, has been slowly declining during the past several years because it is a very crude guideline that does not take into consideration the tax ramifications of different ranges of investors and does not recognize alternate methods of financing. (*See* **gross income multiplier [GIM]**.)

ground area   The area of a building computed from the exterior dimensions of the ground floor. Ground coverage area is the ratio of the floor area of a building divided by the land area.

ground cover   Grass, ivy, and other plants grown to keep dirt from washing away.

ground lease   A lease of land alone, sometimes secured by improvements placed on the land. Also called a *land lease*, the ground lease is a means used to separate the ownership of the land from the ownership of the buildings and improvements constructed on the land. In most areas, it is a net lease that creates a tenancy for years, typically for a term of 55, 75, or 99 years. Ground leases do not generally run for longer than 99 years due to early state laws that held leases of 100 years or longer to be transfers of fee simple title rather than leases.

The lease rent (called *ground rent*) normally is fixed for an initial period of 30 years (calculated as a percentage of the assessed valuation of the land on the date of lease execution), with the balance of the rent to be renegotiated on or before the expiration date of the fixed term. The new rent is usually based on a set percentage of the then-appraised value of the property minus the cost of on-site and off-site improvements. Sometimes the rent increase is determined at the time of execution of the lease, and a graduated lease, with fixed increases at stated intervals, is agreed to.

In some states, a ground lease is used in both residential and condominium developments; however, it is also popular in commercial property development. Because land ownership is separated from improvement ownership, capital gains taxes on land sales may be avoided and financing requirements may be decreased. (*See* **building lease, net lease, percentage lease, renegotiation of lease**.)

groundwater   Water under the surface of the earth, regardless of the geological structure in which it is standing or moving. Groundwater does not include water flowing in underground streams with identifiable beds and banks.

group boycott   A type of antitrust violation in which several brokers agree to refuse to cooperate or to cooperate on less favorable terms with a third broker, often in response to that broker offering a discount brokerage program. (*See* **antitrust laws**.)

grout   A fluid mixture of sand and cement used to fill joints and small spaces in masonry and tile work.

growing equity mortgage (GEM)   A full-term mortgage with an initial payment and interest rate generally equal to the prevailing conventional market rate. The GEM has provisions for gradually increasing payments (from 2½ percent to 7½ percent per year) based on either predetermined increases or increases tied to an index. The increased payments are applied directly to principal and substantially reduce both the term of the loan and the total amount of interest paid. The FHA 245(a) appeals to those who have a limited income but who expect that their monthly earnings will increase. These loans can be insured under FHA Section (b) for one- to four-family homes, Section (k) for those homes that require refinancing and rehabilitation, Section (n) for cooperatives, and Section (c) for condominiums.

guaranteed mortgage certificate (GMC)   A debt instrument, issued by Freddie Mac, to raise money for its activities in the secondary market. Each GMC represents an undivided interest in a large, geographically diversified group of residential mortgages and is unconditionally guaranteed by Freddie Mac. Payment of interest is made to the security holder every six months. Principal is paid once a year.

guaranteed sale program (GSP)   A service offered by some brokers in which they agree to pay the owner of a listed property a predetermined price if the property is not sold within a specified period of time. This enables the owner to purchase a replacement property regardless of how long it takes to sell the listed property.

    The broker generally charges a fee in addition to the sales commission. Brokers should be aware that, under the IRC, the Internal Revenue Service considers that the property acquired through a guaranteed sales program is treated as dealer property. (*See* **dealer**.)

    The guaranteed sale agreement must be drafted well to cover all rights and obligations. State licensing officials take a close look at these programs, due to owner complaints that some brokers refuse to perform their promises.

guarantor   A third party to a contract who promises to make good if the original promissor does not fulfill the promises.

guaranty   A pledge or security made by one person (the guarantor) to ensure that another person (the obligor) will perform his contract or fulfill her obligations to a third person (the obligee). There is a growing tendency among lenders to require a mortgagor to obtain someone who collaterally guarantees the repayment of a secured loan, especially when the borrower is either a new or a financially weak corporation. (*See* **personal judgment**.)

guardian   (*curador*)   A person, appointed by court or by will, given the lawful custody and care of the person or property of another (called a *ward*). The ward might be a minor, an insane person, or even a spendthrift. The guardian may, upon court approval and without necessity of obtaining a real estate license, sell the ward's property, if it is in the best interest of the ward. The grantee would receive valid title under a guardian's deed. A *guardian ad litem* is a person appointed by a court to bring or defend a legal action on behalf of his or her ward.

guest-car ratio (GCR) For purposes of high-density housing planning, the number of parking spaces allotted each living unit of guest use.

guide meridians As used in the government (rectangular) survey method, the survey lines running due north-south, 24 miles apart. Guide meridians correct for the convergence of principal meridians due to the earth's curvature. (*See* **government survey method**.)

H

habendum clause That part of a deed beginning with the words *to have and to hold*, following the granting clause and reaffirming the extent of ownership that the grantor is transferring. The habendum clause defines or limits the extent of ownership in the estate granted as, for instance, a fee simple, life estate, or easement: "To have and to hold unto said Jane Henley, grantee, a life estate in . . ." If there is a discrepancy between the extent of ownership as specified in the granting clause and that specified in the habendum clause, the granting clause prevails. Consequently, a habendum clause is *not* an essential part of the deed. (*See* **quantum**.)

habitable Being in a condition that is fit to live in. A residential landlord has an obligation to keep the leased premises in a habitable condition. If any condition within the premises renders the dwelling unit uninhabitable or poses imminent threat to the health or safety of any occupant, a tenant may terminate the rental agreement by following certain procedures prescribed in the state landlord and tenant code.

Courts are now enforcing implied warranties of habitability against builders of new residences when the defects render the building uninhabitable. (*See* **implied warranty of habitability**.)

habitable room A room used for living purposes, such as a den, bedroom, or kitchen, as opposed to a bathroom or hallway. Usually, habitable rooms are the only ones counted in the number of rooms in a house.

half-section An area of land having 320 acres (128 hectares), constituting $\frac{1}{72}$ of a township.

handicap A protected class defined under the fair housing laws and the Americans with Disabilities Act (ADA) consisting of a physical or mental impairment that substantially limits one or more major life activities (walking, seeing, learning, working), a record of having such an impairment, or being regarded as having such disability. In practice, *disability* is often the preferred term to *handicap*.

Handicap (disability) does not include current illegal use of or addiction to a controlled substance, but a person who is rehabilitated in these areas may be protected. (*See* **Americans with Disabilities Act [ADA], federal fair housing law**.)

hand money *See* **earnest money**.

handyman's special *See* **fixer-upper**.

hangout A balloon loan that occurs when a long-term loan exceeds the term of a lease for the same property. If a lender makes a commitment to a 24-year loan on a property with a 20-year lease, the four-year difference is called a *hangout*. When the terms call for the balance of the loan to be paid upon expiration of the lease, the loan is called a *balloon loan*.

H

hard-money mortgage   Any mortgage loan given to a borrower in exchange for cash, as opposed to a mortgage given to finance a specific real estate purchase. Often, a hard money mortgage takes the form of a second mortgage given to a private mortgage company in exchange for the cash needed to purchase an item of personal property or solve some personal financial crisis. Borrowers, in these cases, would pledge the equity in their property as collateral for a hard money mortgage. (*See* **soft money**.)

hazard insurance   A property insurance policy that indemnifies against loss resulting from physical damage to property due to hazards such as fire, flood, and windstorm. (*See* **insurance**.)

hazardous substance   (*sustancia peligrosa*)   Any material that poses a threat to the environment or to public health. Under Superfund, the Environmental Protection Agency lists hundreds of hazardous substances that are either toxic (lead to death), corrosive (acidic), ignitable (danger from heat or smoke), or reactive (can lead to explosions).

hazardous waste   Materials that are inherently dangerous to handle or dispose of. These include radioactive materials, certain chemicals, explosives, or biological waste. The EPA regulates the disposal of such hazardous wastes.

head casing   The strip of molding placed above a door or window frame.

hearing   An administrative legal proceeding with definite issues of fact to be determined and with the parties having the right to be heard and have counsel present, much the same as at a trial. The rules of evidence are usually less strict than in a trial.

A real estate licensee whose license is in danger of being suspended, revoked, or denied renewal is generally assured the right to a hearing under the state license laws.

hearth   The floor of the fireplace. The front hearth, which extends out into the room, may be made of brick or decorative stone. The back hearth inside the fireplace is usually made of firebrick.

heavy industry   Businesses that require ample property to accommodate their nature and function, such as factories, packing plants, or mills. The term connotes noise, pollution, heavy truck traffic, vibration, and fumes.

hectare   A metric unit of land measurement equal to 2.471 acres, or 100 acres. An acre is 100 square meters, and the prefix *hect-* means "100 times." Thus a hectare is 100 acres.

height, building   Vertical distance measured from the curb or grade level, whichever is higher, to the highest level of a flat roof or to the average height of a pitched roof, excluding penthouse or other roof appendages occupying less than 30 percent of the roof area.

heir   (*heredero*)   A person who inherits under a will or a person who succeeds to property by the state laws of descent if the decedent dies without a will (intestate). State probate codes (laws of descent and distribution) set up the method of determining heirs for distributing an intestate decedent's real property. When real and personal property descend to more than one heir, the heirs take title as tenants in common. The words *heirs and assigns* are no longer necessary to convey or devise title in fee simple. In modern usage, the word *heir* is used to indicate those persons who acquire in any manner (by descent, devise, or bequest) the ownership of any property by reason of the death of the owner. (*See* **collateral heirs**, **descent**, **legacy**.)

heirs and assigns   Heirs are recipients of an inheritance from a deceased owner, whereas assigns are successors in interest to a property. The words *heirs and assigns* are customarily inserted in deeds and wills, and are considered to be words of limitation, not words of purchase. Words of limitation in a conveyance indicate what type of estate is created. Words of purchase indicate who takes the estate. For example, in a conveyance "to *Harry Howe* and his heirs," the words to Harry Howe are words of purchase. The words *and his heirs* are words of limitation indicating a fee simple estate; they would not be present in the transfer of a life estate. Heirs and assigns are also generally responsible for the contracts of their predecessors, such as leases, options, mortgages, and contracts for deed.

hereditament   Every kind of inheritable property, including real, personal, corporeal, and incorporeal; those things appurtenant to the land. An incorporeal hereditament would be the right to receive future rents or insurance proceeds.

hiatus
1. A gap in the chain of title.
2. A space existing between adjoining parcels due to a faulty legal description.

hidden risk   A title risk that cannot be ascertained from an examination of the public records. The most common hidden risks include the following: forgery or lack of delivery in the chain of title (forged mortgage release), corporate forgery (the execution of an instrument not authorized by the appropriate officers), minority of a party to an instrument, death of a principal before execution of an instrument by the attorney-in-fact, conveyance in fraud of creditors, elective share rights of the spouse of a first party who falsely claimed to be single, and potential vulnerability of the subject property to mechanics' liens. All such hidden risks are covered under standard policies of title insurance but not under a standard certificate of title or an attorney's opinion that certifies record title. (*See* **certificate of title, extended coverage, title insurance, Torrens system**.)

highest and best use   An appraisal term meaning that reasonable use, at the time of the property appraisal, which is most likely to produce the greatest net return to the land and/or the building over a given period of time. The use must be legal and in compliance with regulations and ordinances within the police power of the county and the state, including health regulations, zoning ordinances, building code requirements, and other regulations. The highest and best use is determined by evaluating the quantity and quality of income from various alternative land uses. Net return normally is interpreted in terms of money, although consideration may be given to such things as amenities.

For example, vacant land in a central business district currently used as a parking lot may or may not be employed at its highest and best use, depending on whether the surrounding market is ready for further commercial development. A gas station site may be more effective as a fast-food facility or a dry cleaner.

For appraisal purposes, land is always valued as though vacant and available for development to its highest and best use. The estate taxes and the real property taxes paid by an owner of unimproved real estate are usually based on the highest and best use of the land rather than the use to which it is actually devoted. (*See* **appraisal, "as is," dedication, income approach, land economics**.)

highrise   A popular expression for a condominium or apartment building generally higher than six stories. However, there is no national height standard.

high-water mark   That line on the shore reached by the shoreward limit of the rise of medium tides "between the spring and the neap." In most states, this mark, also called *mean high water*, is the seaward boundary of privately owned lands and is the dividing line between public and private property. The shoreline, however, may be determined in a few areas by the high wash of the waves, as usually evidenced by the vegetation line, not the high-water mark. (*See* **shoreline**.)

highway   A roadway generally serving through traffic on a continuous route providing the primary access between communities.

hip roof   Pitched roof with sloping sides and ends.

historic structure   A property listed in the National Register of Historic Places, located in a registered historic district and certified by the secretary of the Department of the Interior as being of historic significance to the district, or located in a historic district designated under an appropriate state or local government statute certified by the Interior Department. The Internal Revenue Code provides certain tax incentives and deterrents to encourage the preservation of historic buildings and structures. There is a 20 percent investment tax credit for qualified rehabilitation expenses in qualified rehabilitated buildings and certified historic structures.

The tax code penalizes an individual who demolishes or substantially alters a historic structure. Demolition costs are not permitted as a deduction, and substantial alterations or completely new improvements are not eligible for any form of accelerated depreciation. (*See* **scenic easement**.)

holdback
1. The portion of a loan commitment that will not be funded until some additional requirement has been attained, such as presale or rental of 70 percent of the units or completion of all building work. (*See* **floor loan**.)
2. In construction or interim financing, a percentage of the contractor's draw held back until satisfactory completion of the contractor's work and assurance of no mechanics' or materialmen's liens. (*See* **retainage**.)

holder (*tenedor*) in due course
A person who has obtained a negotiable instrument (promissory note, check) in the ordinary course of business before it is due, in good faith and for value, without knowledge that it has been previously dishonored and without notice of any defect or setoff at the time it was negotiated.

A holder in due course enjoys a favored position with respect to the instrument because the maker cannot raise certain "personal defenses" in refusing payment. Personal defenses include lack of consideration, setoff, and fraud.

This facilitates trade and commerce because people are more willing to accept such instruments without careful investigation of the maker's credit or the circumstances surrounding the creation of the instrument.

A holder in due course is insulated against a claim by the maker that the promissory note has been paid in part or in full or has been forged. Thus, the maker of the note should have the note marked "paid" and returned to him in order to avoid the risk of the holder's negotiating it to another holder in due course who could force the maker to pay it again. (*See* **negotiable instrument**.)

hold-harmless clause
A contract provision whereby one party agrees to indemnify and protect the other party from any injuries or lawsuits arising out of the particular transaction. Such clauses are usually found in leases in which the lessee agrees to "indemnify, defend, and hold harmless" the lessor from claims and suits of third persons for damage resulting from the lessee's negligence on the leased premises. Hold-harmless clauses are also found in property management contracts when the owner holds the agent harmless for all damages except those caused by the agent's own negligence or fraud. (*See* **exculpatory clause**.)

holding company
A company that owns, directs, or controls the operations of one or more other corporations, usually directly owned subsidiaries; a corporation organized to hold the stock of other corporations, such as a bank holding company.

holding escrow
An arrangement whereby an escrow agent holds the final title documents to a contract for deed. Holding escrows are often suggested as the solution for the problems that arise under a contract for deed when the buyer is ready to pay off the balance owing on the contract but the seller either cannot be found or is not cooperative about executing the deed. Under a holding escrow, the seller, at the time the contract for deed is signed, deposits with the escrow agent an executed deed or assignment of lease and instructs the escrow agent to deliver the conveyance to the buyer when

full payment is made under the contract. Many escrow companies are reluctant to handle holding escrows, even when they are indemnified against loss, because of the following possible complications:

- It may be difficult for the holding escrow to ascertain whether there has been a full payoff, whether the amount deposited in escrow is the correct amount, and whether the buyer is in default under any other terms of the contract for deed.
- Difficulties may arise if the seller dies, particularly in terms of determining the rights of any heirs. Other problems may arise if the seller remarries, and new dower, curtesy, or marital rights must be considered. (*See* **relation-back doctrine**.)
- If the buyer has resold the property still under contract and used a different escrow agent, the seller is asked to draft new documents conveying title directly to the new buyer. Thus, there sometimes are added costs.

While the holding escrow practice is good in theory, these practical problems may prevent its effective use. A good alternative is to establish a collection account with the lending institution where the seller has the existing mortgage. The collecting agent knows how to contact the seller if the buyer wants to quickly pay off the outstanding balance and receive a deed to the property. Also, the buyer can thus be assured that the seller's mortgage payments are being made as long as he makes his contract for deed payments—and vice versa—the seller can be notified if the buyer is in default in making payments. This situation is sometimes called a *true escrow*. (*See* **collection account**, **contract for deed**.)

holding period   The period during which a person retains ownership of a capital asset. Federal tax law provides that if property is held for a specific holding period and then disposed of, the gain is treated as long-term gain and is taxed at favorable capital gains rates. If the property was not held for the specified holding period, any gain on disposition would be a short-term gain and taxed at ordinary income rates. The holding period required to qualify as long-term capital gains is 12 months plus one day.

holdover tenant   A person who stays on the leased premises after the lease has expired. The landlord normally has the choice of evicting the holdover tenant or permitting the tenant to remain and continue to pay rent. The landlord may also elect to treat the holdover tenant as a tenant whose lease would continue from period to period, with the period to be that of the original lease, and for the same rent. The lease, however, would generally not exceed one year, because most state statutes of fraud require that leases for one year or longer be in writing. A holdover tenant usually has no rights whatsoever to the leased property—being deemed little better than a trespasser. (*See* **tenancy at sufferance**.)

H

holiday   (*día inhábil*)   The following is a list of significant holidays recognized by most banks and many businesses, as well as state and federal offices:

New Year's Day	January 1
Martin Luther King Day	Third Monday in January
Lincoln's Birthday	February 12
Washington's Birthday (observed)	Third Monday in February
Washington's Birthday	February 22
Memorial Day (observed)	Last Monday in May
Memorial Day	May 30
Independence Day	July 4
Labor Day	First Monday in September
Columbus Day (observed)	Second Monday in October
Columbus Day	October 12
Election Day	First Tuesday in November
Veterans' Day	November 11
Thanksgiving Day	Fourth Thursday in November
Christmas Day	December 25

Legal public holidays recognized by the federal government are specified in Section 6103(a) of Title 5 of the United States Code.

Usually, whenever an act is to be performed on a particular day that happens to fall on a holiday, the act may be performed on the next business day with the same effect as if performed on the day appointed. This rule is generally not true where the parties have clearly indicated that "time is of the essence" or they are meeting the deadlines for a 1031. In any event, a prudent contract drafter should foresee possible problems and make the appropriate adjustments.

holographic will   A will that is written, dated, and signed in the testator's handwriting, but not witnessed. Some states consider a holographic will to be valid even though it was not witnessed, presumably on the theory that the handwriting can be analyzed to verify authenticity and demonstrate competency.

home equity line-of-credit loan   A mortgage loan (usually in a subordinate position) that allows the borrower to obtain multiple advances of the loan proceeds at the borrower's discretion, up to an amount that represents a specific percentage of the borrower's equity in a property.

home inspection   A professional inspection of a property to ascertain the condition of the improvements. It is normally paid for by the buyer and made a contingency to the buyer's obligation to buy. Some sellers authorize a home inspector to complete a report in the hopes this will make the property more marketable. Buyers and sellers should review the scope of services covered—some inspectors check roofs and foundations, whereas others do not.

home loan   A loan secured by a residence for one, two, three, or four families under either a mortgage or a deed of trust.

Home Mortgage Disclosure Act   (*Ley de Divulgación sobre las Hipotecas de Vivienda*)
See Appendix D.

Home Valuation Code of Conduct (HVCC)   Standards effective May 1, 2009, to ensure that appraisals of one- to four-unit single-family homes are evaluated fairly and without influence by the lender or real estate agents. Replaced by the Appraiser Independence Requirements under the Dodd-Frank Act.

homeowners' association (HOA)   A nonprofit association of homeowners organized pursuant to a declaration of restrictions or protective covenants for a subdivision, PUD, or condominium. Like other nonprofit associations, a homeowners' association has members, not shareholders.

In a typical subdivision development, a developer records a declaration of restrictions, covenants, and easements to ensure the orderly and harmonious development of the subdivision and to protect against future depreciation of values resulting from deterioration of the neighborhood. After sale of the lots has commenced, the developer normally transfers the right to enforce the restrictions, liens, and covenants to the HOA. In connection with condominiums, the association is also responsible for maintaining the common elements, such as the swimming pool and elevators, and for hiring a managing agent to implement its policies.

The Tax Reform Act of 1976 allows two types of housing associations—condominium management associations and residential real estate management associations—to elect to be treated as tax-exempt organizations for taxable years beginning after 1973. However, this tax-exempt status protects the association from tax only on its exempt function income, such as membership dues, fees, and assessments received from member-owners of residential units in the particular condominium or subdivision involved. On any net income that is not exempt function income, the association is taxed at corporate rates but is not permitted the corporate surtax exemption granted to regular domestic corporations.

Currently, some HOAs are incorporated nonprofit associations because an unincorporated association could expose its members to the risk of unlimited liabilities, as damages for personal injuries to others. Another added benefit of a nonprofit corporation is the established body of law that exists, which can be used to guide the corporation's operations.

home ownership   The status of owning the residence in which one lives. There are certain income tax advantages derived from owning a home, such as deduction of real estate taxes and mortgage interest payments, exclusion of capital gain tax on the sale of the residence, and certain casualty losses. (*See* **residence, sale of.**)

homeowners' insurance   A combined property and liability insurance policy designed for residential use. A variety of packaged policies designed for owners of single-family dwellings, for tenants, and for condominium owners. The homeowners' policy can be endorsed for additional coverage, such as inflation guard and workers' compensation (to cover servants or contractors). This policy never covers rising water (i.e., flooding) for which a separate policy must be purchased. (*See* **insurance.**)

Homeowners' Warranty Program (HOW)   A private insurance program that offers a buyer of a new home a ten-year warranty against certain physical defects, such as faulty roofing, heating, electrical services, and plumbing. The one-time insurance premium may be paid by broker, seller, or buyer, or it may be shared.

home rule   The power of local governments to adopt zoning and building ordinances, as well as other land-use regulations.

homestead   A tract of land that is owned and occupied as the family home. In many states, a portion of the area or value of this land is protected or exempt from judgments for debts and protects the family against eviction by general creditors. It protects each spouse individually by requiring that both husband and wife join in executing any deed conveying the homestead property. The homestead value that is exempt from creditors' claims is specifically defined by state law. In some states, a single person may claim a homestead exemption in the same manner as a married couple. Also in some states, the homestead interest attaches by operation of the law, but in others, the homestead interest must be protected by filing a notice as required by local statute. Usually, state laws do not exempt homesteads from annual real estate taxes levied against the property or to a mortgage for purchase money or for the cost of improvements. The rights to occupy the homestead and to enjoy the exemption benefits generally continue for the life of the husband and the wife and the survivor of them and also for minor children. Homestead rights may be released by both husband and wife joining in a deed. Homestead rights in property may be lost by abandonment, as when the home is sold and the householder plans to move to a new home. Intention of the householder is a key factor in the legal establishment of a homestead.

Some states authorize a probate homestead to provide a home for the surviving children and minor children out of the decedent's lands.

H

homogeneous   An appraisal term meaning of the same or similar kind. As used in appraisal, this term describes an area or neighborhood in which the property types or uses are similar and harmonious and the inhabitants have similar cultural, social, and economic backgrounds. A homogeneous neighborhood tends to stabilize property values in the area.

horizontal property acts   The name generally given to the body of laws pertaining to condominiums that permit ownership of a specified horizontal layer of airspace, as opposed to the traditional method of vertical ownership of property from the earth below to the sky above. In a condominium, the horizontal planes appear as the floor and the ceiling, and the vertical planes appear as the walls. Also called *condominium property regimes*.

To ensure that each unit is eligible for the individual rights of private property in terms of taxation and conveyance, a developer generally has to disclose (by way of a declaration) all plans to a state real estate commission or other legal governing body for approval. If approval is given, the governing body usually issues a public report of its findings, which each buyer of an individual unit must read and sign a receipt for. Once the condominium building has been completed, it is turned over to the owners (by way of the owners' association) to operate and manage according to the bylaws established pursuant to general guidelines imposed by the law. (*See* **condominium owners' association**, **condominium ownership**.)

hostile possession   Possession of real property by one person that is in contradiction, or adverse, to the possession of the title owner. The word *hostile* does not imply animosity, only that the possessor's claim neither recognizes the title of the true owner nor is subordinate to that title. Hostile possession is one of the essential elements needed to establish a claim to title under adverse possession. (*See* **adverse possession**.)

hotel   (*hotel*)   As defined in many zoning codes, a building or group of attached or detached buildings containing lodging units in which 50 percent or more of the units are lodging units. A hotel includes a lobby, clerk's desk or counter with 24-hour clerk service, and facilities for registration and keeping of records relating to hotel guests.

Although the reserving of hotel spaces does not require a real estate license, the rental of real property does. The distinction is sometimes rather narrow, especially for resort properties.

house rules   Rules of conduct adopted by the board of directors of a condominium owners' association and designed to promote harmonious living among the owners and occupants. Such rules are usually enforced by the resident manager with the support of the board. Because it is generally easier to change the house rules than to amend the condominium bylaws, condominium associations often use the house rules to regulate the condominium use, as in the rules governing the use of certain common areas such as the picnic grounds, pool, or guest parking, or rules prohibiting pets or loud noises.

Landlords of apartment buildings usually require tenants to abide by the published house rules. The house rules must be fair and apply equally to all tenants. (*See* **landlord-tenant code**.)

Housing for Older Persons Act of 1995 (HOPA)   *See* Appendix D.

housing for the elderly   A project specifically designed for elderly persons (55 years of age or older), which provides living-unit accommodations and common-use space for social and recreational activities; it may also include incidental facilities and space for health and nursing services for the project residents.

housing starts   Housing units actually under construction, as distinguished from building permits issued. The use of national and regional statistics in housing starts is helpful in analyzing real estate and mortgage trends; it is a key economic indicator. (*See* **starts**.)

HR-10 Plan   *See* **Keogh Plan**.

HUD   A federal cabinet department officially known as the U.S. Department of Housing and Urban Development, HUD is active in national housing programs. Among its many programs are urban renewal, public housing, model cities, rehabilitation loans, FHA-subsidy programs, and water and sewer grants. The Office of Interstate Land Sales Registration is under HUD's jurisdiction, as are the Federal Housing Administration (FHA) and Ginnie Mae. HUD also has oversight of Fannie Mae and Freddie Mac, administers the Community Development Block Grant and Section 8 programs, and is responsible for Indian housing. Web site: *www.hud.gov*

HUD programs generally identified by number	
Title	
I	Home Improvement Loans
	Mobile Home Loans
II	Community Development Block Grants (Housing and Community Development Act of 1974)
VI	Equal Opportunity in HUD-Assisted Programs (Civil Rights Act of 1964)
VIII	Fair Housing (Civil Rights Act of 1968)
Section	
8	Lower-Income Rental Assistance (U.S. Housing Act of 1937)
23	Low-Rent Leased Public Housing (U.S. Housing Act of 1937)
202	Direct Loans for Housing for the Elderly or Handicapped (Housing Act of 1959)
203(b) and (i)	One- to Four-Family Home Mortgage Insurance (National Housing Act [1934])
203(v)	Special One- to-Four-Family Home Mortgage Insurance for Veterans
207	Multifamily Rental Housing (National Housing Act [1934])

H

213	Cooperative Housing (National Housing Act [1934])
221(d)(2)	Homeownership for Low- and Moderate-Income Families (National Housing Act [1934])
221(d)(3) and (4)	Multifamily Rental Housing for Low- and Moderate-Income Families (National Housing Act [1934])
223(f)	Existing Multifamily Rental Housing (National Housing Act [1934])
231	Mortgage Insurance for Housing for the Elderly (National Housing Act [1934])
232	Nursing Homes and Intermediate Care Facilities (National Housing Act [1934])
234	Condominium Housing (National Housing Act [1934])
235	Homeownership Assistance for Low- and Moderate-Income Families (National Housing Act [1934])
244	Single-Family Home Mortgage Coinsurance (National Housing Act [1934])
	Multifamily Housing Coinsurance (National Housing Act [1934])
	Graduated Payment Mortgage (Housing Act of 1976)
251	Adjustable Rate Mortgage
312	Rehabilitation Loans (Housing Act of 1964)
701	Comprehensive Planning Assistance (Housing Act of 1954)
Executive Order	
11246	Equal Employment Opportunity (September 24, 1965)
11063	Fair Housing (Title VIII) (Civil Rights Act of 1968)

HUD Code   A standard for the construction of all manufactured homes created by the National Manufactured Housing Construction and Safety Standards Act of 1974 (also known as *Red Label*). (*See* **manufactured housing**.)

HUD-1 form   A form used at closings for all loans that are federally related, including FHA, VA, FDIC-insured funds, and any loans that will be sold to Fannie Mae or Freddie Mac. Exempt closings include cash sales, assumed loans, and seller-financed loans (carryback financing). Since December 2009, the form is three pages, and requires a comparison of charges first disclosed on the Good Faith Estimate (GFE) to those actually charged at closing. The third page requires disclosures about the terms of the loan. (*See* **good-faith estimate [GFE]**.)

hundred percent commission   *See* **one hundred percent commission**.

hundred percent location   Generally refers to the location in the downtown business district that commands the highest land value. This type of location usually reflects the highest rental prices and the highest traffic and pedestrian count. The term sometimes refers to the site that is ideal for the requirements of a specific user.

HVAC   An acronym for the heating, ventilation, and air-conditioning systems in a building.

hypothecate   To pledge specific real or personal property as security for an obligation without surrendering possession of it. For example, a long-term tenant could hypothecate the tenant's leasehold rights as security for a loan. The lender could even use its rights in a receivable mortgage as collateral for some loan to the lender.

In a typical house purchase, the buyers pay a portion of the purchase price with their own cash and borrow the balance from a lending institution. The lender requires the buyers to hypothecate the property or pledge it as security for repayment of the loan, which repayment is accomplished by use of a mortgage or trust deed. The borrowers retain the rights of possession and control, and the lender secures an underlying equitable right in the pledged property. (*See* **pledge**.)

ICSC   *See* **International Council of Shopping Centers (ICSC)**.

idem sonans   Sounding the same. Legally, names improperly spelled need not void an instrument, provided the written name sounds the same as the correctly spelled name and there is no evidence of any intent to deceive by incorrect spelling. An important rule in title insurance practice.

identity theft   The deliberate act of assuming another person's identity by using that person's information, such as birth date, Social Security number, address, name, and bank account information in order to gain access to their credit. On average, the theft may have occurred more than 14 months earlier, and usually, victims have to prove that they did not commit the fraud, regaining their identity and good credit scores. The Fair Credit Reporting Act (FCRA) provides victims specific rights, which include placing "fraud alerts" in the victim's file and free access to all information.

illiquidity   Difficulty in selling an asset for full value on short notice. The lack of assets that can be quickly converted to cash. (*See* **liquidity**.)

illiterate   A person who has not learned to read or write. An illiterate may still enter into contracts.

immediate family member   In lenders' terms, the borrower's spouse, parent, stepparent, legal guardian, grandparent, brother, sister, or child.

impact fees   A municipal assessment against new residential, industrial, or commercial development projects to compensate for the added costs of public services generated by the new construction. Such indirect service requirements would be to cover hook-up costs for water and sewer lines.

implied agency   An actual agency that arises by deduction or inference from other facts and circumstances, including the words and conduct of the parties (i.e., implied in fact through behavior). (*See* **agency, implied listing**.)

implied contract   An unwritten contract inferred from the actions of the parties. Such an agreement is created by neither word nor writing; it is inferred from the conduct of the parties. Also, a contract in which the terms are understood and agreed to but not fully stated in the document. Note that, for obvious reasons, this is not a very businesslike or effective way of transacting real estate business.

A contract implied in law is one that is not considered to have been actually intended by the parties but that the law creates in the interest of fairness and equity. Also called a *quasi contract*.

implied easement   An easement arising by implication from the acts or conduct of the parties. For example, a person acquiring mineral rights on a property also acquires an implied easement to enter the property for the purposes of removing the minerals. (*See* **easement**.)

implied listing   A listing that arises by operation of law as implied from the acts of the parties; in some states, a listing that arises by implication from the conduct of the broker and the seller and may be enforceable even though not in writing. In many other states, however, to be enforceable, all listing contracts must be in writing, and all parties signing them must receive a copy; and no listing agreement will be implied. (*See* **contract**, **exclusive listing**, **implied agency**, **listing**, **statute of frauds**.)

implied warranty of habitability   A legal doctrine that imposes a duty on the landlord to make the leased premises habitable and ready for occupancy and to continue to maintain them in a state of repair throughout the entire term of the lease. This is a reversal of the common-law caveat emptor doctrine, under which the landlord was released of responsibility and the tenant took the premises "as is," regardless of habitability.

Many state landlord and tenant codes specifically provide that the landlord must make all repairs and arrangements necessary to put and keep the premises in a habitable condition. The landlord must protect the tenant from all latent defects—that is, hidden conditions the tenant is not aware of and could not be expected to know.

The implied warranty of habitability has recently been held to apply to the seller or the builder of a new home, who can be held liable for defects that make the dwelling unfit. For example, courts have ruled that the implied warranty of habitability protects the purchasers of new condominium units with defective air-conditioning systems. (*See* **habitable**.)

imply   To indicate, suggest, or communicate something, not by express statement but by conduct or actions that lead to a logical inference. Most real estate transactions must be express, as opposed to implied, and must be in writing.

impound account   A trust account, also called an *escrow account*, established to set aside funds for future needs relating to a parcel of real property. Most mortgage lenders require an impound account to cover future payments for taxes, assessments, private mortgage insurance, and hazard insurance in order to protect their security from defaults, tax liens, and catastrophes. When the property is sold and the buyer assumes the seller's mortgage, the lender does not usually return the escrow account balance to the owner. The sum remains with the lender, and it is the responsibility of the buyer and the seller to prorate the balance between them. Impound accounts are required for FHA loans. Under RESPA, the amount of reserves in the impound account is limited to $\frac{1}{6}$ of the estimated amount of taxes and insurance that will become due in the 12-month period beginning at settlement.

Sometimes, part of the purchase price due the seller may be impounded or put aside by escrow to meet the postclosing expense of clearing title or repairing the structure. (*See* **customer trust fund [CTF]**.)

The issue of use of interest earned on reserve funds is frequently debated. Some, but not all, states require lenders to pay interest to borrowers on money held as reserves.

improved land   Real property whose value has been enhanced by the addition of such on-site and off-site improvements as roads, sewers, utilities, and buildings, as distinguished from raw land.

improvements   (*mejora*)   Valuable additions made to property that amount to more than repairs, costing labor, and capital, intended to enhance the value of the property or extend the useful remaining life. Improvements of land include grading, sidewalks, sewers, streets, utilities, and the like. Improvements to land include buildings, fences, room additions, new roofs, and similar constructions. An improvement could also be an alteration of the land's surface, such as an irrigation channel.

Based on modern appraisal methods, the value of an improvement is generally determined by what it adds to the land in terms of production of income or amenities. A reasonable relationship should exist between a site and the character of the improvement placed on it. An overimprovement, underimprovement, or misplaced improvement detracts from the combined value of a lot and the building on it.

For income tax purposes, improvements must generally be capitalized, with cost recovery deductions taken over a period of years, whereas maintenance and repairs that do not add to the value of the property can be deducted on income property as business expenses in the year incurred. (*See* **basis**, **betterment**, **repairs**, **substantial improvement**.)

imputed interest   Interest implied by law. When an installment contract, such as a land contract or a mortgage note, fails to state an interest rate or sets an unreasonably low rate, the IRS imputes, or assigns, interest at a prescribed rate (computed semiannually). The applicable federal rate depends on the term of the note and is determined by the IRS and published monthly. This rule does not apply to installment sales under $3,000.

Section 483 of the Internal Revenue Code, "Interest on Certain Deferred Payments," and Sections 1271 through 1274, original issue discount rules, prevent the seller from treating as capital gain the part of the selling price that really represented interest on deferred payments. In effect, they prevent deferred payments from being treated wholly as principal. Before the enactment of these sections, parties to a real estate installment sale frequently would omit interest from the contract and raise the purchase price to reflect this omission.

Buyers may deduct for tax purposes, even though no interest is paid, the imputed interest per annum on the unpaid balances. By reallocating the face amount of the note to part interest and part principal (buyer and seller agreement), the buyer may not only carve out an interest deduction but also reduce the basis of the property acquired. (*See* **installment sale**.)

imputed notice   An agent's knowledge that is binding on the principal because of the agency relationship between them. If, for example, the buyer's agent is notified of the seller's acceptance of the buyer's offer, the buyer could not thereafter withdraw the offer even though the buyer had no actual notice yet of the acceptance of the contract.

inactive license   A real estate license in inactive status. In many states, a real estate licensee can place the license in an inactive status. During this time, the licensee may not transact any real estate business, including splitting fees with active licensees for referrals. The licensee usually must continue to pay license fees, although many states charge a lesser fee than for an active license.

inchoate   An incomplete, imperfect interest, begun but not completed. In most states where dower is recognized, a wife's interest in the lands of her husband during his lifetime is an inchoate dower interest. A husband's curtesy right, however, is typically not an inchoate right; it takes effect only upon the wife's death. Also describes a mechanic's lien that has not yet been filed but will take effect when filed and relate back to the visible commencement of work. (*See* **dower**, **mechanic's lien**.)

inclusionary zoning   A land-use concept in which local zoning ordinances require residential developers to include a certain percentage of dwelling units for low-income and moderate-income households as a condition to governmental approval of development of the project. In some areas, developers can pay a fee in lieu of allocating space for low-income or moderate-income units. Certain communities have even tried to impose resale price controls on developers as a condition to approval.

income and expense report   A monthly financial report showing the income from the property, operating expenses, and the amount distributed to the owner.

income approach   An approach to the valuation or appraisal of real property as determined by the amount of net income the property will produce over its remaining economic life. With this method, the market value is equal to the present worth of future net income. Four main steps are used in calculating valuation using the income approach.
1. Estimate the potential annual gross income—that is, the income that would accrue if all units were rented at their market value.
2. Determine the effective gross income by deducting an allowance for vacancy and collection loss.
3. Determine the annual net operating income by deducting the annual expenses of operation.
4. Apply the appropriate capitalization rate to the annual net income.

   The most difficult step in this process is determining the appropriate capitalization rate. This rate must be selected to accurately reflect the recapture of the original investment over the economic life of the improvement, and thus to give the investor an acceptable rate of return on the original investment and provide for the return of borrowed capital. Note that an income property that carries with it a great deal of risk generally requires a higher rate of return than a "safe" investment. The appraiser must use residual techniques to provide for the recapture of the investment in the improvement but not in the land, because the land is not a wasting asset.
   The main advantage of using this approach is that it best approximates the expectations of the typical investor in income-producing property who is looking for a money return on the investment. It is rarely used on single-family residential properties. (*See* **appraisal, band of investment [BOI], built-up method, capitalization [CAP] rate, economic rent, residual process**.)

income averaging   A method of reducing income taxes, especially for an individual taxpayer who earns a disproportionately high amount of money in comparison to the preceding four tax years. Income averaging has been repealed for most taxpayers, although it is still relevant for farmers and fishermen.

income capitalization approach   *See* **income approach**.

income property   (*propiedad generadora de ingresos*)   Property purchased primarily for the income to be derived plus certain tax benefits. Income property can be commercial, industrial or residential.

income statement   *See* **profit and loss statement**.

income tax   (*impuestos de ingreso*)   *See* **basis, depreciation, property tax, residence**.

incompetent   (*inhábil*)   A person who is not legally qualified to perform a valid act; one who lacks the power to act with legal effectiveness; any person who is impaired by reason of mental illness, physical disability, drugs, age, or other cause to the extent that he lacks sufficient understanding or capacity to make or communicate responsible decisions concerning his person. Thus, insane and, in certain cases, intoxicated people are incapable of entering into valid contracts. A corporation not authorized by its articles of incorporation to purchase real property is incompetent to contract for the purchase of real estate. Similarly, an officer not so authorized by the board of directors is incompetent to sell corporate real estate. An illiterate person, however, is not incompetent to contract as long as she understands the nature of her acts. If a person is adjudged incompetent, the court generally appoints a guardian to contract with all persons doing business with the incompetent. (*See* **capacity of parties**, **conservator**, **guardian**, **illiterate**.)

incorporate   To form a corporation by preparing the necessary articles of incorporation and filing them with the appropriate state government business registration division. (*See* **articles of incorporation**, **corporation**.)

incorporation by reference   A method of including all the terms of one document into another document merely by reference. For example, a sales contract may refer to an addendum or an Exhibit A and incorporate the terms of such addendum to the same extent as though it were fully set forth. A short-form mortgage or lease may refer to a previously recorded lengthy document containing the many "boilerplate" provisions of the mortgage or lease transaction. (*See* **boilerplate**.)

incorporeal rights   Intangible or nonpossessory rights in real property, such as easements, licenses, profits, mining claims, insurance claims, and future rents; possessing no physical body.

increment   An increase in quantity or size, commonly used in reference to the development of large subdivisions in phases, or in increments. (*See* **unearned increment**.)

incubator space   An industrial park building divided into small units of different sizes to accommodate young, growing companies that want to combine office and industrial space at one location.

incumbrance   *See* **encumbrance**.

incurable obsolescence   An appraisal term meaning the external or functional obsolescence of an improvement that is not economically feasible to repair or correct. If the loss in value is due to functional obsolescence, it is treated as incurable if it is not profitable to cure it. External obsolescence is generally incurable. (*See* **appraisal**.)

indemnification   (*indemnización*)   An agreement to reimburse or compensate someone for a loss. For example, a buyer of commercial property might require the seller to indemnify the buyer against claims caused by the discovery of hazardous substances on the property. (*See* **hold-harmless clause**.)

indenture deed   A deed in which both grantor and grantee bind themselves to reciprocal obligations. Normally, a deed need only be signed by the grantor (called a *deed poll*), but an indenture deed is signed by the grantee as well, who might thereby agree to assume the mortgage or agree to special covenants. The word *indenture* stems from an ancient custom whereby deeds were made for each of the parties on the same sheepskin and then torn apart on an uneven line. They could later prove genuineness by matching up their indentures. Many leases to be signed by both lessor and lessee also begin with the words "This Indenture . . ." (*See* **deed poll**.)

independent appraisal   An appraisal conducted by a qualified, disinterested person.

independent contractor   One who is retained to perform a certain act, but who is subject to the control and direction of another only as to the end result and not as to how she performs the act. The critical feature, and what distinguishes an independent contractor from an employee or agent, is the degree of control the employer has over such a person's activities. An employer, as defined or interpreted by the FICA and income tax laws, must withhold income tax from and pay Social Security taxes on commissions paid to an employee but does not need to do so in the case of an independent contractor, who must personally pay FICA and taxes.

　　In 1982, under IRS Section 3508, real estate licensees were allowed to retain their independent contractor status, for income tax purposes only. Three conditions for an independent contractor status must exist: (1) a written contract, (2) a real estate license, and (3) payment of the salesperson on the basis of performance, not the number of hours worked.

A person who hires an independent contractor is not usually liable for injuries caused by the negligence of the independent contractor. An employer, on the other hand, is liable for employees' acts within the scope of their employment. Thus, an employer would be liable for the automobile accident of an employee who was driving in the course of conducting company business. In view of the complex issues involved in determining whether real estate salespeople are employees or independent contractors, most brokers carry public liability insurance that covers all their salespeople and office personnel. In addition, many brokers request their salespeople to name the broker as "additional insured" in their personal automobile policies.

Because many licensing laws make brokers responsible for the activities of their salespeople, even if they are treated as independent contractors, many brokers want to exercise a high degree of control over such activities. However, the state licensing laws do not preclude the establishment of independent contractor status for tax purposes, provided the relationship is carefully structured to avoid possible classification of such a person as an employee. A broker should always consult a tax attorney concerning such matters. (*See* **principal broker [PB]**, **salesperson[s]**.)

index lease   A lease that provides for adjustments of rent according to changes in a price index such as the consumer price index. The index used in establishing the escalation must be reliable and bear a close relationship to the nature of the tenant's business. The most frequently used indexes are the consumer price index, also called the **cost-of-living index**, and the wholesale price index. The escalator clause connects the rent to the index, so the index lease is also called an escalation lease. LIBOR is an abbreviation for London Interbank Offered Rate.

index rate   The rate to which the interest rate on an adjustable-rate loan is tied. At set adjustment periods, the borrower's interest rate moves up or down as the index rate changes. Popular indices include the interest rate on one-year U.S. Treasury securities, Treasury constant maturity series, and LIBOR (London Interbank Offered Rate).

indicated value   The worth of a subject property as shown in the three approaches to value: (1) recent sales of comparable properties; (2) cost now less accrued depreciation plus land value; and (3) capitalization of annual net operating income.

indirect costs   (*costos indirectos*)   Development costs not related to the land or the structure, such as legal and architectural fees, financing, and insurance costs during construction.

indirect lighting   The light that is reflected from the ceiling or other object external to the fixture.

individual retirement account (IRA)   A retirement savings program that can be either an "individual retirement account" or an "individual retirement annuity." There are several types of IRAs: traditional, Roth IRAs, SIMPLE IRAs, and SEP IRAs. The traditional and Roth IRAs may be set up by individual taxpayers who are allowed to contribute 100 percent of compensation (self-employment income for sole proprietors and partners) up to a certain amount. Contributions to a Roth are not tax deductible, so qualified distributions are tax-free. Employers may set up SEPs and Simples.

First-time homebuyers (i.e., buyers who haven't owned a home in the past two years) can withdraw up to $10,000 from a retirement account (their own, their parents', or their grandparents') free of the 10 percent penalty but not the burden of paying taxes to apply toward the down payment and closing costs. (*See* **Keogh Plan**.)

indoor air quality   The presence of air pollutants inside a building. The major indoor air pollutants are tobacco smoke, biological contaminants, formaldehyde, carbon monoxide, organic gases (paint, solvents), radon, and asbestos.

As part of due diligence in the purchase of an industrial or commercial building, buyers should consider hiring outside experts to conduct indoor air-quality surveys. The survey could include tenant and employee questionnaires, ventilation studies, and specific contaminant sampling.

Buildings that are sealed to promote energy efficiency also can seal in pollution. Buildings used in a manner inconsistent with original design, old and dirty ductwork, new materials emitting formaldehyde fumes, and damp and dirty areas all contribute to indoor air quality problems. Some experts label the problem "the sick building syndrome," signaled by symptoms such as headaches, fatigue, and upper respiratory problems. (*See* **sick building syndrome [SBS]**.)

indorsement   *See* **endorsement**.

industrial broker   A real estate broker who specializes in brokering industrial real estate.

industrial park   An area zoned for industrial use that contains sites for many separate industries and is developed and managed as a unit, usually with provisions for common services to its users.

Typically, an industrial developer acquires a large parcel of land (usually 400 to 500 acres); obtains industrial zoning; and adds streets, water and sewer systems, and utilities. Then the developer records a declaration of restrictions that sets up a property owners' association and regulates setback lines, landscaping, architectural styles, and so forth. The developer might sell a site to a particular industry that will build its own plant, or the developer might build the plant and lease it to the industry. The advantage of acquiring a site in an industrial park is that it avoids the problems and costs involved in acquiring prepared industrial property and saves money through the sharing of common expenses for items such as sewers, security, utilities, and the like.

infant   *See* **minor**.

infiltration   The gradual alteration of a neighborhood due to displacement of residents or change in the existing uses of the property caused by shifts in the economic, social, and physical forces creating the environment.

inflation guard   An endorsement to an insurance policy that automatically increases coverage during the life of the policy at a certain percentage per quarter, as selected by the insured.

informed consent   Consent to a certain act, given after a full and fair disclosure of all facts needed to make a conscious choice. Only those with adequate reasoning facilities who can appreciate the implications and future consequences of an action can give informed consent. *See* **competent party**.

infrastructure   The constructed physical features of an urban area such as roads, highways, sewage and drainage systems, and utility facilities necessary to support a concentration of the population.

ingress   A way to enter a property; access. The opposite of egress.

inheritance tax   A state "estate" tax imposed on heirs for their right to inherit property. The tax is not levied on the property itself, but rather on the heirs for their right to acquire the property by succession or devise. Therefore, the rates or the deductions may vary depending on the degree of the relationship. (*See* **estate tax**, **federal tax**, **gift tax**.)

At the time of a person's death, a statutory lien usually attaches to all real property interests owned by the decedent, which lien remains in effect until the inheritance taxes have been paid and a "tax clearance" is issued. This applies even if property was held in joint tenancy with right of survivorship.

in-house sale   A sale in which the listing broker is the only broker in the transaction; there is no outside broker involved, as in a cooperative sale. Either the listing salesperson finds the buyer, or another salesperson working for the listing broker finds the buyer. If the buyer is a client of the broker, the issue of dual agency arises. (*See* **dual agency [limited agency]**.)

initials   Abbreviation for a name. Initials are effective as a person's signature so long as the signer intends them to be equivalent to that individual's legal signature.

Any changes to a contract should be initialed by all parties and dated. Usually a notary must initial all erasures on a document; otherwise, the document may not be accepted for recordation. A conservative approach to signing a lengthy document is to have all parties initial each page. This is sometimes done with a will.

In the more formal Torrens system of title registration, the recorder will not generally accept for recordation any document on which the parties have not signed their full names; initials are unacceptable. If an initial is only part of a given name or a party has no middle name, the document should state that fact. Similarly, a power of attorney used to execute documents usually must be signed with the full name of the principal. (*See* **legal name**, **signature**.)

injunction   (*conminación*)   A legal action whereby a court issues a writ that forbids a party defendant from doing some act or compels the defendant to perform an act. An injunction requires the person to whom it is directed to refrain from doing a particular thing, such as violating deed restrictions or house rules prohibiting pets.

in-law apartment   *See* **granny flats**.

inner city   An urban area that is generally recognized as a central residential or commercial part of a city even though it does not necessarily have political, geographic, racial, or economic boundaries.

innocent misrepresentation   A misstatement of material fact given without any intent to deceive. (*See* **misrepresentation**.)

innocent purchaser for value   One who purchases real property without notice, actual or constructive, of any superior rights or interests in the property. The state recording statutes are designed to protect an innocent purchaser for value from the secret claims of a prior purchaser. Also called a *bona fide purchaser for value*. (*See* **possession**, **recording**.)

inquiry notice   Legal notice that is presumed by law when factors exist that would make a reasonable person inquire further. For example, if someone is in possession of the property offered for sale, the purchaser is charged with knowing whatever facts an inspection of the property would have disclosed; purchasers therefore take title subject to the rights of the occupant. (*See* **actual notice**, **constructive notice**, **possession**.)

in-service loan   A program under the National Housing Act's Section 222 mortgage insurance for housing for military personnel under which HUD allows the departments of Defense, Transportation, and Commerce to pay the HUD mortgage insurance premium on behalf of the personnel on active duty under their jurisdiction. The mortgages may finance single-family dwellings and condominiums insured under standard HUD home mortgage insurance programs.

inside lot   Any lot located between the corner lots on a given block; interior lot (see the illustration).

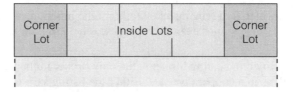

inspection   A visit to and review of particular premises. A purchaser should always inspect the property before closing. Because possession of property gives constructive notice of any claims of ownership, an inspection is an important step in discovering any possible claims by others. An inspection might also reveal any encroachments or unrecorded easements. It is good practice for a broker to inspect the listed premises to ascertain that any representations to prospective buyers are accurate.

Many brokers recommend inserting a clause in the sales contract to the effect that all appliances and electrical and plumbing fixtures are in normal working order and will be inspected by the buyer before closing. The buyer must make such an inspection a few days before the closing. If such a clause is inserted in the contract when the transaction is to be closed in escrow, the escrow company will not close until it has received an inspection approval letter from the buyer. The FHA and VA require that inspections be made before their approval of residential loans in order to ensure that the buyer will not have to make major repairs (wiring, roof, and the like) during the first year of ownership. The VA prohibits buyers from being charged inspection fees, and sellers should be aware that they may have to make repairs before VA approval of the loan application.

A title insurance company issuing an owner's policy may have one of its inspectors search for easements not shown in the public records, building restrictions, and improvements not within the stated lot lines.

A residential landlord generally reserves the right to inspect leased premises after having given appropriate notice. (*See* **access**, **due diligence**.)

installment contract   *See* **contract for deed**.

installment note   A promissory note providing for payment of the principal in two or more definite stated amounts at different times. (*See* **installment sale**.)

installment sale   For income tax purposes, a method of reporting gain received from the sale of real estate when the sales price is paid in installments (i.e., where at least one payment is to be received after the close of the taxable year in which the sale occurs). No down payment is required in an installment sale. Section 453 of the Internal Revenue Code no longer requires two installments of principal (i.e., the buyer could make a down payment of prepaid interest only, and a balloon payment of principal in a later year). If the seller provides any financing, it is an installment sale. Some or the entire purchase price must be paid within a year(s) after the tax year of the sale.

If certain conditions are met, taxpayers can save on taxes by postponing the receipt of an installment and the reporting of such income to future years when their other income may be lower. Thus, a taxpayer can avoid paying the entire tax on the gain in the year of sale. A gain from the installment sale is recognized for any tax year with respect to principal payments received in that tax year in the same ratio as the gross profit from the sale bears to the total "contract price."

In addition to cash received, the sales price includes the market value of any property or notes received from the buyer and any existing mortgage on the property, whether assumed by the buyer or not. The year of sale is the tax-reporting year of the seller, and the date of the sale is the date of title transfer to the property or, under a contract for deed, the date of possession. Note that the installment method of reporting is automatic with respect to qualifying sales of real estate, although the taxpayer can elect not to use the installment method. This can be accomplished by reporting the entire gain on the taxpayer's tax return for the tax year. Principal payments contracted for before the 1997 tax changes are taxed under the lower new rates.

Money received in the year of sale includes option money (even if paid in a prior year), down payment, payment of seller's indebtedness, excess of mortgage over basis, and subsequent principal payments. Mortgages assumed by the buyer are not normally included in computing payments in the year of sale. However, if the amount of the mortgage exceeds the seller's basis in the property, the excess is treated as payment in the year of sale. Note that the rule includes only money paid on the property's purchase price. Payment of interest is not considered to be a payment made on the purchase price but rather a payment made in consideration of the right to defer all or part of such payment; as such, the interest is always taxable.

Because the seller can defer all or a substantial part of the gain until receipt of the unpaid balance of the purchase price, the seller can accept a small cash down payment and thus expand the market of potential buyers. This may also put the seller in a position to negotiate for a higher sales price. In addition, the seller pays income tax only on the profit portion of each installment payment. Only that portion of the principal that represents gain is taxable, and the portion that represents the return of capital investment (basis) is not taxable. The seller thus retains a larger amount of each payment, which can be used for further investments. Interest, of course, is fully taxable as ordinary income.

The three steps in determining tax liability under an installment sale are:
1. Determine the total taxable gain on the transaction
2. Determine the seller's total proceeds from the sale (i.e., that money to be paid directly to seller), but do not include proceeds to others, such as a loan assumption (often called the *contract price*)
3. Determine the amount of gain to be realized each year (the ratio of the total taxable gain to the total "contract price," multiplied by the amount of cash received in that year)

For example, an investor sells a property for $135,000, accepts a down payment of $40,500, and takes back a purchase-money mortgage from the buyer in the amount of $94,500, to be paid over 20 years beginning in the following year. The total gain the investor realizes from the sale is $30,375. Thus, the investor must claim 22.5 percent of the down payment as a capital gain—22.5 percent being the ratio between the $30,375 gain and the $135,000 contract price, or

$$\text{Contract price } \$135,000 \overline{)\begin{array}{c} 0.225 \textbf{ or 22.5\% ratio} \\ 30,375 \qquad\qquad \text{total gain} \end{array}}$$

The investor, therefore, reports an initial capital gain of $9,112.50—22.5 percent of the original down payment:

$$
\begin{array}{ll}
\$40,500.00 & \text{down payment} \\
\underline{\times\ 22.5\%} & \text{ratio} \\
\$9,112.50 & \textbf{initial capital gain}
\end{array}
$$

The investor's capital gains for each of the next 20 years (the mortgage loan period) would be as follows:

$$\text{Number of years } 20 \overline{)\begin{array}{c} \$4,725 \text{ paid to seller each year} \\ \$94,500 \text{ owed to seller after down payment} \end{array}}$$

$$
\begin{array}{ll}
\$4,725.00 & \\
\underline{\times\ 22.5\%} & \text{ratio} \\
\$1,063.13 & \textbf{capital gain each year}
\end{array}
$$

The installment sale method is not allowed for sale of dealer real estate or sale of personal property.

Institute of Real Estate Management (IREM)   *See* Appendix A.

institutional lender   A financial institution such as a bank, insurance company, savings and loan association, or any lending institution whose loan is regulated by law. Such institutions invest depositors' and customers' money in mortgages, as opposed to private lenders such as pension and trust funds or credit unions, which invest their own funds. Institutional lenders are frequently represented by mortgage brokers who act as loan correspondents for out-of-state institutional lenders. Because they are actually lending other people's money, institutional lenders are carefully regulated by government rules.

institutional property An office building owned and occupied by the same company.

instrument (*instrumento*) A formal legal document such as a contract, deed, or will. The term *document* is a more comprehensive term referring to any paper relied on as the basis, proof, or support of anything else.

insulation Pieces of plasterboard, asbestos sheeting, compressed wood-wool, fiberboard, or other material placed between inner and outer surfaces, such as walls and ceilings, to protect the interior from heat loss. Insulation works by breaking up and dissipating air currents.

insulation disclosure A requirement by the Federal Trade Commission that real estate brokers, builders, and sellers of new houses must disclose in their sales contracts the type, thickness, and R-value of the insulation installed in the house. In addition, brokers must show the required facts in all listing and earnest money agreements. (*See* **R-value**.)

insurable interest A right or interest in property that would cause the person who has that right or interest to suffer a monetary loss if the property were destroyed or damaged. Thus, an insurable interest would exist not only for a property owner or lessee but also for any involved mortgagee or other lien creditors as well. To collect damages from an insurance policy, one must be able to prove an insurable interest at the time of loss. (*See* **insurance**, **interest in property**.)

insurable title A title on which a title-insuring company is willing to issue its policy of insurance. (*See* **title insurance**.)

insurance (*seguros*) Indemnification against loss from a specific hazard or peril. Many kinds of insurance are available to cover property or liability against various risks. Fundamentally, insurance may be written on buildings, building contents, and equipment; or it may be written to cover activities such as loss of income resulting from damage or some other unforeseen happening. Insurance can also be obtained to cover the insured's legal liability to other people. Note that when a building is insured under an insurance policy, it is insured against specific risks such as fire, windstorm, and explosion.

Property and liability insurance policies are personal contracts made between an *insurer* and a particular *insured*. Such policies, therefore, do not run with the land and cannot be assigned without the consent of the insurer. If a loss occurs, however, the right to the insurance proceeds may be assigned.

When a loss of property does occur, the policy may be reduced by the amount of the loss. An additional premium is then required to reinstate the policy to the full amount of insurance.

Most insurance policies contain a pro rata liability clause that usually provides that "the insurer is not liable for a greater portion of any loss than the amount insured against bears to the total insurance carried on the property against the peril involved, whether collectible or not." This prevents the owner from collecting a greater amount than the actual loss by carrying policies with several insurance carriers.

Public liability insurance covers the risk an owner assumes when the public may enter the owner's building. A situation that might be covered by such a liability policy would be a claim made for hospital expenses and doctors' bills submitted by a person who was injured in a building and claimed that the injury was due to the landlord's negligence in improper maintenance of the stairs. These policies are usually referred to as *owners'*, *landlords'*, and *tenants' liability insurance*.

Two possible methods may be used to determine the amount of the claim. One is based on the depreciated value, or actual cash value, of the damaged property, and the other is based on the replacement cost. If part of a 30-year-old building is damaged, the timbers and the materials are 30 years old and therefore do not have the same value as new material. In determining the amount of the loss according to actual cash value, the cost of new material would be obtained and reduced by the estimated depreciation the item had suffered while in the building. The alternate method is to cover replacement cost. This would represent the actual amount a builder would charge to replace the damaged property at the time of the loss.

Insurance rates are set by rating bureaus, which are supervised by state authorities. Under this system, the cost of the risk of possible damage is spread over all properties in the state by the establishment of a premium rate based on the losses experienced during the past year (or several years) for the risk involved. Rates are revised by underwriting bureaus and kept current in accordance with the loss ratio and cost of repairing the damage.

If a person owned a $1 million building and thought the building was in such fine condition and so well protected and cared for that it would be impossible to suffer a loss for more than $100,000, the owner might buy a policy for $100,000. The building is underinsured because the policy on a commercial building includes what is called a *coinsurance clause*. This clause requires that in the event of loss, the total insurance carried on the building must equal a stated percentage of the value of the insured building. The penalty for not carrying the proper amount of insurance is a reduction in the amount of the claim the insurance company is required to pay. For instance, most commercial properties include an 80 percent coinsurance clause. If the building owner carries the proper amount of insurance at the time of loss, the claim is paid in full to the limit of the amount of the policy. The purpose of a coinsurance clause is to require the insured to carry the proper amount of insurance so that he or she pays an adequate premium for this coverage.

Residential insurance policies also contain a coinsurance clause. For example, a house costing $100,000 to rebuild today would be insured for $80,000 to meet the 80 percent requirement (note that some policies are increasing this percentage). All losses, total or partial, would be fully paid up to the $80,000 face value. However, if the house is covered for only $40,000, it is insured for only half the minimum. Therefore, if the property loss is total, the homeowner would be reimbursed up to the full face value; but if the loss is partial, the homeowner would be reimbursed either for the actual cash value (i.e., current replacement cost less depreciation) or for half the loss, whichever is greater. The theory is that the company pays only the fraction of loss equal to the fraction of insurance carried. If the loss was partial or totaled $28,000, then reimbursement might be for only $14,000, regardless of the policy's $40,000 face value.

The three most popular types of homeowners' policies are the basic (HO-1), the homeowners (HO-3), and the condominium (HO-65). The HO-3 covers many perils except flood, earthquake, and war. Flood insurance must always be obtained separately.

To obtain hazard insurance, one must have an insurable interest in the property. Both vendor and vendee have an insurable interest in property sold under a contract for deed. Most contracts for deed require that the buyer maintain insurance to a stated amount and make the loss payable to the seller. If the sales contract provides for the assignment and proration of the seller's insurance policy, the transfer should be made at the closing. The seller then signs a form called an *assignment of policy*. This form is not effective until it has been accepted by the insurance company or by its authorized agent. (*See* **coinsurance**, **insurable interest**.)

Real estate brokerage firms should consider carrying errors and omissions (E&O) insurance, professional liability insurance much like a doctor's malpractice coverage. E&O insurance provides protection if the broker is sued for misrepresentation or concealment of a material fact, whether intentional or not.

A property manager is often responsible for securing adequate insurance protection for properties under its management. Some of the most common categories of insurance coverage are standard fire; extended coverage and collateral fire; machinery and equipment; consequential loss, use and occupancy coverage, such as for business interruption and rental income; general liability; and workers' compensation insurance.

Property owners often pay small casualty losses instead of filing a claim against the insurance company in order to avoid rate increases or cancellation. Taxpayers may only deduct personal casualty losses in excess of 10 percent of adjusted gross income for any taxable year. Few taxpayers can benefit, because the amount of a casualty loss not covered by the individual's insurance policy usually does not exceed 10 percent of adjusted gross income. (*See* **builder's risk insurance**, **commercial leasehold insurance**, **errors and omissions [E&O] insurance**, **extended coverage**, **flood insurance**, **homeowners' insurance policy**, **mortgage insurance**.)

intangible property   Anything having no material or physical existence, which cannot be seen or touched; that which derives any value it may have from what it represents. For example, good will is intangible, as are the "sticks" in the bundle of rights.

interest   (*interés*)   The sum paid or accrued in return for the use of money. Interest is usually stated in terms of an annual rate, although the parties may not always call this payment interest, because it may be disguised in the form of points or mortgage prepayment penalties. Interest on a promissory note is usually charged and due in arrears at the end of each payment period (monthly, semiannually, or as required by the lender).

The maximum rate of interest that may be charged on mortgage loans is often controlled by state law, although there are federal exemptions for home mortgage loans. Charging interest in excess of the statutory loan rate is called *usury*, and nonexempt lenders are penalized for making usurious loans. In some states, a lender who makes a usurious loan is permitted to collect the borrowed money, but only at the legal rate of interest. In other states a usurious lender may lose the right to collect any interest or may lose the entire loan amount in addition to the interest. Loans made to corporations and FHA and VA loans are generally exempt from state usury laws.

Note that interest (and real property taxes) related to a building's construction period must be amortized over a ten-year period. Low-income housing continues to be exempt from this capitalization requirement.

Interest rates are quoted for a one-year period. This annual interest amount is divided by 12 to find the interest due for one month. A shortcut to finding one month's interest charge is to multiply the principal balance of the loan by the interest factor.

Mortgage interest payments on acquiring and improving principal residences and second or vacation homes are fully deductible from income for tax purposes so long as the debt does not exceed $1,000,000. In addition, the discount points paid by a homebuyer are tax deductible in the year of purchase. Interest paid on amounts borrowed against the appreciated equity in first or second homes ("home equity debt") may not exceed $100,000 in order for the interest thereon to be deductible in full.

Note the difference between *nominal interest*, the amount (percentage) of annual interest stated in the loan document, and *effective interest*, the amount of interest the borrower actually pays. The difference usually results from the manner in which the debt is collected, such as the use of discount points to increase the gross rate or principal plus interest (add-on) methods. *See* the explanation under Truth-in-lending laws for the difference between interest and annual percentage rate. (*See* **annual percentage rate [APR]**, **block interest**, **compound interest**, **imputed interest**, **points**, **prepaid interest**, **Truth in Lending Act**, **usury**, **variable interest rate**.)

interest in property   A legal share of ownership in property, whether the entire ownership (as in a fee simple interest) or partial ownership (as in a leasehold estate). (*See* **estate**, **insurable interest**.)

interest-only mortgage loans   A mortgage loan under which the borrower pays only the interest on the loan for a period of time, often five to seven years, after which the borrower either pays off the loan in full, refinances, or starts to pay off the principal.

interest rate cap   The maximum interest rate charge allowed on an adjustable-rate loan for any one adjustment period during the life of the loan. In addition, the loan may have a lifetime cap on interest.

interim financing   A short-term loan usually made during the construction phase of a building project; often referred to as a *construction loan*. Proceeds from the interim loan are disbursed in increments as the construction progresses. Long-term or permanent financing is usually arranged to "take out" the interim loan. (*See* **construction loan**, **development loan**, **takeout financing**.)

interim use   The uses to which sites and improved properties may be put until they are ready for a more productive highest and best use.

interlocutory decree   A judicial order that does not take final effect until a specified time or the occurrence of a certain event. Besides divorce decrees, which often have a bearing on the division of real property, condemnation actions frequently involve interlocutory decrees.

intermediary   *See* **qualified intermediary**.

intermediate theory   The legal concept that a mortgage is a lien on property until default, at which time title passes to the lender. (*See* **lien-theory states**.)

internal rate of return (IRR)   (*tasa interna de redimiento*)   A rate of discount at which the present worth of future cash flows is exactly equal to the initial capital investment. An investor in real estate or any other investment is interested in two factors when analyzing a potential investment: the return of the original invested capital and a return on the original investment. Usually this return on investments is expressed as an annual return, or yield. The advantage of using the internal rate of return as a measurement of an investment's worth is that all types of investments—stocks, bonds, real estate, and business ventures—can be analyzed so they can be compared objectively. Internal rate of return is calculated on the basis of the projected cash flows from the initial investment.

   Although use of the IRR is becoming more widespread, it does present some problems. The particular problem with use of the IRR mathematical formula is that it requires the assumption that the investments being analyzed have similar risk factors, and the projected cash flows used as measurements are only as good as the person preparing the projections. Also called **discounted cash flow**. (*See* **Inwood tables**, **present value of one dollar**.)

Internal Revenue Code of 1986 (IRC)   The body of statutes codifying the federal tax laws and administered by the Internal Revenue Service (IRS), an agency that issues its own regulations interpreting those laws.

Internal Revenue Service (IRS)   *See* Appendix A.

International Code Council (ICC)   *See* Appendix A.

International Council of Shopping Centers (ICSC)   *See* Appendix A.

International Facility Management Association (IFMA)   *See* Appendix A.

International Real Estate Federation (IREF)   *See* Appendix A.

Internet   A world-wide electronic network connecting government, academic, and business institutions providing data, news, and opinions. Nearly two-thirds of prospective homebuyers first consult the

Internet, weeks before they approach a real estate licensee. Internet skills, such as e-mail and attachments, among others, are essential to the real estate licensee in the 21st century.

interpleader   A legal proceeding whereby an innocent third party (stakeholder), such as an escrow agent or broker, can deposit with the court property or money that the party holds and that is subject to adverse claims so that the court can distribute it to the rightful claimant.

The distribution of deposit or earnest money held in escrow is often a problem when the buyer and the seller are in dispute over the purchase contract. Generally, the escrow agent will not release the funds until all parties—including the broker—sign a cancellation of escrow form. If one of the parties refuses to cancel the escrow, then no one can recover the deposit money. If the escrow agent cannot get the parties to agree on the disposition of the deposit money, one recourse is to file an interpleader action asking the court to accept the money and distribute it to the rightful claimant. (*See* **escrow**.)

interrogatory   *See* **deposition**.

interstate   An event occurring between two or more states, thus triggering the jurisdiction of federal law, such as the federal securities laws.

Interstate Land Sales Full Disclosure Act   (*Ley Interestatal de Divulgación Completa en la Venta de Tierras*)   A federal law, enacted in 1968, that regulates interstate land sales by requiring registration of real property with the Office of Interstate Land Sales Registration (OILSR) of the U.S. Department of Housing and Urban Development (HUD). It requires disclosure of full and accurate information regarding the property to prospective buyers before they decide to buy. To comply with the act, the developer must prepare a statement of record and register the subdivision with HUD. After the registration is effective, the developer must deliver to the purchaser (and obtain a receipt for) the property report before execution of the purchase agreement. The developer must give prospective buyers a cooling-off period of seven calendar days to consider the material contained in the property report. Many large subdivisions are registered with HUD because HUD regulations apply if the developer uses the mail or any other means of interstate commerce in the sale of lots.

The intrastate exemption to the regulations of the act is limited in scope and very narrowly construed. If the subdivision contains fewer than 300 lots that are sold or leased to residents of the same standard metropolitan statistical area (SMSA) in which the subdivision is located (leeway is given so that 5 percent or less of sales in any one year may be made to residents of another state), the subdivider may apply for the exemption. Some of the more common exemptions from HUD filing requirements are as follows:

- Subdivisions in which there are fewer than 100 lots; if there are fewer than 25 lots, there is a total exemption from the act, not just from the registration and disclosure requirements
- Subdivisions in which all the lots are five acres or larger (inclusive of easements)
- Subdivisions in which the land is improved by a building or in which there is a contract obligating the seller to erect such a building within a period of two years
- Bulk sales of lots to another developer
- Sale to a contiguous owner
- Fewer than 12 sales per year
- Sales to a governmental agency
- Cemetery lots
- Sales of a single-family residential subdivision when the subdivision meets local code standards, title passes within 180 days after the contract, and the seller refrains from promotional techniques such as gifts and dinner programs

HUD considers condominium units to be lots "in the sky," and the developer may have to register a condominium with HUD as well as the local regulatory agency. The risk of noncompliance is greatest in those larger projects in which the developer is building in separate increments but promotes the use of common facilities that may not be completed for more than two years (such as a golf course).

A developer need not register with HUD a condominium in which each unit has been completed before sale. In this regard, the term *completed* means habitable and ready for occupancy. The developer can also avoid registration (and thus not be required to furnish buyers with a property report) if the unit is sold under a contract that obligates the seller to complete construction of the development within two years following the sale, as long as construction is not delayed by conditions beyond the developer's control. Also, the developer need not give a prospective buyer a HUD property report before the buyer signs a reservation, only before the buyer signs a contract to buy.

A registered subdivider who sells on an installment contract must refund any payments over 15 percent of the purchase price (excluding interest owed) if the purchaser defaults on the contract. This requirement can be avoided if the contract requires the subdivider to deliver legal title within 180 days after the execution of the contract.

The three-year statute of limitations for fraud does not begin to run until discovery of the fraud is made or should have been made.

Note that even though a particular subdivider or subdivision may be exempt from registration under the law (e.g., a 60-lot subdivision), it is still unlawful to make false statements regarding such sales by means of interstate commerce. However, if there are fewer than 25 lots, then the subdivider is not subject to any provision of the act. (*See* **property report**, **statement of record**.)

interval ownership   A popular system of time-share ownership in which the owner acquires title to a specific property for a certain week (or weeks) of each year. (*See* **time-sharing**.)

inter vivos trust   A "living" trust, which takes effect during the life of the creator, as opposed to a testamentary trust, which is created within a person's will and does not take effect until the death of the creator. Inter vivos transfers are made between living persons (e.g., deeds or leases).

The inter vivos trust is frequently used to allow the trustee to provide investment services when the trustor is either unwilling or too unsophisticated to administer the assets or as a vehicle for a trustor to dispose of insurance proceeds, pension benefits, and the estate (pour-over trust). The use of an inter vivos trust-owning property can be a way to avoid probate proceedings on the death of the trustor. (*See* **land trust**.)

intestate   (*intestado*)   Dying without a will or having left a will that is defective in form. An intestate decedent's property passes to the heirs according to the laws of descent in the state where such real property is located. These laws of descent vary from state to state and determine who is entitled to the decedent's property, which then must pass through probate in the state. Descent laws do not affect the distribution of jointly held property or life insurance proceeds.

State laws of descent vary greatly: in some states, an unmarried person's estate passes to the deceased's parents; in other states, the decedent's parents may have to share the estate with the intestate person's lineal brothers and sisters. A married person's property may pass to the spouse and children or descendants of children in varying shares; if the deceased left no children or descendants of same, the surviving spouse may be the sole heir in some states or may have to share with the decedent's parents in others. Many states allow a surviving spouse to take a special marital share of the estate, such as dower, curtesy, or an elective share. In states that recognize community property, a surviving spouse legally owns one-half of all community property, so it is only the half-interest owned by the decedent that passes to his or her heirs according to the state laws of descent. (*See* **descent**, **escheat**, **will**.)

intrastate exemption   An exemption from federal securities registration requirements afforded to securities that are offered and sold only to residents of one particular state, where the issuer of the security is a resident of, and doing business within, that state. The exemption applies to a corporation if it is incorporated by and doing business within that state and if the assets and activity of the partnership are also located within that state. Though exempt from the burdensome registration requirements of the Securities and Exchange Commission, the intrastate offering is still subject to the full-disclosure and antifraud provisions of the Securities Act of 1933 and the Securities Exchange Act of 1934. The intrastate exemption is strictly construed and enforced. If one sale or resale—or even an offer—is made to a nonresident, the exemption is lost; the issuer then has to register the entire issue and offer rescission rights to prior purchasers. (*See* **private offering, real property securities registration, Rule 147.**)

intrinsic value   An appraisal term meaning the result of a person's individual choices and preferences for a given geographical area based on the features and amenities the area has to offer. For example, to most people, property located in a well-kept suburb near a shopping center would have a greater intrinsic value than similar property located near a sewage treatment plant. As a rule, the greater the intrinsic value, the more money a property can command upon its sale. Most land speculation is based on this principle of present versus future intrinsic value. What was farmland a few years ago could very well be a booming community today, and the wise investor knows how to spot, buy, and sell such speculative properties at the most advantageous times.

inventory   (*inventario*)
1. An itemized list of property. Many brokers recommend that their clients attach to the sales contract an inventory of property to be included in the sale of a residential property, including a condominium dwelling. Such a procedure lessens misunderstandings concerning which items in the seller's home will pass to the buyer with the sale. Of course, an inventory should definitely be included in the sale of income-producing property, such as a furnished apartment building, and the agent should verify the inventory.
2. A list of goods on hand held for sale in the ordinary course of business. Profits from the sale of inventory goods are taxed as ordinary income. (*See* **bulk sales transfer, dealer.**)

inverse condemnation   An action for just compensation brought by a person whose property has been effectively taken, substantially interfered with, or taken without just compensation. For example, when a governmental authority announces it will condemn an owner's property and then unduly delays in taking the property, the owner can bring legal action to force a condemnation and payment for the taking. Or if the noise of low-flying government aircraft damages the owner's use of the land, there may be inverse condemnation, or a taking of property for which compensation must be paid. Another example is where some public works are undertaken with resultant damage to a private owner, but no condemnation action is taken by a public body. Such cases are called *inverse condemnations* because they are started by an owner who seeks compensation from the condemning agency and the payment is for land not directly condemned. (*See* **condemnation.**)

Courts have held that a zoning action that merely decreases the market value of property does not constitute a compensable taking actionable under a theory of inverse condemnation as long as a reasonably viable economic use exists. An inverse condemnation suit is not available before there has been an actual taking or physical interference with the subject property.

Inverse condemnation is the flip side of eminent domain and occurs when a public entity indirectly "condemns" private property by acting (e.g., a restrictive use regulation like downzoning), or failing to act when it should have, and property loss or damage results. The taking is not by legal action but by conduct. It is irrelevant whether the act or failure to act was negligent.

investment contract   A contract, transaction, or scheme whereby a person invests money in a common enterprise and is led to expect profits solely from the efforts of the promoter or a third party. The sale of real property using investment contracts is deemed to be the sale of a security, thus requiring compliance with federal and state securities laws. (*See* **real property securities registration**.)

investment interest   The amount of interest incurred to purchase or carry investment property. This does not include interest paid on a personal residence or passive-activity interest. Investment property includes that producing income defined as interest, dividends, annuities, or royalties, and any trade or business in which the taxpayer does not materially participate, so long as that activity is not treated as a passive activity. Investment interest is deductible to the amount of the investment income. Any excess investment interest is carried over to the following years.

involuntary conversion   A tax term referring to loss of property through destruction or condemnation. Such a conversion is considered a "sale" and is subject to income tax unless proceeds of the condemnation award or insurance proceeds are reinvested in similar property. If property has been condemned and the owner replaces the property, basis in the replacement property is deemed to be the same as that which is replaced, except that it is increased by any debt assumed above the amount of the condemnation award, and gain is recognized to the extent that the award exceeds the price paid for the replacement property. Under Section 1033 of the Internal Revenue Code, the replacement property for business or investment property must be purchased within two to four years, depending on the type of property at the end of the tax year in which there was a threat of condemnation. (*See* **condemnation**.)

involuntary lien   A lien created by operation of law, such as a real property tax lien, judgment lien, or mechanic's lien.

Inwood tables   A set of interest tables widely used by appraisers, before the popularity of calculators and computers, in computing the present value of an annuity for a number of years at various interest rates. Among their many uses, Inwood tables enable an appraiser to estimate the value of a leasehold interest when the income stream (cash flow) is constant. Also referred to as the *Inwood coefficients*.

    The principle underlying the system is that a series of equal annual payments to be made in the future is not an annuity's present worth. The annuity is worth only the amount that, if deposited today at a fixed rate of interest compounded annually, would provide for the withdrawal at the end of the year of an amount equal to one annual payment. (*See* **present value of one dollar**.)

IRC   *See* **Internal Revenue Code of 1986 (IRC)**.

ironclad agreement   An agreement that cannot be broken by the parties to it.

irrevocable consent   An agreement that cannot be withdrawn or revoked. Most state licensing laws require a nonresident broker to file an irrevocable consent agreeing to be bound to the outcome of lawsuits brought against the broker.

irrigation districts   Quasi-political districts created under special state laws to provide water services to property owners in the district and given the power to levy assessments to finance the districts' operations.

J

jalousie   Adjustable glass louvers in doors or windows used to regulate light and air or exclude rain.

jamb   A vertical surface lining the opening in the wall left for a door or window.

joint and several liability   A situation in which more than one party is liable for repayment of a debt or obligation and a creditor can obtain compensation from one or more parties, either individually or jointly. General partners are jointly and severally liable for partnership debts and obligations, as are the grantee and grantor for any unpaid common expenses in the sale of a condominium unit. Usually a right of contribution exists among persons who are jointly and severally liable, so that the person who is actually forced to repay the debt can try to collect equal amounts from the others who also are liable. (*See* **right of contribution**.)

joint tenancy   An estate or unit of interest in real estate that is owned by two or more natural persons, all owning equal shares with rights of survivorship. The basic idea of a joint tenancy is unity of ownership; title is held as though all owners collectively constituted one person, a fictitious entity. The death of one joint tenant does not destroy the owning unit—it only reduces by one the number of persons who jointly own the unit. The remaining joint tenants receive the deceased tenant's interest by the right of survivorship. Thus, the decedent's interest cannot be transferred by will or descent. As each successive joint tenant dies, the remaining tenants acquire the interest of the deceased. The last survivor takes title in severalty, fully inheritable at the survivor's death by heirs and devisees.

Some form of joint tenancy is recognized in most states, although several states have opted to eliminate the right of survivorship as a distinguishing characteristic. Sometimes called the "poor man's will," the fact that one holds title to property as a joint tenant is no reason for a person not to make a will. Joint tenancy does avoid a formal probate proceeding, however.

Traditionally, four unities are required to create a joint tenancy: unity of title, unity of time, unity of interest, and unity of possession. All unities must be present when title is acquired by one deed, executed and delivered at one time that conveys equal interests to all the grantees, who hold undivided possession of the property as joint tenants.

A joint tenancy can be created *only* by grant or purchase (by a deed of conveyance) or by devise (will)—it cannot be created by operation of law. The grantees or devisees must be specifically named as joint tenants. In most states, a deed or will that is unspecific about the grantees' or devisees' tenancy will pass title to the parties as tenants in common. Typical wording used to create a joint tenancy may be as follows: "To Morton Charles and Seymour Berkowitz, and to the survivor of them, and his or her heirs and assigns as joint tenants, with rights of survivorship, and not as tenants in common."

A combination of interests can exist in one parcel of real estate. For example, if A and B hold title to an undivided one-half as joint tenants, and C and D hold title to the other undivided half as tenants by the entirety, the relation between the two sets of joint tenants is that of a tenancy in common.

A joint tenancy is terminated when any of the essential unities has been terminated by mutual agreement of the parties or by one of the parties selling his or her interest in the joint tenancy. For example, if A, B, and C hold title to certain farmland as joint tenants, and A conveys his interest to D, then D owns an undivided one-third interest, and B and C continue to own an undivided two-thirds interest as joint tenants. D owns the farm as a tenant in common with the joint tenants B and C.

J

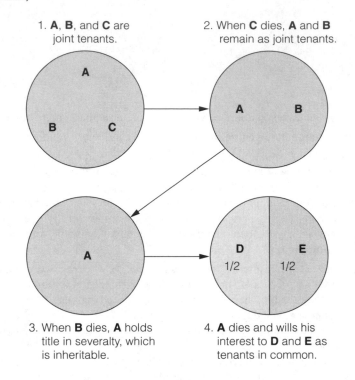

1. **A**, **B**, and **C** are joint tenants.

2. When **C** dies, **A** and **B** remain as joint tenants.

3. When **B** dies, **A** holds title in severalty, which is inheritable.

4. **A** dies and wills his interest to **D** and **E** as tenants in common.

Likewise, if one or more of the joint tenants' interests are defeated by an action of law, such as the appointment of a receiver in bankruptcy or the sale of property to satisfy a judgment, then joint tenancy is broken. In title-theory states, a mortgage is a conveyance of land to the lender. The land is then subject to being reconveyed upon payment of the debt, and a joint tenant in such states who mortgages her interest without the other joint tenants joining the mortgage therefore destroys the existing joint tenancy by removing her interest from the joint tenancy.

Many state laws hold that there is no dower in joint tenancy. Thus, business associates can hold title to a parcel of real estate as joint tenants, and any spouses are not required to join in a conveyance to waive dower and/or homestead rights. A corporation cannot be a joint tenant because it has perpetual existence and—at least in legal theory—never dies.

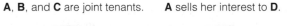

A, **B**, and **C** are joint tenants.   **A** sells her interest to **D**.

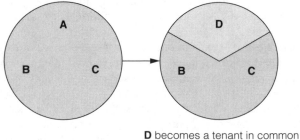

D becomes a tenant in common with **B** and **C** as joint tenants.

Debtors cannot protect themselves from creditors' claims by taking title to property in joint tenancy. The creditor has every right to attach the debtor's interest in jointly held property and force a partition. However, if the joint tenant dies before the creditor seizes that tenant's interest then the creditor loses his interest because the surviving tenant takes the property free from the claims of the decedent's creditors. On the other hand, a creditor of the surviving joint tenant has substantially increased his security.

One principal advantage of joint tenancy is avoiding the delay and expense of probate proceedings because the surviving joint tenant immediately becomes the sole owner of the property. The current value of the property is not included in the total value of the estate on which probate fees are assessed. In addition, the survivor holds the property free from the debts of the deceased joint tenant and from heirs against her interest.

Joint tenants give up the right to dispose of their individual interests by will, thus precluding the use of estate planning to minimize the estate taxes. Although not subject to probate proceedings, joint tenancies are subject to gift taxes, income taxes, and inheritance taxes, in addition to federal estate taxes. A purchaser should discuss these tax consequences with experienced tax counsel before deciding whether to hold title to the property in joint tenancy. In addition, joint tenancy or tenancy by the entirety may not be appropriate for people with children from a prior marriage.

In many states, a property owner can create a joint tenancy (also a tenancy by the entirety with a spouse) by conveying to herself and another as joint tenants without the necessity of conveying through a third person (called a *straw man*). This is a statutory exception to the common-law "four unities" rule that requires the creation of a joint tenancy by one and the same instrument when title to the property is acquired.

If all joint tenants die in a common disaster, the Uniform Simultaneous Death Act in effect treats them as equal tenants in common. Rather than avoid probate, however, the unfortunate effect would be to multiply the number of probate proceedings.

Upon the death of a joint tenant, the survivor(s) should, as a matter of good title practice, record an affidavit of death and a death certificate with the county recorder. This is often required under state inheritance tax laws to obtain a tax clearance. If the property is registered in Torrens, the certificate of title must be amended to reflect such death. (*See* **cotenancy**; **dower**; **gift tax**; **inheritance tax**; **ownership, form of**; **probate**; **property tax**; **severance**; **straw man**; **survivorship, right of**; **title-theory states**; **undivided interest**; **unity [joint tenancy]**.)

jointure   A freehold estate in land for the life of the wife to take effect upon the death of her husband; a life estate in lieu of dower. A jointure or any pecuniary provision that is made for the benefit of an intended wife and in lieu of her dower bars her right to dower provided she assents to the jointure. (*See* **dower**.)

joint venture   (*asociación en participación, contrato de asociación en participación*)   The joining of two or more people in a specific business enterprise, such as the development of a condominium project or a shopping center. The parties may pool their respective resources (such as money, expertise, property, or equipment). There must be an agreement, express or implied, to share in the losses or profits of the venture. Joint ventures are a business form of partnership and for tax purposes are treated as partnerships. The main difference between the two is that a joint venture is a special joining of the parties for a specific project with no intention on the part of the parties to enter into any continuing partnership relationship (a "one-shot partnership"). If the joint parties combine their efforts on several different projects, the relationship becomes more like a general partnership than a joint venture. Also, even though a partner can bind the partnership to a contract, one party to a joint-venture agreement cannot bind the other joint venturers to a contract. (*See* **limited partnership**, **partnership**.)

joist   A heavy piece of horizontal timber to which the boards of a floor or the lath of a ceiling are nailed. Joists are laid edgewise to form the floor support.

judgment   (*juicio*)   The formal decision of a court on the respective rights and claims of the parties to an action or suit. A judgment that has been entered and recorded with the county recorder usually becomes a general lien on the property of the defendant. (*See* **execution, general lien.**)

judgment lien   A purely statutory general lien on real and personal property belonging to a debtor. Usually the lien covers only property located within the county where the judgment is rendered; notices of the lien must be filed in other counties when the creditor wishes to extend the lien coverage. To collect the amount of the judgment, the court is asked to issue a legal document, called a *writ of execution*, directing the sheriff to seize and sell as much of the debtor's property as is necessary to pay the debt and the expenses of the sale. A judgment lien differs from a mortgage in that a judgment lien does not have a specific parcel of real estate given as security at the time that the debtor-creditor relationship is created.

The law in the state where the real estate is located determines priority of liens. A judgment takes its priority as a lien on the debtor's property on one or a combination of the following dates: (1) the date the judgment was entered by the court, (2) the date the judgment was filed for record in the recorder's office, or (3) the date an execution was issued. Judgments are enforced through the issuance of an execution and the ultimate sale of the debtor's real or personal property by a sheriff. When the property is sold to satisfy a debt, the debtor should demand a legal document known as a *satisfaction judgment*, which should be filed with either the clerk of the court or, in some states, with the recorder of deeds so that the record is cleared of the judgment. (*See* **attachment, execution, lis pendens [Lis/P].**)

judgment-proof   Having no assets to satisfy a judgment for money. Under many states' real estate recovery fund procedures, a person defrauded by a real estate licensee can collect damages from the fund only if able to show that the licensee is judgment-proof. (*See* **recovery fund.**)

judicial foreclosure   A method of foreclosing on real property by means of a court-supervised sale. In a judicial foreclosure, there is an appraisal, after which the court determines an upset price below which no bids to purchase will be accepted. (*See* **foreclosure, power of sale, upset price.**)

judicial precedent   A legal term describing the requirements established by prior court decisions (called *case law*). Under the doctrine of "stare decisis," lower courts must follow the prior decisions of higher courts. (*See* **common law.**)

jumbo loan   A residential mortgage loan that exceeds the loan amounts acceptable for sale to Freddie Mac and Fannie Mae. Also called *nonconforming loans*, they may carry higher interest rates and require a larger down payment. As such, they must be packaged and sold differently to underwriters.

junior mortgage   A mortgage, such as a second mortgage, that is subordinate in right or lien priority to an existing mortgage on the same realty. In the event of a foreclosure, second and third mortgage loans are repaid only if funds remain after paying the first mortgage. Because they are riskier, they generally carry a higher interest rate.

Generally, the foreclosure of a senior lien extinguishes all junior liens, whereas the foreclosure of a junior lien has no effect on a senior lien; that is, the purchaser at the junior foreclosure sale buys the property subject to the senior lien. There is no legal limit on the number of junior mortgages that can be placed on a property, but there is a practical limit. A lender would never want the loan amount to exceed the borrower's equity in the secured property. (*See* **secondary financing, second mortgage, subordination clause, wraparound mortgage.**)

Junk Fax Act   *See* Appendix D.

jurat   The clause written at the bottom of an affidavit by a notary public stating when, where, and before whom the affidavit was sworn. (*See* **affidavit**.)

jurisdiction   (*jurisdicción*)   The authority or power to act, such as the authority of a court to hear and render a decision that binds both parties. Real estate matters are usually within the jurisdiction of the court of the county in which the property is located. A state real estate commission or department generally has jurisdiction over the licensing and conduct of real estate salespeople and brokers in the state.

just compensation   An amount of compensation to be received by a party for the taking of property under the power of eminent domain. Under both federal and state constitutions, private property may not be taken for public use without just compensation having first been determined by the court. Determination of just compensation is probably the most difficult problem in condemnation proceedings. A condemnee can generally accept the offered compensation or can request and receive a court hearing for determining the appropriate amount of compensation. (*See* **before-and-after method, condemnation, eminent domain, special benefit**.)

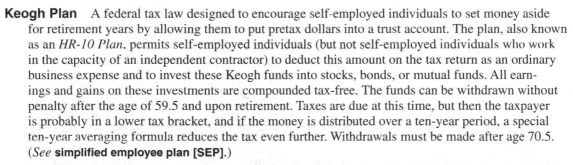

Keogh Plan   A federal tax law designed to encourage self-employed individuals to set money aside for retirement years by allowing them to put pretax dollars into a trust account. The plan, also known as an *HR-10 Plan*, permits self-employed individuals (but not self-employed individuals who work in the capacity of an independent contractor) to deduct this amount on the tax return as an ordinary business expense and to invest these Keogh funds into stocks, bonds, or mutual funds. All earnings and gains on these investments are compounded tax-free. The funds can be withdrawn without penalty after the age of 59.5 and upon retirement. Taxes are due at this time, but then the taxpayer is probably in a lower tax bracket, and if the money is distributed over a ten-year period, a special ten-year averaging formula reduces the tax even further. Withdrawals must be made after age 70.5. (*See* **simplified employee plan [SEP]**.)

key lot   A lot that has added value because of its strategic location, especially when it is needed for the highest and best use of contiguous property; a lot that adjoins the rear property line of a corner lot and fronts on a secondary street. Also, the piece of property that is essential to the development of a project.

key man insurance   A life insurance policy paid for by a company to cover the estimated cost of replacing a key person in the company; it may be either a life or a disability policy or a combination of both. Some lenders require key employee insurance when the borrower is a small corporation that relies primarily on the talents of one executive.

key money   Payment made to secure a leasehold interest. The prospective tenant in essence is buying the key to the premises.

key tenant   A major office-building tenant that leases several floors; a major department store in a shopping center. (*See* **anchor tenant**.)

kickers   Different types of equity participations a lender may seek as a condition for lending money, such as participation in rentals, profits, or extra interest. Serious legal questions are often raised concerning whether such equity participations constitute additional interest in terms of the usury laws.

kiln   A large oven-like chamber used for baking, drying, and hardening various materials such as lumber, brick, and lime.

kiosk   A small structure, usually constructed of wood, with one or more sides open and typically used as a newsstand, jewelry stall, or phone sales, especially in an enclosed mall. Such an enterprise usually pays rent on a fairly high percentage lease basis.

kitchenette   Space, less than 60 square feet, used for cooking and preparation of food.

kiting   *See* **dual contract**.

knockdown   Prepared construction materials that are delivered to the building site unassembled but complete and ready to be assembled and installed.

L

labor and material payment bond   *See* **payment bond**.

laches   An equitable doctrine used by courts to bar or prevent the assertion of a right or a claim because of undue delay or failure to assert the claim or right. Laches is similar to the statute of limitations, which is a legal (as opposed to an equitable) doctrine used to bar a claim asserted after the passing of a statutory period of time. (*See* **statute of limitations**.)

lanai   Popular term in the western or southern states for a balcony, veranda, porch, or covered patio.

land   (*terreno*)   The surface of the earth extending down to the center and upward to the sky, including all natural things thereon such as trees, crops, or water, plus the minerals below the surface and the air rights above. The term *real property* includes the land and all artificial things attached to the land, such as houses, fences, fixtures, and the like, together with all rights appurtenant to the property, such as easements, rents, and profits. In customary usage, the term *land* has become synonymous with real property and real estate. (*See* **improved land, raw land, real estate, real property, registered land, wasteland**.)

land bank   Land purchased and held for future development. In some communities, the government will condemn and land-bank certain scenic property in an effort to prevent adverse development and to control urban or suburban development or sprawl. (*See* **scenic easement**.)

land banker   A developer who improves raw land for construction purposes and maintains an inventory of these types of lots as a function of this ongoing business.

land capacity   The ability of land to handle capital and labor; an important step in determining highest and best use. (*See* **highest and best use**.)

land contract   An installment contract for sale with the buyer receiving equitable title (right to possession) and the seller retaining legal title (record title). (*See* **contract for deed**.)

land description   A description of a particular piece of real property. In the case of a deed, assignment of lease, or mortgage, the description of the property should be a complete legal description. In the case of a sales contract, however, the description need only be sufficient to identify the property; often a street address would suffice for this purpose.

land economics   The scientific study of land and the methods of determining and implementing land's highest and best use.

land grant   A grant of public lands by the government, usually for roads, railroads, or agricultural colleges (thus the term *land-grant college*).

land lease   *See* **ground lease**.

land leaseback   A creative financing device (often used with raw land a developer wants to improve) by which a developer sells the land to an investor, who leases the land back to the developer under a long-term net lease and subordinates the fee ownership to the lender, who provides development financing. The net effect of the land leaseback transaction is to obtain maximum leverage, including 100 percent land financing, and, because the land is subordinated to development financing, probably 100 percent development financing as well. (*See* **sale-leaseback, subordination agreement**.)

landlease communities   Community or park defined as a parcel of land containing two or more manufactured homes in which the homeowner rents the land on which the manufactured home is situated. The owner often provides the pad on which the home is located and hookups to utilities such as electricity, plumbing, and a water supply. (*See* **manufactured housing**.)

landlocked   Real property that has no access to a public road or way, such as parcel *C* in the following figure.

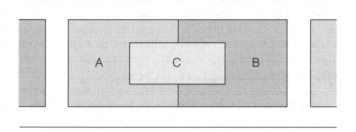

   If parcel C had ever been a part of parcel A or B, a court would grant the owner of C an easement of necessity over the parcel with which it had once been joined. This easement of necessity continues only during the period of necessity. Landlocked parcels are sometimes created as a result of condemnation for a limited-access highway. (*See* **easement by necessity**.)

landlord   (*arrendador, casero, locador*)   The lessor or the owner of leased premises. The landlord retains a reversionary interest in the property, so that when the lease ends the property will revert to the landlord.

landlord's warrant   *See* **distraint**.

landlord-tenant code   *See* **Uniform Residential Landlord and Tenant Act [URLTA]**.

landmark   (*hito, mojón, mojonería*)   A stake, stream, cliff, monument, or other object or feature used to fix or define land boundaries; also a prominent feature of a landscape or property that symbolizes the place; often used in metes-and-bounds land descriptions. (*See* **monument**.)

land poor   The state of being short of money because of owning an excess of real property that does not produce income but results in ongoing out-of-pocket expenses.

land residual technique   A method of real property appraisal similar to the building residual technique of capitalization, except that the amount of income earned by the improvements at the highest and best use of the site (the return on and recapture of the capital investment) is deducted from the annual net income, and the resulting figure (the land residual) is capitalized at the land capitalization rate and is then added to the improvement cost to arrive at the appraised value of the real property. (*See* **income approach, residual process**.)

landscaping   Shrubs, bushes, trees, and the like on the grounds surrounding a structure. Under certain circumstances, landscaping costs can be depreciated generally over 15 years. Generally, however, is that land itself is not depreciable for tax purposes.

land, tenements, and hereditaments   A feudal phrase used to describe all types of immovable realty, including the land, buildings, and all appurtenant rights thereto; the complete ownership of all the bundle of rights in a freehold estate.

land trust   A trust originated by the owner of real property in which real estate is the only asset. As in all trusts, the legal and equitable title to the property is in the trustee's name under a deed in trust. The beneficial interest in the trust property is in the beneficiary, who is usually the trustor (that is, the person who created or established the trust). Generally, only living persons may create a land trust, but corporations as well as living persons can be the beneficiaries. The beneficial interest in real estate held in a land trust is considered personal property. The beneficiary has the rights to the possession, income, and proceeds of sale of such property. Under a land trust agreement, the trustee deals with the property only upon the written direction of the beneficiary. The land trust agreement is executed by the trustor and the trustee. A beneficial interest under a land trust can be transferred merely by assignment, without the necessity of a deed and all its formal requirements. It can be pledged as collateral for a loan without a mortgage being placed on record (through a collateral assignment). Courts have held that real estate held in a land trust cannot be partitioned by the beneficiaries, because their interest is not one in real estate but one in personal property.

A land trust generally continues for a definite term, such as 20 years. At the expiration of the term, if the beneficiary does not extend the trust term, the trustee is usually obligated to sell the real estate and to return the net proceeds of the sale to the beneficiary.

Land trusts are popular among multiple owners who seek protection against the effects of divorce, judgments, or bankruptcies of the other owners. Because ownership is kept private, a land trust is sometimes used for secrecy when assembling separate parcels. Land trusts can also avoid title liens and partition suits, reduce probate expenses, and help nonresidents avoid ancillary probate costs and inheritance taxes in the state where the land is located. If the real property is to be sold, the trustee should execute the contract of sale and the deed. (*See* **deed in trust**.)

land-use intensity   A system of land use under local zoning codes or comprehensive development ordinances designed to relate land, building coverage of the land, and open space to one another. The land-use intensity (LUI) scale provides a series of density ratings (percentages) that include floor area, open space, living space, and recreation space. In applying land-use intensity, the floor area ratio creates a maximum amount of floor area in a building in relation to the land area of the lot upon which the building is to be constructed. Open-space requirements are minimum requirements based on and computed from a percentage of the actual floor area to be developed in a particular zoned lot. The LUI has become an important tool in the development of planned unit developments (PUDs). (*See* **planned unit development [PUD]**.)

land-use map   A map that shows the types and intensities of different land uses. (*See* **zoning**.)

land-use plan   A plan submitted to a local government agency by a developer of a proposed real estate project as part of the permitting process under local comprehensive development ordinances.

lane   A narrow roadway without curbs or sidewalks; generally found in older developments.

large-lot zoning   *See* **acreage zoning**.

larger parcel   A term used in condemnation cases when the court considers the extent of severance damages in situations where a partial taking has occurred. There is usually a requirement of unity of ownership, use, and contiguity. However, it has been held that integrated use, not physical contiguity, is the test of whether condemned land is part of a single tract that would warrant an award of severance damages. (*See* **severance damages**.)

late charge   An added charge a borrower is required to pay for failure to pay a regular loan installment when due. It is generally not treated as interest but as a service charge for the extra work and inconvenience suffered by the creditor. The courts, however, will not enforce excessive late charges (such as 10 percent or more of the unpaid principal), which would be deemed a penalty.

late date order   The commitment to a buyer for an owner's title insurance policy issued by a title insurance company, which covers the seller's title as of the date of the contract; also called *later-date*. At the closing, the buyer orders the title company to record the deed and extend its examination to show the buyer as the present owner of the real property. (*See* **continuation**.)

latent defects   (*defectos ocultos*)   Hidden structural defects, known to the seller but not to the purchaser and not readily discoverable by inspection. The seller or *the broker* who is aware of such defects, such as termite damage, a defective water heater, or a dangerous stairway behind a basement door, must disclose them to the prospective purchaser. Failure to disclose such information is a tacit misrepresentation and grounds for the buyer to rescind the contract. (*See* **"as is," misrepresentation**.)

lateral and subjacent support   The support a parcel of real property receives from the land adjoining it is called *lateral support*. It is not a right in the land of an adjoining owner, rather a right incident to ownership of the property entitled to the support. *Subjacent support* is that support the surface of the earth receives from its underlying strata.

   The basic rules of support are the same for both. In essence, an adjoining landowner (or holder of mineral or other rights beneath the land of another) has a duty to support a neighbor's land in its natural state. This duty of support does not run specifically to any of the improvements on the land but does impose liability for damage to improvements on the neighbor's land if the land would have subsided as a result of a landowner's excavation, even without the weight of the improvements. In general, a property owner can lessen any exposure to liability by giving neighbors adequate notice of intent to perform excavation work on the property so they can take the necessary precautions.

lath   Thin strips of wood or metal nailed to rafters, ceiling joists or wall studs to form groundwork for slates, tiles, shingles, or plaster.

law   (*ley*)   That body of rules by which society governs itself. Real estate law derives from state and federal constitutions, state and federal legislation, regulations of federal and state boards and commissions, county and municipal ordinances, and—most important—court decisions. *Private law* refers to the law that the parties create for themselves in their legal documents. For example, the bylaws and house rules of a condominium set forth detailed private rules of conduct for the owners, and violation of these rules gives the owners legal recourse against the violator. (*See* **common law, practice of law**.)

law day   The date an obligation becomes due; sometimes refers to the closing date. Under common law, the mortgagor had to pay off the mortgage debt by the law day. Failure to pay on time would result in the mortgagor's automatic loss of the mortgaged property to the mortgagee. If payment was made by the law day, the mortgage became void and the mortgagee would be divested of any title to the property pursuant to the defeasance clause. (*See* **defeasance clause**.)

lawful interest   The maximum interest rate permitted by law, with any amount above the statutory rate being deemed usurious. (*See* **interest, usury**.)

leaching cesspool   In plumbing, any cesspool that is not watertight and permits waste liquids to pass into the surrounding soil by percolation. (*See* **septic tank**.)

Lead-Based Paint Hazard Reduction Act (LBPHRA)   A federal law outlining a comprehensive federal strategy for reducing lead paint hazard exposure. The act and enabling regulations require affirmative action on the part of sellers, landlords, real estate agents, and renovators disturbing more than two square feet of old paint in houses built before 1978 to ensure that lead-based paint hazards are addressed in the sale and leasing of homes and apartments constructed before 1978. Each tenant or buyer must be given the HUD booklet *Protect Your Family from Lead in Your Home.*

The law requires disclosure of any tests for lead and/or the possibility of the presence of lead-based paint, but does not require testing, removal, or abatement. The buyer, although not the tenant, must be given the opportunity to test for lead-based paint within ten days or anytime agreed upon, or the opportunity may be waived altogether. Real estate agents are responsible for ensuring seller/lessor compliance under the regulations. Failure to do so can result in fines up to $11,000 per omission.

A rule, effective April 2010, requires that all contractors and maintenance professionals who are renovating housing, child-care facilities, and schools built prior to 1978 that contains lead-based paint be trained to follow protective work practice standards. The rule applies to renovation, repair, or painting activities but not minor maintenance or repair activities, which are defined as less than six square feet of lead-based paint in a room or less than 20 square feet of lead-based paint on the exterior.

Some owners of property built before 1978 are exempt from the disclosures: housing for the elderly, vacation housing, rental property certified as "lead-based paint free," and others. (*See* **x-ray fluorescent device [XRF]**, **lead poisoning**.)

lead lender   Typically, a local lender who funds the initial portion of a large loan and arranges for one or more institutional lenders to fund the balance of the financing. Lead lenders handle servicing of the loan. (*See* **participation mortgage**.)

lead poisoning   A serious illness caused by high concentrations of lead in the body, discovered by a blood test. Lead can cause major health problems, especially learning disabilities in young children. Common sources of lead include lead-based paint, water contamination through lead pipes, and lead solder. (*See* **Lead-based Paint Hazard Reduction Act [LBPHRA]**.)

lease   (*arrendamiento, arriendo, contracto de arrendamiento, locación*)   An agreement, written or unwritten, transferring the right to exclusive possession and use of real estate for a definite period of time. The lessor (landlord) grants the right of possession to the lessee (tenant) but retains the right to retake possession after the lease term has expired (reversionary right). In effect, the lease is a combination of both a *conveyance* (to transfer the right of occupancy) and a *contract* (to pay rent and assume other obligations). It is an exchange of the possession and profits of the land in return for rent. The lessor's interest is called the *leased fee estate* and consists of the right to recover the contract rent plus the reversion. The lessee's interest is called the *leasehold estate* and consists of the right to the exclusive use and occupancy of the leased estate. An "agreement for a lease" contemplates the execution of a lease at a later time.

Historically, landlord-tenant relations developed from early agricultural leases, under which the landlord's obligation was limited to providing the tenant with peaceful possession; in return, the tenant agreed to pay rent. The landlord was not expected to assist in the operation of the land and leased lands were under the exclusive control of the tenant without interference from the landlord. In the simplest terms, the tenant-landlord relationship was a strict possession-rent relationship. If a tenant defaulted in rent payment, eviction would be forthcoming. In a rural setting, this was a workable arrangement.

Today, contract law determines the validity of a lease. Although no special wording is necessary to create the relationship of landlord and tenant, a lease should be in writing. If it is not, the law will write it for the parties involved. Although—depending on the circumstances—the lease may be written, oral, or implied, the provision of the statutes of the state in which the real estate is located must be followed. The lessor, being the owner of the real estate, is usually bound by an implied covenant of quiet enjoyment for the benefit of the lessee. By this covenant, the lessor asserts that the lessee will not be evicted by a person who successfully claims to be the real owner of the premises with a title that is paramount to the lessor's. The requirements for a valid lease are similar to those of a contract and are generally as follows:

Capacity to contract: The parties must be legally capable of entering into a contract. (Note, however, that a minor can generally enter into binding contracts for necessities, of which housing *may* be considered one of the most essential.)

Mutual agreement: The parties must reach a mutual agreement and support it by valid consideration.

Legal objectives: The lease objectives must be legal; that is, it would generally be illegal to lease a building to manufacture and sell methamphetamines, so a lease for such a purpose would be invalid.

Statute of frauds: State fraud statutes generally apply to leases. They usually provide that leases for more than one year (one year plus one day) or leases that cannot be fully performed within one year from the date of making must be in writing. A lease for exactly one year could fall short of the requirements of the statute of frauds if the lease period commences after the date of entering into the agreement. Similarly, a lease for less than one year may fall under the statute of frauds if more than one year elapses between the signing of the lease and its termination date. Regardless of the term, any lease should be put into writing to avoid disputes and misunderstandings between the parties. A lease not in conformance with the statute of frauds is generally considered unenforceable.

Signatures: The lease must be signed by the landlord (and wife, if in a dower state) because the courts consider the lease as a conveyance of real estate. Although it is good practice for the lessee to do so, a lease need not be signed by the lessee because taking possession and paying rent with knowledge of the lease terms constitutes an acceptance of the lease terms. When a lease is signed by two or more tenants, they become jointly and severally liable and can avoid this only by signing separate leases specifying their separate obligations.

Description of premises: A description of the leased premises should be clearly stated and may only include a street address and/or apartment number for residential, apartment, and small commercial properties. Large commercial site leases, on the other hand, must be more detailed, including such things as a floor plan, total square footage, storage areas, parking, and the like. If the lease affects land, as with a ground lease, a legal description should be used.

Use of premises: The lessor may restrict the use of the leased property through provisions included in the lease, particularly important with leases for stores or commercial space. For example, a lease may contain a provision that the property is "to be used for the purpose of a Big Beltbuster Burger Bonanza Bazaar drive-in restaurant, and no other." If the lease does not state a specified purpose, the tenant may use the premises for any lawful purpose.

Term of lease: The term of lease is the period the lease will run and should be stated precisely, preferably with the beginning and ending term dates stated together with a statement of the total period of the lease—for example, "for a term of 30 years beginning June 1, 1968, and ending May 31, 1998." Courts do not favor leases with an indefinite term and will hold that such perpetual leases are not valid unless the language of the lease and the surrounding circumstances clearly indicate that such is the intention of the parties. Leases are controlled by and must be in accord with the statutes of the various states. Some state statutes limit terms of agricultural leases and leases for 100 years or more. Generally the lease term is unaffected by the death of either landlord or tenant.

Possession of leased premises: In most states, the landlord must give the tenant actual occupancy or possession of the leased premises. Thus, if the premises are occupied by a holdover tenant or adverse claimant at the date of a new lease, the landlord owes a duty to the new tenant to bring whatever action is necessary to recover possession and to bear the expense of this action. However, in a few states, the landlord is bound to give the tenant only the right of possession, and then it is the tenant's obligation to bring any necessary court action to secure actual possession. It is this right to exclusive possession that distinguishes a lease from a mere license to use property.

Consideration: Although payment of rent is not essential as long as consideration was granted in the creation of the lease itself, some courts have construed rent as being any consideration that supports the lease, not limiting its definition to the monthly payment of a specified amount. Most courts will not enforce an agreement to reduce or increase the rent during the term for which the lease was originally drawn once the lease is in force. Generally, courts consider the lease a contract and therefore not subject to change unless the changes are in writing and agreed to by both parties. Most modern leases provide for rent to be paid in advance. In addition to the payment of rent, most land leases and long-term leases require that the tenant pay all property charges, such as real estate taxes, special assessments, water and sewer taxes, and all necessary insurance premiums to protect the property. Most leases provide for some form of security, such as contracting for a lien on the tenant's property, by requiring the tenant to pay a portion of the rent in advance, by requiring the tenant to post security, and/or by requiring the tenant to have a third person guarantee the payment of the rent.

There are three main classifications of leases:

1. Leases based on the type of realty involved, such as office leases, ground leases, proprietary leases, residential leases
2. Leases classed according to the term of the lease, such as short-term and long-term leases. Most short-term leases are gross leases requiring the landlord to pay all taxes, assessments, and operating costs (such as most apartment leases). Long-term leases (generally ten years and longer) are often net leases that give the tenant greater rights and responsibilities. Particularly in long-term leases, attention should be given to the rights of both parties in the event of condemnation of the leased premises.
3. Leases classed according to the method of rent payment (such as fixed-rental, graduated, percentage, gross, and net leases)

Generally, leases can be filed for record in the county in which the leased property is located, although most leases are not recorded unless they are for a relatively long term (three years or more) or are security for a mortgage.

Unless prohibited in the lease, a lessee may assign the lease or sublet the premises. A tenant transferring the entire remaining lease term *assigns* the lease as opposed to transferring most but not all of the term *sublets*. Most leases prohibit a lessee from assigning or subletting without the landlord's permission. When a lease is assigned, the assignee becomes the principal obligor, and the lessee assumes the position of a surety.

If the landlord sells the property, the grantee takes title subject to the lease and becomes liable for all lease covenants. Tenants who make improvements to a landlord's property usually do so for the benefit of the landlord. If classified as fixtures, such improvements become part of the real estate. However, a tenant may be given the right to install trade fixtures or chattel fixtures by the terms of the lease. It is customary to provide that such trade fixtures may be removed by the tenant before the expiration of the lease, provided the tenant returns the building to the condition it was at the time of possession.

In leases involving agricultural land, the courts have held that damage or destruction of the improvements does not relieve the tenant from the obligation to pay rent to the end of the term. This ruling has been extended in most states to include leases of land on which the tenant has constructed a building or leases that give possession of an entire building to the tenant. Because the tenant is leasing an entire building, the courts have held that the tenant is also leasing the land on which that building is located. In those cases where the leased premises are only a part of the building (such as office or commercial space or an apartment in an apartment building), upon destruction of the leased premises, the tenant is not required to continue to pay rent. Furthermore, in some states, if the property was destroyed as a result of landlord negligence, the tenant can recover damages from the landlord. Under most commercial and industrial leases, the tenant must maintain and repair the interior and often the exterior of the premises as well.

A lease may be terminated by
- expiration of the term;
- merger of the leasehold and fee estates;
- destruction or condemnation of the premises;
- abandonment;
- agreement of the parties (surrender);
- forfeiture due to default or breach of the leasing terms and conditions (note that under the federal Bankruptcy Act, tenant bankruptcy is no longer a permitted ground for default); and
- commercial frustration of purpose, such as if the proposed use is made illegal (but not if the tenant cannot obtain a needed business license).

(*See* **abandonment, eviction, fixture, flat lease, graduated rental lease, gross lease, ground lease, index lease, landlord, leasehold, lease option, master lease, month-to-month tenancy, net lease, percentage lease, security deposit, surrender, trade fixture, Uniform Residential Landlord and Tenant Act [URLTA], waste.**)

leased fee The interest and rights of the lessor in real estate that the lessor has leased. The lessor has a right to receive rental income and a right to possess the property at the end of the lease. The value of the rental payments plus the remaining property value at the end of the lease period (the reversionary interest) is the leased fee interest, which may be sold or mortgaged subject to the rights of the tenant. In valuing the leased fee, the appraiser usually capitalizes the present value of the income received by the lessor and adds the reversionary value of the land, or land and building, at the expiration of the lease term (the annuity method of capitalization). The reversionary worth of the land is difficult to predict, so it is usually calculated to be the same as its present value, discounted to its present worth by multiplying the value by the appropriate Inwood factor. (*See* **Inwood tables.**)

leasehold A less-than-freehold estate that a tenant possesses in real property. Under a lease, the tenant possesses a leasehold estate and the landlord possesses the reversion estate. Leasehold estates are generally classified as estates in personal property. Some states, however, provide for certain leasehold estates to be considered as real property while also retaining their characteristics as personal property. Under common law, an estate for years was termed a "chattel real" and classified as personal property.

The four principal types of leasehold estates are the estate for years, the periodic tenancy (estate from year to year), the tenancy at will, and the tenancy at sufferance. The estate for years runs for a specific period of time; the periodic tenancy runs for an indefinite number of time periods; the estate at will runs for an indefinite time; an estate at sufferance runs until the landlord takes some action.

Unlike other uses of land, the leasehold is a transfer of the exclusive right to possession, as opposed to the mere privilege to use the land. Thus, a hotel guest is different from a tenant. The difference among various types of authorized usages of property (licenses, easements, profits, and leases) becomes important in terms of the remedies available upon breach of contract. The leasehold tenant can be removed from the property only by strict statutory eviction procedures, whereas a license usually can be revoked at any time.

The term or duration of the leasehold estate varies, depending on the purposes. Many residential apartment leases are short term—that is, for one year or from month to month while ground leases may run for 55 years, even 75 years or longer. For FHA leasehold-mortgage purposes, leases must have a minimum term that exceeds the fixed rental term of the loan. These long-term leases are transferred by assignment of lease rather than by deed. Both the assignor and the assignee of a leasehold estate must sign the assignment of lease, because the assignee assumes the obligations of the assignor under the lease.

Under common law, improvements constructed by the lessee on the leased premises would revert to the landlord at termination of the leasehold estate. Many ground leases, however, specifically provide in the reversion clause for the right of the lessee to remove all improvements at the end of the lease term. This provision simplifies the arrangement of financing and negotiation for lease extension or renewal.

In areas where leaseholds are popular, such as Hawaii and Maryland, common practice makes leasehold estates subject to a recorded declaration of restrictions, usually by reference in the lease to the book and page number of the declaration. A purchaser should examine the lease and all referenced documents well in advance of closing in order to ascertain exactly what is being purchased. (*See* **assignment of lease**, **concession**, **ground lease**, **leasehold mortgage**, **less-than-freehold estate**, **periodic tenancy**, **tenancy at sufferance**, **tenancy at will**.)

leasehold improvements   The improvements to leased property made by the lessee. Such improvements, generally tax depreciable by the lessee, are depreciable over the cost recovery period.

leasehold insurance   *See* **commercial leasehold insurance**.

leasehold mortgage   A mortgage placed on the lessee's interest in the leased premises. Leasehold mortgage financing is a specialized form of secondary financing because the mortgage is subordinate to the position of the fee owner. The prime lenders in leasehold financing are life insurance companies, major mutual savings banks, and major commercial banks.

In the development of a large project, the fee owner sometimes leases the land to a developer and subordinates the fee to the leasehold mortgage. The subordination may be limited to loans of a certain type or term (such as a construction loan but not any refinancing), or the subordination might take place only upon full completion of construction of the proposed improvement. Often, the lender attempts to persuade the fee owner to mortgage the fee along with the leasehold mortgage. (*See* **subordination clause**.)

lease option   A lease clause that gives the tenant the right to purchase the property under specified conditions. Following are some important features of a lease option:

- It usually runs with the land, so that if the lease is assigned, the option to purchase is likewise assigned.
- Usually it does not extend beyond the term of the lease.
- The supporting consideration can be the paid rent. A default in rent may result in termination of the option.
- It can be assigned separately from other provisions in the lease.

The lessor/optionor must be careful to structure the transaction so that the economic reality of the transaction makes it a lease rather than an outright sale. For example: If the total payments under the lease are substantially equal to the purchase price payment under the option, and if the payments are applicable to the purchase price, the IRS may characterize the deal as a sale because the lessee has no other economic choice but to exercise the option.

An option in a lease is inseparable from the integrated lease contract, and therefore an extension of the lease usually prolongs the life of the option, unless the lease states otherwise.

In addition to an option to purchase, other lease options include options to renew and options to extend. Under the latter, the original lease is continued on the same terms, including the extension provision. With an option to renew, the lessee is entitled to a new lease on set terms, not including the original renewal provision. (*See* **option**.)

lease purchase agreement   An agreement in which part of the rent payment is applicable toward a set purchase price. Title is transferred from lessor to lessee when the lessor receives the prearranged total price.

leeward   On or toward the side sheltered from the wind; opposite of windward.

legacy   A disposition of money or personal property by will, as in a bequest. The recipient is called the *legatee*.

legal age   The statutory age at which a person attains majority and is no longer a minor. (*See* **minor**.)

legal description   A description of a piece of real property that is acceptable by the courts of the state where the property is located for use in real property conveyance documents. The description is usually complete enough so that an independent surveyor can locate and identify that specific parcel of land. Oral testimony is not admissible as a way of describing the property more fully, except in certain cases involving fraud or mistake. Such descriptions are usually based on the field notes of a surveyor or civil engineer. Methods of description are lot, block and subdivision; government survey; and metes and bounds.

A legal description is required on all deeds, assignments of leases, and mortgages and is in most contracts for deed. Street addresses, tax-bill descriptions, and general descriptions (the Smith farm) are generally inadequate for use in recorded title documents because such identifying characteristics may not endure indefinitely. Use of such temporary descriptions could lead to obvious difficulties for someone searching the chain of title or trying to locate the property in the distant future. In general, a legal description should be used in any instrument that is to be recorded. If the description is incorrect, then the document may be improperly indexed and thus may not be sufficient constructive notice to a third person under recording laws.

The general rules in case of conflicts in legal descriptions are
- natural or artificial monuments prevail over courses and distances,
- natural monuments prevail over artificial monuments,
- courses govern over distances, and
- stated acreage or area is the least reliable method of describing a parcel.

(*See* **land description**; **lot, block, and subdivision**; **government survey method**; **metes and bounds**.)

legally permissible   Use of property that is allowable by law, as required in the highest-and-best-use analysis. (*See* **highest and best use**.)

legal name   The given name in combination with the surname, or family name. Under common law an insertion, omission, or error in a middle name or initial is immaterial to the validity of a conveyance document.

An application for a real estate salesperson's or broker's state examination or license generally requires applicants to supply their full legal name. The use of initials only is strongly discouraged, especially with common surnames such as Smith, Lee, Brown, and the like. This policy is designed to eliminate confusion and misidentification of applicants with similar names.

legal notice   Notice that is either implied or required by law as a result of the possession of property or the recording of documents. When deeds are recorded, subsequent purchasers are thereby put on notice as to the contents of such documents. Under the recording law, constructive notice is also referred to as *legal notice*.

legal rate of interest   The rate of interest prescribed by state law that prevails in the absence of any agreement fixing the rate. For example, state law may provide for 6 percent interest on monies due after the maturity date of a promissory note. The usury limit is referred to as the *lawful interest*.

legatee   (*legatario*)   A person who receives money or personal property under a will.

legend stock   A security certificate that has a notation on its face indicating that its transferability is restricted. Such stock usually cannot be transferred for a certain period of time or until registered. Securities claiming exemption from SEC registration under the intrastate exemption (Rule 147) or the private offering exemption (Rule 146) must contain a restricted transfer legend. (*See* **Rule 146, Rule 147**.)

lessee   The person to whom property is rented or leased; called a *tenant* in most residential leases.

lessor   The person who rents or leases property to another. In residential leasing, such a person is often called a *landlord*.

less-than-freehold estate   The estate held by a person who rents or leases property. This classification includes an estate for years, periodic tenancy, estate at will, and estate at sufferance. (*See* **freehold, leasehold**.)

let   (*alquilar*)   To rent out.

letter of credit   An agreement or commitment by a bank (issuer) made at the request of a customer (account party) that the bank will honor drafts or other demands of payment from third parties (beneficiaries) upon compliance with the conditions specified in the letter of credit. Through the issuance of its letter of credit, the bank agrees to pay the seller's draft, thereby substituting the bank's credit for that of the buyer. This often takes the form of a letter from a bank in one area of the country to a bank or merchant in another area introducing the person named, vouching for the customer and specifying a sum of money to be extended.

A bank charges a small annual fee for issuing a letter of credit, which is issued only to customers with the highest credit ratings. Unlike direct loans, the bank need not report obligations under letters of credit as liabilities in its financial statements, nor is the bank required to maintain a certain amount of bank reserves to back up its letter of credit obligations.

Article 5 of the Uniform Commercial Code extensively covers the law concerning letters of credit. (*See* **line of credit**.)

letter of intent   (*carta de intención*)   An expression of intent to invest, develop, or purchase without creating any firm legal obligation to do so. It may refer to a specific project, or it may be a general letter of intent without regard to a specific project. The following is the kind of language used in a letter of intent to negate any legal duty to carry out the terms of the letter:

Because this instrument consists only of an expression of our mutual intent, it is expressly understood that no liability or obligation of any nature whatsoever is intended to be created as between any of the parties hereto. This letter is neither intended to constitute a binding agreement to consummate the transaction outlined herein nor an agreement to enter into contract. The parties propose to proceed promptly and in good faith to conclude the arrangements with respect to proposed development, but any legal obligations between the parties shall be only those set forth in the executed contract and lease. In the event that a contract and lease are not executed, we shall not be obligated for any expenses of the developer or for any charges or claims whatsoever arising out of this letter of intent or the proposed financing or otherwise and, similarly, the developer shall not be in any way obligated to us.

letter of patent   A legal instrument transferring title to real property from either the United States or an individual state to the person named in the patent.

letter report
1. A short appraisal report limited to the property characteristics, valuation, and recommendations.
2. A report by a title company as to the condition of title as of a specific date; it gives no insurance on that title, however.

level-payment mortgage   A mortgage scheduled to be repaid in equal periodic payments that include both principal and interest. Payments are credited first against interest on the declining principal balance, so the amount of money credited to principal gradually increases, while that credited to interest gradually decreases. Under most conventional, VA, and FHA loans, the mortgage payments include taxes and insurance in addition to principal and interest. (*See* **amortization, budget mortgage, direct reduction mortgage.**)

leverage   The impact of borrowed funds on investment return. The use of borrowed funds to purchase property with the anticipation that the acquired property will increase in return so that investors will realize a profit not only on their own investment but also on the borrowed funds. The employment of a smaller investment to generate a larger rate of return through borrowing.

The term *high leverage* often is used when the investor has made a very low down payment. Example: Danita purchases a $75,000 condominium unit for $4,000 down with a five-year, interest-only contract for deed for the balance. Danita hopes to sell the property for $85,000, thus making a profit from the use of other people's money. Her expected profit on the purchase price of $75,000 is 13 percent, but the profit on her principal investment of $4,000 is 250 percent, which shows the advantage of leveraging. In addition, Danita can receive the tax benefits of depreciation on the entire improvement (including the leveraged portion). The term *reverse leverage* is used to describe a situation in which an investor pays a higher rate to borrow money than the rate of net income received from the property. Reverse leverage is also called **debt financing**.

levy   To assess; to seize or collect. To levy a tax is to assess a property and set the rate of taxation. To levy an execution is to officially seize the property of a person in order to satisfy an obligation. Usually, sheriffs levy upon and bring within their control the personal property of a judgment debtor. Levying is not a judicial act but a ministerial one. (*See* **attachment, writ of execution.**)

liability
1. In a double-entry accounting system, all amounts appearing on the credit side, including all amounts owed. In a personal financial statement, assets minus liabilities equal net worth. (*See* **asset, net worth.**)
2. Legal responsibility for an act. (*See* **damages.**)

liber   Latin for *book*. Usually refers to the record books at the county recorder's office that contain copies of all recorded documents relating to real estate in that county. When a document is recorded, it is given a liber volume and page number (also called *folio*). Anyone wishing to examine this document can then locate an exact copy of the document by reference to the appropriate liber and page number. (*See* **recording.**)

license (*licencia*)

1. Permission or authority to do a particular act on the land or property of another, usually on a nonexclusive basis. A license is a personal, revocable, and nonassignable right, but unlike an easement, it is not considered an interest in the land itself. If a right to use another person's land is given orally, it is generally considered a license rather than an easement. The landowner may revoke such a right at any time, unless it has become irrevocable by estoppel. A license ceases upon the death of either party and is revoked by the sale of the land by the licensor. For example, a landowner who grants a friend permission to enter his property for hunting purposes thus grants the friend a license to use the land. If an owner mistakenly builds a rock wall across the boundary line so that it encroaches onto the neighbor's property, the owner sometimes pays the neighbor for a license to keep the rock wall in place. This arrangement should be reduced to a formal encroachment agreement that is signed and recorded so that it runs with the land. (*See* **easement, estoppel**.)

2. Formal permission from a constituted authority (such as a state real estate commission) to engage in a certain activity or business (such as real estate brokerage or real estate appraisal). (*See* **inactive license, license laws**.)

licensed appraiser *See* **appraiser**.

licensee A person who has a valid real estate or appraisal license. A real estate licensee can generally be a salesperson or broker, active or inactive, or an individual, corporation, or partnership. Only individuals can be licensed as appraisers.

L

license laws Laws enacted by all states, the District of Columbia, and certain Canadian provinces that provide the states with the authority to license and regulate the activities of real estate brokers, salespeople, and appraisers. Certain details of the laws vary from state to state, but the main provisions of each remain much the same. The general purposes of license laws are to (1) protect the public from dishonest or incompetent real estate practitioners, (2) prescribe certain standards and qualifications for licensing, and (3) raise the standards of the real estate profession.

All states require license applicants to pass an examination designed to test their real estate knowledge and competency regarding federal and state-specific laws pertaining to real estate. Licenses or registration certificates are issued to qualified individuals and generally to partnerships and corporations. These licenses are legal permits to operate a real estate brokerage business as described and permitted by the state law. Each state law must be examined to determine whether a license is required for such activities as appraising, mortgaging, auctioning, or exchanging real estate. State licensing usually preempts attempts by municipal governments to assess local licensing fees.

Licenses are issued for definite terms and must be renewed within specified time limits. Each license is a personal right and terminates upon the death of the individual or the dissolution of the partnership or corporation. While a license or registration certificate is in effect, the activities of each licensed person or entity are subject to the control of the authorized state officials as prescribed by state law. For this reason, every licensed person must be thoroughly familiar with the applicable state license laws. Violation of the license law provisions is usually cause for refusal, revocation, or suspension of a real estate license. A court conviction for acting as a real estate broker or salesperson without a license is generally considered a misdemeanor, punishable by a fine and/or imprisonment.

Each state law exempts certain persons from the license laws. Such exemptions usually include owners dealing with their own property; trustees, executors, receivers, and others operating under court orders; public officials acting in the line of their duties; and, in some cases, attorneys.

Annual continuing education is required in many states to renew or to reactivate a license.

State license laws now exist for certified and licensed real estate appraisers.

lien   (*gravamen*)   A charge or claim that one person (lienor) has on the property of another (lienee) as security for a debt or obligation. A lien always arises from a debt and can be created by agreement of the parties (e.g., a mortgage) or by operation of law (e.g., a tax lien). A lien may be general or specific. A *general lien* applies to all the lienee's real and personal property. A *specific lien* affects only a particular property, such as a mortgaged house. Liens can also be statutory or equitable, voluntary, or involuntary. For example, a mechanic's lien is an involuntary, statutory, special lien, whereas a mortgage is a voluntary, equitable, special lien. However, if the mortgage lien foreclosed and the proceeds from the foreclosure sale did not cover the debt, the resulting deficiency judgment, when recorded, would be a general lien on all the debtor's property. Lien procedure is based on each state's statutes. Liens do not transfer title to the property—until foreclosure, the debtor retains title. Certain statutory liens (mechanics' liens and judgments) become unenforceable after a lapse of time from origination or recording unless a foreclosure suit is filed.

Lien priority is normally determined by the date of recordation. Thus, it is important to record the appropriate document as soon as the lien is created. State property tax liens and assessments, however, take priority over all other liens, even those previously recorded. State law sometimes changes the order of priority, as with mechanics' liens. Because the lien is an encumbrance on the title, the lienor should (at the lienee's expense) execute and record a satisfaction of the lien as soon as the lien is paid so as to remove this cloud on the title. (*See* **encumbrance**, **judgment lien**, **mechanic's lien**, **mortgage**, **subordination**, **tax lien**, **Uniform Commercial Code [UCC]**.)

lien letter   *See* **tax and lien search**.

lien statement   A statement of the unpaid balance of a promissory note secured by a lien on property, plus the status of interest payments, maturity date, and any claims that may be asserted. Also called an **offset statement**. (*See* **certificate of no defense**, **reduction certificate**.)

lien-theory states   Those states that treat a mortgage solely as a security interest in the secured real property with title retained by the mortgagor. The mortgagor has use of the property and is entitled to all rents and profits. The lien theory, or equitable theory of mortgages, regards the debt as the principal fact and the mortgage merely as collateral. It treats the mortgagor as the owner of the equitable title and the mortgagee merely as the holder of a lien for the security of his or her debt. This differs from a title-theory state, where legal title is actually transferred to the mortgagee and is reconveyed back to the mortgagor only when the mortgage debt is satisfied. (*See* **deed of trust**, **defeasance clause**, **title-theory states**.)

life-care facility   A residential development designed to provide medical and skilled nursing care for senior citizens. Residents are offered a continuing care contract, including independent living units at a periodic rent.

life estate   Any estate in real or personal property that is limited in duration to the life of its owner or the life of some other designated person. If the estate is measured by the lifetime of a person other than its owner, it is called a *life estate pur autre vie*. Although classified as a freehold estate because it is a possessory estate of indefinite duration, a life estate is not an estate of inheritance. For example, Hai conveys his home to his son Quan and reserves a life estate for himself. Hai (the life tenant) has a life estate, and Quan has a reversionary interest in the property. When Hai dies, the fee simple property reverts to Quan.

A life estate may arise by agreement of the parties, in which case it is called a *conventional life estate*; or it may arise by operation of law (as with homestead, curtesy or a wife's dower rights), in which case it is referred to as a *legal life estate*.

A life tenant is

■ entitled to possession and ordinary uses and profits of the land, just as though she were the fee owner;

■ obligated to keep the premises in a reasonable state of repair and free from waste so that the realty will later revert to the grantor or the remainderman in approximately unchanged condition in terms of its characteristics and value;

■ obligated to pay the ordinary taxes, interest on encumbrances (not mortgage principal amortization), and a pro rata share of special assessments (along with the remainderman);

■ barred from creating any interest in the property that extends beyond the measuring life; and

■ under no obligation to insure the premises for the benefit of the future interest holders, who have separate, insurable interests and are responsible for obtaining their own insurance.

Life tenants may sell their interest or encumber it subject to any deed restrictions to the contrary, and the interest is subject to execution sale if there is a money judgment against the life tenant. The transferee receives no greater interest than the life tenant had—that is, an estate that ends at the expiration of the measuring life. Thus, it is difficult to sell or mortgage a life estate. The mortgagee of a life tenant's interest would therefore probably require the life tenant to make the mortgagee the beneficiary of a term life insurance policy.

For tax depreciation purposes, a life tenant deducts depreciation over the useful life of the property and not on the tenant's life expectancy. After the death of the life tenant, the remainderman gets the deduction.

Where a taxpayer makes a gift of real property but retains a life estate, the entire value of the property is includable in the deceased taxpayer's estate for federal estate tax purposes.

A life estate is terminated by the death of the person whose existence is the measuring life. Although no probate proceeding is necessary to establish title in the remainderman (the person now entitled to the property), it is good title practice to record a death certificate to show the fact of death. If the life tenant acquires the fee simple title to the property, the life estate is terminated by merger. A deed of surrender is used to merge a life estate with the reversion or remainder interest. (*See* **freehold, pur autre vie, remainderman, waste**.)

life tenant   A person possessing a life estate.

lifting clause   A clause included in a junior loan instrument that allows the underlying mortgage or deed of trust (senior loan) to be replaced or refinanced so long as the amount of the new senior loan does not exceed the amount of the first lien outstanding at the time the junior loan was made. (*See* **subordination agreement**.)

light and air   Owners have no natural right to light and air and cannot complain when a neighbor erects a structure that cuts off their light and air. To eliminate this possibility, some abutting owners attempt to purchase an easement for light and air over the neighbor's property. Such an easement should be granted in writing. For example, an owner with a beautiful view of the mountains might seek to obtain from a neighbor an easement of light and air over the neighbor's property. If the easement had been properly created and recorded, then neither the neighbor nor any successor could build a structure in this airspace. It is not possible to acquire a light and air easement by prescription; that is, a person cannot claim to have acquired a prescriptive right to airspace because he has used the view for the prescriptive statutory period of, for example, 20 years. (*See* **air rights**.)

light industry   A zoning designation for industrial use encompassing mostly unobjectionable light manufacturing, as opposed to those industries that cause noise, air, or water disturbances and pollution. Light industry includes such "clean" industries as bakeries, dry cleaning, and food processing. (*See* **heavy industry**.)

like-kind property   A federal term relating to the nature of real estate rather than its quality or quantity. Only like-kind property qualifies for a real estate exchange and the resulting tax benefit.

Like-kind property is any real property, whether improved or unimproved, held or to be held by the taxpayer for investment or income purposes, thus excluding dealer property and residences. The property need only qualify as like property to the party seeking the tax-deferred benefit of the exchanges of like property. Personal residences are not eligible for exchange treatment as either leg of the exchange.

One property may be improved and the other raw land, or one a shopping center and the other an apartment building. Both properties, however, must be of the same ownership interest. Thus, a fee simple interest is not exchangeable for a leasehold interest. However, an IRS regulation does state that a leasehold interest of 30 years or more is to be deemed a fee simple. The tax court has upheld the exchange of general partnership interests in partnerships with substantially the same kind of underlying assets. Under current regulation, the replacement property must be a U.S. property if the exchanged property is U.S. property; exchange of foreign property for foreign property is allowed. (*See* **condemnation**, **delayed exchange**, **exchange**, **replacement property**.)

limitations of actions   Time within which legal actions must commence or else action is barred. (*See* **laches**, **statute of limitations**.)

limited access highway   A highway with access only at specific intervals, usually by way of ramps. Such a highway is designed to benefit through traffic and to avoid interference from neighboring traffic. Also called a *controlled access highway*.

limited common elements   That special class of common elements in a condominium project that is reserved for the use of one or more apartment(s) to the exclusion of other apartments. This would include assigned parking stalls, storage units, or any common areas and facilities available for use by one or more, but less than all, unit owners.

Any amendment of the condominium declaration that affects the limited common elements requires the unanimous consent of all those to whom the use is reserved. Any addition or alteration to a limited common element usually requires prior approval of the board of directors, which acts on behalf of the apartment owners' association. (*See* **common elements**.)

limited liability company (LLC)   An alternative, hybrid business entity with the combined characteristics and benefits of both limited partnerships and S corporations. Unlike a corporation, however, an LLC does not have perpetual existence. The principal governing document of an LLC is its operating agreement, which is similar to a corporation's bylaws. (*See* **S corporation**.)

limited partnership   A partnership agreement in which one person (called the *general partner*) or a group of persons organizes, operates, and is responsible for the entire partnership venture. The other partnership members are merely investors and have no say in the organization and direction of the operation. These passive investors, called *limited partners*, share in the profits and compensate the general partner for his efforts out of such profits. Unlike a general partnership, in which each member is responsible for the total losses (if any) of the syndicate, limited partners stand to lose only as much as their individual investments—usually nothing more. The general partner, then, is totally responsible for any large-scale losses incurred by the investment. Note, however, that when a limited partner receives cash distributions, either upon dissolution of the partnership or during the investment period, and the partnership's creditor obligations remain unsatisfied, the limited partner may be required to return such distributions in order to satisfy creditor claims.

The limited partnership has been popular in the syndication of real estate ventures because it permits investors with only small amounts of capital to participate in real estate projects that require much capital and management expertise, restricts their potential liability to their contribution, and permits "pass-through" of tax benefits of real property ownership.

The organizer of a limited partnership must take care that the IRS does not treat the partnership as an association taxable as a corporation (resulting in double taxation of income). An experienced real estate tax attorney should carefully draft the limited partnership agreement to assure the partnership of the appropriate tax status, in which all profits or losses pass through the partnership and are taxed only at the individual level. Partnership status thus combines the direct tax advantages of an immediate write-off of losses, if any, plus the elimination of a second tax at the corporate level.

Many states have adopted the Uniform Limited Partnership Act to regulate the formation and operation of limited partnerships. The act requires that a certificate listing the names and investments of each participant in the partnership be filed at the business registration division or county recorder's office. A limited partnership is not effective until a certificate is filed. Because a limited partner's interest is personal property, her death does not dissolve the partnership. Also, judgment and federal tax liens against a partner do not affect the partnership property, although they may affect the partner's right to receive profits.

Under the 1986 Tax Reform Act, limited partnerships are subject to the passive loss rules. Losses from limited partnerships can be used only to offset income from other "passive investments" and cannot be used to shelter income from salary, interest, and dividends, as under previous law. Passive investments are defined as any trade or business in which the taxpayer does not materially participate and any rental activity, whether or not the taxpayer materially participates. Any interest held by a limited partner is automatically treated as passive.

Because the sale of a limited partnership interest involves the sale of a security, it is subject to state and federal laws dealing with the sale of securities and, unless exempt, must be registered with the SEC and the appropriate state securities authorities. (*See* **at-risk rules, double taxation, foreclosure, master limited partnership [MLP], net worth, partnership, passive activity, real property securities registration, safe harbor rule.**)

limited power of attorney   A power of attorney that is restricted to a particular task, such as the transfer of a specific parcel of property. Most lenders and title insurance companies prefer the use of limited or special powers of attorney in real estate transactions as opposed to the use of general powers of attorney. (*See* **power of attorney, special agency.**)

limited principal's license   *See* **direct participation program licenses**.

limited referral agent   A salesperson with an active real estate license who refers prospective buyer or seller leads into the brokerage company in return for a referral fee upon closing. The lead is turned over to a full-time agent, and the referral agent refrains from representing the client any further.

limited service broker   A broker who offers the consumer less than the full line of services usually provided by a real estate broker. Such limited services might include explaining the standard offer form, writing ads, helping a buyer obtain financing, and following up in escrow. They might not include advertising, showing, or holding open houses.

limited warranty deed   A deed that contains warranties covering the time period that the grantor holds title. (*See* **special warranty deed.**)

lineal

1. As it relates to family relationships, describes direct-line descendants, such as children or grandchildren, as opposed to "collaterals" (nephews, cousins, etc.); also applies to living descendants (blood or adopted), however remote from the deceased.
2. As it relates to measurements, applies to a measurement made on a line. The lineal measure of a square that is 4 feet on each side is 16 feet. Lineal measure is also called *linear measure*.

line of credit The maximum amount of money a bank will lend one of its more reliable and credit-worthy customers without the need for a formal loan submission. The borrower is thus assured quick loan service without the delay of a credit review before disbursement of funds. A customer's line of credit is subject to periodic reviews of the customer's credit standing and the overall banking relationship. (*See* **letter of credit**.)

line-of-sight easement A right that restricts the use of land within the easement area in any way that interferes with the view.

line stakes Stakes set along the boundary lines of a parcel of land surveyed by metes and bounds.

lintel A horizontal board that supports the load over an opening such as a door or window.

liquidated damages An amount predetermined by the parties to an agreement as the total amount of compensation an injured party should receive if the other party breaches a specified part of the contract. In building contracts, the parties often anticipate the possibility of a breach (for example, a delay in completion by a set date) and specify in the contract the amount of the damages to be paid in the event of the breach.

To be enforceable, the liquidated damages clause must set forth an amount that bears a reasonable relationship to the actual damages as estimated by the parties; otherwise, the court treats the amount as a penalty for failure to perform. If a defaulting buyer deposited earnest money of over 20 percent of the purchase price and the buyer failed to complete the contract, the courts would probably permit the buyer to recover some of the deposit money on the theory that the seller would be unjustly enriched by keeping it all.

Courts look with disfavor on penalty clauses and tend to declare them void and unenforceable. The clause should therefore specify for what damage the party is being compensated (loss of rent, attorney fees, and the like). As a rule, a court will not enforce a liquidated damage clause in an installment contract or contract for deed if the clause tends to effect a forfeiture of all installment payments made.

A seller who elects to keep deposited earnest money as liquidated damages may be constrained from successfully pursuing other remedies, including additional money damages. For example, if a buyer deposits $1,000 earnest money on a $75,000 house and later defaults, the seller who keeps the $1,000 as liquidated damages and later sells the house for only $70,000 cannot later recover from the first buyer the difference in the two purchase prices.

Some forms for contracts of sale have a special box for the parties to initial if they desire to treat the earnest money as liquidated damages. Some states have statutory guidelines as to what is a reasonable amount for liquidated damages; for example, in California if the amount is more than 3 percent of the sale price, the seller has the burden of proving that such excess is reasonable; otherwise, it would be treated as a penalty and returned to the buyer. (*See* **damages**, **election of remedies**, **unjust enrichment**.)

liquidity (*liquidez*) The ability to sell an asset and convert it into cash at a price close to its true value. Stocks that are traded publicly (not stocks in small or closely held corporations) are a relatively liquid investment. Real estate is traditionally considered a longer-term investment and is not highly liquid.

L

One test of the liquidity of a person (or company) is a ratio that measures the immediate debt-paying ability of that person. It considers cash in hand and anything that can be instantly turned into cash, called *quick assets*. This quick ratio is Quick Assets:Current Liabilities. A 1:1 quick ratio is generally acceptable for a business firm.

lis pendens (Lis/P)   A recorded legal document that gives constructive notice that an action affecting a particular piece of property has been filed in a state or federal court. Lis pendens is Latin for *action pending* and is in the nature of a "quasi lien." A person who subsequently acquires an interest in that property takes it subject to any judgment that may be entered; that is, a purchaser *pendente lite* (pending a lawsuit) is bound by the result of the lawsuit. The theory behind lis pendens is that multiple lawsuits can be avoided if all persons who might become involved with the property are first put on notice that the property is the subject of a lawsuit.

A notice of lis pendens is not the same as placing a lien on, or attaching, real property. It is only notice of a pending action involving title or possession of real property. The action must affect title, or right to possession, of real estate. Thus, it could not be used in a suit to recover attorney fees or real estate commissions. A lien, however, is a charge or security interest against the property; an attachment is a procedure to preserve the property for collection purposes. The end result of filing a lis pendens, however, is the same; that is, the property may not be freely sold or encumbered, and title is thereby effectively rendered unmarketable during the litigation.

The notice of pending action must generally contain the names of the parties, the object of the action, and a description of the affected property. Some states require a court hearing before rendering a lis pendens. From and after the time of recording the notice, the purchaser or encumbrancer of the affected property is considered to have constructive notice of the pendency against the designated parties. An attorney should be consulted before filing a lis pendens; an improperly filed lis pendens could lead to a lawsuit by the property owner for slander of title or malicious prosecution. Such a lis pendens could be removed from the record by filing a "motion to expunge." (*See* **attachment, slander of title**.)

listing   A written employment agreement between a property owner and a real estate broker authorizing the broker to find a buyer or a tenant for certain real property. Listings can take the form of open listings, exclusive-agency listings, or exclusive-right-to-sell listings. Most brokers prefer the exclusive-right-to-sell listing.

Note that net listings, although not specifically illegal, are unenforceable under many state statutes of frauds and therefore are not generally recommended.

A broker should be careful to check the true ownership of the property at the time of listing in order to avoid taking listings signed by unauthorized parties. It is important that all owners of record sign the listing agreement. The broker also has the legal and ethical duty to inspect the listed property to ensure that all information included in the listing agreement is accurate and complete. Owners should not be relied on to confirm the accuracy of technical or detailed matters about which they could not know, such as the legal effect of certain recorded restrictions on the property.

Listings are personal service contracts, and as such they may not be assigned to another broker. This does not, however, prevent the broker from delegating to the sales office the task of procuring buyers for the property.

The time limit included in the listing agreement is extended by implication if negotiations to sell the property are in progress at the time the listing expires.

The listing usually states the amount of commission the seller will pay the broker upon the happening of certain stated conditions. If a listed property is transferred by way of an involuntary sale such as a foreclosure, condemnation, or tax sale, the broker is usually not entitled to a commission.

In a buyer's listing, the buyer employs the broker to locate a property. (*See* **buyer's broker**.)

The broker must give a copy of the listing agreement to all the parties signing it at the time of signing. The broker should not show the listing contract (including MLS listings) to the buyer—the listing is an employment contract strictly between the seller and broker and is confidential. (*See* **exclusive agency, exclusive right to sell, extender clause, implied listing, net listing, offer, open listing, termination of listing**.)

listor A real estate broker or salesperson who obtains the listing on a particular property. In most brokerage companies, the listor receives a certain percentage of the total commission if the property is sold—more if the listor also is responsible for making the sale (the "selling broker"). Also spelled *lister*.

littoral land Land bordering on the shore of a sea or ocean and thus affected by the tide currents. Littoral land is different from riparian land, which borders on the bank of a watercourse or stream. (*See* **riparian rights**.)

livability space ratio For purposes of site planning, the minimum square footage of nonvehicular outdoor area in a development that is provided for each square foot of total floor area.

live load A moving or variable weight that may be safely added to the intrinsic weight of a structure. For example, a modern highrise office building may have a live load capacity of 60 pounds per square foot to accommodate office furniture and equipment.

livery of seisin An ancient ceremony of transferring title to real property. In the Middle Ages, conveyancing was accomplished by a formal process known as an *enfeoffment*, with livery of seisin literally a handing over of the fee with delivery of the seisin (possession of a freehold estate). The transfer was often symbolized by the simple ritual of transferring a handful of the soil, a piece of the turf, or a twig from a tree on the land, performed before a witness. (*See* **deed**.)

living trust An arrangement in which a property owner (trustor) transfers assets to a trustee who assumes specified duties in managing the asset. After payment of operating expenses and trustee's fees, the income generated by the trust property is paid to or used for the benefit of the designated beneficiary. (*See* **land trust, testamentary trust**.)

load (*carga*) The weight supported by a structural part such as a load-bearing wall.

load factor *See* **loss factor**.

loading dock The area, either within an industrial building and adjacent to its loading doors or outside the structure, used for the shipping or receiving of merchandise and the movement of merchandise between the warehouse area and trucks or rail cars.

loan balance table A table showing the balance remaining to be paid on an amortized loan; also called a *remaining balance table*.

loan broker *See* **mortgage broker**.

loan commitment A written pledge by a lender to lend a certain amount of money to a qualified borrower on a particular piece of real estate for a specified time under specific terms. It may be a conditional or qualified commitment, or it may be a firm commitment. It is more formal than a preliminary loan approval. After reviewing the borrower's loan application, the lender usually decides whether to make a commitment to lend the requested funds. This application contains such information as the borrower's name and address, place of employment, salary, bank accounts, credit references, and the like. (*See* **loan submission**.)

loan constant *See* **constant**.

loan correspondent   One who negotiates loans for conventional lending institutions or other lenders. The correspondent often continues to service the loan for the lender and acts as the collecting agent. (*See* **mortgage banker**.)

loan pool   A block of loans held in trust as collateral to support an issue of mortgage-backed securities. The loans may be a special category of mortgage loans, such as all new houses, or it can be a geographically diversified block of loans. The cash flows generated by the assigned loans are passed through to the holders of the securities either as direct pass-through of the principal and interest generated or on a sequential basis. Loan pools provide more than half the funding for residential mortgage loans and are beginning to find limited success funding commercial loans and other forms of debt (such as credit cards and car loans).

loan pooler   A company that assembles large blocks of loans to be held in trust as collateral for the issuance of a series of mortgage-backed securities. Loan poolers are usually large financial institutions with the resources to assemble multimillion-dollar blocks of loans. Even though loan poolers may issue creditworthiness, most poolers seek the credit enhancement of one of the major federal underwriters. (*See* **federal underwriters**.)

loan servicing   *See* **servicing**.

loan submission   A package of pertinent papers and documents regarding a specific property or properties provided to a lender for review and consideration for the purpose of making a mortgage loan. The following papers and documents are generally included: letter of transmittal; appraisal; financial statements; credit reports and/or Dun & Bradstreet reports; application; sales or purchase agreements on existing properties; leases, if applicable; photographs; plat plan and survey; cost breakdown, if applicable; set of plans and specifications on proposed construction; and zoning ordinances, utilities map, strip maps, aerial photographs, and other pertinent information that would help the lender in considering a particular submission.

loan-to-value (LTV) ratio   The ratio of a mortgage loan principal to the property's appraised value or its sales price, whichever is lower. Loan-to-value ratios depend on the individual lender's policy and governmental banking regulations. Lenders feel that the greater the equity a borrower has in a property, the less likely that the borrower will default and lose the property through foreclosure. When private mortgage insurance is used, the lender can sometimes offer 90 to 95 percent loan-to-value ratios (usually restricted to owner/occupants). Investors might qualify for 80 percent financing, FHA ratios are fixed by statute, and a veteran with a VA loan can borrow the purchase price or 100 percent LTV.

lobby
1. A public waiting area or meeting place in hotels, motels, apartment buildings, office buildings, or other similar structures.
2. To work for or against passage of a bill or resolution pending before a legislative body.

local improvement district   A separate legal entity, activated under state law by the inhabitants of a particular geographic area. The district is governed by a board of directors and possesses many of the characteristics of a city, particularly in terms of taxation. As a rule, the district issues its own bonds to finance particular improvements, such as water distribution systems, drainage structures, irrigation works, and a host of other types of developments. To repay the funds borrowed through the issuance of bonds, these districts have the power to assess all lands included in the district on an ad valorem basis.

locational obsolescence   Loss of value caused by negative influence outside the property (e.g., a commercial use abutting a residential property). (*See* **external obsolescence**.)

lockbox   A special locked container placed on the door of a listed property designed to facilitate the broker's showing of that property. The house keys are located inside the lockbox, which can be opened by a code or a magnetic stripe card.

   Lack of ordinary care in installing the lockbox or providing the combination or special key could result in liability for property damage, theft, or personal injury. Some errors and omissions insurance policies now have a special lockbox liability endorsement.

lock-in clause
1. A condition in a promissory note that prohibits prepayment of the note.
2. A contract provision covering the right of buyer and seller to notify the lender to fix the amount of points as of the date of the notice. (*See* **points**.)

locus sigilli   Latin for *place of seal*, using the abbreviated form, L.S., at the end of the signature line in some formal legal documents; used instead of the actual seal. (*See* **seal**.)

loft   (*desván, tapanco*)   Building area that is unfinished; also refers to open space, normally on the first or second floor and typically used for a low-cost manufacturing operation. The tenant pays a lower rent for loft space than for finished space and amortizes the cost of finishing the area over the term of the lease. Banks, savings and loan associations, and retail stores usually rent on a loft-space rate basis.

loop   A looped roadway having two access points off the same roadway.

loss factor   A commercial leasing term, also known as the *load factor* or *partial floor factor*, which is the square-footage difference between the rentable area and the usable area expressed as a percentage. For example, an office-building floor with a rentable area of 10,000 square feet and a usable area of 9,000 square feet has a loss factor of 10 percent—bathrooms, corridors, and elevator shafts use up the 1,000 square feet.

   The loss factor is a simple gauge for a tenant to use in evaluating separate rental sites that may have comparable rents but widely differing loss factors.

loss payee   The person designated on an insurance policy as the one to be paid in case the insured property is damaged or destroyed. A secured lender often requires a borrower to carry adequate insurance on property used as security and to name the lender as the loss payee.

lost-grant doctrine   A rarely used rule of real property law relating to the claim of title to real property against the sovereign. Tracing its roots to the field of incorporeal hereditaments, its application to realty has been recognized in the United States largely in claims relating to lands allegedly held under now lost grants from the Spanish Crown before the extension of American sovereignty over such territories. The lost-grant doctrine is similar to adverse possession in that the possession must be actual, open, and exclusive. For a claim against the sovereign, however, a higher degree of proof is required (for example, a chain of conveyance and payment of taxes). The claimant need only show the legal possibility of a lost grant, not its actual existence. (*See* **adverse possession**.)

lot, block, and subdivision   A description of real property that identifies a parcel of land by reference to lot and block numbers appearing on maps and plats of recorded subdivided land. For example, the description might read: "Lot 6, Block 8, Breezy Hills Subdivision, Serene County, Anystate, according to the plat thereof on file and of record in the office of the Registrar of Deeds in and for the said county and state."

   A *lot* is an individual parcel of land intended to be conveyed in its entirety to a prospective buyer. A *block* is typically a group of contiguous lots bounded by streets, as in a city block. Blocks are separated by roads or by other manmade or natural features such as creeks or ditches.

lot split   The division of land by separating its ownership or otherwise dividing it into several parcels. Lot splitting is typically regulated by local ordinances. Also called *land division*.

lottery   A system by which one pays a price for a chance to win a prize. In tight credit markets, sellers sometimes look to the lottery method to sell their real property. Many states have specific provisions in their real estate license acts preventing real estate brokers from selling real estate by means of a lottery or offering prizes for the listing or selling of real estate.

   The U.S. Code, Title 18, Section 1302 prohibits any reference, in any publication that uses the U.S. mail, to a lottery or a similar enterprise. The offering of real estate under a lottery cannot be transmitted by mail or published by mail. Violation of this act could bring a fine of not more than $1,000 or imprisonment of not more than two years, or both. For a second offense, imprisonment is not more than five years.

louver   Slats or fins over an opening, pitched so as to keep out rain or snow yet permit ventilation. A finned sunshade on a building; the diffusion grill on fluorescent light fixtures. Also spelled *louvre*.

love and affection   Usual consideration when a gift is intended, it is different from valuable consideration. The difference between the two is important in those areas of the law requiring a valuable consideration, such as under the recording acts, which protect the rights of bona fide purchasers for value. A common example of a grant deed supported by love and affection is a gift transfer of the family home by a father to his son "for love and affection." (*See* **consideration**, **gift deed**, **valuable consideration**.)

low-E glass   Window glass that has been covered with a thin, virtually transparent metallic coating that filters solar radiation and blocks harmful ultraviolet rays of the sun. Low E glass windows improve thermal performance by suppressing radiative heat flow.

lowrise   A two-story or three-story building.

luminous ceiling   A ceiling emitting light from its entire surface through the use of fluorescent light above translucent glass or plastic.

lump-sum payment   Repayment of a debt by a single payment, including principal and accrued interest. A straight note may provide for periodic interest payments with one lump-sum principal payment.

M

Maggie Mae   The trademark owned by the MGIC Mortgage Marketing Corporation, a mortgage insurance company, for the first, nonfederal secondary market for conventional mortgages.

Magnusen-Moss Warranty Act   *See* **warranty**.

MAI   Member, Appraisal Institute. *See* Appendix B.

mail, use of   *See* **acceptance**.

main line   The principal or through track of a railroad line on which traffic moves through yards or between stations. The main line is operated by timetable or train order and governed by block signal indication.

maintenance (*mantenimiento*)   The care and work put into a building to keep it in operation and productive use; the general repair and upkeep of a building. Deferred maintenance contributes to a building's loss in value. (*See* **deferred maintenance**.)

maintenance fee   A charge or lien levied against property owners to maintain their real estate in operation and productive use, especially in condominiums. In condominiums, the amount of the maintenance fee is usually determined by the board of directors upon review of the budgets. There are usually two budgets. The first is designed to anticipate the month-by-month needs with totals by category for the year. Monthly financial statements compare the actual receipts and disbursements with the operating budget figures, giving a clear financial picture on which to base management decisions.

A *five-year capital budget*, prepared or updated yearly, is designed to anticipate major expenditures such as painting the building, purchasing association insurance for the common areas, recarpeting corridors, and replacing any items of substantial cost. A reserve fund is established to cover these expenditures. This reserve fund money is kept in regular savings accounts or higher yield time certificate deposits, and is withdrawn for disbursements when the need arises. (*See* **operating expenses**.)

majority   The age at which a person is no longer a minor and is thus able to enter freely into contracts. In most states, the age of majority for contract purposes is 18. (*See* **minor**.)

maker   The person (borrower) who executes a promissory note and thus becomes primarily liable for payment to the payee (lender). The maker of a check is known as the *drawer*.

malfeasance   Commission of an act that is clearly unlawful; especially applicable to acts of a public official.

mall   A landscaped public area set aside for pedestrian traffic. Malls are popular features of large retail shopping centers. They are now also being created in established downtown retail areas to revitalize existing businesses and are being built in suburban areas to generate new business.

management agreement   A contract between the owner of income-producing property and the individual or firm managing that property. The management agreement establishes the scope of the agent's authority, as well as duties, compensation, termination procedures, payment of expenses, and other matters. In addition to the essential elements of a valid contract, the written management agreement should contain, at minimum, the legal description of the property to be managed, hold-harmless clauses, scope of services, rate and schedule of compensation, accounting and report requirements, the starting date, the termination date, and any provisions for renewal options. (*See* **property management**.)

management survey   A detailed analysis of the economic, physical, and operational aspects of a property, with recommendations as to changes and improvements that could enhance the property's profitability.

mandamus   An emergency writ issued from a court ordering a public official to perform a certain activity. For example, a court might order a reluctant public official to issue a real estate license if the complainant is qualified, or it might order a governmental agency to issue a building permit.

mansard roof   An architectural style in which the top floor or floors of a structure are designed to appear to be the roof. Such a roof has two slopes on each of the four sides of the building, with the upper slope less steeply inclined. (*See* **Roof Designs** [in Appendix G].)

mantel   The decorative facing placed around a fireplace. Mantels are usually made of ornamental wood and topped by a shelf.

M

manufactured housing   A type of housing unit factory-constructed according to standards of the Federal Manufactured Home Construction and Safety Standards (HUD, Title 6) on a permanent chassis and containing at least 320 square feet. Fewer than 5 percent are ever moved a second time. Manufactured housing offers a cost-effective solution to rising housing costs in many parts of the country, even though many communities have instituted zoning legislation restricting factory-built housing. However, both Fannie Mae and Freddie Mac buy mortgage loans secured by a manufactured home on the secondary market under certain, well-defined conditions: at the very least, the home must be a single-family dwelling that is classified as real property in that community and the home must be permanently affixed to the foundation in accordance with the manufacturer's requirement for anchoring, support, stability, and maintenance.

Manufactured Housing Institute (MHI)   *See* Appendix A.

maps and plats   Surveys of particular pieces of land showing monuments, boundaries, area, ownership, and the like, prepared by registered surveyors or civil engineers. Subdividers must generally submit maps and plats of proposed subdivisions with their applications for recordation and registration (if under the Torrens system) of the subdivisions. Thereafter, when lots are sold in a subdivision, the legal description need only refer to the subdivision, lot, and block number, which may be taken from the recorded map. (*See* **tax map**.)

margin   The amount added to the index rate that represents the lender's cost of doing business (includes costs, profits, and risk of loss of the loan) in an adjustable-rate loan. Generally, the margin stays constant during the life of the loan. (*See* **adjustable-rate loan**.)

marginal land   Land that is of little value because of some deficiency, such as poor access, inadequate rainfall, or steep terrain. Modern land reclamation and development techniques have successfully converted some marginal lands into attractive and functional developments. Former desert land, for instance, has been successfully developed into attractive subdivisions.

marginal release   Notation of a satisfaction or release of mortgage by a county recorder, as evidenced by a note of its liber (book) and page number on the margin of the recorded mortgage.

marginal tax rate   The ordinary rate of income tax charged on the last dollar of income; often used when making calculations for investment decisions.

marina   A docking and mooring facility for boats that is generally equipped with repair facilities, gas, supplies, and other conveniences; a boat basin.

marital deduction   The deduction against federal estate tax equal to 100 percent of the assets passing to the surviving spouse. (*See* **estate tax**, **federal**.)

mark   A symbol used for a signature. (*See* **X**.)

market   (*mercado*)   A group of properties that would each be competitive to a given typical buyer.

marketable title   Good or clear salable title reasonably free from risk of litigation over possible defects; also referred to as *merchantable title*. A marketable title is one that (1) is free from undisclosed encumbrances; (2) discloses no serious defects and does not depend on doubtful questions of law or fact to prove its validity; (3) will not expose a purchaser to the hazard of litigation or embarrassment in the peaceful enjoyment of the property; and (4) would be accepted by reasonably well-informed and prudent persons, acting on business principles and willful knowledge of the facts and their legal significance with the assurance that they could in turn sell or mortgage the property at market value.

Marketable title does not necessarily mean a perfect title, just one that is free from plausible or reasonable objections. A court of law would order the buyer to accept it if asked to decree specific performance of the sales contract.

Title would not be marketable if there were a significant risk of litigation—the buyer cannot be forced to buy a lawsuit along with the property. An unmarketable title does not mean that the property cannot be transferred, but it does mean that certain defects in the title may limit or restrict its ownership, and the purchaser cannot be forced to accept a conveyance that is materially different from the one bargained for or "marketed" in the contract of sale.

If the buyer inserts a contract provision that the seller must deliver title "free from all defects or encumbrances," the seller should be aware the buyer could probably reject title even if only a small or insignificant encroachment or defect existed. Unless the contract provides otherwise (in a "subject to" clause), any of the following could render title unmarketable: easements, restrictions, violations of restrictions, zoning ordinance violations, existing leases, encroachments (except slight ones), and outstanding mineral and oil rights.

A burdensome zoning ordinance does not generally render title unmarketable. However, if a seller incorrectly represents that a zoning ordinance would not prohibit a purchaser's required use when in fact it would, a zoning ordinance may be equivalent to a lien or encumbrance. Furthermore, the seller's failure to inform the buyer of a zoning ordinance violation may constitute actionable fraud or entitle the purchaser to rescind the contract.

Questions of marketable title must be raised by the purchaser before acceptance of the deed. Once accepting the deed, the buyer's only recourse is to sue on the covenants of warranty, if any, contained in the deed. (*See* **merger, "subject to" clause, unmarketable title, warranty deed**.)

market conditions   Features of the marketplace, including (but not limited to) interest rates, demographics, employment levels, vacancy rates, and absorption levels.

market data approach   *See* **direct sales comparison approach**.

marketing period   The period of time between the start of marketing and the final closing. The popularity of the sale is related to the shortness of the marketing period.

market value   (*valor de mercado*)   The most probable price a property should bring in a competitive and open market under all conditions requisite to a fair sale under guidelines published by federal lending institutions (Fannie Mae, Freddie Mac). Such conditions include the assumption that the buyer and the seller acted prudently and knowledgeably and that the price is not affected by undue stimulus. Implicit in this definition are the consummation of a sale as of a specified date and the passing of title from seller to buyer under the following conditions:
- Buyer and seller are typically motivated.
- Both parties are well-informed or well-advised, and they are acting in what they consider their own best interest.
- A reasonable time is allowed for exposure in the open market.
- Payment is made in terms of cash in U.S. dollars or in terms of comparable financial arrangements.
- The price represents the normal consideration for the property sold unaffected by special or creative financing or sales concessions granted by anyone associated with the sale. (*See* **fair market value**.)

master deed   The principal conveyance document used by the owners of land on which condominiums are located. The master deed, together with a declaration, must generally be submitted when recording or registering the condominium pursuant to state laws. (*See* **declaration**.)

master form instrument   An instrument containing various forms such as covenants and other clauses in a mortgage or deed of trust recorded with the county registrar as a master form instrument. Such an instrument need not be acknowledged (notarized and witnessed). It is indexed under the name of the person recording it. Thereafter, any of the provisions of a master form instrument may be incorporated by reference in any mortgage or deed of trust if the reference states that the master is recorded in the county and it gives the recording date, file number, volume, and page. Such a reference should also state that a copy of the master was furnished to the person executing the mortgage or deed of trust.

master lease   The dominant lease in a building or development. For example, a developer might lease land from a fee owner, construct a building or condominium, and then sublease space to others. The subleases generally have provisions that conform to the terms of the master lease because the sublease is subject to the terms of the master lease. (*See* **sublease**.)

master limited partnership (MLP)   A limited partnership formed under state partnership law where the limited partnership's interests are registered to be publicly traded; also called a *publicly traded limited partnership*. The partnership interests are issued to a "master" limited partner, who then arranges for the sale of the units to the public.

master plan   (*plan urbano maestro*)   A comprehensive plan to guide the long-term physical development of a particular area. (*See* **general plan**, **zoning**.)

Master Senior Appraiser (MSA)   *See* Appendix B.

master switch   An electrical wall switch that controls more than one fixture or outlet in a room.

material fact   Any fact that is relevant to a person making a decision. Real estate licensees must disclose all material facts to their clients, especially facts about the condition of the property, such as known structural defects, building code violations, and hidden dangerous conditions. The use of seller disclosure statements, now mandated in a number of states, shifts much of the disclosure burden from the real estate licensee to the seller.

    Brokers are often placed in the no-win situation of trying to evaluate whether a certain fact is material enough that it needs to be disclosed to a prospective buyer, such as the fact that a murder occurred on the property ten years ago or that the neighbors throw loud parties. It is sometimes difficult to distinguish between "fact" and "opinion." The statement "real property taxes are low" is different from "real property taxes are $500 per year." Even though brokers act in good faith, they may still be liable for failure to exercise reasonable care or competence in ascertaining and communicating pertinent facts that the broker knew or "should have known."

    Under fair housing law guidelines the fact that an occupant of property has AIDS is not deemed to be a material fact. A broker who fails to disclose this fact is not liable for concealment of a material fact. (*See* **misrepresentation**, **puffing**.)

materialman   The supplier of materials used in the construction of an improvement. The materialman is entitled to a lien on the property for monies overdue, whether due from the owner or the prime contractor. The materialman must file a lien within the time specified by state law. This is usually measured from the completion date. (*See* **mechanic's lien**.)

maturity   (*vencimiento*)   The time when a debt, such as a mortgage note, becomes due and extinguished if paid in accordance with the agreed on schedule of payments. (*See* **curtail schedule**.)

mean   The average of a set of numbers. The mean of 1, 3, 7, and 9 is 5. (*See* **median**.)

meander line   An artificial line used by surveyors to measure the natural, uneven, winding property line formed by rivers, streams, and other watercourses bordering a property. The meander line is primarily a device to measure area, not to delimit title or determine a boundary line. Surveyors sometimes use straight lines on courses approximating the natural line. In a conveyance of land described as bounded by a meander line, the true boundary is the stream or waters.

mean high water   *See* **high-water mark**.

measurement tables Understanding U.S. measurements and their metric equivalents is useful to real estate professionals. The Metric Conversion Act of 1975 regulates the conversion from the U.S. system to the International Metric System. Some of these conversions are shown here.

Unit	U.S. Measurement	Metric Equivalent
mile	5,280 feet; 320 rods; 1,760 yards; 80 chains	1.609 kilometers
rod	5.50 yards; 16.5 feet	5.029 meters
square mile	640 acres; 102,400 sq. rods	2.590 square kilometers
acre	4,840 sq. yards; 160 sq. rods; 43,560 sq. feet	4.047 sq. meters; 0.405 hectares
acre foot	43,560 cubic feet	1,234 kiloliters
square yard	9 sq. feet	0.836 square meters
square foot	144 sq. inches	0.093 square meters
chain	66 feet; 100 links; 4 rods	20.117 meters
kilometer	0.62 mile (3,280 ft., 10 in.)	1,000 meters
hectare	2.47 acres	10,000 square meters

Acre Equivalent

One acre equals a rectangle of the following size:

Length (Feet)*		Width (Feet)*
16.5	by	2,640.0
33.0	by	1,320.0
50.0	by	871.2
66.0	by	660.0
75.0	by	580.8
100.0	by	435.6
132.0	by	330.0
150.0	by	290.4
208.7	by	208.7

* Note: Multiply by 0.3048 to arrive at the equivalent measurement in meters.

M

M

Conversion from U.S. System to Metric and Vice Versa			
	Multiply	**By**	**To Find**
LENGTH	inches	25	millimeters
	feet	30	centimeters
	yards	0.9	meters
	miles	1.6	kilometers
	millimeters	0.04	inches
	centimeters	0.4	inches
	meters	1.1	yards
	kilometers	0.6	miles
AREA	square inches	6.5	square centimeters
	square feet	0.09	square meters
	square yards	0.8	square meters
	square miles	2.6	square kilometers
	acres	0.4	square hectometers (hectares)
	square centimeters	0.16	square inches
	square meters	1.2	square yards
	square kilometers	0.4	square yards
	square hectometers (hectares)	2.5	acres
MASS	ounces	18	grams
	pounds	0.45	kilograms
	short tons	0.9	megagrams (metric tons)
	grams	0.035	ounces
	kilograms	2.2	pounds
	megagrams (metric tons)	1.1	short tons
LIQUID VOLUME	ounces	30	milliliters
	pints	0.47	liters
	quarts	0.95	liters
	gallons	3.8	liters
	milliliters	0.034	ounces
	liters	2.1	pints
	liters	1.06	quarts
	liters	0.26	gallons

measure of damages   The rule of law set by statute or case law as to the amount of damages a plaintiff can recover against a defendant for a breach of contract or other civil wrong. (*See* **benefit of bargain, damages**.)

mechanic's lien   (*gravamen de constuctor*)   A statutory lien created in favor of materialmen and mechanics (and architects and designers in some states) to secure payment for materials supplied and services rendered in the improvement, repair, or maintenance of real property. This right did not exist in common law. Note that materialmen are *suppliers*, whereas mechanics are *laborers*.

The mechanic's lien provides security to those who perform labor or furnish materials in the improvement of the real property (but usually not public property) based on the "enhancement of value" theory. Because the real estate has been enhanced in value by the labor performed and the materials furnished, the parties performing the work or supplying materials should be given a right of lien on the real estate on which the work was done. The lien accrues in favor of subcontractors, materialmen, and laborers independently of the original contractor, and not by way of subrogation to the rights of the latter. Thus, any person furnishing labor or material for the improvement of real estate can assert a mechanic's lien, provided there is a valid contract. The lien is for work and materials that become a permanent part of the building only, and thus does not cover certain costs for furnishing tools or office overhead like telephone, stationery, and other similar expenses.

The mechanic's lien attaches to the improvement, as well as to the interest of the owner of the real property who contracts for the improvement, including the equitable interest of a buyer under a contract for deed. The term *owner* also includes a lessor whose lease requires the erection of buildings, even though only the lessee contracted for the building.

Usually such a lien is relied on to cover situations in which the owner has not paid for the work, or when the general contractor has been paid but has, in turn, not paid the subcontractors or suppliers. The work must have been done under a contract (express or implied) with the owner or owner's authorized representative.

Mechanics' liens are controlled by the requirements of the statute of the state where the real estate is located. In some states, mechanics' liens may be given priority over previously recorded liens, such as mortgages. The claimant must take steps to enforce a lien within a certain time, usually one or two years after the filing of the lien claim, or the lien will expire. Enforcement usually requires a court action to foreclose the lien through the sale of the real estate to produce money to pay the lien.

The effective date of the lien is usually the time of visible commencement of operations—that is, when enough work is performed to give notice that the real property is being improved or is about to be improved. If the property is transferred after the lien is effective, but before the filing of the notice of lien, the mechanic's lien has priority. Thus, a good-faith purchaser for value who is without notice of the visible commencement of operations takes title subject to the possibility of a subsequent notice of lien. A prudent purchaser should obtain proper title insurance (an extended coverage policy) as protection against this type of risk.

In many states, mechanics' and materialmen's liens have priority over all other liens of any nature, except (1) liens in favor of any branch of the government; (2) mortgages, liens, or judgments recorded or filed before visible commencement of operations; and (3) mortgages recorded before the date of completion, under which all or a portion of the monies advanced and secured up to that time have been used to pay for the improvement. The mortgage must include such a statement.

Once a mechanic's lien has been paid off, a written notice (generally called a *satisfaction of lien*) should be filed in the proper court at the expense of the lienee (owner). If the liened property is registered under the Torrens system, the satisfaction of lien must be filed with the registrar of titles.

Usually, an owner of property can find protection against mechanics' liens for work authorized by a lessee or vendee (under contract for deed) by posting or recording a "notice of nonresponsibility." In effect, this notice would inform the contractor that he would have to look solely to the person authorizing the work for payment. (*See* **inchoate, notice of completion, notice of lien, notice of nonresponsibility**.)

median   The middle figure in a set of numbers. If sales prices were $70,000, $90,000, and $180,000, the median would be $90,000. Some lenders define eligible income as being 80 percent or less of the area median income. (*See* **mean**.)

mediation   (*mediación*)   An alternative process of dispute resolution in which an independent third party works with two disputing parties to help them resolve their differences. If successful, the mediation should be reduced to an enforceable written agreement. If mediation is not successful, the next step often is binding arbitration. (*See* **arbitration**.)

meeting of the minds   Mutual assent or agreement between the parties to a contract regarding the substance of the contract. If the parties by their words and acts manifest an intention to be bound to a contract, they can be held accountable. Thus, while parties may not intend to bind themselves to a contract, they may be deemed bound in law because of their outward indications of assent. There can be no contract unless there is a meeting of the minds; that is, there must be a valid offer that is properly accepted. (*See* **estoppel**, **offer and acceptance**.)

megalopolis   A large densely populated metropolitan area, consisting of a number of major urban areas, such as the Eastern Seaboard area, which includes New York City; Washington, D.C.; Philadelphia; Boston; and smaller surrounding cities. (*See* **metropolitan statistical area**.)

menace   The threat of violence used to obtain a contract. Like duress and undue influence, menace is a ground to void a contract. (*See* **duress**.)

merchantable title   *See* **marketable title**.

merchants' association   An organization for shopping center tenants structured to facilitate joint advertising, promotion, and other activities beneficial to the entire center.

merger   (*fusión*)   The uniting or combining of two or more interests or estates into one.

   An easement may be extinguished upon the merger of a servient and a dominant estate. Example: Samir, the owner of lot 1, the servient estate, gives Sonja, the owner of the adjacent lot 2, the dominant estate, an easement to cross over 1. Subsequently Sonja acquires title to 1. If Sonja later sells 2 to Milan, the easement is not revived; it has been merged into 1 and would have to be created anew.

   As a rule, when a greater and a lesser estate become vested in the same person, the lesser estate merges into the greater estate. For example, if a landlord sells property to a tenant, there is a merger of the leasehold estate with the original freehold estate. Obviously, the lease is terminated, and the tenant is relieved of the duty to pay rent. This is also true when the tenant inherits the leased fee.

   When a deed is delivered pursuant to a contract for deed, all terms of the contract for deed are merged into and superseded by the deed, unless otherwise provided in the contract or the deed. Thus, a vendor who wants representations, warranties, or restrictions in the contract for deed to continue and survive the deed must insert them in the deed or specify which covenants and conditions in the contract are to survive delivery of the deed or assignment of the lease. In essence, the contract merges into the deed and ceases to exist. Also, when a sales contract calls for something to be done *after* closing and delivery of the deed, such as the installation of a sewer system, this requirement would usually survive the deed and be enforceable; that is, matters collateral to the conveyance are not merged.

   A merger clause in a contract states that this writing constitutes the entire agreement between the parties; all other prior negotiations and representations are not a part of the contract. (*See* **survival clause**.)

meridian   One of a set of imaginary lines running north and south used by surveyors for reference in locating and describing land under the government survey method of property description. (*See* **government survey method.**)

mesne conveyance   An intermediate or middle conveyance; any conveyance between the first conveyance and the most recent conveyance in the chain of title.

mesne profits   Profits derived from the wrongful possession of land. Usually mesne profits are recoverable by the lawful owner.

messuage   A house and the adjacent buildings and land used by the household.

metes and bounds   (*medidas y límites*)   A common method of land description that identifies a property by specifying the shape and boundary dimensions of the parcel, using terminal points and angles. A metes-and-bounds description starts at a well-marked point of beginning and follows the boundaries of the land by courses and metes (measures, distances, compass direction) and bounds (landmarks, monuments) and returns to the true point of beginning. Generally, however, in verifying such a description, monuments prevail over courses and distances. A description that fails to enclose an area by returning to the point of beginning is defective. If there is any discrepancy in the distance between monuments and linear measurements, the actual measured distance between the monuments prevails. An example of a metes-and-bounds description is as follows:

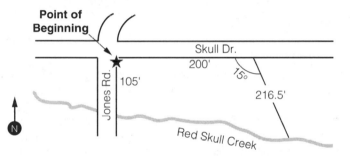

A tract of land located in Red Skull, Virginia, is described as follows: Beginning at the intersection of the east line of Jones Road and the south line of Skull Drive; thence east along the south line of Skull Drive 200 feet; thence south 15° east 216.5 feet, more or less, to the center thread of Red Skull Creek; thence northwesterly along the center line of said Creek to its intersection with the east line of Jones Road; thence north 105 feet, more or less, along the east line of Jones Road to the place of beginning.

When used to describe property within a town or city, a metes-and-bounds description may begin as follows:

Beginning at a point on the southerly side of Kent Street, 100 feet easterly from the corner formed by the intersection of the southerly side of Kent Street and the easterly side of Broadway; thence . . .

When used to describe land in rectangular survey states, a metes-and-bounds description may begin as follows:

That part of lots 7, 8, and 9 in Block R of Lightwater's Subdivision in the NW1/4 of the SE1/4 of Section 16, Township 39 north, Range 12 east of the 5th principal meridian bounded and described to wit as follows, beginning . . .

(*See* **legal description, monument, point of beginning [POB].**)

meth labs   The places where illegal methamphetamines are manufactured, which can include all types of buildings and enclosures, ranging from RVs to motels and apartments to upscale residential houses. Chemicals used to make methamphetamines and the by-products from the process are highly toxic, leaving the buildings and the grounds surrounding them more contaminated than many federally designated toxic waste sites. Production of one pound of methamphetamine can create between five to seven pounds of toxic waste while releasing poisonous gases into the atmosphere.

metropolitan statistical area (MSA)   The area in and around a major city. For example, the Chicago metropolitan area is often construed to include certain areas in western Indiana as well as the surrounding suburbs in Illinois.

mezzanine   (*entresuelo*)   An intermediate floor between two main stories of a building or between the floor and ceiling of a one-story structure. A mezzanine usually covers a relatively small portion of the total floor space.

middleman   A person who brings two or more parties together but does not conduct negotiations. One limited exception to the rule that a real estate broker cannot collect a fee from both parties without their prior approval is the so-called middleman exception. The middleman exception, in which the broker merely brings the parties together to negotiate their own contract, does not apply if the broker exercises any discretion or authority to negotiate for the principal. In actual practice, true middleman status occurs only in rare situations. (*See* **facilitator**, **finder's fee**.)

midrise   A four- to seven-story building.

mile   A linear measurement of distance equal to 1,760 yards or 5,280 feet or 1.609 kilometers. (*See* **measurement tables**.)

military clause   A provision in some residential leases allowing a tenant in military service to terminate the lease in case of transfer, discharge, or other appropriate circumstances. Sample language follows.

It is expressly agreed that if the lessee herein should receive official orders relieving him or her from duty at Fort Shafter or from active duty in the army or ordering him or her to live in service quarters, he or she may terminate this lease upon written notice of intention to do so. Such termination shall become effective 30 days after the date of the service of the notice upon the lessor. If the date of such termination falls between the days on which rent becomes due there shall accrue on the first day of the rental period in which termination takes effect a proportionate part only of the rent due but for such termination. (*See* **Soldiers and Sailors Civil Relief Act [SSCRA]**.)

mill   One-tenth of one cent. Some states use a mill rate to compute property taxes and sales taxes. Example: If the mill rate is 52 and the property is assessed at \$40,000, the tax would be 0.052 × \$40,000, or \$2,080. This tax can also be quoted or computed as \$52 per \$1,000. *See* **tax rate**.)

mineral rights   Rights to subsurface land and profits. Normally, when real property is conveyed, the grantee receives all right and title to the land, including everything above and below the surface, unless excepted by the grantor. (*See* **oil and gas lease**.)

minimum lot area   A zoning ordinance requirement establishing a minimum lot size upon which a building may be erected.

minimum property requirements   The minimum requirements for a property to be livable, soundly built, and suitably located as to site and neighborhood before the FHA underwrites a residential mortgage loan. A broker, in estimating the seller's closing costs, should consider repair expenses to comply with these requirements. Parties in an FHA loan cannot avoid meeting FHA standards by using an "as is" clause.

minimum rent   The smallest amount of rent from a tenant under a lease with a varying rent schedule; base rent.

ministerial acts   Acts that can be performed without creating an agency relationship, although such actions may require a real estate license. They are routine acts performed for the customer that do not involve judgment, discretion, or advice. For example, a licensee representing a seller may work with the buyer, as customer, by showing the property, finding a lender, and doing paperwork necessary for closing. In most states, a real estate license is required for these activities, even though they do not rise to client-level actions.

miniwarehouse   A structure containing self-storage units. A miniwarehouse is typically found in an industrial park and is designed to provide small, secure storage (10 to 200 sq. ft.) for use by individuals and small businesses. Operators must follow legal procedures in disposing of goods (old records or files for example) that appear to have been abandoned by the renter. Commonly referred to as a *ministorage facility*.

minor   (*menor de edad*)   A person under the legal age of majority; a legal infant who is not a completely competent legal party. The legal age of majority is set by state law and may vary depending on the purpose of the law, such as the legal age to drive, drink, or enter into contracts. Most contracts, except those for necessities such as food and clothing, entered into by a minor are generally voidable at his or her option. However, if the minor does not disaffirm the contract within a reasonable time after attaining majority, then the contract becomes fully enforceable against him or her. For example, if a minor lists property with a broker, the broker could not collect an earned commission if when the broker finds a ready, willing, and able buyer the minor decides to repudiate the listing contract. In any event, a minor could not sell the property without court approval, because such a person has neither the legal capacity to transfer title to property nor the power to make a valid will.

Even if the minor misrepresents his or her age, the minor can still disaffirm the contract, although misrepresentation may lead to an action in damages for fraud.

A deed by a minor is voidable, although a minor may be a grantee and may receive realty by gift or inheritance. A minor is generally deemed incapable of appointing an agent to sell his or her property; thus any power of attorney executed is void.

If land owned by a minor must be sold for the minor's maintenance or for investment, court proceedings to appoint a guardian must be instituted, in which case the minor becomes a ward of the court. The court can grant the guardian a special license to sell the property if the guardian posts a bond (the guardian does not need a real estate license).

Generally, title by adverse possession cannot be established against a minor unless the adverse possession continues for the prescription period *after* the minor reaches majority. (*See* **guardian, majority, voidable.**)

minority   A subgroup that appears to be outnumbered by other groups and often used to categorize people of a different language, sex, color, nationality, religion, culture, ethnicity, or lifestyle. In the context of fair housing laws, minority referred to consumers who have been discriminated against historically and for whom such discrimination is now prohibited. The term *minority* is misleading, because sometimes the minority may become the majority, in terms of numbers. The preferred term today is *protected classes*, any group designated as such by HUD against whom real estate licensees or sellers may not discriminate. Federal fair housing laws prohibit discrimination based solely on race, color, religion, national origin, sex, familial status, or disability (handicap). For example, white males are clearly in the minority (terms of numbers) but they have not been designated a protected class.

misdemeanor A crime, less serious than a felony, usually punishable by fine or imprisonment for one year or less. (*See* **felony**.)

misnomer A mistake in a name. To correct a misnomer in a deed, the proper procedure is to prepare and record a correction of deed so as to avoid future title disputes. A corporation misnamed in a deed does not constitute material error if the corporation can be reasonably identified, as when the deed states "Abby, Ltd.," when the real name is "Abby, Limited." A seller can be compelled to execute a correction of deed if his or her deed to the grantee contains a covenant of further assurance. (*See* **covenant**.)

misplaced improvement A poorly located improvement; an improvement that is poorly planned in that it either is too costly or does not conform to the best use of the site. A modern dwelling constructed among a group of Victorian mansions is an example.

misrepresentation A false statement or concealment of a material fact made with the intention of inducing some action by another party. A court will grant relief in the form of damages or rescission if the misrepresented fact is material to the transaction. Misrepresentation can be an affirmative statement, such as "This house does not have termites." It can also be a concealment of a material fact known to one party who knows the fact is not reasonably ascertainable by the other party. An example is a seller who knows of a serious defect in the support beams, yet does not disclose this fact to the buyer. This failure to disclose is sometimes called "negative fraud." However, if the buyer clearly does not believe or rely on the misrepresentations, or makes his or her own inspection and relies only on this investigation, the contract cannot be rescinded on a defense of misrepresentation.

Statements of opinion are not normally material facts. For example, "This house is a great buy at $50,000, because it is worth much more than that," is a statement of opinion, often known as "puffing." Note the difference between the statements "The taxes are low" and "The taxes are $500" where actual taxes are $1,000. It would be no defense to a broker that the seller told the broker the taxes were $500—this is information the broker should verify. However, if the person making the representation possesses some superior knowledge, then the representation, even though opinion, is treated as fact. If a builder, for instance, says, "The foundation appears to be properly laid," he or she may be liable if in fact it is not.

Courts have held that a broker who represents that he or she does not think the property is on filled land may be liable if it turns out the land is filled and the buyer suffers damages. Although misrepresentations usually are oral or written statements, they could be a nod of the head, pointing out false boundaries, or displaying a forged map—in other words, any action that may convey a false message. Common subjects for misrepresentation lawsuits are statements regarding easements, sewer connections, high water, proposed special assessments, number of legal units, and condition of roof.

A person need not actually intend to misrepresent a fact. A broker or salesperson would be liable if he or she *knows* or *should have known* of the falsity of a statement. Thus, if a broker makes a negligent misrepresentation of a material fact to induce the buyer to buy, and the buyer relies on this fact to the buyer's detriment, then the broker is liable. The seller is also liable because the statement was made by the seller's agent within the scope of authority of the agency. If the broker fails to disclose a material fact, an aggrieved buyer usually has a successful case against the broker when:

- The broker has knowledge of facts unknown to or beyond the reach of the buyer that materially affect the value or desirability of the property, and the broker fails to disclose these facts.
- The broker intends to defraud the buyer by such nondisclosure.
- The buyer suffers actual damages as a result of the misrepresentation.

Some consequences of misrepresentation are:

- The real estate licensee can have his or her license suspended or revoked.
- The defrauded party can collect damages or have the contract rescinded.
- The seller may not have to pay a commission to a misrepresenting broker.
- Under the federal Interstate Land Sales Act, a misrepresenting broker may be jointly and severally liable to the purchaser.
- The buyer may be able to keep the property and sue the seller for the difference between the purchase price and the lesser actual value.
- The buyer may be able to collect damages for expenditures made in reliance on the misrepresentation.

(*See* **"as is," fraud, innocent misrepresentation, latent defects, puffing, scope of authority**.)

mistake   An error or misunderstanding. A contract is voidable if there is a mistake that is mutual, material, unintentional, and free from negligence, such as both parties honestly contracting for a different lot in a subdivision (mistake of fact). Innocent mistakes seldom serve to void a contract. A party cannot claim "mistake" to get out of a contract on the basis that he or she did not read the contract he or she signed and was therefore mistaken as to its material terms; neither ignorance nor poor judgment is a mistake of fact. Nor can a party claim mistake in not knowing the legal consequences upon signing the contract (mistake of law). (*See* **adhesion contract**.)

When there is an ambiguity known by one party who fails to explain the mistake to the innocent party, the innocent party's interpretation generally will prevail.

miter   In carpentry, the ends of any two pieces of board of corresponding form cut off at an angle and fitted together in an angular shape.

mitigation   Methods used to reduce the sources of environmental hazards and to limit their impact on the environment and to human life. For example, radon mitigation consists of properly installing a system of pipes and fans to reduce radon levels.

mitigation of damages   A principle of contract law that refers to the obligation of an injured party to take reasonable steps to reduce or eliminate the amount of entitled damages for that party. For example, a landlord may have a duty to try to locate a replacement tenant for space vacated or abandoned by a prior tenant in breach of the lease.

mixed use   The use of real property for more than one use, such as a condominium building that has residential and commercial units. It could combine retail, office, and residential, or industrial, office, and residential.

MLS   *See* **multiple listing service (MLS)**.

mobile home   Prefabricated trailer-type housing units built prior to June 15, 1976, but often incorrectly applied to manufactured housing. (*See* **manufactured housing, mobile-home park**.)

mobile-home park   An area zoned and set up to accommodate mobile or manufactured homes and provide water hookups and sewage disposal for each home. The mobile home park contains all utilities, streets, parking, and amenities. Parks and communities built before 1980 are often called mobile home parks. (*See* **landlease communities**.)

model home   A house built as part of a land development program to demonstrate style, construction, and possible furnishings of similar houses to be erected and sold. A model home, also known as a *demonstration home* or a *spec home*, is an excellent selling aid if properly handled and is often sold with some of the furnishings after it has served its purpose. The first house completed in the development may be used as the model and is generally the last to be sold.

modification
1. The influence on land use and value resulting from man-made improvements to surrounding parcels.
2. A change to a contract. A contract can be modified at any time with the consent of both parties.
3. A change to a building design as required by law, such as a requirement under the Americans with Disabilities Act to make a public-accommodation building more accessible to persons with disabilities. (*See* **Americans with Disabilities Act [ADA]**.)

modification and assumption agreement   A written agreement to change the interest rate when the due-on-sale provision of the mortgage is enforced upon a change of ownership. It also releases the previous mortgagor from personal liability under the mortgage.

modified accelerated cost recovery system (MACRS)   A method of depreciation allowing for depreciating assets over a longer period of time than provided by the accelerated cost recovery (ACR). The 1986 Tax Reform Act (TRA '86) replaced ACR with MACRS, which maintains the ACR structure but lengthens the cost recovery periods for most depreciable assets. Effective for property placed in service after December 31, 1986, the recovery period is 27.5 years for residential rental property and 39 years for nonresidential real property. The accelerated method is no longer available for real estate; straight-line is the only allowable method. (*See* **declining-balance method**, **straight-line method**.)

    The current depreciation rules do not distinguish between new or used property, nor is any salvage value considered. Component depreciation is barred except as new components are actually added after the initial acquisition. The depreciation method used for additions or improvements is identical to that used for the underlying property. For both residential rental property and nonresidential real property, a midmonth convention now applies. That is, no matter when the property is placed in service, it is deemed to have been placed in service at the middle of the month. (*See* **component depreciation**.)

    TRA '86 also created an alternative depreciation system (ADS), which must be used for property that is used predominantly outside the United States, for property leased to a tax-exempt entity or financed with tax-exempt bonds, and to calculate the portion of depreciation treated as a tax preference for the purposes of the corporate and alternative minimum tax. ADS real property is depreciated over 40 years. Taxpayers may elect to use ADS even if they do not fall into one of the foregoing categories. (*See* **tax preference**.)

modular construction   A highly engineered method of producing six-sided buildings (four walls plus a ceiling and a floor) or building components in an efficient and cost-effective manner in a controlled manufacturing (factory) environment; also called *prefabricated housing*. Modular methods expedite construction because the house itself can be built in the factory while the building site is being prepared, thus potentially eliminating costly delays.

    There are no federal codes of standards for modular construction. Modulars have been used for office buildings, hotels, strip malls, schools, factories, and storage in addition to single-family and multi-family residences. Some courts have held that the sale of an unattached modular home is the sale of personal property, and thus no written listing or real estate license is required to earn a commission. (*See* **factory-built construction**.)

module   A common dimensional element that influences the placement of window mullions, ceiling tiles, light fixtures, columns, electrical distribution systems, partitions, and the like. The module selected may greatly enhance the flexibility of office design.

mold
1. The cornice; wood molding applied to cover the junction of roof boards and outside wall. On the interior, the picture mold is placed where a wall joins a ceiling.
2. A simple life form lacking the ability to photosynthesize, therefore not requiring sunlight to grow, that releases alcohols, ketones, and hydrocarbons as well as spores, that can cause allergic, respiratory, and sinus problems in some people. Most molds thrive in moisture levels above 55 percent and can spread rapidly in many airtight homes. Mold is one of the many environmental issues that impact real estate transactions on a regular basis. There are no federal requirements to disclose mold infestations, and few states require disclosure. Buyers should be reminded that not only do they have the right to discover, they have a burden to discover.

money market fund   A form of mutual fund that trades primarily in short-term debt obligations, such as certificates of deposit (CDs), commercial paper, Treasury bills, and other U.S. government securities. (*See* **disintermediation**.)

month-to-month tenancy   A periodic tenancy whereby the tenant rents for one period at a time. In the absence of a rental agreement (oral or written), a tenancy is generally considered to be month-to-month or, in the case of boarders, week-to-week. Under such a tenancy, the estate continues renewing for an indefinite period of time until either lessor or lessee gives the statutory notice of termination. This notice, as outlined by the various state statutes, must generally be given at least one rental period before termination. In other words, if the rent is due each month, one month's notice must be given; if the rent is due each week, one week's notice must be given; and so forth. In some states, the required notice can be given at any time during the month.

A month-to-month tenancy may be created when a tenant holds over after the lease term expires. When no new lease agreement has been made, the landlord may elect to evict the tenant or acquiesce in the holdover tenancy. Acceptance of rent is usually considered conclusive proof of landlord acquiescence. The courts customarily rule that tenants holding over will do so for a term equal to the term of the original lease, provided the period is for one year or less. Some courts have ruled that a holdover tenancy will never exist for longer than one year. If the original lease, then, was for six months and the tenancy is held over, the courts usually consider that the holdover is for a like period—that is, six months. However, if the original lease was for five years, the holdover tenancy would not exceed one year (the statute of frauds period). Some written leases stipulate that in the absence of a renewal agreement, a tenant who holds over does so as a month-to-month tenant. This is usually a valid agreement. (*See* **lease, periodic tenancy, rent**.)

monument   A visible marker, either a natural or artificial object, set by the government or surveyors, used to establish the lines and boundaries of a survey. Monuments include artificial immovables, such as stakes, iron pins, or posts, and metal or stone markers, as well as natural objects, such as marked trees, streams, and rivers. A possible problem with natural monuments is that they sometimes move from their original locations. An example of an intangible monument would be the corner of a section in a government survey system. Although not visibly identifiable, it can still be accurately located by survey.

The use of monuments is essential to the accuracy of a metes-and-bounds description, which commences with a point of beginning at a monument (such as an iron pin or the intersection of two streets). In a dispute over who owns a particular property, monuments prevail if courses or distances, as set forth in a metes-and-bounds description in deeds or other documents, show otherwise. (*See* **metes and bounds**.)

M

moral character   The ability on the part of the person licensed to serve the general public in a fair and honest manner.

moral turpitude   An act of baseness, vileness, or depravity in private social duties (that is, duties one owes to a fellow person or to society in general); contrary to the accepted customary rule of right and duty between persons; conduct contrary to justice, honesty, modesty, or good morals. For example, embezzlement, perjury, robbery, or larceny is generally a crime of moral turpitude, whereas failure to pay income tax, speeding, or possession of small amounts of marijuana probably is not. Thus, felonies are crimes of moral turpitude.

   Note that state licensing authorities may refuse to issue a license to any person convicted of a crime involving moral turpitude unless that person has received a full and free pardon or presents satisfactory proof of living an upright and moral life for a specified period of time. (*See* **felony**.)

moratorium

1. A temporary suspension of payments due under a financing agreement in order to help a distressed borrower recover and thus avoid a default and foreclosure.
2. A temporary suspension of issuing building permits pending governmental study of more restrictive zoning controls, as with condominium conversions. This may especially happen with regard to shoreline development and no-growth policies and is sometimes called a *zoning freeze*.

more or less   A phrase indicating that the dimension or size given is approximate when describing real property. Slight variation from the true size has no effect on the enforceability of the contract, but a material or gross discrepancy could justify a rescission of the contract. Buyers should hire a surveyor to determine the exact boundaries to protect their own interests. Some courts have ruled that the phrase "more or less" indicates a sale in gross as opposed to a sale by the acre. (*See* **sale by the acre**.)

mortgage   (*hipoteca, contrato de hipoteca*)   A legal document used to secure the performance of an obligation. The term *mortgage*, which is derived from the French words *mort* meaning "dead" and *gage* meaning "pledge," is appropriate in that the pledge is extinguished only after the debt is paid. In the usual real estate transaction, the buyer seeks to borrow money to pay the seller the difference between the down payment and the purchase price. When the lender (mortgagee) lends the money, the buyer/borrower (mortgagor) is required to sign a promissory note for the amount borrowed and to execute a mortgage to secure the debt.

   A valid mortgage requires both a debt and a pledge. The mortgage note creates a personal liability for payment on the part of the mortgagor; the mortgage creates a lien on the mortgaged property as security for the debt. Although the note and the mortgage may appear in the same document, it is customary to have separate instruments. Once the debt is satisfied or becomes unenforceable—for example, when the statute of limitations expires—the mortgage is no longer effective security. The mortgage document is lengthy, containing a number of clauses such as provisions for acceleration, subordination, release schedule, defeasance, and waivers. Also included are covenants to pay taxes, to keep the premises in repair, and to maintain adequate insurance. If the mortgagor fails to pay taxes or insurance premiums, the mortgagee can advance these costs and add the amount to the mortgage debt.

   Most mortgages contain an assignment-of-rents clause that allows the lender to collect rents in the event of default if the borrower continues to collect rental income from the property without paying on the note.

   In effect, the mortgage provides that the lender can depend on possessing the property if the borrower defaults in paying the note. Although not always the case, the mortgaged property is *usu-*

ally the property that the borrower purchases with the loan proceeds. Therefore, upon default by the borrower (mortgagor), the lender (mortgagee) can bring foreclosure proceedings to sell the property and retain that part of the proceeds representing the monies still due on the note. If the proceeds of sale are less than the amount owed, in most states the mortgagee would obtain a deficiency judgment against the mortgagor for the difference.

Contract law applies to mortgages: the mortgage must be in writing, name the parties (who must be competent to contract), include a legal description of the mortgaged property, state a consideration, contain a mortgaging clause, state the debt, and be signed by the borrower (mortgagor). In addition, mortgagors should state their marital status, regardless of sex, spouses should always sign because of homestead rights in the property. The mortgage is usually acknowledged and then recorded, with priority of the lien determined by the date of recordation. The mortgage is recorded because it creates rights and interest in real property. The mortgage note, however, need not be recorded because it represents only a personal obligation. The number of signatures on the note does not have to conform to the number of persons signing the mortgage.

Some states recognize the mortgagee as the owner of the mortgaged property, subject to defeat upon full payment of the debt or performance of the obligation. Such states recognize the mortgage document as a conveyance of property and are called *title theory states*. Those states that interpret the mortgage purely as a lien on real property are called *lien theory states*.

Upon default, under the lien theory, the mortgagee is required to foreclose, offer the property for sale, and apply the funds received from the sale to reduce the debt. As protection to the mortgagor, some state laws give the mortgagor a statutory period within which to redeem after the foreclosure sale. Whether a state follows the title theory or lien theory of mortgages, the security interest of the mortgagee in the land is legally classified as personal property and can only be transferred with the transfer of the debt that the mortgage secures.

When property is sold, the existing mortgages may be assumed, made subject to (unless restricted by a due-on-sale clause) or paid off. When paid in full, the mortgagor should be sure to have the note returned "canceled" and to record a satisfaction of mortgage or release of mortgage as notice that the mortgage is no longer a lien on the property.

Mortgages take on a variety of forms. Some are the adjustable-rate mortgage loan, the graduated-payment mortgage, the wraparound mortgage, the shared appreciation mortgage, the flexible loan insurance payment, and the buydown mortgage. These and other types of mortgages—such as blanket mortgages, budget mortgages, open-end mortgages, package mortgages, participation mortgages, and purchase-money mortgages—are discussed under their respective headings. (*See* **acceleration clause, alternative mortgage instrument, certificate of no defense, deed of trust, defeasance clause, deficiency judgment, foreclosure, marginal release, mortgage lien, promissory note, redemption period, satisfaction of mortgage, subordination clause, waiver.**)

mortgage-backed security (MBS)   A security guaranteed by pools of mortgages and used to channel funds from securities markets to housing markets. Ginnie Mae has a popular MBS program recognized for its low risk and high yield. The Ginnie Mae MBS security is a pool of VA and FHA mortgages put together as a bond. Freddie Mac and Fannie Mae also have MBS programs. (*See* **collateralized mortgage obligation [CMO], guaranteed mortgage certificate [GMC], participation certificate [PC].**)

mortgage banker   A person, corporation, or firm not otherwise in banking and finance that normally provides its own funds for mortgage financing as opposed to savings and loan associations or commercial banks that use other people's money—namely that of their depositors—to originate mortgage loans. Although some mortgage bankers do supply permanent long-term financing, the majority specialize in supplying short-term and interim financing, either through their own resources or by borrowing from commercial sources. It is said that what a mortgage banker lends, it must sell.

The activities of mortgage bankers have been greatly expanded due to the development of the mortgage correspondent system. Under this system, a mortgage banker or mortgage banking company seeks to originate numerous loan transactions and then sell these mortgages at a discount to large investors, such as insurance companies, commercial banks, and retirement and pension funds. Mortgage bankers are a major source of construction loans and are very active in lending money on commercial real estate such as shopping centers and office buildings.

Most of the funding for mortgage banking is from the secondary mortgage market. A typical mortgage banking arrangement not involving the secondary market would be set up as follows:

1. A local mortgage banker negotiates a commitment with a savings and loan association (in New York, for example) to sell $5 million of loans within a certain time.
2. Loans are made to individuals.
3. The local mortgage banker services the loans for the association.
4. The loans are sold to the New York investor under the terms of the previously arranged commitment.

In addition, these loan administrators are specialists in originating FHA and VA loans in areas where mortgage money is tight. They generally sell such mortgages for an origination fee to financial institutions in other parts of the country where funds are not as tight. Typically, then, they are not the ultimate lenders in the mortgage transactions; the mortgage banker's objective is ultimately to sell the loan in the secondary mortgage market at a profit while personally underwriting the risk. This is in contrast to the mortgage broker, who does not act without the principal's consent. The mortgage banker normally remains in the picture and services the underlying mortgage for major investor clients. Such services include collecting monthly payments, disbursing the funds to pay taxes and property insurance, supervising the loan, preventing delinquencies, and taking proper remedial action in the event of delinquency. (*See* **loan correspondent**, **origination fee**, **servicing**, **warehousing**.)

mortgage broker   A person or firm that acts as an intermediary between borrower and lender; one who, for compensation or gain, negotiates, sells, or arranges loans and sometimes continues to service the loans; also called a *loan broker*. Loans originated by the mortgage broker are usually closed in the lender's name and are usually serviced by the lender. This is in contrast to mortgage bankers, who not only close loans in their own names but continue to service them as well. Many mortgage brokers are also licensed as real estate brokers and provide these financing services as supplements to their realty services, being careful to avoid any conflicts of interest.

mortgage constant   *See* **constant**.

mortgage discount   *See* **discount points**, **points**.

mortgagee   (*acreedor hipotecario*)   In a mortgage transaction, the party who receives and holds a mortgage as security for a debt; the lender; a lender or creditor who holds a mortgage as security for payment of an obligation.

mortgage for future advances   *See* **open-end mortgage**.

mortgage insurance   (*seguro hipotecario*)   An insurance plan that pays off the mortgage balance in the event of the death or, in some plans, disability of the insured mortgagor. In essence, mortgage insurance is decreasing-term life insurance. The premiums are paid with the regular monthly mortgage payment. (*See* **Federal Housing Administration [FHA]**, **private mortgage insurance [PMI]**.)

mortgage insurance premium   *See* **Federal Housing Administration (FHA)**, **private mortgage insurance (PMI)**.

mortgage lien   A lien or charge on the property of a mortgagor that secures the underlying debt obligation. The mortgage lien is a voluntary lien created by the property owner, as opposed to the tax lien, which is an involuntary lien imposed by law. As with other liens affecting real property, the mortgage lien receives its priority through recording. Until recorded, the mortgage generally operates only as a contract between the parties and creates no lien affecting any recorded mortgage or lease. Whether a recorded mortgage is titled "first mortgage," "second mortgage," or "third mortgage," it has priority over all subsequently recorded mortgages or other liens, unless it is subordinated to such subsequent liens. As with all liens, a mortgage lien becomes junior to any state real estate tax liens or liens for special assessments. The mortgage lien does not affect property that is registered in Torrens until such time as the mortgage itself is registered with the registrar of titles and noted on the certificate of title.

Sometimes a mortgage is intended to secure future advances the mortgagee (the lender) may make to the mortgagor (the borrower), as in a construction loan, when obligatory progress payments are made as various stages in the construction are completed. Such future advances would be superior in priority to mortgages or other liens taking effect between the date of recording of the mortgage and the future advance only where the future advance relates to the same transaction or series of transactions and the mortgage specifically refers to this particular advance as being secured by the previously recorded liens. (*See* **advance**, **anaconda mortgage**, **lien**, **recording**, **subordination agreement**.)

mortgage participation certificate   *See* **Federal Home Loan Mortgage Corporation (FHLMC)**.

mortgage pool   A common fund of mortgage loans in which one can invest.

mortgage spreading agreement   A contract that extends a prior mortgage lien to properties not previously covered. This gives added security to the lender and is often used when the mortgagor seeks additional financing.

mortgage subsidies   A method of financing where a homebuilder permits a purchaser of a new home to occupy the home for a period of time (e.g., six months) without monthly payments. The money saved goes toward a down payment, into a savings account to act as a reserve to help make the monthly payments after permanent financing is in place or into a fund to buy down the interest rate of permanent financing. A builder may offer a lowered monthly payment, or subsidy, for a certain period of months. (*See* **buydown**, **creative financing**.)

mortgaging out   Obtaining 100 percent of the monies needed to acquire or develop a project.

mortgagor   (*deudor hipotecario*)   The one who gives a mortgage as security for a debt; the borrower; usually the landowner, though it could be the owner of a leasehold estate; the borrower or debtor who hypothecates or puts up property as security for an obligation. (*See* **hypothecate**.)

mortmain   The transfer of real property to a church, school, or charitable organization for perpetual ownership. Mortmain statutes limit the percentage of an estate that can be bequeathed to such institutions.

most favored tenant clause   A provision in a lease that assures a tenant that any negotiating concessions given to other tenants will also be given to this tenant. Such a clause is especially helpful in the early stages of renting a building because the tenant is assured that later tenants will not get better concessions.

motel   A structure designed to provide convenient rental quarters for transients with parking provided at or near the room. Motels sometimes have common guest facilities such as dining rooms, meeting rooms, pools, or lounges.

Mother Hubbard clause   *See* **anaconda mortgage**.

MSA   Master Senior Appraiser. *See* Appendix B.

mudroom   A vestibule or small room used as the entrance from a play yard or alley. The mudroom frequently contains a washer and dryer.

mudsill   The lowest horizontal component of a structure, such as a foundation timber placed directly on the ground or foundation.

mud tunnel   Access routes for subterranean termites.

mullion   Thin vertical strips inside the window sash that divide the window glass into panes.

multiple-asset exchange   An exchange of property for income tax purposes, usually involving two businesses, in which the values of many related assets—land, buildings, machinery, goodwill—are added together to reach a composite figure on which to compute the exchange.

  Even if the individual component values differ in a multiple-asset exchange, income tax on any gain realized from the transaction can be deferred if the composite values are the same. For example, company A exchanges all of its operating assets for like-kind assets of company B. The following breakdown of each company's assets occurs:

	Company A	Company B
Land	$150,000	$100,000
Buildings	175,000	200,000
Machinery	75,000	50,000
Goodwill	50,000	100,000

M

  Traded on an asset-by-asset basis, A would be taxed on boot valued at $75,000—the $25,000 difference in the building values, plus the $50,000 difference in goodwill values. However, classified as a multiple-asset exchange, both composite values are the same and no boot is involved. Note that multiple-asset exchanges are generally complicated and are subject to many tax laws and rulings too detailed and specific for this discussion. (*See* **boot**, **exchange**.)

multiple dwelling   A tenement house. Any structure used for the accommodation of two or more families or households in separate living units. An apartment house.

multiple listing service (MLS)   A service in which member brokers pool their listings and offer cooperation and compensation to other member brokers. Usually, the MLS is operated by a local association of REALTORS®, but not always. The contractual obligations between the member brokers of a multiple listing organization vary widely. Most provide that upon the sale of the property, the commission is divided between the listing broker and the selling broker. The terms for division of the commission can vary from broker to broker.

  Under most multiple listing organizations, the broker securing the listing is not only authorized but also usually obligated to turn the listing over to the MLS within a definite period of time so that it can be distributed to the other member brokers. The length of time the listing broker has to offer the property exclusively, without notifying the other member brokers, varies widely.

  Both the broker and the seller benefit from the multiple listing service. The broker makes available a sizable inventory of properties to sell and to be sold and is assured a portion of the commission if she lists the property or participates in the sale. The seller also gains because all members of the multiple listing organization become aware of this property and can offer it to their prospective buyers. (*See* **contingency listing**, **cooperating broker**, **listing**, **office exclusive**, **pocket listing**, **subagent**.)

multiple regression   A mathematical technique used to estimate the value of a subject property based on known variables and prices for comparable properties. Often used in mass appraisals for single-family residences.

municipal ordinance   *See* **ordinances**.

muniment of title   A legal document evidencing title to real property. An example is a deed or contract, which is proof of ownership and enables an owner to defend his or her title. To register property in the Torrens system, an applicant must file with his or her application a file plan, an abstract of title, and all original muniments of title within his or her control mentioned in the schedule of documents.

muntin   (*entrepaño de puertas y ventanas*)   The narrow vertical strip that separates two adjacent window sashes.

mutual agreement   The consent of all parties to the provisions of a contract. The voluntary cancellation of a contract by all parties is called *mutual rescission*.

mutuality of consent   A meeting of the minds; a mutual assent of the parties to the formation of the contract. (*See* **offer and acceptance**.)

Mutual Mortgage Insurance Fund   One of four FHA insurance funds into which all insurance premiums and other specified FHA revenues are paid, and from which any losses are met.

mutual savings banks   Savings institutions that issue no stock and are mutually owned by their investors who are paid dividends, not interest. These institutions operate similarly to savings and loan associations and are located primarily in the northeastern section of the United States.

Although mutual savings banks offer limited checking account privileges, they are primarily savings institutions and are active in the mortgage market, investing in loans secured by income property, as well as in residential real estate. Most of their real estate investment is now in mortgage-backed securities, not so much in VA and FHA loans, as in the past.

With the savings association collapse in the 1980s, the federally chartered savings bank emerged alongside the mutual savings banks. One difference is that the savings banks have always been insured by FDIC, the same as commercial banks, not the FSLIC. (*See* **savings banks**.)

mutual water company   A water company organized by or for water users in a given district, with the object of securing an ample water supply at a reasonable rate. Stock is purchased by and issued to users.

M
N

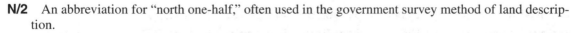

N

N/2   An abbreviation for "north one-half," often used in the government survey method of land description.

naked title   Bare title to the property, lacking the usual rights and privileges of ownership. A trustee in a deed of trust securing instrument may hold the title to a secured property, but only such title as is needed to carry out the terms of the lien document. (*See* **deed of trust**.)

name, change of   Use of a new name. A person may change his name merely by using another name with the intention to make that the legal name, as long as the change is not done with fraudulent intent. However, because of potential identification problems, most parties changing their names go through a formal name change procedure that usually involves filing a petition with the proper state authorities. They may also be required to publish the change in the local newspaper for a statutory period of time. A name change can also be embodied in a divorce decree permitting a woman to resume use of her maiden name or that of another former husband. A corporation can change its name by an amendment to its articles of incorporation, which must be filed in the state of incorporation.

People who change their names should be sure that the new name is properly noted at the registrar of titles if they own registered property and at the recorder's office if they own any other recorded properties. For example, a recorded document should be amended to read, "Cathy Jones, being the same person who acquired title as Cathleen J. Arbuckle."

If a person uses one name as a grantee of property and then grants the same property under another name, there will be a potential defect in the recorded title. When the second deed is recorded, it will not be recorded in the proper chain of title and therefore will not give constructive notice to the world of its contents. For example, if Patty Lee, a single woman receiving title as such and later changing her name through marriage, should convey title as Patty Wilson, there would be a defect in the record title. Patty Lee should convey title as "Patty Wilson, formerly known as Patty Lee." An appropriate entry would therefore be made in the grantor-guarantee index so that a title company searching the title could see that the new deed was derived from the chain of title in which Patty Lee was the grantee.

It is helpful to title searchers for a married woman to continue using the name given by her parents. For instance, Patty Ann Lee would become Mrs. Patty Ann Wilson or Mrs. Patty Lee Wilson, not Mrs. Robert Wilson. (*See* **chain of title**, **legal name**.)

name, fictitious   *See* **fictitious company name**.

name, legal   *See* **legal name**.

name, reservation of   The exclusive right to the use of a trade name or a corporate name. This right may be reserved by any person intending to organize a corporation or change the name of an existing corporation. Reservation of a name is usually made by filing an application with the proper state authorities and paying the appropriate fee.

The National Association of REALTORS® has zealously protected the exclusive use of its trade name, REALTOR®.

NARELLO   Former name for ARELLO. (*See* **Association of Real Estate License Law Officials** in Appendix A.)

narrative report   A complete appraisal report in which the appraiser presents all information pertinent to the property and the market for the property, along with analysis, opinions, and conclusions leading to an estimate of value. The report is quite lengthy compared to the short form (or check report) and the letter report. (*See* **letter report**.)

National Affordable Housing Management Association (NAHMA)   *See* Appendix A.

National Apartment Association (NAA)   *See* Appendix A.

National Association of Exclusive Buyer Brokers (NAEBA)   *See* Appendix A.

National Association of Hispanic Real Estate Professionals (NAHREP)   *See* Appendix A.

National Association of Home Builders (NAHB)   *See* Appendix A.

National Association of Housing and Redevelopment Officials (NAHRO)   *See* Appendix A.

National Association of Independent Fee Appraisers (NAIFA)   *See* Appendix A.

National Association of Industrial and Office Parks (NAIOP)   *See* Appendix A.

National Association of Master Appraisers (NAMA)   *See* Appendix A.

National Association of Real Estate Appraisers (NAREA)   *See* Appendix A.

National Association of Real Estate Brokers (NAREB)   *See* Appendix A.

National Association of Real Estate Investment Trusts (NAREIT)   *See* Appendix A.

National Association of Real Estate License Law Officials   *See* **Association of Real Estate License Law Officials (ARELLO)** in Appendix A.

National Association of REALTORS® (NAR)   *See* Appendix A.

National Association of Residential Property Managers (NARPM)   *See* Appendix A.

National Association of Review Appraisers and Mortgage Underwriters (NARA/MU)   *See* Appendix A.

National Association of Securities Dealers (NASD)   *See* Appendix A.

National Do Not Call Registry   A national registry maintained by the Federal Trade Commission (FTC) of telephone numbers whose owners do not wish to receive telemarketing calls. Created to offer consumers a choice regarding telemarketing calls, the free registration at *www.donotcall.com* is generally accurate about 31 days after the number is registered and is active for five years. The National Do Not Call Registry does not limit calls by political organizations, charities, or telephone surveyors. Nor does it limit calls by any telemarketer or seller to a consumer with whom it has an established business relationship for up to 18 months after the consumer's last purchase, delivery, or payment—even if the consumer's number is on the do-not-call registry. The company may also call for up to three months after the consumer makes an inquiry, submits an application to the company, or has given the company written permission. If the consumer has specifically asked the company not to call, then the company may not call. A real estate licensee may call a for sale by owner only if the licensee has a buyer who is actually interested in the property. If the for sale by owner is listed on the do-not-call registry, the licensee may not call to solicit the listing. (*See* also **Junk Fax Act**.)

National Environmental Protection Act (NEPA)   The law viewed as the national charge for the protection of the environment, passed in 1969 in response to the growing public demand for cleaner water, air, and land. NEPA established the Environmental Protection Agency (EPA), which has developed programs and activities that affect, protect, and improve environmental quality. *See* **Environmental Protection Agency (EPA)** in Appendix D.

National Flood Insurance Program (NFIP)   A federal program created in 1968, in response to the rising cost of taxpayer-funded disaster relief for flood victims and the increasing amount of damage caused by floods. The Mitigation Division, a component of the Federal Emergency Management Agency (FEMA), manages the NFIP, and oversees the floodplain management and mapping components of the program. *See* **flood insurance**.

natural affection   A phrase describing that feeling presumed to exist between close relatives (such as father and son and husband and wife). In contract law, such affection is regarded as "good consideration," as opposed to "valuable consideration." To support a contractual promise and make the contract enforceable, however, there must be a valuable consideration. (*See* **consideration**, **gift deed**.)

natural person   An individual; a private person, as distinguished from an artificial entity such as a corporation or partnership.

navigable waters   A body of saltwater or freshwater capable of carrying a commercial vessel and large enough to ebb and flow (a "highway for commerce"). The U.S. Army Corps of Engineers has jurisdiction over navigable waters. With nonnavigable waters, the bordering landowners have what are called *riparian rights*. (*See* **riparian rights**.)

N

negative amortization   A financing arrangement in which the monthly payments are less than the true amortized amounts and the loan balance increases over the term of the loan rather than decreases; an interest shortage that is added to unpaid principal. In some cases, the interest shortage is added back to the loan and payable at maturity. For example, amortized payments for the first six months of a 30-year adjustable mortgage loan would be based on a 3 percent rate, but interest would be charged against equity at 8 percent, and such interest rate charged would fluctuate every six-month period. In some loans, the negative amounts may be made up by applying such deficits against the borrower's down payment equity.

negative cash flow   A situation in which cash expenditures to maintain an investment (taxes, mortgage payments, maintenance) exceed the cash income received from the investment. Assume that an investor in a $70,000 condominium apartment pays $10,000 down and finances the balance through a contract for deed that provides that for payment of the $60,000 balance in $600 monthly payments (all expenses included). Assume further that the apartment rents for only $400 a month. In this case, the owner would have an out-of-pocket monthly loss of $200, a negative cash flow. The reason some investors voluntarily purchase a real estate investment that operates on a negative cash flow basis is that they expect that upon sale of the property, the favorable yield on their investment will come in the form of appreciated value. (*See* **tax shelter**.)

   Under the 1986 Tax Reform Act, rental real estate activities are considered "passive investments," and losses generated can only be used to offset other passive income. Individuals with adjusted gross incomes (AGI) of $100,000 or less may deduct up to $25,000 of net losses from rental of residential or commercial property against regular income. This deduction phases out for taxpayers with AGIs between $100,000 and $150,000. Also known as *negative carry*.

negative easement   An easement, such as a building restriction or a view easement, that has the effect of preventing the servient landowner from doing an act otherwise permitted.

negative leasehold   *See* **contract rent**.

negligence   (*negligencia*)   The failure to use ordinary or reasonable care under the circumstances.

negligent waste   *See* **permissive waste**.

negotiable instrument   Any written instrument that is transferable by endorsement or delivery so as to vest legal title in the transferee. Common examples of negotiable instruments are checks, publicly traded stocks, and promissory notes. Negotiability, here, is the quality that allows these instruments to circulate as money does. To be negotiable, a promissory note, for example, must be an unconditional promise, made in writing by one person to another and signed by the maker engaging her to pay on demand, or at a fixed or determinable time, a certain sum of money *to order* or *to bearer*. It is essential to use words of negotiability such as "pay to Bob Reininski," or "order," or "bearer." Note that only the person (or persons) whose name appears on the instrument is liable for it. Thus, a principal is not liable unless his name appears on the instrument.

   One who takes a negotiable instrument in good faith for a valuable consideration and without notice of any defect is a *holder in due course*, against whom the maker of the note cannot assert personal defenses (such as lack of consideration) in order to refuse payment.

   Under the Uniform Commercial Code, a transferor implies certain warranties concerning the negotiable instrument, such as that it is genuine and is what it purports to be; that the transferor has good title; that all involved parties have the capacity to contract; and that the transferor does not know of any fact that would impair the validity of the contract or make it valueless. (*See* **endorsement, holder in due course, Uniform Commercial Code [UCC]**.)

negotiation   The transaction of business aimed at reaching a meeting of the minds among the parties; the act of bargaining. A real estate sale illustrates the negotiation process: The first offer received for property often is considered merely an intention to deal. Thereafter follows a series of counteroffers leading to the consummation of the transaction. Usually, however, negotiation takes place only if the broker's efforts have proceeded to the point where the prospect is considered a likely purchaser.

Most listing forms contain a safety clause, also called an **extender** or **override clause**, allowing the broker to recover a commission for a specified time after termination of the listing if the listed property is sold to anyone with whom the broker was negotiating before the listing ended. This applies, *provided that* the broker has registered the names of such persons with the seller at the time the listing ended. In this regard, negotiation means more than putting the parties in touch; it means actually transacting business, bargaining, and arousing sufficient interest to effect a purchase and sale.

In commercial lease situations, concessions (such as temporary free rent) are negotiable points in the lease terms that are decided in favor of the prospective tenant.

Real estate commission rates are not fixed by law but are the subject of negotiation between the parties. (*See* **procuring cause**.)

neighborhood   (*vecindario*)   Contiguous areas showing common characteristics of population and homogeneity of land use.

neighborhood shopping center   A group of retail buildings, usually 15 to 20, providing a variety of convenience stores (barbershop, dry cleaning), having common parking and management and catering to 1,000 or more families.

net after taxes   The net operating income after deducting all charges, including federal and state income taxes.

net income   (*ingreso neto*)   The sum arrived at after deducting from gross income the expenses of a business or investment, including taxes, insurance, and allowances for vacancy and bad debts. Net income is what the property will earn in a given year's operation. It is generally calculated before accounting for depreciation. (*See* **cash flow**, **net operating income [NOI]**.)

net lease   (*arrendamiento neto*)   A lease, usually commercial, in which the lessee not only pays the rent for occupancy but also pays maintenance and operating expenses such as taxes, insurance, utilities, and repairs. The rent paid is "net" to the lessor. This kind of lease is popular with investors who want to obtain a steady stream of income without having to handle the problems associated with management and maintenance. Commercial or industrial leases, ground leases, and long-term leases are typically net leases.

Because the common interpretations given to the term *net lease* are so broad, it is essential to review the lease document to determine what expenses the tenant is to pay. In a true net lease, the tenant is responsible for expenses relating to the premises exactly as if the tenant were the owner. Examples of such expenses are real estate taxes; special assessments; insurance premiums; all maintenance charges, including labor and materials; cost of compliance with governmental health and safety regulations; payment of claims for personal injury or property damage; and even costs of structural, interior, roof, and other repairs.

It is helpful to distinguish between the net rent, called *base rent*, and the total of base rent and expenses, called *effective rent*. (*See* **gross lease**, **percentage lease**, **triple-net lease**.)

net listing   An employment contract in which the broker receives as commission all excess monies over and above the minimum sales price agreed on by broker and seller. Because of the danger of unethical practices in such a listing, its use is discouraged in most states and is illegal in many. (*See* **listing**.)

net-net-net lease   *See* **triple-net lease**.

N

net operating income (NOI) (*ingreso neto de operación*)   The balance remaining after deducting from gross receipts all fixed expenses, operating expenses, replacement reserves, and allowance for vacancy and bad debts, but before deducting any debt service, income taxes, or depreciation. (*See* **cash flow, net income.**)

net proceeds   The cash received after paying all liens and expenses.

net spendable income   The money remaining each year after collecting rents and paying operating expenses and mortgage payments.

netting out   A slang expression that describes the amount of money the seller wants to receive on a sale of property; the amount that can be put in the seller's pocket after expenses and payment of liens. The broker's commission, however, is typically calculated on the gross sales price, not the seller's net price.

net usable acre   That portion of a property that is suitable for building. A 20-acre parcel may have 20 gross acres and only 15 net usable or buildable acres. Density requirements under local zoning regulations are often based on the net usable acreage of the property.

net worth (*patrimonio neto*)   The value remaining after deducting liabilities from assets. Many private real estate syndicates establish their own suitability standards for prospective investors, often requiring that an investor maintain a minimum net worth. The Dodd-Frank Act created new accredited investor regulations that affect real estate syndications. (*See* **limited partnership, safe harbor rule.**)

net yield   That portion of gross yield that remains after all costs, such as loan servicing and reserves, are deducted.

new town   A modern concept of urban planning characterized by a development that offers a complete range of services, including housing, recreation, schools, and churches, as well as a thoroughly planned and controlled balance of land use. The new town is usually a new municipality built in a previously undeveloped area close to an existing municipality, such as Foster City, California, or Reston, Virginia. It is intended to be self-governing and relatively self-contained.

   The "new town in town" is a concept for a new town located within a city area, such as in an urban renewal clearance area. A prime example is Roosevelt Island, linked to New York City by a five-minute aerial tramway ride.

NHP Foundation (NHPF)   A nonprofit organization committed to providing affordable, multifamily housing to those with low-to-moderate incomes. NHPF combines commercial bank financing, permanent tax-exempt bonds, and low-income-housing tax credits to build, rehabilitate, and provide affordable housing to more than 20,000 residents in 17 communities across the United States.

"no action" letter   A written opinion from the staff of the Securities and Exchange Commission (SEC). "No action" letters cover many items, including informing an applicant that—based on facts presented in the request for opinion—the SEC will not require that a proposed project register as a security. If a project is classified as a security, it is subject to various complicated restrictions and regulations. It is advantageous, then, for project developers to avoid having their projects considered a security in order to avoid these regulations. A developer of a proposed resort condominium may seek an interpretation from the SEC that its project does not involve the offering of a real estate security. The developer will do this in the form of a request for a "no action" letter in accordance with the procedure set forth in regulations under the Securities Act of 1933. A developer might also request a "no action" letter to certify that its project is exempt from registration under the federal interstate land sales subdivision regulations. (*See* **real property securities registration.**)

no-compete clause   *See* **noncompetition clause.**

"no deal/no commission" clause   A clause in a listing contract that stipulates paying a commission *only if and when title passes*. This nullifies the generally accepted principle that a broker earns commission when the broker has brought an acceptable "ready, willing, and able" buyer to the seller for the price and under the terms specified in the listing agreement.

nominal consideration   A consideration bearing no relation to the real value of a contract used so as not to reveal the true value of the property being conveyed; in name only, and not having any relation to actual market value. A deed often recites a nominal consideration, such as "ten dollars and other valuable consideration," rather than the full selling price. Such nominal consideration makes it clear that the grantee is a purchaser rather than a donee (receiver of a gift) and thus is protected under the state's recording act as a subsequent good-faith purchaser.

A broker must not be a party to the naming of a false consideration in any document, unless it is the naming of an obviously nominal consideration. To do so would be not only unethical but also a cause generally for suspension or revocation of the broker's license. (*See* **dual contract**, **recording**.)

nominal interest rate   The stated interest rate in a note or contract, which may differ from the true or effective interest rate, especially if the lender discounts the loan and advances less than the full amount. (*See* **effective interest rate**.)

nominee   One designated to act for another as a representative in a limited sense. A nominee corporation is sometimes used to purchase real property when the principals do not wish to be known. Care should be taken in structuring a purchase through the nominee corporation so that there are no adverse tax consequences, such as double taxation to the nominee corporation and then to the shareholders.

The term *nominee* is not a synonym for *assignee*. Especially if the purchase is based on seller carry-back financing, the real buyer may not be able to get specific performance of the sales contract to the nominee on the grounds that there is no real mutuality of agreement and by reason of indefiniteness. Nominee status is simply a name substitution—no legal rights are transferred. On the other hand, assignee status is a substitution of legal rights. Therefore, in most cases, use of the word *assignee* rather than *nominee* better achieves the parties' intended result of effectively transferring legal rights to the ultimate purchaser.

The nominee form is often used by a real estate syndicator who is the buyer but not the ultimate purchaser. It is also used in a Section 1031 exchange situation for acquiring the replacement property.

The offer should always identify the offeror; that is, neither the phrases *buyer nor nominee* nor *buyer nor assignee* should be used in the deposit receipt portion of the offer. Otherwise, the named buyer could simply walk away from the deal and tell the seller to look to the nominee for recovery. Most courts would thus rule the contract illusory and unenforceable. (*See* **assignment**, **straw man**.)

nonassignment clause   *See* **assignment**.

nonassumption clause   *See* **due-on-sale clause**.

noncompetition clause   A provision in a contract or lease prohibiting a person from operating or controlling a nearby business that would compete with one of the parties to the contract; also called *a "no-compete" clause*. The courts will enforce this kind of provision as long as it is reasonable as to time and location. In addition, if insertion of a noncompetition clause gives the contract added value, such value is generally considered ordinary income to the benefited party. This value, then, is capitalized by the maker of the clause and amortized over the life of the covenant. Noncompetition clauses are frequently found in percentage leases for shopping centers where a shoe store tenant, for example, agrees that the center will not establish a competing shoe store across the street. Such clauses have come under close scrutiny with regard to federal and state antitrust laws.

nonconforming use   (*uso inconforme*)   A permitted use of real property that was lawfully established and maintained at the time of its original construction but that no longer conforms to the current zoning law. The nonconforming use might be the structure itself, the lot size, use of the land, or use of the structure. The use will eventually be eliminated, although the nonconforming use status does not necessarily have to be discontinued upon the sale or lease of the property. By allowing the use to continue for a reasonable time, the government can assure itself that the use will not continue indefinitely and, at the same time, avoid having to pay just compensation for taking the property through condemnation.

When purchasing a nonconforming structure, a buyer should be made aware that in case of substantial destruction by fire or otherwise, the zoning statutes may prohibit reconstruction of the structure. In such a case, a buyer should discuss the possibilities of purchasing demolition insurance from an insurance agent. A nonconforming use can also terminate upon abandonment of the property. (*See* **variance**.)

nondisclosure   (*discreción*)   The failure to reveal a fact, with or without the intention to conceal it. (*See* **misrepresentation**.)

nondisturbance

1. A mortgage clause stating that the mortgagee agrees not to terminate the tenancies of lessees who pay their rent in the event that the mortgagee forecloses on the mortgagor/lessor's building. Without such a clause, a lessee whose lease was signed subsequent to the mortgage could have the lease terminated by a foreclosure action. (*See* **attornment**.)
2. When a seller chooses to keep mineral rights to conveyed property, a nondisturbance agreement is made between seller and buyer to the effect that the seller will not interfere with any building or development on the surface of the land itself.

nonhomogeneic   The fact that all properties are unique, even similar houses in a tract subdivision, each with its own "bundle of rights." All buyers, all sellers, and all transactions are also nonhomogenic, thus explaining why property has value and all transactions are different.

nonjudicial foreclosure   The process of selling real property under a power of sale in a mortgage or deed of trust that is in default. In many states, but not all, the lender cannot then obtain a deficiency judgment. Also, some title insurance companies are reluctant to issue a policy unless a court has judicially foreclosed the mortgagor's interest. (*See* **foreclosure**, **power of sale**.)

nonprofit corporation   A corporation formed for a nonprofit purpose, such as a charity or a political, fraternal, educational, or trade organization. These organizations, sometimes referred to as *eleemosynary corporations*, do not have shareholders (as do profit-making corporations). They only have members who, although not personally liable for corporate debts, also have no right to corporate dividends or assets. The properties of nonprofit corporations are controlled, and their affairs are conducted by a board of directors. Such corporations may make contracts and acquire and dispose of real or personal property in their own names. The special tax rules covering nonprofit corporations are found in IRC Section 501.

nonrecourse loan   A loan in which the borrower is not held personally liable on the note. The lender of a nonrecourse loan generally feels confident that the property used as collateral is adequate security for the loan. Also called a **dry mortgage**. (*See* **deficiency judgment**, **dry mortgage**, **exculpatory clause**.)

Nonrecourse financing is used in real estate syndications to enable the limited partners to add their proportionate share of the mortgage to their tax basis for the purpose of computing depreciation deductions or taking other losses in a real estate syndication.

normal wear and tear   The physical deterioration that occurs with the normal use of a property without negligence, carelessness, accident with, or abuse of the premises, equipment, or chattels by the occupants or their guests. The tenant of residential property is not responsible for loss in value due to normal wear and tear. Therefore, the landlord cannot hold back the security deposit for such damage. As defined in the Uniform Residential Landlord and Tenant Act, normal wear and tear is deterioration or depreciation in value by ordinary and reasonable use. This specifically excludes, however, items that are missing from the dwelling unit. Normal wear and tear is a major cause of property depreciation, along with functional and economic obsolescence.

An important element in determining the reasonableness of a unit's wear and tear is the length of the tenant's residency. For instance, if the same renter has inhabited an apartment for three years, it may be reasonable to expect that the walls need painting and that the carpeting needs cleaning.

nosing   The rounded outer face of a stair tread.

notary public   A public officer who functions as an official witness. The duties of notaries are to administer oaths; to attest and certify documents by their signature and official seal, giving them credit and authenticity; to take acknowledgments of deeds and other conveyances; and to perform certain official acts, such as protesting rates and bills. Without a seal, the notarization is void. One who has a beneficial interest in a document cannot act as a notary public to the same document. In some states, the notary must post a fidelity bond. (*See* **acknowledgment**.)

note   A document signed by the borrower of a loan and stating the loan amount, the interest rate, the time and method of repayment, and the obligation to repay. The note serves as evidence of the debt. When secured by a mortgage, it is a *mortgage note*, and the mortgagee is named as the payee. In a trust deed, the note is usually made payable to the bearer or the holder. The note may also contain some of the same provisions as are found in the mortgage or trust deed document, such as prepayment or acceleration. (*See* **debenture**, **promissory note**.)

notice   (*notificación*)   Information that may be required by the terms of a contract. When two parties agree to terminate a one-year lease, for example, usually written notice must be given by one of the parties 30 days before its termination. Though notice can be oral, it is always advisable to give notice in writing, so that it can be proved that necessary notice was given.

Contracts frequently contain a standard paragraph covering the details of proper notice, such as "Notices, requests, or demand by either party shall be in writing and shall be given personally or by Registered or Certified Mail, postage prepaid, addressed to seller and buyer at the addresses set forth herein. Notice shall be deemed given when mailed." (*See* **actual notice**, **constructive notice**, **imputed notice**, **inquiry notice**, **legal notice**, **notice of default**.)

notice of assessment   A notice issued by the state or local taxing agency to the owner of real property specifying the assessed valuation of the property. For example, assume that the market value of a home is $170,000, of which $40,000 is allocated to the fee simple land and $130,000 to the improvements. Assume further that under local law, the assessed value is 70 percent of the market value. Thus, the assessed valuation for the improvements would be $91,000, and the assessed valuation of the land would be $28,000. (*See* **assessed valuation**, **conveyance tax**, **property tax**.)

notice of completion   A document filed in some states to give public notice that a construction job has been completed and that mechanics' liens must be filed within a specified time to be valid. The owner or the general contractor may publish the notice of completion, though the notice generally may not be published by the contractor until after the contractor has made a written demand on the owner to publish and the owner has failed to do so.

If within the specified period a mechanic does not file a notice of lien in writing in the office of the clerk of the appropriate court where the property is situated, then lien rights will be waived. Note that recording or filing the notice of lien is generally not enough to create a lien. The lien must be recorded with the clerk of the appropriate circuit court, and a hearing must be held to establish whether probable cause exists to enforce the lien. (*See* **mechanic's lien**, **notice of lien**.)

notice of consent   A legal procedure that allows a state official to receive legal process for nonresidents. As a condition of doing business in a state, an out-of-state subdivider or broker, for example, often must file a notice of consent. (*See* **irrevocable consent**.)

notice of default   A notice to a defaulting party announcing that a default has occurred. The defaulting party is usually provided a grace period for curing the default. Notices of default are frequently provided for in contracts for deed and mortgages and are sometimes required by operation of law. Care should be taken to make the grace period at least five *business* days; otherwise a defaulting party receiving a notice of default sent on Thursday before a long holiday weekend might not have sufficient time to cure the default.

Under a contract for deed, in order to avoid a forfeiture of the property through inadvertent default, the prudent purchaser inserts a clause requiring that notice of default be given along with a grace period for correction of the default. Such notice should be in writing and sent to the defaulting party by registered or certified mail, return receipt requested, at an address specified in the contract. (*See* **default**, **grace period**.)

notice of dishonor   A document issued by a notary public at the request of a note holder who has been refused payment of the note by its maker. The notice is legal evidence that the note is unpaid.

In a law action of the holder against the endorser or drawer, the notice of dishonor is an essential element, unless waived (as it usually is in most mortgage notes). Related rights of the holder are "presentment" (to demand payment of the amounts due) and "notice of protest" (to obtain an official certification of the nonpayment).

N

notice of lien   A specific written notice required in some states in an application for a mechanic's lien. Notice of lien must be made to the appropriate court where the property is located. A copy of the notice must be served on the owner and on any other interested persons in the same manner as provided by law for the service of a summons. The notice is usually posted on the improvement and must set forth the amount of the claim; the labor or material furnished; a sufficient description of the property; and the names of the parties who contracted for the improvement, the general contractor, the owners of the property, and any other person or persons with an interest in the property. Service of a proper notice of lien on any one of several joint owners is generally deemed to be service on all owners. The notice of lien must be filed within a certain time period after the date of completion of the improvement against which it is filed.

The lien attaches only after the court has determined there to be probable cause to believe there is basis for the mechanic's claim. In response to recent U.S. Supreme Court decisions supporting an individual's constitutional right to notice and a hearing before being deprived of property rights, many states now require a probable cause hearing. (*See* **mechanic's lien**, **notice of completion**.)

notice of nonresponsibility   A legal notice designed to relieve a property owner of responsibility for the cost of improvements ordered by another person (such as a tenant). Owners usually give notice that they will not be responsible for the work done by posting notice in some conspicuous place on the property, and by recording a verified copy in the public records. (*See* **mechanic's lien**.)

notice of pendency   *See* **lis pendens (Lis/P)**.

notice to quit   A written notice given by a landlord to the tenant stating that the landlord intends to regain possession of the leased premises and that the tenant is required to leave and yield up the property. The notice to quit can stipulate that the tenant must quit either at the end of the lease term or immediately if there is a breach of lease or if the tenancy is at will or by sufferance. Usually a notice to quit based on nonpayment of rent gives less time to correct the default than a notice to quit based on damage to the premises or some other grounds. This term sometimes refers to the notice given by tenants to the landlord that they intend to give up possession on a stated day.

novation (*novación*)   The substitution of a new obligation for an old one; substitution of new parties to an existing obligation, as when the parties to an agreement accept a new debtor in place of an old one. For example, in the assumption of a loan, the lender may release the seller and substitute the buyer as the party primarily liable for the mortgage debt. Novation requires intent to discharge the original contract and, being a new contract, requires its own consideration and other essentials of a valid contract. Note, however, that unless there is a novation, a tenant assigning a lease to another still remains liable for the original lease. (*See* **assignment**.)

nuisance   Conduct or activity that results in an actual physical interference with another's reasonable use or enjoyment of his or her property for any lawful purpose. A *private nuisance* affects only a limited number of people, whereas a *public nuisance* affects the community at large—such as excessive noise from jet planes. If a use is considered a nuisance, the injured party can seek an abatement of the nuisance either by way of damages or by injunction, such as restraining a neighbor from operating an open garbage dump. Common examples of nuisances are activities resulting in unreasonable noise, odors, and fire hazards. (*See* **attractive nuisance**, **encroachment**, **trespass**.)

null and void (*nulo*)   Having no legal force or effect, of no worth; unenforceable; not binding. Discriminatory restrictive covenants contained in a deed or other instrument are null and void. (*See* **void**.)

nuncupative will   An oral will declared by the testator just prior to death, made before witnesses and shortly afterward reduced to writing by the witnesses. Such a will is not valid in most states and is usually limited to military personnel or to disposition of personal effects. (*See* **holographic will**.)

nut   A slang term referring to the carrying charge on a property, such as the monthly nut for an investment piece of real estate. (*See* **debt service**.)

oath   A solemn pledge made before a notary public or other officer. A person taking an oath is often referred to as "affiant." An oath often takes the form of an appeal to a Supreme Being to attest to the truth of a statement, for example: "You do solemnly swear that the contents of this affidavit, which you subscribe to, are true as therein stated." In all cases, the notary must require the affiant either to raise his hand or to place it on a Bible before administering the oath. If for personal or religious reasons the affiant objects to the term *swear*, an affirmation is permissible. (*See* **affirmation**.)

obligation bond   A bond signed by a mortgagor in excess of the loan amount, executed to serve as a safeguard to the lender against nonpayment of taxes, insurance premiums, or any overdue interest that may accrue over the life of the loan.

obligor   A promisor; one who incurs a lawful obligation to another (the obligee). The maker of a promissory note is an obligor. In a performance bond, the contractor is the obligor. One who guarantees the performance of the obligation is a surety; also called a *guarantor*. (*See* **surety**.)

observed condition   (*condición observada*)   An appraisal method used to compute depreciation. To arrive at a total depreciation figure, the appraiser first considers physical deterioration, functional obsolescence (both curable and incurable), and external obsolescence and then subtracts each of these figures from the reproduction (or replacement) cost new of the subject property improvements.

obsolescence   (*obsolescencia*)   A cause of depreciation in a property. Functional obsolescence is a loss of value due to a structural defect, such as outmoded plumbing or inadequately designed fixtures. An example of functional obsolescence is one bathroom in a five- or six-bedroom house. External obsolescence is the diminished utility, or loss in value, from causes in the neighborhood but outside the property itself, such as a change in zoning, loss of job opportunities, and other external detrimental conditions.

occupancy agreement   An agreement to permit the buyer to occupy the property before the close of escrow in consideration of paying the seller a specified rent, usually on a daily prorated basis. An occupancy agreement should be in writing to avoid possible friction between buyer, seller, and broker over the right to early occupancy and the amount of rent to be paid. It is not prudent for the buyer to be allowed occupancy before the close of escrow without a written occupancy agreement; in most cases, it would be prudent to first have the buyer waive any contingencies to the purchase. The buyer in this situation should take out a homeowners' insurance policy, or at least receive an endorsement on the seller's policy in order to be properly covered. Disputes between sellers and buyers who occupy early have been a fertile area for litigation, especially as to the habitable condition of the premises. (*See* **early occupancy**.)

occupancy permit   (*permiso de ocupación*)   A permit issued by the appropriate governing unit to establish that a property is habitable and meets necessary health and safety standards.

occupancy rate   (*tasa de ocupación*)
  1. The ratio of space rented relative to the amount of space available for rent.
  2. The rent received divided by the income possible from full occupancy.

offer   (*oferta*)   A promise by one party to act or perform in a specified manner, provided the other party acts or performs in the manner requested. An offer demonstrates an intention to enter into a contract, as opposed to merely inviting offers from others, as with a listing contract. An offer creates the power of acceptance in the other party. The sales contract transmits to the seller a prospective buyer's offer to purchase the seller's property (also called a **proposition**).

All offers should be dated. This is especially important if an offer does not contain a specific expiration date. The courts usually declare that an offer should remain open, unless withdrawn, for a reasonable time. This requires evidence of the time and date at which an offer was made.

If the parties anticipate that the acceptance will be communicated by way of electronic transmission, it is best to include a clause stipulating that acceptance is deemed effective at the time it is sent.

offer and acceptance   The two components of a valid contract; a meeting of the minds. An offer is a manifestation of an intention to enter into an agreement. In a real estate contract, the offer must be communicated to the offeree and must be definite and certain, with all terms reduced to writing. The offer creates the power of acceptance in the person to whom it is communicated. Upon acceptance and notice by the offeree of all terms of the offer, a valid contract is created. Unless the offer is in the form of an option, the offeror can revoke the offer at any time before the offeree has communicated acceptance to the offeror, but the revocation usually is not effective until received by the offeree. Immediately upon an effective revocation, the offeree no longer has the power to accept the contract. An offer may be terminated by lapse of time, communication or notice of revocation, qualified acceptance (as in a counteroffer), rejection, death, or insanity of either the offeror or offeree.

Acceptance of an offer must be definite, unambiguous, and unqualified. If acceptance is in any way qualified or changes the terms of the offer, then such acceptance constitutes a counteroffer, and a contract can be created only when this counteroffer is accepted by the original offeror. In real estate transactions, the acceptance should be in writing and signed by the party to be bound. It is also advisable that the time of acceptance be indicated. There is a presumption in commercial transactions that an offer made in writing normally must be accepted in writing.

Most offers to purchase real property are made in the sales contract. There is no legal requirement that the offer be accompanied by an earnest money deposit, although this is the usual case. It is common for the offeror, usually the prospective buyer, to give the offeree a limited time in which to accept the offer. The offeror could, nevertheless, withdraw the offer at any time during this period because an offer can be revoked at any time prior to notification of acceptance. An exception is a case where the offeror's agreement to hold the offer open is supported by independent consideration, such as in an option. If accepted *after* the deadline, the acceptance would constitute a counteroffer.

A written offer mailed to the offeree is accepted and a contract is created when the offeree places the acceptance in the mail. Therefore, the offeror cannot revoke the offer after the offeree has mailed the acceptance but before the acceptance is received by the offeror. The rationale is that the offeror has chosen the mail as the agent, and when the offeree delivers to the agent (i.e., puts the acceptance in the mail), it is deemed to be effectively communicated to the offeror, even if the acceptance is lost in the mail. (*See* **acceptance**, **counteroffer**, **earnest money contract**, **meeting of the minds**, **mutuality of consent**, **option**.)

offering sheet   A one-page loan summary that describes the loan's important features. This summary assists the investor in evaluating the purpose of the mortgage loan being submitted by the loan correspondent.

offeror   (*oferente*)   The party who makes an offer to an offeree.

offer to lease   A document used to create an agreement for the lessor to lease commercial space to a lessee on specified terms and conditions. Upon closing, the lessor and lessee sign a formal lease document.

offer to sell   Broadly defined in most condominium and subdivision statutes to include any inducement, solicitation, or attempt to encourage a person to buy property or acquire an interest in property.

Under the various licensing laws, one who offers to sell, buy, or rent real estate or any options on real estate—for others and for a consideration—is required to have a valid real estate license.

Under state and federal securities law, an "offer to sell" is any specific discussion of an investment that is available for purchase. The law may limit the number of such offers or the manner in which they are offered in nonregistered securities transactions.

office building   A building usually divided into individual offices, used primarily by companies to conduct business.

In general, an office building is appraised like any other income property. Office building appraisal, however, is a complex process involving special problems. An appraiser must particularly consider the economic background of the area in which the building is located. Specific factors usually include population growth, monthly industrial payrolls, total bank clearances, building permits over a period of years, school enrollment, public utilities, transportation facilities, rentals of comparable properties, percentage of vacancies, and the nature of tenancies. (*See* **appraisal**.)

office exclusive   A listing retained by one real estate office to the exclusion of other brokers; a listing in which the seller refuses to submit the listing to a multiple listing service. The seller in essence wants only the listing broker to show the property.

In certain cases, the MLS may write to the seller, enumerating the advantages of MLS and requesting that the seller reconsider listing with the MLS. A copy of any such letter must be sent to the listing broker. An office exclusive listing does not relieve the listing broker from the obligation to cooperate fully with other members in selling the property, but does not require sharing compensation. This is in accordance with the bylaws of the board of REALTORS® and the Code of Ethics of the National Association of REALTORS®. (*See* **multiple listing service [MLS]**, **Code of Ethics**.)

Office of Equal Employment Opportunity Commission (EEOC)   The federal agency that is in charge of administering the federal laws that make it illegal to discriminate against a job applicant or employee because of the person's race, color, religion, national origin, sex (including pregnancy), age (40 or older), disability, or genetic information.

Office of Interstate Land Sales Registration (OILSR)   The federal agency that regulates interstate land sales. The agency was established as part of HUD in 1969 to prevent abuse, such as fraud and misrepresentation, perpetrated on the public in the promotion and sale of recreational property across state lines.

Office of the Comptroller of the Currency (OCC)   A federal agency within the U.S. Treasury Department that regulates nationally chartered banks.

Office of Thrift Supervision (OTS)   (*Oficina Supervisora del Ahorro*)   Formerly, a branch of the U.S. Treasury Department that replaced the Federal Home Loan Bank Board as regulator of the thrift industry. Section 312 of the Dodd-Frank Act required that the OTS merge with the Office of the Comptroller of the Currency (OCC), the Federal Deposit Insurance Corporation (FDIC), the Federal Reserve Board of Governors, and the Consumer Financial Protection Bureau (CFPB) in July, 2011. The OTS no longer exists.

office park   *See* **business park**.

off-record title defect   A defect in title to real property that is not apparent from an examination of public records. A recorded document may not effectively transfer title to property if it was forged, was never delivered to the grantee, or was signed by an incompetent party. A party whose signature has been forged on a deed still retains legal title to the property and can enforce the title even against a good-faith purchaser for value who records the forged deed. A certificate of title does not reveal or insure against such off-record risks. A buyer should obtain title insurance to protect against losses incurred as a result of off-record risks. (*See* **certificate of title**, **hidden risk**, **title insurance**.)

offset statement
1. A statement by an owner or lienholder to the buyer as to the balance due on existing liens against property being purchased.
2. A statement by a tenant of a rental property to a buyer, setting forth the terms of the rental agreement, including the rent and amount of security deposit.

off-site costs   Developer's costs for sewers, streets, and utilities incurred in the development of raw land but are not connected with the actual construction, or on-site costs, of the building.

off-site management   Property management functions that can be performed away from the premises being managed. These activities include accounting for rents collected and paying bills. (*See* **on-site management**.)

off-street parking   Parking spaces located on private property, usually on an area provided especially for such use; provides vehicular parking spaces with adequate aisles for maneuvering to provide access for entrance and exit.

oil and gas lease   A grant of the sole and exclusive right to extract oil and/or gas from beneath the surface of land. Such a lease is generally for a designated term of years and is subject to a payment of royalties in the event of production, the commencement of drilling operations on or before a specified date, and the performance within a specified time of a certain amount of development work. Typically, an express or implied easement is granted to enter the property in order to drill. (*See* **implied easement, profit a prendre, royalty**.)

one hundred percent commission   A commission arrangement between a real estate broker and a salesperson, treated as an independent contractor, in which the salesperson receives the full net commission on certain real estate sales, provided the salesperson meets specified sales quotas and/or pays the broker for specified administrative overhead costs. The state real estate commission closely scrutinizes such arrangements to be certain that there is continued compliance with the licensing law requirement of adequate supervision of all salespeople by the managing broker.

one hundred percent location   *See* **hundred percent location**.

on-frame modular   A combination of modular construction constructed on nonremovable steel frames. Generally, these are not built to HUD Code (red label). (*See* **HUD Code, manufactured housing, modular construction, factory-built construction**.)

online auction   The use of the Internet to transact the bidding and sale of real estate, consisting of both distress properties and voluntary sales. (*See* **auction**.)

on or before   A phrase in a contract referring to the time for performance of a specified act, such as the payment of money or the closing of a transaction. Such a provision in a promissory note may be so written as to permit prepayment without penalty. If, for example, a seller wants a transaction to close in tax year 2013, the seller should not permit the contract to have the closing set for "on or before January 1, 2014."

on-site improvement   The construction of a building or other improvement within the boundaries of a property, thus increasing the property's value.

on-site management   Those property management functions that must be performed on the premises being managed. Examples of on-site management functions are showing rental units, making repairs, and handling evictions.

open and notorious possession   Possession sufficiently clear that a reasonable person viewing the property would know that the occupant claimed some title or interest in it. Property is not lost to adverse possession unless the owner has notice, actual or constructive, of the occupant's claim to the property. The construction of buildings or the fencing and cultivating of land would suffice as open and notorious possession, whereas the mere posting of a No Trespassing sign probably would not. (*See* **adverse possession**.)

open-end mortgage   An expandable loan in which the borrowers are given a limit up to which they may borrow, with each incremental advance to be secured by the same mortgage. The advances may be in amounts up to but not exceeding the original borrowing limit. This practice reduces closing costs on future loans under the same mortgage and minimizes refinancing costs and appraisal costs. An open-end mortgage usually contains more favorable terms than a home improvement loan, which charges a much higher interest rate and must be repaid in a relatively short time. Note that the interest rate on new money under the open-end mortgage may be the current market rate at the time of disbursement. The lender of an open-end mortgage should require a lien search or title update before each incremental advance to ensure that no intervening recorded liens have priority over the mortgage. Also called a *mortgage for future advances*, this type of loan is sometimes used by farmers to meet their seasonal operational expenses, much like a line of credit. (*See* **advance, equity mortgage**.)

open house   (*demostración especial, casa abierta*)   The common real estate practice of showing a listed home to the public during established hours. (*See* **signs, site office**.)

open housing   Housing offered on the market without any discrimination based on race, sex, color, handicap, familial status, religion, or national origin. Both federal and state antidiscrimination laws are designed to ensure that housing is made available to all who can afford it. (*See* **discrimination**, **federal fair housing law**.)

open housing law   *See* **federal fair housing law**.

open listing   A listing given to any number of brokers who can work simultaneously to sell the owner's property. The first broker to secure a buyer who is ready, willing, and able to purchase at the terms of the listing earns the commission. In the case of a sale, the seller is not obligated to notify any of the brokers that the property has been sold.

Unlike an exclusive listing, an open listing need not contain a definite termination date. The listing terminates after a reasonable time, usually whatever is customary in the community. Either party can, in good faith, terminate the agency at will. Note, however, that some state license laws require all listings to contain definite expiration dates.

This type of listing is often used by contractors or builders. Unless stated otherwise, a listing is treated as an open listing in the form of a unilateral contract. (*See* **procuring cause**.)

open mortgage   A mortgage that may be repaid in full at any time over the life of the loan without levy of a prepayment penalty by the lender.

open space   (*espacio abierto*)
1. A certain portion of the landscape that has not been built upon and that is sought either to be reserved in its natural state or used for agricultural or recreational purposes, such as parks, squares, and the like.
2. Park land within a subdivision, usually designated as such by a developer as a condition for receiving a building permit from the city or county. HUD provides funds to communities for up to 50 percent of the cost of acquiring, developing, and preserving land for parks, recreation, conservation, science, and historic uses.

open space act   A tax law designed to encourage the preservation of qualified lands through the application of a current-use assessment. Certain types of agricultural land, timberland, open space, or unused lands qualify for a lower assessment, which results in a significant reduction in assessed valuation, in turn resulting in lower taxes.

Once classified, the land must not be applied to any other use; unauthorized change of use will result in removal from classification, in which case an additional tax will be imposed. This additional tax is the difference between the amount of tax paid as open space and the amount that would have been paid if the land had not been classified. (*See* **real property taxes**.)

open wall systems   Wall components constructed in a factory environment. These systems include exterior sheathing installed at the factory, but the interior wall is left open so that local officials can inspect the insulation, wiring, and plumbing. Drywall is installed at the site. (*See* **factory-built construction**.)

operating budget   An itemized statement of income, expenses, net operating income before debt service, and cash flow. Expenses consist of fixed costs such as employee salaries, taxes and insurance premiums, and a cash reserve fund for variable expenses such as repairs, supplies, and replacements.

A property manager for an investment property typically is charged with developing an operating budget to give the owner an idea of the cash yield to expect from the property during a fixed period (typically a year). The budget is also helpful as a guide to the manager for the future operation of the property and as a measure of past performance. The property manager should be conservative in forecasting income for future periods. The budget should incorporate the owner's long-term goals for the property.

operating expense ratio   The ratio of operating expenses to potential gross income.

operating expenses   (*gastos de operación*)   Those recurring expenses essential to the continuous operation and maintenance of a property. Operating expenses are generally divided into the following categories: fixed expenses such as real property taxes and building insurance; variable costs such as utilities, payroll, administration, and property management fees; and reserves for replacement. Operating expenses do not include items such as mortgage payments, capital expenditures, and depreciation. (*See* **maintenance fee**.)

operating statement   *See* **profit and loss statement**.

operation of law   A term that describes the way in which rights and (sometimes) duties belong to a person by the mere application to a particular transaction of established rules of law, without any act by the person. For example, a purchaser of land bordering a nonnavigable stream has certain riparian rights. These rights are not given by contract, but they pass automatically to the buyer by operation of state law.

opinion of title   An opinion by a person competent in examining titles, such as a title attorney, as to the status of the record title of a property. An opinion of title is not a guarantee of title. Examiners assert only that they are competent in examining titles and that they have used care and diligence in examining the abstract of title. (*See* **abstract of title**, **certificate of title**, **title insurance**.)

option   (*opción, contrato de opción*)   An agreement to keep open, for a set period, an offer to sell or lease real property. An option can be used, for example, to give the buyer time to resolve questions of financing, title, zoning, and feasibility before committing the buyer to purchase. Options are frequently used in the land assemblage process. The option must be supported by its actual consideration, separate and independent of the purchase price of the property. Mere recital of consideration alone is not sufficient except in a lease-option in which the provisions of the lease are themselves sufficient consideration to support the option.

An option merely creates a contractual right; it does not give the optionee any estate in the property. At the time the option is signed, the owner does not sell, nor does the buyer purchase, the property. Although the owner is obligated to sell if given notice by the buyer, the buyer is not obligated to purchase. An option to buy is also known as a *call*; an option to sell is known as a *put*.

An option must contain all the essential terms of the underlying contract of sale. A binding contract is created immediately upon the optionee's decision to exercise the option. Necessary information includes names and addresses of the parties, date of the option, consideration, words granting the option, date the option expires, a statement of purchase price, and principal terms. Often a copy of the purchase agreement is attached and incorporated by reference. An option agreement often includes a statement as to the method of notice by which the option is to be exercised, provisions for forfeiture of option money if the option is not exercised, and acknowledged signatures of optionor and optionee (only the optionor must sign). Unless prohibited by its terms, the option is usually assignable.

If the option fails to cover all the material terms and leaves room for future agreement, then the option will not be enforceable. For example, if the option agreement detailed the parties, the property, the price, and the method of payment but omitted the interest rate on the mortgage, a court would not enforce the contract. Thus, the parties should consult an experienced real estate attorney before entering into an option agreement.

Because a broker often does not earn a commission on an option until the option is exercised, the distinction between an option and a contract to buy and sell has a practical importance. If both parties are obligated to perform (i.e., there is *mutuality of obligation*), then the agreement is a *contract for sale*. If just one party is obligated to perform, then it is an *option*. An option is thus a unilateral contract in which the optionor/offeror promises to make the offer irrevocable for a certain time in return for the optionee/offeree's performance of payments of the option money. When the optionees give the appropriate notice of intent to exercise the option, they in effect accepts the offer, and there is then a bilateral contract for sale with both parties bound to perform. The option money is usually applied toward the purchase price, but the parties must cover this point in the option contract itself.

If the optionee does not exercise the option, most options provide that the optionor keep the option money and that neither party be obligated to perform. Time is of the essence in an option agreement; thus the option automatically expires if not exercised before the termination date. Death of the optionor or optionee usually does not affect the option. The optionee or heirs can still exercise the right to purchase. The contract is also binding on the optionee's heirs and assigns.

An option should be recorded, because the rights of the optionee will relate back to the date of the option and take priority over all intervening rights of third parties with notice of the option. Good title practice requires that a release of option be recorded in the event a recorded option is not exercised. Otherwise, the lapsed option constitutes a cloud on the title. Because of this risk, many options contain a defeasance clause stating that the recorded option will automatically cease to be a lien on the property upon expiration of the option exercise date.

Different types of options include the standard fixed option; the step-up option, where the purchase price increases during set stages of the option period; and the declining-credit option, where the percentage of the option price that may be credited toward the purchase price decreases as time passes (opposite of the full-credit option).

Because an option is not an interest in land, most lenders will not accept an option as security for a mortgage. Similarly, an optionee does not receive just compensation if the underlying property is taken in a condemnation proceeding. In addition, an optionee does not usually have sufficient standing to seek zoning changes.

One who buys and sells options without the exercise thereof must usually obtain a real estate license, except in isolated cases and when buying and selling are not done to evade the licensing requirements. Of course, if the option is exercised, then no license is required to sell the property—the optionee becomes the owner of the property, and owners need not be licensed to sell their own property. The real estate broker should be sure the listing covers the right to and disbursement of a commission upon the broker's negotiating an option, rather than an outright sale, during the option period. The listing should also address whether the commission is based on the option consideration (regardless of exercise of the option) or on the full purchase price only if exercised.

If a tenant pays rent with the understanding that an option to purchase is present and if that tenant eventually exercises that option, the option may provide that a certain part of all rents paid may be applied to the purchase price. However, failure to exercise the option does not entitle the tenant to a refund of the portion that would have been applied to the purchase price had the property been purchased.

On the other hand, where the rent or a portion thereof is applied to the purchase price and the tenant has the right to purchase the property for a nominal amount at the end of the lease, there is a strong possibility that the Internal Revenue Service will construe this arrangement *not* as a lease with option to buy but as a disguised real estate contract and sale. In such a case, the lease rent payments would not be deductible; they would be treated as installment payments, which the "tenant" must capitalize and take deductions for in the form of depreciation deductions. The "landlord" runs the risk of being taxed on the entire gain unless the transaction can qualify for installment reporting. (*See* **call**, **expansion option**, **holding period**, **lease option**.)

option listing   A listing in which the broker also retains an option to purchase the property for the broker's own account. In view of the body of litigation involving breach of fiduciary duties by brokers who conceal offers from buyers until after the broker has exercised the option, full and fair disclosure must be given to the seller.

option to renew   A lease provision giving the tenant the right to extend the lease for an additional period of time on set terms. (*See* **option**.)

oral contract   A verbal contract. Typically, all real estate contracts must be in writing except leases made for a period of one year or less. However, even short-term leases should be in writing to lessen the chances of dispute between lessor and lessee. (*See* **statute of frauds**.)

ordinances   (*ordenanzas*)   The rules, regulations, and codes enacted into law by local governing bodies, which generally enact ordinances regulating such things as building standards, motor vehicle standards, and subdivision requirements. For example, many areas have enacted ordinances that ban the posting of Sold signs on recently sold real estate. (*See* **building codes**, **signs**.)

ordinary and necessary business expense   An expense incurred in the normal course of business, such as rent or expenditures for supplies, as opposed to expenses for a specific project or venture. Under federal income tax laws, ordinary and necessary business expenses may be deducted in the year they are incurred, rather than spread over two or more years as with a capital expenditure. (*See* **capital expenditure**, **repairs**.)

ordinary gain   A gain or profit for which income tax must be paid at ordinary income rates. Long-term capital gains are taxed at a lower rate, even though other ordinary income is subject to a higher maximum rate.

organizational expenses, partnership   Partnerships and partners cannot claim deductions under the partnership provisions for amounts paid or incurred to promote the sale of (or to sell) partnership interests (called *syndication expenditures*) or for amounts (except as noted below) incurred to organize a partnership.

   Syndication expenditures are those connected with the issuing and marketing of interests in a partnership. Examples are commissions, professional fees, and printing costs.

   However, a partnership may elect to capitalize its organizational expenditures and to amortize and deduct these expenses apportioned over a period of not less than 60 months commencing with the month that the partnership begins business. (*See* **syndication**.)

orientation   (*orientación*)   Placement of a house on its lot with regard to certain considerations: the house's exposure to the sun's rays, to prevailing winds, privacy from the street and neighbors, and protection from outside noises, to name a few.

oriented strandboard (OSB)   A building material manufactured from waterproof heat-cured adhesives and rectangular-shaped wood strands layered at right angles, similar to plywood. All model building codes in the United States and Canada allow OSB panels for the same uses as plywood on a thickness-by-thickness basis. The engineered wood panel shares many of the same strength and performance characteristics as plywood. Not only is OSB widely used in residential and commercial construction, it is also used in upholstered furniture.

origination fee   The finance fee charged by a lender for making a mortgage. An origination fee covers initial costs, such as preparation of documents and credit, inspection, and appraisal fees. The origination fee is generally computed as a percentage of the face amount on the loan. For example, the lender's fee for originating a $100,000 loan might be 2 percent, or $2,000. If expressed as points, the origination fee may be tax deductible, as is interest on borrowed money. In VA and FHA transactions involving existing structures, such a fee cannot exceed 1 percent of the total mortgage amount. Where a lender makes inspections and partial disbursements during construction of a structure, both VA and FHA permit an origination fee in excess of 1 percent. (*See* **finance fee points**.)

"or more" clause   A provision in a mortgage, trust deed, or contract for deed that allows for a larger monthly payment without a prepayment penalty. There may be a limitation, however, on how much can be paid under an "or more" clause. (*See* **prepayment penalty**.)

ostensible agency   An actual agency relationship that arises by the actions of the parties rather than by express agreement. For example, an owner knows a broker is showing the owner's vacant lot to prospective buyers without authority to do so. Unless the owner takes steps to stop such unauthorized showings, the law considers that third parties have just cause to believe the broker to be the owner's agent. Thus, the owner could become liable for certain acts of the "owner's broker." This situation is an *ostensible agency* because on the surface an agency appears to exist. Once this type of agency is created, the owner is prevented (by estoppel) from denying its existence. (*See* **agency by estoppel**, **Implied agency**.)

outparcel   A tract of land adjacent to a larger tract of which it was originally an integral part. The outparcel has at least one boundary that is not common to the larger tract. An example is land that was part of and is adjacent to a shopping center and that is or can be improved for use as a separate site by a tenant, a bank, or fast-food restaurant.

outside of closing   The payment of certain closing costs to someone directly, and not through the closing process, as reflected by the notation *POC* on the settlement statement.

outstanding balance   The amount of a loan that remains to be paid. An outstanding note is one in which there is still a liability.

overage   Added rent; in retail store leases, the lessee often sets a minimum base rent, with a percentage of the volume of business the store does over a certain amount constituting additional rent. This overage should be treated as excess income by the lessee. (*See* **percentage lease**.)

overall rate (OAR)   (*tasa global*)   The direct percentage ratio between net annual operating income and sales price. Calculate the overall rate by dividing the net income by the price.

overburdening   *See* **easement**.

overflow right   The right to flood another person's land. It may be either a temporary or a permanent right.

overhang   The part of a roof that extends beyond the exterior wall.

overimprovement   (*sobremejora*)   An improvement that by reason of its excessive cost is not the highest and best use of the site on which it is placed. An example of an overimprovement is a $500,000 home in a neighborhood containing mostly $100,000 homes. The term also refers to over-improving an existing property. (*See* **highest and best use**, **superadequacy**.)

overlapping loan   *See* **wraparound mortgage**.

override
1. A provision in a listing agreement that protects a broker's right to a commission for a reasonable time after the agreement expires if the owner sells the property to a prospect with whom the broker negotiated during the time the listing was in effect. (*See* **extender clause**.)
2. A commission paid to managerial personnel, such as principal brokers, on sales made by the managers' subordinates. This override is usually calculated as a percentage of the gross sales commissions earned by the salespeople under the managers' supervision.
3. A rental amount paid by a tenant on monies generated by the tenant's business in excess of certain amounts; such as $0.01 per gallon of gas sold in excess of 50,000 gallons each month by a gas station tenant.

overriding loan   *See* **wraparound mortgage**.

overriding royalty   A royalty fee retained by a lessee of an oil and gas lease when the property is subleased.

owelty   Money paid by a favored cotenant to the other members of the tenancy where there is a physical partition of a tenancy into unequal shares. Such payments are usually court-ordered.

owner occupant   (*dueño/inquilino*)   A property owner who physically occupies the property; the opposite of an absentee landlord or owner. An owner/occupant can usually get preferred mortgage rates over an investor/owner.

owner of record   The person who appears in the public record as the owner of a particular property or mortgage.

owner's duplicate certificate   *See* **transfer certificate of title (TCT)**.

ownership, form of   A broker is often asked by buyer clients to advise them on the appropriate form of ownership of real property. The form of ownership is important because

- the existing form of ownership determines who must sign the various documents involved in the sale, such as listing, contract of sale or deed; and
- the form of ownership affects many future rights of the parties. How one takes title to property may have consequences involving income taxes, real property taxes, gift taxes, estate and inheritance taxes, transferability, exposure to creditors' claims, and probate (or its avoidance).

A broker should be able to discuss various methods of owning property, such as joint tenancy, tenancy in common, tenancy by the entirety, tenancy in severalty, community property, partnership trust, and corporate forms of ownership, but should not recommend a specific ownership form because to do so would constitute the illegal practice of law. The broker should recommend that the client consult experienced tax or legal counsel, especially if there will be multiple owners, to determine the most advantageous form of ownership for the client. For example, when husband and wife are to take title to property, it may be appropriate for them to hold it as tenants by the entirety, if recognized in that state. However, in certain circumstances—especially if the husband and wife are in a high income tax bracket—this form could be disadvantageous from a tax viewpoint, because the estate tax on jointly held property might be much higher than if title were held in another form. Therefore, a broker who fails to recommend experienced legal or tax counsel may be doing a client a disservice. (*See* **absentee owner**, **community property**, **estate**, **grantee**, **joint tenancy**, **tenancy by the entirety [entireties]**, **tenancy in common**, **tenancy in severalty**, **partnership**.)

owners', landlords', and tenants' liability insurance   *See* **insurance**.

owner's policy   A title insurance policy, the proceeds of which are payable to the property owner. The coverage is usually less extensive than the lender's policy. If there is a lender's policy, the owner can obtain a combined owner/lender policy for minimal added expense. (*See* **title insurance**.)

P

package mortgage   A method of financing in which the loan that finances the purchase of a home is also secured by personal items such as a washer, a dryer, a refrigerator, an air conditioner, and other specified appliances. The mortgage instrument describes the real property and declares the enumerated home accessories to be fixtures and, thus, part of the mortgaged property. As in a budget mortgage, the monthly payments include principal, interest, and pro rata payments for the appliances.

Some lenders feel that the use of a package mortgage results in fewer defaulted loans, feeling that a buyer can pay for essential furnishings over an extended period of time without an additional down payment, rather than exhaust resources by buying them outright. The package mortgage is popularly used in the sale of new subdivision homes and in the sale of condominiums, especially in resort areas. Most package mortgages also require the mortgagor to sign and file a financing statement in accordance with the provisions of the Uniform Commercial Code. In a package mortgage, the interest is paid only on the remaining balance and not on the original debt as in the typical consumer installment loan. (*See* **budget mortgage**, **financing statement**.)

pad
1. The area in a land lease park allocated for the placement of a manufactured home.
2. A foundation or site particularly suited for a specific type of improvement, such as a convenience store pad.

paired sales analysis   A procedure used in the direct-sales comparison approach in which property sales are paired by similar property characteristics. The sales price is adjusted to reflect a particular difference in one characteristic, such as an adjustment for date of sale (market conditions).

panelized construction   Buildings constructed on-site with prebuilt factory products such as completed sections of walls, floors, beams, trusses, roofs, and other housing parts, delivered to a construction site, where they are assembled into one housing unit. (*See* **factory-built construction**.)

panic peddling   The illegal practice of soliciting sales or rental listings by making written or oral statements that create fear or alarm, transmit written or oral warnings or threats, solicit prospective renters or buyers of a protected class, or act in any other manner to induce or attempt to induce the sale or lease of residential property, either
- through representations regarding the present or prospective entry of one or more minority residents into an area; or
- through representations that would convey to a reasonable person under the circumstances, whether or not overt reference to minority status is made, that one or more minority residents are or may be entering the area.

Vigorous solicitation of sellers in a rapidly changing neighborhood is called **panic peddling**. (*See* **blockbusting**, **federal fair housing law**, **protected class**.)

paper   A business term referring to a mortgage, note, or contract for deed, which is usually taken back from the buyer by a seller when real property is sold. Land developers frequently sell subdivided lots by way of ten-year contracts for deed with down payments as low as 5 percent. They then sell these contracts, or "paper," at a discount to a lender, or pledge them as security for a loan. (*See* **contract for deed**, **discount**, **mortgage**, **note**.)

par   Average; equal, face value. The accepted method of comparison, such as "this loan is two points above par."

paragraph 17   The mortgage provision most frequently encountered that contains a due-on-sale clause; paragraph 17 of the Fannie Mae/Freddie Mac Uniform Instrument. In a tight money market, it is difficult to sell a single-family residence if the mortgage loan includes a due-on-sale clause. (*See* **due-on-sale clause**.)

parapet   That part of the wall of a house that rises above the roof line.

parcel   (*parcela*)   A specific portion of a larger tract; a lot.

parity clause   A provision that allows for a mortgage or trust deed to secure more than one note and that provides that all notes be secured by the same mortgage without any priority or preference. The term *parity* also means two investments having equal value.

parking ratio   The relationship between the number of off-street parking spaces and the number of building units in a particular development. Local zoning codes often specify minimum ratios.

parkway   A major collector roadway, usually containing a median strip, with landscaped, setback, park-like areas on each side of the right-of-way, generally heavily planted with trees for its entire length.

parol evidence rule   A rule of evidence designed to achieve a degree of certainty in a transaction and to prevent fraudulent and perjured claims. Although the word *parol* means oral, in this context it refers to evidence that is extrinsic to, or outside and separate from, the writing. When parties to a real estate contract put their agreement into final written form, the parol evidence rule prevents the admission into court of evidence of any prior or contemporaneous oral or written negotiations or agreements that vary or contradict the terms of the written contract.

   Thus, if the buyer and the seller orally agree that the buyer will pay the broker's commission, but the final contract of sale states that the seller will pay, then the written contract prevails, and evidence of the prior oral agreement is inadmissible. Note that the rule does not prohibit proof of oral contracts entered into after the formal written contract.

   There are many exceptions to the parol evidence rule. For example, parol evidence is always admissible to show that the parties did not in fact intend to create a contract, to show that the contract was illegal in its inception, to show that there were certain conditions leading to the creation of a contract, or to clarify any ambiguities in the contract. In other words, a party can still challenge the validity of a contract, as opposed to trying to vary, change, or add new terms to it.

parquet floor   A floor made of short pieces of hardwood laid in various patterns; not a strip floor.

partial eviction   A situation in which the landlord's negligence renders part of the premises unusable to the tenant for the purposes intended in the lease. (*See* **constructive eviction**, **eviction**.)

partial floor factor   *See* **loss factor**.

partially amortized   A loan repayment schedule wherein payments on principal are insufficient to amortize the loan over its term. At maturity, the remaining principal balance is due in full. (*See* **balloon payment**.)

partially disclosed principal   A situation in which a party to a transaction (such as a seller) knows, or has reason to know, that the agent to the transaction is working on behalf of a principal, but the seller is unable to discern the principal's identity. A buyer's broker is not required to disclose the name of the buyer-client. (*See* **undisclosed agency**.)

partial reconveyance   An instrument filed when a certain portion of encumbered real property is released from a mortgage or trust deed lien. (*See* **blanket mortgage**, **partial-release clause**.)

partial-release clause   A mortgage provision under which the mortgagee agrees to release certain parcels from the lien of the blanket mortgage upon payment by the mortgagor of a certain sum of money. The clause is frequently found in tract development construction loans. A mortgagee cannot be compelled to release a portion of the realty from the lien of the mortgage unless it is provided for in the mortgage. Thus, in the absence of a partial-release clause, purchasers from a mortgagor/developer cannot compel the mortgagee to release their lot from under the lien of the developer's mortgage upon the payment of a proportionate part of the debt. In addition, where the terms of a purchase-money note restrict the purchaser's right to prepay all or part of the amount due, the purchaser will want the right to obtain releases of portions of the mortgaged property or the substitution of other collateral for the released property. The mortgagee should insist that the mortgagor be free from any default at the time of the release.

Many states require the partial release of condominium units and subdivision parcels from any blanket lien before the original conveyance of the unit. (*See* **blanket mortgage, release clause**.)

partial taking   In condemnation, the taking of only part of a privately owned property for public use. Special benefits or damages to the part remaining must be considered in determining the just compensation to be paid for the partial taking. (*See* **before-and-after method, condemnation, severance damages, special benefit**.)

particleboard   A building material made of a mixture of wood particles and a binding agent, resulting in a less expensive substitute for solid wood or plywood.

participating broker
1. A brokerage company or its sales agent who obtains a buyer for a property that is listed with another brokerage company. Usually called a *cooperating broker* or *cobroker*, the participating broker normally splits the commission with the seller's broker in an agreed on amount.
2. A broker who assists the listing broker on behalf of the seller, whether or not the broker is an agent of the seller, the listing broker, or the buyer. Sometimes, condominium developers list their condominiums for sale with several brokerage companies, which are referred to as the *participating brokers in the project*. (*See* **cooperating broker, subagent**.)

participation certificate (PC)   A mortgage-backed security sold by Freddie Mac to fund its purchases of mortgages and represent ownership interest in pools of mortgages purchased by Freddie Mac and serviced by the sellers. PCs are freely transferable, so they may be sold among investors in much the same way as bonds. (*See* **mortgage-backed security [MBS]**.)

participation mortgage   (*hipoteca con participación*)
1. A mortgage in which the lender participates in the income of the mortgaged property beyond a fixed return, or receives a yield on the loan in addition to the straight interest rate. The lender may share in a percentage of the income of the property and the profits of the mortgagor or can take an equity position in the project. It is sometimes called an "equity kicker" or "hybrid mortgage." Lenders need to be cautious about environmental hazards on the property, for the Environmental Protection Agency might consider the lender's participation enough of an ownership interest to create lender liability under Superfund regulations. (*See* **Comprehensive Environmental Response, Compensation, and Liability Act [CERCLA], Environmental Protection Agency [EPA]**.)

   Lenders generally use participation mortgages in connection with commercial loans as a hedge against inflation and to increase their total yield on the loan. An example of this is a lender's participation in gross rents over a fixed base of 90 percent. These participations usually occur when an institutional lender, such as a life insurance company, makes loans on commercial properties or multifamily units during periods of high interest rates and tight money. There is some disagreement on the question of whether the lender's participation in the income stream or equity of a project actually constitutes additional interest as related to the state's usury law. (*See* **kickers**.)
2. A loan in which several lenders fund the loan. (*See* **piggyback loan**.)

parties   The principals in a transaction or judicial proceeding. For example, the buyer and the seller (not the broker) are the parties to a sales contract; the plaintiff and the defendant are the parties to a lawsuit. (*See* **third party**.)

partition   (*partición*)
1. An interior wall.
2. The dividing of cotenants' interests in real property. During co-ownership, one of the several owners may want to sell the property, and the other owners do not want to. If the parties cannot reach agreement, an action in partition is often the solution. Partition is a means by which people in an undesirable common relationship can free themselves of the relationship incidental to such common ownership.

   A suit in equity may be brought by any one or more of the owners holding title as tenants in common or as joint tenants requesting a partition of the property. If it appears that a "partition in kind" cannot be made without great prejudice to the owners, the court orders the sale of all or part of the property. The verified petition for partition fully describes the property and specifically sets forth the rights of all interested parties. The petitioner should immediately file a lis pendens against the property to give constructive notice of the pending action.

   The court can appoint a commissioner to investigate and advise as to the best course of partition. If directed by the court, the commissioner has power to make deeds of partition or to sell the property. The court in equity can remove any clouds on title (such as an unreleased lien or encumbrance), to vest titles by decree, to cause the property to be divided among the parties as they agree, or by the drawing of lots, to divide and allot portions of the premises to some or all of the parties and order a sale of the remainder, or to sell the whole and use the proceeds to make everyone equal in the general partition.

   A joint tenancy may be terminated by an action for partition, but a tenancy by the entirety cannot be terminated by partition. The common elements of a condominium usually cannot be partitioned under most state statutes.

   By clear agreement among the parties, the right to partition may be limited or modified. Reasonable restraints on the right of partition are valid, but they must be in writing under the statute of frauds. For example, it is not uncommon for joint owners to agree that each has a right of first refusal in the event one wants to transfer his interest.

   When a partition is decreed, a mortgagee's lien attaches to that portion of the land set apart to the mortgagor, the person who originally took the loan. In some cases, the fact of partition might trigger an acceleration clause in the mortgage.

   Because procedures are lengthy and expensive legal matters, tenants may choose to negotiate the division among themselves or conduct an auction sale of the property. This can be done even if the tenants are the only bidders and a third party acts as auctioneer. (*See* **acceleration clause, cloud on title, cotenancy, lis pendens [LIs/P], owelty**.)

partner   *See* **general partner, partnership**.

partnership   An association of two or more persons who carry on a business for profit as co-owners as defined in the Uniform Partnership Act, in force in most states. Under this act, a partnership can hold title to real property in the name of the partnership, holding by tenancy in partnership. An advantage to this form of ownership is that the partnership itself does not pay taxes. It must file a partnership information return (Form 1065) showing how much income it distributed to each partner. The partners, however, are responsible for paying their own individual tax.

   Under certain conditions, individual state license laws may permit a partnership to obtain a real estate broker's license. (*See* **co-ownership, double taxation, joint venture, general partnership, limited partnership, tenancy in partnership**.)

P

party driveway　A driveway located on both sides of a property line and used in common by the owners of each abutting property. It is best for the owners to hold a written agreement detailing the rights and duties of both parties, rather than for them to rely solely on the general law of easements. (*See* **easement**.)

party to be charged　The person referred to in the statute of frauds as the one against whom the contract is sought to be enforced; the one who is being sued (the defendant) and thus being charged with the obligations of the contract that person has signed; the one to be bound or held to the contract. (*See* **statute of frauds**.)

party wall　(*pared medianera*)　A wall located on or at a boundary line between two adjoining parcels and used, or intended to be used, by the owners of both properties in the construction or maintenance of improvements on their respective lots. This wall is often designed to serve simultaneously as the exterior wall of two adjacent structures, built and maintained under a recorded agreement. Both neighbors need to agree on their respective rights so that both properties become more marketable.

A party wall may be created by agreement, deed, or implied grant. Though it is most often centered, the party wall may be located entirely on one lot. Typically, a perimeter wall joining two attached houses and giving structural support to both, a party wall is most frequently encountered in row or tract houses in highly developed urban areas where property owners wish to make full use of the width of their lots and to share the building and maintenance costs. The duty to repair a party wall falls equally on both owners, and the owners may not use their rights to the wall in such a way as to damage their neighbor.

Each owner holds in severalty that cross-portion of the wall on his tract subject to an easement, called a *cross-easement*, by the other owner for use of the wall as a perimeter wall of each owner's respective building and for its support. Because a party wall involves an easement, the agreement should be in writing, as required by the statute of frauds. The right to a party wall can also arise by prescription, as where a surveyor's error causes a wall to encroach on adjoining land and such encroachment continues for the prescriptive period.

When one property owner decides to build, that owner may enter into a party-wall agreement with neighbors. For example, under a typical agreement, owner A will build first, and then at such time as neighbor B decides to build on his lot and use the wall, B will pay A for one-half the cost of the wall. A party wall is also used, for example, if A owns two lots and builds a house on each, with one wall dividing the two houses and serving as the perimeter wall of each. (*See* **common wall**, **prescription**.)

passive investor　An investor who invests only capital and does not take an active role in the packaging, building. or managing of a project; the opposite of an active investor. (*See* **limited partnership**.)

passive loss　Loss from a passive activity. The Tax Reform Act of 1986 eliminated the prior practice of allowing losses and credits from passive investments to offset other sources of income (also called **tax shelter**). The law now disallows deductions of passive activity losses and passive activity credits against other active sources of income, but they are allowed against passive activity gains. Losses or credits disallowed in any year may be carried forward to the succeeding year and treated as a deduction or credit allocable only to passive activities. Carrybacks are not permitted. Any unrealized losses from an activity are allowed in full upon a taxable disposition of the activity. There is a limited exception (up to $25,000 offset) for real estate rental activities in which an individual taxpayer actively participates.

A passive activity is any activity that involves the conduct of any trade or business in which the taxpayer does not materially participate and any rental activity. A taxpayer is deemed to be materially participating in an activity only if the taxpayer is involved in the operation on a regular, continuous, and substantial basis. Any interest held by a limited partner is generally treated as passive because limited partners do not participate in management. Passive income does not include interest, dividends not derived in the ordinary course of business, or gain or loss from the disposition of property producing interest or dividends. (*See* **tax shelter**.)

passive waste *See* **permissive waste**.

pass-through Tax advantage of a partnership, limited liability company, or S corporation that permits income, profits, losses, and deductions—especially depreciation—to "pass through" the legal structure of the partnership directly to the individual investors. Also called *flow-through*. The pass-through is also found in real estate investment trusts. (*See* **limited partnership**.)

pass-through security A security issued by Ginnie Mae to mortgage investors. Cash flows from the underlying block of individual mortgage loans are "passed through" to the holders of the securities in a pro rata share, including loan prepayments. With a mortgage-backed security, the timely payment of principal and interest is guaranteed by Ginnie Mae. (*See* **mortgage-backed security [MBS]**.)

patent (*patente*) The instrument that conveys real property from the state or federal government to an individual.

patio home A land-conserving, small-lot housing design in which part of the home is built close to, or at, the lot line. A patio is built on the side of each home. Facing that patio, to preserve privacy, is the windowless wall of the next home. (*See* **party wall**, **planned unit development [PUD]**, **zero lot line**.)

pavilion A projecting wing or partially connected portion of a building.

payee The person to whom a debt instrument, such as a check or promissory note, is made payable; the obligee; the receiver. (*See* **maker**.)

payment bond A surety bond by which a contractor assures an owner that material and labor furnished in the construction of a building will be fully paid for, and that no mechanics' liens will be filed. The payment bond protects subcontractors and materialmen from nonpayment by the prime contractor. Also known as a *labor and material payment bond*. (*See* **completion bond**, **performance bond**.)

payoff The payment in full of an existing loan, usually at the time of refinancing or upon the sale or transfer of a secured property. Escrow will contact the mortgagee seeking the "payoff figures."

payor The party who makes payment to another. (*See* **obligor**.)

pedestrian traffic count A systematic study and analysis of the number and kinds of people passing by a particular location, which determines the potential buying power in a given area. A pedestrian traffic count is especially important in planning, developing, and leasing shopping centers.

penalty A punishment imposed for violating a law or an agreement. Sometimes a court will not enforce a liquidated damages clause as a penalty for breach of contract if the amount of damages is so excessive that it bears no true relationship to the real damages suffered upon the breach. In such a case, the court treats the damages clause as a penalty and, therefore, not enforceable. The court then awards the proper measure of damages to the party who was injured. (*See* **liquidated damages**.)

P

pension fund
1. An institution holding assets invested in long-term mortgages and high-grade stocks and bonds to accumulate funds with which to provide individuals with retirement income according to a prearranged plan. Pension funds are a fertile source of funds for real estate financing. Because pension funds are not taxed on earnings, they can accept a lesser yield on an investment.
2. A pension or profit-sharing plan. A practice among attorneys and real estate brokers as well as other professional businesspeople is to incorporate individually and set up their own pension and profit-sharing plans because of favorable tax treatment given to qualified plans. (*See* **Keogh Plan, simplified employee plan [SEP], Savings Incentive Match Plan for Employees [SIMPLE]**.)

penthouse   (*penthouse*)   A structure on the roof of a building used to store mechanical equipment or, more commonly, an apartment on the top floor of a building. Generally, when the area of a penthouse used to store mechanical equipment exceeds 20 percent of the area of the roof or when the penthouse is to be occupied by people, the penthouse is considered another story. A penthouse apartment normally sells for a premium above the prices of most other apartments in the building.

per autre vie   *See* **pur autre vie**.

percentage lease   A lease whose rental is based on a percentage of the monthly or annual gross sales made on the premises. Percentage leases are common with large retail stores, especially in shopping centers. An underlying concept of the percentage lease is that both the landlord and the tenant should share in the locational advantages of the leased premises. There are many types of percentage leases: the straight percentage of gross income, without minimum (uncommon); the fixed minimum rent plus a percentage of the gross; the fixed minimum rent against a percentage of the gross, whichever is greater; and the fixed minimum rent plus a percentage of the gross, with a ceiling to the percentage rental (among others).

The Institute of Real Estate Management, the International Council of Shopping Centers, the Urban Land Institute, and other real estate management organizations publish percentage lease tables (see sample table that follows), which can be used as general guides when negotiating lease terms. For example, the percentage ranges of bowling lanes might be 8 to 10 percent; for cocktail lounges, 7 to 10 percent; and for movie theaters, 10 to 12 percent.

Most percentage leases are based on a percentage of gross sales, not gross profits, because of the difficulty in determining what a "profit" is. Utmost care must be taken to adequately and fully define *gross sales*. It is particularly necessary to differentiate the applicability of the percentage to credit sales, sales made at other store locations, credit card discounts, mail orders, trade-ins, gift certificates, and interstore transactions. The definition of *gross income* usually excludes sales and excise taxes. A generally acceptable definition of *gross sales* is "the gross amount of all sales made in, from, or at the leased premises, whether for cash or on credit, after deducting the sales price of any returned merchandise where a cash refund is given."

The landlord should consider protective provisions to cover the following: tenant's obligation to act in good faith; tenant's obligation not to compete by opening a nearby store; periodic reports of sales volume; landlord's right to inspect books and records; tax participation clause; landlord's prohibition of assignment or subletting without consent; and recapture of the premises.

The percentage rent requires detailed auditing procedures, which are difficult to apply to small business operations, difficult to enforce, and do not apply to personal service businesses such as real estate brokers or attorneys. (*See* **base rent, gross rent, net lease, noncompetition clause, recapture clause, shopping center**.)

P

Sample Percentage Lease Rates

	%		%
Auto accessories	3–4	Grocery stores (individual)	3
Books and stationery	5–7	Hardware	5
Bowling lanes	8–9	Leather goods	5–6
Cocktail lounges	8	Motion picture theaters	10–11
Department stores	3–4	Office supplies	4–6
Dime stores	4–5	Parking lots and garages	40–60
Drug stores (individual)	4–6	(attendant)	
Electrical appliances	5–6	Photography	7 9
Furniture	5–8	Restaurants	6–7
Gas stations, cents per gallon	1Z\x–2	Women's dress shops	6–7
Grocery stores (chain)	1–2		

perch   The measurement equal to 16.5 feet in length; also called a **rod** in land surveying.

percolation test   A hydraulic engineer's test of soil to determine the ability of the ground to absorb and drain water; a perk test. This information helps to determine the suitability of a site for certain kinds of development and for the installation of septic tanks or injection wells for sewage treatment plants. A subdivider registering the subdivision with HUD must include a percolation report in the application.

Water beneath the surface that is not confined to a known and well-defined channel or bed is called *percolating water*; if it is so confined, it is termed a *subterranean lake* or *stream*.

perfect escrow   An escrow in which all the documents, funds, and instructions needed to close the transaction are in the hands of the escrow agent.

perfecting title   The process of eliminating any claims against a title, such as having a wife execute a quitclaim deed to release any possible dower claim. To "perfect" is to show of record, as in filing a UCC financing statement or recording an affidavit of a surviving joint tenant.

performance bond   A bond, usually posted by one who is to perform work for another, ensuring that a project or undertaking will be completed as per agreement or contract. A performance bond is frequently requested of a contractor to guarantee a project's completion. The bond usually provides that if the contractor fails to complete the contract, the surety company can itself complete the contract, or pay damages up to the limit of the bond. A performance bond is normally combined with a labor and materials bond, guaranteeing the owner that all bills for labor and materials contracted for and used by the contractor will be paid by the surety company if the contractor defaults. Thus, the performance bond is the best device to protect the owner against mechanics' liens filed by subcontractors. A performance bond typically costs about 1 percent of the total construction cost. A contractor must have a good record to obtain such a bond. (*See* **completion bond**, **payment bond**, **surety**.)

periodic costs   The fixed property expenses (like taxes and insurance) that occur on a regular but infrequent basis.

periodic tenancy   A leasehold estate that continues from period to period, such as month to month or year to year. All conditions and terms of the tenancy are carried over from period to period and continue for an uncertain time until proper notice of termination is given. The periodic tenancy is thus characterized by this element of continuity. If a yearly rent is reserved, the tenancy is one from year to year whether the rent is paid monthly or quarterly. This reservation of rent distinguishes a periodic tenancy from a tenancy at will.

A periodic tenancy may arise by express agreement of the parties, but it usually arises by implication in situations in which no definite time of possession has been set but rent has been fixed at a certain amount per week, per month, or per year. (*See* **month-to-month tenancy**, **notice**, **tenancy at will**.)

permanent financing   A long-term loan, as opposed to an interim short-term loan. Certain lenders specialize in lending short-term money to finance the construction of condominiums, shopping centers, or other major projects. Other lenders specialize in lending long-term money to "take out" the interim or construction lender. In the past, permanent loans typically ranged from 20 to 30 years at fixed interest rates. Today a variable interest rate may be used or a rate may be set for an initial period and then renegotiated.

With construction loans, there is often a tri-party agreement covering the permanent lender, interim lender, and borrower so that there is a joint use of documents; the interim lender agrees not to assign the loan to another lender; and the interim loan is assigned to the permanent lender within a stated time upon completion of construction and satisfaction of specified conditions. (*See* **takeout financing**.)

permanent reference mark   *See* **benchmark**.

permissive waste   The failure of lessees or life tenants to maintain and make reasonable repairs to the real property under their control. Also called *negligent* or *passive waste*. For example, permissive waste occurs when a tenant fails to keep the property adequately protected during winter, resulting in damaged plumbing and improvements. In such a case, the landlord may sue for damages or, in some cases, seek an injunction to prevent further waste. (*See* **waste**.)

person   (*persona*)   Statutes vary as to the definition of *person* because a legal person is not always necessarily an individual but may also be a corporation, a government or governmental agency, a business trust, an estate, a trust, an association, a partnership, a joint venture, two or more persons having a joint or common interest, or any other legal or commercial entity. (*See* **natural person**.)

personal assistant   A person who works for another licensed real estate agent who employs the assistant to perform tasks such as handling paperwork, setting up appointments, coordinating marketing efforts, and managing the personal affairs of the top producer. If the personal assistant is not licensed, the employing licensee needs to establish clear guidelines for what the assistant can and cannot do, consistent with state license laws. Generally, these assistants must be treated as employees because they do not fall under the safe harbor rules for independent contractors. (*See* **independent contractor**.)

personal liability   The obligation to satisfy a debt to the extent of one's personal assets. Shareholders in a corporation and limited partners in a limited partnership syndication are usually protected against personal liability for debts of the corporation or syndication. A borrower under a nonrecourse loan also avoids personal liability on the loan (the lender must look solely to the sale of secured property for recovery of amounts owed). A guarantor is personally liable for the default of the borrower. (*See* **nonrecourse**.)

personal property   Things that are tangible and movable; property that is not classified as real property, such as chattels (also called *personalty*). Title to personal property is transferred by way of a bill of sale, as contrasted with a deed for real property.

Items of personal property frequently become the object of dispute between buyer and seller, most often due to whether an item is considered a fixture or due to the seller's attempt to substitute a similar item. Some cautious buyers insert a clause in their purchase contracts to the effect that the buyer gets the appliances "as currently installed and used in the premises."

A tree is real property while it is rooted in the ground, but when severed, it is transformed into personal property. When lumber is assembled, however, and used as material to construct a house, it once again becomes a fixture, or real property. (*See* **fixture**, **real property**, **Uniform Commercial Code [UCC]**.)

personal representative   The title given to the person designated in a will or appointed by the probate court to settle the estate of a deceased person. Before the uniform probate court rules, such person was called an *executor* or *administrator*.

personalty   *See* **personal property**.

personal value   *See* **subjective value**.

per stirpes   To take a share under the law of descent by right of representation, as opposed to taking per capita, or in one's individual right. Example: Assume Samir dies without a will, leaving $60,000. He leaves no wife but has two surviving children, Aida and Nina, plus two grandchildren by a deceased third child. Aida and Nina take their per capita share of one-third each. The two children of the deceased child would take per stirpes (by right of representation) equally of the deceased child's one-third share. Each grandchild, then, takes a one-sixth share, or $10,000. (*See* **descent**, **intestate**.)

per-unit cost method   A method of computing a property management fee based on the direct cost of managing a specific number of rental units.

pest control report   *See* **Wood Destroying Insect Inspection Report**

petition   (*solicitud*)   A formal request or application to an authority, such as a court, seeking specific relief or redress of some wrong. Petitions frequently encountered in real estate include a petition to a court of equity for partition of real estate; a petition filed in circuit court by a respondent in a state discrimination hearing; a petition to the local zoning board for a zoning change.

Phase I audit   An initial evaluation of a property site to determine potential contamination or noncompliance with environmental laws and regulations, often required by lenders for commercial and industrial properties.

Formal standards have not been determined. The preliminary standard suggested by the American Society of Testing and Materials suggests that the Phase I environmental site assessment should be done by or under the supervision of an environmental consultant and should include review of public records, site reconnaissance (for evidence of hazardous waste, underground storage tanks, leaks, and suspicious features), interviews with current owners and operators, evaluation, and report preparation. About 20 percent of the properties require a more detailed Phase II assessment to determine the scope of contamination. Phase III assessment involves corrective actions, including removal. (*See* **Comprehensive Environmental Response, Compensation, and Liability Act [CERCLA]**.)

physical deterioration   A reduction in utility or value resulting from an impairment of physical condition, which deterioration can be divided into either curable or incurable types. A form of depreciation caused by the action of the physical elements, such as wind or snow, or just ordinary wear and tear.

Two common methods of calculating physical depreciation are the observed condition method and the straight-line or age-life method. (*See* **depreciation [appraisal]**.)

physical life   (*vida físca*)   The actual age or life span over which a structure is considered habitable, as opposed to its economic life. (*See* **economic life**.)

pier

1. A column, usually of steel reinforced concrete, evenly spaced under a structure to support its weight. In a house, foundation piers are formed by drilling holes in the earth to a prescribed depth and pouring concrete into them. Foundation piers that support some structures, such as bridges, may be above the ground.
2. May also refer to the part of a wall between windows or other openings that bears the wall weight.

piggyback   As it relates to industrial properties, a system in which truck trailers loaded with merchandise are placed aboard rail flatcars to be hauled by railroad between two points.

piggyback loan   A type of financing that seeks to avoid private mortgage insurance (PMI). The first mortgage at 80 percent of value and a second (or third) mortgage are "piggybacked" onto the first loan. Often all loans are from the same lender. Because the loans are made at the same time, there are fewer closing costs. Another advantage is that interest paid on the second loan reduces taxable income while the PMI payments do not. (*See* **participation mortgage**.)

pilaster   An upright, architectural member or vertical projection from a wall, on either one or both sides, used to strengthen the wall by adding support or preventing buckling.

pitch   The slope of a roof measured as the vertical distance in inches (rise) divided by the horizontal distance in feet (span).

PITI   (*PITI*)   Abbreviation for principal, interest, taxes, and insurance, originally found in an all-inclusive mortgage payment. Monthly payments can also include private mortgage insurance (PMI), mortgage insurance premiums (MIP), flood insurance, and homeowners' association dues.

place   A cul-de-sac serving more than three lots and exceeding 125 feet in length.

placement fee   A fee charged by a mortgage broker for negotiating a loan between lender and borrower. (*See* **mortgage broker**.)

plain language law   A federal or state law that requires certain consumer contracts to be written in a clear and coherent manner, using words with common everyday meanings and appropriately divided and captioned by its various sections. Some states, such as Hawaii and New York, require real estate rental agreements and consumer loan agreements to be written in plain language. (*See* **adhesion contract**.)

plaintiff   A person who brings a lawsuit; the complainant. (*See* **defendant**.)

planned unit development (PUD)   A relatively modern concept in housing designed to produce a high density of dwellings, maximum use of open spaces, and greater flexibility for residential land and development, usually resulting in lower-priced homes and minimum maintenance costs. PUDs are often specifically provided for in zoning ordinances or are listed as a conditional permitted use, sometimes called *planned development housing*.

Local government approval of the proposed PUD zone is required. A nonprofit community association is organized to provide for maintenance of the common areas. The developer records a declaration of covenants and restrictions and records a subdivision plat reserving common areas to the members of the association but *not* to the general public.

The PUD concept is really an "overlay" zoning, which enables a developer to obtain a higher density (and sometimes a mixed use for commercial and industrial) than is permitted by the underlying zoning. Because the buildings are usually clustered together, there is more green area left open for parks and recreation.

For example, compare the two illustrations on page 329. The first is a rendition of a conventional-design subdivision, containing 368 housing units. Note that it uses 23,200 linear feet of street and leaves only 1.6 acres open for parks. Contrast this with the second figure, the PUD. Both subdivisions are equal in size and terrain. However, by minimally reducing lot sizes and clustering them around limited-access cul-de-sac streets, the number of housing units remains nearly the same—366; the street areas are reduced—17,000 linear feet; and open space is drastically increased—23.5 acres. In addition, using modern building designs, this clustered plan could be modified to comfortably accommodate 550 patio homes or 1,100 townhouses.

A PUD differs markedly from a condominium. In a PUD, the unit is a lot; thus the PUD owners own the land beneath their houses. Also in a PUD, there is no direct interest in the common areas; the community association is in corporate form, and the PUD is created by covenants in the deed or master lease. In a condominium, the unit is a space of air, and there is a percentage of ownership interest in the common areas, so owners do not directly own the land beneath their units. The association of owners is usually unincorporated, and the condominium is created by recording a declaration pursuant to state condominium laws. PUDs are also used in resort housing and even shopping center projects.

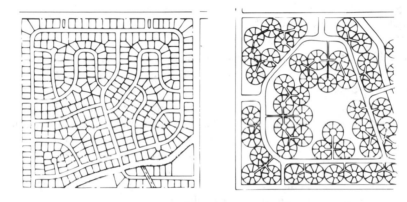

A de minimis PUD, as defined by most underwriters, is one in which the community association has little or no effect on the property's value. Fannie Mae and Freddie Mac also use this term. Fannie Mae's definition of a PUD is as follows: "A planned unit development that has a minimal amount of common property and improvements (which have little effect on the value of individual units in the development) to the point that the owner's association has minimal financing responsibility for maintaining the common property and improvements." Because the PUD aspect has a negligible effect on the value of the individual unit, both Fannie Mae and Freddie Mac permit appraisers to use the Uniform Residential Appraisal Report (URAR) in appraising the unit, rather than their special condo/PUD appraisal forms. Many underwriters, in interpreting the term "little effect on value," use 2 percent or less as a rule of thumb. (*See* **density zoning**.)

planning commission   An official agency usually organized on the city, county, or regional level to develop a master plan and control the use, design, and development of land.

plans and specifications   Plans including all the drawings pertaining to a development under consideration, such as the building, the mechanical and electrical drawings, and the like. Specifications include the written instructions to the builder containing all the information pertaining to dimensions, materials, workmanship, style, fabrication, colors, and finishes, which supplement the details appearing on the working drawings. (*See* **working drawings**.)

plant (*complejo*)   The storage facility of a title insurance company in which it has accumulated complete title records of properties in its area. The plants also store the original title reports (called starters) prepared by the company and sometimes those prepared by other companies as well. Many of the larger title insurance companies maintain their own title plants, or record rooms, containing copies of all recorded instruments. These title plants often file hundreds of newly recorded documents per day, and many have developed effective computerized systems of indexing by parcel of land. This reduces some of the difficulties found in searching titles in the grantor-grantee indexes, especially with parties having common surnames. Some plants have computers that are hooked up to the computer at the government recording office, so the title plant has the recording information the instant a new document is entered on record.

plaster finish   The last thin layer of fine-grain plaster applied as a decorative finish over several coats of coarse plaster on the lath base. Finishing plaster usually has a high ratio of lime to sand, whereas coarser plasters have more sand. Plaster is pasty when applied to the wall, but it hardens as it dries. In newer buildings, plasterboard or gypsum board is often used instead of plaster, because it does not have to harden.

plat book   A public record of maps of subdivided land showing the division of the land into blocks, lots, and parcels, and indicating the dimensions of individual parcels.

plate   A horizontal piece that forms a base for supports. The sill or sole plate rests on the foundation and forms the base for the studs. The wall plate is laid along the top of the wall studs and forms a support base for the rafters.

plat map   A map of a town, section, or subdivision indicating the location and boundaries of individual properties. Generally, a plat illustrates such details as lots, blocks, sections, streets, public easements, and monuments. A plat may also include dates and scales, engineering data such as the location of floodplains, restrictive covenants, elevation, and names of adjoining owners. Plats and platting are generally an important part of subdivision procedures that often require the subdivider to submit a preliminary plat for consideration. The subdivider later files a final plat after improvements have been completed and approved by the appropriate officials.

plaza   A public square or meeting place usually in the center of an area, frequently a shopping complex.

pledge   The transfer or delivery of property to a lender to hold as security for repayment of a debt. A hypothecation, such as a mortgage, differs from a pledge in that hypothecated property is put up as security but possession is not surrendered, as in a pledge.

   Some savings and loan associations lend an amount over their authorized limit when the borrower, the seller, or some other person pledges sufficient funds to cover such excess amount. The pledge account is like a savings account, although the pledgor cannot withdraw funds except in accordance with the pledge agreement. The lender thus has the benefit of more effective asset management.

   A common form of pledge relates to corporate stock certificates delivered to a lender.

pledged account mortgage (PAM)   *See* **graduated-payment mortgage (GPM)**.

plot plan   A plan showing the layout of improvements on a property site; a plot. The plot plan usually includes location, dimensions, parking areas, landscaping, and the like.

plottage value   The increased usability and value resulting from the combining or consolidating of adjacent lots into one larger lot. Plottage is also called **assemblage**, although the latter is more often used to describe the process of consolidation. The term is often used in eminent domain matters to designate the added value given to lots that are contiguous. (*See* **assemblage**.)

POC   *See* **outside of closing**.

pocket license card   Evidence of real estate licensure, sometimes called a "wallet card," issued by the state real estate licensing agency. This card should be carried by a licensee at all times and should be presented when requested by any person with whom the licensee is dealing with regard to real estate.

pocket listing   A listing retained by the listing broker or salesperson and not made available to other brokers in the office or to other multiple listing service members. This practice is strongly discouraged by the profession and is forbidden by many brokers' offices. Under MLS rules, a member *must* generally report any new listing, within a short time—two or three days after obtaining such a listing—unless the seller has directed otherwise as part of the listing agreement. (*See* **multiple listing service [MLS]**.)

point of beginning (POB)   (*punto de inicio*)   The starting point in a metes-and-bounds description of property; usually a street intersection or a specific monument. To be complete, a legal description of a property must always return to the point of beginning to describe the area accurately. (*See* **metes and bounds**.)

point of switch   In the case of one rail track separating from another and diverging (for example, a spur track leaving a drill track); the initial point at which the separation occurs.

points   (*puntos porcentuales*)   A generic term for a percentage of the principal conventional loan amount; a rate adjustment factor. A lender often charges a borrower some service charge points for making the loan. Each point is equal to 1 percent of the loan amount. In the initial stages of a loan application, because the lender does not know what loan amount will be approved, it is more convenient to state the charge as a set percentage of the loan amount. Points are sometimes justified to cover lender expenses in originating the loan and to offset any losses when the mortgage is sold in the secondary mortgage market. Points can be used to increase the lender's yield or to "buy down" the rate. In conventional financing, the points may be paid by the buyer or the seller.

The term *points* takes on numerous meanings in everyday practice and is a common source of confusion. Although used interchangeably, the terms *points* and *discount charges* are not synonymous. A point is technically a unit of measure. It measures not only the amount of "discount" but also other costs such as mortgage insurance premiums and origination fees. The borrower should insist on each cost item being properly identified.

The sales agreement should address the issue of who is paying points. Sellers paying points should be aware that they may have to pay more than originally anticipated due to such variables as an appraisal at a value lower than the sellers originally thought; property repairs, as required per FHA, calling for building permit fees and other costs; and market changes that may cause a higher point structure.

Points are a onetime charge paid for the use of money. Deductibility for federal tax law varies. Points paid as compensation for the use of borrowed money qualify as interest for tax purposes rather than as payment for the lender's services. These points are similar to a prepayment of interest and are to be treated as paid over the term of the loan for purposes of the prepaid interest rule. This also applies to charges that are similar to points, such as a loan processing fee or a premium charge. Note, however, that discount charges paid by the seller for an FHA loan are not interest and therefore are not deductible.

Homeowners who have refinanced existing loans solely to get a lower interest rate cannot fully deduct the points charged in connection with paying off their loans. The points must be amortized over the term of the loan.

Under federal truth-in-lending laws, the borrower's payment of points must be reflected in the annual percentage rate and fully disclosed to the consumer. (*See* **annual percentage rate [APR]**, **buydown**, **discount points**, **Federal Housing Administration [FHA]**, **prepaid interest**.)

P

police power   The constitutional authority and inherent power of a state to adopt and enforce laws and regulations to promote and support the public health, safety, morals, and general welfare. Such laws must be uniform in operation and nondiscriminatory, and cannot be advantageous to any one particular person or group. In essence, it is an authority derived from individual state constitutions, which also vest the power in counties, cities, and municipalities to adopt and enforce appropriate local ordinances and regulations that are not in conflict with general laws. Some examples of police power are the right to tax, the right to regulate land use through a general plan and zoning, the right to require persons selling real estate to be licensed, the right to regulate pollution, environmental control, and rent control.

     Traditional concepts of police power have been broadened in recent years to include the furtherance of the aesthetic beauty of the community. For example, courts have upheld an ordinance restricting advertising in state parks, and have upheld the regulation of the appearance of a community through design review boards.

     Also derived from police power is the right to damage or destroy private property (without compensation to the owner) when such an act is necessary to protect the public interest. This may happen, for example, when a condominium unit is on fire and the fire department must destroy an adjoining unit to extinguish the fire and save the rest of the building. Although the government would not be required to compensate an owner for such destruction, a valid claim may be filed against the insurance policy covering the burning unit or against the owner's own policy. Although police power permits the state to regulate the use of an individual's property in order to protect public health, safety, and welfare, such regulation has its limits. If it goes too far, it is recognized as a "taking," which requires that the state pay just compensation to the individual affected. (*See* **condemnation, eminent domain, escheat, general plan.**)

porte cochere   A roofed structure extending from the entrance of a building over an adjacent driveway to shelter persons getting into or out of vehicles.

portfolio loan   A loan originated and maintained by the lending institution and not sold in the secondary mortgage market. The lender is not restricted by the qualification requirements set by the secondary mortgage market. These loans eventually are sold after becoming "seasoned." (*See* **secondary mortgage market.**)

positive cash flow   (*flujo de efectivo positivo*)   The number of dollars remaining after collecting rental income and paying operating expenses and mortgage payments. If more money is owed than is earned, it is called *negative cash flow* or an *alligator*.

possession   (*posesión*)   The act of either actually or constructively possessing or occupying property. Possession imparts constructive notice that the party in possession may have certain rights. Therefore, when someone is in possession of property under a claim of ownership and a buyer purchases the property from the owner of record, the purchaser for value is not protected under the recording laws, in that possession imparts constructive notice in much the same way the recording of a deed. It is said that the purchaser should have inquired into the claims of the person in possession (sometimes called *inquiry notice*). In addition, possession of a property often cures an indefinite description in deeds, leases, contracts of sale, and the like. The right to possess real property typically passes to the buyer upon the closing of a sales transaction. (*See* **constructive notice, inquiry notice, occupancy agreement, recording.**)

possibility of reverter   A possibility that property granted under a deed may revert back to the grantor if the grantee breaches a condition subject to which the property was granted. For example, Napoleon Baker deeds his farm to Steve Stowe and his heirs, so long as Stowe does not permit the consumption of alcohol on the property. Upon Stowe's breaching the condition by allowing alcoholic beverages on the property, the property would automatically revert back to Baker. The modern view is that a possibility of reverter is an estate in land and can be sold and devised. (*See* **fee simple defeasible**.)

postdated check   A check that on its face is dated later than the actual date of signing and therefore is not negotiable until the later date arrives, because a bank cannot make payment before the stated date. Such a check is valid, provided it was not postdated for an illegal purpose. The person to whom a postdated check is delivered is deemed to acquire title as of the date of delivery, not the date of the check. It is poor practice for a broker to accept a postdated check as a deposit. It is preferable to draw up a promissory note that provides for recovery of costs and attorney fees by the prevailing party if the deposit is not paid on time. A broker, upon accepting a check or promissory note, must disclose this fact to the principal. Note that an escrow company usually will not accept a postdated check, although it may hold a properly dated check for one day before cashing.

potable water   (*agua potable*)   Water that can be safely and agreeably used for drinking. A public offering statement used in the sale of subdivided land must disclose whether potable water is available.

pour-over trust   *See* **inter vivos trust**.

power of attorney   (*carta de personería*)   A written instrument authorizing a person, the attorney-in-fact, to act as the agent on behalf of another to the extent indicated in the instrument. Also called a *warrant of attorney* or a *letter of attorney*. Highlights of pertinent general practice with respect to the use of powers of attorney for the sale or purchase of real estate are as follows:

- An attorney-in-fact may not need a real estate license to sell the owner's property. An exception to this would occur if the attorney-in-fact is engaged in real estate development or brokerage and is purposely evading the licensing law.
- Good title practice requires that the power of attorney be recorded; otherwise, the document signed by the attorney-in-fact, such as a deed, is not effective against third parties. The power of attorney must be acknowledged to be recorded. A notice of revocation is needed to revoke a recorded power of attorney.
- Good title practice requires that the parties use a "special" or limited power of attorney rather than an all-inclusive general power of attorney to convey real estate. The power of attorney is strictly construed and thus must specifically authorize the attorney-in-fact to carry out the full transaction. Also, the time limit must not have expired. A power to *sell* does not carry with it the power to *convey*.
- Any instrument signed with a power of attorney should be executed as follows: "John Frank by John Neil, his attorney-in-fact." The agent's name should never be signed first. The agent may type in the principal's name.
- One spouse can be the attorney-in-fact for the other spouse for the purchase of property, but this may interfere with homestead, dower, or curtesy rights in the sale of property. An agent cannot validly act if the agent has an adverse interest in the transaction.
- Normally, death of either the principal or the attorney-in-fact automatically revokes the power of attorney. Most title companies are extremely cautious with power of attorney documents because of the revocation-by-death rule. A durable power of attorney is still effective after the principal becomes incompetent or disabled.
- Under the equal dignities rule, the power of attorney must be in writing, because the real estate documents to be signed under the power of attorney must be in writing.
- When the transaction is to be closed in escrow, an original and three copies of the power of attorney should be forwarded to escrow. (*See* **attorney-in-fact**, **equal dignities rule**, **practice of law**.)

P

power of sale   A clause in a mortgage authorizing the holder of the mortgage to sell the property at public auction without a judicial action in the event of the borrower's default. The proceeds from the public sale are used to pay off the mortgage debt first, and any surplus is paid to the mortgagor. A power-of-sale clause is also found in trust deeds, giving the trustee authority to sell the trust property under certain circumstances. Powers of sale are not used in all states.

The power of sale is a matter of contract and cannot be validly exercised unless all the terms of the mortgage are complied with.

Generally, when dealing with land registered in the Torrens system, the certificate of title must note that there is a power of sale contained in the mortgage. Otherwise, no subsequent document, such as a deed or assignment of lease executed pursuant to the power of sale, will be accepted for registration. (*See* **certificate of title**, **foreclosure**, **Soldiers and Sailors Civil Relief Act [SSCRA]**, **Torrens system**.)

practice of law   Rendering services that are peculiar to the law profession, such as preparing legal documents, giving legal advice and counsel, or construing contracts by which legal rights are secured. A broker's license can be suspended or revoked for the unlawful practice of law, whether or not fees are charged. The broker also has an ethical duty to recommend that legal counsel be obtained when the interest of either buyer or seller requires it.

There is universal uncertainty as to whether the broker's use of certain forms constitutes the practice of law. Whereas it is permissible for the broker to help complete certain standard forms, such as a sales contract, the broker has a duty to do so with accuracy and with certainty. Such completion of forms is permissible only where it is incidental to the broker's earning a commission and not where the broker makes a separate charge for filling in the form. In most states, the broker may not prepare documents such as contracts for deed, deeds, options, mortgages, and certain leases but may assist with the completion of an attorney-approved document.

preapproved loan   A pending loan in which all the underlying documents are in file and there is a strong probability that no credit or income issues will stop the loan from closing. It does not necessarily mean that the file has been underwritten by the lender who will commit to provide the funds for closing. (*See* **prequalified loan**.)

preclosing   A preliminary meeting preceding the formal closing where documents are prepared, reviewed, and signed, and where estimated prorations are made well in advance of the closing date. Preclosings are common in the conversion of entire apartment buildings to condominiums because there may be hundreds of separate units to close finally within one day.

precuts   Building components delivered to the construction site unassembled and coded to indicate step-by-step instructions. Precuts require skilled labor on-site, and construction can cost more than factory-built homes. (*See* **factory-built construction**.)

predatory lending   A variety of unscrupulous lending practices by the lender to make loans secured by a home or car with the intention that the borrower will be unable to repay the loan, thus allowing the lender to repossess the home or the car to resell at a profit. The practices, falling somewhere between appropriate risk-based pricing and outright fraud, are designed to take advantage of unwary borrowers—often the low-income, uninformed, or elderly. Real estate licensees should not be a party to these schemes.

preemption
1. A clause sometimes inserted in a deed of subdivided land either retaining the right of first refusal for the developer or giving that right to the owner of an adjacent lot who may exercise the right when the property is offered for sale. Also contained in some condominium docu-

ments in which any condo owner has the right of first refusal upon the resale of another unit in the building. (*See* **right of first refusal**.)

2. A legal doctrine in which one law is superior to another. For example, federal lenders make the argument that, under the Supremacy Clause of the U.S. Constitution, the federal laws concerning validity of due-on-sale clauses preempt any state laws or court cases to the contrary. The OCC and the FHLBB have adopted regulations preempting state usury laws under certain conditions.

prefab housing   *See* **modular housing, panelized construction, factory-built construction**.

preliminary costs   Those costs incurred in conjunction with, but prior to, actual commencement of the main project. Examples are costs for feasibility studies, soil tests, financing commitments, and preliminary legal matters.

preliminary report   A title report made before issuance of a title insurance policy or the opening of escrow. A preliminary report or policy of title insurance reports only on those documents having an effect on the title and should not be relied on as being an abstract. An abstract of title, on the other hand, reflects all instruments affecting title from the time of the original grant and also includes a memorandum of each instrument, and makes no attempt to determine which documents currently affect record title. The "preliminary" is not a binder or commitment that the title company will thereafter insure the title to the property, although this commitment may be obtained at an added cost. (*See* **abstract of title, title report**.)

premises

1. A specific section of a deed that states the names of the parties, the recital of consideration, and the legal description of the property. (*See* **deed**.)
2. The subject property, such as the deeded property or the leased unit. This generally includes the dwelling unit, appurtenances, grounds, facilities held out for the use of tenants, and any other area or facility whose use is promised to the tenant. *Premises* is sometimes synonymous with *land*.

premium   (*prima*)

1. The consideration given to invite a loan or a bargain, such as the consideration paid to the assignor by the assignee of a lease or a contract such as an option. In leasing property, sometimes part of the rent is capitalized and this premium is paid in a lump sum at the time the lease is signed.
2. The amount paid for insurance coverage. The unearned premium is the portion that must be returned to the insured upon cancellation of the policy.

prenuptial agreement   *See* **antenuptial agreement**.

prepaid expenses   Expenses that are paid before they are currently due, also called *prepaids*. Most fire insurance premiums are paid one year in advance. Rent is normally paid one month in advance. At closing, the seller is normally credited with prepaid expenses and charged for prepaid income, such as rent received.

prepaid interest   The paying of interest before it is due. Prior to 1975, the prepayment of interest was a tax-saving technique because the IRS allowed a taxpayer to deduct the prepayment of interest under certain circumstances. The Internal Revenue Code, however, now provides that interest cannot be deducted as prepaid but must be deducted over the life of the loan when and as earned. Mortgage service points are also subject to the prepayment rules. However, mortgage service points paid in connection with the financing of a principal residence may be deducted in the year paid, if payment of points is an established business practice in the area, and if the amount paid does not exceed the amount generally charged in the area. (*See* **points**.)

prepaid items   A lump-sum payment to establish a reserve or impound account. This payment is often referred to as *prepaid items* and includes the first year's mortgage insurance, first year's hazard insurance, and prorated taxes and insurance. (*See* **impound account**.)

prepayment   Early payment of a debt.

prepayment penalty   The amount set by the creditor as a penalty to the debtor for paying off the debt before it matures; an early-withdrawal charge. The prepayment penalty is charged by the lender to recoup a portion of interest that the lender had planned to earn when the loan was made. It covers the lender for initial costs to set up the loan, to service it, and to carry it in the early years of high risk. This punitive device also may represent the loss of income to the lender for the time the mortgage is paid off and the funds remain uncommitted. The reason most lenders are willing to allow prepayment after five years without penalty is that much of the total note's interest has been paid in by that time.

Typical language concerning prepayment is, "Additional principal payments may be made with any monthly installment, but prepayments made in any calendar year in excess of 20 percent of the original amount of this note shall be subject to a charge of 1 percent of such prepayments." Some states limit the prepayment penalties a lender may charge, and other states prohibit them altogether. Some loans contain a prepayment and coasting clause, under which the buyer can pay before the money is due and then "coast" so long as there is a surplus built up. The amount of penalty varies, but it is often an amount equal to the interest that would have been paid on the balance for a specified period of, for example, 90 days.

Real estate loans with savings and loan institutions can be prepaid at any time and by law the penalty may not exceed a certain percentage of the prepayment amount, unless limited further by state law. The amount of the prepayment penalty is usually specified in the promissory note. The current trend is to treat excessive prepayment penalties as being usurious and thus not enforceable. A reasonable prepayment charge, however, is not considered interest, because it is payable only in connection with the borrower's exercise of an option given by the lender. Prepayment penalties are not permitted on FHA, VA, or conforming loans.

Some lending institutions waive the penalty if the borrower refinances with the same lender. Others may waive it, provided the sources of funds to pay off the loan come from personal means as opposed to refinancing with another lender. On the other hand, some lenders do exercise their penalty provisions even in the event of any involuntary payment, such as receipt of condemnation or insurance proceeds.

Conforming loans purchased by Fannie Mae and Freddie Mac may not charge a prepayment penalty. The trend is toward eliminating the prepayment penalty, as in certain federal credit union rules.

prepayment privilege   The right of the debtor to pay off part or all of a debt, without penalty or premium or other fee, prior to maturity, such as in a mortgage or agreement of sale. Lenders are legally permitted to apply the prepayment in a variety of ways, some of which are more beneficial to the borrower than others. For example, if a debtor prepays part of the loan, the payment may be applied to the last payments falling due. Thus, if in January the debtor prepays for six months, she still has to make the February payment, and the large payment is credited against the final six monthly installments of the loan.

No right to prepay exists unless agreed to, for example, as when monthly payments are in a stated amount "or more" or "not less than," such as "$200 or more per month." Absence of a statement granting right to prepay a mortgage is called a *closed mortgage*. A statement granting a right to prepay is called an *open mortgage*. If no right to prepay is stated in the contract and the seller will not consent to a prepayment, the buyer cannot force a prepayment by purposely defaulting on several installments, tendering the balance due with interest to the date of payment, and arguing that the default in the mortgage automatically triggered the acceleration clause. Courts have ruled that an acceleration clause is for the benefit of the creditor, and the creditor can elect whether or not to enforce it.

An increasingly popular practice is to state a time period in the first part of the mortgage during which there can be no prepayment. This is generally known as a "lock in." Note that a lender may not charge a prepayment penalty on any FHA-insured or VA-guaranteed loan. (*See* **acceleration clause, installment sale, lock-in clause, "or more" clause**.)

prequalified loan   A pending loan in which a loan officer opines that, based on a preliminary interview and a credit report, the borrowers will be able to meet the loan requirements—assuming the borrowers are telling the truth about their financial situation and income status. (*See* **preapproved loan**.)

presale   A prior-to-construction sales program by a developer. Often a developer is required to presell a certain percentage of units before a lender will commit to finance construction of a condo project. In some states, presales in a condominium project may be made only after the developer obtains a preliminary public report. Such presales are not binding until the purchaser receives the final public report. The more recent marketing trend is away from the presale program and toward selling under a final public report during the construction period, especially if the lender is participating in the profits of the project as a joint venturer.

prescription   (*prescripción*)   Acquiring a right in property, usually in the form of an intangible property right such as an easement or right-of-way, by means of adverse use of property that is continuous and uninterrupted for the prescriptive period established by state statute. Use of land is adverse when it is made under a claim of right. Therefore, there is no adverse use if the owner has granted permission, if the user has paid for the use, or if the user has admitted that the owner has a superior right in the property.

Prescription is often used interchangeably with the term *adverse possession*, which more strictly refers to the acquiring of *title* to lands. As in adverse possession, the essential elements are that the prescriptive right be adverse; under claim of right; continuous and uninterrupted; open, notorious, and exclusive; with the knowledge and acquiescence of the servient owner; and continuing for the full prescriptive period. "Continuous" means that the property is used on a regular basis. There is usually no prescription against the state or against Torrens-registered property. (*See* **adverse possession, easement**.)

presentment   *See* **notice of dishonor**.

present value of one dollar   A doctrine based on the fact that money has a time value. The present worth of a payment to be received at some time in the future is the amount that, at a given fixed interest rate, grows to the amount of the payment over the projected term. The present value of one dollar receivable one year from now is equal to one dollar less the loss of interest for one year. For example, if interest is 6 percent a year, then the value of the dollar to be received next year is 94 cents today.

Tables (such as the Inwood tables) have been devised to set forth a list of mathematical factors to be used to discount money to be received in the future at various interest rates over various periods of time. These tables are most frequently used to compute the value of a lessor's reversionary interest, especially in long-term lease valuations. They are also used to determine the appropriate conveyance tax on the initial issuance of a ground lease. The present value of one dollar is also used in computations related to the value of a building in determining the present value of the assigned leases. (*See* **internal rate of return [IRR]**, **Inwood tables**.)

preservation district   A zoning district established to protect and preserve parkland, wilderness areas, open spaces, beach reserves, scenic areas, historic sites, open ranges, watersheds, water supplies, and fish and wildlife, and to promote forestry and grazing.

presumption   A rule of law that provides that a court will draw a particular inference from a certain fact or evidence unless and until the truth of such inference is disproved or rebutted. For example, the date on a deed is presumed to be the date of delivery, and a transfer to two or more people with no tenancy stated is presumed to be a tenancy in common with equal interests. (*See* **adverse possession**, **delivery**, **possession**.)

prevailing party   The person who wins a lawsuit. Some contracts provide that, in the event of a lawsuit arising under the contract, the prevailing party is entitled to be reimbursed for reasonable attorney fees incurred.

prevailing rate   A general term to describe the average interest rate that banks and lending institutions are currently charging on mortgage loans.

price   (*precio*)   The quantity of one thing that is exchanged for another. The amount of money paid for an item; the consideration; the purchase price. There is a distinction between market price and market value. (*See* **asking price**, **market value**.)

price-fixing   The illegal practice of conspiring to establish fixed fees or prices for services rendered or goods sold; a violation of antitrust laws. In recent years, the setting of attorney fees by local bar associations and commission percentages and management fees by local realty associations has been successfully attacked as price-fixing and thus a violation of the Sherman Antitrust Act. (*See* **antitrust laws**.)

prima facie evidence   A legal term used to refer to evidence that is good and sufficient on its face ("at first view") to establish a given fact or prove a case. Unless it is rebutted or contradicted, prima facie evidence proves a case; presumptive evidence.

  For example, the fact that a homeowner lists the home for sale without ever occupying the home is prima facie evidence of intent not to be an owner-occupant despite obtaining an owner-occupant loan. The burden of proof then switches to the homeowner.

primary mortgage market   (*mercado hipotecario primario*)   The market in which lenders originate loans and make funds available directly to borrowers, bear the risk of long-term financing, and usually service the loan until the debt is discharged. (*See* **secondary mortgage market**.)

prime contractor   *See* **general contractor**.

prime rate   The minimum interest rate charged by a commercial bank on short-term loans to its largest and strongest clients (those with the highest credit standings). Prime rate is often used as a base rate for other business and personal loans. Prime rates are determined in part by the rates banks have to pay for the money they lend to their prime rate borrowers. Interest rates obtainable on other types of loans and the return on investments, such as federal government securities, also have considerable influence on the setting of prime rates. The supply of money and the demand for loans causes the prime rate to fluctuate, sometimes on a daily basis. The decisions of the Federal Reserve Bank to increase or decrease the supply of money cause prime rates to increase or decrease, as does the Federal Reserve Bank's discount rate.

  On many large loans, the interest rates float with the prime rate. For example, the interest rate may be stated as 3 percent (or three "points") above the prime rate, determined as of the first banking day of each month. In a very volatile money market, such as where the prime rate changes six or seven times in a month, some lenders structure their loans using the daily prime rate average for the month. Many interim construction loans have the interest rate tied to the prime rate; thus, large increases in the prime rate during construction can have a destructive effect on the profits of a real estate development. (*See* **float**.)

prime tenant   A tenant (or related group of tenants) who is the largest single occupant of a building. Such occupancy is usually for 25 percent or more of the building's rental area. The prime tenant may be the principal tenant of a property by virtue of name and reputation. A tenant who occupies the largest amount of floor space leased, or who possibly owns the building it occupies, is also considered a prime tenant. In a sublease situation, the original lessee is sometimes referred to as the *prime tenant*. (*See* **AAA tenant**.)

principal

1. One of the main parties to a transaction. For example, the buyer and the seller are principals in the purchase of real property. (*See* **parties**.)
2. In a fiduciary relationship, the person who hires a real estate broker to represent her in the sale of property. The phrase "principals only," often found in real estate ads, is meant to exclude real estate agents from contacting the owners of the property. (*See* **fiduciary**.)
3. The capital sum. Interest is paid on the principal. An amortized payment includes interest and principal.

    (Note: Do not confuse *principal* and *principle*. Principles are rules like codes of behavior or ethics.)

principal broker (PB)   Under some state license laws, the licensed broker directly in charge of and responsible for the real estate operations conducted by a brokerage company. Also called the *designated broker*, **broker-in-charge**, or *supervising broker*. (*See* **trust fund account**.)

principal meridian   The prime meridian intersecting the reference marker of a survey used as a reference line for numbering ranges. (*See* **base line, description, legal description, metes and bounds**.)

principal residence   A structure that has been actually and physically occupied by the taxpayer. Taxpayers selling their principal residence receive special preferential tax treatment: exclusion (i.e., no tax) of up to $250,000 for an individual return and up to $500,000 for married filing jointly if they own and have occupied the residence for two of the past five years. Foreign sellers may be exempt from the FIRPTA withholding rules if the buyer uses the home as a principal residence. (*See* **Foreign Investment in Real Property Tax Act [FIRPTA]; residence, sale of**.)

principles of appraisal   The theories and economic concepts that explain the rationale of market behavior affecting value. Appraisal principles include the theories of anticipation, change, competition, balance, substitution, supply, and demand.

prior appropriation   A theory of water law based on the principle, restated as "first in time is first in right," that regards the right to divert water from a water source. The theory is that if available water were equally divided among all potential users, there would not be an adequate supply to produce anything; but if the water were concentrated in a few, then at least something would be produced. (*See* **correlative water right**.)

priority   (*prioridad*)   The order of position, time, or place. The priority of liens is generally determined by the order in which the lien documents are recorded, except that real property tax liens have priority even over recorded liens. Thus, the old adage "prior in time is prior in right." (*See* **recording**.)

private mortgage insurance (PMI)   (*seguro hipotecario privado*)   A special form of insurance designed to permit lenders to increase their loan-to-market-value ratio, often up to 97 percent of the market value of the property. Many lenders are restricted to 80 percent loans by government regulations, special loss reserve requirements, or internal management policies related to mortgage portfolio mix. A lender, however, may lend up to 95 percent of the property value if the excess of the loan amount over 80 percent of value is insured by a private mortgage guaranty insurer. Mortgages insured by private companies are sometimes called *conventional guaranteed mortgages*.

The mortgage insurance company issues a commitment to insure the lender under a policy carrying 20 percent of the loan balance. Upon receipt of the certificate of insurance, the lender may increase the loan amount to a higher percentage of the value of the property. The borrower pays the premiums for the insurance, usually a percentage at closing and monthly amounts thereafter.

For loans originated after July 1, 1999, the private mortgage insurance must terminate when the borrower reaches a 22 percent equity position based on the original value of the property at the time the loan originated with no allowance for either appreciation or depreciation.

Most policies cover the top 20 to 25 percent of the loan, which is viewed to be the risk portion of the higher-ratio loan. Unlike the FHA, which requires the insurance to be maintained throughout the life of the loan, policies on privately insured loans permit the lender to discontinue insurance coverage when the lender is confident the risk level has been sufficiently reduced. This determination is made on a case-by-case basis. State and federal laws affect the lender's obligation to terminate the insurance once the borrower has achieved the stated amount of equity in the property.

Upon default of an insured mortgage loan, the insurer can either buy the property from the lender for the balance due or it can let the lender foreclose and then pay the lender's losses up to the amount of the insurance. Many insurers elect the first alternative, especially because lenders prefer it. The lender must notify the insurer if the loan is in default for more than four months.

Private mortgage insurance has dampened the appeal of FHA and VA loans, due to the private insurer's lower administration costs and fees and faster processing. About seven private mortgage insurance companies belong to a trade association—the Mortgage Insurance Companies of America. (*See* **Federal Housing Administration [FHA]**, **piggyback loan**, **Veterans Affairs [VA] loan**.)

private offering   An offering of a real estate security that is exempt from registration with state and/or federal regulatory agencies because it does not involve a public offering. In 1974, the Securities and Exchange Commission adopted guidelines (called *Rule 146*) in the hopes of bringing more certainty to what constitutes a private offering and thus does not require registration. Note, however, that even though the private offering security may be exempt from the SEC's expensive and burdensome registration requirements, it is still subject to the full disclosure and antifraud provisions of the securities laws. (*See* **antifraud provisions**, **intrastate exemption**, **Rule 146**.)

privity   The mutual or successive relationship to the same rights of property, as in privity of contract (mortgagor-mortgagee or assignee-assignor) or privity of estate (landlord-sublessee or heir-ancestor). A succession in rights. (*See* **assignment of lease**.)

PRM   *See* **benchmark**.

probate   The formal judicial proceeding to prove or confirm the validity of a will, to collect the assets of the decedent's estate, to pay the debts and taxes, and to determine the persons to whom the remainder of the estate is to pass. The will is presented to the probate court, and creditors and interested parties are notified to present their claims or to show cause of why the provisions of the will should not be enforced by the court (sometimes called *surrogate's court*). Existence of a will does not avoid probate; it does, however, specify the disposition of the testator's property rather than have it pass by intestate succession under the laws of the state where the decedent was domiciled.

Title to any interest in land vests immediately in the heirs or the named devisees. This transfer, however, is not a final sale, in that it is subject to some limitations:

- The title is subject to the personal representative's right to possess the real estate.
- The title is subject to valid claims against the decedent's estate. If claims are found valid, the property could be sold and any proceeds split.
- The title is subject to the surviving spouse's right to elect against the will.
- The title is subject to all liens and encumbrances existing as of the date of death.
- The validity of the will may be attacked.
- The title is subject to estate and inheritance taxes that attach to all property of the deceased.

Even if the decedent dies without a will (intestate), the estate is still subject to a probate action. The court determines the rightful heirs, pays legal claims of creditors, and appoints an administrator to distribute the real and personal property according to the court's decree.

To claim an interest in the decedent's estate, a creditor must assert the claim within a specified period of time or be forever barred. An exception to this, however, is that a secured creditor, such as a mortgagee, may foreclose upon the decedent's property held as security even though she has not previously filed a claim.

The executor or administrator of an estate (also called the **personal representative**) must file a final accounting in court, showing all income, expenses, and the remaining assets. This person is discharged upon court approval of the final accounting. When this process has been completed, the real property is fully transferable, free from debts, claims, or taxes of the decedent.

A broker entering into a listing agreement with the executor or administrator of an estate in probate should be aware that the amount of commission is fixed by the court, and that commissions are payable only from the proceeds of sale. Thus, a broker is not entitled to a commission unless the court approves the sale. This is true even if the broker produces a ready, willing, and able buyer. Both the sale itself and the payable commissions are subject to court confirmation. (*See* **administrator, estate tax, executor, intestate, testator, will**.)

proceed order   A written order to a general contractor to proceed with a change in contract requirements, subject to a later equitable adjustment of the contract price and/or completion time as specified in the contract. (*See* **change order**)

proceeds-of-loan escrow   An escrow in which the lender deposits the loan proceeds pending the closing of a real estate transaction. Such a step is particularly important in cases where the loan commitment is due to expire before the closing date.

procuring cause   That effort that brings about the desired result. Also called the *predominant efficient cause* or the *contributing cause*.

Under an open listing, the broker who is the procuring or effective cause of the sale is the one entitled to the commission. A broker can be the procuring cause even though it is only indirectly through the broker's efforts that the property is sold. For example, if the broker sent a prospect to the owner's home and then sold the property, the broker is considered to have been the procuring cause of the sale.

With the exclusive-right-to-sell contract, the broker is entitled to a commission if the property is sold "by you, by me, or by anyone else," thus eliminating most procuring cause controversies. Procuring cause issues sometimes arise, however, in disputes between the cooperating broker acting as a subagent and the listing broker where both advise the buyer without knowledge of the other's involvement. Issues also arise when more than one buyer's broker works with the buyer. Procuring cause disputes should, if at all possible, be resolved between the offices involved.

Several state REALTOR® boards have adopted guidelines by which procuring cause disputes may be settled. Procuring cause panels try to determine from all the facts who it was that initiated and carried forth the sequence of events that resulted in a successful transaction.

profit   A nonpossesory right to take the soil, minerals, or products of the land of another; contains an implied access easement.

profitability   *See* **break-even point**, **capital gain**.

profit and loss statement   (*estado de pérdidas y ganancias*)   A detailed statement of the income and expenses of a business that reveals the operating position of the business over a certain time. Commonly referred to as a *P&L*, *operating statement*, or **income statement**.

A property manager is charged with the responsibility of preparing P&L statements on a regular basis. Most such statements list only the gross receipts rather than itemized sources of income and the total of all operating expenses instead of individual expenditures. (*See* **balance sheet**.)

profit a prendre   A right to take part of the soil and produce of the land, such as the right to take coal, fruit, or timber. Because a profit is an interest in land, it can be created only by written grant or by prescription, not by custom or oral agreement. The basic difference between an easement and a profit is that an easement confers only the right to use another's land, whereas a profit confers the right to *remove* the soil or products thereof. An easement that is necessary for the full enjoyment of a profit a prendre is called an *ancillary easement*.

A profit a prendre is different from a natural resource lease in which the owner leases the property to a developer and retains the right to receive a royalty payment, as in an oil or gas lease arrangement with a royalty of one-sixth of the net sales price of the amounts extracted.

pro forma   In form only; not necessarily official.

pro forma statement   A projection of future income and expenses or other results. A projected annual operating statement that shows expected income, operating expenses, net operating income, and taxable income and loss. A pro forma statement is frequently found in a prospectus for an offering of a real estate security, such as a limited partnership to own income property. A pro forma statement should be clearly labeled as a projection and distinguished from operating figures, which are based on actual past performance.

progression   (*progresión*)   A principle of appraisal, which states that the worth of a lesser object is increased by being located among better objects. The opposite of regression. (*See* **direct sales comparison approach**, **regression**.)

progress payments
1. Payments of money scheduled in relation to the completion of portions of a construction project. Progress payments are required of buyers of many new condominium projects, whereby the buyer pays the down payment incrementally into escrow, with a certain amount due at the time of purchase, loan approval, completion of the building, and closing.
2. Construction loan funds usually disburse as the construction progresses and not in one lump sum at the start of the work. The lender, on behalf of the owner, normally retains a small percentage of each progress payment to the contractor until the lender is satisfied that the work is completed according to specifications. (*See* **retainage**.)

project   (*proyecto*)
1. A dwelling or dwellings generally composed of five or more single-family units.
2. A planned development such as a condominium project or a shopping center project.

promissory note   (*pagaré*)   An unconditional written promise of one person to pay a certain sum of money to another, or order, or bearer, at a future specified time. The words or *order* or *or bearer* are important to make the instrument negotiable because these words enable the instrument to be endorsed and transferred. If it is negotiable, the maker should be sure to execute and sign only one note and not any copies. The maker usually initials any copies. The Uniform Commercial Code sets the standards for drafting an enforceable and negotiable promissory note.

A broker who accepts a promissory note as a deposit from a prospective purchaser must generally disclose to the seller that the buyer's deposit is in the form of a promissory note. The broker who does not inform the seller risks license suspension or revocation. This requirement stems from the agent's common-law duty to inform the principal of all facts relating to the subject matter of the agency that would affect the principal's interest. It is preferable that the broker accept a promissory note rather than a "hold check" (a check that the buyer instructs the broker to hold instead of cashing) or a postdated check. It is good practice to insert a clause in the note to the effect that the prevailing party in any dispute over the note is entitled to costs of collection, including attorney fees.

In real property financing, the promissory note, which is sometimes called the *mortgage note*, serves as evidence of the debt for which the mortgage on the property is the security. If the security is insufficient to cover the indebtedness, the holder of the note can obtain a deficiency judgment against the debtor for the balance unless the note is labeled a nonrecourse note. (*See* **negotiable instrument, note, postdated check**.)

promulgate   To publish; to print. The state real estate commission may promulgate rules and regulations or it may promulgate approved forms for brokers to use.

property   (*propiedad*)   The rights or interests a person has in the thing owned but not, technically, the thing itself. These rights, commonly called the *bundle of rights*, include the right to possess, to use, to encumber, to transfer, and to exclude. In modern understanding, however, property has come to mean the thing itself to which certain ownership rights are attached. Property is either real or personal. (*See* **intangible property, personal property, real property**.)

property management   (*administración de inmuebles*)   That aspect of the real estate profession devoted to the leasing, managing, marketing, and overall maintenance of the property of others. The property manager strives to maintain the investment and income in the property and to maintain the physical features of the building. In some states, persons performing such functions for others and for a fee must either hold real estate licenses or special property manager licenses. This generally excludes janitors or custodians working for only one specific property.

A property manager may be a member of a real estate office or property management company that manages several properties for various owners. A property manager's primary duties include securing and keeping tenants, providing financial records and accounts, and providing upkeep and maintenance of the property. In essence, the property manager markets space. The property manager performs three basic functions:

1. Fiscal management—financial affairs
2. Physical management—structure and grounds
3. Administrative management—files and records

The individual building manager may be employed by a property manager or directly by the owner of the building, usually on a straight salary basis, to supervise the daily operations of the building. Condominium resident managers normally reside in one of the apartment units on the premises.

While the property manager has a fiduciary responsibility to the principal (the owner), the manager also owes honesty, fair dealing, and accountability to the residents of the building. Whereas the owner expects the greatest net return on investment, the residents expect the most efficient functioning of the building. To fulfill these respective responsibilities, the property manager must possess a working knowledge of property maintenance, leasing, accounting, income tax, insurance, real estate law (especially contracts and agency principles), and human relations.

Property managers' fees are usually based on a percentage of gross income (after deducting for vacancies and other rent losses) without taking into account operating expenses.

Some of the more important provisions found in a properly drafted management agreement are the responsibilities of the management agency, the scope of the manager's authority to rent and operate the premises (e.g., whether the manager can grant concessions), the length of the agreement, the fee, and the identity of the parties and the property (usually not a legal description). (*See* **management agreement**.)

property report   (*informe sobre la propiedad*)   A disclosure document required under the federal Interstate Land Sales Full Disclosure Act where applicable to the interstate sale of subdivided lots. The property report is in the form of questions and answers, and covers such matters as topography, accessibility of public transportation and schools, soil conditions, existence of liens and encumbrances, recreational facilities, whether special assessments will be charged, and other similar information. A prospective purchaser must be given a copy of the property report at least 48 hours before committing to purchase, unless the purchaser acknowledges in writing receipt of the report and inspection the property. If a property report is not received at least 48 hours before purchase, the purchaser has seven calendar days to reconsider and cancel. Failure to provide the purchaser with a copy of the property report gives the purchaser the right to rescind the transaction at any time and have his or her money refunded plus interest. (*See* **Interstate Land Sales Full Disclosure Act**.)

property residual technique   (*técnica de remanente de propiedad*)   An appraisal technique similar to the building residual technique and the land residual technique of capitalization, except that the net income is considered to be attributable to the total real property. The income is capitalized into an indicated value as a whole, based on the premise that the land and the particular improvements on the land are producing income as an overall balanced economic unit. (*See* **building residual technique, land residual technique**.)

property tax   Tax levied by the government against either real or personal property. Real property has traditionally been a favorite subject of taxation due to its immobility and consequent ease to locate, evaluate, and tax. The right to tax real property in the United States rests exclusively with state and local governments. The U.S. Constitution prohibits the federal government from taxing land.

The general real estate tax is made up of the taxes levied on real estate by various governmental agencies and municipalities. These include the city, town, village, and county. Other taxing bodies are the school districts or boards. These include local elementary and high schools, junior colleges, and community colleges. Drainage districts, water districts, and sanitary districts are also taxing bodies. Municipal authorities operating recreational preserves such as forest preserves and parks are also authorized by the legislatures of the various states to levy real estate taxes.

General real estate taxes are levied for the general support or operation of the governmental agency authorized to impose the levy. These taxes are known as *ad valorem taxes* because the amount of the tax varies in accordance with the value of the property being taxed. Education receives about 45 percent of real estate taxes, with the balance divided among welfare, highways, and public services (police, fire, hospitals).

Under most state laws, certain real estate is exempt from real estate taxation. Common examples are property owned by the government, religious organizations, educational institutions, and hospitals—provided such property is used for tax-exempt purposes. Other state laws allow special exemptions to reduce the real estate tax for homeowners, veterans, and the elderly. Some states offer reductions to attract businesses or to encourage the use of agricultural land.

The tax is regressive in nature. That is, there is no relation between the owner's income or ability to pay and the tax rate. Thus low-income families tend to spend a larger share of their income for property taxes.

The general tax rate may be quoted as dollars per $1,000 of assessed valuation or mills (one-thousandth part of a dollar, $0.001) per dollar of assessed value. For example, a property assessed at $20,000 with a tax rate of $2.10 per $100 of assessed valuation will be taxed $420, computed as follows:

$$\$20,000 \div \$100 = 200$$
$$R \times \$2.10 = \$420$$

The same tax quoted at a millage rate is 21 mills per dollar; this is $21 per $1,000 assessed value.

Property is valued or assessed for tax purposes by county and township assessors. The land is usually appraised separately from the building. The building value is usually determined from a manual or set of rules covering unit cost prices and rates of depreciation. Some states require assessments to be a certain percentage of true or market value and for property to be reassessed periodically. Property owners claiming that errors were made in determining the assessed value of their property may present their objections, usually to the local board of appeal or board of review.

In some jurisdictions, when it is necessary to correct general inequalities in statewide tax assessments, uniformity may be achieved by using an equalization factor. Such a factor may be used in counties or districts where the assessments are to be raised or lowered. When the equalization factor is used, the tax rate is applied to the equalized assessment. For example, to increase the assessed value of a property that has been valued by the assessor at $10,000, an equalization factor of 1.4 for the county in which the property is located is multiplied by the original assessment. With a tax of $3.10 per $100 of equalized value, the tax would be $434, computed as follows:

$$\$10,000 \times \$1.40 = \$14,000$$
$$\$14,000 \div \$100 = 140$$
$$140 \times \$3.10 = \$434$$

In most states, the general real estate tax becomes a lien on January 1 of the tax year. In some states, the tax is payable within a month or two after it becomes a lien. Many states permit the tax to be paid in two installments.

The taxes for a condominium unit are assessed against each individual unit. It is not necessary to assess and tax the common elements individually because the market value of each unit reflects not only the value of the unit itself but also the proportionate value of ownership in the common elements.

Real property taxes are deductible items for income tax purposes. However, the deduction does not extend to special assessment taxes for improvement districts. Because tax laws change and some situations are special, a tax authority should be consulted before taking any deductibility.

proposition   The instrument used to submit an offer; similar to proposed offer to purchase in some states. (*See* **offer**.)

proprietary lease   A written lease in a cooperative apartment building, between the owner/corporation and the tenant/stockholder, in which the tenant receives the right to occupy a particular unit. It differs from the typical landlord-tenant lease in that the tenant is also a stockholder in the corporation that owns the building.

P

Unlike a standard rental agreement, there is no fixed rental amount. The tenant pays a proportionate part of the carrying charges of the corporation. When a particular unit is sold, the proprietary lease is assigned to the buyer along with the seller's stock certificate. (*See* **cooperative ownership**.)

proprietorship   Ownership of a business or income property. (*See* **sole proprietorship**.)

prorate   (*prorratear*)   To divide or distribute proportionately. With the exception of principal payments on a mortgage, most real estate expenses such as rent, insurance—which is frequently prepaid for several years' coverage—and the like are paid in advance. Some expenses, however, such as real property taxes and interest on a mortgage, are paid in arrears. Upon closing a real estate transaction, these various expenses are prorated between the buyers and the sellers to ensure that each is responsible for the operating expenses of the property during their ownership. For example, if sellers who pay the fire insurance policy for a three-year period were to sell the property after the second year, they would be credited with a prorated amount equal to the cost of the remaining year. The buyer then is responsible for insuring the property and thus receives the benefit of the policy for that last year. Expenses are usually prorated as of either the date of closing or the date of possession.

In certain cases, a seller might negotiate a provision into the sales contract to the effect that any buyer credits would be applied against the balance due on a purchase-money mortgage taken back by the seller.

Some of the most common items to be prorated are sewer charges, interest on loans, insurance premiums, rent, mortgage impounds, utilities, and real property taxes. (*See* **closing [settlement]**, **escrow**.)

prospect   A party who may be interested in buying or selling real property; a potential buyer; a customer.

prospectus   A printed statement distributed to describe and give advance information on a business, venture, project, or stock issue. If a real estate project is offered as a security, the prospectus must fully disclose all material aspects and investment features of the project that conceivably could affect an investor's decision whether to invest. The term is generally limited to a publicly offered security (registered). In a private offering, the disclosure statement is called a *private placement memorandum*. (*See* **private offering, red herring**.)

protected class   Any group of people protected from discrimination by federal, state, or local law. Such laws include fair housing, equal employment, and credit opportunities. State and local laws may add, but never delete, protections found in federal laws. *See* **minority**.

protective bid   *See* **bid**.

protest   *See* **notice of dishonor**.

proxy   (*poderhabiente*)   A person temporarily authorized to act or do business on behalf of another. Also refers to the document giving such person the power to act for another—a power of attorney.

Proxies are frequently used in voting or for quorum purposes in condominium association meetings. The proxy is not an irrevocable commitment, and the submission of a proxy merely ensures that the owner's vote will be cast if the owner cannot attend the meeting. (*See* **power of attorney**.)

public land   Land owned by the federal government and available for purchase by a private citizen when no longer needed for government purposes. Public land is administered by the U.S. Department of the Interior's Bureau of Land Management. The General Services Administration participates in the sale of public land that is already fully developed.

public offering statement   The document prepared by a subdivider in accordance with individual state subdivision laws requiring disclosure of all material facts about a subdivision to be offered for sale to the public. No sale is valid unless the purchaser receives a copy of the current public offering statement, is given a reasonable time in which to examine it, and signs a receipt for it.

A public offering statement is not current unless all amendments are incorporated. Therefore, a subdivider who experiences a material change in the project must stop all sales until the proper regulatory agency accepts the amendment and incorporates it into a new public offering statement.

public sale   An auction sale for the public that has been informed by notice or by invitation so as to have the opportunity to engage in competitive bidding at a place to which the public has access. (*See* **deed of trust, foreclosure, mortgage, tax deed, tax lien**.)

PUD   *See* **planned unit development (PUD)**.

puffing   Exaggerated or superlative comments or opinions not made as representations of fact and thus not grounds for misrepresentation, such as, "This property is a really good buy." One test used is whether a reasonable person would have relied on the statement. A statement such as, "The apartment has a fantastic view," is puffing because the prospective buyer can personally assess the view, whereas a statement such as "The apartment has a fantastic view of the lake," when in fact all its windows face the street, would be misrepresentation. (*See* **caveat emptor, misrepresentation**.)

punch list   A discrepancy list showing defects in construction that need some corrective work to bring the building up to standards set by the plans and specifications. A punch list may be compiled by the property owner and/or by the original architect in a final inspection of the building, noting discrepancies in the building plans and other construction flaws. With a punch list in hand, the building contractor may then proceed to correct the defects.

punitive damages   Exemplary or vindictive court-awarded damages to an injured party, as opposed to compensatory damages, which are damages awarded to repay an injured person for actual losses suffered. The purpose of punitive damages is to punish the perpetrator, not to reward the injured party. The general rule is that no money damages are recoverable for purely mental suffering due to breach of a contract. Also, punitive damages are not covered under errors and omissions insurance and may not be awarded unless there has been some actual damage.

A broker may be liable to a defrauded client for punitive damages if the broker retains a salesperson known to have a propensity for defrauding the real estate consumer.

P

pur autre vie   For another's life. A life estate pur autre vie is a life estate that is measured by the life of a person other than the grantee. For example, George grants to Harry a life estate in his mansion for the life of Sally. Although an estate pur autre vie is not strictly an estate of inheritance, it is generally considered a freehold estate that can pass to heirs, at least until the death of the measuring life. (*See* **life estate**.)

purchase agreement   *See* **contract of sale**.

purchase-money mortgage (PMM)   A mortgage given as part of the buyer's consideration for the purchase of real property, and delivered at the same time that the real property is transferred as a simultaneous part of the transaction. It is commonly a mortgage taken back by a seller from a purchaser in lieu of purchase money. Although the purchase-money mortgage may be used to purchase the property, it is usually used to fill a gap between the buyer's down payment and a new first mortgage or a mortgage assumed, as when the buyer pays 10 percent in cash and gets an 80 percent first mortgage from a bank, and then the seller takes back a purchase-money second mortgage for the remaining 10 percent.

When a seller agrees in a contract of sale to take back a purchase-money mortgage for part of the purchase price, the terms and conditions of the mortgage (such as interest rate and duration) must be set forth in detail; otherwise, the contract might not be enforceable due to incompleteness or uncertainty.

Depending on state law, a deficiency judgment may or may not be permitted upon default of a purchase-money mortgage. In some states, a purchase-money mortgage is exempt from the state's usury ceiling.

Technically speaking, any mortgage on real property executed to secure the purchase money by a purchaser of the property contemporaneously with the acquisition of the legal title thereto is a purchase-money mortgage. Thus, the fact that a mortgage is made to a person other than the seller does not prevent its being a purchase-money mortgage.

purchaser's policy   A title insurance policy, also called an **owner's policy**, generally furnished by a seller to a purchaser under a real estate sales contract or contract for deed, insuring the property against defect in record title. (*See* **title insurance**.)

pyramiding   A process of acquiring additional properties through refinancing properties already owned and then reinvesting the loan proceeds in additional property.

pyramid zoning   A zoning ordinance that permits a more restricted zone classification (light industrial) in a less restricted zone (heavy industrial). (*See* **zoning**.)

quadrangle   A square tract of land in the U.S. Government Survey System measuring 24 miles on each side.

quadraplex (quad)   A four-unit residential building designed to provide each unit with privacy and a separate entrance.

quadrominium   A four-unit condominium project.

qualification   The process of reviewing a prospective borrower's credit and payment capacity before approving a loan. Brokers who assist a seller in reviewing a prospective buyer's qualification to purchase a property in which the seller is carrying back financing should be aware of the possible application of the federal Truth in Lending Act, the Equal Credit Opportunity Act. and the Real Estate Settlement Procedures Act (RESPA).

qualified acceptance   An acceptance, in law, that amounts to a rejection of an offer and is a counteroffer; an acceptance of an offer upon certain named conditions, or one that has the effect of altering or modifying the terms of the offer. Because the qualified acceptance does not comply with the terms of the offer, it is not an acceptance of the offer. (*See* **counteroffer**.)

qualified buyer   A buyer who has demonstrated the financial capacity and creditworthiness required to afford the offered price. Many real estate licensees advise buyers to be prequalified by a lender before starting their property search.

qualified fee   An estate in fee that is subject to certain limitations imposed by the owner. For example, a grantor may convey his farm to a grantee with the stipulation that the grantee not build a liquor store on the premises. In the event that the grantee builds a liquor store on the property, the farm reverts to the grantor. A qualified fee can also be granted in a will where a testator leaves property to a spouse "so long as she (he) does not remarry." Also called a *base fee*, *defeasible fee*, or a *fee deter-*

minable. In modern practice, a qualified fee includes all types of defeasible fees, a fee simple subject to a condition subsequent among them. (*See* **fee simple defeasible**.)

qualified intermediary The individual or company (disinterested third party) who acts as the facilitator of a 1031 exchange. A qualified intermediary, sometimes called an accommodator, should not be related to the exchanger and is permitted to receive a fee. The intermediary first acquires the relinquished property from the exchanger and then acquires the replacement property and transfers it to the exchanger. Today, this is the most common method of working a three- or four-way 1031 exchange.

quantity survey *(estudio de costos)* A method of estimating construction cost or reproduction cost; a highly technical process used in arriving at the cost estimate of new construction and sometimes referred to in the building trade as the *price takeoff method*. A quantity survey involves a detailed estimate of the quantities of raw materials (lumber, plaster, brick, cement) used, as well as the current price of the material and the installation costs, and also includes indirect costs, such as building permit, land survey, and overhead. An example of what such a survey would include is 10,000 concrete slabs at $2 per slab, 1,500 doorknobs at $5 each and so on. These factors are added together to arrive at the total cost of a structure. Quantity survey is a time-consuming method and is most frequently used by contractors and experienced estimators. (*See* **unit-in-place method**.)

quantum A term used in describing the amount or quantity of an estate as measured by its duration and not its quality; for example, an estate for life, or for 55 years, or forever. The quantum of an estate is generally found in the habendum clause. (*See* **habendum clause**.)

quantum meruit The legal theory, also called **unjust enrichment**, under which a person can recover the reasonable value of services rendered in the absence of any agreement between the parties. In many states, a real estate broker may not sue the seller for a commission in the absence of a written agreement.

quarter-section A land-area measure used in connection with the government (rectangular) survey of land measurement. A quarter-section of land is 160 acres, or 2,640 feet by 2,640 feet. Historically, it is the area of land originally granted to a homesteader.

   Note that when lands throughout the United States were originally surveyed, lakes, streams, and other features were sometimes encountered that resulted in fractional pieces of land less than a quarter-section. These pieces were called *government lots* and were identified by a specific lot number, which became the legal description for that parcel of land. (*See* **government survey method**.)

quash To annul or to set aside, as in quashing a summons or an administrative complaint.

quasi Latin for "as if"; similar to; almost like. Commonly used in real estate with such terms as *quasi contract*, *quasi-judicial*, and *quasi corporation*. A quasi contract can arise to prevent an unjust enrichment, such as when a landowner mistakenly pays taxes on his or her neighbor's property.

quick assets Assets that are quickly and easily convertible into cash; liquid assets. (*See* **liquidity**.)

quiet enjoyment The right of an owner or lessee legally in possession of property to uninterrupted use of the property without interference from the former owner, lessor, or any third party claiming superior title. (*See* **covenant**.)

quiet title action A court action intended to establish or settle the title to a particular property, especially where there is a cloud on the title. All parties with a possible claim or interest in the property must be joined in the action. A quiet title action is frequently used by an adverse possessor to substantiate the title, because having official record title makes it easier to market the property. Once the judgment or decree of the court has been recorded, proper record notice of the claimant's right and interest in the property is established.

Q

A quiet title action can generally be used to extinguish easements; remove any clouds on title; release a homestead, dower, or curtesy interest; transfer title without warranties; clear tax titles; or simply release an interest when the grantor may have some remote claim to the property. The seller who holds a forfeited contract for deed, which the buyer had recorded, sometimes brings a quiet title action to clear the cloud on title produced by the recorded contract for deed, especially where the buyer refuses to release or quitclaim the interest. (*See* **cloud on title**.)

quitclaim deed   A deed of conveyance that operates, in effect, as a release of whatever interest the grantor has in the property; sometimes called a *release deed*. The quitclaim deed contains similar language to a deed, with the important exception that rather than using the words *grant and release*, it contains language such as "remise, release, and quitclaim." Grantors therefore do not warrant title or possession. Grantors only pass whatever interest they may have, if any. In effect, a grantor forever quits whatever claim he or she had, if in fact any existed.

The quitclaim deed transfers only whatever right, title, and interest the grantor had in the land at the time of the execution of the deed and does not pass to the grantee any title or interest subsequently acquired by the grantor. Thus the grantee cannot claim a right to any after-acquired title. (*See* **after-acquired**.)

Although a quitclaim deed may not vest any title in the grantee, it is not inferior to the other types of deeds with respect to that which it actually conveys. For example, if a grantor executes and delivers a warranty deed to one person and subsequently executes and delivers a quitclaim deed to the same property to another person, the grantee under the quitclaim deed prevails over the grantee under the warranty deed, assuming he or she is first to record the deed.

A quitclaim deed is not commonly used to convey a fee but is usually restricted to releasing or conveying minor interests in real estate for the purpose of clearing title defects or clouds on the title. It may also be used to convey lesser interests such as life estates and to release such interests as a remainder or reversion.

A title searcher regards a quitclaim deed in the chain of title as a red flag, and most title companies will not guarantee titles derived out of a quitclaim deed—at least not without further explanation.

Quitclaim deeds also are often used between close relatives, such as when one heir is buying out the other, or where a seller is in such poor financial shape that it is inconsequential to the buyer whether he or she is getting any warranties. (*See* **cloud on title**, **deed**.)

quorum   (*quórum*)   The minimum legal number of people required to be present before a specified meeting can officially take place or authorized business can be transacted.

radon   (*radón*)   A colorless, odorless, naturally occurring gas produced from the decay of natural radioactive minerals in the ground found in buildings in every state and territory. Radon is a carcinogen implicated in lung cancer deaths. Indoor levels are measured as picocuries per liter of air (pCi/L). The EPA suggested action level is 4. In most states, brokers must disclose known radon problems and the presence of mitigation systems.

A 48-hour test may be used during a real estate transaction. Mitigation consists of sealing cracks, and installing PVC pipe into the ground that exits the building through the highest level. A small fan draws the ground air and radon through the pipe and into outdoor air where the radon dissipates. (*See* **mitigation**.)

rafter   One of a series of sloping beams that extend from the exterior wall to a center ridgeboard and provide the main support for the roof.

range

1. An open land area for grazing.
2. A series of mountains.

range line   A measurement, used in the government survey system, consisting of a strip of land six miles wide, running in a north-south direction. (*See* **government survey method**, **township**.)

range of value   The market value of a property usually stated as a variable amount between a low and a high limit. Licensees often estimate a range of value as a first step in working with an owner to determine an appropriate listing price.

rate of return   The relationship (expressed as a percentage) between the annual net income that is generated by a business and the invested capital (or the appraised value or the gross income) of the business. The rate of return is the percentage yield to the investor based on the property's production of income. (*See* **internal rate of return [IRR]**.)

ratification   The adoption or confirmation of an act already performed on behalf of a person without prior authorization. In agency law, a principal by his or her actions may ratify the previously unauthorized acts of an agent. Upon reaching legal age, a person can ratify a contract made during his or her minority. (*See* **scope of authority**.)

raw land   Unimproved land; land in its unused natural state before grading, construction, subdividing, or improvements such as streets, lighting, and sewers.

"ready, willing, and able"   A phrase referring to a prospective buyer of property who is legally capable and willing and financially able to consummate the transaction. Traditionally, the broker earns a commission upon procuring a "ready, willing, and able" buyer on the listing terms, regardless of whether the seller actually goes through with the sale. The broker is not entitled to a commission if the contract is subject to conditions not contemplated in the listing agreement unless and until the conditions have been satisfied or waived. The buyer is not "ready and willing" when he or she enters into an option with the seller, but the buyer is "ready and willing" when the option is exercised. A corporation not yet formed cannot be a "ready, willing, and able" buyer. (*See* **contingency**, **qualified acceptance**.)

The "able" requires that the buyer be financially able to comply with the terms of the sale in both initial cash payment and any necessary financing. Generally, the broker is not required to show that the purchaser has actual cash or assets to pay off the mortgage, so the seller implicitly approves the buyer as "able" when the seller accepts an offer from a buyer. However, there is case law to the effect that the broker does have the added responsibility to find out whether in fact the buyer is "able." If the buyer turns out to be financially unable, the broker is generally not entitled to a commission. (*See* **commission**.)

real estate   (*bienes raíces*)   The physical land at, above, and below the earth's surface including all appurtenances, i.e., any structures. Although for all practical purposes, the term *real estate* has become synonymous with *real property*, technically speaking, the term *real property* is the most inclusive and includes the land, plus structures, plus any and every interest in land whether corporeal or incorporeal, freehold or nonfreehold. (*See* **land**, **real property**.)

R

real estate agent   A term commonly used to refer to a licensed salesperson working for a licensed broker, even if the salesperson has already obtained an individual broker's license. (*See* **broker**.)

Real Estate Brokerage Council   *See* Appendix A.

real estate commission/department   A state governmental agency whose primary duties include making rules and regulations to protect the general public involved in real estate transactions, granting licenses to real estate brokers and salespeople, and suspending or revoking licenses for cause.

real estate contract   *See* **contract for deed.**

real estate education, research, and recovery fund   A special state fund, in some states, either supported by a portion of the real estate licensing fees or by a special fee, used to encourage real estate education and to provide a source of financial relief for persons injured by the fraudulent practices of a judgment-proof licensee. (*See* **recovery fund**.)

Real Estate Educators Association (REEA)   *See* Appendix A.

real estate investment conduit   *See* **real estate investment trust (REIT)**.

real estate investment trust (REIT)   (*fideicomiso de inversiones en bienes raíces*)   A method of pooling investment money from at least 100 investors, providing favored tax treatment for certain business trusts by exempting from corporate tax certain qualified REITs that invest at least 75 percent of their assets in real estate and that distribute 95 percent or more of their annual real estate ordinary income to their investors. The real estate investments are primarily office buildings, apartment buildings, and shopping centers or mortgages. *See* **real estate mortgage trust (REMT)**.

Similar to a mutual fund, REIT shares sell like stock on the major exchanges investing in real estate directly, through either properties or mortgages. As a part owner of real property, the shareholder pays normal income tax on the ordinary income from the trust and receives capital gains treatment for any capital gains distribution.

Some advantages of the REIT are avoidance of corporate tax (thus no double taxation), centralized management, continuity of operation, transferability of interests, diversification of investment, and the benefit of skilled real estate advice. Some of the disadvantages are that investments are passive in nature and usually restricted to very large real estate transactions; losses cannot be passed through to the investor to offset other income, as is the case with syndications; and usually the trust must be registered with the Securities and Exchange Commission, a burdensome and expensive process. (*See* **real estate mortgage trust [REMT]**.)

R

real estate mortgage investment conduit (REMIC)   A special tax vehicle for entities that issue multiple classes in investor interests backed by a pool of mortgages. Generally a conduit entity (for tax purposes), the income of the REMIC is passed through to investors and reported on their individual income tax returns. Complex rules cover qualification as a REMIC and transfers to and liquidations of the entity. If the qualification requirements are met, a partnership, trust, or similar entity is granted pass-through REMIC status. The entity qualifies as a REMIC only if it meets two tests: (1) Substantially, all assets at the close of the fourth month ending after the "startup day" and each quarter ending thereafter must consist of qualified mortgages and permitted investments. (2) All interests in the REMIC must consist of one or more classes of regular interests and a single class of residual interests. *See* **real estate mortgage trust (REMT)**.

real estate mortgage trust (REMT)   A type of REIT that buys and sells real estate mortgages (usually short-term, junior instruments) rather than real property. Major sources of income for REMTs are mortgage interest, origination fees, and profits earned from buying and selling mortgages.

A related trust is the *combination or hybrid trust*, which combines real estate equity investing with mortgage lending, thus earning profits from rental income and capital gains, as well as mortgage interest and placement fees. (*See* **real estate investment trust [REIT]**; **real estate mortgage investment conduit [REMIC].**)

real estate owned (REO)   A term used by lenders to describe real property involuntarily acquired by them through foreclosure. Lenders often use brokers to market their REO properties.

Real Estate Settlement Procedures Act (RESPA)   A federal law, enacted in 1974 and later revised, that ensures that the buyer and the seller in a real estate transaction receive information of all settlement costs when the purchase of a one-to-four-family residential dwelling is financed by a federally related mortgage loan. Federally related loans are broadly defined to include loans made by lenders whose deposits are insured by federal agencies, insured by the FHA or VA, administered by the Department of Housing and Urban Development, or intended to be sold by the lender to Fannie Mae or a similar federal agency. RESPA effectively covers most institutional loans.

Note that RESPA regulations apply to first mortgage loans only. RESPA requires that loans covered by the act comply with the following items:

Special information booklet: A lender must give every loan applicant a copy of the HUD-published booklet *Shopping for Your Home Loan*, which provides the borrower with general information about settlement (closing) costs and explains the various RESPA provisions. It includes a line-by-line discussion of the Uniform Settlement Statement.

Good-faith estimate of settlement costs: Upon application or within three business days of the completed application, the lender must provide the borrower with a good-faith estimate of the settlement costs the borrower is likely to incur. This may take the form of a specific figure or a range of costs based on comparable past transactions in the area. The borrower is free to hire and pay for any attorney or title company. However, if the lender is using a particular attorney or title company to conduct the closing, the lender must reveal any business relationship and give an estimate of that individual's charges. Charges that change prior to settlement may trigger a three-day waiting period. The lender may require up to two months' worth of taxes, insurance premiums, and other charges to be escrowed (impounds). (*See* **good-faith estimate [GFE].**)

Uniform Settlement Statement: Loan closing information must be prepared on a standardized HUD form designed to detail all financing particulars of the transaction. The statement must itemize all charges imposed by the lender and other charges paid out of the closing proceeds. Certain charges may not change from the original good-faith estimate (GFE) without triggering a three-day waiting period before closing. Charges incurred by the buyer and the seller, contracted separately and outside the closing, do not require disclosure. Items paid for before the closing must be clearly marked as such on the statement and omitted from the totals. Lenders must retain these statements for two years after the date of closing—unless the loan (and its servicing) is sold or otherwise disposed of. Note that the Uniform Settlement Statement may be changed to allow for local custom; that is, certain lines may be deleted if they do not apply in the area. Upon the borrower's request, the settlement agent must permit the borrower to inspect the settlement statement, to the extent that the figures are available, one business day before closing. In addition, lenders may not impose a fee for preparation of the Uniform Settlement Statement or any statement required under the Truth in Lending Act. (*See* **HUD-1 form.**)

Prohibition against kickbacks: RESPA explicitly prohibits the paying of kickbacks or unearned fees, such as when an insurance agency pays a kickback to a lender for referring one of the lender's recent customers to the agency or when a lender pays a real estate licensee for referring buyers to the lender. Exempted, however, are payments made pursuant to cooperative brokerage or referral arrangements, or agreements between real estate salespeople and brokers.

R

RESPA is administered and enforced by the Consumer Financial Protection Bureau (CFPB). RESPA does not apply to loans secured by mortgaged property larger than 25 acres, to installment land contracts (contracts for deed), or to certain construction loans, home improvement loans, and loans on property where the primary purpose of purchasing is future resale. (*See* **computerized loan origination [CLO]**, **Consumer Financial Protection Bureau**, **controlled business arrangement**, **rebate**.)

realized gain   The profit made on the sale of a capital asset; usually the difference between the net sales price (amount realized) and the adjusted tax basis of the property. The recognized gain is that portion of the realized gain subject to tax.

real property   (*propiedad inmueble*, *bienes inmuebles*)   The earth's surface, the air above, and the ground below, as well as all appurtenances to the land including buildings, structures, fixtures, fences, and improvements erected upon or affixed to the same, excluding growing crops. The term *real property* includes the interests, benefits, and rights inherent in the ownership of real estate (the bundle of rights). (*See* **bundle of rights**, **property**.)

That which is not real property is personal property. It is important to distinguish between the two, because the law treats real property and personal property differently:

Instruments affecting *real property* must be in writing and should be recorded, whereas instruments affecting *personal property* may be oral or written, ordinarily need not be recorded, and can be transferred merely by delivery.

Tax laws make many important distinctions between *real* and *personal* property.

The law of the state where the *real property* is located governs the acquisition and transfer of title to land, including important matters such as rules of descent and probate. *Personal property*, on the other hand, is movable and is governed by the laws of the jurisdiction in which it is located.

Under common-law principles, leaseholds are treated as *personal property*, commonly referred to as "chattels real," although for some purposes (e.g., taxation, condominium), certain long-term leaseholds have been classified by statute as *real property*.

Court-ordered judgment liens may attach to *real property* only. Usually, *personal property* must be sold to pay debts before realty can be levied.

(*See* **land**, **leasehold**, **property**, **real estate**.)

real property securities registration   The process of disclosure and notification to proper government agencies of an issuer's intended real property security offering. All real property securities, unless exempt, must be registered with the federal Securities and Exchange Commission (SEC) and usually with a securities commission in the states in which the securities will be offered for sale.

The two most frequently claimed exemptions are the *intrastate exemption* and the *private offering exemption*. An offering directed solely to residents of a single state where the issuer is also a resident and doing business is exempted from registration with the SEC under the intrastate exemption, although it must register with the state, unless it is also exempt from state registration requirements as a private offering. The private offering rules exempt an offering that is of a limited scope and directed to such a selected type of investor that the prospective purchasers do not need the protection afforded by the SEC disclosure requirements (i.e., investors sophisticated and wealthy enough to withstand a loss of invested funds and knowledgeable enough to evaluate fully the risks of the investment). The Securities and Exchange Commission's Rule 146 further defines the limits of this private offering exemption.

In some circumstances, the SEC regards the offering of condominiums to be real property securities—for example, when the units are offered with emphasis placed on the economic benefits derived from the rental of the units or where there is a rental pool or mandatory rental agreement. The developer of an unregistered (with the SEC) condominium must carefully instruct all salespeople to avoid any representation as to rental income that a purchaser may receive. Sample instructions are as follows:

> Developer advises that no representations or references will be made to either purchasers or prospective purchasers concerning rental of the apartment, income from the apartment, or any other economic benefit to be derived from the rental of the apartment, including but not limited to any reference or representation to the effect that developer or the managing agent of the project will provide, directly or indirectly, any services relating to the rental or sale of the apartment, or as to possible advantages from the rental of an apartment under federal or state tax laws. Rental of the apartments and the provision of management services in connection therewith are and shall be the sole responsibility of the purchaser.

If the condominium is offered for sale in other states, the securities laws (blue-sky laws) of these states must be reviewed to determine whether registration in those states is necessary. For instance, the California commissioner of corporations has ruled that the California offering of Hawaii condominium units coupled with a voluntary rental pool constitutes the offering of a real property security under the laws of California. (*See* **absentee owner, antifraud provisions, intrastate exemption, investment contract, private offering, red herring, rental pool, Rule 10B5, Rule 146, Rule 147, underwriter.**)

Realtist   *See* Appendix B.

REALTOR®   *See* Appendix B.

REALTOR-ASSOCIATE® (RA)   *See* Appendix B.

REALTORS® Institute   *See* Appendix A.

REALTORS® Land Institute (RLI)   *See* Appendix A.

REALTORS® National Marketing Institute (RNMI)   *See* Appendix A.

realty   Land and everything permanently affixed thereto; the opposite of personalty. (*See* **land, personal property, property, real estate, real property**.)

reappraisal lease   A lease that provides for periodic reevaluation of property, with the rent set as a percentage of the appraised value.

reasonable time   A fair length of time that may be allowed or required for an act to be completed, considering the nature of the act and the surrounding circumstances. It is best to state a definite time for performance of a contract; otherwise, the courts imply a "reasonable time," which could vary considerably from case to case.

> If the parties state in their contract a definite time for performance and add that "time is of the essence," then a court would not allow a reasonable time to perform after the expiration of the definite time stated.

> A lender's decision to exercise a due-on-sale clause must be made within a reasonable time after the event that triggers the clause. (*See* **offer and acceptance**.)

rebate   A reduction of a stipulated charge. In certain states, it is permissible for a broker to rebate a portion of the broker's commission to a principal in the real estate transaction. The rationale is that the payment is not for the performance of any act for which a real estate license is required. It is simply a refund or reduced commission. However, full disclosure to all parties is required if the seller's broker is going to rebate part of the commission to the buyer. (*See* **Real Estate Settlement Procedures Act [RESPA]**.)

recapture   To tax at the same rate as the previous deduction (i.e., ordinary tax). All depreciation or cost recovery taken on depreciable real property in excess of the amount allowed under the straight-line

R

method is subject to the recapture provisions of the Internal Revenue Code, which have the effect of taxing this excess at ordinary income rates, all in the year of the sale. These provisions are designed to prevent the taxpayer from taking advantage of both accelerated depreciation and capital gain treatment.

Even though excess depreciation may be taxed at ordinary rates when the property is sold, a knowledgeable investor realizes that dollars saved in taxes in the early years of investment can earn substantial income before those same dollars go to pay taxes at the time of the recapture of the excess depreciation. In addition, if a tax-deferred exchange should take place, the tax on the excess depreciation taken is deferred.

recapture clause   A clause usually found in percentage leases, especially in shopping center leases, giving the landlord the right to terminate the lease, and thus recapture the premises, if the tenant does not maintain a specified minimum amount of business. The tenant may try to negotiate a provision that keeps the lease in effect by increasing the minimum rent to the amount the owner would have received had the expected sales volume been achieved.

A recapture clause may also be used to give a ground lessee the right to purchase the fee after a set period of time has elapsed, or the landlord may have the option to regain the premises if the tenant gives notice of its intention to assign or sublet to another or surrender a portion of the lease space or term.

A recapture provision in an office lease gives the lessor the right to recover any space that the tenant is unable to occupy or sublease.

recapture rate   An appraisal term describing that rate at which invested capital will be returned over the period of time prudent investors would expect to recapture their investment in a wasting asset. (*See* **capitalization [CAP] rate**.)

recasting   The process of redesigning existing loans, especially where there is a default. The term of the loan may be extended, with the interest rate adjusted periodically to alleviate the pressure on the borrower. Care must be taken to avoid the risk of intervening liens attaining priority over the recast loan. In some cases, the lender may prefer to go along with a delinquent construction loan until the building is sold because a modification and recasting of the loan might jeopardize lien priorities. (*See* **forbearance**.)

receipt   (*recibo*)   A written acknowledgment of having received something. Many purchase contracts serve as a receipt, in addition to being the offer to purchase and acceptance form. Thus, brokers should not sign the receipt portion of a contract unless they have in fact received the buyer's deposit. (*See* **constructive receipt**, **deposit**.)

receiver   An independent party appointed by a court to impartially receive, preserve, and manage property that is involved in litigation, pending final disposition of the matter before the court. Such a case might be a bankruptcy action or a case where a subdivider is enjoined from selling an unregistered subdivision. In some states, a receiver is appointed during the statutory redemption period after the foreclosure sale. Receivers would not need a real estate license to sell real estate under their control, but such sales would require court approval.

reciprocal easements   Easements typically arising upon the development of a planned subdivision, in which easements and restrictions are created as covenants limiting the use of the land for the benefit of all the owners in the entire tract.

reciprocity   The practice of mutual exchanges of privileges. Some states have reciprocal arrangements for recognizing and granting licenses to licensed brokers and salespeople from other states.

recital of consideration A statement of what constitutes the consideration for a particular transaction. Although technically a deed does not require consideration to pass title to real property, it is good practice to recite some consideration, especially to support any covenants or promises in the deed. The consideration recited in the deed need not be the actual consideration and is frequently stated as a nominal amount, such as "for $10 and other good and valuable consideration." (*See* **nominal consideration**.)

reclamation The process of converting wasted natural resources into productive assets, such as desert land reclaimed through irrigation or swampland that is filled in.

recognition A precise tax term meaning that the transaction is a taxable event. If a gain or loss is "recognized," the gain is taxable and the loss is deductible. Usually, recognition occurs at the time of the sale or exchange. Some exceptions are involuntary conversion and some sales between related parties.

recognition clause A clause found in some blanket mortgages and contracts for a deed used to purchase a tract of land for subdivision and development. The clause provides for protection of the rights of the ultimate buyers of individual lots in case of default under the blanket mortgage by the developer. It is similar to a nondisturbance clause in a commercial office building mortgage.

reconciliation
1. The final step in an appraisal process, in which the appraiser brings together the estimates of value received from the direct sales comparison, cost, and income approaches to arrive at a final estimate of value for the subject property. Previously called *correlation*.
2. The balancing of entries in a double-entry accounting system.

reconveyance The act of conveying title in property back to the original owner. Under a deed of trust, the trustor (borrower/mortgagor) conveys title to a third-party trustee as security for a debt. When the debt is paid off, the property is then reconveyed by the trustee to the trustor by means of a reconveyance deed. (*See* **deed of trust**.)

recording The act of entering into the book of public records the written instruments affecting the title to real property, such as deeds, mortgages, contracts for sale, options, and assignments. Many public records apart from the real estate recording system have a bearing on the quality of title, such as public records regarding probate, marriage, taxes, and judgments. All documents must be drawn and executed in conformity with the provision of the recording statutes of the state in which the real estate is located.

    Individual state recording acts require that all instruments in writing affecting any estate, right, title, or interest in land should be recorded in the county where the land is located. Recordation serves constructive notice to everyone interested in the title to a parcel of real estate notice of the various interests of all parties. In addition, the recording acts give legal priority to those interests that are recorded first.

    The system of recording creates a hierarchy of claims against a property with priority to be determined by the order in which the claims are recorded. Except for certain governmental tax liens, which automatically take first priority, the order of recorded priority will not be disturbed unless there is subordination or the recordation of a release. Priority of property tax liens, mechanics' liens, and special assessment liens are not determined by date of recordation because they are considered matters of public record. Other tax liens, such as for income tax and payroll tax, must be recorded to take priority over subsequent recorded interests. (*See* **constructive notice**.)

    The act of recordation raises a presumption (rebuttable) that the instrument has been validly delivered and that it is authentic. Proper recordation protects both innocent purchasers who act in ignorance of an unrecorded instrument and the grantee if the deed is altered or lost. Any conveyance *not* properly recorded is generally *void* as against any subsequent purchaser, lessee or mortgagee, donees, or beneficiaries under a will; interests that arise by operation of law rather than by recordable document, such as dower, curtesy, and homestead rights; prescriptive and implied easements; and title by adverse possession. (In the case of adverse possession, however, the adverse possessor's physical possession of the property ordinarily would have provided constructive notice to the subsequent purchaser of the possessor's interest in the property and thus the possessor would not be in "good faith.")

Failure to record a document does not impair its validity as between the parties thereto and all other parties having notice of its existence. However, if a recorded contract is void for some reason, the mere fact that it is recorded will not make it valid. Under the Torrens system of land registration, however, documents must be properly registered to be effective.

Each county has a public recorder's office, known variously as the *county recorder's office*, *county registrar's office*, or *bureau of conveyances*. The person in charge is generally known as the *recorder*, *registrar*, or *commissioner of deeds*. When a copy of the deed is recorded, the recorder cross-indexes it under the names of both grantor and grantee. Anyone can access these records. The registrar usually charges a flat fee per document or per page. (*See* **chain of title**, **constructive notice**, **conveyance tax**, **grantor-grantee index**, **notary public**, **priority**, **registrar [recorder]**, **subordination agreement**, **subsequent bona fide purchaser**, **Torrens system**.)

record owner   The owner of property as shown by an examination of the records; the one having record title.

record title   Title as it appears from an examination of the public records. (*See* **chain of title**, **title insurance**.)

recourse note   A debt instrument with which the lender can take action against the borrower or endorser personally in addition to foreclosure of the property covering the lender's mortgage. (*See* **deficiency judgment**, **nonrecourse loan**.)

recovery fund   A state-regulated fund generally defined and described in the state real estate license law used as a source of money to indemnify buyers and sellers of real estate who have suffered losses due to a real estate licensee's misrepresentation or fraudulent acts (usually not negligent acts). The recovery fund essentially underwrites the payment of otherwise uncollectible court judgments against a real estate licensee.

Generally, to seek money from the recovery fund, an injured person must first obtain a court judgment and then attempt to collect the money by discovering and executing upon the licensee's assets. If the licensee is judgment-proof, or has insufficient assets to satisfy the judgment, the aggrieved person can file a verified claim in the court in which he obtained the judgment and apply to the court for an order directing payment out of the recovery fund. The court may then order the commission to pay out of the recovery fund an amount not to exceed a specified amount per aggrieved person or transaction. Upon payment from the fund, the wrongdoer's license is usually terminated.

It has been held that a real estate licensee is not an aggrieved person for purposes of recovering from the fund if the claim is based on an unsatisfied judgment against another licensee in a claim of fraudulent real estate transaction. (*See* **real estate education, research, and recovery fund**.)

recreational lease   A contract in which the lessor (usually a developer) leases recreational facilities (tennis courts, gyms, swimming pools) to a tenant for a stipulated time and rent consideration. Recreational leases are found in townhouse developments and subdivisions but primarily in residential condominium projects. Typically, these leases are long-term, triple-net leases with a rental index increase tied to the consumer price index.

Recreational leases in condominiums have been the subject of much litigation from discontented lessees, especially where rents sharply increased in short periods of time. Many leases were successfully challenged as being unconscionable, and both federal and state statutes have been proposed to help curb developer abuses in this area.

rectangular survey method   *See* **government survey method**.

reddendum clause   A clause in a conveyance that reserves something for the grantor, such as rent payable to a lessor or an interest in a life estate to a remainderman.

redemption, equitable right of   The right of mortgagors who have defaulted on the mortgage note to redeem or get back their title to the property by paying off the entire mortgage note before the foreclosure sale. The equitable right of redemption comes into existence immediately upon execution of the mortgage and continues to exist until the mortgage is satisfied and discharged by payment or until the right of redemption is cut off by foreclosure sale. After the property has been sold at a foreclosure sale, however, the mortgagor has no right of redemption, unless state law grants a statutory redemption period. (*See* **foreclosure**.)

redemption period   A period of time established by state law during which a property owner has a right to redeem real estate after a foreclosure or tax sale by paying the sales price, interest, and costs, available in some states. During the redemption period (which may be one year or longer), the court may appoint a receiver to take charge of the property, collect rents, pay operating expenses, and so on. If the defaulting owner can raise the necessary funds to redeem within the statutory period, the redemption money is paid to the court.

Historically, the right of redemption is inherited from the ancient chancery proceedings in England in which the court sale ended the equitable right of redemption. In many states, a statutory redemption period, which begins after the sale, is provided by state law to give the mortgagor a further opportunity to regain title to his or her land.

redevelopment   The improvement of cleared or undeveloped land, usually in an urban renewal area.

redevelopment agency   A quasigovernmental agency whose primary purposes are to develop property or improve housing opportunities in urban renewal areas and to relocate residents displaced by the redevelopment of the area. The redevelopment agency usually has the power of eminent domain and often condemns smaller parcels and assembles these lots into one large development project. The redevelopment agency might enter into a development agreement with a professional developer and restrict the amount of profit the developer can derive from the project.

R

red flag   A condition that warns a reasonably observant person of a potential problem, thus suggesting further investigation. A broker who spots uneven floors or water-stained ceilings is on notice to inquire about soil settlement and roof leakage problems. (*See* **material fact, misrepresentation**.)

red herring   A preliminary prospectus for the sale of a security that is filed with the Securities and Exchange Commission but the registration of which has not yet become effective. The term derives from the red printing along the left margin of the prospectus stating that a registration statement has been filed but is subject to change and that the securities covered in the prospectus may not be sold before the registration statement becomes effective.

rediscount rate   The rate of interest charged by the Federal Reserve Bank for loans to member banks; also called the **discount rate**. The rediscount rate has an indirect effect on the interest rates charged by member banks to the public and the supply of funds for loans.

red label   *See* **HUD code, manufactured housing**.

redlining   (*redlining*)   A practice by some lending institutions that restricts the number of loans, or the loan-to-value ratio in certain areas of a community. The usual justification for redlining is that the lender wants to limit the risks in an area that is deteriorating. The lender discriminates against a whole class of risks rather than distinguishing among individual risks.

A redlining policy based on the fact that a certain area of a community is becoming racially integrated is illegal and in violation of Title VIII of the federal Civil Rights Act and the Community Reinvestment Act. For example, it is illegal redlining for a lending institution to require a higher down payment because the home the borrower is buying is located in a racially mixed area. The racial composition of the neighborhood where the loan is to be made is always an improper underwriting consideration.

Under the Home Mortgage Disclosure Act, lenders must disclose information as to how they determine their pattern of making loans in given geographic areas. A related area of concern is insurance redlining, which may be covered under the provision in the federal fair housing law prohibiting conduct that would tend to make housing unavailable.

The Office of Thrift Supervision has also issued a regulation prohibiting redlining. It states that refusal to lend in a particular area solely because of the age of the homes or the income level in a neighborhood may be discriminatory in effect, given that minority persons are more likely to purchase used housing and to live in low-income neighborhoods. (*See* **federal fair housing law.**)

reduction certificate   An instrument that shows the current amount of the unpaid balance of a mortgage, the rate of interest, and the date of maturity. A reduction certificate is normally required from a mortgagee when a prospective purchaser is to assume or to take title subject to an existing mortgage. The mortgagee, then, cannot later claim that the mortgage amount or terms were different from those stated in the certificate. A reduction certificate is similar to a certificate of no defense except that it is executed by the mortgagee. The reduction certificate is useful because only the original amount of the loan is a matter of public record. Any reduction of principal is known only between the parties. The instrument is usually acknowledged, but need not be recorded. It is also called a *statement of condition from the lender*, or a **beneficiary statement** in a deed of trust situation. (*See* **certificate of no defense.**)

reentry   The repossession of real property in accordance with a legal right reserved when the original possession was transferred. The grantor of a fee simple subject to a condition has the right to reentry upon the breach of that condition. In essence, reentry is a power of termination.

The right of reentry should be distinguished from the right of entry that a landlord possesses to go in and inspect the leased premises. (*See* **right of reentry.**)

referee   A disinterested, neutral party appointed by a court to arbitrate, investigate, find facts, or settle some dispute or legal matter. A referee in bankruptcy acts as a temporary administrator of a bankrupt's assets, which may be sold to satisfy the claims of creditors. (*See* **bankruptcy.**)

referral   The act of recommending or referring; a sales lead. A client who has been obtained through the efforts or recommendation of another person. A broker can usually compensate or split commissions with a person who refers a client only if that person is licensed as a real estate broker. If the person is a licensed salesperson, the referral fee must be paid through the salesperson's supervising broker. Although a seller can pay a referral fee to anyone, the person receiving the fee may be deemed to be acting as a real estate salesperson; if that is the case, that person must have a real estate license. (*See* **finder's fee.**)

R

referral agency
1. A licensed brokerage company in which licensed salespeople agree to perform no other brokerage service but to obtain leads on prospective buyers and sellers. These leads are then assigned to other agents, and the referral agency receives a fee upon a sale. (*See* **limited referral agent**.)
2. A brokerage company participating in a national or regional network of relocation services.

refinance   To obtain a new loan to pay off an existing loan; to pay off one loan with the proceeds from another. Properties are frequently refinanced when interest rates drop and/or the property has appreciated in value. Sometimes, a buyer purchases a property by way of a contract for deed with the expectation of either selling the property before the balance under the contract for deed becomes due or refinancing at better terms and interest rates than exist at the time the agreement of sale is entered into.

Income properties are frequently refinanced by investors seeking additional capital with which to purchase other investment properties. Large real estate holdings are often amassed in this manner, a technique known as *pyramiding through refinancing.*

Fannie Mae, a federally chartered secondary purchaser of home loans, will refinance a loan it holds for a new purchaser, usually at less than the market rate. A form of wraparound mortgage, this new loan would take the place of a second mortgage sometimes used to cover the difference between a purchase price and an assumable mortgage.

reformation   A legal action necessary to correct or modify a contract or a deed that has not accurately reflected the intentions of the parties, due to some mechanical error, such as a typographical error in the legal description. If one of the parties will not execute a correction deed, the other party can seek a court order reforming such a deed, also called a *reformation deed.* A grantor under a general warranty deed usually agrees to perform any necessary act of reformation pursuant to the covenant of further assurance. (*See* **correction deed**.)

regional shopping center   A large shopping center containing from 70 to 225 stores and more than 400,000 square feet of leasable area.

registered land   Land that is registered in the Torrens system. (*See* **Torrens system**.)

registrar (recorder)   The person usually having the duty to maintain accurate official records of all deeds, mortgages, contracts for deed, and other instruments relating to real estate titles filed for recordation; often associated with the Torrens system of title registration. (*See* **recording**.)

regression   (*regresión*)   A principle of appraisal stating that, between dissimilar properties, the worth of the better property is adversely affected by the presence of the lesser-quality property. Thus, in a neighborhood where the homes average in the $100,000 range, a better-built structure, which in another neighborhood would be worth at least $140,000, would tend to be valued closer to $100,000. The principle of progression is the opposite. (*See* **direct sales comparison approach**, **over-improvement**, **progression**)

regular system (REG)   A system of recordation of documents affecting land not registered in the Torrens system; also known as the *unregistered system.* Although the recording fees in the regular system are generally greater than in the Torrens system, the requirements for recordation are typically less stringent. (*See* **recording**.)

regulation   (*reglamento*)   A rule or order prescribed for management or government, as in the rules and regulations of the real estate commission. In many states, once the commission's regulations are approved by the governor following a public hearing, they have the force and effect of law.

R

Regulation A   A special exemption from standard SEC registration of a security issue where the aggregate amount of the offering is less than $1.5 million. Even if the issue qualifies under Regulation A, the developer still must file a short-form registration with the regional SEC office and provide prospective purchasers with an offering circular containing much of the same information contained in a formal prospectus. Thus, Regulation A is not really an exemption from registration but a simpler form of registration. (*See* **real property securities registration**.)

Regulation B   A Federal Reserve System regulation covering the Equal Credit Opportunity Act. (*See* **Equal Credit Opportunity Act [ECOA]**.)

Regulation D   An SEC regulation containing a set of rules exempting from registration certain limited security offerings.

Regulation Q   A federal regulation, phased out in 1986, which allowed certain federal agencies to establish different interest rates on savings deposits for commercial banks and thrift (savings and loan) institutions.

Regulation T   A federal regulation, administered by the Federal Reserve Board, governing the extension of credit arrangements for the extension of credit by securities brokers and dealers. The Federal Reserve Board lists only certain securities upon which security dealers can extend credit, and then restricts the amount of credit that may be extended by means of margin requirements. The Federal Reserve Board has effectively exempted condominium securities from Regulation T.

Regulation Z   (*reglamento Z*)   *See* **Truth in Lending Act**.

rehabilitate (rehab)   To restore to a former or improved condition, such as when buildings are renovated and modernized. Rehabilitation may include new construction, buildings, or additions, but it is usually performed without changing the basic plan, form, or style of a structure. In urban renewal projects, neighborhood rehabilitation is the restoration to good condition of deteriorated structures, neighborhoods, and public facilities, and structural rehabilitation; additionally, it may extend to street improvements and such amenities as parks and playgrounds.

    The Internal Revenue Code provides for certain tax benefits in connection with the rehabilitation of older real property.

reinstatement   To bring something back to its prior position, as in restoring a lapsed insurance policy or restoring a defaulted loan to paid-up status. A borrower in default under a deed of trust can avoid a foreclosure sale by reinstating the loan and bringing it to a current status before foreclosure. Afterward, in some states, the borrower has a one-year statutory right of redemption, but the entire debt would have to be paid, not just the amount in default. (*See* **deed of trust**.)

reinsurance   A contract by which the original insurer (the ceding company) obtains insurance from another insurer (the reinsuring company) against loss on the ceding company's original policy. The reinsurance company takes on all the rights, duties, and liabilities of the ceding company under the original policy.

reissue rate   A reduced charge by a title insurance company for a new policy if a previous policy on the same property was recently issued.

REIT   *See* **real estate investment trust (REIT)**.

related parties   Parties standing in a certain defined relationship to each other; parties may be related by blood, by fiduciary relationships, or by ownership interest in a corporation. Under the Internal Revenue Code, any loss on the sale of property between family relations may be nondeductible. In addition, the gain may be treated as ordinary income in the case of a sale or exchange of depreciable property between certain related parties. The sole test is the relationship of the parties and not the fairness of the sales price or rental. Under the tax law, related parties include all entities more than 50 percent owned, directly or indirectly, by the taxpayer. (*See* **imputed interest**, **installment sale**.)

The tax law does permit installment sales between certain related parties (children, parents, spouses), provided the property is not resold or transferred within two years of the original sale. Installment treatment is denied, however, if depreciable property is sold to other specified related persons. For installment sales between related parties where the payments are contingent in amount, but where their fair market value is ascertainable, basis is recovered ratably, and the buyer cannot increase basis in the property before the seller includes the amount in income.

relation-back doctrine   A doctrine establishing the effects of the grantor's death on an escrow transaction. In a valid escrow, there is an irrevocable deposit of the executed deed, purchase money, and instructions into the escrow pending performance of the escrow conditions. Under the relation-back doctrine, death of the grantor does not terminate the escrow or revoke the agent's authority to deliver an executed deed. When the escrow conditions are performed, title passes to the grantee, and the deed can be formally delivered to the grantee without any probate court approval. Delivery of deed to the grantee relates back to the date it was originally deposited with the escrow agent, and it is as though the grantor made delivery to the grantee before the grantor's death. Otherwise, an action for specific performance would have to be brought against the grantor's heirs. In addition, delivery of a deed into escrow also cuts off the rights of any of the sellers attaching creditors and thus passing clear title as of the date of the escrow. (*See* **delivery, equitable conversion, escrow**.)

release   (*liberación*)   The discharge or relinquishment of a right, claim, or privilege. Because a formal release is a contract relieving a person from any further legal obligation, it must contain a valuable consideration. Releases involving real property transactions should be acknowledged and recorded, and should also note the liber and page number of the document released. (*See* **quitclaim deed**.)

release clause
1. A provision found in many blanket mortgages enabling the mortgagor to obtain partial releases of specific parcels from the mortgage upon a payment larger than the pro rata portion of the loan. Most mortgagees insert a clause that no partial release will be issued if the mortgagor is in default under the mortgage.

   For example, as the developer sells off the subdivided lots, a portion of sales proceeds partially satisfies the mortgage. In return, the mortgagee executes and records a release of the particular parcel sold, so that the purchasers can obtain clear title. Usually the release clause contains a formula for the release payments, such as the payment of a sum that is in the proportion that the area of the land to be released bears to the total area of the land under the blanket mortgage. For example, if five parcels were covered under the blanket mortgage, the lender might require the payment of one-fourth of the loan before releasing one parcel. (*See* **blanket mortgage, partial release clause**.)
2. In a purchase agreement, a contingency provision allowing the seller to continue to market the property and accept other offers. Upon acceptance of an offer from another buyer, the original buyer has a period of time, such as 72 hours, in which to waive the contingency, such as the sale of the buyer's present home, or to release the sellers from the agreement so they can sell to the second buyer. (*See* **contingency**.)

release deed   *See* **deed of reconveyance**.

reliction   The gradual recession of water from the usual watermark and, therefore, an increase of the land. When land once covered by water becomes uncovered, the uncovered land is treated as alluvion, and the rules of accretion apply to the ownership of this new land. This new land usually belongs to the riparian owner. (*See* **accretion**.)

relinquished property   The first property transferred in a delayed tax-deferred exchange; the up-leg property. The property for which the exchange is made is called the *replacement property*. (*See* **delayed exchange**.)

relocation clause   A lease provision giving the landlord the right to relocate a tenant. The landlord may want this right when an older building is renovated or, when smaller tenants are relocated, to provide flexibility in accommodating larger tenants' expansion requirements.

relocation company   A company retained by large corporations to help their employees move from one location to another. A primary function of this service is to purchase the transferee's home so that the transferee has the funds to locate new housing and does not have to worry about the uncertainties of first selling the present home. The employer corporation usually pays all the costs incurred by the relocation company in its buying and reselling of the employee's present home.

The relocation company's offer to purchase is usually based on two or more independent fee appraisals. Once the relocation company has purchased the property, it is concerned with effectively marketing the property with a combination of sales price, carrying costs, closing costs, and costs of repair and improvements as they relate to the estimated cost of the company's services. They expect that the listing broker will market the property in a variety of ways, including utilizing the multiple listing service (MLS) and the Internet.

remainder estate   A future interest in real estate created at the same time and by the same instrument as another estate, and limited to arise immediately upon the termination of the prior estate. Whereas a reversion is an estate retained by the grantor when conveying a lesser estate, a *remainder* is a future estate created by the grantor in favor of some third party.

A remainder may be vested or contingent. It is *vested* if the only uncertainty is the actual date of the termination of the prior estate; it is *contingent* when there is some other uncertainty. For example, *H* wills (devises) his farm to his son as a life estate, with the remainder going to his son's living children. If there are no children, then the estate goes to *H*'s brother *J. J*, who has a contingent remainder, which ceases if *H*'s son dies leaving a child.

A gift of a remainder interest in real property is subject to federal gift-tax rules. Because it does not qualify as a "present interest," the remainder interest does not qualify for the $10,000 annual exclusion. The IRS computes the value of the remainder interest by using tables based on the life expectancy of the donor and a discount factor of 6 percent. (*See* **remainderman**, **reversion**, **rule against perpetuities**.)

R

remainderman   One entitled to take an estate in remainder. For example, B owns a property in fee simple and conveys the property to "C and, upon C's death, to D and her heirs." D has a remainder estate, which is vested because the estate *automatically* passes to D and her heirs upon the death of C. Although having only a future interest, the remainderman still has some present rights, such as the right to bring court action against the current possessor for committing waste. (*See* **life estate**.)

remediation
1. The process of remedying or curing a condition, such as sealing or removing lead-based paint or installing a radon mitigation system.
2. The process of implementing a plan to clean up a site that has been identified as containing hazardous substances. The Phase III audit is the stage in which a remediation plan is developed and executed. (*See* **Comprehensive Environmental Response, Compensation, and Liability Act [CERCLA], mitigation**.)

remedy   *See* **election of remedies**.

remise   To give up; to remit. Typical language found in a quitclaim deed. (*See* **quitclaim deed**.)

REMT   *See* **real estate mortgage trust (REMT).**

rendering   An artist's or architect's interpretation, in perspective, of a completed development, usually done in color or ink.

renegotiable rate mortgage (RRM)   A short-term loan secured by a long-term adjustable-rate mortgage, with interest renegotiated at the time of established automatic renewal periods. Although the RRM models itself after the Canadian Rollover Mortgage, there is a big difference: Under the Canadian plan, the mortgage itself is renewed rather than short-term interest adjustments of a long-term mortgage. Since introduction of the adjustable-rate loan, many of the original restrictions on RRM no longer apply. (*See* **adjustable-rate loan.**)

renegotiation of lease   The review of an existing lease after a specified period of time to negotiate the lease terms anew. The most common reason for renegotiating a lease is to establish a new annual rent for an additional period based on changed economic conditions. Many leases provide that renegotiated rent is to be based on mutual agreement and, failing that, by an independent appraisal based on a rate of return to the fee owner equal to some specific rate fixed when the lease is first negotiated. An alternative method uses outside indicators by which the rent increases at set intervals (e.g., U.S. Labor Department cost-of-living indicator). If listing a leasehold, a broker should be careful to verify the renegotiation period and terms, if any. (*See* **ground lease**, **leasehold.**)

renewal option   A lease covenant that gives the lessee the right to extend the lease term for a certain period, on specified terms, provided the tenant is not in default. The landlord, however, usually cannot enforce an automatic renewal clause against the tenant without also giving prior notice of the renewal. The covenant should state whether the option to renew is transferable if the lease is assigned. (*See* **extension.**)

renovation, repair, and painting rule (RRP)   An EPA requirement that firms performing renovation, repair, and painting projects that may disturb lead-based paint in homes built before 1978, child-care facilities, or schools be certified by the EPA. Such renovators must be trained by EPA-approved training providers to follow lead-safe work practices, such as containing the work area, minimizing dust, and thoroughly cleaning up. Renovators must provide owners and occupants of child-care facilities and parents and guardians of children under six the pamphlet *Renovate Right: Important Lead Hazard Information for Families, Child Care Providers, and Schools.*

rent   (*alquiler, ronta*)   Fixed periodic payment made by a tenant or an occupant of property to the owner for the possession and use, usually by prior agreement of the parties. Most leases state that rent is due in advance. Unless the lease specifies otherwise, the rent must be paid to the landlord at the leased premises. If the landlord makes an expressed or implied authorization for the rent money to be mailed to her, delivery to the post office constitutes payment, and the landlord suffers the risk of any subsequent delay or loss. (*See* **contract rent.**)

rentable area   As standardized by the Building Owners and Managers Association International, for an office on a multiple-tenancy floor, the area is computed by measuring to the inside finish of permanent outer building walls, or to the glass line if at least 50 percent of the outer building wall is glass, to the office side of corridors and/or permanent partitions, and to the center of partitions that separate the premises from adjoining rentable areas. No deductions are made for columns and projections necessary to the buildings. (*See* **usable area.**)

rental agent (leasing agent)   Any person who for compensation or other valuable consideration acts or attempts to act as an intermediary between a person seeking to lease, sublease, or assign a housing accommodation and a person seeking to acquire a lease, sublease, or assignment of a housing accommodation. Some states may require a special rental agency or property management license.

R

rental agreement   A written or oral agreement that establishes or modifies the terms, conditions, rules, regulations, or any other provisions concerning the use and occupancy of a dwelling unit and premises; a lease on residential property. Certain states have "plain language" laws, which require rental agreements to be written in clear, understandable, everyday language and appropriately captioned and paragraphed. (*See* **lease**.)

rental pool   A rental arrangement whereby participating owners of rental apartments agree to have their units available for rental as determined by the rental agent, and then share in the profits and losses of all the rental apartments in the pool according to an agreed-on formula. Some plans base payment of profits on the number of days the unit was available for rental. If a condominium is offered for sale and the offer includes participation in a rental pool arrangement, that condominium offering is considered an "investment contract" and therefore a security. Consequently, the offeror must have the condominium registered with the SEC as a security. After a project has been sold, the owners can form a rental pool without the need for SEC registration. (*See* **real property securities registration**.)

rent control   Regulation by state or local governmental agencies restricting the amount of rent or the rental increase; such regulation has been upheld as a valid exercise of the state's police power in the jurisdictions that currently employ rent controls.

Two major themes in rent control have emerged nationwide:
1. The use of rent control to regulate the quality of rental dwellings, with controls to be implemented only against those units that do not conform to applicable building codes, as in the case of New York City
2. The use of rent control across the board to remedy high rents caused by the gross imbalance between supply and demand in housing, such as is seen in Massachusetts and California

An interesting merger of the two themes has occurred in New Jersey, where the enabling statute leans heavily toward quality control, while local jurisdictions have enacted rent control ordinances to cope with emergency housing shortages and inflated rents in Fort Lee and in other towns close to New York City.

rent escalation   Adjustment of rent by the lessor to reflect changes in cost of living or property maintenance costs. (*See* **index lease**.)

rent roll   A list of tenants showing the unit occupied and the rent paid by each. Certified rent rolls are independently verified and are sometimes required by lenders.

rent-up
1. The process of filling a new building with tenants.
2. The requirement of a lender, typically a leasehold mortgagee, that the mortgagor (developer/owner) achieve the leasing of a stated amount of space in the building as a prerequisite to a permanent lender's "taking out" the interim construction lender. The developer must present certified rent rolls, which are usually checked by the lender's servicing agent. If the developer does not meet the rent achievement amount, a floor loan for a reduced amount has to be disbursed and gap financing sought. (*See* **floor loan**, **gap financing**.)

REO   *See* **real estate owned (REO)**.

repairs   Current expenditures to restore to an original condition; minor alterations made to maintain the property rather than to extend the useful life of the property. Generally, the cost of repairs is not tax-deductible for the homeowner.

For income-producing property, the cost of repairs normally is tax deductible as a business expense. Repairs involving changes in either the material form of the building or the renewal of any substantial part of it that results in an increase in the asset's useful life may be treated as capital expenditures increasing the basis of the property. An example would be a new addition or a replacement of carpeting or roof. (*See* **capital expenditure**.)

There is no legal requirement that repairs be made by the lessee or lessor. The landlord normally is not obligated to make any repairs whatsoever in the leased premises unless the lease provides to the contrary. However, under some states' residential landlord-tenant codes, the landlord has a specific duty to keep the premises in a habitable condition; and the lessee must return the property in the same condition as it was leased, less reasonable wear and tear. To eliminate disputes, the lease should specify who is responsible for the various types of repair. Tenants are not under a duty to make extraordinary repairs, however, unless they willfully or negligently caused the damage.

The parties should specify in the sales contract, when applicable, the items the seller should repair before the closing. Sellers of property to be purchased with a VA or FHA loan should be aware that their net sales proceeds will be reduced by the cost of any repairs required by VA or FHA.

replacement cost	(*costo de reposición*)	The cost of constructing a building with current materials and techniques that is identical in functional utility to the structure being appraised and that is designed in accordance with current materials, styles, and standards. Functional obsolescence is generally not considered, because replacement presumes replacing the building's utility at current building standards. (*See* **reproduction cost**.)

replacement property	The property exchanged for in a tax-deferred exchange. The replacement property must be identified and acquired within strict time limitations from the date of sale of the relinquished property. (*See* **delayed exchange**.)

replevin	Legal proceedings brought to recover possession of personal property unlawfully taken, as when a landlord has unlawfully taken the personal belongings of the tenant due to the tenant's failure to pay the rent. (*See* **distraint**.)

reporting requirements	Internal Revenue Service rules that require the settlement agent to report sales or exchanges of all real property or a statement of exemption. Responsibility to file the IRS Form 1099S lies with the settlement agent, the one preparing the closing statement. If there is no settlement agent, the order of responsibility as to who must submit the report is attorneys, title companies, mortgage lenders, and real estate brokers.

reproduction cost	(*costo de reproducción*)	The current cost of building a replica of the subject structure, using the same materials and construction standards. Most appraisers estimate reproduction cost by the comparative cost method, in which estimates are made on the basis of the current cost to construct buildings of similar size, design, and quality. Other methods are the quantity-survey method and the unit-in-place method. Comparisons are usually made on a square-foot or cubic-foot basis.

Reproduction cost is not synonymous with replacement cost. *Reproduction cost* refers to exact duplication; *replacement cost* refers to a building that has the same functional ability but possibly is of different size, materials, or design. After arriving at the reproduction cost for a new building, deduct the amount of accrued depreciation due to physical, functional, and economic causes to complete the appraisal. (*See* **cost approach**, **replacement cost**.)

rescind	(*rescindir, revocar*)	To annul, cancel a contract. One may rescind a contract and revoke an offer. (*See* **rescission**, **revocation**, **revoke**.)

rescission	The legal remedy of canceling, terminating, or annulling a contract and restoring the parties to their original positions; a return to the status quo. Contracts may be rescinded due to mistake, fraud, or misrepresentation; there is no need to show any money damage. When seeking to rescind a contract with a defaulting buyer, the seller must return all payments made by the buyer, minus a fair rental for the time the buyer has been in possession. This is not true, however, under a contract for deed. Sellers often insert a forfeiture clause authorizing them to keep all payments if the buyer defaults. Courts, however, are reluctant to enforce such a forfeiture clause—especially where it is in the nature of a penalty—and often order rescission instead.

Sometimes, purchasers are given a "cooling-off" period during which they can rescind the contract for any reason whatsoever. For instance, the purchaser of subdivided land, which is or should have been registered with HUD, is given a rescission period of seven calendar days from the time of receipt of the property report. In addition, in VA and FHA financing, the buyer is given a right to cancel should the purchase price exceed the official valuation by an FHA or a VA-approved appraiser. There is also a right of rescission under the federal Truth in Lending Act and most state time-sharing laws. (*See* **contract for deed, forfeiture, Interstate Land Sales Full Disclosure Act, Truth in Lending Act**.)

rescission clause
1. A specific clause occasionally found in a contract for deed that requires the seller to return all the buyer's payments, minus the cost and a fair rental value, if the buyer defaults. Because such a clause may overfavor the buyer, it is not in many contracts for deed.
2. A clause in a contract, required by some state subdivided land sales laws, that informs purchasers of their rescission rights as provided by state law.

reservation   The creation, on behalf of the grantor, of a new right issuing from what was granted. A reservation thus is something that did not exist as an independent right before the conveyance. For example, Smith conveys to Jones a ten-acre parcel "reserving to Smith a life estate therein." A right or interest cannot be reserved in favor of a third party.

Title to all property passes to the grantee, but a use may be reserved in the grantor. In an exception, title to a portion is retained by the grantor. (*See* **exception**.)

reservation money   Money used as an earnest money deposit to hold a property being offered for sale. Sometimes a prospective buyer asks a broker to hold reservation money pending the offering of a particular property for sale. When the property goes on the market, the broker uses the reservation money to bind the sale. (*See* **earnest money deposit**.)

reserve for replacements   (*reserva para substitución*)   A typical entry in an operating statement to provide for the replacement of short-life items, such as air-conditioning units, carpeting, and appliances; an allowance that is necessary to maintain a projected level of income.

reserve fund   Monies a lender often requires a borrower to set aside as a cushion of capital for future payment of items such as taxes, insurance, and deferred maintenance. Sometimes a reserve fund is called an *impound account* or *customer's trust fund*. Replacement reserves should be maintained, especially when the owner is installing items having a short life expectancy—for example, appliances, furniture, or carpeting in a furnished apartment.

residence   (*residencia*)   One's home or place of abode. *Residence* is defined differently for tax, license, and education qualification purposes. A person can have several residences but only one domicile. A residence includes such things as a trailer, a cooperative, a condominium, or even a household. (*See* **domicile, dwelling**.)

residence property   Raw land or improved property with buildings designed for human occupation, such as single-family homes or condominium units.

residence, sale of   The Taxpayer Relief Act of 1997 made major changes in the tax treatment of gain from the sale of one's principal residence. Where the owner has resided in the principal residence for two of the last five years, the act provides for a capital gains tax exclusion of up to $500,000 for married taxpayers filing jointly and $250,000 for those filing singly. Taxpayers are no longer required to buy another property, and there is no age requirement. Essentially, this provision can be used over and over again. If the taxpayer occupied the property for two years total (need not be continuous), it would be irrelevant that the taxpayer had rented out the property for a portion of the five-year period.

There is a two-year waiting period once the taxpayer has claimed an exclusion. The waiting period can be waived and the exclusion prorated if the taxpayer sells due to unforeseen circumstances such as health reasons or required job relocation. A taxpayer who sells the principal residence before occupying it for the required two years (out of the last five), or before two years have passed since claiming a previous exclusion, will be forced to pay the tax on any gain. If there is a loss, there is no allowable deduction.

resident manager   A salaried agent of the owner employed to manage a single building. If merely acting as custodian or caretaker, a resident manager generally does not need to be licensed under state real estate license laws. (*See* **property management**.)

residual
1. That which is left over, such as the residual value of property after its economic life is completed.
2. Deferred commissions—that is, commissions earned but for which payment is put off for a stated period. (*See* **deferred commission**.)

residual process   An appraisal process, used in the income approach, to estimate the value of the land and/or the building, as indicated by the capitalization of the residual net income attributable to it. (*See* **appraisal, building residual technique, capitalization, land residual technique, property residual technique**.)

Resolution Trust Corporation (RTC)   Created in 1989 as a part of the Financial Institutions Reform, Recovery, and Enforcement Act (FIRREA) for the purpose of receiving and disposing of the assets of failed savings associations. In 1995, its duties, including insurance of deposits in thrift institutions, were transferred to the Savings Association Insurance Fund (SAIF). (*See* **Financial Institutions Reform, Recovery, and Enforcement Act [FIRREA]; loan pools, Savings Association Insurance Fund [SAIF]**.)

resort property   Property that lends itself to vacationing, recreation, and/or leisure enjoyment because of either its natural resources or beauty (mountains, lakes, or sea) or its improvements (tennis courts, golf courses, manmade ski hills).

Resource Conservation and Recovery Act (RCRA)   *See* Appendix D.

RESPA   *See* **Real Estate Settlement Procedures Act (RESPA)**.

respondeat superior   A principle of agency law that states that the employer (principal) is liable in certain cases for the wrongful acts of an employee (agent) committed during the course of employment, so long as those acts of the agent were performed within the scope of the agent's authority. (*See* **scope of authority, vicarious liability**.)

restraint of trade   Contracts or combinations that are designed to eliminate or stifle competition, to create a monopoly, to control prices, or otherwise to hamper or obstruct the free operation of business. Restraint of trade is generally illegal under federal and state antitrust laws. (*See* **antitrust laws**.)

restraint on alienation   A limitation or condition placed on the right to transfer property. Restraints can take the form of conditions and covenants in deeds or restraints on use of the property. Restrictions placed on the vesting of an estate until some remote time are regulated by the rule against perpetuities, which requires the vesting of contingent interests to take place, if at all, within the period of lives-in-being plus 21 years.

R

One "stick" in the bundle of rights in the ownership of real property is the right to convey; therefore, the courts will not enforce any unreasonable restrictions placed by the grantor on this right. For example, a condition in a deed that the grantee may sell only to tall people would be an unreasonable restraint on alienation and, hence, the condition—but not the deed—is void. Restraints based on race, religion, sex, handicap, familial status, and ancestry are void under antidiscrimination laws.

Some state courts have held that the automatic exercise of a due-on-sale clause by a mortgagee upon a sale of the property covered by the mortgagee is an illegal restraint on alienation. Some courts have refused to enforce the due-on-sale clause, holding that the lender must show some impairment to its security in order to exercise its due-on-sale clause. (*See* **rule against perpetuities**.)

restriction   A limitation on the use of property. Private restrictions are created by means of covenants, conditions, and restrictions (CC&Rs) written into real property instruments, such as deeds and leases. Restrictions are usually enforced by means of court injunction. Restrictions can be terminated by a quitclaim deed executed by the necessary parties. It is always best to consult a title company to determine whose signatures are necessary on the deed. Restrictive covenants that discriminate by restricting the conveyance to or use by individuals of a specified race, color, sex, religion, handicap, familial status, marital status, or ancestry are void.

Private restrictions can be found in deed restrictions, mortgage restrictions, and/or declarations of restrictions used in developments such as subdivisions, PUDs, shopping centers, and industrial parks. Examples of CC&Rs include restricting the number and size of structures to be placed on the land, the cost of structures, fence heights, setbacks, against use of the property for the sale of intoxicating beverages, and the like. Restriction language should be precise because interpretations frequently differ. (*See* **building line**.)

Public restrictions are created by means of zoning ordinances. Unlike private restrictions, they must tend to promote the public health, welfare, and safety. Restrictive covenants tending to create a monopoly on any line of commerce or to lessen competition are generally illegal. For example, a restriction stating that the grantee cannot conduct any business except a funeral parlor on the deeded property may be in violation of the law. (*See* **building restrictions**, **declaration of restrictions**, **deed restrictions**, **restrictive covenant**.)

restrictive covenant   (*pacto restrictivo*)   A private agreement, usually contained in a deed or a lease, restricting the use and occupancy of real property (sometimes called *private zoning*). Such a covenant is said to *run with the land* and binds all subsequent purchasers, their heirs, and assigns. It also normally covers such things as lot size, building lines, type of architecture, and uses to which the property may be put.

Restrictive covenants may generally be terminated by obtaining quitclaim deeds from all benefiting owners. However, this may be impractical, because the termination must be unanimous, and the consent of the underlying mortgagees may be required as well. The covenants may also be terminated by acquiescence of repeated violators and by merger of the burdened and benefiting properties. Often, subdividers specify that deed restrictions will expire after a set length of time, or such expiration also may be specified by state law. This is done to avoid tying up land use needlessly in the distant future. Restrictive covenants are strictly construed against persons seeking to enforce them. All ambiguities, then, are resolved against the restriction and in favor of the person seeking the free and unrestricted use of the property.

resubdivision   The act of taking an existing subdivision and either replatting it (that is, changing the lots from the old grid pattern to the more modern irregular lots) or dividing it even further (that is, taking 20-acre lots and dividing them into 5-acre parcels). For purposes of county subdivision approval and state and federal land sales registration, a resubdivision is the same as a new subdivision. (*See* **subdivision**.)

resulting trust   A trust that is implied by law, resulting from the acts or relationships of the parties involved. A situation, for example, in which M supplies the money to buy a certain highrise apartment building, with title taken in P's name for convenience, would be a resulting trust in which P holds the property in trust for M.

retainage   A portion or a percentage of payments withheld by the landowner until the construction contract has been satisfactorily completed and the period for filing mechanics' liens has expired (or when the lien has been released by the contractor and subcontractors). Likewise, the contractor holds back a portion of its payments to subcontractors until the subcontractor's work has been completed and a waiver of any mechanics' liens has been obtained.

    The amount of retainage is often 10 percent of each progress payment. In some situations, rather than taking the retainage out of the progress payments, the owner simply pays the last one or two payments into escrow for release when the lien period has expired. Retainages are also called **holdbacks**.

retaining wall
1. Any wall erected to hold back or support a bank of earth.
2. Any enclosing wall built to resist the lateral pressure of internal loads.

retaliatory eviction   An act whereby a landlord evicts a tenant in response to some complaint made by the tenant. Many state laws, as well as the Uniform Residential Landlord and Tenant Act, provide that the landlord cannot evict the tenant, demand an increase in rent, or decrease tenant services for any of the following reasons:
- if the tenant has complained in good faith to the proper authorities of conditions that constitute a violation of a health law or regulation;
- if the authorities have filed a notice or complaint of a health or building code violation resulting from a tenant's complaint; or
- if the tenant has in good faith requested necessary repairs.

    The tenant would generally be entitled to damages for such an eviction.

    However, even after a complaint is made by the tenant, a landlord can still evict a tenant for good cause, such as nonpayment of rent or violation of the building rules. (*See* **Uniform Landlord Tenant Act [ULTA]**.)

return-of-capital method   *See* **deferred-payment method**.

revenue stamp   *See* **federal revenue stamp**.

reverse annuity mortgage (RAM)   A form of mortgage that enables elderly homeowners to borrow against the equity in their homes so they can receive monthly payments needed to help meet living costs. Under this plan, the inflow and outflow of funds is in reverse to the standard conventional loan. The homeowner receives periodic (not necessarily equal) payments based on accumulated equity; the payments are made directly by the lender or through the purchase of an annuity from an insurance company. In most cases, interest is added to the principal periodically, relieving the borrower of making any mortgage payments. The loan comes due either upon a specific date or upon the occurrence of a specific event, such as the sale of the property or the death of the borrower.

reverse leverage   A situation that arises when financing is too costly—when the total yield on a cash investment is less than the interest rate on borrowed funds. Web site: *www.reversemortgage.org* (*See* **negative cash flow**.)

reversion   The estate remaining in the grantor or the estate of a testator, who has conveyed a lesser estate from the original. A future estate in real property created by operation of law when a grantor conveys a lesser estate than he has. Because a reversion is created by operation of law, no express words of creation are needed. The residue left in the grantor is called a *reversion*, which commences in possession in the future upon the end of a particular estate granted or devised, whether it be freehold or less than freehold. For example, Adam grants Eve a life estate. Upon her death, the estate reverts to Adam.

A grantor may stipulate a condition in a deed that would result in the reversion of the property to the grantor if not in compliance. For example, Adam grants Eunice the property and in the deed stipulates that Eunice may not use the premises as a restaurant. If she does, title automatically reverts to the grantor. Such a condition creates what is called a possibility of reverter in the grantor. In some states, the courts will not enforce a *possibility of reverter*. They would, however, enjoin Eunice from violating the condition and could even award the grantor damages for breach of the condition. In effect, the courts tend to interpret the condition more like a covenant. (*See* **covenants and conditions**, **remainder estate**.)

Under common-law principles, all improvements placed by the lessee on the leased premises would revert to the lessor upon the expiration of the lease. Some statutes, however, provide that at the termination of any residential lease, or at the expiration of the lease term, the lessee may remove all improvements on the lot that were constructed at the cost of, or otherwise paid for by, the lessee, without having to make any compensation to the lessor so long as the lessee does not damage the property in doing so. (*See* **leasehold**, **renegotiation of lease**.)

reversionary factor   A mathematical factor found in present worth tables used to convert a single, lump-sum future payment into present value, given the proper discount rate and time period. Frequently used to determine the value of the lessor's leased fee interest.

reversionary value   The expected worth of a property at the end of the anticipated holding period. Present worth tables are used to determine the current value of a reversion.

reverter   *See* **possibility of reverter**.

review appraiser   An appraiser who analyzes the written reports of other appraisers to determine validity of the data and the conclusions. Often the review appraiser works for a bank, insurance company, or the government.

revocation   The act of terminating, canceling, or annulling an offer, as when a seller revokes a broker's agency by canceling the listing. A broker or salesperson's license is revocable for cause. It is important to distinguish between the *power* of an agent to revoke and the *right* to revoke an agency contract. Unless the agency is coupled with an interest, the principal always has the power to revoke; but if the principal has no justifiable grounds to revoke, the principal may be liable for money damages. Revoke an offer, rescind a contract. *See* **rescission**.

revoke   The process of terminating, canceling, or annulling an offer. (*See* **rescind**.)

rider   An addition, amendment, or endorsement ("special endorsement") annexed to a document and incorporated into the terms of the document. Riders are frequently attached to insurance policies, usually to provide some extended coverage, such as fire liability coverage as a rider to a comprehensive personal liability policy. Buyers under a contract of sale often request that a rider be attached to the seller's insurance policy so that the buyer is also covered (called a *contract of sale rider clause*). It is usually good practice to have the parties initial a rider addendum to a sales contract to establish officially its authenticity.

ridgeboard   A heavy horizontal board set on edge at the apex of the roof to which the rafters are attached.

right of contribution   The right of one who has discharged a common liability to recover from another liable party his or her pro rata share. For instance, a right of contribution exists in favor of one cotenant who pays taxes or other liens against the entire property. The cotenant (tenant in common or joint tenant) is entitled to an equitable lien on the cotenants' shares. The cotenant may enforce this lien by foreclosure on their shares. (*See* **joint and several liability, tenancy in common**.)

right of first refusal   (*derecho de primera opción*)   The right of a person to have the first opportunity to either purchase or lease real property. Unlike an option, however, the holder of a right of first refusal has no right to purchase until the owner actually offers the property for sale or entertains an offer to purchase from some third party. At that point, the holder may match the offer. If the owner first offers the property to the party holding the right of first refusal, and this person refuses, then the owner is free to offer to any third party at that price or higher.

In a lease situation, a right of first refusal might give the tenant the right either to purchase the property, if offered for sale, or to renew the lease or lease adjoining space. This right of first refusal is clearly more advantageous to the tenant than it is to the landlord because this property is less marketable than one without such a right. However, it may encourage the tenant to make improvements that the tenant might not otherwise have made.

Under an option to purchase, the tenant can decide whether or not to exercise the option at a fixed price during the option period. In a right of first refusal, however, the holder can exercise the right only if the owner has offered to sell or lease the property or has entertained a bona fide offer by a third person to purchase or lease the property. A key to the difference between an option and a right of first refusal is to determine which party has the right to initiate the sale or lease. In both an option and a right of first refusal, the holder has no interest in the land or equitable estate until the option or right is exercised.

In some condominiums, the association of unit owners retains the right of first refusal on any sale of a unit. Some state laws give a right of first refusal to a tenant whose apartment is to be converted into a condominium unit. In HUD-FHA–regulated condominiums and in condominiums eligible for Fannie Mae financing, however, restrictions such as a right of first refusal are not permitted. Rights of first refusal are common in agreements between partners, shareholders, joint owners (where the ultimate effect is to act as a waiver of the right of partition), landlords, and tenants. (*See* **option, preemption clause**.)

right of reentry   The future interest left in the transferor of property who transfers an estate on condition subsequent. If the condition is broken, the transferor has the right and the power to terminate the estate. Unlike a possibility of reverter, however, the transferor must take affirmative steps to terminate the estate, such as filing a suit in court; otherwise the condition may be discharged. For example, Adam grants Alice some property on the condition that Alice does not raise pigs on the property. If Alice raises pigs, Adam must actually reenter and take the premises; that is, there is no automatic reverter. (*See* **fee simple defeasible, possibility of reverter, reversion**.)

right of survivorship   The distinctive characteristics of a joint tenancy (also tenancy by entirety) by which the surviving joint tenant(s) succeeds to all right, title, and interest of the deceased joint tenant without the need for probate proceedings. (*See* **joint tenancy; survivorship, right of; tenancy by the entirety [entireties]**.)

right-of-way (R/W)
1.   The right or privilege, acquired through accepted usage or by contract, to pass over a designated portion of the property of another. A right-of-way may be either private, as in an access easement given a neighbor, or public, as in the right of the public to use the highways or streets or have safe access to public beaches. A gas company, for example, might send out

one of its right-of-way agents to negotiate the purchase of easements from owners of land to be crossed to gain access to gas lines.

2. Land that is either owned by a railroad or over which it maintains an easement for operating on its trackage in accordance with government safety regulations and industry standards. (*See* **access**.)

right, title, and interest   A term often used in conveyance documents to describe the transfer of all that the grantor or assignor is capable of transferring. In a quitclaim deed, the grantor transfers all right, title, and interest in a property without making any representations as to the extent of such right, title and interest, if any.

right-to-sell clause   *See* **due-on-sale clause**.

right-to-use

1. The legal right to use or occupy a property.
2. A contractual right to occupy a time-share unit under a license, vacation lease, or club membership arrangement. (*See* **bundle of rights**, **time-sharing**.)

riparian lease   An agreement covering the terms of leasing lands situated between the high-water mark and the low-water mark.

riparian rights   Those rights and obligations that are incidental to ownership of land adjacent to or abutting on watercourses such as streams and lakes. Examples of such rights are the right of irrigation, swimming, boating, fishing, and the right to the alluvium deposited by the water. Riparian rights do not attach except where there is a water boundary on one side of the particular tract of land claimed to be riparian. Such a real property right in water is a right of use, or a *usufructuary right*. The right is held in common with other riparian owners to make reasonable use of the waters that flow past, provided such use does not alter the flow of water or contaminate the water. In addition, an owner of land bordering on a nonnavigable stream owns the land under the watercourse to the center of the watercourse.

If the body of water is in movement, as a stream or river, the abutting owner is called a *riparian owner*. If the water is not flowing, as in the case of a pond, lake, or ocean, the abutting owner is called a *littoral owner*. The word *riparian* literally means "riverbank." (*See* **littoral land**.)

riser   The vertical face of the step that supports the tread. The riser is the part of the step facing a person walking up the stairs.

risk capital   Capital invested in a speculative venture, thus being the least secure and offering the greatest chance of loss. However, risk capital often yields the greatest rate of return. The concept of risk capital is often discussed in defining whether an offering is a security.

risk factor   The portion of a rate of return on an investment that is assumed to cover the risk associated with that investment. The greater the risk, the higher the capitalization rate.

risk of loss   Responsibility for damages caused to improvements. The Uniform Vendor and Purchaser Risk Act, adopted in many states, covers the standard real estate sales contract situation. Unless the terms of the contract provide otherwise, the vendor cannot enforce the contract and the vendee can recover all monies paid if a material part of the real estate is destroyed without fault of the purchaser or is taken by eminent domain, *provided neither legal title nor possession has passed* to the vendee.

A more difficult question arises upon complete destruction by fire, flood, or tornado if the buyer decides not to rescind and elects to seek specific performance of the contract; that is, the buyer wants the seller to rebuild the house and sell the property as promised. Most courts will order the seller to transfer title to the destroyed premises and to assign the insurance proceeds to the buyer. They usually do not require the seller to rebuild and absorb all the carrying charges until completion.

As a practical matter, most sales contracts should transfer possession to the buyer upon closing. Where legal title or possession has passed to the vendee and all or part of the realty is destroyed without fault of the vendor or is taken by eminent domain, the vendee cannot recover any monies paid in, and he is not relieved of the duty to pay the full purchase price. The risk of loss passes to the vendee when either title or possession passes, and the vendee should protect himself by securing proper insurance. If the buyer takes possession before closing and there is no rental agreement, then the buyer may assume the risk of loss. If, however, there is a rental agreement, the buyer would not assume the risk of loss unless the contract so provides. (*See* **Uniform Vendor and Purchaser Risk Act**.)

RNMI   *See* **REALTORS® National Marketing Institute**.

road   A collector roadway in a rural district, generally without full improvements such as curbs and sidewalks.

rod   A measure of length containing 5½ yards or 16½ feet; also, the corresponding square measure.

rollover
1. Refers to tax provisions that enable the taxpayer to defer paying taxes in certain situations such as the exchange of real property or involuntary conversion.
2. In a financing sense, the practice of rewriting a new loan at the termination of a prior loan, such as a three-year mortgage with a rollover provision to grant a new loan at different terms at the end of the three years using a rollover note. This clause is often in adjustable-rate loans.

roof boards   Boards nailed to the top of the rafters, usually touching each other, to tie the roof together and form a base for the roofing material. The boards, or roof sheathing, can also be constructed of sheets of plywood.

roofing felt   Sheets of felt or other close-woven, heavy material placed on top of the roof boards to insulate and waterproof the roof. Like building paper, roofing felt is treated with bitumen or some other tar derivative to increase its water resistance. Roofing felt is sometimes applied either with a bonding and sealing compound or with intense heat, which softens the tar and causes it to adhere to the roof.

roofing shingles   Thin, small sheets of wood, asbestos, fiberglass, slate, metal, clay, or other material used as the outer covering for a roof. The tiles are laid in overlapping rows to completely cover the roof surface. Shingles are sometimes used as an outer covering for exterior walls.

roof inspection clause   A clause sometimes inserted in a real estate sales contract specifying that the seller must provide the buyer with a certified report of the kind and condition of the building's roof. If the roof is found to be faulty, it must then be repaired at the seller's expense.

rooming house   A house where bedrooms, as such, are furnished to paying guests.

root title   The conveyance or instrument that starts the chain of land title; the original source of title.

row house   One of a series of individual homes having architectural unity and a common wall between units and the land in front of, under, and behind the house is individually owned. Row houses found in the older neighborhoods of old cities, such as Philadelphia and Baltimore, are owned differently from modern townhouse communities that are more often set up as condominium ownership.

royalty
1. The money paid to an owner of realty for the right of depleting the property of its natural resources, such as oil, gas, minerals, stone, builders' sand and gravel, and timber. Usually, the royalty payment is a stated part of the amount extracted, such as ⅙ or ⅛ of the oil and

gas removed, or six cents per ton of sand and gravel taken away, or a given price per cubic yard of material extracted. The royalty payment is a combination of rent and depreciation (depletion charge).

2. A franchise fee.

Rule 10-B5   A rule of the Securities and Exchange Commission (SEC) enacted under the antifraud provisions of the Securities Act of 1934. The rule makes it unlawful for anyone to employ schemes, issue untrue or misleading statements of material facts, or engage in any activity to fraudulently deceive anyone when buying or selling any security.

Even if an offering of securities is exempt from registration under the intrastate or private offering exemptions, the issuer nevertheless is subject to the antifraud provisions of both federal and state securities laws. In other words, the issuer's failure to state a material fact would give a purchaser of the security the right to rescind the transaction and recover all money paid plus interest from the date of purchase. (*See* **antifraud provisions**.)

Rule 146   A rule of the Securities and Exchange Commission (SEC) adopted in 1974 designed to provide more objective standards for determining when offers or sales of securities are transactions "not involving any public offering" that thus would be exempt from the registration process. For example, the act should not apply when there is no public offering. It also addresses the issue of whether the consumer needs the protection afforded by the disclosure required under the Securities Act.

Under the "rich and smart" concept, Rule 146 permits an unlimited number of offers, provided the issuer knows in advance that offerees are sophisticated (smart) enough in real estate investments to evaluate the risk themselves, are represented by an independent adviser having such experience, and are wealthy enough to bear the risk of loss. The rule places a limit of 35 on the number of sales (not offers) made under $150,000, with no limit on sales above that amount. All purchasers must certify in writing that they are buying for investment only, and not for resale. (*See* **legend stock**, **private offering**, **real property securities registration**.)

Rule 147   A rule adopted in 1974 by the Securities and Exchange Commission (SEC) to clarify the intrastate or local offering exemption from registering a security with the SEC. The rule establishes guidelines for determining when one is a resident of a state, especially with regard to legal entities such as corporations and partnerships. A local issuer seeking to raise money for a local project might not be exempt if it has substantial assets (such as real estate holdings) in another state. The rule also sets forth restrictions on the further transfer of exempt securities to nonresidents of the issuer's state for at least nine months from the date of the last sale by the issuer and receipt of all money of any part of the securities issue ("coming to rest"). (*See* **intrastate exemption**, **legend stock**.)

rule against perpetuities   A rule of law designed to require the early vesting of a future contingent interest in real property and thus prevent the property from being made inalienable for long periods of time. The effect of the rule is to destroy future interests that impede the vesting of property rights for longer than the prescribed period, which is usually no later than 21 years after some life or lives-in-being at the creation of the interest. For example, in a conveyance "to George Allen for life, then to his son, Butch Allen, for life, and remainder to Butch's children who reach age 24," the remainder violates the rule because it is possible that the remainder will not vest until after 21 years of some life-in-being; that is, George and Butch could die when Butch's only child is one year old. The rule applies only to contingent interests.

Rule of Five   A rule of thumb used by subdividers to approximate subdivision costs. Generally, ⅕ (20 percent) of the final total sales price is allocable to land acquisition cost; ⅕ (20 percent) goes to improvement costs such as engineering, grading, roads, legal fees; ⅕ (20 percent) goes to miscellaneous costs such as interest and carrying charges plus unsold lots; and ⅖ (40 percent) covers administration costs, advertising, sales commissions, and the profit.

Rule of 72   A rule of thumb in financing stating that the interest rate at which a single sum will double can be found by dividing into the number 72 the years during which the money is growing. Example: If the money is growing during an eight-year period, a financier would use this calculation: $72 \div 8 = 9\%$. If the money is growing at a known percentage, say 9 percent, the investor can figure the time to double: $72 \div 9\% = 8$ years.

Rule of 78s   A method of computing refunds of unearned finance charges on contracts that include precomputed finance charges so that the refund is proportional to the monthly unpaid balances at the time of the refund. Under this rule, on a 12-month contract, the creditor would retain $^{12}/_{78}$ of the total finance charge for the first month, $^{11}/_{78}$ for the second month and so on. If the creditor held a 12-month contract for only 6 months, it would be entitled to $^{57}/_{78}$ of the total finance charge ($12 + 11 + 10 + 9 + 8 + 7 = 57$). In turn, the consumer would be entitled to the remaining $^{21}/_{78}$ of the finance charge.

Under the truth-in-lending laws, the creditor must identify the method of computing any unearned portion of the finance charge if the obligation is prepaid. Most creditors identify their rebate method as the Rule of 78s.

run with the land   A phrase describing rights or covenants that bind or benefit successive owners of a property. An example is a restrictive building covenant in a recorded deed that would affect all future owners of the property. Unlike an easement in gross, an easement appurtenant runs with the land and thus passes to a succeeding owner even if it is not specified in the deed. For example, the covenant will not run with the land if the grantee agrees, as part of the consideration to a transaction, to repair a building located on land owned by grantor Leonard. This is because it merely places a duty on the grantee. The promise does not touch and concern the land conveyed from the grantor to the grantee—it is only a personal covenant for the grantor's benefit. (*See* **appurtenance**.)

rural   A land-use classification pertaining to rustic areas, as opposed to urban areas; land devoted to the pursuit of agriculture.

Rural Housing Service (RHS)   A federal agency under the U.S. Department of Agriculture, providing loans for housing located in open country and in all rural communities with populations under 10,000, and in most towns with populations between 10,000 and 20,000 that are outside standard metropolitan statistical areas (SMSAs) and have a serious lack of mortgage credit.

Various credit programs are available to help purchase or operate farms, provide new employment and business opportunities, enhance the environment, and acquire homes. Most programs fall into two categories: *guaranteed loans*, in which the loan is made and serviced by a private lender and guaranteed for a specified percentage by the FmHA; and *insured loans*, which are originated, made, and serviced by the agency. Discounts, or points, are not allowed with such loans, and preference is given to eligible veterans.

rurban   Pertaining to those fringe areas situated outside but adjacent to cities where the land use is transitioning from rural to urban.

R-value   A special rating or method of judging the insulating value of certain insulation products. The Federal Trade Commission requires sellers of new homes to disclose in their sales contracts certain insulation data such as type, thickness, and R-value. (*See* **insulation, low-E glass**.)

R

safe harbor rule

1. An area of protection. For example, the IRS has outlined certain standards for real estate brokers to meet in treating their salespeople as independent contractors. So long as brokers meet these criteria, they are in a "safe harbor" and not subject to attack by the IRS for failing to withhold taxes from employees. (*See* **independent contractor**.)

2. IRS standards for a delayed 1031 exchange in which an intermediary can hold title pending the identification and acquisition of the replacement property within set time limits. (*See* **delayed exchange**.)

safety clause (listing)   *See* **extender clause**.

SAIF   *See* **Savings Association Insurance Fund (SAIF)**.

sale by the acre   The sale of land described in the sales contract and instrument of conveyance documents by stating the exact area of land (for example, 269 acres). Under a sale-by-the-acre contract, the buyer does not take the risk of any deficiency, nor does the seller take the risk of any excess.

Sometimes large acreage is sold by stating the approximate rather than the exact acreage, such as "269 acres more or less" (i.e., a sale in gross). In such a case, neither party would receive any compensation if there were a slight variance in the exact amount of acres actually conveyed. However, if there is an unusually large excess or deficiency, a court could grant equitable relief to the injured party.

A proper legal description is necessary in the real estate sales contract and all subsequent conveyance documents. (*See* **legal description**, **more or less**.)

sale-leaseback   A real estate financing technique whereby a property owner sells the property to an investor or lender and, at the same time, leases it back. The lease used is usually a full net lease that extends over a period of time long enough for investors-lenders to recover their funds and to make a fair profit on the investment. The arrangement allows original property owners to "pull out" their equity from the property and the rents paid to the investors are fully deductible expenses in the year in which they incur.

Thus, a seller/lessee enjoys many benefits: retaining possession of the property while obtaining the full sales price and, in some cases, keeping the right to repurchase the property at the end of the lease; freeing the capital that was frozen in equity; maintaining an appreciable interest in realty, which can be capitalized upon by subleasing or mortgaging the leasehold; and getting a tax deduction for the full amount of the rent, equivalent to taking depreciation deductions for both the building and the land. In addition, a lease appears as an indirect liability on a firm's balance sheet, whereas a mortgage shows up as a direct liability and adversely affects the firm's debt ratio in terms of obtaining future financing.

The advantages to the investor/landlord in this type of arrangement include a fair return on and of investment in the form of rent during the lease term, and ownership of a depreciable asset already occupied by a reliable tenant. The investor is buying a guaranteed income stream that can probably be sheltered through the proper use of depreciation allowances, and the risk can actually be managed by the amount of rent the investor requires.

When the lease includes an option for the tenant to repurchase the property at the end of the lease term, it is called a *sale-leaseback-buyback*. However, care must be taken to establish the buyback price for the fair market value at the time of sale; otherwise, the arrangement is considered a long-term installment mortgage, and any income tax benefits that might have been enjoyed during the term of the lease will be disallowed by the Internal Revenue Service. (*See* **subordinated sale-leaseback**.)

sale of leased property   A transaction in which an owner of property who has given a lease to one person may sell the leased property to another. The buyer, however, takes the property subject to the existing lease. The deed evidencing the sale usually states that it is "subject to existing leases and rights of present tenants," and this clause means that the seller cannot deliver actual possession of the property. Unless the seller has reserved the lease rents, the buyer does, however, have the right to collect rent due after the sale and to exercise any right of forfeiture for nonpayment of rent given under the lease. (*See* **lease, leasehold, right of first refusal**.)

sales-assessment ratio   The ratio of the assessed value of real property to its selling price.

sales associate   A licensed salesperson or broker who works for a broker. (*See* **salesperson**.)

sales contract   *See* **contract of sale**.

sales kit   An assortment of information about property to be sold. The kit is selected and organized to familiarize the salesperson with the property being presented to a prospect and to help the prospect visualize the property. The sales kit may be in the form of a small loose-leaf book of typewritten pages; a large loose-leaf book including maps and pictures; or an elaborate zippered briefcase with photographs, building plans, maps, and other statistical data. Increasingly, licensees package the information into a slide presentation e-mailed to the buyer or on a Web site with a special access code for the prospective buyer.

salesperson(s)   Any licensed person who, for compensation or valuable consideration, is employed either directly or indirectly by a licensed real estate broker to perform certain acts: to sell, offer to sell, buy, offer to buy; negotiate the purchase, sale, or exchange of real estate; lease, rent, or offer to rent any real estate, or to negotiate leases thereof or improvements thereon. All 50 states have laws controlling the licensing of persons who sell, rent, or manage real estate. Several states have eliminated the salesperson's license and require all licensees to be broker-qualified. Most states, but not all, require that the salesperson work for a period of time under the supervision of a real estate broker or other person authorized to supervise real estate salespeople.

A salesperson's license is issued on the basis of an applicant's character, integrity, and abilities, which must include a reasonable knowledge of real estate law, customs, and usage. Additionally, many states now require a criminal background check and/or fingerprinting.

Generally, license laws distinguish between the real estate broker and the salesperson, and they limit the latter's activities. For example, a salesperson cannot act as an agent for another person, nor can salespeople list or advertise property under their own name. Salespeople can carry out only those responsibilities assigned to them by the supervising broker.

Salespersons are engaged by brokers as either employees or independent contractors. The agreement between broker and salesperson should be set down in a written contract that defines the obligations and responsibilities of the relationship. Whether a broker is employing a salesperson or the salesperson is operating under the broker as an independent contractor determines the broker's relationship with the salesperson and liability to pay and withhold taxes from that salesperson's earnings. (*See* **broker, independent contractor, license laws**.)

S

salvage value
1. The estimated amount for which an asset can be sold at the end of its useful life for pre-1981 property. The salvage value of an asset (improvement) limits the total amount of claimable depreciation, because it provides a floor below which the improvement cannot be depreciated. (*See* **depreciation, useful life.**)
2. The value of a structure to be relocated to another site. Normally used in highway condemnations where large areas must be cleared.

sandwich lease   A leasehold estate in which the sandwich party leases the property from the fee owner or another lessee and then sublets to the tenant in possession, thereby maintaining a middle, or "sandwich," position. The sandwich party is the lessee of one party and the lessor of another; thus the sandwich party is neither the fee owner nor the end user of the property. It is a lease occupying a position within three or more leasehold interests in a property.

sanitary sewer system   A sewer system that carries only domestic water, usually an underground pipe or tunnel to carry off wastes and effluents.

satellite city   A rare term denoting independent municipalities in the natural growth path of a nearby larger city, distinct from the larger city and generally called suburbs.

satellite tenant   A smaller shopping center tenant that is relatively dependent on the ability of a larger anchor or prime tenant to attract business into the center—for example, a small shoe repair shop in a center containing a major department store.

satisfaction   The payment of a debt or obligation such as a judgment. The time when the vendee pays in full under a contract for deed and the vendor transfers legal title is *satisfaction* or *fulfillment*.

satisfaction judgment   *See* **judgment lien.**

satisfaction of mortgage   A certificate issued by the mortgagee when a mortgage is paid in full. Upon payment in full of the debt secured by a mortgage, the mortgage is "satisfied." This document is a *discharge* or *release of mortgage*, or a *satisfaction piece*. It describes the mortgage, recites where it is recorded, certifies that it has been paid, and consents that the mortgage be discharged of record. Clear record title is almost as important as clear actual title and may be more important in some particular real estate transactions. Therefore, the evidence of the satisfaction must be recorded. (*See* **marginal release.**)

savings and loan association (S&L)   A financial institution whose principal function is to promote thrift and home ownership, also called a *savings association*. Depositors earn interest on their deposits, often at a higher rate than is offered at commercial banks. The S&L invests some of these deposits in residential mortgage loans, enabling more people to purchase and/or repair their homes. Savings associations are active participants in the home loan mortgage market.

All savings associations must be chartered, either by the federal government or by the state in which they are located. Associations are regulated on a national level by the Federal Reserve Board. The Federal Deposit Insurance Corporation (FDIC) insures deposits for all federal savings and loan associations and all federal savings banks.

Savings associations are primarily local in nature because they are usually mutually owned and locally managed. Some capital stock and mutual associations, however, are large, statewide associations, with billions of dollars in assets and hundreds of offices.

Although savings associations have gravitated from a regulated to a deregulated savings market, the primary concern of savings associations continues to be granting loans not only for real estate purposes but also for home repairs, construction, and improvement. Associations offer a wide variety of new savings accounts and services, including consumer loans, trust services, debit and credit

S

cards, and interest-bearing checking accounts. (*See* **building and loan association, disintermediation, Federal Savings and Loan Association, Office of Thrift Supervision [OTS], Federal Deposit Insurance Corporation [FDIC].**)

Savings Association Insurance Fund (SAIF)   A fund that formerly insured deposits of savings and loan associations. In 2005, SAIF was merged with the Bank Insurance Fund (BIF) to create one insurance fund called Depositors Insurance Fund (DIF). (*See* **Federal Deposit Insurance Corporation [FDIC], Federal Savings and Loan Insurance Corporation [FSLIC], Depositors Insurance Fund [DIF].**)

savings banks   Originally organized by state charters for the purpose of providing depository safety for workers paid in cash. Most were mutually owned by the depositors—who were paid dividends, rather than interest—and remained primarily in the northeast part of the country. By the mid-1980s, federal savings bank charters were issued to groups of troubled savings and loan associations in an effort to provide a method of saving the associations from bankruptcy. Federal charters are required to have deposit insurance with the Depositors Insurance Fund and the FDIC, same as commercial banks. State charters can join the federal deposit insurance fund if they are eligible.

Savings Incentive Match Plan for Employees (SIMPLE)   A type of contribution savings plan especially useful for those with relatively modest self-employment earnings, although not just for self-employeds. SIMPLEs may be structured as individual retirement accounts (IRAs) or as 401(k) plans for a company with 100 or fewer employees. SIMPLE deposits are tax deductible, self-employment earnings up to $8,000. After 2005, the SIMPLE limit increased to $10,000. The employer can match 100 percent of compensation, and the contributions are immediately and fully vested.

SBA   *See* **Small Business Administration (SBA).**

scarcity   A lack of supply of some type of real property, the supply of which cannot readily be increased. Scarcity results in increased value when demand exceeds supply. (*See* **supply and demand.**)

scenic easement   An easement created to preserve a property in its natural state. For example, the state may acquire (through a condemnation proceeding) a scenic easement over certain choice property to preserve its aesthetic quality and, in effect, to prevent a developer from building on the property. A landowner might purchase a scenic easement over a neighbor's property to preserve the view.

Because of drastic increases in assessments and taxes, some owners of large tracts of land that possess some scenic or natural beauty attempt to make a gift of a scenic easement over part of the property to the county or state. If the gift is accepted, the landowner can possibly get a charitable deduction for tax purposes and a reduction in the real estate tax assessment. A charitable deduction, for income tax purposes, may be taken for contribution of a scenic easement or other partial interest in real estate to be used for public enjoyment, historical preservation, or the preservation of wild areas. The Federal Highway Beautification Act offers incentives to states to acquire scenic or open-space easements to protect the view of historical sites or unusual scenery. (*See* **condemnation, historic structure.**)

schematics   Preliminary architectural drawings and sketches often prepared at the planning stages of a project; basic layouts not containing the final details of design. Schematic drawings may include a site plan, dimensional plan of each typical unit, elevations, typical lobby and floor, mechanical facilities, and commercial-use areas. Developers often use an architect's schematics of a proposed building or development for initial publicity.

scope of authority   A rule of agency law holding that principals are liable to third parties for all wrongful acts of their agent committed while transacting the principal's business. It is not necessary that the principal actually authorize the act; it is sufficient if the agent had apparent (ostensible) or implied authority to act on behalf of the principal. The principal is not liable for acts of the agent committed *outside* the scope of the agent's authority, nor can the broker collect for services rendered outside the scope of that authority. (*See* **ostensible authority**.)

In some states, an act is within the scope of authority if it was primarily to further the principal's interests rather than the agent's interest. A third person who knows he is dealing with an agent has a duty to ascertain the scope of the agent's authority.

The seller of real property is liable for the affirmative misrepresentations made by the broker in the scope of the agent's authority, even though the seller was unaware that the broker had made them. For example, when the broker has knowledge of a defective condition in the house (e.g., a weak foundation), the innocent sellers are usually liable to the buyer if the broker does not disclose the defect to the buyer. This is because the knowledge of the agent is imputed to the sellers, who are treated as though they knew of it. (*See* **agency, respondeat superior**.)

S corporation   A small domestic corporation that has elected to be treated more like a partnership for tax purposes (designated IRS Form 2553). The S corporation, once called a *subchapter S corporation*, allows a business to operate in corporate form and yet not pay a corporate tax, thus avoiding the double-tax feature of corporate ownership. Stockholders are taxable on their individual share of the corporation's income, whether or not it is distributed to them. Similarly, stockholders can report their share of the corporation's ordinary losses and deduct them on an individual personal tax return. Though there is no limitation on the amount of corporate income for an S corporation, there can be no more than 100 shareholders.

S corporations are not subject to the corporate alternative minimum tax or the rule that requires most corporations to recognize their gain or loss on liquidating sales and distributions just as though the assets had been sold. Other major advantages of an S corporation include limited personal liability, ease of transferability of ownership shares, centralized management, and comparative ease of formation.

Its basic disadvantage is that aggregate losses may be passed through to the individual shareholders only equal to the amount of cash paid for the stock plus any loans made to the company. Thus, the S corporation's most efficient application for real estate investment ownership is for projects designed to be other than tax shelters. (*See* **limited liability company [LLC]**.)

seal   An embossed impression on paper caused by a metal die used to authenticate a document or attest to a signature, as with a corporate or notary seal. The corporate seal contains the name of the corporation, the date, and the state of incorporation. Sometimes the parties use the initials L.S. after a signature, which in Latin is for *locus sigilli*—"under seal" or "in place of seal."

Under early common law, a seal took the place of reciting the consideration in a contract. Except as a means of authentication, the common-law effect of this seal has been abolished in most states. Thus, where necessary, a party must still prove that consideration was paid. It is good practice to require the seal of a corporation executing a contract, for it is evidence that the instrument is the act of the corporation, executed by duly authorized officers or agents. Under the Uniform Commercial Code, use of a seal has no effect on the transaction; it "does not constitute the writing . . . and the law with respect to sealed instruments does not apply."

sealed and delivered   A phrase indicating that a transferor has received adequate consideration as evidenced by the voluntary delivery. The word *sealed* adds more weight because under old conveyancing law, an official seal served as a substitute for consideration. Today, the term is generally a mere formality and of no legal consequence. (*See* **seal**.)

seasoned loan   A loan borrowed by someone who has a stable and consistent history of payments under the terms of the loan. The term indicates that the mortgage or land contract is not a new one and thus may be a good purchase risk.

S

second   As used in a mete-and-bounds legal description, $\frac{1}{60}$ of a degree or $\frac{1}{3600}$ part of a circle. A second is denoted by the symbol ". For example, an angle of 97° 00' 25" would read "ninety-seven degrees, zero minutes, twenty-five seconds." (*See* **degree**.)

secondary financing   A junior mortgage placed on property to help finance the purchase price, such as a purchase-money second mortgage taken back by the seller to assist a purchaser who has difficulty in making a large down payment.

Most governmental loan programs (FHA, VA) permit secondary financing but with certain restrictions.

secondary mortgage market   (*mercado hipotecario secundario*)   A market for the purchase and sale of existing mortgages, and designed to provide greater liquidity for selling mortgages; also called *secondary money market*, not to be confused with secondary financing. Secondary (or resale) mortgage market lenders or investors buy mortgages as long-term investments, as opposed to other types of securities (such as government and corporate bonds).

Fannie Mae and Freddie Mac purchase many existing mortgages, thus freeing more money for mortgagees to lend. Ginnie Mae is also active in the secondary mortgage market, especially where federally subsidized projects are involved.

Mortgage pools are created when lenders package mortgages and sell securities that represent shares in these pooled mortgages. The pooled mortgages are actually removed from the balance sheets of the originators of the pools, and the buyers of the securities become the joint owners. The regular mortgage payment and any prepayments are collected by the originators (who usually continue to service the mortgages) and are distributed to the holders of the securities. (*See* **Fannie Mae**, **Freddie Mac**, **Ginnie Mae**, **Maggie Mae**.)

second-generation leasing   A term used in the shopping center industry to describe a leasing of space in buildings already constructed and previously occupied by other tenants.

second mortgage   A mortgage (or trust deed) that is junior or subordinate to a first mortgage; typically, an additional loan imposed on top of the first mortgage, taken out when the borrower needs more money. The degree of risk is determined by the margin between the appraisal value and the total prior liens on the property inasmuch as the second mortgage can be wiped out by the foreclosure of any senior mortgage or lien holder (such as a mechanic's lien or tax lien).

Because the risk involved to the lender is greater with the second mortgage, the lender's conditions are usually more stringent, the term is shorter, and the interest rate is higher than for the first mortgage. Second mortgages usually involve separate closing costs for appraisal, title report, credit check, drafting and recording documents, and other procedures.

Second mortgages may contain a provision stating that they will remain subordinate to any subsequent first mortgage as long as the new mortgage amount does not exceed the present first mortgage. Such a lifting clause permits the mortgagor to "lift out" the first mortgage and refinance it with another first mortgage without altering the junior position of the second mortgage.

In the event of default under the prior mortgage, the second mortgagee can elect to redeem the first mortgage and foreclose under the second mortgage or add the amount advanced to the second mortgage. The second mortgagee should request that it receive a notice of any default under the first mortgage. If the second mortgage is in default, the first mortgagee can also foreclose on the mortgagor because its security has also been threatened. The second mortgagee can thus exert great pressure on the borrower to pay, yet in doing so, it takes the risk that the net proceeds of a foreclosure sale will not be enough to repay the second mortgage after extinguishing the first mortgage note.

Before considering a second mortgage, the parties should check state usury provisions and local laws restricting banks and savings and loan associations from granting second mortgages or limiting the amount loaned or the interest that may be charged. (*See* **junior mortgage**.)

S

secret profit   Refers to a broker making an undisclosed profit at the seller's expense—for example, when the broker has an undisclosed relative buy the listed property and then resell it to a buyer whose earlier offer was never presented to the seller. The seller can sue the broker in an action to "disgorge" the profit. Also called **overage**. (*See* **dual agency [limited agency], overage**.)

section(s)   (*sección*)   As used in the government survey method, a land area of one square mile, or 640 acres. A section is $\frac{1}{36}$ of a township.

Section 8 Program   A federal rent subsidy program for low-income and moderate-income tenants divided into two programs: tenant-based and project-based. Section 8 allows families to choose privately owned rental housing. The public housing authority generally pays the landlord the difference between a HUD-determined payment standard and the fair market rent, which must be reasonable. It is also referred to as Section 8 Housing Choice Voucher Program.

Section 203(b)   The centerpiece of home mortgage insurance offered by the Federal Housing Administration. Homeownership opportunities are more available for first-time homebuyers and other borrowers who would not otherwise qualify for a conventional mortgage on affordable terms. Section 203(b) is also available to those who live in underserved areas where mortgages may be harder to obtain. FHA's Mutual Mortgage Insurance Fund, totally sustained by borrower premiums, protects lenders.

Section 1031 exchange   *See* **exchange, like kind**.

Section 1244 corporation   A corporation qualified under Section 1244 of the Internal Revenue Code. To qualify, a corporation must be a "small business corporation," which means it has a paid-in capital of $1 million or less. Shareholder in a Section 1244 corporation may treat any loss on their capital stock investments as an ordinary loss rather than a capital loss, an important consideration when the corporate form of ownership is being used in a speculative venture and there is a strong risk of loss.

secured party   The person having the security interest, such as the mortgagee, the vendee, or the pledgee.

Securities and Exchange Commission (SEC)   An independent regulatory agency, part of the federal executive branch, that administers federal laws on securities (i.e., stocks and bonds). The SEC aims to protect investors and to ensure that the securities markets function fairly and honestly. It can enforce securities laws through sanctions and its decisions can be reviewed by the United States Court of Appeals. (*See* **real property securities registration**.)

security   (*valor*)   Evidence of obligations to pay money or of rights to participate in earnings and distribution of corporate, trust, or other property. A security is usually where investors subject their money to the risks of an enterprise over which they exercise no managerial control.

   Both state and federal law regulates securities. To prevent fraud and to protect the public against unsuspected schemes, transactions in which promoters go to the public for risk capital are monitored. (*See* **blue-sky laws, real property securities registration**.)

security agreement   (*contrato de garantía*)   A security document that creates a lien on personal property (chattels), including chattels intended to be affixed to land as fixtures; known as a *chattel mortgage* before the adoption of the Uniform Commercial Code (UCC). Rather than record the security agreement, the UCC provides for filing a notice on a short form called a *financing statement* (Form UCC1). To perfect a security interest, the financing statement should be recorded. It therefore appears on a title report as a lien affecting the real property under search. Brokers frequently come into contact with security agreements in the sale of business opportunities. (*See* **financing statement, Uniform Commercial Code [UCC]**.)

security deposit   Money deposited by or for the tenant with the landlord, to be held by the landlord for the following purposes: (1) to remedy tenant defaults for damage to the premises (accidental or intentional), for failure to pay rent due or for failure to return keys at the end of the tenancy; (2) to clean the dwelling so as to place it in as fit a condition as when the tenant commenced possession, considering normal wear and tear; and (3) to compensate for damages caused by a tenant who wrongfully quits the dwelling unit. The security deposit is not regarded as liquidated damages, but rather is a fund held in trust for the tenant that the landlord can use to offset damages caused by the tenant. It is not taxable to the landlord until applied to remedy any tenant defaults. Neither can the tenant take the deposit as a tax deduction. Some states require security deposit monies to be placed in an interest-bearing account in trust for the lessee.

The tenant's claim to the security deposit monies is superior to all claims of the landlord's creditors. An exception is claims of a trustee in bankruptcy.

Although the Uniform Residential Landlord and Tenant Act (adopted by many states) preserves the security deposit, it limits the amount (one month's rent) and prescribes penalties for its misuse. Depending on state law, the landlord must return security deposits to tenants within a specified time period and account for all claims to any part of the deposits; disputes over security deposits may be handled expeditiously in small claims court, and the law provides for penalties in the event a landlord fails to comply with the regulations. The act does not limit the prepayment of rent, as distinguished from security deposits; nor does it require the landlord to pay interest on the security deposits.

The lease should clearly specify whether a payment is a security deposit or an advance rental. If it is a security deposit, the tenant is not entitled to apply it as discharge of the final month's rent. If it is an advance rental, the landlord has to pay taxes on it when received. Many state laws specifically state that the security deposit is not to be construed as payment of the last month's rent by the tenant. When the lessor sells the property, the sales contract should cover the appropriate accounting of security deposit monies (i.e., debit seller and credit buyer). (*See* **normal wear and tear, Uniform Residential Landlord and Tenant Act [URLTA].**)

The security deposit should not be confused with an earnest money deposit in the sales situation. (*See* **deposit, earnest money.**)

seed money   *See* **front money**.

seisin   Actual possession of property by one who claims rightful ownership of a freehold interest therein. A person is seized of property when in rightful possession with the intention of claiming a freehold estate. Seisin (pronounced "seize-in") is now generally synonymous with ownership. The concept is derived from feudal times, when individual ownership was not allowed. A medieval English landowner was said to be seized of his estate, for the king was considered the owner of all lands in England. Also spelled *seizen*. (*See* **livery of seisin**.)

A general warranty deed contains the covenant of seisin in which the grantor warrants that she has the estate or interest she purports to convey. Both title and possession at the time of the grant are necessary to satisfy the covenant. In the event of a breach, the purchaser may recover expenses up to the amount paid for the property. (*See* **delivery, dower, freehold**.)

seizure   The taking of property by the government when the property is being used to conduct illegal activities such as drug dealing. Under the federal rule, the government seizes the property and then brings a legal action to cause a forfeiture of title followed by a sale of the property. To block forfeiture, innocent owners must prove that they knew nothing of the illegal activities of the tenant using the property. (*See* **Drug Enforcement Act**.)

S

self-help   The nonjudicial remedies an owner employs to regain possession of property. For example, a landlord whose tenant is in default may attempt to cut off the utilities, forcibly enter the premises, or change the locks to force the tenant to pay the rent or move out. Most courts disapprove of self-help remedies and require landlords to follow statutory procedures for eviction. (*See* **eviction**.)

seller financing   Financing provided by the owner/seller of real estate, who takes back a secured note. (*See* **deed of trust**, **land contract**, **purchase-money mortgage [PMM]**.)

seller's market   An economic situation that favors the seller because the demand for property exceeds the supply.

selling broker   The broker who procures the buyer. Usually refers to the cooperating broker, although in an in-house sale, one broker is sometimes both the listing broker and the selling broker. Do not confuse with the seller's broker (the listing broker).

semiannual   Occurring twice each year, as in semiannual tax payments. (*See* **biannual**.)

semidetached dwelling   A residence that shares one wall with an adjoining building. (*See* **party wall**.)

SEP   *See* **simplified employee plan (SEP)**.

separate property   Property held individually, as opposed to community property or property held jointly. (*See* **ownership, form of**.)

septic tank   A sewage settling tank in which part of the sewage is converted into gas and liquids before the remaining waste is discharged by gravity into a leaching bed underground. Many local planning commissions require a developer to provide a sewage disposal system rather than use septic tanks because of the fear of pollution. Unlike cesspools, however, septic tanks are generally acceptable sanitary systems for low-density developments. (*See* **cesspool**, **disposal field**, **sanitary sewer system**.)

sequestration order   A writ authorizing the taking of land, rents, and/or profits owed by a defendant in a pending or concluded suit, for the purpose of forcing the defendant to comply with a court order. An example would be to hold rental monies by court order pending the outcome of litigation.

service life   *See* **economic life**.

service of process   The legal act of notifying the defendant of an impending lawsuit and the delivery to the defendant of the summons and complaint in the action. Service is usually made on the defendant by the sheriff's delivery of a certified copy of the summons and the plaintiff's complaint. If the defendant cannot be found within the state, the court may authorize service by certified mail or by publication, usually in a local newspaper, at least once each week for four successive weeks or longer.

    Under many state license laws, out-of-state brokers applying for registration must irrevocably appoint the public official in charge of real estate registration as their agent to receive any lawful process in any noncriminal proceeding relating to their real estate activities. Some states require that out-of-state subdividers or foreign corporations comply with a similar regulation in order to qualify to do business in that state.

servicing   As specified in a servicing agreement, a mortgage banker's duties performed for a fee as loan correspondent. Such duties generally include collecting payments that include interest, principal, insurance, and taxes on a note from the borrower in accordance with the terms of the note. It can also include such operational procedures as accounting, bookkeeping, preparation of insurance and tax records, loan payment follow-up, delinquency follow-up, and loan analysis. The servicing agreement between an investor and a mortgage loan correspondent is generally written, and it stipulates the rights and obligations of each party. The servicing fee ranges between 0.05 and 0.50 percent of the outstanding loan.

servient estate Land on which an easement or other right exists in favor of an adjacent property (called a *dominant estate*); also referred to as a *servient tenement*. If property A has a right-of-way across property B, then B is the servient estate.

   The servient owner may not use the property in such a way as to interfere with the reasonable use of the dominant owner. (*See* **easement, equitable servitude**.)

servitude A burden or charge on an estate. A *personal servitude* (such as a license) attaches to the person its establishment benefits and terminates with the person's life. A *real servitude* (such as an easement) benefits the owner of one estate, who enjoys the use of a portion of a neighboring estate. A real servitude runs indefinitely with the land. (*See* **easement, equitable servitude**.)

set-aside letter A letter from a lender to the contractor of a project to the effect that the lender will set aside money for the contractor and thus induce the contractor to finish a troubled project.

setback Zoning restrictions on the amount of land required surrounding improvements; the amount of space required between the lot line and the building line. These restrictions, called *setbacks* and *sideyard restrictions*, may be contained in local zoning regulations, or they may be established by restrictive covenants in deeds and under subdivision general plans normally noted on the recorded subdivision plat.

   Setback provisions are designed to keep buildings away from streets and to ensure that occupants have more light and air and less noise, smoke, dust, danger of spread of fire, and in some cases, a better view at street intersections. It is important to clarify what is meant by a "building"— that is, whether the provision includes eaves, steps, bay windows, porch, awnings, walls, or fences. (*See* **zero lot line**.)

setoff The claim a debtor can make against a creditor that reduces or cancels the amount the debtor owes. (*See* **holder in due course**.)

settlement (*1. liquidación; 2. transacción, contrato de transacción*)
   1. The act of adjusting and prorating the various credits, charges, and settlement costs to conclude a real estate transaction. Many brokers refer to this process as the *closing* rather than the *settlement*. (*See* **closing [settlement]**.)
   2. The act of compromising in a dispute or a lawsuit. Such an act is usually not an admission of liability. (*See* **conciliation**.)

settlement act *See* **Real Estate Settlement Procedures Act (RESPA)**.

settlement statement *See* **closing statement**.

several tenancy *See* **tenancy in severalty**.

severalty Sole ownership of real property. (*See* **tenancy in severalty**.)

severance The act of removing something attached to land or of terminating a relationship. When a fence is removed, there is a severance of the fence from the real property. The fence thus changes from real property (fixture) to personal property.

   When one joint tenant transfers her interest, there is a severance of the joint tenancy. The other joint tenant and the new transferee are then tenants in common in the property. Only divorce or joint conveyance by husband and wife can sever a tenancy by the entirety.

severance damages A recognition for the loss of value in the remaining property caused by the partial taking of real property under the state, federal, or local government's power of eminent domain.

Severance damages are compensable to the property owner if the partial taking lowers the property's highest and best use or otherwise limits the use of the remainder of the property.

In some states, the value of the special benefit, if any, conferred on the portion not taken is offset against or deducted from severance damages. However, if the benefit is greater than the severance damages, then the benefit is not deducted from the value of the portion taken. In a federal government taking, special benefits can offset the portion taken. (*See* **before-and-after method**, **condemnation**, **larger parcel**, **special benefit**.)

shake shingle   Shingle composed of split wood, most frequently used as roofing or siding material.

shall   In common statutory language, meaning that which is required by law.

shared appreciation mortgage (SAM)   A form of participation mortgage in which the lender shares in the appreciation of a property mortgaged if and when the property is sold. For a reduction in the current market interest rate by up to 40 percent in some cases, the borrower agrees to share with the lender the appreciation in the home's (or commercial property's) value in proportion to the interest reduction. The normal standard is a ten-year limit, with guaranteed long-term financing at the going rate after that, or sharing in proceeds when the house or commercial property is sold. Participating lenders need to be careful about potential liability for cleanup of hazardous conditions under Superfund regulations. (*See* **Comprehensive Environmental Response, Compensation, and Liability Act [CERCLA]**.)

shear wall   Permanent structural wall that provides lateral stability.

shell lease   A lease in which a tenant leases the unfinished shell of a building, as in a new shopping center, and agrees to complete construction by installing ceilings, plumbing, heating, air-conditioning systems, and electrical wiring. The landlord and tenant under a shell lease should agree on who will pay the real property taxes against the premises. Many shell leases provide that all improvements remain the tenant's personal property and that the tenant must pay the taxes assessed against the improvements.

sheriff's deed   A deed given by a court to effect the sale of property to satisfy a judgment. (*See* **deed**.)

Sherman Antitrust Act   The 1890 act that is the principal federal statute covering competition, which is defined by most courts as "that economic condition in which prices are determined by market forces without interference from private concerns and there is reasonable freedom of entry into most businesses." Section I of the Sherman Antitrust Act, which is enforced by the Federal Trade Commission, provides that "every contract, combination in the form of trust or otherwise, or conspiracy in restraint of trade or commerce among the several states or with foreign nations is declared to be illegal." (*See* **Clayton Antitrust Act**, **antitrust laws**.)

shingles   *See* **roofing shingles**.

shoe molding   A thin strip of wood placed at the junction of the baseboard and the floorboards to conceal the joint. The shoe molding improves the aesthetics of the room and helps seal out drafts.

shopping   The practice of negotiating a deal and then attempting to find another deal with better terms.

shopping center   A modern classification of retail stores, characterized by off-street parking and clusters of stores, subject to a uniform development plan and usually with careful analysis given to the proper merchant mix. After World War II, shopping centers were developed in the once-open tracts of suburban land as retail and consumer service stores followed their customers to suburban areas.

Neighborhood centers usually consist of a supermarket, variety store, service station, and a few smaller specialty shops. They are designed to serve the immediate neighborhood. The most simple and common design for a shopping center is the "strip center," with stores built in a line and facing the street or parking area and an anchor store at each end (such as a supermarket and a large drugstore).

Community centers usually contain supermarkets, department stores, variety stores, drugstores, and apparel shops. They are larger than neighborhood centers and designed to serve the entire community.

Regional centers are large planned centers, sometimes enclosed malls, containing many national chains and up to 50 or more stores. Easy access, free parking, and large selections have made regional shopping centers a way of life in many suburban areas.

A shopping center lease is usually a net lease with the rental determined on a percentage basis. The applicable percentages vary greatly among the types and sizes of retail stores, with the large department stores paying a lower per-square-foot minimum rent and a lower percentage than smaller stores. All tenants must belong to a merchants' association, which promotes the shopping center through institutional advertising. Stores must be operated during established hours and limited to the use specified in the lease. Tenants must pay a pro rata share of taxes, maintenance, and insurance; agree to keep their books open for audit; and sometimes use a special type of register to assure the landlord that the gross sales upon which the percentage ratio is based are accurately being recorded. The landlord may go as far as employing spot buyers to make sure that sales are properly recorded on the register.

Most shopping center leases contain some form of "radius clause" that might forbid the landlord to rent premises to the tenant's competitors within a specified radius of the shopping center or that might prevent the tenant from opening another store within a specified radius of the center. However, these noncompetition clauses have come under attack by the Federal Trade Commission as unreasonable restraints of trade, illegal under the Sherman Antitrust Act. (*See* **percentage lease, recapture clause, tenant mix.**)

shore land   *See* **beach**.

shoreline   The dividing line between private land and public beach on beachfront property. The U.S. Supreme Court has ruled that the "mean high-water mark" should determine the shoreline boundary. Some coastal states, however, now treat as public land that shoreline property up to the high wash of the waves, as may be evidenced by the vegetation line.

The prudent seller of shoreline property carefully describes the land area in approximate language (such as "approximately 10,000 square feet," or "10,000 square feet, more or less"), and the prudent buyer requires that the property be resurveyed to ascertain the proper land area in view of these court cases.

A cautious seller may insert in a sales contract protective language such as the following:

Buyer acknowledges that the property being sold is a beachfront lot and accepts the premises subject to the possibility of dispute with regard to exact location of the shoreline boundary of the property. Buyer agrees to make no claim against the seller on account of any such dispute or any decrease in the area of the property resulting from the resolution of any such dispute.

(*See* **access, beach, environmental impact statement [EIS]**.)

shoring   The use of timbers to prevent the sliding of earth adjoining an excavation. Shoring is also the use of timbers as bracing against a wall for temporary support of loads during construction.

short-form document   A brief document that refers to a contract such as a mortgage (called a *fictitious mortgage*), lease, option, or sales contract and simply recites that a contract has been made between the parties covering certain described premises. This satisfies the requirements of recordation yet keeps secret the essential terms and conditions of the transaction. A short-form lease, for example, might contain language such as the following: "This lease has been made upon the rents, terms, covenants, and conditions contained in a certain collateral agreement or lease between the parties hereto and bearing even date herewith."

short rate   A higher periodic rate charged for a shorter term than that originally contracted. The increased premium charged by an insurance company upon early cancellation of a policy to compensate the insurer for the fact that the original rate charged was calculated on the full period of the policy. This increased charge enters into a buyer's decision whether to assume the seller's existing homeowners' hazard insurance policy or to cancel it and obtain a new policy.

short sale   A sale of secured real property that produces less money than is owed the lender; also called a *short pay*, in that the lender releases its mortgage or trust deed so that the property can be sold free and clear to the new purchaser. In essence, the lender decides to cut its losses by agreeing to a negotiated sale rather than experiencing the delay and expense of a foreclosure action, with the possible result of owning the asset and thus carrying a "real estate owned" on its books. Short sales have become more common after the 2009 housing crisis. Lenders often require that the brokers adjust their commissions before the sale takes place—even though the lender is not on the title, it is often positioned to call the shots. (*See* **foreclosure**.)

short-term capital gain   A tax term for gain from the sale or exchange of a capital asset held for one year or less. Short-term capital gains (net of short-term capital losses) are taxed at ordinary income tax rates. (*See* **capital gain**.)

should   Common statutory language meaning that which is recommended but not required by law.

sick building syndrome (SBS)   A label given to indoor air quality problems in commercial and industrial buildings that lead to symptoms that affect at least 20 percent of building occupants during the time they spend in the building and which go away when they leave the building and cannot be traced to specific pollutants or sources within the building. Symptoms may include headaches, fatigue, and skin and eye irritations. Suspect pollutants usually include formaldehyde, which is used in carpets, paints, and pressed wood; pesticides; heated fragrance oils, which are petroleum-based, biological organisms; and combustion-promoted pollutants. Buildings sealed to promote energy efficiency contribute to the problem. (*See* **building-related illness [BRI]**.)

siding   (*revestimiento exterior*)   Boards nailed to the vertical studs, with or without intervening sheathing, to form the exposed surface of the outside walls of the building. Siding may be made of wood, metal, or masonry sheets.

sight-line   A view channel or plane. The CC&Rs of some subdivisions contain provisions designed to preserve maximum sight lines on lots having a view potential.

signage   Slang term for signs, typically referring to whether there are any restrictions of the size or placement of signs on the property.

signature   (*firma*)   Use of any name, including a trade or fictitious name, upon an instrument, or any word or mark used as and intended to be a written signature. To be valid, a signature may be handwritten, typed, printed, stamped, or made in any manner, including pencil. To be acceptable for recordation, however, a document usually must be signed in black ink and include one's full legal name (i.e., the name used to sign checks). A party who cannot write can sign by using a mark, such as "John *X* (his mark) Brown." This mark signature is referred to as "amanuensis." All but the *X* may be typed, but the *X* itself must be affixed by the one signing. In some states, signatures on deeds or contracts for deed must be witnessed.

Under the statute of frauds, a real estate sales contract must be "in writing and signed by the person to be charged therewith." This signature need not appear at the end of the document, though it customarily does. If a statute requires that a document be *subscribed*, however, it must be signed at the end. For example, witnesses to a will (at least two) must generally subscribe their names at the end of the will and in the presence of the testator, who has already signed above their names.

The signature of an attorney-in-fact is not valid on a real estate contract unless his authority is by way of a written power of attorney (under the equal-dignities rule). The power of attorney should also be recorded when the parties intend to record the documents. The proper form of signature is for the attorney-in-fact to place first the name of the principal, and then sign his own name as attorney-in-fact: "John Fred Principal, by John William Agent, his attorney-in-fact."

A listing agreement need be signed only by the party to be charged. Thus, a broker who obtains from the husband a listing that the wife does not sign still has an enforceable employment contract against the husband. All co-owners, including a husband and wife, selling property must sign the necessary transfer documents, though it is not necessary that they all sign one document; that is, they could convey by separate deeds.

For written leases to be valid, it is necessary that the lessors sign because they are conveying possession. Though it is not necessary that lessees sign the document if they accept its terms and take possession of the leased premises, it is preferable that both lessors and lessees read and sign the instrument to prevent disputes from arising between the parties.

When signing a document, fiduciaries should indicate the capacity in which they are signing. For example, a guardian should sign as follows: "Angelo Domini, as legal guardian of Charlie Sanchez, a minor." Likewise, a trust document should be signed: "Angelo Domini, as trustee for the Charlie Sanchez Trust, and not individually." (*See* **electronic signature, legal name, seal**.)

signs   (*letreros*)   Printed display boards frequently used to indicate the availability of real estate on the market. Many communities expressly prohibit the display of For Sale, Sold, and For Rent signs to prevent blockbusting, protect existing home values, and eliminate the overall impression of too many properties for sale in the area. Although in a case based on First Amendment rights to free speech, the U.S. Supreme Court has invalidated at least one local ordinance that banned the use of For Sale signs in the community. Generally it is illegal to place signs, such as "Brookshire Condo Complex—Turn Right Three Blocks," on public property or a public right-of-way.

As a mode of advertising, signs must comply with all advertising regulations such as federal truth-in-lending laws and real estate license laws. Generally, an owner's consent is required before placing a For Sale sign on the property.

silent partner   (*socio capitalista*)   An inactive partner in business. (*See* **limited partner**.)

silent second   An unrecorded second mortgage, typically held secret from the underlying first mortgagee.

sill   The lowest horizontal member of the house frame, which rests atop the foundation wall and forms a base for the studs. The term can also refer to the lowest horizontal member in the frame for a window or door.

SIMPLE   *See* **Savings Incentive Match Plan for Employees (SIMPLE)**.

simple interest   Interest computed on the principal balance only and not additionally on unpaid but previously earned interest. (*See* **add-on interest, compound interest**.)

simplified employee plan (SEP)   A type of pension plan into which both the employer and the employee can contribute that is simpler to set up and operate than most Keoghs and can be used by the self-employed. Since 2003, self-employeds can deduct investment contributions up to, but not more than, the ceiling for profit-sharing Keoghs. Employees must be included in the plan. SEP-IRA allows the taxpayer to set up the plan early in the year and take the deduction for the previous year.

S

single agency   The practice of representing either the buyer or the seller but not both in the same transaction. The single-agency broker may be compensated indirectly through an authorized commission split or directly by the principal who employed the agent to represent him or her.

A single-agency broker does not act as a dual agent when one of the broker's buyer clients wants to purchase an in-house listing. Instead, the broker recommends that one of the parties (usually the buyer) either find another broker or continue in the transaction unrepresented. (*See* **dual agency [limited agency]**.)

single-family residence   (*vivienda unifamiliar*)   A structure maintained and used as a single dwelling unit, designed for occupancy by one family, as in a private home; opposite of a condominium, apartment building, or PUD. A subdivider often restricts use of subdivided lots to single-family residences. It is advisable to further restrict the property to single-family *detached* residences if the subdivider intends to preclude the possibility of someone's using the property for a duplex dwelling.

According to the typical landlord-tenant code, "notwithstanding that a dwelling unit shares one or more walls with another dwelling unit, it shall be deemed a single-family residence if it has direct access to a street or thoroughfare and does not share hot-water equipment or any other essential facility in service with any other dwelling unit."

Although zoning ordinances can validly limit the number of occupants or restrict occupancy to a single family, the ordinance cannot be arbitrary and discriminatory in its definition of "family." For example, a commercial boarding house may be properly excluded from single-family residential zones, whereas a communal living situation (for example, several elderly couples sharing housing) may not be declared improper. Some ordinances include as a "family" unmarried people and their children living together as a family unit as well as small groups living together in extended families.

single licensing   A state law requirement that all real estate agents have the same license rather than the traditional method of licensing salespersons and brokers. Colorado was the first state to adopt such a single license requirement.

single-load corridor   A building term used to describe a building design in which the apartment units are located on only one side of the corridor, with a wall spanning the other side. The alternative is a double-load situation with apartments on both sides of the corridor, as in many hotels.

sinking fund   (*fondo de amortización*)   A fund created to amass enough money gradually to satisfy a debt or to meet a specific requirement; a fund designed to accumulate money to a predetermined amount at the end of a stated period of time, such as a fund set up to repay debentures. The sinking fund method of depreciation contemplates periodic investments of equal amounts of money in a compound-interest-bearing account wherein the investment, plus the compound interest, replaces the improvement at the end of its economic life.

Example: Assume a retail operator enters into a 20-year lease for a store with an option to buy for $100,000 at the end of the lease term. In order to have $100,000 at the end of the term, the operator would have to set aside each year in a sinking fund the principal amount of $3,024, assuming a 5 percent return compounded annually ($100,000 × 0.03024, the factor in a sinking fund table for a 20-year, 5-percent compound return). Also called the **reinvestment method**. A condominium association may set up a maintenance reserve fund in this fashion. (*See* **amortization**.)

SIOR   *See* **Society of Industrial and Office REALTORS®** in Appendix B.

site   The position, situation, or location of a piece of land.

site office   A temporary place of realty business other than the principal place of business or branch office, from which real estate activities are conducted that relate to a specific piece of real property (open house), real estate condominium project, or real estate subdivision. The office must be situated on or adjacent to the specific property, condominium project, or subdivision to be considered a site office, and it must comply with respective city and county requirements pertaining to temporary land use. Usually a brokerage company does not need a special license to operate a site office, nor does it need a broker in charge of the office.

situs
1. The preference by people for a certain location.
2. The place where something exists or originates; the place where something (as a right) is held to be located in law.

sky lease   A lease of the air rights above a property. (*See* **air rights**.)

skylight   (*tragaluz*, *claraboya*)   An opening in a roof that is covered with glass and is designed to admit light.

slab   A flat, horizontal reinforced concrete area, usually the interior floor of a building but also an exterior or roof area.

slander of title   A tort or civil wrong in which a person maliciously makes disparaging, untrue statements concerning another's title to property, thus causing injury. The disparaging statement may be oral or written, but it must be conveyed to some third person(s). Some statements are privileged, notably a lis pendens pleading filed in the appropriate court. Willful failure to remove a satisfied judgment lien may be grounds for a slander of title action.

sleeper note   A promissory note in which the interest and principal are payable together on a future date.

slum clearance   The clearing of old, decrepit buildings so the land may be put to a better, more productive use. This is most often done to eliminate substandard and often unsanitary living conditions. HUD is active in slum clearance, often replacing dilapidated structures with new, low-income housing. (*See* **urban renewal**.)

Small Business Administration (SBA)   A federal agency created to take over the small business function of the Reconstruction Finance Corporation. The SBA is supervised by an administrator appointed by the president. Its function is to administer the federal government's program for the preservation and development of small business concerns. Among other things, the SBA is authorized to make loans to small businesses to finance plant construction, conversion, or expansion, including the acquisition of land. These loans may be made either directly or in participation with private lenders. Before the SBA can make a direct loan, it must try to get a private lender to participate in the loan.

Small Business Liability Relief and Brownfields Revitalization Act   *See* Appendix D.

small claims court   A division of the district court whose jurisdiction is limited to cases of claims not exceeding a certain amount, for example, $1,000 exclusive of interest and costs. The purpose of the small claims court is to provide an inexpensive and speedy forum for the disposition of minor controversies. A key feature of these courts is that attorneys usually are not allowed to participate in the proceedings.

 If landlord and tenant disagree about the right of the landlord to claim and retain the security deposit or any portion of it, either the landlord or the tenant may commence an action in the small claims division of the district court. (*See* **security deposit**.)

SMSA   *See* **standard metropolitan statistical area (SMSA)**.

snob zoning   *See* **acreage zoning**.

Society of Industrial and Office REALTORS® (SIOR)   *See* Appendix A.

Society of Real Estate Appraisers (SREA)   *See* Appendix A.

soffits
1. The external underside of eaves, beams, overhangs.
2. The finished space between the ceiling and cabinets, often found in kitchens.

soft money
1. The money to be financed under a purchase-money mortgage as a part of the purchase price.
2. Tax-deductible items such as carrying charges (interest, real estate taxes, and ground rents) incurred while holding unimproved property or during construction. Soft money does not increase the equity position, as would the payment of hard dollars. (*See* **carrying charges**.)

soil bank   A program administered by the Commodity Stabilization Service of the U.S. Department of Agriculture in which farmers contract to divert land from production of unneeded crops to conservation uses. Such individuals receive an annual rent from the government for this land.

solar easement   An easement designed to protect an owner's access to light and the rays of the sun. There is no common-law right to light and air on one's property. Therefore, if an owner's solar heating system is rendered ineffective because of shadows cast by a neighbor's tree or a proposed nearby condominium, the owner would be left with no legal remedy except to try to negotiate a purchase of an easement to restrict blocking out the sun.

Some jurisdictions are attempting to legislate solar easements to encourage property owners to use more efficient energy systems. California has a statute declaring vegetation shading a solar collector a "nuisance." Other communities offer incentives to builders who protect solar access in their designs. For example, a builder might receive a density bonus of up to 20 percent for incorporating solar access into plans of streets, lots, and buildings.

solar heating   A natural system of heating using the energy of the sun. Both local and federal tax incentives are offered to encourage homeowners to use such energy-efficient systems.

Soldiers and Sailors Civil Relief Act (SSCRA)   *See* Appendix D.

sole proprietorship   A method of owning a business in which one person owns the entire business and reports all profits and losses directly on a personal income tax return, as contrasted with corporate, joint, or partnership ownership.

A sole or individual proprietorship is easy to organize and flexible to operate and is frequently used in real estate brokerage. Individual proprietors may run a brokerage company if they have a valid broker's license. Proprietors may use their own name or a fictitious name previously registered as required by state law.

There is a growing tendency for sole proprietors to incorporate and thus take advantage of certain tax and fringe benefits, such as those provided by pension and profit-sharing plans.

sole tenancy   *See* **tenancy in severalty**.

space plan   Preliminary drawing by an architect, which lays out the floor plan of a leased space to meet the tenant's requirements.

spec home
1. A home built on speculation. (*See* **speculation**.)
2. A model home. (*See* **model home**.)

special agent   One authorized by a principal to perform a particular act or transaction, without contemplation of continuity of service as with a general agent. The real estate broker is ordinarily a special agent appointed by the seller to find a ready, willing, and able buyer for a particular property. An attorney-in-fact under a limited power of attorney is a special agent. (*See* **agent**, **agency**, **general agent**.)

special assessment   A tax or levy customarily imposed against only those specific parcels of realty that will benefit from a proposed public improvement, as opposed to a general tax on the entire community. Because the proposed improvement will enhance the value of the affected homes, only those affected owners must pay this special lien.

Special assessments differ from property taxes in that the latter are levied for the support of the general functions of government, whereas special assessments are levied for the cost of specific local improvements such as streets, sewers, irrigation, and drainage. Common examples of special assessments are water, sidewalk, and sewer assessments, or other special improvements, such as parks and recreational facilities. In some instances, special assessments are periodically levied by improvement districts; in other instances, they are levied only by the city and county for a particular work or improvement.

Owners often either pay the special assessments in installments over several years or pay the balance in full. When a sales contract is involved, it should specify which party is responsible for payment of assessments, if any, at the time of closing. Typically, however, the seller pays for all improvements substantially completed by the closing date because of the increased property value generally resulting from the improvement. Improvements not substantially completed but authorized or in progress are usually assumed by the buyer. In any event, this matter is open to negotiation between buyer and seller.

Special assessments are generally apportioned according to benefits received, rather than by the value of the land and buildings being assessed. This apportionment is frequently called the *assessment-roll spread.* For example, in a residential subdivision, the assessment for installation of storm drains, curbs, and gutters is made on a front-foot basis. The property owner is charged for each foot of his or her lot that abuts the street being improved.

For income tax purposes, real estate taxes are currently deductible. Special assessments, however, are not directly deductible because they increase the value of the property and thus, like any other capital expenditure, add to the cost or basis of the property. The assessment is generally not eligible for depreciation, however. In some cases, a special assessment is deductible if the investor/taxpayer can prove that all or part of the assessment is made for maintenance, repairs, or interest charges. (*See* **insurance**, **property taxes**.)

special benefit   The value added to a specific property or a limited number of properties as a result of some government improvement. In determining the just compensation for a property that is partially taken by condemnation, some courts consider the market value of the property taken plus severance damages less any special benefits. Other courts may consider just compensation to be the difference, if any, between the before value and the value of the remainder property, recognizing any special benefits. Thus, if the state takes a portion of a property for an improvement and the improvement actually increases the value of the remaining land, then the court in a condemnation proceeding may consider the value of the special benefit and reduce the just compensation accordingly. (*See* **before-and-after method**, **just compensation**, **severance damages**.)

special conditions   Specific provisions in a real estate sales contract that must be satisfied before the contract is binding. Typical conditions are those subject to the following:
- Buyer obtaining a $95,000 first mortgage at an interest rate not to exceed 7 percent to be amortized for no longer than a 30-year period
- Buyer furnishing seller with a satisfactory written credit report within [number of calendar days] of acceptance of this offer
- Any repairs [or additions] being completed as agreed before closing and approved in writing by buyer and seller by [date]
- Buyer's acceptance of written inventory furnishings, plants, and the like

- All appliances, electrical and plumbing fixtures and systems being in good working order on closing
- Seller furnishing a Wood Destroying Insect Inspection Report from a reputable pest control company, showing no active, visible infestation of termites or other wood destroying insects in improvements

(*See* **contingency**, **Wood Destroying Insect Inspection Report**.)

special lien   A lien or charge against a specific parcel of property, such as a mortgage, an attachment, or a mechanic's lien. Also called a **specific lien**. A general lien, on the other hand, is a charge against all property of the debtor. (*See* **general lien, lien**.)

special-purpose property   (*propiedad para uso especial*)   A combination of land and improvements with only one highest and best use because of some special design, such as a church, nursing home, school, post office, or hospital.

special-use permit   Permission from the local zoning authority granting a land use that is identified as a special exception in the zoning ordinance. For instance, a zoning ordinance for a residential area might authorize certain special uses for churches, hospitals, or country clubs, provided a permit is first obtained. A special use differs from a variance in that the latter is an authorized violation of the zoning ordinance, whereas the special use is a permitted exception. The standards for a variance are much more difficult than the standards for a special-use permit. (*See* **nonconforming use, variance**.)

special-use zoning   *See* **conditional use zoning**.

special warranty deed   A deed in which grantors warrant or guarantee the title only against defects arising during the period of their tenure and ownership of the property and not against defects existing before that time. Such a deed is usually identified by the language "by, through, or under the grantor, but not otherwise." A special warranty deed is often used when a fiduciary such as an executor or trustee conveys the property of the principal because the fiduciary usually has no authority to warrant against acts of his predecessors in title. This is sometimes used when one spouse conveys property to the other spouse as part of a divorce decree.

specifications   Written instructions to a building contractor containing all the necessary information regarding the materials, dimensions, colors, and other features of a proposed construction. Specifications supplement the plans and working drawings. (*See* **plans and specifications**.)

specific lien   *See* **special lien**.

specific performance   An action brought in a court of equity in special cases to compel a party to carry out the terms of a contract. The basis for an equity court's jurisdiction in breach of a real estate contract is the fact that land is unique and mere legal damages would not adequately compensate the buyer for the seller's breach. The courts cannot, however, specifically enforce a contract to perform personal services, such as a broker's agreement to find a buyer; nor can they enforce an illegal agreement, an ambiguous contract, or a contract in which there is inadequate consideration.

If a seller refuses to sell to a buyer under a contract of sale, the buyer can request a court specifically to enforce the contract and make the seller deed the property under threat of contempt of court. Similarly, a buyer can have a judge enforce performance of a conveyance by the heirs of a deceased seller under a contract of sale.

In some jurisdictions, a seller can force a defaulting buyer to purchase the property, especially if land values have declined. In most cases, however, a seller would have a difficult time proving that the legal remedy of money damages would not be adequate relief, and the seller *must* show this inadequacy to obtain specific performance relief.

speculator
1. One who analyzes a real property market and acquires properties with the expectation that prices will greatly increase, at which time the speculator can sell at a large profit. Many states have enacted legislation against certain land speculation. Some states impose a land gains tax on the gain derived from the sale or exchange of land held less than a set period of time ("antispeculation tax"). The greater the gain and the shorter the time the land is held before the sale, the greater the tax.
2. An owner/builder who constructs homes ("spec homes") expecting to find willing buyers when the homes are *completed* (rather than have a specific buyer ready at the time construction begins). This practice is often called *building on spec.*

spendthrift trust   A trust created to provide a source of money for the maintenance and support of a designated beneficiary and, at the same time, to secure the property from being wasted or depleted by the beneficiary's improvidence or irresponsibility. Income-producing real property is sometimes the subject of a spendthrift trust containing provisions against alienation of the trust fund by the voluntary act of the beneficiary or by creditors.

spin-off   The transfer of a company's assets to a recently formed subsidiary. To control a specific real estate development, a corporation sometimes trades part of its assets to a new corporation in exchange for stock in the new corporation, which is then distributed to the stockholders of the parent company.

spite fence   A fence that is erected and is of such height or type as to annoy a neighbor. Some states have spite fence statutes, which limit the height of fences to, say, ten feet. There is some dispute as to whether a maliciously erected fence under the statutory height can be abated.

split-fee financing   A form of joint venture participation in which the lender actually purchases the fee land under the proposed development project and leases it to the developer. The lender also finances the improvements to be constructed on this leasehold.

split-level   A house in which two or more floors are usually located directly above one another, and one or more additional floors, adjacent to them, are placed at a different level.

split-rate   Capitalization rates applied separately to land and improvements, to determine the value of each.

splitting fees   The act of sharing compensation. A broker can generally split a commission only with the buyer or the seller, with another licensee in the broker's own state, or with a broker from another state who did not participate in any negotiations within the first broker's state. Paying any remuneration to an unlicensed person for referring a client is illegal and could result in suspension or revocation of the broker's license. If the broker wishes to split fees with a licensed salesperson, the money must pass through the salesperson's employing broker. (*See* **cooperating broker, finder's fee**.)

spot loan   A loan on a particular property, usually a condominium unit, by a lender who has not previously financed that particular condominium project. Because of the great amount of background work and investigation required to investigate the entire condominium project and to inspect all relevant documents, many lenders are unwilling to lend money for a single unit in a large condominium development. Other lenders make spot loans for reimbursement of their legal and other service fees required to analyze the loan.

spot survey   A survey that illustrates the locations, sizes, and shapes of buildings, improvements, and easements located on a property, as well as those on any neighboring property that may encroach on the surveyed property. A lender may require a spot survey and a legal description of the land as a prerequisite to financing a project, especially a large development.

spot zoning   A change in the local zoning ordinance permitting a particular use inconsistent with the zoning classification of the area; the reclassification of a small area of land in such a manner as to disturb the tenor of the surrounding neighborhood, such as a change to permit one multiunit structure in an area zoned for single-family residential use; also called a **variance**.

     Spot zoning is not favored in the law. If the change affects only a small area and is not in harmony with the comprehensive general plan for that area (such as a chemical factory in a residential neighborhood), spot zoning is open to attack and will not be permitted by the courts. A permissible spot zone might allow a small grocery store or convenience shop to give easy access to the surrounding residential areas. Also called *contract zoning*.

spreading agreement   An agreement to "spread" or extend an existing mortgage lien to encompass several properties, in order to give the lender additional security on the loan. (*See* **blanket mortgage**.)

spur track   That segment of rail track, usually privately owned by the industry using it, which leads off a drill track or main line and services an industrial plant or site.

square   In the government (rectangular) survey of land description, an area measuring 24 miles by 24 miles; sometimes referred to as a *quadrangle*.

square-foot method   (*método de metros cuadrados*)   A method of estimating a building's construction, reproduction, or replacement costs whereby the structure's square-foot floor area is multiplied by an appropriate construction cost per square foot.

squatter's right   The right of a person in adverse possession of real property. A squatter's possession must generally be actual, open, notorious, exclusive, and continuous for a period of time prescribed by statute. (*See* **adverse possession**.)

SREA   *See* **Society of Real Estate Appraisers**.

staging

1. Temporary scaffolding used to support workers and materials during construction.
2. A process by which the real estate licensee or a staging specialist assists the seller in selecting, designing, rearranging, or modifying the home in order to better show it to buyers, hopefully, to produce a better sale price; also called *prepping a property*.

staging area   An area, either outside at a construction site or inside a building, usually close to its loading doors, where material, apparatus, equipment, or merchandise is collected or assembled before it is moved to where it will finally be used or stored.

staking   A method of identifying the boundaries of a parcel of land by placing stakes or pins in the ground or by painting marks on stone walls or rocks. While staking shows the corners of the property, it does not provide the complete dimensions of the property (or the existence of possible encroachments), as would a boundary survey.

standard metropolitan statistical area (SMSA)   An important designation given by the federal Office of Management and Budget to counties with at least one central city of 50,000 or more residents. In New England, SMSAs consist of groups of cities and townships rather than entire counties. The SMSA designation is often used as a qualifying standard for governmental grants, such as the Community Development Block Grant.

     Under the Interstate Land Sales Act, subdivisions containing fewer than 300 lots if the purchaser's principal residence is within the same SMSA as the subdivision may be eligible for a special exemption for registration requirements.

standard parallel   In the government (rectangular) survey system of land description, one of a series of east-west lines, generally spaced 24 miles apart and located north and south of, and parallel to, the base lines. Such parallels establish township boundaries at 24-mile intervals and correct inaccuracies due to the curvature of the earth; also called **correction lines**.

Standards of Practice   A set of ethical criteria formulated by the Professional Standards Committee of the National Association of REALTORS®. Such Standards of Practice are amplifications of certain articles of the REALTORS® Code of Ethics. A charge of an alleged violation of the Code of Ethics by a REALTOR® that has been filed should read as an alleged violation of one or more articles of the code. A Standard of Practice may be cited only in support of the charge that the article was violated. (*See **Uniform Standards of Professional Appraisal Practice [USPAP]**.*)

standby fee   A substantial sum paid by a borrower at the time of issuance of a standby commitment letter, as a charge for the lender's risk and responsibility in committing to the loan. The standby fee is forfeited if the loan is not closed within a specified time. Most courts uphold the forfeiture of the standby fee as a lawful damage provision and not as an unlawful penalty. (*See **standby loan**.*)

standby loan   An arrangement whereby the lender agrees to keep a certain amount of money available to the borrower, usually a developer, for a specified period of time. Thus, a standby loan is like an option on a loan because the developer has the right to borrow the money but is not obligated to do so. In fact, the terms of the standby commitment are usually onerous to discourage the developer from exercising the loan, so it amounts to a commitment to make a loan in the future, if the borrower cannot get better financing elsewhere. Standby loans are usually made by noninstitutional lenders and are usually short term, from 18 to 24 months. The standby fee is typically 2 to 3 percent of the loan per year. Developers should be careful to specify those conditions that will excuse their performance under the terms of the standby loan agreement, such as condemnation of a building site or refusal of a building permit.

standing loan

1. A commitment by interim or construction lenders to keep the money they have already funded in the project for a specified period of time after the expiration of the interim loan, usually until permanent takeout financing is secured. For instance, a lender might agree to provide an interim construction loan for one year and a standing loan for two years from the date of termination of the one-year loan. This usually enables the borrower to build and rent a shopping center or office building before obtaining permanent financing, thus improving the chance of obtaining favorable permanent financing.
2. A straight mortgage (i.e., one that calls for payments of interest only with no amortization during its term and the entire principal becoming due at maturity). The entire principal "stands" until satisfaction. (*See **straight note**.*)

Starker exchange   *See* **delayed exchange**.

starter

1. Reference to an earlier title report on a particular piece of real property. Many title companies have copies of earlier policies in their title plants; if there is a starter on a property, the title searcher can avoid having to search back to the original source of title again. The searcher need only search all relevant records for items affecting the title from the date of the starter up to the date of the search.
2. A person's first residence or other real estate investment. (*See* **pyramiding**.)

starts   A term commonly used to indicate the number of residential units begun within a stated period of time. (*See* **housing starts**.)

startup costs   *See* **front money**.

S

state-certified appraiser   An appraiser certified or licensed according to certification requirements set by the state, which are consistent with those formulated by the Appraisal Qualification Board of the Appraisal Foundation and approved by the Appraisal Subcommittee of the federal Financial Institutions Examination Council. The certificate may be residential or general.

statement of condition   *See* **reduction certificate**.

statement of record   A document that must be filed with a HUD registration of subdivided land intended to be sold using any means of interstate commerce. The lengthy and detailed statement of record requires information dealing with the property, the site, and the developer, including such information as the name and address of each person having an interest in the property, a legal description of the property, general terms and conditions of contracts including prices, descriptions of access to the property and public utilities, and all encumbrances. In addition, copies of the corporation or partnership documents of the developer and other instruments relating to the property are required. In support of the statement of record, the developer must also provide financial statements (certified in certain cases). (*See* **Interstate Land Sales Full Disclosure Act**.)

state revenue stamp   *See* **transfer tax (conveyance fee)**.

statute   A law enacted by Congress (federal law) or by a state legislature (state law), as opposed to judicial or common law; statutory law as opposed to case law.

statute of frauds   State law that requires certain contracts to be in writing and signed by the party to be charged (or held) to the agreement in order to be legally enforceable. Most state statutes of frauds are based on the original English Statute for Prevention of Frauds and Perjuries (1677). Statutes of frauds generally require that all contracts for the sale of land or any interest therein (and some listings) be written. Oral leases for a period not exceeding one year, however, are generally valid and enforceable. The law does not require a single, formal contract; the writing could consist of a memorandum of the contract or several items of correspondence, so long as the material terms agreed on are stated. In one case, the commission terms were jotted on the back of the broker's business card and initialed by the seller. The writing can even be a subsequent confirmation of an earlier oral contract ("this letter is to confirm our prior telephone understanding").

It is generally held that a valid written agreement can be canceled by a subsequent oral agreement. This is so because the statute of frauds deals only with the *making* of a contract.

The parties to an oral real estate contract may have a valid contract (i.e., one containing all the essential elements), but the contract is not enforceable if it is not in writing. The statute of frauds relates to the remedy only and not to the inherent validity of the contract. Thus, the parties to a fully executed or performed oral agreement cannot thereafter assert the statute of frauds to seek rescission of the contract. The statute may be pleaded only as an affirmative defense to a lawsuit seeking enforcement of the oral contract.

The purpose of the statute of frauds is to prevent the perpetration of fraud by seeking enforcement of an executory contract that was never in fact made; it is not designed to prevent the performance of oral contracts. Thus there are exceptions to the statute of frauds, mostly where the assertion of the statute of frauds as a defense against an oral contract would in itself amount to a fraud or result in unjust enrichment or unconscionable injury. In some instances, part performance of an oral agreement will take the case out of the statute of frauds. For example, a contract will be "taken out" of the statute of frauds if the buyer, in reliance on a seller's oral promise to sell the property, pays part or all of the purchase price, enters into possession, and makes substantial improvements on the property. In such a case of part performance, some courts refuse to allow the seller to assert the statute of frauds as a defense against the buyer's action to force the seller to fulfill the terms of the oral agreement to sell.

The Uniform Commercial Code states that contracts for the sale of personal property in excess of $500 must be in writing. If a seller wishes to retain a fixture (regardless if under $500), this fact must be clearly stated in the contract, because a fixture is considered to be real estate. (*See* **estoppel, parol evidence rule, unenforceable contract.**)

statute of limitations   (*ley de prescripción*)   That law pertaining to the period of time within which certain actions must be brought to court. The law is intended to protect the vigilant against stale claims by requiring the prompt assertion of claims; thus an action must be brought (i.e., the complaint filed) within a specified time of the occurrence of the cause of action. After the time period expires, the claim is said to be "outlawed" and may not be enforced in court. The theory behind the statute of limitations is that there must be some end to the possibility of litigation. It is said that stale witnesses and stale records produce little truth and result in accidental justice, if any.

If a partial payment is made before the time period has expired, then the full period starts running anew. If the payment is made afterward, then the debt is not revived and remains outlawed or barred. (*See* **laches.**)

statutory law   Law created by the enactment of legislation, as opposed to case law created by judicial decision.

steering   The illegal practice of channeling homeseekers interested in equivalent properties to particular areas, either to maintain the homogeneity of an area or to change the character of an area to create a speculative situation. This practice makes certain homes unavailable to homeseekers on the basis of a protected class, and on these grounds, it is prohibited by the provisions of the federal Fair Housing Act. Steering is often difficult to detect, however, because the steering tactics can be so subtle that homeseekers are unaware that their choice has been limited. Steering could be a licensee's use of a word, phrase, or act that is intended to influence the choice of a prospective property buyer on a discriminatory basis. It is estimated that more than 80 percent of the suits filed by the Department of Justice against real estate licensees for violation of the federal fair housing law have involved steering. (*See* **blockbusting, federal fair housing law, minority, protected class.**)

stepped-up basis   The new basis of property acquired from a decedent, equal to the value as finally determined by the IRS of the property transferred on the date of death, or on an alternate valuation date for federal estate tax purposes (six months after the date of death), or the fair market value where no estate tax return is filed. (*See* **basis**; **estate tax, federal.**)

step-up lease   A lease with fixed rent for an initial term and a predetermined rent increase at specified intervals and/or increases based on periodic appraisals. Because the main purpose of a step-up lease is to hedge against inflation, its term tends to be longer than that of a fixed lease. It covers increases due to inflation as well as increased taxes, insurance premiums, and maintenance costs (often keyed to federal cost of living indexes). A lease that includes specified rent decreases is a step-down lease. (*See* **graduated rental lease.**)

stick-built on-site   A term for an on-site builder who builds with raw materials that are delivered to the construction site—that is, "built from scratch." The materials are then measured, cut, and assembled by skilled craftspeople. (*See* **systems-built.**)

stigmatized property   A property regarded as undesirable because of events that occurred there; also called *psychologically impacted property*. Some conditions that typically stigmatize a property are a previous murder, gang-related activity, proximity to a nuclear plant, and even the alleged presence of ghosts. State law sometimes addresses the circumstances under which a real estate broker must disclose certain stigmas attached to a property. Under federal guidelines, the fact an occupant of the property has AIDS does not require disclosure.

S

straight-line method   A method of depreciation, also called the *age-life method*, computed by dividing the adjusted basis of a property by the number of years of estimated remaining useful life. The cost of the property is thus deducted in equal annual installments. For example, if the depreciable basis is $100,000 and the estimated useful life is 25 years, the annual depreciation deduction is $4,000 for each year during the useful life of the asset. (*See* **age-life depreciation**, **depreciation**, **recapture of depreciation**, **salvage value.**)

straight note   A promissory note evidencing a loan in which payments of interest are only made periodically during the term of the note, with the principal payment due in one lump sum upon maturity. A straight note is usually a nonamortized note made for a short term, such as three to five years, and is renewable at the end of the term. A mortgage that secures a straight note is a term mortgage or straight-term mortgage.

straw man   (*testaferro*)   One who purchases property for another so as to conceal the identity of the real purchaser; a dummy purchaser; a nominee; a front.

　　At one time, it was necessary for an owner who wanted to change a title to joint tenancy from severalty to convey the property to a straw man, who would then convey it back to the owner and joint tenant. Many states no longer require that the joint tenancy be created at the same time by one and the same instrument. Thus, an owner can convey to himself and another party as joint tenants, or convey to herself and a spouse as tenants by the entirety without using a straw man.

　　Where several tracts of land are being assembled for development, confidentiality may be important—hence the desirability of nominees and straw men. However, a federal court has held that if the nominee misrepresents the identity of the principal, with knowledge that the seller would not have negotiated if in possession of the true facts, the seller may set aside the transaction. In addition, if the nominee or straw man exercises any managerial control over the property, then he may be held to be the real owner for tax purposes.

　　If a broker or a salesperson attempts to use a straw man to purchase property listed by the broke or the salesperson, this relationship with the buyer must be specifically disclosed in writing to the seller. Failure to do so may result in license suspension or revocation.

　　In a presale of a condominium, a developer normally must attain a certain percentage of purchases before a lender commits to lend money; straw men are sometimes used to meet this minimum requirement, though this practice is clearly against the lender's policy and would be illegal in connection with VA and FHA loans. (*See* **joint tenancy.**)

street   A fully improved through roadway serving local or minor collector traffic.

strict foreclosure   *See* **foreclosure**.

stringer
　　1. One of the sloping enclosed sides of a staircase that supports the treads and risers.
　　2. A horizontal beam that connects the uprights in a frame.

structural alterations   Any change in the supporting members of a building, such as bearing walls or partitions; columns, beams, or girders; or any structural change in the roof, but not normally including extension or enlargement of the building. (*See* **nonconforming use.**)

structural defects   In residential homes, actual damage to the load-bearing portion of a home that affects its load-bearing function and vitally affects the use of the home for residential purposes. This includes damage from shifting soil from causes other than earthquake or flood.

structural density   The ratio of the total ground floor area of a building to the total land area. The average density for a general-purpose industrial building is about one-third.

structure (*cimbra*, *estructura*)   Something built or constructed; an improvement. A structure in local building codes is usually "anything that is more than 18 inches off the ground and cannot be lifted by a person without mechanical aid," or "any production or piece of work, artificially built up or composed of parts and joined together in some defined manner." As a rule, a structure can be built only after a building permit is obtained.

     An interesting question arises from a poorly drafted restriction against building any structure without developer approval, e.g., whether a swimming pool, fence, or tennis court is a structure.

stucco (*estuco*)   A cement or plaster wall covering that is installed wet and dries into a hard surface coating. There have been a number of lawsuits involving property defects caused by certain synthetic stucco materials. (*See* **exterior insulation and finish systems [EIFS]**.)

stud   In wall framing, the vertical members to which horizontal pieces are attached. Studs are placed 16 to 24 inches apart and serve as the main support for the roof and/or the second floor.

studio   *See* **efficiency unit or apartment.**

subagent   An agent of a person who is already acting as an agent for a principal. The original agent can delegate authority to a subagent where such delegation is either expressly authorized or customary in the trade. For example, it is customary for listing brokers to delegate certain functions of a ministerial nature to subagents, such as to show property and solicit buyers.

     Many multiple listing services were based on the theory that a listing is an offer of subagency to members and that members who work on such listings do so as subagents of the listing broker. That changed to an offer of cooperation and compensation in 1993.

     Where it is clear that the principal has authorized the agent to appoint subagents, the relation of principal and agent also exists between the principal and the subagent. A subagent who is lawfully appointed represents the principal in like manner with the prime agent. Some courts hold that the prime agent is not responsible to third persons for acts of the subagent. (*See* **agency**.)

subagreement of sale   An agreement of sale (contract for deed) between the original vendee of an agreement of sale and a new purchaser. Under such an agreement, there is no contractual relationship between the new purchaser (subvendee) and the owner of the property (original vendor).

     An assignment of agreement of sale is a transfer to the new buyer of the original vendee's right, title, and interest in that agreement. A subagreement of sale, however, is an entirely new contract, strictly between the original vendee and the new buyer. Because the original vendor usually reserves the right to consent to all transfers by the vendee, the subagreement of sale should not contain any provisions that are prejudicial to the original vendor; otherwise, the vendor can withhold consent and delay the transaction closing.

     Because of the complications that can arise with a subagreement of sale, many attorneys recommend that the new parties enter into an entirely new contract clearly detailing the rights and obligations of all parties, and that they set up a collection account to handle all the payments. (*See* **collection account**, **contract for deed**.)

subchapter S corporation   *See* **S corporation**.

subcontractor   A builder or contractor who enters into an agreement with a developer or the prime contractor to perform a special portion of the construction work, such as electrical, plumbing, or air-conditioning installation. The subcontractor does not deal directly with the owner; however, if not paid by the prime contractor, the subcontractor can assert a mechanic's lien against the property within a certain time after a notice of completion is published. (*See* **contractor**.)

S

subdivider   An owner whose land is divided into two or more lots and offered for disposition. Under the Uniform Land Sales Practices Act, a subdivider may also be the principal agent of an inactive owner. A subdivider who later puts improvements on the property becomes a developer.

subdivision   (*fraccionamiento, subdivisión*)   Land that is divided or is proposed to be divided for the purpose of disposition into two or more lots, parcels, units, or interests. *Subdivision* usually refers to any land, whether contiguous or not, if two or more lots, parcels, units, or interests are offered as part of a common promotional plan of advertising and sale. The law would thus apply to the sale of a ¹⁄₂₅ undivided interest in a large parcel of land.

   A developer of a subdivision must first comply with the subdivision regulations of the county or municipality in which the property is located. Upon local approval and posting of any required improvement completion bonds, the subdivider usually must then register the subdivision with the proper state agency before beginning to sell. In certain cases, the subdivider must also register the subdivision under the federal Interstate Land Sales Full Disclosure Act. (*See* **restriction**.)

subdivision registration law   Laws requiring subdivision registration to protect prospective purchasers from the deceptive practices and abuses once common in the unregulated sale of greater numbers of unimproved lots. There are usually many exemptions from registration, such as if the consumer is adequately protected by other regulations (condominium law, local building codes), or if there are only a few purchasers or lots.

   If the subdivision contains fewer than 100 lots, and if any means of interstate commerce is used to dispose of the lots (such as the U.S. mail), the subdivider may have to register the subdivision with the federal Department of Housing and Urban Development (HUD). If each lot is 20 acres or more in size (inclusive of easements), the subdivision is exempt from the HUD requirements.

   To register a subdivision, the subdivider must submit a form application to the proper state regulatory agency containing such things as a legal description of the property; names, occupations, and interests of applicant's officers and directors; current title policy; copies of all proposed documents the prospective purchaser is to sign; a statement of zoning; advertising material; the proposed public offering statement; and a current financial statement.

   If the registration is accepted, the subdivider can then sell the lots using a public offering statement, which is designed to disclose fully and accurately to a prospective purchaser all material and relevant facts concerning the subdivision. As with any disclosure device, there is a constant interplay between the subdivider, who considers the public offering statement as a marketing tool, and the attorney preparing it, who considers it as an insurance document against later lawsuits for failing to disclose accurate material facts.

   If the subdivider does not use the current public offering statement, the regulatory agency can issue a cease-and-desist order to stop all selling and revoke the registration. It is generally unlawful for anyone to sell or offer an interest in nonexempt, subdivided lands without first registering the subdivision, delivering a current public offering statement to the prospective purchaser and giving that person reasonable opportunity to examine it and sign a formal receipt for it.

   An injured purchaser can usually recover the consideration paid plus interest from the date of payment, property taxes paid, costs, and reasonable attorney fees less any income received. The scope of liability under these laws is very broad and will generally cover not only the subdivider but also all officers, employees, real estate salespeople, and brokers, who are jointly and severally liable unless they can sustain the burden that they did not know the existence of facts by reason of which the liability is alleged to exist. (*See* **Interstate Land Sales Full Disclosure Act**.)

subflooring   Boards or plywood sheets nailed directly to the floor joists serving as a base for the finish flooring. Subflooring is usually made of rough boards, although some houses have concrete subflooring.

S

subjacent support   The support that the surface of the earth receives from its underlying strata. (*See* **lateral and subjacent support**.)

subjective value   The amount a specific person might pay to possess a property; also called *personal value*. Contrast with *objective value*, or what a reasonable person might be expected to pay for the same property.

subject property   A reference to the real property under discussion, or the real property under appraisal.

"subject to" clause   The clause in a contract for sale setting forth any contingencies or special conditions of purchase and sale, such as an offer made and accepted subject to obtaining financing, approving leases, securing certain zoning, and similar requirements. The seller might sell the property subject to existing leases, certain liens, specific restrictions, or other limitations. If exceptions are not noted in the "subject to" clause, any encumbrance will render the title unmarketable and the seller can be forced to clear the encumbrance. (*See* **contingency**, **special conditions**.)

"subject to" mortgage   A grantee taking title to a real property "subject to" a mortgage is not personally liable to the mortgagee for payment of the mortgage note. In the event that the grantor/mortgagor defaults in paying the note, however, the grantee could lose the property, and thus the equity, in a foreclosure sale.

Example: If Dudley owned a farm valued at $75,000 and had an existing $50,000 mortgage with the Bank of Upson, he could sell the property to Eugene for $75,000 subject to the mortgage. Eugene's payments would be used to meet the mortgage payments. If Eugene were to default, however, he would merely lose the property; the bank would not be able to sue Eugene for any mortgage deficiency.

To avoid this dilemma, most mortgages now contain acceleration clauses giving the mortgagee the options of whether to declare the debt due when the property is sold, to allow assumption (usually with an assumption fee) or to permit the mortgagor to sell subject to the mortgage. This special acceleration clause is often called an *alienation* or *subject to* clause. The purchaser should request an estoppel or reduction certificate from the lender to ensure that no defaults have occurred; that all installments of the loan and interest have been paid; and that the interest rates, terms, and unpaid balance of the loan are as represented by the seller.

In the usual contract for deed or the wraparound mortgage, the sale is also "subject to" the mortgage.

Real estate brokers sometimes buy property subject to existing mortgages when they expect to resell the property shortly and do not want to be named parties on too many mortgages. In such cases, brokers must be especially careful to disclose to the sellers all the ramifications of selling subject to the mortgage. (*See* **assumption of mortgage**, **reduction certificate**.)

sublease   (*subarrendamiento, contrato de subarrendamiento*)   A lease given by a lessee for a portion of the leasehold interest, while the lessee retains some reversionary interest. The sublease may be for all or part of the premises, for the whole term or part of it, as long as the lessor retains some interest in the property. Leases normally contain a clause prohibiting subletting without prior consent of the lessor. The lessee remains directly liable to the lessor for the rent, which is usually paid by the sublessee to the lessee and then from the lessee to the lessor. The sublessee does not have a contractual obligation to pay rent to the original lessor.

If the lessee transfers her entire interest in the lease, however, this is called an *assignment of lease*. In an assignment, the transferee comes into privity of estate with the lessor, which means that each is liable to the other on the covenants in the original lease that run with the land. (*See* **assignment of lease**, **sandwich lease**.)

submittal notice   Written notice by a broker to a seller, with whom the broker has a listing agreement, stating that the broker has shown the seller's property and indicating the prospect's name, address, and the selling price quoted. Such a notice registering a prospect is especially important in open listing situations to avoid problems with regard to procuring cause.

subordinated sale-leaseback   A financing device used by developers of unimproved land that is either being purchased or is already owned by the developer. To raise capital, the developer sells the land to an investor who in turn leases it back to the developer. The developer then seeks financing for the improvements, and the lessor-investor agrees to subordinate the lease to the mortgage.

subordination agreement   An agreement whereby a holder of a prior superior mortgage agrees to subordinate or give up her priority position to an existing or anticipated future lien. Subordination agreements are frequently used in development projects where the seller of the land to be developed takes back a purchase-money mortgage and agrees to subordinate the mortgage or become subject to a construction loan, thereby enabling the developer/purchaser to obtain a first mortgage loan to improve the property. The subordination agreement thus alters the normal rule of giving priority to the first recorded mortgage. As a result, the construction mortgage, even though recorded after the existing purchase-money mortgage, becomes the first mortgage.

Many interim lenders refuse to lend any money in the absence of a subordination clause in all prior loans or other agreements. Thus, most presale purchase contracts for proposed condominium units have a clause subordinating the apartment purchaser's right to buy the apartment (equitable lien) to any future interim construction mortgage given by the developer. Thus on default, the lender could wipe out the purchase contract if it wanted to do so.

A developer of leasehold property will often try to get the fee owner to subordinate the fee to a construction loan. In this situation, subordinating is really a misnomer, because one cannot subordinate the fee to a leasehold mortgage. What the fee owner is really doing is agreeing to encumber the fee. Sometimes a fee owner will partially subordinate the fee, in which case the landlord/owner is saying to the lender that in the event of foreclosure, no ground rent will be due; the owner is not risking the fee, just the ground rent.

Some states have statutes requiring specific forms and certain disclosures of subordination agreements. It might be considered the unauthorized practice of law for the broker to draft a subordination clause.

subordination clause   A clause in which the holder of a mortgage permits a subsequent mortgage to take priority. *Subordination* is the act of yielding priority. This clause provides that if a prior mortgage is paid off or renewed, the junior mortgage will continue in its subordinate position and will not automatically become a higher or first mortgage. A subordination clause is usually standard in a junior mortgage because the junior mortgagee gets a higher interest rate and is often not concerned about the inferior mortgage position. A sample subordination clause might read: "This mortgage shall be and remain subordinate to the present first mortgage or any renewal thereof, or in event of its payment, to any new mortgage, provided the excess, if any, of said mortgage over the amount of the present first mortgage be applied in reduction of the principal of this mortgage."

A broker should take care to point out to a client the implication to all parties of any subordination clauses contained in the mortgage documents and to recommend that an attorney check to be sure that the preliminary subordination language in the contract of sale between buyer and seller is definite, certain, and unambiguous. (*See* **leasehold**, **mortgage**, **second mortgage**.)

subpoena   A legal process ordering a witness to appear and give testimony under penalty of law. Anyone refusing to obey the court order can be jailed.

subpoena duces tecum   A court order to produce books, records, and other documents.

subprime loan   A loan made to persons with lower credit ratings than acceptable in regular loans, based on the fact that lenders can negotiate the interest rate and discount in their efforts to make substantial profits. However, the risk is greater and requires careful underwriting to be successful. Recent improvements in technology with credit scoring and appraisals have given lenders the necessary tools to undertake these loans. (*See* **A, B, C, D paper**; **credit scoring**.)

subrogation   (*subrogación*)   The substitution of a third person in place of a creditor to whose rights the third person succeeds in relation to the debt. For instance, a title company that pays a loss within the scope of its policy is subrogated to any claim that the buyer has against the seller for a loss. Insurance policies typically contain subrogation clauses. Whenever a payment is made from a state real estate education, research, and recovery fund to satisfy a judgment, the fund is subrogated to the rights of the injured party.

If the Department of Veterans Affairs makes advances to the mortgagee due to the default of the veteran-mortgagor, the VA is subrogated to the rights of the mortgagee against the mortgagor to the extent of these advances.

subscribe   To place one's signature at the end of a document. Most documents do not need to be subscribed. For example, in a promissory note, it is sufficient to write, "I, George Smith, hereby promise to pay Tash Lee $100,000." Some statutes, however, require subscribing witnesses (i.e., witnesses who sign at the end of the document after the principal's signature). In many states, it is essential to the validity of a will that there be two disinterested subscribing witnesses. (*See* **signature**.)

subscription   An agreement to buy a new securities issue.

subsequent bona fide purchaser   One who purchases an interest in real property without notice, actual or constructive, of any other superior rights in the property. The recording laws are designed to protect subsequent purchasers for value when they deal with the property without notice of prior unrecorded interests. Thus, a conveyance that is not recorded is void as against any subsequent purchaser (lessee, mortgagee) who, without having actual notice of the unrecorded conveyance, records another. Possession of property under an unrecorded deed imparts constructive notice to a subsequent purchaser who records a deed. The subsequent purchaser would not then be bona fide and is not protected by the recording act. Also unprotected would be a subsequent donee or a devisee under a will, because neither is a purchaser. (*See* **constructive notice**, **recording**.)

subsidized housing   Residential housing assistance to private landlords who rent to low-income families. The housing choice voucher program is administered by the U.S. Department of Housing and Urban Development. (*See* **Section 8 Program**.)

subsidy
1. Monetary grants by the government or other entity made to reduce the cost of one or more of the housing components—land, labor, management, materials—to lower the cost of housing to the occupant. (*See* **subsidy rent**.)
2. In a buyer's market, a seller or developer might offer some subsidy incentives. (*See* **buydown**.)

subsidy rent   The difference between the developer's cash out-of-pocket annual costs allocable to a particular tenant's space and the tenant's minimum rental. Some shopping center developers subsidize the rent of certain specialized tenants, such as banks or post offices, in the hopes of attracting more customers to the center complex. In reality, both the developer and the other tenants are subsidizing the rent, because the cash deficit on that tenant must be made up from other tenants before the developer can make any profit at all. (*See* **shopping center**.)

The Housing and Urban Development Act of 1968 and subsequent amendments, the 1969 Housing Act and the 1970 Emergency Home Finance Act, contain a number of programs enabling low-income families to rent or purchase shelter under subsidized programs. These laws reflect congressional concern with meeting a growing population's needs for housing, setting up an urban policy, and encouraging and supporting sound real estate development, including new community and intercity development. *See* **Section 8**, **subsidized housing**.

substantial improvement   For tax purposes, it might be deemed to be any improvement made to a building at least three years after the building was placed in service; over a two-year period, the amounts added to the capital account of the building (not repairs) must be at least 25 percent of the adjusted basis of the building as of the first day of that period.

substitution   A principle of value stating that the maximum value of a property tends to be set by the cost of acquiring, through purchase or construction, an equally desirable and valuable substitute property, assuming no costly delay is encountered in making the substitution.

substitution of collateral   Provision in a mortgage to permit the mortgagor to obtain a release of the original collateral by replacement with other collateral acceptable to the mortgagee.

substitution of eligibility   *See* **certificate of eligibility**.

subsurface easement   An easement permitting the use of belowground space for such purposes as power lines, sewers, tunnels; also called a *subsurface right*.

suburb   A town or community located near, and economically linked to, a central city.

successors and assigns   Words of limitation used in deeds that reference the third parties to whom the rights in the property may subsequently be transferred. (*See* **heirs and assigns**.)

sufferance   *See* **tenancy at sufferance**.

summary possession   A legal process, also called *actual eviction*, used by a landlord to regain possession of the leased premises if the tenant has breached the lease or is holding over after the termination of tenancy. Summary possession proceedings are based on the theory that a landlord-tenant relationship existed and that the tenant is wrongfully holding possession of the demised premises after termination of tenancy by reason of forfeiture or termination under conditions or covenants of lease, including proper notice.

Among the usual specified grounds for summary possession are nonpayment of rent, abandonment, holdover tenancy, and violation of governmental or landlord use regulations. Generally, for nonpayment of rent, notice and demand for rent must be given before commencing the summary proceeding. (*See* **eviction**.)

summation approach   The value derived by adding the estimated value of improvements to the estimated value of the site as of the date of the appraisal. (*See* **cost approach**.)

summons   (*convocatoria*)   A legal notice that a lawsuit has been started against a defendant and unless the defendant answers the complaint within the specified time (usually 20 days), a default judgment will be entered against the defendant.

sum-of-the-years'-digits (SOYD) method   A method of depreciation designed to provide the greatest depreciation in the early years of ownership, eliminated as an acceptable method of accelerated depreciation by the Economic Recovery Tax Act of 1981. (*See* **depreciation**.)

sump   A pit or reservoir used for collecting and holding water (or some other liquid), which is subsequently disposed of, usually by a pump.

superadequacy   Functional obsolescence caused by an improvement or structural component whose cost exceeds its value; an overimprovement (for example, gold faucets in a kitchen; high ceilings in an office).

Superfund   The nickname given to the Comprehensive Environmental Response, Compensation, and Liability Act of 1980, as amended by the Superfund Amendment and Reauthorization Act of 1986 (SARA). Superfund focuses on the cleanup of releases of hazardous substances on property. It creates significant legal exposure based on strict liability for owners, landlords, and sometimes, lenders. (*See* **Comprehensive Environmental Response, Compensation, and Liability Act [CERCLA].**)

supervisory broker   *See* **principal broker (PB)**.

supply and demand   (*oferta y demanda*)   An economic valuation principle stating that market value is determined by the interaction of the forces of supply and demand in the appropriate market as of the date of the appraisal. This principle is that price varies directly with demand and inversely with supply (i.e., supply is low, price is high). Alternatively, when supply is high and there is little demand, price is low.

support deed   A deed used to convey property that specifies that, as consideration, the buyer will support the grantor for the rest of the grantor's life. If proper support ceases, the courts will disallow the deed.

surcharge   (*recargo*)
1. Additional rent charged to tenants who consume utility services (gas, water, electric) in excess of the amounts allowed in the terms of the lease.
2. An additional charge imposed by the Federal Reserve Bank on member banks that borrow money too frequently.

surety   One who becomes a guarantor for another. Surety companies typically execute surety agreements in the form of completion and performance bonds on contractors. The surety does not insure against loss, but rather provides an assurance to the owner that the contractor is financially sound and professionally capable, efficient, and reliable; otherwise the surety company would not bond the contractor. Under the bond, the contractor is the principal, the owner is the obligee, and the bonding company is the surety.

The bond premium is more of a service charge than a buildup fund against loss. If the bonded contractor fails to complete the job, the surety of a completion bond will step in and guarantee its satisfactory completion. If, on the other hand, the owner defaults, the surety under a performance bond would have the same defenses as the contractor and might not be compelled to complete the contract.

In an assumption of mortgage, the grantee of the mortgagor becomes personally and primarily liable to the mortgagee for any deficiency judgment after a foreclosure sale, with the mortgagor standing in the position of a surety. The lessee under an assigned lease is, in essence, a surety.

Some states require brokers to post surety bonds with the state real estate commission. (*See* **performance bond**, **subrogation**.)

surety bond   *See* **fidelity bond**.

surface water   Diffused storm water, as contrasted to a concentrated flow within a stream. In most instances, property owners have the right to let water flow through their yard and onto the lot below as long as it is in sheet form and is not artificially concentrated by them onto the party below. Under the common law, landowners can take any steps (regrading, paving) to protect their land, even if this construction had an adverse effect on a neighbor's land.

surmortgage   A type of writ used in some states that specifies that a defaulting mortgagor must show cause why the mortgagee should not foreclose in order to prevent such a procedure.

S

surrender   A premature conveyance of a possessory estate to a person having a future interest, as when a lessee surrenders a leasehold interest to the owner of the reversion interest, the lessor, before the normal expiration of the lease—as opposed to an abandonment of the lease.

If the surrender is accepted by the lessor, then the lessee is no longer liable for rent. However, if the tenant abandons the premises without a formal surrender, the landlord can usually collect either the rent due for the entire period of the rental agreement, or the rent for the time it takes to rerent the dwelling unit at a fair rental *plus* the difference between the fair rental and the rent the tenant had been paying, *plus* a fee for rerenting.

Note that an oral surrender agreement is generally valid only if the unexpired rental period is one year or less. If the balance is for longer than one year, an oral agreement is unenforceable. (*See* **statute of frauds**.)

If the parties recorded the lease, they should execute and record a written surrender agreement to clear the title in the event the lease terminates before its normal expiration.

A surrender clause in a lease controls what happens to the improvements at the termination of the lease.

survey   The process by which boundaries are measured and land areas determined; the on-site measurement of lot lines, dimensions, and position of houses in a lot, including the determination of any existing encroachments, easements, party walls, and compliance with setback requirements.

A broker should check the property at the time of the listing to see whether survey stakes are visible. If not, the broker should inform the seller that a survey may be required at the seller's expense. (Occasionally, buyer will elect to have the property resurveyed at their own expense.) The survey may reveal easements and encroachments that the public records do not reveal. If there is any discrepancy between the new survey and the original survey, the seller should be required both to remedy the discrepancy and to pay for the cost of the survey.

Lenders frequently require an accurate survey before lending money to finance acquisition of or construction on certain properties. Large construction loans require a "date-down" survey as the construction progresses to ensure that the new building does not encroach beyond the building or lot lines.

There are three major types of surveys. The *geodetic survey* measures the shape and size of the earth. *Cadastral surveys* determine the boundaries of parcels for defining ownership. *Topographic surveys* measure the features of the earth's surface (hills, valleys) and the location of roads. In interpreting a survey, compass readings are "bearings," linear measurements are "distances," and directions of a line are "courses."

S

survival of deed   *See* **merger**.

survivorship, right of   The special feature of a joint tenancy whereby all title, right, and interest of a decedent joint tenant in certain property passes to the surviving joint tenants by operation of law, free from claims of heirs and creditors of the decedent. Upon the death of a joint tenant, the property is released of the decedent's interest, and the remaining joint tenants share equally in the entire property. Under the Uniform Partnership Act, adopted by many states, the surviving partners have certain rights in property held as tenancy in partnership. Upon the death of a tenant in common, however, all the decedent's right, title, and interest pass according to the will or, if the person dies without a will, to that persons' heirs according to the laws of intestacy. (*See* **joint tenancy, partnership, right of survivorship, tenancy by the entirety [entireties], tenancy in partnership.**)

suspension   A period of enforced inactivity. The real estate commission has the power, after a hearing, to suspend a real estate license for a violation of the licensing law. During the period of the suspension, the licensee is prohibited from engaging in real estate activities for the purpose of earning a commission or fee. A suspended broker may not employ any salespeople during the period of the suspension; the salespeople must transfer their licenses to other firms if they wish to continue in their real estate activities.

sweat equity   A popular expression for equity created in a property by the performance of work or labor by the purchaser or borrower. It directly increases the value of the property.

sweetheart contract   A slang expression to describe a situation where a developer hires a thinly disguised subsidiary company to manage the developer's project. Most state condominium laws regulate the use of sweetheart contracts and make them subject to cancellation by the homeowners' association.

swing loan   A short-term loan, also known as a *bridge loan*, used to enable the purchaser of a new property to purchase that property on the strength of the equity from the property the purchaser is now selling. (*See* **bridge loan**.)

switchpoint   *See* **point of switch**.

syndication   A descriptive term for a group of two or more people united for the purpose of making and operating an investment. A syndication is not a form of legal ownership but rather a term used to describe multiple ownership of an investment. It is essentially a combination of money and management and is frequently treated as a real estate security.

A syndication may operate in the form of a REIT, corporation, general partnership, limited partnership, or even as tenancy in common. Some of the parties take an active role in the creation and management of the investment, while others assume a passive role, usually limited to supplying capital.

Most real estate syndications are organized as limited partnerships with the syndicator acting as general partner and the investors being limited partners. This enables the partnership to act as a conduit to pass through high depreciation deductions directly to the individual investors and thus avoid the double taxation aspects of corporate ownership. Syndication frequently offers the small investor a chance to participate in a real estate investment that will be managed by experienced persons. The Internal Revenue Code provides that amounts paid to organize a partnership or promote the sale of interests are not deductible. (*See* **limited partnership**.)

Syndication also refers to the process of aggregating and distributing listing data for display on the Internet using the services and technology of a national syndicator.

S

systems-built   A term used by premium-home builders to describe factory-built construction to avoid the stigma attached to manufactured or prefab homes. (*See* **stick-built on-site**.)

T

tacking
1. Adding or combining successive periods of continuous occupation of real property by adverse possessors, thus enabling one not in possession for the entire required statutory period to establish a claim of adverse possession. For one person's possession to be tacked to that of another, each of the possessions must be continuous and uninterrupted, and the parties must have been successors in interest, such as ancestor and heir, landlord and tenant, or seller and buyer. (*See* **adverse possession**.)
2. A carryover of holding periods for tax purposes. For example, in a tax-deferred exchange or a replacement of principal residences, the holding period of a new replacement property or principal residence includes the holding period of the formerly held property. (*See* **residence**.)

take down   To borrow or draw against funds committed by a lender earlier, as in a construction loan. (*See* **progress payments**.)

take-down search   *See* **bring-down search**.

"take-it-or-leave-it" contract   *See* **adhesion contract**.

take off   The estimation of materials needed to construct a building.

takeout financing   Long-term permanent financing. In the usual large construction project, the developer obtains two types of financing. The first is the interim loan, a short-term loan to cover construction costs. Before lending any money, however, the interim lender normally requires a commitment by a permanent lender to agree to "take out" the interim lender, in which the lender pays off the construction loan and leaves the developer with a permanent long-term loan when the building has been completed. Such a commitment, called a *takeout commitment* or a *takeout letter*, typically is the second phase of financing a development. (*See* **end loan**, **interim financing**, **permanent financing**, **standby loan**.)

taking   Reference to the "takings clause" of the Fifth Amendment, which states the following: "Nor shall private property be taken for public use, without just compensation." (*See* **condemnation**, **eminent domain**, **police power**.)

tandem plan   A mortgage subsidy program offered by Congress from time to time through Ginnie Mae. When assistance is needed, Ginnie Mae is authorized to purchase certain mortgages at below-market interest rates so that borrowers (builders and developers of non-profit public housing) can be granted low-interest loans. Ginnie Mae then sells these loans in the secondary market at deep discounts, the discount loss being the amount of the subsidy. When these programs are available, they are offered through, or "in tandem" with, local mortgage lenders, generally administered under a contract with Fannie Mae and Freddie Mac. (*See* **Fannie Mae**, **Freddie Mac**, **Ginnie Mae**.)

tax abatement   A reduction, for a stated period of time, of the taxes of a property owner. A municipality may grant an abatement as incentive for developers to build and buyers to buy as a stimulus to the economy. A downside is higher property taxes when the abatement is lifted.

tax and lien search A title search issued to cover property registered in the Torrens system. Because the Torrens certificate of title does not reflect certain encumbrances such as real property taxes, city and county assessments, and federal tax liens or bankruptcies, the tax and lien search is used to provide this information. The report issued by a title insurance company is sometimes called a *lien letter*. (*See* **Torrens system.**)

tax base (*base gravable*)
1. For property tax purposes, the assessed valuation of all real property within an area subject to taxes. This would exclude exempt church- or government-owned property.
2. For income tax purposes, the net taxable income.

tax bracket The rate at which a taxpayer pays tax on income above a set amount. Individual tax rates are structured on a graduated basis.

tax certificate The document issued to a person as a receipt for paying the delinquent taxes on real property owned by another, entitling the person to receive a deed to the property if the property is not redeemed within a specified period. (*See* **tax deed.**)

tax clearance A form required by the state to be filed by a decedent's estate when real property is owned in that state. The form is used to verify that there are no outstanding inheritance tax liens on the property.

tax credit A dollar-for-dollar offset against taxes due. Sometimes, the IRS uses tax credits as incentives to develop low-income housing, historic properties, or housing for the elderly, or to encourage businesses to make alterations in compliance with the ADA accessibility rules.

tax deed The instrument used to convey legal title to property sold by a governmental unit for nonpayment of taxes. The property may be sold at public auction after proper notice if the tax lien has remained unpaid for a set period of time. The defaulting taxpayer usually has a period after the tax sale in which to redeem the property by paying the purchase price and costs plus interest. The tax deed is presumptive evidence of the propriety and validity of the sale, and it must generally be recorded. (*See* **redemption period, tax lien.**)

tax-deferred exchange A transaction in which some or all of the realized gain from the exchange of one property for another may not have to be immediately recognized for tax purposes. Under Section 1031 of the Internal Revenue Code, the exchange is not a tax-free transaction; the payment of taxes is simply deferred to a later transfer.

　　Both the property received and the property given in exchange must be held for productive use in trade or business or for investment (not a principal residence), and both properties must be "of a like kind." (*See* **delayed exchange, exchange, like-kind property**.)

tax-escalation clause *See* **tax stop clause.**

tax-free exchange *See* **exchange.**

tax lien (*gravamen de tributación*) A statutory lien imposed against real property for nonpayment of taxes that remains on the property until the taxes are paid, even if the real estate is conveyed to another person. The *local* tax lien for unpaid real property taxes generally has priority over all other liens on the property, whether or not such liens were recorded before the recording of the state tax lien. Owners of out-of-state properties should take care to keep current on paying real property taxes, or they may find that through inattention, they have lost title to their property sold at a tax sale.

　　A *federal* tax lien results from a failure to pay an Internal Revenue tax, including income tax, estate tax, and payroll tax. A federal tax lien is a general lien on all property and rights to property of the person liable, but its priority depends on the number of liens previously recorded when notice is recorded. (*See* **federal tax lien, inheritance tax, lien, tax deed.**)

T

tax map   A map drawn to scale showing the location of real property, tax keys, size, shape and dimensions, and so on, for convenience of identification, valuation, and assessment. These maps are usually kept in tax map books, prepared and held by local tax departments.

tax participation clause   A clause in a commercial lease that requires the tenant to pay a pro rata share of any increases in taxes or assessments above an established base year.

tax preference   An item that may be included when calculating the taxpayer's alternative minimum income tax.

tax rate   The rate that is applied to the assessed value of a property to arrive at the amount of annual property tax. The tax rate is established according to assessed valuation, which varies depending on land use. (*See* **mill**, **notice of assessment**, **property tax**.)

Tax Reform Act of 1986   A landmark federal law passed in 1986 that made comprehensive changes in taxation. In addition to eliminating preferential tax treatment of capital gains, and decreasing the use of tax shelters, the law amended the rules for qualifying as a real estate investment trust and the taxation of REITs. It lengthened the cost recovery periods for most depreciable assets. Effective for property placed in service after December 31, 1986, the recovery period is 27.5 years for residential rental property and 39 years for nonresidential real property. The accelerated method is no longer available for real estate; straight-line is the only allowable method. (*See* **accelerated cost recovery system (ACRS)**, **declining-balance method**, **straight-line method**.)

The Tax Reform Act also created an alternative depreciation system (ADS), which must be used for property that is used predominantly outside the United States, for property leased to a tax-exempt entity or financed with tax-exempt bonds, and to calculate the portion of depreciation treated as a tax preference for the purposes of the corporate and alternative minimum tax. ADS real property is depreciated over 40 years. Taxpayers may elect to use ADS even if they do not fall into one of the foregoing categories. (*See* **tax preference**.)

Tax Relief Act of 1997   Tax rules that provided for tax relief for persons selling their personal home, investment property, farms, and small businesses. The act changed the rules for capital gains taxes when selling a primary residence. If the owners live in and occupy the home for two of the previous five years, there is no tax on gains up to $250,000 for singles and up to $500,000 for couples filing jointly.

tax roll   Public records showing all taxable property, tax amounts, assessed valuations, and millage rates.

tax sale   The sale of real property by a governmental unit to satisfy unpaid real property tax liens, frequently followed by a statutory period of redemption. (*See* **tax deed**, **redemption period**.)

tax search   A specific part of a title search that determines whether there are any unpaid taxes or special assessments that may be a lien against the property under search.

tax shelter   A phrase often used to describe some of the tax advantages of real estate or other investments, such as noncash deductions for cost recovery (depreciation), interest, taxes, and postponement or even elimination of certain taxes. The tax shelter not only may offset the investor's tax liability relevant to the real estate investment but also may reduce the investor's other ordinary income, which reduces overall tax liability.

Tax reform in 1986 significantly limited the use of tax shelter losses to reduce taxable income from other sources such as salary, interest, and dividends. The passive loss rule disallows the deduction of passive activity losses against other active sources of income. Profits and losses from passive activities, including rental activities, are first netted against each other. Passive investments are defined as any trade or business in which the taxpayer does not materially participate and any rental activity, whether or not the taxpayer materially participates. Limited partnerships generally are passive activities under the 1986 law. (*See* **passive loss**.)

tax stamps   *See* **transfer tax (conveyance fee)**.

tax stop clause   A lease article providing that the lessee pay any increase in taxes over a base or initial year's taxes; also referred to as a *tax-escalation clause*. The lease should state that this added amount will be deemed additional rent.

TCT   *See* **transfer certificate of title (TCT)**.

TDR   *See* **transfer of development rights (TDR)**.

teaser rate mortgage   An adjustable-rate mortgage with an interest rate initially set below the market rate. Prior to the housing crisis of 2009, many borrowers who did not qualify for a loan at market rate were lured into a larger mortgage loan than they could ultimately afford, leading to defaults when the rates adjusted upward.

Telephone Consumer Protection Act   A law designed to restrict unsolicited calls by telemarketers. Under the Federal Trade Commission rules, cold call telephone solicitation to those who are registered on the National Do Not Call Registry is prohibited. Any solicitation calls are limited to the hours of 8:00 am to 9:00 pm. Real estate licensees may contact a for-sale-by-owner seller only if the licensee has an actual buyer interested in the property. A licensee may contact a company's expired listing owner up to 18 months after the listing expired. Also, facsimile solicitations are strictly prohibited unless the advertisements were solicited by the parties contacted. (*See* **National Do Not Call Registry**, **Junk Fax Act**.)

tenancy at sufferance   (*posesión por tolerancia*)   A tenancy (or estate) that exists when a tenant wrongfully holds over after the expiration of a lease without the landlord's consent, as where the tenant fails to surrender possession after termination of the lease. A tenancy at sufferance is the lowest estate in real estate, and no notice of termination may be required from the landlord to evict the tenant. This kind of tenancy is designed to protect the tenant from being classified as a trespasser on one hand and to prevent the tenant's acquisition of title by adverse possession on the other hand. The relationship exists not by express consent of the landlord but by implication. Tenants have only naked possession and no estate that they can transfer.

     Different from a tenancy at will, under a tenancy at sufferance, the landlord has not consented to the continuation of the tenant's possession. Even though acting wrongfully, the tenant at sufferance is not considered a trespasser because the tenant originally entered the property with the landlord's consent. Upon consent of the landlord, a tenancy for years for the same term (usually not for more than one year due to the tenancy at sufferance) can be converted into a tenancy at will, a periodic tenancy, or a tenancy for years for the same term (usually not for more than one year due to the statute of frauds). (*See* **holdover tenant**, **summary possession**.)

tenancy at will   A tenancy (or estate) in which a person holds or occupies real estate with the permission of the owner, for a term of unspecified or uncertain duration (i.e., there is no fixed term to the tenancy).

     The main features of the tenancy are its uncertainty of duration and its continuing permissive status. The tenancy is not assignable, though it is usually permissible for the tenant to sublet the premises; an attempted assignment typically terminates the tenancy. Unlike a tenancy at sufferance, all the duties and obligations of a landlord-tenant relationship exist in a tenancy at will, and notice of termination is required by either party.

     In common law, either party could terminate at any time. Most modern statutes now require a specific notice period, such as 30 days. Unlike other leasehold estates, a tenancy at will is also termi-

T

nated by death of either landlord or tenant, or by sale of the property (the sale results in conveyance of the reversion).

tenancy by the entirety (entireties)   A special joint tenancy between a lawfully married husband and wife, which places all title to property (real or personal) into the marital unit, with both spouses having an equal, undivided interest in the whole property. In essence, each spouse owns the *entire* estate; neither spouse owns a fractional share, but the property ownership is, instead, an indivisible entirety. Upon the death of one spouse, the survivor succeeds to the entire property to the exclusion of heirs and creditors of the deceased spouse and without the need for probate. Tenancy by the entireties is sometimes called a "poor man's will." Unlike a joint tenancy, neither spouse can convey interest or force a partition during the lifetime of the other, without the consent of the other spouse.

Tenancy by the entirety property ownership exists in less than one-third of the United States. Based originally on the common-law theory that husband and wife are one person, this theory has been abandoned under modern law, which recognizes women's rights in property separate from their husbands.

Both spouses can also voluntarily convert the tenancy into a tenancy in common or a joint tenancy. The tenancy by the entirety may be severed only by mutual agreement, divorce, or joint conveyance; it may not be severed by any attempt of one spouse to transfer that spouse's interest. Although an attempted unilateral transfer is ineffective, the transferor may still be liable to the transferee for money damages for breach of contract. Where divorce severs the tenancy by entirety, the parties become tenants in common (even where the entire purchase price was paid by one party). Upon the death of a spouse, the survivor should record an "affidavit of surviving tenant by the entirety" reflecting the fact of death. (*See* **gift tax**; **joint tenancy**; **ownership, form of**; **property tax**; **survivorship, right of.**)

tenancy for life   A freehold estate of uncertain duration, which is not an estate of inheritance; a life estate. (*See* **life estate**.)

tenancy for years   A less-than-freehold estate (or tenancy) in which the property is leased for a definite, fixed period of time, whether 60 days, any fraction of a year, a year, or ten years. In most states, such a tenancy can be created only by express agreement, which should be written if the tenancy is longer than one year. The tenancy for years must have a definite term, beginning and ending on dates specified in the lease. In the absence of a statute or agreement, the tenancy is considered personal property and passes to the tenant's heirs upon the tenant's death. The tenancy ends on the last day of the term of the lease with no need for the parties to give notice of termination. A tenant who continues in possession is a *holdover tenant* or a *tenant at sufferance*. Most ground leases and commercial leases are tenancies for years. (*See* **leasehold**.)

T **tenancy in common**   A form of concurrent ownership of property between two or more persons, in which each has an undivided interest in the whole property. Each cotenant holds an estate in land by separate and distinct titles, and cotenants are entitled to the undivided possession of the property, according to their proportionate share and subject to the rights of possession of the other tenants. Interest is considered equal unless the conveyance document indicates otherwise. No special wording is required to create the tenancy. It is the most common form of co-ownership unless another intent is clearly specified.

Unlike a joint tenancy, there is no right of survivorship in a tenancy in common. If one of the cotenants dies, the interest passes to the deceased's heirs or beneficiaries and not to the surviving tenants in common, and the property interest of a tenant in common is subject to probate. Dower rights may exist in property held in common.

Tenants in common can sell their interest in the property without the consent of the cotenants, but they cannot transfer the entire property without the consent of all cotenants. If one of the common owners wishes to sell the entire property and the other cotenants do not, the co-owner can bring an action for partition and seek to have the property divided up in kind or sold at auction with the owners paying their individual share of the proceeds.

Cotenants have the right to possess all portions of the property and to retain profits from their own use of the property, though they must share net rents received from third parties. Tenants in common cannot be charged for use of the land nor may one cotenant charge rent for other cotenants' use of the land. If one cotenant pays taxes or assessments due above her share, then the cotenant generally has a lien on the interest of each cotenant for the pro rata share.

As a rule, a tenant in common's interest is not considered acceptable security by a lender because the mortgagee has the additional expense in a foreclosure action of forcing a partition proceeding to recover on its security interest.

As with joint tenancy, if one cotenant in good faith makes improvements to the real property without the permission of the other, that cotenant should be compensated for the improvement in a partition action. The standard used is either the percentage of improvement cost attributable to the other cotenant or the proportionate share of the increased value of the property.

One problem with tenancy in common is the element of uncertainty connected with the fact that the interest of a deceased cotenant is subject to probate. For example, suppose A, B, and C hold lakefront property as an investment as tenants in common. A, a single person, dies intestate. He had 12 brothers and sisters and both parents living. One sister dies shortly thereafter, leaving a husband and six children. To sell the property to a developer, the other tenants in common may have to get the signatures of all A's brothers and sisters, parents, and guardian for the minors to release every possible interest. Property so encumbered is referred to as "heirs' property."

Tenants in common assume the risk that their individual interest in the property will be imperiled by the failure of cotenants to pay their share of taxes, debt service, and other carrying charges. In addition, there is a risk of bankruptcy or involuntary sale or partition of the property to enforce a judgment lien or income tax lien against the interest of one cotenant in the property. (*See* **cotenancy**; **grantee**; **joint tenancy**; **owelty**; **ownership, form of**; **partition**; **property tax**; **tax lien**; **undivided interest**.)

tenancy in partnership   A partnership is an association of two or more persons for the purpose of carrying on a business as co-owners and sharing in the profits and losses. Generally, a partnership is not a legal entity and from a technical, common-law standpoint, a partnership cannot own real estate. The title must be vested in the partners as individuals, not in the firm. Most states have adopted the Uniform Partnership Act, under which partnership realty may now be held in the partnership name.

The features of a tenancy in partnership as they affect each partner are generally as follows:

- A partner has an equal interest in the property and an equal right of possession of the property, but only for partnership purposes.
- A partner's right is not assignable, except in connection with the assignment of the rights of all partners; thus a purchaser can acquire only the whole title.
- A partner's right is not subject to attachment or execution except on a claim against the partnership itself, and there can be no homestead exemption claim. The entire property, however, can be sold on execution sale to satisfy a partnership creditor. The partner's interest cannot be seized or sold separately by a personal creditor, but a partner's share of the profits may be obtained by a personal creditor by an action called a "charging order."
- Upon the death of a partner, the decedent's rights in the partnership real estate vest in the surviving partner(s), though the decedent's estate is reimbursed for the value of his

interest. The partner's interest in the partnership firm is all that passes to the adminis-trator as personal property upon his death intestate.

- The heirs have a right in the partnership but not in the specific partnership property. If there are no surviving partners, the decedent's rights in the property vest in a legal representative. The vesting in the surviving partner or partners and in the legal repre-sentative of the last surviving partner conveys no greater right on them than to possess the partnership property for a partnership purpose.
- A partner's right to specific partnership property is not subject to dower, curtesy, or family allowances.
- Because this property is owned by the partnership, no tax exemption applicable to an individual partner will be available to the partnership or its property.
- The partnership's property and its income or losses are subject to partnership income tax treatment. (*See* **partnership**.)

tenancy in severalty　　Ownership of property vested in one person alone, rather than held jointly with another; also called *several tenancy* or *sole tenancy*. A husband or wife could each own property as a tenant in severalty, although the rights may be impacted by dower and curtesy. The owner's title is thus severed from any other person. When the sole owner dies, the property is probated and passes to the heirs or devisees. A corporation, state, or county often holds title and property in severalty. (*See* **ownership, form of**.)

tenant　　(*arrendatario, inquilino, locatario propietario*)　　In general, one who exclusively holds or possesses property, such as a life tenant or a tenant for years; commonly used to refer to a lessee under a lease. A tenant's occupancy, although exclusive, is always subordinate to the rights of the owner. *Tenant* refers to an occupant, not necessarily a renter.

tenant alternative costs　　The costs of construction and remodeling needed to make the premises us-able by a particular tenant. These costs may be paid by the owner or the tenant or may be shared by both as a result of negotiations.

tenant contributions　　All costs for which the tenant is responsible over and above the contract rent specified in the lease. Area maintenance is an example.

tenant improvements　　*See* **construction allowance**.

tenant mix　　The selection and location of retail tenants so as to maximize the income to the lessor and stimulate business in general. Stores in a shopping center complex should be situated so that pedes-trian traffic stimulated by one business benefits the others, and yet competition does not become a detriment.

tenant union　　A local organization of residential tenants working for their common interests and rights.

tender　　An unconditional offer by one of the parties to a contract to perform her part of the bargain. For example, when a seller brings an action seeking enforcement under a sales contract of the buyer's obligation to pay the purchase price, the seller must first make a tender of the deed. In some states, this is done by placing it into escrow. This is required because the buyer's duty to pay is a concurrent condition of the seller's duty to tender the deed. Likewise, a tender of performance by the buyer, for example, by depositing the purchase money into escrow, places the seller in default if she refuses to accept it and deliver a deed.

Where money is owed, a tender of the amount owed discharges any lien that is security for the debts, releases sureties, and stops debts from accruing interest.

When parties to a contract clearly show an intent not to perform—that is, where there is an anticipatory repudiation or where the seller has already sold the property to a third party—then no tender is necessary because it would be a useless act. The parties may seek appropriate remedies, including recovery of damages for breach of performance. Sellers should not try to resell the property until they can establish that a valid tender has been made or that the other party has repudiated the contract. (*See* **backup offer, bilateral contract**.)

tenement   A common-law real estate term describing those real property rights of a permanent nature that relate to the land and pass with a conveyance of the land, such as buildings and improvements; those things affixed to the land. Tenements include not only land but also corporeal and incorporeal rights in real property. In more modern usage, the term refers to apartment buildings, especially the more run-down, old buildings in urban areas. (*See* **hereditament**.)

tenure   A common-law term indicating the manner in which land is held, such as a fee simple or leasehold. The manner or system of holding lands or tenements in subordination to some superior right, which in feudal times was the primary characteristic of real property ownership.

term   (*plazo, término*)
1. A length of time. For example, a *mortgage term* is the length of time (as set forth in the mortgage) in which the mortgage loan must be paid off. A *lease term* is the length of time (as set forth in the lease) in which the tenant can rightfully occupy the premises—for example, 60 days, ten years, life. An *option term* is the time stipulated in the option agreement for the optionee to exercise rights under the agreement.
2. A provision or condition in a contract.

termination of listing   The cancellation of a broker-principal employment contract. If a listing contains no specific termination date, it is terminated after a reasonable time. The seller can revoke this type of listing at any time before the broker produces a ready, willing, and able buyer on the listing terms. If, however, the listing does contain a specific termination date (usually required of all exclusive listings), the seller cannot revoke the listing before that date without liability for the broker's expenses (advertising the property, for example) incurred in marketing the property. Courts, and most state regulations, do not look favorably on provisions for automatic extension of the listing period—that is, "thirty days and continuing thereafter indefinitely until written cancellation is given."

A listing is basically an agency contract and can be terminated under general agency and contract principles as follows:
- Death or insanity of principal or agent
- Expiration of listing period
- Mutual agreement
- Sufficient written notice
- Completion of performance under the agreement; thus, under an open listing the sale by one broker would terminate the agency for all brokers
- Condemnation or destruction of the subject property
- Bankruptcy of either party
- Abandonment of the agency by the broker (broker might be liable for damages)
- Revocation by the principal (broker may recover damages)
- A change in law that prohibits the current use of the property

(*See* **extender clause, listing**.)

termination statement   A document recorded to cancel a financing statement filed under the provisions of the Uniform Commercial Code.

termite inspection   *See* **Wood Destroying Insect Inspection Report**.

termite shield   A metal sheet laid into the exterior walls of a house near ground level, usually under the sill, to prevent termites from entering the house. Termite shields should be affixed to all exterior wood in the house and around pipes entering the building. Shields are generally constructed with an overhanging lip to allow for water runoff.

term mortgage   A short-term mortgage securing a loan that requires interest-only payments until the maturity date, at which time the entire principal is due and payable. (*See* **straight note**.)

terre tenant   One who has actual possession of the land.

testamentary trust   A trust established by will.

testator   (*testador*)   A person who makes a last will and testament; one who dies leaving a will is said to have died *testate*. Devisees inherit real property, taking title to the property subject to any liens in favor of the creditors of the estate. (*See* **probate, will**.)

testimonium clause   A clause found in a legal document beginning "In Witness Whereof . . ." and then citing the act and date of execution of the document.

thin capitalization   Excessively high ratio of debt to equity in a corporation's capital structure, resulting in the Internal Revenue Service's treatment of at least some of the debt capitalization as equity and the consequent loss of the tax benefits of debt.

thin market   A real estate market in which there are few buyers and sellers and a slow turnover of properties. This makes it difficult to obtain reliable comparable sales information. Also called a *limited market*. (*See* **direct sales comparison approach**.)

third party   (*tercero*)   A person such as a broker or escrow agent who is not party to a contract but who may be affected by it; one who is not a principal to the transaction. For example, the for–sale-by-owner seller is the unrepresented third party when the real estate licensee represents the buyer in the transaction.

tideland   *See* **beach**.

tidewater land   Land beneath the ocean from the low-tide mark to a state's outer territorial limits.

tie-in contract   A contract in which one transaction depends on another. For example, a developer might agree to sell a choice property only if the buyer also agrees to buy a less desirable property from the developer or agrees to list the property for sale with the developer's brokerage company. Such tie-in arrangements may violate state and federal antitrust regulations. (*See* **antitrust laws**.)

tier   A row of townships extending east and west. (*See* **government survey method**.)

tight money market   An economic situation in which the supply of money is limited and the demand for money is high, as evidenced by high interest rates.

"time is of the essence"   A contract clause that emphasizes punctual performance as an essential requirement of the contract. Thus, if any party to the instrument does not perform within the specified time period (the "drop-dead" date), that party is in default, provided the nondefaulting party has made a valid tender of performance. If no tender is made, then the clause may be waived. The clause may also be waived by the subsequent acts of the parties such as accepting tardy payments or signing escrow instructions that allow for extensions of time in which to perform.

   In equity, time is not regarded as of the essence to a contract unless there appears a clear intention to make it so. The concept cuts both ways—the purchasers are expected to make prompt payments, while the sellers must also take timely steps to enforce their rights if the purchaser defaults. Time is of the essence in option contracts; that is, the option is no longer valid if not exercised by the option date. (*See* **reasonable time, tender, waiver**.)

time–price differential The difference between a property's purchase price and the higher total price the same property would cost if purchased on an installment basis (including finance charges). Under the Truth in Lending Act, a lender must disclose the time-price differential, as well as all finance charges of any kind in an installment contract.

time-share ownership plan (TSO) A form of ownership in which a number of individuals hold legal title to a particular condominium unit or other real estate as tenants in common, entitling them to the use of the property for a specified time each year. There is usually a "separate use agreement" among the tenants in common that details the rights and obligations of each owner, including any privileges to exchange units in other resort areas.

   Also known as interval ownership, ownership may be for a specified number of years, after which time all time-share owners become tenants in common and are free to enter into a new interval agreement, sublet the property, or sell it.

time-sharing (*tiempo compartido*) A modern approach to communal ownership and use of real estate that permits multiple purchasers to buy undivided interests in real property (usually in a resort condominium or hotel) with a right to use the facility for a fixed or variable time period. Common expenses are prorated among the owners. Sometimes, time-sharing programs have a reservation system or a rotation-of-unit system in which tenants in common can occupy their unit at different times of the year in different years. Other time-sharing programs sell specific time periods of each year. Some time-sharing programs are based on the purchase or lease of the property (ownership programs); others are based on mere licenses to use the property (right-to-use or license contracts). (*See* **rental pool**.)

   The time-sharing industry is often regulated by states that require special disclosure reports, escrow accounts, licensing of agents, review of promotional material, and complete disclosure of the details of any exchange program in which time-share units can be exchanged for other properties. Among the tough questions have been the procedures for billing real property taxes, tax delinquencies, and the assessment valuation problem (i.e., whether the building is valued at the same figure as a similar building that is not time-share or at an amount determined by the cost and number of time-share interests).

   The Uniform Real Estate Time-Share Act covers all aspects of time-sharing and has already been adopted in several states. Residential time-share units are subject to the antidiscrimination provisions of the federal Fair Housing Act.

time value of money An economic principle that the worth of a dollar received today is greater than the worth of a dollar received in the future.

title (*título*) The right to or ownership of land; the evidence of the right to an estate. Title to property encompasses all in the bundle of rights that an owner possesses; the totality of rights and property possessed by a person. Title may be held individually, jointly, in trust, or in corporate or partnership form. *Title* is a common term used to denote the facts that, if proved, would enable a person to recover or retain possession of something.

   If one owns real property outright, that person is said to *have title to it*. Titles are either original or derivative. Original title can be vested only in the state. This means a title gained through discovery, occupancy, conquest, or cession to the state. All other titles are derivative, and these are vested in individuals. Such titles may be divided into titles by descent (no will) and titles by purchase (deed, land contract, will). (*See* **cloud on title**, **color of title**, **evidence of title**, **insurable title**, **marketable title**, **record title**.)

title by estoppel *See* **estoppel by deed**.

T

title insurance   (*seguro contra vicios en un título de propiedad*)   A comprehensive indemnity contract under which a title insurance company warrants to make good a loss arising through defects in title to real estate or any liens or encumbrances. Unlike other types of insurance, which protect a policyholder against loss from some future occurrence (such as a fire or auto accident), title insurance in effect protects a policyholder against loss from some occurrence that has already happened, such as a forged deed somewhere in the chain of title. Fannie Mae and Freddie Mac require title insurance on every loan they buy.

The title company will issue a policy if satisfied with the investigation of the public records and all other material facts. Generally, a title insurance policy protects the insured against losses arising from such title defects ("hidden risks") as the following:

- Forged documents such as deeds, releases of dower, mortgages
- Undisclosed heirs; lack of capacity (minors)
- Mistaken legal interpretation of wills
- Misfiled documents, unauthorized acknowledgments
- Confusion arising from similarity of names
- Incorrectly given marital status; mental incompetence

In addition, and most important, the title company will agree to defend the policyholder's title in court against any lawsuits that may arise from defects covered in the policy. A title insurance policy generally consists of three sections:

- The agreement to insure the title and indemnify against loss
- A description of the estate and property being insured
- A list of conditions of and exclusions to coverage

These uninsured exclusions generally include such title defects as the following:

- Rights of parties in possession, not shown in the public records, including unrecorded easements
- Any facts that an accurate survey would reveal (e.g., encroachments)
- Taxes and assessments not yet due or payable
- Zoning and governmental restrictions
- Unpatented mining claims
- Certain water rights

Title indemnity is made as of a specific date. Except with certain policies, a one-time premium is paid, and coverage continues until the property is conveyed to a new owner (including a conveyance to an insured's wholly owned corporation). It does not run with the land. Coverage is thus limited to the tenure of the named insured, and certain of the insured's successors by operation of law.

An *owner's policy* is issued for the benefit of the owner, the owner's heirs and devisees or, in the case of a corporation, its successors by dissolution, merger, or consolidation; but the policy is not assignable. For an added premium, title companies will issue an extended coverage owner's policy for certain properties to cover possible title defects excluded from standard coverage. Such title defects may include the rights of parties in possession, questions of survey, and unrecorded liens.

A *lender's policy* is issued for the benefit of a mortgage lender and any future holder of the loan. It protects the lender against the same defects that an owner is protected against under an owner's policy (plus additional defects), but the insurer's liability is limited to the mortgage loan balance as of the date of the claim, and liability under a lender's policy reduces with each mortgage payment, and is voided when the loan is completely paid off and released. Because of this reduced liability, a lender's policy usually costs less than an owner's policy. Under a mortgagee policy, the loss payable is automatically transferred to the holder of the mortgage.

T

Upon foreclosure and purchase by the mortgagee, the policy automatically becomes an owner's policy, insuring the mortgagee against loss or damage arising out of matters existing before the effective date of the policy. In addition to these policies, title companies also issue policies to cover the leasehold interests of a lessee, a lender under a leasehold mortgage, or a vendee under a contract for deed.

In the event of loss under a mortgagee's policy, the insurer pays the mortgagee the balance due on the loan, and the owner is thereby relieved from making further payments. The owner will lose the property and the investment unless he or she has obtained an owner's policy for only a slightly higher premium.

If an insured property appreciates in value (as when an expensive improvement is made), it is good practice to increase the amount of title insurance to cover possible increased losses. Newer policies have an "inflation guard" endorsement to cover appreciation.

Nearly 2,000 title companies belong to the American Land Title Association (ALTA) and use standardized ALTA title insurance policies. (*See* **American Land Title Association [ALTA]**, **certificate of title**, **closing protection letter**, **extended coverage**, **hidden risk**, **leasehold mortgage**, **reissue rate**, **Torrens system**.)

title, marketable   *See* **marketable title.**

title paramount   A **superior title.**

title plant   *See* **plant.**

title report   Preliminary report of the current record title to a property. Unlike an abstract of title, a title report shows only the current state of the title, along with the recorded objections to clear title such as unpaid mortgages and easements. The title insurance policy is issued based on the title report. The insurer incurs no liability under a preliminary report. (*See* **certificate of title**, **title insurance**.)

title search   (*investigación del título*)   An examination of the public records to determine what, if any, defects there are in the chain of title; usually performed by an experienced title company or abstracter. Before an institutional lender will lend money secured by real estate, it will order a title search at the expense of the borrower to assure itself that there are no liens superior to its mortgage on the property.

The title searcher begins the examination with the original source of title, which often dates from a government patent grant or award of title, or 40–60 years earlier, depending on local custom. After examining the original source of title, the searcher then "runs the title" in the recorder's office and searches the records in other governmental offices, such as the tax offices and assessment offices (for sewer or street assessments that may be in effect). Title searchers are often confronted with spelling differences in similarly sounding names. In this regard, there is the legal "rule of idem sonans," which allows the rebuttable presumption that names that sound alike refer to the same person despite minor inconsistencies in spelling.

After conducting its title search, a title company will issue a title abstract, a preliminary report, a certificate of title, a continuation certificate of title, or a title insurance policy. Some of these various documents give title opinions, whereas others merely state the facts disclosed by the search. (*See* **abstract of title**, **bring-down search**, **certificate of title**, **chain of title**, **clearing title**, **federal tax lien**, **grantor-grantee index**, **title insurance**.)

title-theory states   States in which the law considers the mortgagee to have legal title to the mortgaged property (usually in the form of a trust deed), and the mortgagor to have equitable title. Title-theory states, also called *conveyance* or *transfer theory states*, follow the common-law approach that a mortgage is a conveyance defeasible upon a condition subsequent. The condition to the defeasance is the payment of the mortgage debt when it becomes due. Thus, in receiving a mortgage, the creditor takes title to the property; the debtor regains ownership when the debt is repaid. Under title theory, a mortgagee has the right to possession and rents of the mortgaged property upon default. A mortgagee in a lien-theory state must foreclose to assert the same rights. (*See* **lien-theory states**.)

Title XI   The portion of real estate appraisal reform amendments that are included in the Financial Institutions Reform, Recovery, and Enforcement Act of 1989 that provides for state licensing and certification of appraisers. (*See* **Financial Institutions Reform, Recovery, and Enforcement Act) [FIRREA].**)

tolling   The suspension or interruption of the running of the statute of limitations period. For example, the running of the statute of limitations regarding adverse possession may be suspended during the time the record owner is mentally incompetent.

tongue and groove   A method of joining two pieces of board wherein one has a tongue cut in the edge and the other board has a groove cut to receive the corresponding tongue. The method is used to modify any material prepared for joining in this fashion, as tongue-and-groove lumber.

topography   (*topografía*)   The nature of the surface of the land; the contour.

topping-off   The highest point in a building's construction. This is sometimes signified by securing a tree branch to the topmost point in the project.

Torrens system   A legal system for the registration of land, used to verify the ownership and encumbrances (except tax liens), without the necessity of an additional search of the public records. The purpose of the Torrens Act is to conclusively establish an indefeasible title to the end that those dealing with such property are assured that the only rights or claims of which they need take notice are those so registered. The Torrens system of registration is the title itself; it differs from a title insurance policy, which is only evidence of title. In other words, a person does not acquire title to Torrens-registered real property unless that person registers the title.

The distinctive feature of registered property is that title does not pass, and encumbrances (such as mortgages) are not effective against the property until such encumbrances or conveyances are noted on the registered certificate of title. A party who suffers loss through an error made by the governmental registrar can recover damages from the state through an assurance fund. The registrar, however, will not personally defend against litigation or reimburse the landowner for litigation expenses, which is one reason why most mortgagees require title insurance, even for Torrens-registered titles.

Under the Torrens system, the landowner initially petitions a state court to register a property, giving notice to all interested parties. After a search of title is filed with the court, there is generally a hearing to determine the status of the title and the court's determination is made in the form of a court decree. The procedure is similar to a quiet title suit. The initial use of the Torrens system is optional. But once property is registered, all subsequent transfers must follow the registration procedures.

Approximately ten states have adopted the Torrens system, which is popular in Canada, Australia, and Great Britain. In some states, Torrens-registered property is not subject to a general judgment lien, nor can title be lost through adverse possession. (*See* **tax and lien search, transfer certificate of title [TCT].**)

tort   A negligent or intentional wrongful act arising from breach of duty created by law and not contract; violation of a legal right; a civil wrong such as negligence, libel, nuisance, trespass, slander of title, false imprisonment. For example, an escrow agent who negligently or intentionally fails to comply with the escrow instructions may be liable in a tort action for the damages caused by its negligence. The escrow agent may also be liable for breach of its contract for failure to perform according to its agency.

town house A type of dwelling unit normally having two floors, with the living area and kitchen on the base floor and the bedrooms located on the second floor; a series of individual houses having architectural unity and a common wall between each unit. Town houses, or row houses, are very popular in cluster housing, and often employ the use of party walls and shared common grounds. Townhouse developments are often planned unit developments (PUDs), with each owner possessing fee title to the structure and the land underlying the structure; many are organized in the condominium form of ownership. The surrounding land, including sidewalks, open spaces, and recreational facilities, is normally owned in common with others. The townhouse concept is a hybrid of the single family home and the apartment, and is sometimes used in areas that have height restrictions preventing highrises. (*See* **planned unit development [PUD]**.)

township (*distrito municipal, sexmo*) A division of territory, used in the government (rectangular) survey system of land description, that is six miles square; contains 36 sections, each of which is one mile square; and consists of 23,040 acres. (*See* **government survey method**.)

track record
1. The previous operating results of a sponsor (or developer) or a real estate project. In making a credit check, the creditor looks at the debtor's track record or past history of paying other creditors.
2. The history of a real estate syndicator. This history is required to be disclosed in a public or private placement offering.

tract A lot or parcel of land; a certain development. Generally refers to a large area of land.

tract house A house mass-produced according to the plans of the builder, as one of many residences in a subdivision that are very similar in style, materials, and price. It is distinguished from a custom home, which is built to the specifications of the homeowner.

tract index An index of records of title according to the description of the property conveyed, mortgaged, or otherwise encumbered or disposed of. (*See* **chain of title**.)

trade fixture An article of personal property annexed or affixed to leased premises by the tenant as a necessary part of the tenant's trade or business. At the termination of a lease, a tenant must leave most fixtures in the premises; however, trade fixtures are removable by the tenant before expiration of the lease, and the tenant is responsible for any damages caused by their removal. However, a tenant cannot usually remove replacement fixtures—that is, improvements installed to replace worn-out ones. For instance, if a tenant installs a new bar to replace an old bar in a tavern the tenant leases, the tenant cannot remove the bar upon termination of the lease. If the tenant fails to remove trade fixtures within a reasonable time of lease expiration, the fixtures will be considered abandoned and become the property of the landlord. (*See* **fixture**.)

trade-in An agreement by a developer or a broker to accept from a buyer a designated piece of real property as a part of the purchase price of another property. The usual scenario is this: A homeowner agrees to purchase another home and the builder of the other home or the selling broker agrees to purchase the owner's present home at a specified price if the home has not sold for that price or more within a certain time. This arrangement guarantees that the owner will have the necessary financial resources to purchase the new home. (*See* **guaranteed sale program [GSP]**.)

trade usage A uniform course of conduct followed in a particular trade, calling, occupation, or business. Any practice or method of dealing having such regularity of observance in a place, vocation, or trade as to justify an expectation that it will be observed with respect to the transaction in question.

trading on the equity The practice of agreeing to buy real estate and then assigning the purchase agreement to another buyer before closing takes place; thus turning a profit by "selling the paper."

trading up   Buying or exchanging for something more expensive than what is currently owned.

trailer park   *See* **mobile-home park**.

transaction broker   A nonagency relationship allowed in states that have designed a category of service where the agent represents neither the buyer nor the seller in the transaction, treating both as customers. Also called **facilitation** or **nonagency relationship**.

transfer   *(traspaso)*   *See* **deed, delivery, exchange**.

transfer certificate of title (TCT)   A duplicate Torrens system certificate of title. Under the Torrens system of registration of title to property, the court issues an original certificate of title in the owner's name once the owner has established rightful title to the property. The certificate is issued in duplicate and shows the owner's name, the date of registration, the Torrens documentation number, and all encumbrances on the title. The original certificate is then recorded, and a duplicate copy is given to the owner (or it is sometimes held by the mortgagee). When selling the property, the original owner delivers a typical deed along with a transfer certificate of title. The original certificate and the owner's duplicate are then canceled, and the registrar issues the grantee a new transfer certificate of title. (*See* **certificate of title, Torrens system**.)

transfer of development rights (TDR)   A concept of land-use planning that looks at land development rights as being a part of the bundle of individual rights of land ownership. Under this concept, any one of these rights may be separated from the rest and transferred to someone else, leaving the original owner with all other remaining rights of ownership. By viewing development rights as a separable economic entity, communities have considerable power to direct growth, preserve landmarks or unique environmental features, and maintain adequate amounts of open space. All of this is done without placing undue financial burden on the community or on the owners of the lands that will remain undevelopable in the community interest. TDR may be implemented in a variety of ways, but the result is that the owner of the development rights will be reimbursed by the person acquiring the rights for the rights that are given up.

     TDR has been proposed or adopted in some fashion to promote various community values in several areas of the country. New York and Chicago have used it to preserve landmarks. It was proposed to preserve the ecologically fragile Phosphorescent Bay in Puerto Rico. Southampton, New York, has adopted TDR to encourage construction of moderate- and low-income housing. The State of New Jersey and counties in Virginia and California have developed proposals to use TDR as a primary system of land-use regulation and preservation of open space.

transfer tax (conveyance fee)   A state tax imposed on the transfer or conveyance of realty or any realty interest by means of deed, lease, sublease, assignment, contract for deed, or similar instrument. One purpose of the tax is to acquire reliable data on the fair market value of the property to help establish more accurate real property tax assessments. Generally, the seller, the grantor, or the lessor is liable for the tax.

     The federal revenue tax on conveyances of real estate was repealed effective December 31, 1967. Following the repeal of the federal tax, most states now mark the amount of tax on the first page of the document rather than actually affixing stamps.

     Each state that has enacted a real estate transfer tax has established the amount of its tax, the procedures used to determine the taxable consideration, and those deeds or transactions that are exempt from the transfer tax. Generally, but not always, when the real estate is transferred subject to the unpaid balance of an existing mortgage made by the seller before the time of transfer and being assumed by the buyer, the amount of the assumed mortgage may be deducted from the full consideration to determine the taxable consideration.

T

The tax usually is payable at the time of the recording of the deed from the county recorder of the county in which the deed is to be recorded. In many states, a transfer declaration form must be signed by both buyer and seller or their agents. Often, this form must provide information such as the legal description of the property conveyed; the address; the date and type of deed; the type of improvement; and whether the transfer was an arms' length transaction, between relatives, or a compulsory transaction per court order.

When the transaction is exempt, the document normally must be accompanied by a form certificate explaining the grounds for the exemption. Some transfers, such as a deed of easement, are totally exempt and the grantor is not required to file even an exemption certificate. Generally exempt from the tax are mortgages, correction deeds, transfers of realty if the tax was paid when the underlying contract for deed was recorded, transfers between husband and wife or parent and child, and transfers in which the actual consideration is $100 or less. Also, deeds exempted from the tax may include gift deeds; correction deeds; conveyances to or from or between governmental bodies; deeds of easement; deeds by charitable, religious, or educational institutions; deeds securing debts or releasing property as security for a debt; partition deeds; tax deeds; and deeds pursuant to mergers of corporations and those from subsidiary to parent corporations for cancellation of stock.

transit-oriented development (TOD)   A type of community planning that includes mixed-use residential and commercial areas within walkable areas, very often centered around public transportation such as train stations, bus stops, or bicycle paths. These developments are intended to promote healthier lifestyles, and to lower air pollution and greenhouse gas emissions by reducing household driving.

tread   The horizontal surface of a stairstep resting on the riser. The tread is the part stepped on.

treble damages   Damages provided for by statute in certain cases, as in an antitrust suit; actual damages may be tripled. For example, a court may have the power to treble damages when a landlord wrongfully and willfully retains all or part of a tenant's security deposit.

trespass   Any wrongful, unauthorized invasion of land ownership by a person having no lawful right or title to enter on the property. Trespass can occur on the land, below the surface or even in the airspace. Certain trespasses are privileged, such as trespasses to prevent waste, to serve legal process, and to use reasonable airspace for flights by aircraft.

The unauthorized possession of real property is a mere trespass and cannot ripen into ownership unless all elements of adverse possession are present. Because a tenant is entitled to the exclusive possession of the leased premises, not only against third parties but the landlord as well, any unauthorized entry by either the landlord or a third party would constitute trespass.

Generally, a landowner is not liable for injuries suffered by a trespasser whose presence is not known. A landlord who knows of the trespass, however, must not create conditions or do anything that may imperil the trespasser. (*See* **adverse possession**, **attractive nuisance**, **encroachment**, **nuisance**, **self-help**.)

trim   Wood or metal interior finishing pieces such as door and window casings, moldings, and hardware.

triple A tenant   A commercial tenant with a top credit rating, especially desirable as an anchor tenant in a shopping center. (*See* **AAA tenant**.)

triple-net lease   A net-net-net lease where, in addition to the stipulated rent, the lessee assumes payment of all expenses associated with the operation of the property. This includes both fixed expenses, such as taxes and insurance, and all operating expenses, including costs of maintenance and repair. In some cases, the triple-net tenant even pays the interest payments on the lessor's mortgage on the property leased.

T

Strictly speaking, the term *triple-net lease* (also known as a *net-net-net lease*) is redundant because "net lease" adequately describes the situation. Rather than rely on labels, however, the parties must examine the provisions of the lease to discover the extent of the tenant's responsibilities.

triplex   A building composed of three dwelling units.

truck well   A depressed area abutting a loading dock (either inside or outside a building) deep enough to permit direct loading from the floor of the building onto the bed of a truck that has backed into the well.

true escrow   *See* **holding escrow**.

truss   A type of roof construction employing a rigid framework of beams or members, which supports the roof load and usually achieves relatively wide spans between its supports.

trust   (*fideicomiso*)   An arrangement whereby legal title to property is transferred by the *grantor* (or *trustor*) to a person called a *trustee*, to be held and managed by that person for the benefit of another, called a *beneficiary*. The grantor and trustee initially may be the same person as in a trust agreement (i.e., a "declaration of trust"). The beneficiary holds equitable title. Trusts may be created by express agreement or by operation of law, and may be actual or constructive. For purposes of estate planning, there are inter vivos (or living) trusts and testamentary trusts. (*See* **inter vivos trust**, **land trust**, **living trust**, **testamentary trust**.)

trust beneficiary   The person for whom a trust is created. The beneficiary is the party who receives the benefits or proceeds of the trust and may be the same person as the grantor.

trust deed   *See* **deed of trust**.

trustee   (*fiduciario*)
1. One who holds property in trust for another as a fiduciary and is charged with the duty to protect, preserve, and enhance the value and the highest and best use of the trust property. Care should be taken to set forth in the trust agreement the powers and responsibilities of the trustee.
2. One who holds property in trust for another to secure the performance of an obligation. In those states using trust deeds as security devices, the trustee holds bare legal title to the property pending the borrower/trustor paying off the underlying debt or promissory note. The trustee is usually a lending institution, trust company, or title insurance company. Some states employ a public trustee to hold title in trust for the lender. The two main functions of a trustee in a trust deed are to sell the property at public auction if requested by the beneficiary when the debt is not paid and when the trust deed contains a power of sale, and to execute a reconveyance (release) when requested to do so by the beneficiary when the debt has been paid off. Many financial institutions have set up an auxiliary corporation to act as trustee in a deed of trust situation. In such a case, the corporation is more a common agent than a true trustee.

trustee in bankruptcy   (*síndico*)   One appointed by the court to preserve and manage the assets of a party in bankruptcy.

trust fund account   An account set up by a broker, attorney, or other agent at a bank or other recognized depository, into which the broker deposits all funds entrusted to the agent by the principal or others; also called an **earnest money** or **escrow account**. The trust fund for a brokerage firm account must designate the principal broker as trustee and must provide for withdrawal of the funds upon demand.

A principal broker may generally permit a broker-in-charge of a branch office to have custody and control of trust funds on behalf of the principal broker on transactions transpiring at said branch office. The principal broker and broker-in-charge are usually held jointly responsible for any trust funds the principal broker authorizes the broker-in-charge to handle. Because a broker is liable for the acts of the salespersons, the broker is liable to a buyer if one of the salespersons embezzles earnest money deposited in a trust fund account. Note also that if a broker deposits earnest money in the broker's own personal bank account or spends it, the broker may be guilty of commingling, a violation of most state license laws. Most license laws, however, allow a broker to keep a small amount of personal funds in a client trust account in order to keep the account open. The broker cannot use trust fund monies to offset even a valid debt owed by the client to the broker. (*See* **client trust account**, commingling.)

Truth in Lending Act (TIL)   (*Ley de Veracidad en los Préstamos*)   A body of federal law effective July 1969 as part of the Consumer Credit Protection Act, implemented by the Federal Reserve Board's Regulation Z, and amended in 1982 and later by the Truth in Lending Simplification and Reform Act. The main purpose of TIL is to ensure that borrowers and customers in need of consumer credit are given meaningful information with respect to the cost of credit so they can more readily compare the various credit terms available to them. TIL law creates a disclosure device only and does not establish any set maximum or minimum interest rates or require any charges for credit. In addition, some states have adopted their own truth-in-lending laws.

All real estate credit is covered by Regulation Z when it is extended to a natural person (the customer) and does not apply to business, commercial, or agricultural transactions. Personal property credit transactions over $25,000 are exempt from Regulation Z, as is the extension of credit to the owner of a dwelling containing more than four family housing units or a construction loan to a builder (this is considered a business purpose). However, if the extension of credit is secured by real property or by personal property used or expected to be used as the principal dwelling of the consumer (manufactured home), then the transaction is covered by Regulation Z. The credit offered must either involve a finance charge or, by written agreement, be payable in more than four installments.

The finance charge and the annual percentage rate (APR) are the two most important disclosures required. They provide a quick reference for consumers, informing them how much they are paying for credit and its relative cost in percentage terms. Note that a cushion or tolerance of $5 is given if the transaction is less than $1,000 and $10 if it is more than $1,000. (*See* **annual percentage rate [APR]**.)

Finance charge: The finance charge is the total of all costs the customer must pay, directly or indirectly, for obtaining credit, and includes such costs as interest, loan fee, loan-finder's fee, time-price differential, discount points, service fee, and premium for credit life insurance if it is a condition for granting credit. Real estate purchase costs that would be paid regardless of whether credit is extended are not included in the finance charge, provided these fees are bona fide, reasonable in amount, and not excluded for the purpose of evading the law.

Annual percentage rate (APR):   Under Regulation Z, the APR is not interest, although interest is figured in along with the other finance charges in computing the annual percentage rate. The APR is the relationship of the total finance charge to the total amount to be financed computed to the nearest one-eighth of 1 percent.

Disclosure statement: The disclosure statement for real estate transactions must contain the following information: total dollar amount of the "finance charge," the annual percentage rate, the number, amounts, and timing of payments, the total of payments, the amount charged for any late payments, the fact that the creditor may acquire a security interest in the property, prepayment privileges or penalties, and more. If the required disclosures were not made or a notice of rescission was not given to a borrower, the borrower's right to rescind continues for a period of three years after the date of consummation of the transaction or upon sale of the property, whichever occurs first.

Right to rescind: The borrower has a limited right to rescind or cancel a credit transaction. This rescission is intended to protect the homeowner from losing his or her home to unscrupulous sellers of home improvements, appliances, or furniture, who secure the credit advance by taking a second mortgage on the purchaser's home. In most situations, the borrower has the right to cancel the transaction (in writing) by midnight of the third business day (including Saturdays) following the date of consummation of the transaction, delivery of the notice of right to rescind, or delivery of all material disclosures, whichever is later. The right to rescind does not apply to the initial loan to purchase or construct the consumer's principal dwelling.

Creditors: This law requires compliance by all creditors who regularly extend credit. A person "regularly extends" credit only if that person extended credit more than 25 times (or more than five times for transactions secured by a dwelling) in the preceding calendar year. Owner/occupants of a single-family home ordinarily do not have to comply with the disclosure requirements of Regulation Z even when selling under a contract for deed payable in more than four installments. Brokers who are operative builders, subdividers, brokers selling property on their own account (except for the sale of their own permanent dwelling), or brokers taking a second mortgage as a commission may be deemed to be creditors and thus must comply with the law.

Advertising: Regardless of who the advertiser may be, Regulation Z also affects all advertising to aid or promote any extension of consumer credit, including window displays, fliers, billboards, multiple-listing cards if shown to the public, and direct mail literature.

Certain credit terms, when mentioned in an ad, trigger the required disclosure of other items. The purpose of this requirement is to give the prospective purchaser a complete and accurate picture of the transaction being offered. The trigger terms and required disclosures are shown in the following table:

Column A Trigger Terms	Column B Required Disclosures
Appearance of any of these items in Column A requires inclusion of everything in Column B: • The amount or percentage of down payment • The amount of any installment • The finance charge in dollars or that there is no charge for credit • The number of installments • The period of repayment	 • The amount or percentage of down payment • The terms of repayment • The annual percentage rate and whether increase is possible

Any advertisement that mentions an interest rate but omits the APR or omits the words *annual percentage rate* is in violation. Any advertisement that includes any trigger term (Column A) without all of the required disclosures (everything in Column B) is in violation.

General terms such as "small down payment OK," "FHA financing available," or "compare our reasonable rates" do not trigger required disclosures. When advertising an assumption of mortgage, the ad can state the rate of finance charge without any other disclosure. The finance charge, however, must be stated as an annual percentage rate, using that term and stating whether increase is possible. For example, "assume 7 percent mortgage" is improper, whereas "assume 7½ percent annual percentage rate mortgage" is permissible. The interest rate can be stated in advertisements in conjunction with, but not more conspicuously than, the annual percentage rate. Also, "annual percentage rate" is usually spelled out but it is permissible to abbreviate it to *APR*. Bait advertising is prohibited; thus, an advertisement offering new homes at "$1,000 down" is improper if the seller normally does not accept this amount as a down payment, even if all the other required credit terms are disclosed in the ad.

Creditors should keep records of all compliance with the disclosure requirements of the federal Truth in Lending Act for at least two years after the date disclosures are required to be made or action is required to be taken. Truth in ending requires advance disclosure of any variable rate clause in a credit contract that may result in an increase in the cost of credit to the customer.

Where joint ownership is involved, the right to receive disclosures, and notice of the right of rescission, the right to rescind, and the need to sign a waiver of such right applies to each consumer whose ownership interest is subject to the security interest.

Penalties: The penalty for violation of Regulation Z is twice the amount of the finance charge or a minimum of $100, up to a maximum of $1,000, plus court costs, attorney fees, and any actual damages. Willful violation is a misdemeanor punishable by a fine up to $5,000 or one year's imprisonment, or both. The Federal Trade Commission is in charge of enforcing Regulation Z. (*See* **annual percentage rate [APR]**, **finance charge**, **Rule of 78s**.)

tsunami damage   Damage caused by tidal-wave action. Owners of property located in flood zones must obtain insurance to cover flood and tsunami damage because the federal government no longer compensates fully for this type of damage. Lending institutions now require flood insurance in order to complete a mortgage loan transaction involving any building or its apartments located in a designated flood or tsunami zone. Thus, an owner attempting to sell a beachfront resort condominium might run into a problem when reselling the unit, unless the condominium association takes out enough insurance to conform to the new federal requirements. (*See* **flood insurance**.)

turnkey project   A development term meaning the complete construction package from groundbreaking to building completion. All that is left undone is to "turn over the keys" to the buyer. Some governmental housing projects are turnkey projects with a private developer completing a housing development that is then totally purchased by a government agency for use as low-income family housing. A turnkey job is different from a "package deal," which typically includes the financing as well.

A turnkey lease is one in which the landlord agrees to give the leased premises to the tenant in a ready-to-occupy condition. (*See* **build-to-suit**.)

turnout   *See* **point of switch**.

turnover
1. The frequency with which real property in a given area is sold and resold.
2. The rate at which tenants move into and out of a rental building. A high turnover rate results in added expenses to the landlord.

ultra vires   Describes acts of a corporation that are beyond its legal powers as set forth in its articles of incorporation.

unbalanced improvement   An improvement that is not the highest and best use for the site. It may be either an overimprovement or an underimprovement. (*See* **appraisal**.)

unconscionability   A legal doctrine whereby a court will refuse to enforce a contract that was grossly unfair or unscrupulous at the time it was made; a contract offensive to the public conscience. The Uniform Residential Landlord and Tenant Act expressly provides that courts may refuse to enforce an unconscionable rental agreement either in whole or in part. Under the Uniform Commercial Code, unconscionable contracts are also expressly rendered unenforceable.

under-floor ducts   Floor channels that provide for the placement of required telephone and electrical lines; this placement allows flexibility in space planning and furniture arrangement in commercial office buildings.

underground storage tanks (USTs)   A tank and any underground piping connected to the tank having 10 percent or more of its volume beneath the surface of the ground. These tanks were made of steel to store petroleum and other hazardous materials. Many are leaking, causing groundwater contamination. Laws pertaining to UST regulation include the Resource Conservation and Recovery Act (RCRA), the Hazardous and Solid Waste Amendment Act, and the Superfund Amendment and Reauthorization Act (SARA). The Leaking Underground Storage Tanks (LUSTs) Trust Fund was set up to oversee cleanups by responsible parties and to pay for cleanups at sites where the owner is unknown, unwilling, or unable to respond.

underimprovement   (*mejora insuficiente*)   An improvement that, because of its deficiency in size or cost, is not the highest and best use of the site. Usually, a structure that is of lesser cost, quality, and size than typical neighborhood properties—for example, a single-family home in an area zoned for six-unit dwellings. (*See* **overimprovement**.)

underlying financing   A mortgage or deed of trust that takes precedence over subsequent liens, such as contracts for deed or mortgages on the same property. In taking a listing, a broker should check the terms of any underlying financing documents affecting the property, especially noting any pre-payment penalty provisions.

undersigned   The person whose name is signed at the end of a document; the subscriber.

undertenant   One who holds property under one who is already a tenant, as in a sublease; a subtenant.

underwater loan   A term indicating a higher loan balance than what can be realized by the sale of the property. This may occur because the security for the loan has depreciated, or in other cases, the borrower may have overencumbered the loan in the first place.

underwriter
1. In insurance, a person who selects risks to be solicited and then rates the acceptability of the risks solicited. For example, a local title company usually buys insurance from a larger title company (the underwriter) for all or part of the liability of the policies that it originates.
2. As applied to real property securities, a person who has purchased securities from the issuer with the intention to offer, or who actually sells or distributes, the securities for the issuer.

For example, if a syndicator retains a securities firm to sell its limited partnership units, that firm is an underwriter. Underwriters may have to be registered in their state and/or with the Securities and Exchange Commission as an underwriter or broker/dealer.

3. A person working for a lender who reviews a loan application and makes a recommendation to the loan committee.

underwriting   The analysis of the extent of risk assumed in connection with a loan. Underwriting a loan includes the entire process of preparing the conditions of the loan, determining the borrower's ability to repay, and subsequently deciding whether to give loan approval.

undisclosed agency   A situation where an agent deals with a third person without notifying that person of the agency. Even if the broker is instructed not to reveal the name of the client, the agent must still indicate agency status. Otherwise, agents who sign their own name to any contract without disclosing the agency become fully liable for any breach or failure to perform on the contract. To avoid liability, brokers must declare the agency on the contract so it is clear that all parties intended to bind the principal and not just the agent.

undistributed taxable income   Income received by an S corporation that, although it is not distributed to the shareholders, is taxed as part of the shareholders' income. (*See* **S corporation**.)

undivided interest   That interest a co-owner has in property that carries with it a right to possession of the whole property along with the other co-owners. The undivided interests may be equal, as in a joint tenancy, or unequal, as sometimes in a tenancy in common. No owner has the right to any specific part of the whole. Thus, each owns a fractional share of the entire parcel, not a specified piece of it. For example, if Julio owned nine-tenths undivided interest in a ten-acre parcel of land, he would not own nine acres—all owners with undivided interests have the right to complete possession. In other words, there is no physical division of the land between the co-owners.

One cotenant cannot convey or encumber a specific part of the property. To acquire a right to a specific part of a property, a co-owner must petition the court for a partition or division of the property.

Condominium owners have a specified undivided interest in the common areas according to their percentage of common interest. There is no limit to the number of persons who may own an undivided interest in real property.

Each of the co-owners has a separate economic right in a property. Thus, if part of the parcel is arid and part is fertile, it would be unlikely, in a partition action, for a court to partition the property into equal geographic areas.

The sale of undivided interests is specifically covered under the Uniform Land Sales Practices Act, which regulates the mass marketing of undivided interests in land. For example, if a developer sells a $\frac{1}{275}$ tenancy in common interest in a large parcel of land, this act may be taken as an attempt to evade the subdivision registration law. (*See* **Interstate Land Sales Full Disclosure Act**; **ownership, form of.**)

undue influence   Strong enough persuasion to completely overpower the free will of another and prevent that person from acting intelligently and voluntarily, as in a case where a broker guilty of blockbusting has induced someone to sell in fear of a change in the racial character of the community. Undue influence usually requires a close or confidential relationship like parent-child, broker-seller, attorney-client, or trustee-beneficiary. A person who has been unduly influenced to sign a contract can void the contract.

unearned income   Income derived from sources other than personal services. Rents, dividends, and royalties would fit into this tax category, whereas wages, tips, and commission money would not.

unearned increment   An increase in value to real property that comes about from forces outside the influence and control of the property owner, such as a favorable rezoning or a favorable shift of population in the neighborhood.

unencumbered property   A property that is free and clear of liens and other encumbrances; a "free and clear" property.

unenforceable contract   A contract that was valid when made but either cannot be proved or will not be enforced by a court. An unenforceable contract is not merely one that is void or illegal. A contract may be unenforceable because it is not in writing, as may be required under the state statutes of frauds, or because the statute of limitations period has elapsed. The contract is nevertheless valid for certain purposes, such as evidence of a preexisting debt. Also, certain government contracts may not be enforceable against the government; that is, they are enforceable to the extent the government permits it. (*See* **statute of frauds**.)

unethical   Lacking in moral principles; failing to conform to an accepted code of behavior. Real estate agents can lose their licenses for not abiding by a code of conduct as set forth in most state licensing laws. (*See* **Code of Ethics**.)

unfair and deceptive practices   Sales practices that do not involve deception but are still illegal under the regulations of the Federal Trade Commission (FTC). A sales practice is unfair if it offends public policy; is immoral, unethical, oppressive, or unscrupulous; or causes injury to consumers. This concept applies to practices such as inducing purchases by intimidation and scare tactics, substitution of products, or wrongful refusal to return deposits or refunds.

The FTC can enjoin unfair and deceptive practices, issue complaints and prosecute, issue cease-and-desist orders, and impose fines.

unfinished office space   Space in a "shell" condition excluding dividing walls, ceiling, lighting, air-conditioning, floor covering, and the like. In leasing unfinished office space, the landlord often provides the building with standard items and/or a construction allowance.

uniform and model acts   Laws proposed for adoption in the individual states. Such uniform laws are approved by the National Conference of Commissioners on Uniform State Laws, and many have been adopted in one or more states. Some examples are the Uniform Commercial Code, Uniform Condominium Act, Uniform Consumer Credit Code, Uniform Fraudulent Conveyances Act, Uniform Land Sales Practices Act, Uniform Land Transactions Act, Uniform Partnership Act, Uniform Real Estate Time-Share Act, and Uniform Residential Landlord and Tenant Act.

Uniform Appraisal Dataset (UAD)   A standardized form that defines all fields required for specific appraisal forms and standardizes definitions and responses for a key subset of fields. Effective September 1, 2011, the form is required by the Federal Housing Finance Agency (FHFA) for any appraisal submitted to Fannie Mae and Freddie Mac.

Uniform Building Code (UBC)   A national code published by the International Conference of Building Officials and used mostly in the western states. Adopted in part by more than 1,000 municipalities throughout the United States, it is now being replaced by the codes developed by the International Code Council. (*See* **International Code Council**.)

Uniform Commercial Code (UCC)   A body of law that attempts to codify and make uniform throughout the country all law relating to commercial transactions, such as conditional sales contracts, pledges, and chattel mortgages. The UCC also covers personal property transactions, including negotiable securities and commercial paper.

The main relevance of the UCC to real property is in the area of fixtures, as covered in Section 9 of the code. Where a chattel is purchased on credit or is pledged as security, a security interest is created in the chattel by the execution of a security agreement. Rather than recording the agreement, the creditor would file a financing statement in the recorder's office. If the financing statement has been properly filed, the creditor, upon default, can repossess the chattel and remove it from the property. (*See* **bulk sales transfer**, **financing statement**, **security agreement**.)

Uniform Commercial-Industrial Appraisal Report (UCIAR)   A standard appraisal report form for appraising commercial and industrial property.

Uniform Electronics Act (UETA)   A uniform model law recommended by the National Conference of Commissioners on Uniform State Laws that allows documents and signatures to be communicated by e-mail or facsimile without the necessity of being linked to a paper document. UETA created standards for electronic signatures and permits a notary public and other authorized officers to act electronically, without the use of a stamp or seal. All parties must agree to conduct the transaction electronically.

uniformity   An appraisal term used in tax assessment practice to describe assessed values that have the same relationship to market value and thus imply the equalization of the tax burden.

Uniform Land Sales Practices Act (ULSPA)   *See* **Interstate Land Sales Full Disclosure Act**.

Uniform Land Transactions Act (ULTA)   A uniform model law proposed by the National Conference of Commissioners on Uniform State Laws, which covers a wide range of real estate transactions, including sales, conveyances, mortgages, and leases. The law has not yet gained wide support. One of the more important financing proposals urges the elimination of the present distinctions among mortgages, deeds of trust, and contracts for deed.

Uniform Limited Partnership Act (ULPA)   A model act, adopted in whole or in part by many states, that establishes the legality of the limited partnership form of ownership and provides that realty may be held in the name of the limited partnership. (*See* **limited partnership**.)

Uniform Partnership Act (UPA)   A model act, adopted in whole or in part by most states, that establishes the legality of the partnership form of ownership and provides that real estate may be held in the partnership's name. (*See* **partnership**.)

Uniform Residential Appraisal Report (URAR) (Form 1004)   An appraisal form; since May 1, 1987, the form adopted for use by the U.S. Department of Housing and Urban Development, the Department of Veterans Affairs, and the Farmers Home Administration, in addition to the Freddie Mac and Fannie Mae.

Uniform Residential Landlord and Tenant Act (URLTA)   A uniform act intended to provide some consistency in regulating the relationship of landlord and tenant in residential leases. A number of states have adopted all or parts of the Uniform Residential Landlord and Tenant Act or have enacted similar legislation.

Rental agreements: Unless otherwise specified in a lease or rental agreement, the act considers a tenant to have a periodic tenancy. If either the landlord or the tenant signs and delivers a written rental agreement, it is considered accepted by the other party, even without that party's signature, if the other party either pays rent or accepts rent without objecting to the agreement. If no specific amount of rent is agreed on, the rent due is considered to be the fair rental value of the unit. The rental agreement may not contain certain provisions: the tenant does not have to agree to forgo rights or remedies under the act, to authorize any person to confess judgment on a claim arising from the rental agreement, or to pay the landlord's attorney fees. A rental agreement may limit the landlord's liability for fire, theft, or breakage with respect to common areas, but the tenant does not have to agree to limit the landlord's liability. In the case of a legal dispute between a landlord and a tenant, the court may refuse to enforce an agreement, or any portion

U

thereof, that it finds to be unconscionable—that is, so grossly unfair as to violate the public conscience.

Condition of the premises: Within five days after the tenant takes possession of the premises, the lessor and the lessee must make a joint inventory detailing the condition of the premises and any of the furnishings or appliances supplied by the landlord. A fully signed copy of this document must be given to each party.

Security deposits: The maximum security deposit the landlord may receive is one month's rent on an unfurnished unit and one and one-half month's rent on a furnished unit, but it may require an additional half-month's rent on either furnished or unfurnished units as a pet fee. When the tenancy ends, the deposit can be applied to any accrued rent or damages to the premises. An itemized list of damages must be given to the tenant, and any balance remaining must be returned to the tenant within the time specified in the act. If the landlord fails to return the deposit, the tenant has the right to recover the money due, together with damages in an amount equal to one and one-half times the amount wrongfully withheld, plus reasonable attorney fees. A tenant is prohibited from deducting any portion of the security deposit from the final month's rent. If a tenant does so, the landlord is entitled to recover the rent as though the security deposit had not been deducted.

Use of the property: The landlord may establish rules concerning the use and occupancy of the property, if such rules are equally applicable to all tenants. Any later rule that substantially modifies the rental agreement is enforceable against the tenant only if signed by the tenant. Unless otherwise agreed, the tenant may use the premises only as a dwelling unit. The tenant may not unreasonably withhold consent from the landlord for entry to the premises.

Landlord's obligations: After giving reasonable notice, the landlord may enter the premises at reasonable hours to inspect the unit, make necessary repairs or improvements, supply service, or show the unit to prospective buyers or tenants. Only in cases of extreme emergency may the landlord enter without prior permission from the tenant.

The landlord is obligated to make all repairs necessary to keep the premises fit for habitation by complying with local building and housing codes in providing and maintaining in good operating condition all electrical, heating, plumbing, and similar systems, and other facilities and appliances (such as elevators) supplied by him or her. The landlord must also provide for the upkeep of the common areas, and for trash and garbage receptacles. Running water and a reasonable amount of hot water and heat during the required months must be supplied by the landlord unless the building is not required by law to be equipped for these purposes, or unless the tenant has exclusive control over the installations supplying water and heat. The tenant may agree in writing, however, to pay for any or all utility services.

These landlord duties do not apply if compliance is prevented by conditions beyond the landlord's control. If the property is sold, the landlord is relieved of liability as of the date of sale, with the exception of the duty to return security deposits. The previous landlord's duties and liabilities are thus assigned to and assumed by the new owner.

Tenant's obligations: The tenant must comply with local building and housing code provisions affecting health and safety, such as keeping the unit clean and safe for habitation and disposing of trash and garbage. All plumbing fixtures, elevators, and other facilities provided by the landlord, as well as electrical, plumbing, heating, and air-conditioning systems, must be used in a reasonable manner by the tenant. The tenant also must not willfully destroy or damage the premises, or allow others to do so, and must not disturb a neighbor's quiet enjoyment of the premises.

Termination of the tenancy: If the tenant is guilty of significantly failing to comply with the terms of the rental agreement in maintaining the premises, the landlord should provide the tenant with the nature of the breach and state that the rental agreement will terminate in 30 days if the tenant does not begin a good-faith effort to repair the breach within the time specified in the notice.

The landlord may terminate the lease within three days after giving notice, if the tenant still has not paid rent. If the tenant's noncompliance can be remedied by the repair or replacement of damaged items, and the tenant does not make such repairs within a reasonable time after the written notice is given, the landlord may enter the unit and have the necessary work performed and then charge the tenant. The landlord does not have the right to a lien on the tenant's household goods, however.

If the tenant abandons the unit, the landlord must make a reasonable effort to rerent the unit at a fair rental price. The tenant's obligation for rent continues until either the rental agreement expires or the unit is rerented, whichever occurs first. However, if the landlord does not try to rerent the unit, or if the landlord accepts the abandonment as surrender of the premises, the rental agreement is terminated when the landlord has notice of the abandonment.

If the landlord is guilty of significant failure to perform his duties, the tenant may also terminate the rental agreement by giving the landlord 30 days' notice of contract breach unless the landlord makes a good-faith effort to remedy the breach within the time specified by the notice. The tenant also has the right to sue for damages and obtain a court injunction directing the landlord to correct the breach. If the landlord's noncompliance is willful, the tenant may also recover reasonable attorney fees. Whenever a rental agreement is terminated through noncompliance on the landlord's part, the tenant is always entitled to recover the security deposit and any prepaid rent.

If the landlord willfully fails to deliver possession of the unit, the tenant's obligation to pay rent stops until possession is delivered. The tenant may either terminate the rental agreement or sue for performance, and obtain possession, reasonable damages, and attorney fees.

If the landlord negligently fails to supply heat, running water, or some other essential service, the tenant may give written notice of the contract breach to the landlord, and the tenant may then take appropriate measures to obtain the services and deduct the cost from rent payments (the so-called rent and deduct statutes), sue for damages based on the decrease in the fair rental value of the unit, or procure substitute housing until the breach is remedied. If substitute housing is obtained, the tenant's obligation for rent ceases during the landlord's period of noncompliance. The cost of such housing may be recovered, not to exceed the amount of periodic rent, along with reasonable attorney fees, if the tenant files suit against the landlord. When the cost of the necessary repairs is small, and the landlord fails to comply within a reasonable time after written notice has been given, the tenant may have the work performed, present an itemized bill to the landlord, and deduct the cost of repairs from the next rent payment.

If the dwelling unit is damaged or destroyed by fire or other casualty to such extent that enjoyment of the premises is impaired, the tenant may immediately vacate the premises and notify the landlord in writing of the intention to terminate the rental agreement as of the day of vacating. In cases where portions of the dwelling are still habitable, the tenant may vacate the damaged part of the dwelling and any liability for rent is reduced in proportion to the decrease in the fair rental value of the unit.

If the landlord illegally excludes the tenant from the premises or willfully diminishes tenant services, the tenant has the right to either recover possession or terminate the rental agreement. The tenant may also recover reasonable damages and attorney fees.

U

A landlord is prohibited from increasing the rent or decreasing the services of a tenant who has made a complaint to the landlord or to a governmental agency, or who has joined a tenant's union.

Exemptions: The Uniform Residential Landlord and Tenant Act would not, however, usually apply in the following situations:

- A person occupying property under a contract for deed
- Residence at a public or private institution for the purpose of receiving education, counseling, healthcare, or a similar service
- Occupancy by a member of a fraternal organization in a structure operated for the benefit of the organization
- Transient occupancy in a hotel or motel
- Occupancy by an employee of the landlord, when the employee's right to occupy is conditional upon his or her employment
- Occupancy by an owner of a condominium unit or holder of a proprietary lease in a cooperative
- Agricultural leases
- Rental of mobile-home lots, unless the landlord also furnishes the mobile home

(*See* **house rules, lease, repairs, security deposit, surrender.**)

Uniform Settlement Statement   The standard RESPA form, or HUD-1, required to be given to the borrower, lender, and seller at or before settlement by the settlement agent in a transaction covered under the Real Estate Settlement Procedures Act. The lender must retain its copy for at least two years.

Uniform Simultaneous Death Act   A statute adopted in most states designed to cover the situation where two joint tenants die in a common disaster. In essence, the statute provides that the parties died as tenants in common with equal shares. Typical language is as follows:

> Where there is no sufficient evidence that two joint tenants died otherwise than simultaneously, the property so held shall be distributed one-half as if one had survived and one-half as if the other had survived. If there are more than two joint tenants and all of them have so died, the property thus distributed shall be in the proportion that one bears to the whole number of joint tenants.

Naturally, if there are several joint tenants and all but one die in a common disaster, the statute does not apply, and the surviving joint tenant continues to own the entire property, now as tenant in severalty. (*See* **joint tenancy.**)

Uniform Standards of Professional Appraisal Practice (USPAP)   A set of ten standards developed in 1987, now updated annually, by an ad hoc committee composed of representatives of several appraisal associations in response to congressional criticism that the appraisal industry lacked uniform standards. The standards, which deal with the development and communicating of appraisals and analyses, are overseen by the Appraisal Standards Board of the Appraisal Foundation and have been adopted by most state appraiser regulatory bodies.

Uniform Vendor and Purchaser Risk Act   A law adopted in many states to determine which party bears the risk of loss if the property is damaged or destroyed before legal title passes to the vendee under a contract for sale. Unless the purchase agreement provides otherwise, the risk of loss does not pass from vendor to vendee until either legal title or possession has passed to the vendee. Once title or possession passes to the vendee, the vendee must pay the full purchase price if all or part of the property is destroyed without fault of the vendor or is taken by eminent domain. Unfortunately, the act does not address the question of what the parties do after loss when the vendee elects not to rescind but, rather, insists on the vendor rebuilding and specifically performing the contract obligations. (*See* **risk of loss**.)

unilateral contract   (*contrato unilateral*)   A contract in which one party makes an obligation to perform without receiving in return any express promise of performance from the other party. One party gives a promise in exchange for an act; that party is not obligated to perform on that promise unless the other party decides to act. An example is an open listing contract, where the seller agrees to pay a commission to the first broker who brings a ready, willing, and able buyer. The contract actually is created by the performance of the act requested of the promisee, not by the mere promise to perform. Note that a unilateral contract contains a promise on one side, whereas a bilateral contract contains promises on two sides.

Before the act is performed, the promise of the promisor is a mere unilateral offer. When the act is performed, this unilateral offer and the performed act give rise to a unilateral contract. The broker makes no promise to perform or to do any acts such as advertising. The broker can enter into a unilateral contract and thus bind the seller only by actual performance—that is, by producing a buyer. (Many standard exclusive-right-to-sell listings are now written as bilateral contracts wherein the broker agrees to use reasonable efforts to locate a buyer and the seller agrees to pay a commission if the property is sold by the broker, the seller, or anyone else.)

The classic example of a unilateral contract is a newspaper notice offering a reward for the return of a lost dog. The offeree is under no obligation to look for the dog, but if the offeree does in fact return the dog, then the offeror owes the reward money. Listing agents, through multiple listing services (MLS), offer cooperation and compensation to participating brokers, but none of them are obligated to produce a ready, willing, and able buyer. An option, in which the seller agrees to sell for a certain period of time at set terms, provided the buyer performs by paying the specified option price, is also a unilateral contract. (*See* **bilateral contract**.)

unimproved property   Land without buildings, improvements, streets, and so on. The fact that property is unimproved must be clearly stated in all disclosure statements in promoting subdivided land. (*See* **raw land**, **subdivision**.)

unincorporated association   An assembly of people associated for some religious, scientific, fraternal, or recreational purpose. Members of such associations are not personally liable for debts incurred in the acquisition or leasing of real property used by the association, unless they specifically assume liability in writing. The association itself normally does not hold title to property; any title is held through a trustee. Therefore, it is important when dealing with unincorporated associations, such as churches, that the broker check to see whether the person representing the association has actual authority to convey title to the property. Most condominium owners' associations are unincorporated.

The Internal Revenue Code allows two types of housing associations to elect to be treated as tax-exempt organizations—condominium management associations and residential real estate management associations. However, this tax-exempt status protects the association from tax only on its exempt-function income, such as membership dues, fees, and assessments received from member/owners of residential units in the particular condominium or subdivision involved. For example, on any net income that is not exempt-function income, the association is taxed at corporate rates but is not permitted the corporate surtax exemption granted to regular domestic corporations. (*See* **condominium owners' association**, **cooperative ownership**.)

U

unit   A part of the property intended for any type of independent use and with an exit to a public street or corridor, commonly referring to the individual units in a condominium, exclusive of the common areas. A unit normally consists of the walls and partitions, which are not load-bearing, within a condominium's perimeter walls; the inner decorated or furnished surfaces of all walls, floors, ceilings, doors, windows, or panels along the perimeters; and all original fixtures. The particular condominium declaration should be consulted for the exact definition of the unit.

unit-in-place method   An appraisal method of computing replacement cost; also called the *segregated cost method*, which uses prices for various building components, as installed, based on specific units of use such as square footage or cubic footage. These cost figures include the cost of labor, overhead, and profit. For example, insulation may cost $0.07 per square foot, drywall $1.50 per square yard, painting $0.08 per square foot, and so on. The total in-place cost of each unit (unit value) is multiplied by the number of such units in the building to determine the total replacement cost for the entire building. Sample building components are roof, floor, concrete, electrical, plumbing, and parking area. (*See* **quantity survey**.)

unit value   Value or price related to a unit of measurement; for example, $20 per square foot, $200 per front foot, and so on.

unity (joint tenancy)   A concurrence of certain requirements. Under common-law rules, the creation of a joint tenancy requires four unities: interest, title, time, and possession. That is, the tenants must have one and the same equal interest; the interests must arise from the same conveyance instrument from the same grantor; they must commence at one and the same time; and the property must be held by one and the same undivided possession.

By statute in many states, however, an owner of property can convey to himself or herself and another as joint tenants, thus altering the common-law rule requiring unity of title. In a tenancy in common, the only unity is that of possession. (*See* **joint tenancy.**)

universal agent   A general agent; one authorized to act on behalf of another. For example, an attorney-in-fact under a general power of attorney. (*See* **general agent**.)

universal design   The concept of designing products and environments to be usable by all people, to the greatest extent possible, without the need of adaptation or specialized design.

unjust enrichment   The circumstances in which a person has received and retains money or goods that in fairness and justice belong to another. A lawsuit may be necessary to recover such money or goods. (*See* **quasi.**)

unlawful detainer action   A legal action that provides a method of evicting a tenant who is in default under the terms of the lease; a summary proceeding to recover possession of property. (*See* **summary possession.**)

unmarketable title   A title to property that contains substantial defects such as undisclosed encroachments, building code violations, easements, or outstanding dower. A title acquired by adverse possession is usually not marketable until a quiet title suit is brought. (*See* **marketable title.**)

In some cases, a title insurance company might insure a title even though there are some remote claims to the title. The title is then insurable though not marketable. This can cause problems should a subsequent title examiner object to the title and effectively prevent a resale of the property. Because no actual loss has occurred, the coverage under the original title insurance policy is not applicable.

unreasonably withheld consent   Many legal documents, such as leases and contracts for deed, contain a transfer clause that states in effect that the property may be transferred only with the owner's consent, "which consent shall not be unreasonably withheld." There is no acceptable definition of what is unreasonable. For example, it might be reasonable for a lessor to refuse to transfer a lease to a new tenant whose business would directly compete with another tenant in the same shopping center complex (i.e., poor tenant mix).

In a contract for deed situation, it would generally be unreasonable for the vendor to refuse an assignment or to demand a share in the profits where the assignee is as good a credit risk, if not better, as the assignor-vendee.

To avoid lawsuits, it would be best to set forth some criteria for reasonable consent in the transfer clause itself. (*See* **assignment**.)

unrecorded deed   A deed that is valid between grantor, grantee, and anyone with notice of the ownership of the property. An unrecorded deed is different from a wild deed (one not properly recorded). (*See* **wild deed**.)

unregistered system   *See* **regular system (REG)**.

unsecured   Describes a debt instrument, such as a debenture, that is backed only by the debtor's promise to pay. (*See* **debenture, nonrecourse**.)

upgrades   Changes in design or improvements to property after the purchase but before the closing date, such as added appliances, carpeting, or reconstructed roof. The purchaser would absorb the costs for such improvements.

up-leg   The replacement property purchased in a Section 1031 tax-deferred exchange; typically, the taxpayer trades up in an exchange. (*See* **exchange**.)

up-ramp   An inclined or sloping roadway or walk leading from one level to another, often employed to gain access from ground level to the floor level of a dock-high building for either personnel or vehicles.

upset date   A date stipulated in a contract that specifies when a building must be ready for occupancy or when the buyer has the option to rescind the agreement.

upset price   A minimum price set by a court in a judicial foreclosure, below which the property may not be sold by a court-appointed commissioner at public auction; the minimum price that can be accepted for the property after the court has had the property appraised. The upset price should not exceed the reasonable market value of the property at the time of foreclosure. It sometimes happens that the upset price is so high that there are no bidders and the entire process leading up to the public auction must be repeated. The resulting delay and expense are reasons why many attorneys provide for nonjudicial foreclosure proceedings under a power of sale provided in the mortgage instrument. (*See* **auction, bid, foreclosure**.)

upside down   A financial condition in which there is not enough equity in the property to pay the outstanding liens; also known as an "underwater mortgage." (*See* **short sale**.)

upzoning   A change in zoning classification from a lower to a higher use. (*See* **downzoning**.)

urban enterprise zone   Patterned after a British model, an enterprise zone is a depressed neighborhood, usually within an urban area, in which business enterprises are given tax incentives (reduced property taxes) and exemptions from many governmental restrictions (no rent control) in an attempt to stimulate new business activity, provide jobs, and revitalize the area. The emphasis is on removing government financial burdens rather than providing direct government subsidies.

Urban Land Institute (ULI)   *See* Appendix A.

urban renewal   A process of upgrading deteriorated neighborhoods through clearance and redevelopment, rehabilitation, and the installation of new public improvements, or through modernization of existing ones. Urban renewal activities may be funded with a combination of federal and local funds, or strictly with private monies.

U

For example, the FHA 229(d)(3) program insures mortgages for rent-subsidized housing projects in approved urban renewal areas and subsidizes mortgage interest for qualified housing sponsors. (*See* **new town**, **slum clearance**, **transit-oriented development**.)

urban sprawl   The unplanned expansion of a municipality over a large geographical area.

usable area   On a multitenancy floor, the gross area minus core space. Core space includes the square footage used for public corridors, stairwells, washrooms, elevators, electrical and janitorial closets, and fan rooms. On a single-tenant floor, the usable area is the gross square footage, excluding building lobby and all penetrating shafts (that is, ducts, stairwells, and elevators).

useful life   That period of time over which an asset, such as a building, is expected to remain economically feasible to the owner. Because the annual amount of tax depreciation results from an apportionment of the investment in the building over its useful life, it has traditionally been important to ascertain correctly the proper useful life; the shorter the life, the more the annual deductions. The IRS now dictates the useful life of both new and used property acquisitions.

use tax   A tax imposed on the purchaser or importer of tangible, personal property for resale, use, or consumption.

use value   The subjective value of a special-purpose property, designed to fit the particular requirements of the owner but having little or no use to another owner. Also called *value-in-use*, it includes the valuation of amenities attaching to a property.

U.S. Geological Survey (USGS)   An agency within the U.S. Department of the Interior with responsibility for conservation, geological surveys, and mapping of lands within U.S. boundaries. (*See* **benchmark**.)

U.S. League of Savings Associations   The former name of America's Community Bankers, a national trade association for savings and loan associations and cooperative banks.

usufructuary right   The right to the use, enjoyment, and profits of property belonging to another, such as an easement or profit a prendre. (*See* **easement**.)

usury   (*usura*)   The act of charging a rate of interest in excess of that permitted by law. Some states have set a specific interest limit, charging more than what would be usury, while others have what is known as a *floating interest rate*, usually pegged each month at a certain percentage above a fluctuating economic indicator, such as the interest rate on long-term Treasury notes or Federal Reserve discount rates. A lending contract that charges a usurious interest rate may be void or voidable in certain states. Deliberately charging or receiving usurious interest rates on loans is known as *loan sharking*, a crime that may be considered either a misdemeanor or a felony. In some states, the penalty for usury is that the lender is not entitled to any interest and must apply all interest collected to reduce the principal balance of the loan.

Certain transactions are exempt from state usury laws, such as VA and FHA transactions. Under the federal Depository Institutions Deregulation and Monetary Control Act of 1980, the federal government preempted state usury ceilings for federally related conventional residential first mortgage loans unless a state enacts overruling legislation. (*See* **interest**.)

utilities   The basic service system required by a developed area, such as telephone, electricity, water, and gas. Utility easements are usually gross easements running on, over, or under the property.

utility   (*utilidad*)   *See* **diminished utility**, **value**.

utility room   A room, often located on the ground floor, that is designed for use as a laundry or service room.

utility value   The value in use to an owner-user, which includes a value of amenities attaching to a property; also known as subjective value. (*See* **subjective value**.)

vacancy factor   (*porcentaje de vacancia*)   An allowance or discount for estimated vacancies (unrented units) in a rental project. The vacancy rate is the ratio between the number of vacant units and the total number of units in a specified project or area. The vacancy and loss in rent are vital when assembling an investment income analysis of a property, such as an apartment building.

Current statistics on vacancy factors can be obtained from the U.S. Census Bureau, regional housing reports published by the Department of Commerce, and local utility companies.

vacate   To give up occupancy or surrender possession.

vacation home   A residence, usually in a resort or vacation area; often a second home for recreational purposes. Federal tax laws limit the business-type deductions an owner may claim relating to rental of a second home if the owner's personal use exceeds the 14 days or 10 percent of the number of days it is actually rented, whichever is greater. If the personal use limitation is exceeded, deductions for cost recovery, maintenance, and utilities can be deducted only for the rental portion of the year, and then only to the extent that rental income exceeds interest and real property taxes. (*See* **absentee owner**, **rental pool**.)

valid   Legally sufficient or effective, such as a valid contract; a contract that must in all respects comply with the provisions of contract law. A valid contract should be executed with proper formalities, satisfy legal requirements, have sufficient legal force to stand against attack, and be for a legal purpose.

valuable consideration   The granting of some beneficial right, interest, or profit, or the suffering of some legal detriment or default by one party in return for the performance of another, usually as an inducement for a contract. Historically, the law of conveyances has distinguished between valuable consideration and good consideration, which is love and affection with no pecuniary measure of value, such as a father might use as consideration to grant an estate to his son or daughter.

Valuable consideration is always sufficient to support a contract, whereas good consideration may in some cases be insufficient. Modern courts speak only in terms of consideration and would find love and affection to be no valid consideration. For example, a father might agree to transfer title to real property to his son in consideration for the son's abstention from smoking, drinking, and associating with persons of questionable moral character before age 21. If the son does agree to forbear, at the age of 21, the son can enforce the contract because he has provided valuable consideration; that is, he gave up a right in return for his father's promise.

However, if the father had agreed to convey title to the property in consideration of the love and affection that the son has for him, the son would not be able to force the father to transfer the property to him. Although it would be sufficient to pass title if stated in the deed, it is not enough to support the contract because the son has not given up any rights or made any promises. (*See* **consideration**, **love and affection**, **specific performance**.)

valuation date   *See* **date**.

value   (*valor*)   The power of a good or service to command other goods in exchange for the present worth to typical users and investors of future benefits arising out of ownership of a property; the amount of money deemed to be the equivalent in worth of the subject property. The four essential elements of value are demand, utility, scarcity, and transferability (DUST). Cost does not equal value, nor does equity.

There are various types of value, such as market value, tax assessed value, book value, insurance value, use value, par value, rental value, and replacement value. By far, the type of value used for the largest number of real estate transactions is market value.

In addition, many factors influence the value of a particular property and, generally, location is most important. Other factors are size and shape, utility, access, and exposure. For example, the south and west sides of business streets are usually more valuable because pedestrians seek the shady side of the street and display merchandise is not damaged by the sun. (*See* **appraisal**, **assessed valuation**, **conformity**, **contribution**, **going-concern value**, **indicated value**, **intrinsic value**, **market value**, **subjective value**.)

value added (*valor agregado*) The anticipated increase in property value expected from fixing a condition causing accrued depreciation.

variable interest rate A modern approach to financing in which the lender is permitted to alter the interest rate under a loan, with a certain period of advance notice, based on an agreed basic index, such as the prime rate. Although the monthly payment stays the same, the portion of the payment credited to paying off the unpaid principal varies according to the current interest rate. The constant payment of the variable interest rate is in contrast to the fluctuations of the adjustable-rate mortgage loan payments. Consider the following example:

> The sum of $50,000 payable in monthly installments of $400 each, including interest on the unpaid balance at the rate of 7 percent per year or 2 percent higher than the prime interest rate in effect at the Bank of Primo, whichever is greater (such rate to be established once each year on the first banking day of each calendar year), provided that the interest rate shall not exceed the maximum rate permitted by law.

A variation of this concept is the one-year maturity/20-year amortization mortgage loan. At the end of the year, the loan is renegotiated at the then-current interest rate, and the remaining principal balance and new interest payments are spread over a 19-year period. This process continues every year the loan is outstanding. (*See* **adjustable-rate loan**.)

variable-payment plan A mortgage repayment plan that allows a person to make small payments early in the loan term, increasing in future years, presumably as the mortgagor's income increases. This is also called the **flexible-payment mortgage**, the design of which is to help borrowers qualify for loans by basing repayment schedules on salary expectations. The variable index may be external (interest rate on government bonds) or internal (tied to the rate paid on the lender's savings deposits). (*See* **flexible-payment mortgage**.)

variance (*permiso de uso condicionado*) Permission obtained from governmental zoning authorities to build a structure or conduct a use that is expressly prohibited by the current zoning laws; an exception from the zoning laws. A variance gives some measure of elasticity to the zoning game.

The applicant usually must describe how the applicant would be deprived of the reasonable use of the land or building if it were used only for the purpose allowed in that zone; how the request is due to unique circumstances and not the general conditions in the neighborhood; and how the use sought will not alter the essential character of the locality or be contrary to the intent and purpose of the zoning code.

Examples include requesting apartment use in a single-family residential area and asking to build a structure larger than permitted. (*See* **nonconforming use**.)

vendee The purchaser of realty; the buyer. The buyer under contract for deed.

vendor The seller of realty. The seller under contract for deed. In some cases, the vendor may not be the owner—but might be the holder of an option.

vendor's lien   The equitable lien of the grantor on the land conveyed in the amount of the unpaid purchase price. Unlike a mortgage, it is not an absolute interest in the property but is only an equitable right to rely on in case all the purchase money is not paid.

veneer   A layer of material covering a base of another substance, such as mahogany veneer on other less valuable wood, or brick exterior finish over wood framing.

vent   A small opening to allow the passage of air through any space in a building, as for ventilation of an attic or the unexcavated area under a first-floor construction.

venture capital   Unsecured money directed toward an investment. Because of the risks involved, it usually commands the highest rate of return for its investment.

venue   The place where the cause of action arose or the jury is selected and the trial is brought; from the Latin word meaning "to come." An acknowledgment contains a statement of the county and state where the acknowledgment is taken and where the officer taking the acknowledgment is appointed—the venue.

verify   To confirm or substantiate by oath. Claims made to small claims court must be verified. In real estate appraisal, the confirmation of price, financing terms, motivation, and other details of a transaction in a market data study. (*See* **affirmation**.)

vested interest   A present right, interest, or title to realty, which carries with it the existing right to convey, even though use of possession is postponed to some uncertain time in the future. For example, when Hosea grants Evita a life estate in his ranch, the property reverts to Hosea upon the death of Evita. The reversion is a vested interest.

vestibule   A small entrance hall to a building or to a room.

Veterans Affairs (VA) loan   (*Préstamo V.A.*)   A government-sponsored mortgage assistance program, also called *GI loans*. Under the Servicemen's Readjustment Act of 1944, as amended in 1952, 1974, 1978, 1980, and 1987, eligible veterans and unremarried widows or widowers of veterans who died in service or from service-connected causes may obtain partially guaranteed loans for purchasing or constructing homes or refinancing existing mortgage debts. VA loans are administered by the Department of Veterans Affairs.

The main purpose of the GI loan is to assist veterans in financing the purchase of reasonably priced homes, including condominium units and manufactured homes, with little or no down payment, relatively easy qualification criteria, and a comparatively low rate of interest. The VA program encourages private lending institutions to make what are often very high loan-to-value mortgages by guaranteeing part of the loan in the event of default.

Eligibility can be determined by contacting any Department of Veterans Affairs Regional Office or through most VA-approved lending institutions. Generally, an eligible veteran is one who served a minimum of 181 days of active duty between September 16, 1940, and September 7, 1981. The minimum requirement is 90 days of active duty during specifically designated wartime periods. Enlisted members of the armed forces who began service after September 7, 1980, or any commissioned officer who began active service after October 16, 1981, must complete a total of two years of active service to be eligible. Certain reserve and National Guard personnel with six years' service are also eligible. A special provision allows active-duty personnel with less than two years' service to obtain a VA-guaranteed home loan after 181 days, so long as they are still on active duty.

> ***Entitlement and loan guaranty:***   The VA does not impose maximum loan limits, only the maximum possible guaranty on a loan. Under Public Law 110-389, The Veterans' Benefits Improvement Act of 2008, the maximum loan guaranty depends on the location of the county in which the property is located and by considering both the county's median home price and the Freddie

Mac conforming loan limit. The guaranty is 50 percent of a home loan up to $45,000 and up to $22,500 for loans between $45,001 and $56,250. The guaranty is 40 percent of the loan amount, with a maximum of $36,000 for loans between $56,251 and $144,000. For loans between $144,001 and $417,000, the guarantee is 25 percent of the loan amount. For loans greater than $417,000, the guaranty is the lesser of 25 percent of the VA county loan limit or 25 percent of the loan amount. The VA's loan limit chart is updated yearly.

The VA must list all foreclosed properties with real estate brokers.

The VA will only lend money to Native Americans on trust land or to supplement a grant for a specially adapted home for certain eligible veterans who have a permanent and total service-connected disability(ies). Usually, veterans make application with VA-approved lending institutions of their choice, which consider veterans' applications knowing the loans will be at least partially guaranteed against loss by the VA.

Interest rate and loan limits: Since 1992, the VA issues its guarantee for loans at an interest rate agreed upon between borrower and lender. The loan period can be for any number of years up to a maximum term of 30 years. Two factors limiting the length of the mortgage are (1) the term of the loan, which cannot exceed the dwelling's remaining useful economic life as determined by a VA appraisal; and (2) that the loan can be only for the remaining fixed rental period on a ground lease property.

VA sets no maximum loan amount except those imposed by the secondary market (i.e., Fannie Mae and Ginnie Mae). Usually, lenders loan up to four times a veteran's available entitlement with no down payment so long as the veteran has sufficient income and has sufficient credit, and the loan does not exceed the appraised value of the property (the certificate of reasonable value) or the purchase price, whichever is less. Loans are made in increments of $50. VA recognizes FHA appraisals but not conventional appraisals. VA requires that the real estate sales contract on a property include a provision (usually in the form of an addendum) that should the property appraise for less than the sales price, the seller agrees to refund the buyer's good-faith deposit and cancel the contract if the veteran does not wish to complete the purchase of the property.

Under certain conditions, secondary financing is permitted at the time a VA-guaranteed loan is made.

Closing costs may not be financed in the loan, so the veteran must be prepared to pay cash for all closing costs, except those paid by the seller, up to 4 percent of the sales price and for the difference between the sales price and the maximum loan amount. There is no prohibition against placing secondary financing on the property after the VA mortgage is closed and VA has issued the VA guarantee to the lender.

Loan fees, discount points, and funding fees: An allowable fee is up to 1 percent origination fee, although some lenders may choose to itemize the actual costs associated with preparing and process the loan application documents. The lender cannot charge for both. Since 1992, discount points may be paid by the veteran borrower but may not be added to the loan amount. The funding fee varies with the loan amount and may be financed.

Programs: VA-guaranteed home loans are granted for constructing or purchasing a home or refinancing existing mortgage debt. In all cases, however, VA requires veterans to certify that they occupy or intend to occupy the property as their home. This certification must be given at the time of loan application and again at closing. The veteran is subject to criminal prosecution for making false certifications, although after fulfilling the owner/occupancy requirement, the veteran would be allowed to rent the home or sell it while retaining the VA loan.

There are two types of VA loans—level payment mortgages and graduated-payment mortgages. The level payment or "traditional" VA loan has for some years had a maximum loan-to-value ratio of 100 percent for properties where the sales price or the appraisal (whichever is less) does not exceed four times the amount of entitlement the veteran has available. The structure of the graduated payment program is virtually identical with that of the FHA-245 loan program. As with the FHA graduated mortgage, the VA GPM requires a higher down payment than the level payment loan and is designed for young homebuyers just starting out. It enables these veterans to qualify to buy a home sooner than if they had to earn the income necessary to qualify for a loan with higher payments.

Assumptions: VA loans are no longer fully assumable. For loans underwritten after March 1, 1998, assumptions are not permitted without prior underwriting approval by the lender or VA. While older loans are still freely assumable, the seller remains fully liable unless a release of liability is obtained.

A veteran may sell a home purchased with a VA-guaranteed loan to anyone, including a nonveteran. The veteran can choose to remain liable for the VA loan or may seek a release of liability on the loan if the person assuming the loan is financially qualified to make the mortgage payments. Release of liability is different from restoration of entitlement. If the person assuming the loan is an eligible veteran, that person can substitute the entitlement for that of the seller. Upon substitution, which also requires the veteran-purchaser to qualify to release the veteran-seller of liability, the veteran-seller then has entitlement reinstated to allow the use of a VA loan privilege in a future home purchase. Veterans need to obtain releases from both the lender and the VA.

Anyone assuming the loan must pay a one-half percent user fee. Buyers assuming a VA-guaranteed loan must also undergo a creditworthiness check. If a purchaser does not meet these standards, the veteran can request that the VA approve the assumption, as long as the veteran agrees to be secondarily liable for the loan.

veto clause A clause in a shopping center lease that gives the tenant, usually an anchor tenant, the right to bar any lease between the landlord and another tenant. Such clauses are generally held invalid under modern antitrust interpretation.

vicarious liability Liability created not because of a person's actions but because of the relationship between the liable person and other parties. For example, real estate brokers are vicariously liable for the acts of salespeople while acting on their brokers' behalf even if the brokers did nothing to cause liability. (*See* **respondeat superior**.)

villa A one-story residence often owned as a condominium and usually built in units of two or four, and may include enclosed parking and a yard.

violation An act, deed, or condition contrary to the law or permissible use of real property.

visual rights The right to prevent a structure (e.g., a billboard) from being erected where it would obstruct a scenic view or interfere with clear vision at a traffic intersection.

vocation One's regular calling or business. The work in which a person is regularly employed. In most states, one can be a real estate broker or salesperson as a part-time vocation.

void Having no legal force or binding effect; a nullity; not enforceable. A void agreement is no contract at all. A void contract need not be disaffirmed, nor can it be ratified. A contract for an illegal purpose (for example, gambling) is void. Under many state and local discrimination laws, any restrictive covenant that discriminates on the basis of race, sex, color, religion, marital status, or ancestry may be void (although the nondiscriminating portions of the document in which it is contained may still remain valid). (*See* **unenforceable contract**.)

voidable   A contract that appears valid and enforceable on its face but is subject to rescission by one of the parties who acted under a disability. This includes such disabilities as being a minor or being under duress or undue influence; that which may be avoided or adjudged void but which is not, in itself, void. A voidable contract is one that is *able* to be *voided*. *Voidable* implies a valid act that may be rejected by an act of disaffirmance, rather than an invalid act that may be confirmed. For example, if a minor contracts to buy a diamond ring, the contract can be voided by the minor because of lack of sufficient age. If, however, the minor elects to enforce the contract, the contract is valid and the other party cannot assert the minor's lack of age as a defense.

In cases of fraud against the buyer of real estate, the buyer may affirm or disaffirm the contract within a reasonable time after the truth is discovered. For the duration of a license suspension, a broker's listings are voidable because of the inability to perform contractual obligations. (*See* **minor, void**.)

voluntary deed   *See* **deed in lieu of foreclosure**.

voucher system   In construction lending, a system of giving subcontractors a voucher that they may redeem with the construction lender in lieu of cash. The voucher system is the opposite of a fixed disbursement schedule where the lender forwards certain amounts of capital under a fixed schedule to subcontractors.

wains   *See* **baseboard**.

wainscoting   Wood lining of an interior wall. Wainscoting is also the lower part of a wall when finished differently from the wall above.

waiver   (*remisión de deuda*)   To give up or surrender a right voluntarily. The waiver is a common defense to a breach of contract suit, so it is good practice to insert a clause into every contract that stipulates that no waiver, modification, or amendment of any provision in the document will be valid unless it is in writing and signed by the party against whom the enforcement is sought. In some cases, the law prohibits a person from waiving certain rights granted by statute. For example, a provision in a contract is generally void if it purports to bind any prospective purchaser of subdivided lands to waive compliance with the protections afforded under state subdivision registration laws. Also void may be agreements to waive rights provided under a landlord-tenant code.

In building construction, the general contractor usually retains a portion of the final payment to the subcontractors until they present waivers of their mechanic's lien rights—called a *waiver of lien*.

The general rule is that a contingency placed in a contract for one person's benefit can be waived by that person for any reason. For example, a buyer who agrees to buy a farm contingent on favorable soil tests can decide to waive the contingency and purchase the farm even if the soil tests are negative.

walk-through   A final inspection of a property just before closing. This assures the buyer that the property has been vacated, that required repairs have been satisfactorily completed, and that otherwise the property is in essentially the same condition that it was when the buyer made the offer. If damage has occurred, the buyer might ask that funds be withheld at the closing to pay for the repairs.

V
W

walk-up   An apartment building that has several levels and no elevator.

wallboard   A board used as the finishing covering for an interior wall or ceiling. Wallboard can be made of plastic laminated plywood, asbestos/cement sheeting, plywood, molded gypsum, plasterboard, or other materials. Wallboard is applied in thin sheets over the insulation and is often used today as a substitute for plaster walls although it can also serve as a base for plaster.

wall sheathing   Sheets of plywood, gypsum board, or other materials nailed to the outside face of the wall studs to form a base for the exterior siding.

wall stud   *See* **stud**.

wall-to-wall carpeting   Carpeting that fully covers the floor area in a room. When a seller lists property to include wall-to-wall carpeting, the broker should take care to verify that there is, in fact, wall-to-wall carpeting to avoid the common problem that occurs when the seller removes the furniture and the buyer discovers gaps in the carpeting. In most cases, wall-to-wall carpeting is treated as a fixture, but to avoid disputes, the buyer and the seller should specify in their sales contract whether the wall-to-wall carpeting will pass to the buyer.

Wall-to-wall carpeting meeting minimum FHA standards is now accepted as finished flooring in proposed or existing homes and multifamily properties and is considered part of the real property.

ward   *See* **guardian**.

warehouse   (*bodega*)   A building used to store merchandise and other materials or equipment. As an investment, a warehouse is considered low-risk, a relatively low rate of return, and is usually operated under a net lease. Such properties are usually classified as industrial. (*See* **miniwarehouse**.)

warehousing   A line of credit normally extended by a commercial bank to a mortgage banker. A mortgage banker initially often borrows short-term money to fund mortgage loans and pledges the loans as collateral.

The banker then warehouses a number of such loans (much as a wholesaler warehouses clothing or furniture) to be sold at a later date to a large financial institution. When the loans are sold, the mortgage banker generally receives the value of the warehoused mortgage loans, plus a 1 percent origination charge and a commitment for an approximately 0.5 percent servicing fee over the life of the loan.

warranty   A promise that certain stated facts are true; a guaranty by the seller, covering the title as well as the physical condition of the property. In contract law, a warranty is basically a written or oral undertaking or stipulation that a certain fact in relation to the subject matter of the contract is or will be as it is stated or promised to be.

A warranty is different from a representation in that a representation is a statement made in the course of negotiations leading up to the sale, but not incorporated into the contract. In addition, a warranty must always be given contemporaneously with, and as a part of, the contract, whereas a representation precedes and induces the contract.

To prove a breach of warranty, a buyer must prove that the situation in violation of the warranty was in effect as of the date of closing (such as when the seller asserts that adequate water is available for drinking purposes when in fact it is not). A breach of warranty action can result only in damages being awarded by a court, not rescission as with a misrepresentation.

Upon the breach of a warranty, the contract remains binding, and only damages are recoverable for their breach. Upon a false representation by the seller, the purchaser may elect to avoid the contract and recover the entire price paid.

Currently, the courts tend to enforce an implied warranty of fitness and merchantability against builders and sellers of new homes, including condominium units. This rejection of the common-law caveat emptor doctrine has not yet been applied to the resale of older homes. (*See* **caveat emptor**, **implied warranty of habitability**.)

The Magnusen-Moss Warranty Act is a federal law requiring the full and fair disclosures of any warranty, whether the manufacturer's or the seller's, on any consumer product in the home. The law covers separate items of equipment attached to real property, such as air conditioners, furnaces, and water heaters. The act is administered by the Federal Trade Commission.

warranty deed   A deed in which the grantor fully warrants good clear title to the premises; also called a *general warranty deed*. The usual covenants of title are covenant of seisin, covenant of quiet enjoyment, covenant against encumbrances, covenant of warranty forever, and covenant of further assurance. A warranty deed warrants the title, not the quality of construction of the real property. A warranty deed is used in most real estate deed transfers and offers the greatest protection of any deed. (*See* **deed**.)

waste   (*desperdicio*)   An improper use or abuse of property by a landowner who holds less than the fee ownership, such as a tenant, life tenant, mortgagor, or vendee. Waste thus impairs the value of the land or the interest of the one holding the title or the reversion (for example, the lessor).

The term *waste* includes ameliorating waste, which is the unauthorized alteration by the occupant of improvements on the land—even though such changes in fact increase the value of the property. Although the tenant is usually not liable for ameliorating waste (because it increases the worth of the future interest), the owner of the future interest does not have to pay for the improvement.

Waste could occur through failure to pay property taxes, insurance, or mortgage payments, as well as by making material changes to the original use of the property, such as converting from residential to heavy industrial. In essence, any act on the land that substantially impairs the security value of the real estate is considered waste. Other examples of affirmative or voluntary waste are cutting timber, removing minerals, or destroying buildings. (*See* **permissive waste**.)

wasteland   Land deemed to be unfit for cultivation; unproductive, unimproved, barren land such as lava land. An owner may be able to apply to the local tax agency to classify his or her property as wasteland for the purposes of real property tax.

waste line   A pipe that carries waste from a bathtub, shower, basin, or any fixture or appliance, except a toilet.

wasting asset   Property such as timber, an oil well, a quarry, or a mine, the substance of which is depleted through drilling and exploitation. Also refers to rights such as patent rights and franchises for a fixed term. (*See* **depletion**.)

water   In its natural state, water is real property. When it is severed from the realty and reduced to possession by putting it in containers, it becomes personal property.

There are three classifications of water: *Surface water* is water diffused over the land surface or contained in depressions, resulting from rain, snow, or that which rises to the surface from springs. Surface water is distinguishable from water flowing to a fixed channel, which constitutes a *watercourse*, or water collected in an identifiable body, such as a river or lake. The extraordinary overflow of rivers and streams is known as *floodwater*. (*See* **correlative water right**, **littoral land**, **riparian rights**.)

watercourse   A running stream of water following a regular course or channel and possessing a bed and banks.

waterfront property   Real estate (improved or unimproved) abutting on a body of water such as a canal, lake, or ocean. (*See* **littoral land**, **riparian rights**.)

W

watershed The drainage area contributing to the water found in the abutting stream; the drainage basin. Many municipalities restrict owners from filling in or otherwise disrupting water flow in a watershed area.

water table The natural level at which water is located, be it above or below the surface of the ground.

way A street, alley, or other thoroughfare or easement permanently established for passage of persons or vehicles.

way-growing crop *See* **emblement**.

wear and tear The gradual physical deterioration of property, resulting from use, passage of time, and from weather. Only property subject to wear and tear is eligible for cost recovery. Generally, a tenant must return the leased premises to the landlord in good condition, ordinary wear and tear excepted. (*See* **normal wear and tear**.)

weep hole One of several small holes left in a wall to permit surplus water to drain, as used in a retaining wall or foundation.

wet column A column containing plumbing lines facilitating the installation of sinks, drinking fountains, and like things.

wetlands Land areas where groundwater is at or near the surface of the ground for enough of each year so as to produce a wetland plant community, such as swamps, ponds, estuaries, and marshes. Because these areas are so susceptible to flooding, they are subject to many federal, state, and local controls, including environmental protection and zoning for special preservation and conservation.

    The Natural Resources Conservation Service (NRCS) identifies wetlands on agricultural lands, and farmers can rely on a single wetlands determination. The EPA and the U.S. Corps of Engineers share Section 404 enforcement authority.

widow's quarantine That period of time after the husband's death that a widow may remain in the house of her deceased husband without being charged rent. In the meantime, she is entitled to her reasonable sustenance out of his estate. (*See* **dower**.)

wild deed A deed appearing in the chain of title in which the first party (grantor) has no recorded interest in the subject property. If the grantor is a stranger to the chain of title, the deed does not give constructive notice of its existence. However, actual knowledge of its existence puts one on notice that this first party may have had a legitimate interest in the subject property under an unrecorded instrument. (*See* **chain of title**; **name, change of**.)

will (*testamento*) A written instrument disposing of probate property (tenancy in severalty or tenancy in common) upon the death of the maker (the testator). A will takes effect only upon the testator's death, and thus can be revoked or amended at any time during the testator's life. The testator must generally be of sound mind and of adult age and must declare the writing to be a last will and testament and sign it, usually in the presence of two or more credible persons who subscribe their names as witnesses to the will. A witness must generally be a person other than a beneficiary under the will. The testator often designates an executor or personal representative and, where there are minor children, usually nominates a guardian. No one should attempt to write a will without first consulting an attorney.

    When a person dies either without a will or with a defectively executed will, the decedent's property passes to the heirs according to the laws of intestacy. A surviving spouse may be able by law to elect to take a one-third life estate as dower or curtesy, an elective share, or some other survivorship portion given by statute in lieu of the spouse's share provided in the will, if any. (*See* **descent**, **holographic will**, **intestate**, **probate**, **testator**.)

W

window jamb trim   A thin vertical strip of molding covering the junction of the vertical members of the window frame and the jamb.

window sash   (*marco de ventana*)   The movable frame that holds the window glass. Sash windows move vertically; they may be either a single, in which only the lower half of the window opens, or a double, in which both the upper and lower portions are movable.

wipeout   A decrease in property value caused by public action, such as planning regulations, denial of permit, and governmental uses of land, that creates nuisance-like results. A wipeout includes the effect on the public when governments permit private action that in turn creates negative impacts.

withholding   The process of holding back money earmarked for the payment of taxes. (*See* **Foreign Investment in Real Property Tax Act [FIRPTA]**, **independent contractor**.)

without recourse   A form of qualified endorsement relieving the maker of personal liability. In a promissory note secured by a mortgage on real property, a without-recourse note means that the mortgagee can satisfy only the claim against the property; that is, the mortgagee cannot sue the defaulting mortgagor for a deficiency judgment. (*See* **nonrecourse loan**.)

witness   (*dar fe*)   The act of signing one's name to a contract, deed, will, or other document for the purpose of attesting to its authenticity and proving its execution by testifying, if required. As a rule, witnesses are not necessary to the validity of a real estate contract. A will, however, must usually be witnessed by at least two disinterested third persons. (*See* **subscribe**.)

Women's Council of REALTORS®   *See* Appendix A.

Wood Destroying Insect Inspection Report (NPMA-33)   A report approved by HUD for FHA and VA loans, consisting of inspection for wood-destroying insects, including termites, carpenter ants, carpenter bees, and reinfesting wood-boring beetles. The report does not include mold, mildew, or non-insect-wood-destroying organisms. It is not a warranty and is valid for 90 days from the time of the inspection. FHA and VA loans require treatment for any active infestation. The report includes suggestions for eliminating conditions that promote insect infestation. (*See* **termite inspection**, **pest control report**.)

workers' compensation law   A state law requiring all employers to provide insurance coverage for their employees for work loss of employment due to work-related illness or injury. This law may apply to real estate brokers, regardless of whether the brokers consider their salespeople to be employees or independent contractors. Thus, a salesperson who is injured on the job is covered for specified medical expenses and lost wages. A broker who does not carry the requisite insurance may be subject to civil penalties, including suspension or revocation of the broker's real estate license. (*See* **independent contractor**.)

working capital   Liquid assets available for the conduct of daily business.

working drawings   The final-stage drawings by an architect that show the lighting layout, electrical plugs, telephone outlets, and similar items, and that detail the precise method of construction. (*See* **blueprint**, **plans and specifications**.)

work letter   A detailed addition to a lease defining all improvement work to be done by the landlord for the tenant and specifying what work the tenant will perform at her own expense.

workout plan   An attempt by a mortgagee to assist a mortgagor in default to work out a payment plan rather than proceed directly with a foreclosure. Some possible workout plans could include extending the loan term, accruing interest, or reducing the interest rate. (*See* **forbearance**.)

worthier title doctrine   A common-law doctrine holding that where a testator devised to an heir exactly the same interest in land as the heir would take by the laws of descent, then the latter was regarded as worthier, and the heir took title by descent rather than by devise.

wraparound mortgage   A method of financing in which the new mortgage is placed in a secondary or subordinate position; the new mortgage includes both the unpaid principal balance of the first mortgage and whatever additional sums are advanced by the lender. Sometimes called an *all-inclusive loan*, an *overriding loan*, or an *overlapping loan*.

In essence, it is an additional mortgage in which another lender refinances a borrower by lending an amount over the existing first mortgage amount, without cashing out or disturbing the existence of the first mortgage. The wraparound combines two or more debts and is treated as a single obligation (like a "consolidated loan"), and the wrap, or secondary, mortgagee pays the obligations of the first mortgage from the total payments received.

The difference between the interests of the two mortgage notes is the *arbitrage*. While the wraparound lender makes the debt service payments on the first mortgage, the lender does not assume liability for this first lien. A default on the wraparound mortgage usually results in a default on the underlying mortgage.

For example, assume a property is worth $300,000 with an existing first mortgage in the amount of $100,000 at 7 percent interest with 15 years remaining on the term. The owner desires to raise an additional $100,000 in capital. Under conventional financing, the owner would have to refinance the building for $200,000, probably at a higher interest rate, say 11 percent, and use $100,000 to pay off the existing first mortgage and the balance for the new needs.

By using a wraparound mortgage, the owner can obtain a lower interest rate, say 9 percent. The actual amount advanced to the borrower under the wraparound mortgage is $100,000, and the new lender makes the payments on the underlying $100,000 first mortgage at 7 percent and receives payments from the owner on the newly negotiated 9 percent $200,000 wraparound or overriding mortgage.

The first mortgage cannot contain an alienation clause ("due-on-encumbrance") because this could effectively preclude the use of the wraparound mortgage. The wraparound mortgage is attractive in condominium conversions, where the existing mortgage usually has a rate that is lower than the current market interest rate.

Because the usury ceiling laws in many states apply to second liens but not to residential first liens, many state laws have been amended to define wraparound loans as first liens, following the definition created by the Federal Home Loan Bank Board. Thus, institutional lenders can make wraparound loans. (*See* **all-inclusive deed of trust**, **arbitrage**.)

write-off
1. Clearing an asset off the accounting books, as with an uncollectible debt.
2. A tax deduction. (*See* **tax shelter**.)

writ of attachment   *See* **attachment**.

writ of execution   A court order authorizing and directing an officer of the court (sheriff, police officer) to levy and sell property of the defendant to satisfy a judgment. The officer may be required to give prior notice of the sale and first attempt to sell enough personal property to pay the judgment before executing the levy. Generally, the title of a purchaser at an execution sale relates back to the date of judgment and is free from any lien created after the attachment.

When there is insufficient property within the district in which the judgment was rendered, the plaintiff can obtain a writ of execution from a higher court covering all property of the defendant, wherever situated in the state. (*See* **attachment**, **levy**.)

writ of garnishment   *See* **garnishment**.

W

X

1. A mark that may substitute for a signature in some cases. An individual who cannot write his name can indicate the intention to sign by marking an *X* in the place for signature. A witness would then write the name of the signer alongside the *X*. When a person appearing before a notary cannot sign his name, the notary must first satisfy herself as to the identity of the person by requiring some proof of identification. The notary would then have the person place an *X* on the document, after which the notary would indicate that it is the mark of the person, for example, "*X* (mark of Charlie Smith)." (*See* **signature**.)
2. A mark found on some maps in the form "*X* marks the spot where . . . "

x-bracing   Cross-bracing in a partition.

x-ray fluorescent device (XRF)   A handheld device used to detect the levels of lead in any underlying layers of lead-based paint.

xylotomous   Capacity of an organism to bore into wood; a characteristic of termites.

yard   (*yarda*)
1. A unit of measurement equaling three feet.
2. The open, unoccupied space on the plot between the property line and the front, rear, or side wall of a building. There are three main types of yard:
   - *Front yard*—The yard across the full width of the plot facing the street extending from the front line of the building to the front property line. On a corner lot, both yards facing a street are considered front yards.
   - *Back yard*—The yard across the full width of the plot opposite the front yard, extending from the rear line of the building to the rear property line.
   - *Side yard*—The yard between the side line of a building and the adjacent side property line, extending from the front yard to the back yard. (*See* **setback**.)

year-to-year tenancy   A periodic tenancy in which the rent is reserved from year to year. Sufficient notice (if not specified in the contract, then a reasonable time) must be given to terminate this tenancy. Where the tenant holds over after the first year, he or she normally creates another year-to-year tenancy. (*See* **periodic tenancy**.)

yield   (*rendimiento*)   The return on an investment or the amount of profit, stated as a percentage of the amount invested; the rate of return. In real estate, *yield* refers to the effective annual amount of income that is being accrued on an investment. The yield on income property is the ratio of the annual net income from the property to the cost or market value of the property. The yield, or profit, to a lender is the spread or differential between the cost of acquiring the funds lent and the interest rate charged.

yield capitalization   In the income approach to appraisal, a process whereby cash flows are projected over a holding period to include the proceeds of sale at the end of the holding period, and cash flow is discounted at a selected yield rate to estimate current value of the cash flows. The yield rate may be compared with yields from other investments. (*See* **internal rate of return**.)

X
Y

yield spread premium (YSP)   Upfront loan charge expressing the difference between the market interest rate and the (generally higher) interest rate charged to the buyer. The premium was often used to reduce the amount of money buyers needed to bring to closing. Unfortunately, YSP became a way for mortgage brokers to increase their fees. The Dodd-Frank Act prohibits yield spread premium bonuses because they increase the total cost of the loan.

yield to maturity   A method of financing repayment in which a borrower pays a certain percentage of actual funds borrowed each year (such as interest only) and pays the loan off in full at the end of its maturity.

yuppie   Slang for young, upwardly mobile professionals; young singles or couples with high job skills and good prospects for steady income advances. The term faded in prominence after the 1990s recession.

zero lot line   A term generally used to describe the positioning of a structure on a lot so that one side rests directly on the lot's boundary line. Such construction is generally prohibited in many areas by setback ordinances unless, of course, it is a part of a special space-conserving project. (*See* **party wall, patio home, planned unit development [PUD]**.)

zone condemnation   The demolition and clearance of entire areas to make way for new construction, especially in slum clearance projects.

zoning   (*zonificación*)   The regulation of structures and uses of property within designated districts or zones. Zoning laws are enacted in the exercise of police power and are upheld as long as they may reasonably protect the public health, safety, morals, and general welfare of an area. Because there are no national zoning standards, counties and/or municipalities generally enact their own zoning ordinances pursuant to an enabling act of the state. Zoning laws are generally enforced through building permits that must be obtained before one can build on a parcel of land. A permit is not issued unless the proposed structure conforms to the permitted zoning, among other requirements, including the implementation of a master plan. Where zoning and private restrictions conflict, the more restrictive must be followed. (*See* **master plan**.)

Zoning regulates and affects such things as use of the land, lot sizes, types of structure permitted, building heights, setbacks, and density (the ratio of land area to improvement area). Some of the more typical zoning classifications of real property are (1) residential, such as single-family homes, townhouses, multifamily apartments, and condominiums; (2) commercial, such as retail shopping centers and highrise office buildings; (3) industrial, such as warehouses, loft buildings, and industrial parks; and (4) special-purpose, such as hotels, motels, schools, and mobile home parks.

Requests for rezoning may have to be directed toward a special zoning appeals board or other administrative body because the change can usually be accomplished only by passage of a special ordinance.

Purchasers of property must be aware of the zoning requirements; that is, zoning regulations do not render the title unmarketable where they differ from what the purchaser thought they were. Consequently, the broker has an obligation to ascertain whether the contemplated use of the property conforms to existing zoning. However, violations of zoning regulations do render the title unmarketable. Where the zoning permits single-family dwellings only and the seller has a duplex, the title is therefore rendered unmarketable unless the buyer agrees to accept title under those conditions. Also, where either the seller or the broker misrepresents the actual permitted zoning use, the buyer can rescind the transaction on the basis of the misrepresentation.

Where the downzoning (for example, from urban to conservation) of an area results in lowering the property values, the state is not responsible to make just compensation payments to the owners

Y

(as it is when property is condemned under the power of eminent domain). Some special types of zoning are as follows:

- *Bulk zoning*: Controls density and avoids overcrowding by regulating setback, building height, and percentage of open area
- *Aesthetic zoning*: Requires that new buildings conform to specific types of architecture
- *Cumulative zoning*: Permits higher uses (e.g., residential) to exist on land zoned for lower uses (industrial), but lower uses cannot occupy higher-zoned land
- *Incentive zoning*: Requires that street floors of office buildings be used for retail establishments
- *Directive zoning*: Encourages zoning as a planning tool to use land for its highest and best use

(*See* **airport zoning, buffer zone, cluster zoning, commingling, conditional-use zoning, density zoning, downzoning, general plan, inclusionary zoning, land-use intensity, nonconforming use, special-use permit, spot zoning, urban enterprise zone, variance.**)

zoning estoppel   A rule that bars the government from enforcing a new downzoning ordinance against a landowner who had incurred substantial costs in reliance on the government's assurances that the landowner had met all the zoning requirements before the new downzoning took place.

Organizations

American Arbitration Association (AAA)

www.adr.org

A trade association with international participation offering education and training, publications, and the resolution of a wide range of disputes through mediation, arbitration, elections, and other out-of-court settlement techniques.

American Institute of Real Estate Appraisers (AIREA)

www.appraisalinstitute.org

A professional organization formerly affiliated with the National Association of REALTORS® and merged in 1991 with the Society of Real Estate Appraisers into the Appraisal Institute. Designations: Member, Appraisal Institute (MAI) and Residential Member (RM) designations. (*See* **Appraisal Institute**)

American Land Title Association (ALTA)

www.alta.org

An association of land title companies whose collective objectives include using uniform ALTA title insurance forms to provide standardization in the transfer of ownership within the free enterprise system. ALTA members provide information and education to consumers and government regulators working with legislation affecting the land title evidencing industry, and to its own members. ALTA members may provide abstracts, issue title insurance, or act as agents for title insurance underwriting companies.

American National Standards Institute (ANSI)

www.ansi.org

A private, nonprofit organization (501[c]3) that administers and coordinates the U.S. voluntary standardization and conformity assessment system. ANSI promotes and facilitates voluntary consensus standards and conformity assessment systems.

American Resort Development Association (ARDA)

A national trade association for real estate professionals involved in development of recreation and second homes by representing the interstate land development industry in matters related to land development. The mailing address is 1200 L Street, N.W., Washington, D.C. 20005; (202) 371-6700.

American Society of Appraisers (ASA)

www.appraisers.org

A professional organization of appraisers engaged in the appraisal of both real and personal property. Designations: Accredited Member (AM), Accredited Senior Appraiser (ASA).

American Society of Farm Managers and Rural Appraisers

www.asfmra.org

A professional association representing professionals in financial analysis, valuation, and management of agricultural and rural resources, including farm management. Certifications: Accredited Farm Manager (AFM), Accredited Rural Appraiser (ARA), Real Property Review Appraiser (RPRA), Accredited Agricultural Consultant (AAC).

American Society of Home Inspectors (ASHI)

www.ashi.org

A professional organization of home inspectors of members from the United States and Canada, meeting the needs of its membership by building public awareness of home inspections, and promoting excellence and exemplary practice within the profession under ASHI's Standards of Practice and Code of Ethics.

Appraisal Foundation

www.appraisalfoundation.org

A self-regulated organization created for the purpose of developing appraisal standards and appraiser qualifications by the Financial Institutions Reform, Recovery, and Enforcement Act of 1989 (FIRREA). The five-member Appraiser Qualification Board approves the education, experience, and testing requirements for state certification of appraisers. The Appraisal Standards Board establishes minimum standards for appraisers.

Appraisal Institute

www.appraisalinstitute.org

A professional real estate organization formed as a result of the merger of the American Institute of Real Estate Appraisers and the Society of Real Estate Appraisers. Designations: Member, Appraisal Institute (MAI) and Senior Residential Appraiser (SRA).

Appraisal Institute of Canada (AIC)

www.aicanada.ca

A Canadian self-regulating body protecting the public interest by maintaining high standards, practices, and professional conduct in real estate appraisal; Designations: Canadian Residential Appraiser (CRA); Accredited Appraiser Canadian Institute (AACI); Professional Appraiser (P.App).

ASIS International

www.asisonline.org

A professional association of industrial security personnel. Certification programs: Certified Protection Professional (CPP), Professional Certified Investigator (PCI), and Physical Security Professional (PSP).

Association of Real Estate License Law Officials (ARELLO)

www.arello.org

A professional organization of real estate commissioners and real estate administrators from all 50 states, three Canadian provinces, Guam, Puerto Rico, and the Virgin Islands. A joint committee of ARELLO and the National Association of REALTORS® (NAR) has drafted several model license laws since the early 1960s, since adopted by the various states.

BOMI International

www.bomi.org

An independent institute for property and facility management education. Designations: Real Property Administrator (RPA), Facilities Management Administrator (FMA), Systems Maintenance Administrator (SMA), and Systems Maintenance Technician (SMT).

Building Owners and Managers Association International (BOMA)

www.boma.org

An international professional organization of 100 North American and nine overseas affiliates and the primary information source for office building development, leasing, building operating costs, energy consumption patterns, local and national building codes, legislation, occupancy statistics, and technological developments. Its members are building owners, managers, developers, leasing professionals, medical office building managers, corporate facility managers, asset managers, and the providers of the products and services needed to operate commercial properties.

Bureau of Land Management (BLM)
www.blm.gov

An agency within the U.S. Department of the Interior; administers 261 million surface acres of America's public lands, located primarily in 12 western states. The BLM sustains the health, diversity, and productivity of the public lands for the use and enjoyment of present and future generations.

CCIM Institute
www.ccim.com

A professional organization of real estate practitioners specializing in commercial real estate, affiliated with the National Association of REALTORS®. Designation: Certified Commercial Investment Member (CCIM).

Chinese American Real Estate Professional Association (CAREPA)
www.carepa.org

A national association of Chinese American real estate professionals seeking to further home ownership in the Chinese American communities and to conduct a high, ethical real estate practice in Chinese American communities.

Commercial Real Estate Development Association (NAIOP)
www.naiop.org

A national trade association representing the interests of developers and owners of industrial, office, and related commercial real estate throughout North America through communication, networking, and business opportunities for all real estate related professionals.

Community Associations Institute (CAI)
www.caionline.org

A not-for-profit research and educational organization offering education for creating, financing, operating, and maintaining the common facilities and services in condominiums, townhouse projects, planned unit developments, and open-space communities. Certification (with National Board of Certification for Community Association Managers) (NBC-CAM) the Certified Manager of Community Associations (CMCA). Designations: Association Management Specialist (AMS); Professional Community Association Manager (PCAM); Accredited Association Management Company (AAMC); Large-Scale Manager (LSM); Reserve Specialist (RS); Community Insurance and Risk Management Specialist (CIRMS); College of Community Association Lawyers (CCAL).

Council of Real Estate Brokerage Managers
www.crb.com

A not-for-profit affiliate of the National Association of REALTORS®, whose goal is to improve standards and professionalism in real estate brokerage management by offering training and education to brokers and owners of real estate companies. Designation: Certified Real Estate Brokerage Manager (CRB).

Council of Residential Specialists
www.crs.com

The largest not-for-profit affiliate of the National Association of REALTORS® whose goal is to recruit, train, and enhance members' continuing competency through superior educational opportunities. Designation: Certified Residential Specialist (CRS).

Counselors of Real Estate (CRE)
www.cre.org

A not-for-profit worldwide organization established exclusively for real estate advisors with opportunities for professional development, knowledge, sharing, and networking opportunities. Designation: Counselor of Real Estate (CRE).

Department of Housing and Urban Development (HUD)
www.hud.gov

A U.S. government agency created in 1965, consolidating older federal agencies to administer federal housing and community programs and urban development, and fair housing laws. HUD plays a major role in fostering home ownership by underwriting loans for lower- and moderate-income families through its mortgage insurance programs such as the Federal Housing Administration (FHA), Ginnie Mae, and the Community Development Block Grant (CDBG). Designations: Area Management Brokers (AMBs).

Department of Veterans Affairs (VA)

www.va.gov

A federal cabinet-level department established to serve as the principal advocate for America's veterans and their families. Among its tasks, the VA administers the partially guaranteed loans for purchasing or constructing homes by eligible veterans and unmarried widows or widowers.

Environmental Protection Agency (EPA)

www.epa.gov

A federal agency created in 1970 to coordinate government action on behalf of the environment by a variety of research, monitoring, standard-setting, and enforcement activities. The EPA coordinates and supports research and antipollution activities by state and local governments, private and public groups, individuals, and educational institutions. It also monitors the environmental impact of other Federal agencies and is specifically charged with making public its written comments on environmental impact statements (EIS).

Fair Isaac Corporation

www.myfico.com

A for-profit company best known for developing the FICO scores as a method of determining the likelihood that credit users will pay their bills, by condensing a borrower's credit history into a single number. Lenders use FICO scores, computed by data provided by each of the three credit bureaus—Experian, TransUnion, and Equifax—to determine loan availability.

Fannie Mae

www.fanniemae.com

A government-sponsored enterprise charted by Congress to expand the flow of mortgage money by creating a secondary market for home mortgages.

Farm Credit

www.farmcreditnetwork.com

A nationwide network of borrower-owned lending institutions and affiliated service entities that lend to agricultural producers, cooperatives, and certain farm related business. Unlike commercial banks, the system banks do not accept deposits and instead provide financial and human resources necessary to underwrite, distribute, and maintain a primary and secondary market in Farm Credit Debt Securities.

Farm Credit Administration (FCA)

www.fca.gov

An independent agency in the U.S. government responsible for regulating and examining the banks, associations, and so on that collectively comprise the Farm Credit System, including the Federal Agricultural Mortgage Corporation (Farmer Mac) in order to promote a safe, sound, and dependable source of credit and related services for agriculture and rural America.

Farm Service Agency (FSA)

www.fsa.usda.gov

An agency created by the merger of several other agencies under the U.S. Department of Agriculture responsible for administering farm income-support programs, conservation cost-sharing programs and farm loan programs through field service centers located throughout the United States. Each state FSA is led by a state executive director (SED).

Federal Agricultural Mortgage Corporation (Farmer Mac)

www.farmermac.com

A government-sponsored, stockholder-owned, publicly traded company regulated by the Farm Credit Administration (FCA) that provides a secondary market for first mortgage agricultural and rural housing real estate loans. Working with the USDA, Farmer Mac purchases loans from agricultural lenders, sells instruments backed by these loans, and seeks to maintain a sufficient liquidity reserve, and surplus funds with appropriate interest-rate risk.

Federal Deposit Insurance Corporation (FDIC)

www.fdic.gov

An independent agency of the federal government that seeks to promote public confidence in the U.S. financial system by insuring deposits in banks and thrift institutions for up to $100,000 by identifying, monitoring, and addressing risks to the deposit insurance funds and by limiting the effect on the economy and the financial system when a bank or thrift institution fails.

Federal Emergency Management Agency (FEMA)
www.fema.gov

A former independent agency that became part of the new Department of Homeland Security in March 2003 responsible for disaster mitigation, preparedness, response, and recovery planning.

Federal Financial Institutions Examination Council (FFIEC)
www.ffiec.gov

An interagency of federal regulatory agency representatives organized to promote uniformity among commercial banks, savings associations, and credit unions by prescribing uniform principles, standards, and report forms for the federal examination of financial institutions by the Board of Governors of the Federal Reserve System (FRB), the Federal Deposit Insurance Corporation (FDIC), the National Credit Union Administration (NCUA), the Office of the Comptroller of the Currency (OCC), and the Consumer Financial Protection Bureau (CFPB).

Federal Housing Administration (FHA)
www.hud.gov/fha

A federal agency that neither builds homes nor lends money directly; rather it insures loans on real property made by approved lending institutions.

Federal Housing Finance Agency (FHFA)
www.fhfa.gov

The Federal Housing Finance Agency regulates the 12 Federal Home Loan Banks created in 1932 to improve the supply of funds to local lenders that, in turn, finance loans for home mortgages. The FHFA ensures the safety and soundness of these banks, their access to the capital markets, and the accomplishment of their congressionally defined housing finance mission. As of 2008, FHFA is the regulator and conservator of Fannie Mae and Freddie Mac.

Federal Reserve System ("the Fed")
www.federalreserve.gov

The nation's central bank that helps stabilize the economy by careful handling of the money supply and credit available in the country. The system functions through a seven-member Board of Governors and 12 Federal Reserve District Banks. The Fed is responsible for supervising the Truth in Lending Act, the Equal Credit Opportunity Act, and the Community Reinvestment Act.

Federal Trade Commission (FTC)
www.ftc.gov

A federal agency created to investigate and eliminate unfair and deceptive trade practices or unfair methods of competition, and false and misleading advertising in interstate commerce.

The FTC has very broad antitrust and consumer protection authority.

Financial Industry Regulatory Authority (FINRA)
www.finra.org

A nonprofit, self-regulatory organization registered with the U.S. Securities and Exchange Commission that governs the practices of broker-dealer firms in the over-the-counter (OTC) market. FINRA has federal authority to discipline securities firms and individuals in the securities industry who violate the rules by fining, suspending, or expelling them from the industry. It has authority over securities salespeople such as those selling real estate securities, resort condominiums with rental pools, and tax shelters in programs providing a direct "pass-through" of tax benefits, limited partnerships and REITs, but not stock in ordinary corporations.

Freddie Mac
www.freddiemac.com

A quasi-governmental, federally chartered corporation that is one of America's largest buyers of home mortgages from insured depository institutions and HUD-approved mortgage bankers, including commercial banks, mortgage banks, savings institutions, and credit unions. Freddie Mac is operating under a conservatorship under the direction of the Federal Housing Finance Agency (FHFA).

General Services Administration (GSA)
www.gsa.gov

An independent, central management federal agency that sets federal policy for procurement and real property management and information resources management (i.e., it manages, leases, and sells buildings belonging to the U.S. government). The GSA supplies products and communications for U.S. government offices, provides transportation and housing to federal employees, and develops government-wide cost-minimizing policies.

Ginnie Mae
www.ginniemae.gov

A government corporation that guarantees federally insured or guaranteed loans—mainly loans insured by the Federal Housing Administration (FHA) or guaranteed by the Department of Veterans Affairs (VA). Other guarantors or issuers of loans eligible as collateral for Ginnie Mae mortgage-backed securities (MBS) include the Department of Agriculture's Rural Housing Service (RHS) and the Department of Housing and Urban Development's Office of Public and Indian Housing (PIH).

Independent Community Bankers of America (ICBA)
www.icba.org

A trade association representing community banks of all charter types whose members provide financial services to their communities and customers. It implements a broad range of advocacy and progressive, entrepreneurial, and service-oriented strategies.

Institute of Real Estate Management (IREM)
www.irem.org

A professional real estate management association serving both multifamily and commercial real estate sectors, an affiliate of the National Association of REALTORS®. Designations: Certified Property Manager® (CPM), the Accredited Residential Manager (ARM), and the Accredited Management Organization (AMO).

Internal Revenue Service (IRS)
www.irs.gov

A bureau of the Department of the Treasury whose role is to help taxpayers understand the tax laws passed by Congress, while ensuring that all pay their fair share of the taxes.

International Code Council (ICC)
www.iccsafe.org

A nonprofit organization dedicated to developing a single set of comprehensive and coordinated national model construction codes.

International Council of Shopping Centers (ICSC)
www.icsc.org

A global trade organization of shopping center owners, managers, and major tenants that functions as a medium for the interchange of information about shopping center practices and operations. Designations: Certified Shopping Center Manager (CSM); Certified Leasing Specialist (CLS); Certified Marketing Director (CMD); Senior Level Certified Shopping Center Manager (SCSM); Accredited Shopping Center Manager (ASM); Senior Level Certified Shopping Center Marketing Director (SCMD); Accredited Marketing Director (AMD).

International Facility Management Association (IFMA)
www.ifma.org

An international professional organization for facility management that conducts research, provides educational programs, and recognizes facility management degree and certificate programs. Designation: Certified Facility Management (CFM).

International Real Estate Federation (IREF)
www.fiabci.com

An international association of real estate professionals who provide essential commercial information about local markets to professional real estate associations. Designation: Certified International Property Specialist (CIPS).

Manufactured Housing Institute (MHI)

www.manufacturedhousing.org

A national trade organization serving all segments of the factory-built housing industry by providing industry research, promotion, education, and government relations programs.

National Affordable Housing Management Association (NAHMA)

www.nahma.org

A nonprofit organization for affordable housing by advocating on behalf of multifamily property owners and managers providing quality affordable housing. The membership—multifamily property owners, managers, and industry stakeholders—support legislative and regulatory policies that promote the development and preservation of decent and safe housing by providing technical education and information between government and industry. Designations: Certified Professional of Occupancy (CPO); Housing Credit Certified Professional (HCCP).

National Apartment Association (NAA)

www.naahq.org

A professional organization serving the interests of multifamily housing owners, managers, developers, and suppliers and provides education and training opportunities for both multisite managers and on-site staff. NAA works with the National Multi Housing Council to monitor legislation and regulations at the federal level. Designations: Certified Apartment Property Supervision (CAPS); Certified Apartment Manager (CAM); Certified Apartment Maintenance Technician (CAMT); National Apartment Leasing Professional (NALP); Certified Apartment Supplier (CAS).

National Association of Exclusive Buyer Agents (NAEBA)

www.naeba.org

An independent alliance of real estate professionals who provide client-level services only to buyer clients and whose real estate companies do not accept seller-property listings.

National Association of Hispanic Real Estate Professionals (NAHREP)

www.nahrep.org

A national trade association of real estate professionals who want to increase the rate of sustainable homeownership by empowering those who serve the Hispanic real estate community.

National Association of Home Builders (NAHB)

www.nahb.org

A trade association consisting of more than 205,000 residential homebuilding and remodeling industry members. Designations: Certified New Home Sales Professional (CSP); Registered in Apartment Management (RAM); Certified Leasing Professional (CLP); plus many others.

National Association of Housing and Redevelopment Officials (NAHRO)

www.nahro.org

A professional organization of officials who administer HUD programs such as public housing, Section 8, and others to advocate for providing adequate and affordable housing for all Americans, including those with low and moderate incomes.

National Association of Independent Fee Appraisers (NAIFA)

www.naifa.com

A professional association of appraisers seeking to raise standards in the appraisal industry and to gain recognition for its members. Designations: Independent Fee Affiliate (IFA); Independent Fee Affiliate Senior (IFAS); Independent Fee Affiliate Counselor (IFAC).

National Association of Real Estate Appraisers (NAREA)

www.narea-assoc.org

One of the largest professional associations of appraisers. Designations: Certified Real Estate Appraiser (CREA), Certified Commercial Real Estate Appraiser (CCREA).

National Association of Real Estate Brokers (NAREB)

www.nareb.com

The oldest trade association of minority professionals in the real estate industry, consisting of local boards in principal cities throughout the United States; the members are called Realtists. The organization is open to any real estate licensee committed to achieving the ideals of the Realtist organization: democracy in housing.

National Association of Real Estate Investment Trusts (NAREIT)

www.reit.com

A professional organization representing REITs and publicly traded real estate companies worldwide and whose members are real estate investment trusts (REITs), academics, investors, industry professionals, and other businesses that own, operate, and finance income-producing real estate, and firms and individuals who advise, study, and service these businesses.

National Association of Real Estate License Law Officials

See **Association of Real Estate License Law Officials (ARELLO)**.

National Association of REALTORS® (NAR)

www.realtor.org

The largest real estate organization in the world with more than one million members including REALTORS® and REALTOR®-ASSOCIATES® representing all branches of the real estate industry. The national organization functions through local boards and state associations. Active brokers admitted to membership in state and local NAR boards are allowed to use the trademark REALTOR®. Salespeople are admitted on a REALTOR®-ASSOCIATES® active status. NAR members subscribe to a strict Code of Ethics.

National professional organizations directly affiliated with NAR include the following: REALTORS® National Marketing Institute (formerly known as the National Institute of Real Estate Brokers, or NIREB); Commercial Investment Real Estate Institute (CIREI); Society of Industrial and Office REALTORS® (SIOR); Institute of Real Estate Management (IREM); REALTOR® Land Institute (RLI), Real Estate Securities and Syndication Institute (RESSI); American Society of Real Estate Counselors (ASREC), Women's Council of REALTORS® (WCR); and the American Chapter of the International Real Estate Federation.

National Association of Residential Property Managers (NARPM)

www.narpm.org

A professional association of real estate professionals who specialize in managing single-family and small residential properties. Designations: Professional Property Manager (PPM); Master Property Manager (MPM).

National Association of Review Appraisers and Mortgage Underwriters (NARA/MU)

www.naramu.org

A nonprofit, national organization whose members review appraisals and underwrite mortgages, one of the largest "consumers" of appraisals in the nation. Designations: Certified Review Appraiser (CRA) and Registered Mortgage Underwriter (RMU).

National Investment Center for the Seniors Housing and Care Industry (NIC)

www.nic.org

An independent, nonprofit organization facilitating efficient capital formation for the seniors' housing and care industries through research, networking, and providing business and financial information to lenders, investors, developers/operators, and others interested in meeting the housing and healthcare needs of senior citizens in the USA.

Office of Equal Employment Opportunity Commission (EEOC)

www.eeoc.gov

A federal commission that enforces federal laws prohibiting employment discrimination.

Office of Interstate Land Sales Registration (OILSR)

A federal agency that regulates interstate land sales to prevent abuse, such as fraud and misrepresentation, perpetrated on the public in the promotion and sale of recreational property across state lines. It is now part of the Consumer Financial Protection Bureau (CFPB).

Office of the Comptroller of the Currency (OCC)
www.occ.treas.gov

A federal agency within the U.S. Treasury Department that charters, regulates, and examines approximately 2600 national banks, 66 federal branches, and agencies of foreign banks in the United States.

Real Estate Buyers Agent Council (REBAC)
www.rebac.net

An affiliate of the National Association of REAL-TORS® whose goal is to promote buyer representation skills and services. Designations: Accredited Buyers Representative (ABR®) and Accredited Buyers Representative Manager (ABRM).

Real Estate Educators Association (REEA)
www.reea.org

A professional organization established by and for real estate educators, including individuals and institutions. REEA is international in scope and represents every aspect of real estate education from degree programs, proprietary school, to publishers, etc. Designation: Distinguished Real Estate Instructor (DREI).

Real Estate Negotiation Insitute (RENI)
www.negotiationexpertise.com

A negotiation training and coaching company serving real estate professionals, it offers the designations Certified Negotiation Expert (CNE) and Master Certified Negotiation Expert (MCNE).

Realnet Learning Services
www.realnetlearning.com

A for-profit company that offers specialized training for real estate agents. Designation: Certified Buyers Representative (CBR).

REALTORS® Institute
www.realtor.org

A series of classes leading to the professional designation Graduate, REALTORS® Institute (GRI), which may be earned by any member of a state-affiliated Board of REALTORS® who successfully complete prescribed courses approved by the state Board of REALTORS®. State associations generally sponsor the GRI courses covering law, finance, investment, appraisal, office management, and salesmanship.

REALTORS® Land Institute (RLI)
www.rliland.com

A professional organization formerly known as the Farm & Land Institute, now an affiliate of the National Association of REALTORS® (NAR) focused on land brokerage transactions of five specialized types: farms and ranches, undeveloped tracts of land, transitional and development land, subdivision and wholesaling of lots, and site selection and assemblage of land parcels. Individual members frequently engage in other land specialties such as agribusiness, appraisal, consulting, and management. Designation: Accredited Land Consultant (ALC).

Resolution Trust Corporation (RTC)

A now defunct agency created as a part of FIRREA for the purpose of receiving the assets of failed savings associations and to dispose of repossessed property through direct sales and auction sales.

Rural Housing Service (RHS)
www.rurdev.usda.gov/LP_Subject_HousingAnd-CommunityAssistance.html

The successor to Farmers Home Administration (FmHA), it is responsible for administering many rural housing programs, not all serving low and very low income people. Since it has a national office but no field staff, the programs are administered by the USDA's Rural Development staff.

Securities and Exchange Commission (SEC)
www.sec.gov

An independent regulatory agency that administers the laws and rules that protect investors, maintain fair and orderly markets, and facilitate capital formation.

Small Business Administration (SBA)

www.sba.gov

An independent federal agency in the executive branch created to provide management and financial assistance to small businesses, primarily by either making loans directly or guaranteeing loans through financial institutions. The loans may be used for working capital, machinery and equipment, acquisition of real estate, and expansion.

Society of Industrial and Office REALTORS® (SIOR)

www.sior.com

A professional organization affiliated with the National Association of REALTORS® (NAR), whose members specialize in the marketing of industrial and office properties. Designations: Specialist, Industrial and/or Office Real Estate (SIOR).

Urban Land Institute (ULI)

www.uli.org

An independent, nonprofit research and educational organization composed of individuals working in private enterprise and public service to improve the quality and standards of land use and real estate development. Certifications: Real Estate Development Certification; Real Estate Development Financing Certification.

Women's Council of REALTORS® (WCR)

www.wcr.org

An organization originally founded by women for women within the National Association of REALTORS® and whose purpose today is to expand its members' knowledge of the real estate business and provide an opportunity for sharing experiences and exchanging information.

Designations

Note: Terms in *italics* denote organizations listed in Appendix A.

AAC   Accredited Agricultural Consultant, see *American Society of Farm Managers and Rural Appraisers*

AACI   Accredited Appraiser Canadian Institute, see *Appraisal Institute of Canada (AIC)*

AAMC   Accredited Association Management Company, see *Community Associations Institute (CAI)*

ABR®   Accredited Buyers Representative, see *Real Estate Buyers Agent Council*

ABRM   Accredited Buyers Representative Manager, see *Real Estate Buyers Agent Council*

AFM   Accredited Farm Manager, see *American Society of Farm Managers and Rural Appraisers*

ALC   Accredited Land Consultant, see *REALTORS® Land Institute*

AM   Accredited Member, see *American Society of Appraisers (ASA)*

AMBs   Area Management Brokers, see *Department of Housing and Urban Development (HUD)*

AMD   Accredited Marketing Director, see *International Council of Shopping Centers (ICSC)*

AMO   Accredited Management Organization, see *Institute of Real Estate Management (IREM)*

AMS   Association Management Specialist, see *Community Associations Institute (CAI)*

ARA   Accredited Rural Appraiser, see *American Society of Farm Managers and Rural Appraisers*

ARM   Accredited Residential Manager, see *Institute of Real Estate Management (IREM)*

ASA   Accredited Senior Appraiser, see *American Society of Appraisers (ASA)*

ASM   Accredited Shopping Center Manager, see *International Council of Shopping Centers (ICSC)*

CAM   Certified Apartment Manager, see *National Apartment Association (NAA)*

CAMT   Certified Apartment Maintenance Technician, see *National Apartment Association (NAA)*

CAO   Certified Appraisal Organization, see *National Association of Master Appraisers (NAMA)*

CAPS   Certified Apartment Property Supervision, see *National Apartment Association (NAA)*

CAS   Certified Apartment Supplier, see *National Apartment Association (NAA)*

CBR   Certified Buyers Representative, see *Realnet Learning Services*

CCAL   College of Community Association Lawyers, see *Community Associations Institute (CAI)*

CCIM   Certified Commercial Investment Member, see *CCIM Institute*; *REALTORS® National Marketing Institute (RNMI)*

CCREA   Certified Commercial Real Estate Appraiser, see *National Association of Real Estate Appraisers (NAREA)*

CFM   Certified Facility Management, see *International Facility Management Association (IFMA)*

CIPS   Certified International Property Specialist, see *International Real Estate Federation*

CIRMS   Community Insurance and Risk Management Specialist, see *Community Associations Institute (CAI)*

CLP   Certified Leasing Professional, see *National Association of Home Builders (NAHB)*

CLS   Certified Leasing Specialist, see *International Council of Shopping Centers (ICSC)*

CMCA   Certified Manager of Community Associations, see *Community Associations Institute (CAI)*

CMD   Certified Marketing Director, see *International Council of Shopping Centers (ICSC)*

CNE   Certified Negotiation Expert, see *Real Estate Negotiation Institute (RENI)*

CPM   Certified Property Manager®, see *Institute of Real Estate Management (IREM)*

CPO   Certified Professional of Occupancy, see *National Affordable Housing Management Association (NAHMA)*

CPP   Certified Protection Professional, see *ASIS International*

CRA   Canadian Residential Appraiser, see *Appraisal Institute of Canada (AIC)*

CRA   Certified Review Appraiser, see *National Association of Review Appraisers and Mortgage Underwriters*

CRB   Certified Real Estate Brokerage Manager, see *Council of Real Estate Brokerage Managers*

CRB   Certified Residential Broker, see *REALTORS® National Marketing Institute (RNMI)*

CRE   Counselor of Real Estate, see *Counselors of Real Estate (CRE)*

CRS   Certified Residential Salesperson, see *REALTORS® National Marketing Institute (RNMI)*

CRS   Certified Residential Specialist, see *Council of Residential Specialists (CRS)*

CSM   Certified Shopping Center Manager, see *International Council of Shopping Centers (ICSC)*

CSP   Certified New Home Sales Professional, see *National Association of Home Builders (NAHB)*

DREI   Distinguished Real Estate Instructor, see *Real Estate Educators Association (REEA)*

FMA   Facilities Management Administrator, see *BOMI International*

GRI   Graduate, REALTORS® Institute, see *REALTORS® Institute; National Association of REALTORS®*

HCCP   Housing Credit Certified Professional, see *National Affordable Housing Management Association (NAHMA)*

IFA   Independent Fee Affiliate, see *National Association of Independent Fee Appraisers (NAIFA)*

IFAA   Agricultural Appraiser Specialist, see *National Association of Independent Fee Appraisers (NAIFA)*

IFAC   Independent Fee Affiliate Counselor, see *National Association of Independent Fee Appraisers (NAIFA)*

IFAS   Senior Appraiser Specialist for Non-Residential and Income Properties, see *National Association of Independent Fee Appraisers (NAIFA)*

LSM   Large-Scale Manager, see *Community Associations Institute (CAI)*

MAI   Member, Appraisal Institute, see *Appraisal Institute; American Institute of Real Estate Appraisers (AIREA)*

MCNE   Master Certified Negotiation Expert, see *Real Estate Negotiation Institute (REN)*

MPM Master Property Manager, see *National Association of Residential Property Managers (NARPM)*

NALP National Apartment Leasing Professional, see *National Apartment Association (NAA)*

P.App Professional Appraiser, see *Appraisal Institute of Canada (AIC)*

PCAM Professional Community Association Manager, see *Community Associations Institute (CAI)*

PCI Professional Certified Investigator, see *ASIS International*

PPM Professional Property Manager, see *National Association of Residential Property Managers (NARPM)*

PSP Physical Security Professional, see *ASIS International*

RAM Registered in Apartment Management, see *National Association of Home Builders (NAHB)*

Real Estate Development Certification See *Urban Land Institute (ULI)*

Real Estate Development Financing Certification See *Urban Land Institute (ULI)*

Realtist see *National Association of Real Estate Brokers (NAREB)*

REALTOR® See *National Association of REALTORS® (NAR)*

REALTOR- ASSOCIATE® (RA) See *National Association of REALTORS® (NAR)*

RM Residential Member, see *American Institute of Real Estate Appraisers (AIREA)*

RMU Registered Mortgage Underwriter, see *National Association of Review Appraisers and Mortgage Underwriters*

RPA Real Property Administrator, see *BOMI International*

RPRA Real Property Review Appraiser, see *American Society of Farm Managers and Rural Appraisers*

RS Reserve Specialist, see *Community Associations Institute (CAI)*

SCSM Senior Level Certified Shopping Center Manager, see *International Council of Shopping Centers (ICSC)*

SCMD Senior Level Certified Shopping Center Marketing Director, see *International Council of Shopping Centers (ICSC)*

SIOR Specialist, Industrial and/or Office Real Estate, see *Society of Industrial and Office REALTORS® (SIOR)*

SMA Systems Maintenance Administrator, see *BOMI International*

SMT Systems Maintenance Technician, see *BOMI International*

SRA Senior Residential Appraiser, see *Society of Real Estate Appraisers (SREA)*

SRA Senior Residential Appraiser, see *Appraisal Institute*

SREA Senior Real Estate Analyst, see *Society of Real Estate Appraisers (SREA)*

SRPA Senior Real Property Appraiser, see *Society of Real Estate Appraisers (SREA)*

Abbreviations of Terms

A

a/c	air-conditioning
ac; A	acre
ACM	asbestos-containing material
ACRS	accelerated-cost recovery system
ADR	asset-depreciation range system
ADS	alternative depreciation system
ADT	average daily traffic
AFD	agreement for deed
AFR	applicable federal rate
AIR	Appraiser Independence Requirements
AITD	all-inclusive trust deed
a.k.a.	also known as
ALJ	administrative law judge
AMB	area management broker
APR	annual percentage rate
ARM	adjustable-rate mortgage
ATCF	after-tax cash flow

B

BA	bathroom
BD	bedroom
BFP	bona fide purchaser
BID	business improvement district

BHC	bank holding company
BIC	broker-in-charge
BIF	bank insurance fund
BRI	building-related illness
BTU	British thermal unit

C

CAM	common area maintenance
Cap	capitalization
CB	carry back
CBD	central business district
CBS	concrete block and stucco
CCD	Census County Division
CC&Rs	covenants, conditions, and restrictions
CD	certificate of deposit
CF	cash flow
CFC	chlorofluorocarbons
CFD	contract for deed
CLO	computerized loan origination
CLTV	combined loan to value
CMA	comparative market analysis
CMO	collateralized mortgage obligation
Co.	company
CO	carbon monoxide
COB	close of business

COC	certificate of completion
COF	cost of funds
CON	connected (sewer)
COCR	cash on cash return
COO	certificate of occupancy
CPA	Certified Public Accountant
CPI	consumer price index
CRA	credit rating agency
CRV	certificate of reasonable value
CSM	certified survey map
CT	conveyance tax
CTL	cash-to-loan ratio
CZC	comprehensive zoning code

D

DCF	discounted cash flow
DCR	debt coverage ratio
d/b/a	"doing business as"
DBH	diameter breast-high
DCRR	discounted rate of return
DLUM	detailed land-use map
Dog	bad investment
DOS	due-on-sale clause
DOT	deed of trust; Department of Transportation
DP	down payment
DPC	debt previously contracted
DR	dining room
DRM	direct reduction mortgage
DSCR	debt service coverage ratio
DT	depth tables

E

EA	exclusive agency
EBA	exclusive buyer agent
EC	extended coverage
EIFS	exterior insulation and finish systems
EIS	environmental impact statement
EM	earnest money deposit
EMAC	enclosed mall air-conditioned

E&O	errors and omissions insurance
ERA	environmental risk audits
ESA	environmental site assessment
ESOP	employee stock owner-ship plan

F

FAR	floor area ratio
FB	full bath
FFE	furniture, fixture, and equipment
FH	flood hazard
FICB	federal intermediate credit banks
FIFO	first in, first out (accounting)
FLB	federal land bank
FLIP	Flexible Loan Insurance Program
FMR	fair market rent
FMV	fair market value
FP	file plan
FRM	fixed-rate mortgage
FS	fee simple
FRBO	for rent by owner
FSBO	for sale by owner

G

GBA	gross buildable area
GCR	guest-car ratio
GEM	growing equity mortgage
GIT	gross income tax
GLA	gross leasable area; gross living area
GMC	guaranteed mortgage certificate
GP	general plan
GPARM	graduated payment adjustable-rate mortgage
GPM	graduated-payment mortgage
GRM	gross rent multiplier
GSE	government-sponsored enterprise
GSP	guaranteed sales program

H

HBU	highest and best use
HELOC	home equity line of credit

HEPA	high-efficiency particulate acquisition
HML	hard money lender
HOA	homeowners' association
HOW	Homeowners' Warranty Program
HMIS	hazardous material identification system
HRS	hazard rank system
HVCC	Home Valuation Code of Conduct
HSF	heated square feet
HUD	U.S. Department of Housing and Urban Development
HVAC	heating, ventilation, and air-conditioning

I

IFA	independent fee appraiser
IRA	individual retirement account
IRC	Internal Revenue Code
IRR	internal rate of return
IRS	Internal Revenue Service
IS	information systems
IT	information technology

J

J/T	joint tenant

K

Kit	kitchen

L

L	leasehold
L#	liber number (book number)
LA	living area
LR	living room
LAL	limit on artificial accounting losses
LDD	local development district
LH	leasehold
LHA	local housing authority
LIBOR	London Interbank Offering Rate
LIFO	last in, first out
LIR	land-use intensity rating
Lis/P	lis pendens

LLC	limited liability company
L.P.	land patent
LOC	line of credit
LOI	letter of intent
L/O	lease option
L/P	lease purchase
LP	limited partnership
LPOA	limited power of attorney
LS	landlord seller; locus sigilli (Latin—"place of seal")
LSR	livability space ratio
LTV, L/V	loan-to-value
LUI	land-use intensity
LUL	land use law
LUMS	land utilization marketing study
LUST	leaking underground storage tank

M

MBR	master bedroom
MBS	mortgage-backed security
MACRS	modified accelerated cost recovery system
MF	multifamily
MGRAD	minimum guidelines and requirements for accessible design
MGRM	monthly gross rent multiplier
MIP	mortgage insurance premium
MIS	management information system
MLP	master limited partnership
MLS	multiple listing service
MPR	minimum property requirement
MRB	mortgage reserve bond
MSA	metropolitan statistical area
MSDSs	material safety data sheets
MUD	municipal utility district

N

n/a	not available or not applicable
NC	not connected (sewer)
NLA	net leasable area

NNN	triple-net lease		**POC**	paid outside of closing
NOI	net operating income		**PRD**	planned residential development
NOL	net operating loss		**PRM**	permanent reference marker
NOO	nonowner occupant		**PRP**	potentially responsible party
NOW	negotiable order of withdrawal		**PSC**	participation sale certificate
NPL	national priorities list		**PUD**	planned unit development
NRA	net rentable area			
NRV	net realizable value		**R**	
NSF	not sufficient funds		**R**	REALTOR®

O

OAR	overall rate
OER	operating expense ratio
O/F	owner financing
OE&T	operating expenses and taxes
OIR	official interpretation rulings
OL&T	owners', landlords', and tenants' liability insurance
OO	owner occupant
ORE	owned real estate
OTC	over the counter

P

PAM	pledged account mortgage
PB	principal broker
PC	participation certificate
PCB	polychlorinated biphenyls
PCi/L	picocuries per liter of air
PD-H	planned development housing
PE	professional engineer
P&I	principal and interest
P&L	profit and loss
P&S	purchase and sale agreement
PITI	principal, interest, taxes, and insurance (monthly payments)
PMI	private mortgage insurance
PMM	purchase-money mortgage
POA	power of attorney
POB	point of beginning

R

R	REALTOR®
RA	REALTOR-ASSOCIATE®
RAM	reverse annuity mortgage
REA	reciprocal easement agreement
REC	real estate commission
REIT	real estate investment trust
REO	real estate owned
Rm	room
ROI	return on investment
RRM	renegotiable rate mortgage
RS	revenue stamp
RTO	rent to own
RV	recreational vehicle
R/W	right-of-way

S

S	section
SAM	shared appreciation mortgage
SBLN	setback line
SBS	sick building syndrome
SF	square feet
SFH	single-family house
SFR	single-family residence
S&L	savings and loan association
SMSA	standard metropolitan statistical area
SOYD	sum of the years' digits
SS	scilicet (Latin—"namely")

T

T/B	tenant buyer
T/C	tenant in common

TCT	transfer certificate of title		**V**	
TDD	telecommunication devices for deaf		**VA**	U.S. Department of Veterans Affairs
TDI	temporary disability insurance		**VOCs**	volatile organic compounds
TDR	transfer of development rights		**VRM**	variable-rate mortgage
T/E	tenancy by the entirety		**v.**	versus
TSO	time-share ownership		**W**	
U			**WROS**	with right of survivorship
UBIT	unrelated business income tax		**W/W**	wall to wall
UCC	Uniform Commercial Code		**Y**	
UCR	usual, customary, and reasonable		**YSP**	yield spread premium
UFFI	urea-formaldehyde foam installation		**YTD**	year-to-date
URAR	Uniform Residential Appraisal Report		**Z**	
USPAP	*Uniform Standards of Professional Appraisal Practice*		**Z**	zone
UST	underground storage tank			

List of Laws

Agricultural Foreign Investment Disclosure Act (AFIDA) (1978)

A federal law requiring foreign persons who have an interest in U.S. agricultural land of more than one acre to file certain disclosure information with the Secretary of Agriculture.

Americans with Disabilities Act (ADA) (1992) *(Ley sobre los estadounidenses incapacitados)*

A federal law designed to eliminate discrimination against individuals with disabilities by mandating equal access to jobs, public accommodations, government services, public transportation, and telecommunications.

Bankruptcy Abuse Prevention and Consumer Protection Act of 2005 (BABCPA)

A federal bankruptcy reform act intended to provide consumer protection while combating fraud and abuse.

CAN-SPAM Act of 2003

A federal law that sets rules for commercial email, establishes requirements for commercial messages, gives recipients rights to opt out of certain electronic communications, and includes penalties for violations. Its full name is the Controlling the Assault of Non-Solicited Pornography And Marketing Act of 2003.

Chemical Safety Information, Site Security and Fuels Regulatory Relief Act (1999)

An amendment and clarification of the Clean Air Act requiring facilities dealing with chemicals to hold public meetings about their risk management plans, including a summary of the worst-case off-site consequences, and exempts certain facilities from these requirements.

Civil Rights Act of 1866

A federal act prohibiting all racial discrimination, without exception, affirmed in 1968 in *Jones v. Alfred H. Mayer Company*. Enforcement of 1866 is through federal courts, not HUD.

Civil Rights Acts of 1968

A federal law to follow the Civil Rights Act of 1964 providing protection for civil rights workers and prohibiting discrimination in the sale, rental, and financing of housing based on race, color, religion, and national origin. Protections have since been expanded to include sex, familial status, and handicap.

Clayton Antitrust Act

A federal statute passed in 1914 to clarify and supplement the Sherman Antitrust Act of 1890.

Clean Air Amendments and the Resource Recovery Act (1970)

A comprehensive federal law regulating air emissions from area, stationary, and mobile sources and authorizing the U.S. Environmental Protection Agency (EPA) to establish air standards to protect public health and the environment. This law has been amended in 1977 and 1990 to set new goals/dates and to address problems such as acid rain, ground-level ozone, stratospheric ozone depletion, and air toxics.

Clean Water Act (CWW) (1977)

A federal law amending an earlier law of 1972, establishing the basic structure for regulating discharges of pollutants into U.S. waters by giving the EPA authority to implement pollution control programs such as setting water-quality standards for all contaminants in surface waters and making it illegal to discharge pollutants into navigable waters without a permit.

Coastal Zone Management Act (1972)

A federal law passed in 1972, recognizing the national interest in the effective planning, management, beneficial use, protection, and development of the saltwater and Great Lakes coastal zones. The act calls for states to plan and develop management programs for the land and water resources of their coastal zones.

Community Reinvestment Act (CRA) (1977)

A federal act that requires lenders to meet the credit needs of the communities in which they do business by expanding credit to low- and moderate-income people. Lenders are required to submit reports to demonstrate that they are loaning money in the neighborhoods in which they take deposits. Enforced by Federal Deposit Insurance Corporation (FDIC).

Comprehensive Environmental Response, Compensation, and Liability Act (CERCLA) (1980)

A federal law commonly known as Superfund placing a tax on the chemical and petroleum industries. The tax money is placed in a trust fund to clean up abandoned or uncontrolled hazardous waste sites and providing broad Federal authority to respond directly to releases of hazardous substances that could endanger public health or the environment. The EPA cleans up orphan sites when the potentially responsible parties cannot be identified or when they fail to act. The EPA works with state environmental protection or waste management agencies and is authorized to identify, monitor, and respond to activities in every state.

Consumer Credit Protection Act (a.k.a. Truth in Lending Act) (1969)

A federal act requiring most lenders and extenders of consumer credit to disclose the true cost of the loan and to place limits on wage garnishments and excessive interest rates. Employees are protected from discharge because their wages have been garnished for any one debt. The Wage and Hour Division (WHD) of the Department of Labor's (DOL) Employment Standards Administration (ESA) administers this Act.

Controlled Substances Act (1976)

A federal law consolidating numerous laws regulating the manufacture and distribution of narcotics, stimulants, hallucinogens, anabolic steroids, and chemicals used in the illicit production of controlled substances providing the legal foundation against the abuse of drugs and other substances.

Dodd-Frank Wall Street Reform and Consumer Protection Act (Dodd-Frank Act) (2010)

A sweeping federal reform act adopted in response to the late-2000s recession. Among other changes in financial regulation, Dodd-Frank created the Consumer Financial Protection Bureau, which may independently write rules for financial institutions as well as oversee the enforcement of federal laws intended to ensure the fair, equitable and nondiscriminatory access to credit for individuals and communities.

Emergency Planning and Community Right-to-Know Act (EPCRA) (1986)

The national legislation on community safety allowing local communities better protection of public health, safety, and the environment from chemical hazards by requiring specific disclosures. Communities are required to develop, implement, and exercise emergency plans and to identify additional required resources.

Endangered Species Act (ESA) (1973)

An act providing a program for the conservation of threatened and endangered plants and animals and the habitats in which they are found. Lists are maintained and policies implemented by the U.S. Fish and Wildlife Service and the Department of the Interior. The EPA decides to register a pesticide in part on the risk of adverse effects on endangered species as well as on the environmental.

Equal Credit Opportunity Act *(Ley de igualdad de oportunidades para obtener crédito)*

The federal law that ensures that consumers applying for credit are evaluated for business reasons, such as income, expenses, debt, and credit history, and not on the basis of race, color, religion, national origin, sex, receipt of public assistance, and marital status. The act applies to all who regularly extend or arrange for credit; and in certain circumstances may include real estate licensees. The overall enforcing agency for ECOA is the Federal Trade Commission.

Fair and Accurate Credit Transaction Act (2004)

A federal law implemented by the Federal Trade Commission to reduce identity theft and to help victims recover their losses.

Fair Credit Billing Act (1974)

The federal law that pertains to "open end" credit accounts, revolving accounts such as credit cards and department store accounts, but not installment contracts. The law offers protections against unauthorized charges, those incorrectly charged as to wrong date or amount, nonposted payments and credits, and so forth. The consumer must follow certain guidelines to complain, and the creditor must respond quickly. Generally enforced by the Federal Trade Commission.

Fair Credit Reporting Act (1970)

The federal law that applies to business practices by the consumer reporting agencies (CRAs) that gather and sell information about consumers regarding where they live and work and how they pay bills, as well as information about being sued, arrested, or filed for bankruptcy. The act is designed to promote accuracy and to ensure privacy of the information used in consumer reports. Generally enforced by the Federal Trade Commission (FTC).

Fair Debt Collection Practices Act (1996)

An amendment to the Consumer Credit Protection Act to prohibit abusive practices by debt collectors and to promote consistent actions by individual states to protect consumers against debt collection abuses. A debt collector may use mail, telephone, telegrams, faxes, or even a personal visit but not during inconvenient places or times, i.e., not before 8:00 AM or after 9:00 PM unless agreed to by the consumer. Generally enforced by the state Attorney General's office and/or the Federal Trade Commission.

Fair Housing Amendment Act of 1988

An amendment to the federal Fair Housing Act that expanded coverage to prohibit discrimination based on disability or on familial status (presence of a child under 18 or a pregnancy); new administrative enforcement procedures; design and construction accessibility provisions for certain new construction of multifamily dwellings. Generally enforced by local and state equal opportunity commissions and the Department of Housing and Urban Development (HUD).

Federal Deposit Insurance Act of 2005

A reform act that merged the Bank Insurance Fund (BIF) and the Saving Association Insurance Fund (SAIF) into a new fund called the Deposit Insurance Fund (DIF).

Federal Unemployment Tax Act (FUTA)

A federal regulation requiring employers to file federal (and often state) unemployment tax returns for employees to provide unemployment compensation to workers who have lost their jobs.

Federal Insecticide, Fungicide and Rodenticide Act (FIFRA) (1996)

The federal law authorizing the EPA to study the consequences of pesticide usage and to require users (farmers, utility companies, etc.) to register when purchasing pesticides to ensure that pesticides are properly labeled according to specifications and will not cause unreasonable harm to the environment. Later legislation requires uses to take certification exams and requires that all pesticides used in the U.S. must be registered, i.e., licensed by the EPA to ensure proper labeling and use.

Federal Insurance Contributions Act (FICA)

A federal regulation requiring employers to pay retirement fund taxes (Social Security) for employees.

Financial Institutions Reform, Recovery, and Enforcement Act (FIRREA) (1989) *(Ley de Reforma, Recuperación y Ejecución de las Institutiones Financieras)*

A comprehensive law to provide guidelines for the regulation of financial institutions by creating the Savings Association Insurance Fund (SAIF) and the Bank Insurance Fund (BIF), both administered by the restructured Federal Deposit Insurance Corporation (FDIC). FIREEA also created the Appraisal Foundation requiring the use of state-certified or state-licensed appraisers to appraise properties involving federal insurance or federally regulated industry. Much of the act has been superseded by the Dodd-Frank Act.

Foreign Investment in Real Property Tax Act (FIRPTA)

A federal law that applies to foreign persons who dispose of U.S. real property interests to pay an income tax on any gain from the sale of the property.

Freedom of Information Act (FOIA) (1966)

The federal law that permits "any person" to make requests for government information. Citizens are not required to either identify themselves or explain why they want the information. All branches of the federal government are obligated to comply with the requests unless the information is deemed confidential, classified, or related to national security.

Home Mortgage Disclosure Act (HMDA) (1975) *(Ley de Divulgación sobre las Hipotecas de Vivienda)*

A federal law requiring lenders to provide data about the types of loan applications received and action taken by their institutions each year to determine if they are serving the housing needs of their communities; to assist public officials in distributing public-sector investments in order to attract needed investment; and to identify possible discriminatory lending patterns. The rule-writing authority was transferred to the Consumer Financial Protection Bureau (CFPB) in 2011.

Housing for Older Persons Act of 1995 (HOPA)

The amendment to the Fair Housing Act that eliminates the requirement that age 55 and older housing must have "significant facilities and services" designed for the elderly and that the facility has been designated by HUD. However, it still retains the requirement that at least 80 percent of the occupied units must be occupied by someone over age 55. These properties will not violate the act if they include families with children so long as they comply with the other policies and procedures demonstrating intent to be 55 and older housing.

Internal Revenue Code (IRC)

The body of statutes codifying the federal tax laws and administered by the Internal Revenue Service (IRS), a federal agency that issues its own regulations interpreting those laws.

Interstate Land Sales Full Disclosure Act (1968) *(Ley Interestatal de Divulgación Completa en la Venta de Tierras)*

The federal law that requires all land promoters to comply with antifraud provisions by including information about the owners of the land being subdivided and sold, physical properties of the land, availability of utilities, and the status of access to the land. Registration is required with the Office of Interstate Land Sales Registration (OILSR) of the U.S. Department of Housing and Urban Development (HUD) and applies to any offers of 25 or more undeveloped lots promoted through the U.S. Mail or any other interstate commerce.

Junk Fax Prevention Act (2005)

The federal law that prohibits sending unsolicited advertisements to any business and residential fax machine without the express invitation or permission of the recipient, unless there is an established business relationship (EBR) between the parties.

Lead-Based Paint Hazard Reduction Act (LBPHRA) (1978)

The federal act that seeks to control exposure to lead-based paint hazards, specifically mentioning protection of children under the age of six by requiring sellers, landlords, real estate licensees, and renovators of properties built before 1978 to make certain disclosures.

National Environmental Protection Act (NEPA) (1969)

The basic national charter for protection of the environment that created the Environmental Protection Agency (EPA). Its authority allows it to establish policy, set goals, and provide means for carrying out the policy. Such actions may include new highway construction, harbor dredging or filling, nuclear power plant construction, large-scale aerial pesticide spraying, river channeling, new jet runways, munitions disposal, and bridge construction among others.

National Flood Insurance Act (1968, and amended)

A federal law passed in 1968 and amended several times since then creating the National Flood Insurance Program (NFIP) designed to provide an insurance alternative to disaster assistance to meet the escalating costs of repairing damage to buildings and their contents caused by floods. Communities must adopt and enforce a floodplain management ordinance to participate. Federally related loans trigger a flood insurance requirement. The program is administered by Federal Emergency Management Agency (FEMA).

National Manufactured Housing Construction and Safety Standards Act (1976)

A federal law establishing construction standards for manufactured homes that are entirely factory-built to HUD standards, including built on a nonremovable steel chassis, of at least 320 square feet.

Noise Control Act and the Marine Protection Research and Sanctuaries Act (1972)

www.epa.gov/history/topics/nca/02.htm

The act assigning responsibility to the EPA to coordinate all federal programs in noise research and control and authorizing citizen lawsuits. The EPA is required to recommend aircraft noise regulations to the Federal Aviation Agency, which retains final authority. In addition, the EPA has authority to label noise-generating products, encourage reduction of noise, and can fine or imprison manufacturers or importers for nonconforming or mislabeled products.

Occupational Safety and Health Act (OSHA) (1970)

The federal law passed to ensure worker and workplace safety by requiring employers to provide workers a workplace free from recognized hazards to safety and health, such as exposure to toxic chemicals, excessive noise levels, mechanical dangers, heat or cold stress, or unsanitary conditions. OSHA is enforced by the U.S. Department of Labor.

Oil Pollution Act (OPA) (1990)

The federal law that streamlined and strengthened the EPA's ability to prevent and respond to catastrophic oil spills. A trust fund financed by a tax on oil is available to pay for cleanups if the responsible party cannot or will not. Owners of oil storage facilities and vessels are required to submit plans on how they will respond to large discharges.

Pollution Prevention Act (PPA) (1990)

The law that focuses industry, government, and public attention on reducing pollution through cost-effective changes in production, operation, using raw materials, recycling, source reduction, and sustainable agriculture.

Real Estate Settlement Procedures Act (RESPA)

A federal law that requires lenders to provide consumers information of all closing costs when the purchase of a one to four family residential dwelling is financed by a federally related mortgage loan.

Regulation A

A special exemption from standard SEC registration of a security issue where the aggregate amount of the offering is less than $1.5 million. Even if the issue qualifies under Regulation A, the developer still must file a short-form registration with the regional SEC office and provide prospective purchasers with an offering circular containing much of the same information contained in a formal prospectus. Thus, Regulation A is not really an exemption from registration but a simpler form of registration. (*See* **real property securities registration**.)

Regulation B

A Federal Reserve System regulation covering the Equal Credit Opportunity Act. *See* **Equal Credit Opportunity Act [ECOA]**.

Regulation C

Implements the Home Mortgage Disclosure Act (HMDA).

Regulation D

An SEC regulation containing a set of rules exempting from registration certain limited security offerings.

Regulation Q

A federal regulation, phased out in 1986, which allowed certain federal agencies to establish different interest rates on savings deposits for commercial banks and thrift (savings and loan) institutions.

Regulation T

A federal regulation, administered by the Federal Reserve Board, governing the extension of credit arrangements for the extension of credit by securities brokers and dealers. The Federal Reserve Board lists only certain securities upon which security dealers can extend credit, and then restricts the amount of credit that may be extended by means of margin requirements. The Federal Reserve Board has effectively exempted condominium securities from Regulation T.

Regulation Z *(reglamento z)*

Regulation to implement the Consumer Credit Protection Act to promote more informed use of consumer credit by requiring certain disclosures about its terms and cost and giving consumers the right to cancel certain transactions that involve a lien on the principal dwelling. It prohibits certain acts or practices in connection with credit secured by the consumer's principal dwelling. In addition, it addresses credit card disputes and requires that a maximum interest rate is stated on variable-rate loans secured by the principal dwelling.

Resource Conservation and Recovery Act (RCRA) (1976)

The law giving the U.S. EPA authority to control hazardous waste from the "cradle-to-grave" including the generation, transportation, treatment, storage, and disposal of hazardous waste, and managing nonhazardous wastes. Amendments in 1984 and 1986 required phasing out land disposal of hazardous waste in addition to a comprehensive underground storage tank program.

Rule 10B5

A rule of the Securities and Exchange Commission (SEC) enacted under the antifraud provisions of the Securities Act of 1934 addressing "insider" trading.

Rule 146

Called the private offering or private placement exemption, adopted by the Securities and Exchange Commission (SEC) in 1974, Rule 146 is designed to provide more objective standards for determining when offers or sales of securities are transactions "not involving any public offering" that thus would be exempt from the registration process.

Rule 147

Adopted in 1974 by the Securities and Exchange Commission (SEC) to clarify the intrastate or local offering exemption from registering a security with the SEC.

Safe Drinking Water Act (SDWA) (1974)

The federal law passed to protect the quality of U.S. drinking water whether from above ground or underground sources by authorizing the EPA to establish safe standards of purity and allowing state governments to encourage water safety.

Sherman Antitrust Act

A federal act passed in 1890 making it a felony to create monopolies in any part of trade or commerce between states, and any contracts to form monopolies are illegal.

Soldiers and Sailors Civil Relief Act (SSCRA)(2003)

The law that expanded and improved the former Soldiers' and Sailors' Civil Relief Act of 1946 that offers financial protections or civil obligations to service members and relieves stress on family members. Protected obligations include credit card debt, mortgage payments, pending trials, taxes, and lease terminations.

Small Business Liability Relief and Brownfields Revitalization Act (2002)

The federal law that enables certain contaminated industrial or commercial properties to become economically viable by allowing prospective purchasers and their lenders relief from liability for past contamination that they did not cause, providing that they meet certain criteria.

Superfund Amendments and Reauthorization Act (SARA) (1986)

The act reauthorizing CERCLA to continue its cleanup activities and adding site-specific amendments, definitions, clarification, and technical requirements. It also authorizes the Emergency Planning and Community Right-to-Know Act. Owners, landlords, and sometimes lenders may be exposed to significant legal liability.

Toxic Substances Control Act (TSCA) (1976)

The federal act that authorizes the EPA to track industrial chemicals produced or imported to the United States and to ban the manufacture and import of those chemicals if deemed an environmental or human-health risk.

Telephone Consumer Protection Act (TCPA) (2003)

The federal law that allows the Federal Communications Commission (FCC) and the Federal Trade Commission (FTC) to establish a national do-not-call registry that applies to all telemarketers (with some limited exceptions) and covers both interstate and intrastate telemarketing calls. Register at *www.donotcall.gov* or toll-free at 888-382-1222.

English-Spanish Key Terms

accession
accesión

accessory building
edificación complementaria

accrued depreciation
depreciación acumulada

acre
acre

act of God
caso fortuito, fuerza mayor

adjunction
adjunción

adjustable-rate mortgage (ARM)
hipoteca con tasa ajustable

adverse possession
prescripción adquisitiva

age, effective
edad de vigencia

air rights
derechos aéreos

alienation
enajenación

alienation clause
cláusula de enajenación

allocation method
método de asignación

allodial system
sistema alodial

Americans with Disabilities Act
Ley sobre los estadounidenses incapacitados

amortization
amortización

antitrust laws
leyes antimonopolios

appeal
apelación

appraisal
avalúo

appraiser
valuador, tasador

arbitration
arbitraje

arcade
galería

area
área

arm's-length transaction
transacción donde se guarda distancia

asbestos
asbesto

asking price
precio demandado

assessment
tasación

association
asociación

assumption of mortgage
adquisición de hipoteca

attachment
embargo

attorney-in-fact
apoderado, mandatario

auction
subasta

auctioneer
martillador

avulsion
avulsión

balcony
balcón

balloon payment
pago mayor

bankruptcy
quiebra, bancarrota

basement
sótano

bearing wall, structural wall
muro de carga

benchmark
punto de referencia

beneficiary
beneficiario, fideicomisario

bid
licitación

block
manzana

blockbusting
rompe cuadras

bond
bono

book value
valor en libros

branch office
sucursal

breach of contract
violación de contrato

break-even point
punto de equilibrio

broker
corredor

brokerage
corretaje

building codes
reglamentos de construcción

building permit
permiso de edificación

building residual technique
técnica de remanente de construcción

building restrictions
limitaciones de construcción

business day
día hábil

cadastral map
plano catastral

cancellation clause
cláusula resolutoria

capital gain
ganancia de capital

capitalization
capitalización

capitalization (CAP) rate
tasa de capitalización

capital loss
pérdida de capital

casing
marco

caveat emptor
caveat emptor

CC&Rs
CC&Rs

certificate of reasonable value
certificado de valor razonable

certificate of title
certificado de título

certify
certificar

cesspool
fosa séptica

chain of title
cadena de título

change
cambio

check
cheque

chimney, fireplace
chimenea

cistern
cisterna, aljibe

client
cliente

closing (settlement)
cierre

closing statement
declaración de cierre

Code of Ethics
código de ética

cold call
llamada en frío

cold canvass
búsqueda en frío

commercial property
propiedad comercial

competitive market analysis (CMA)
análisis del mercado comparativo o competitivo

compound interest
interés compuesto

condominium
condominio

condominium owners' association
asociación de propietarios de condominios

contract
contrato

contract for deed
contrato por escritura

contract of sale
contrato de compraventa

contribution
contribución

conveyance
traspaso

corporation
corporación

cost approach
cálculo de costos

counteroffer
contraoferta

counterpart
contraparte

credit
crédito

date
fecha

datum
nivel de referencia

dead-end street
calle sin salida

debit
debe

debtor
deudor

decree
decreto

deed
escritura

deed restrictions
limitaciones en la escritura

demand
demanda

demography
demografía

Department of Housing and Urban Development (HUD)
Departamento de la Vivienda y del Desarrollo Urbano

deposit
depósito

depreciation
depreciación

descent
sucesión

developer
desarrollador

devise
legado

disability
incapacidad

discount
rebaja

document
documento

dominant estate (tenement)
dominante, predio dominante

down payment
abono inicial

drainage
drenaje

draw
giro

duress
coacción

dwelling
morada, vivienda

earnest money
arras

easement
servidumbre

easement by necessity
servidumbre por necesidad

easement by prescription
servidumbre por prescripción

economic life
vida económica

economic rent
renta económica

ejectment
acción reivindicatoria

elasticity
elasticidad

endorsement
endoso

environmental impact statement (EIS)
informe de impacto ambiental

Equal Credit Opportunity Act (ECOA)
Ley de igualdad de oportunidades para obtener crédito

escrow
depósito en garantía

eviction
evicción; desalojo, desahucio lanzamiento

exclusive listing
renta exclusiva

executor
albacea

extension
prórroga

external obsolescence
obsolescencia externa

facade
fachada

Fair Housing Act
Ley de Igualdad de Vivienda

farm area
área de cultivo

feasibility study
estudio de viabilidad

Federal Deposit Insurance Corporation (FDIC)
Corporación Federal Aseguradora de Depósitos

Federal Home Loan Mortgage Corporation (FHLMC)
Corporación Federal de Préstamos Hipotecarios para Viviendas

Federal National Mortgage Association (FNMA)
Asociación Nacional Hipotecaria Federal

Federal Reserve System ("the Fed")
Sistema de la Reserva Federal

fee simple
pleno dominio

Financial Institutions Reform Recovery, and Enforcement Act (FIRREA)
Ley de Reforma Recuperación y Ejeción de las Institutioners Financieras

floor load
carga total

franchise
franquicia

gable
gablete

gap in title
inmatriculación

Government National Mortgage Association (GNMA)
Asociación Gubernamental Hipotecaria Nacional

gradient
pendiente, declive

graduated-payment mortgage
hipoteco con pagos graduados

gross income
ingreso bruto

gross income multiplier
multiplicador de ingreso bruto

gross rent multiplier
multiplicador de alquiler bruto

guardian
curador

hazardous substance
sustancia peligrosa

heir
heredero

holder
tenedor

holiday
día inhábil

Home Mortgage Disclosure Act
Ley de Divulgación sobre las Hipotecas de Vivienda

hotel
hotel

improvements
mejora

income property
propiedad generadora de ingresos

income tax
impuestos de ingreso

incompetent
inhábil

Indemnification
indemnización

indirect costs
costos indirectos

Injunction
conminación

instrument
instrumento

insurance
seguros

interest
interés

internal rate of return (IRR)
tasa interna de rendimiento

Interstate Land Sales Full Disclosure Act
Ley Interestatal de Divulgación Completa en la Venta de Tierras

intestate
intestado

inventory
inventario

joint venture
asociación en participación, contrato de asociación en participación

judgment
juicio

jurisdiction
ámbito de competencia, jurisdicción

land
terreno

landlord
arrendador, casero, locador

landmark
hito, mojón, mojonería

latent defects
defectos ocultos

law
ley

lease
arrendamiento, arriendo, contrato de arrendamiento, locación

legatee
legatario

let
alquilar

letter of intent
carta de intención

license
licencia

lien
gravamen

liquidity
liquidez

load
carga

loft
desván, tapanco

maintenance
mantenimiento

market
mercado

market value
valor de mercado

master plan
plan urbano maestro

maturity
vencimiento

mechanic's lien
gravamen de constructor

mediation
mediación

merger
fusión

metes and bounds
medidas y limites

mezzanine
entresuelo

minor
menor de edad

mortgage
hipoteca, contrato de hipoteca

mortgagee
acreedor hipotecario

mortgage insurance
seguro hipotecario

mortgagor
deudor hipotecario

muntin
entrepaño de puertas y ventanas

negligence
negligencia

neighborhood
vecindario

net income
ingreso neto

net lease
arrendamiento neto

net operating income (NOI)
ingreso neto de operación

net worth
patrimonio neto

nonconforming use
uso inconforme

nondisclosure
discreción

notice
notificación

novation
novación

null and void
nulo

observed condition
condición observada

obsolescence
obsolescencia

occupancy permit
permiso de ocupación

occupancy rate
tasa de ocupación

offer
oferta

offeror
oferente

Office of Thrift Supervision (OTS)
Oficina Supervisora del Ahorro

open house
demostración especial, casa abierta

open space
espacio abierto

operating expenses
gastos de operación

option
opción, contrato de opción

ordinances
ordenanzas

orientation
orientación

overall rate
tasa global

overimprovement
sobremejora

owner/occupant
dueño/inquilino

parcel
parcela

participation mortgage
hipoteca con participación

partition
partición

party wall
pared medianera

patent
patente

penthouse
penthouse

person
persona

petition
solicitud

physical life
vida física

PITI
PITI

plant
complejo

point of beginning (POB)
punto de inicio

points
puntos porcentuales

positive cash flow
flujo de efectivo positivo

possession
posesión

potable water
agua potable

power of attorney
carta de personería

premium
prima

prescription
prescripción

price
precio

primary mortgage market
mercado hipotecario primario

priority
prioridad

private mortgage insurance (PMI)
seguro hipotecario privado

profit and loss statement
estado de pérdidas y ganancias

progression
progresión

project
proyecto

promissory note
pagaré

property
propiedad

property management
administración de inmuebles

property report
informe sobre la propiedad

property residual technique
técnica de remanente de propiedad

prorate
prorratear

proxy
poderhabiente

quantity survey
estudio de costos

quorum
quórum

radon
radón

real estate
bienes raíces

real estate investment trust (REIT)
fideicomiso de inversiones en bienes raíces

real property
propiedad inmueble, bienes inmuebles

REALTOR®
REALTOR®

receipt
recibo

redlining
redlining

regression
regresión

regulation
reglamento

Regulation Z
reglamento Z

release
liberación

rent
alquiler, renta

replacement cost
costo de reposición

reproduction cost
costo de reproducción

rescind
rescindir, revocar

reserve for replacements
reserva para substitución

residence
residencia

restrictive covenant
pacto restrictivo

right of first refusal
derecho de primera opción

secondary mortgage market
mercado hipotecario secundario

section
sección

security
valor

security agreement
contrato de garantía

settlement
liquidación, transacción, contrato de transacción

siding
revestimiento exterior

signature
firma

signs
letreros

silent partner
socio capitalista

single-family residence
vivienda unifamiliar

sinking fund
fondo de amortización

skylight
tragaluz, claraboya

special-purpose property
propiedad para uso especial

square-foot method
método de metros cuadrados

statute of limitations
ley de prescripción

straw man
testaferro

structure
cimbra, estructura

stucco
estuco

subdivision
fraccionamiento, subdivisión

sublease
subarrendamiento, contrato de subarrendamiento

subrogation
subrogación

summons
convocatoria

supply and demand
oferta y demanda

surcharge
recargo

tax base
base gravable

tax lien
gravamen de tributación

tenancy at sufferance
posesión por tolerancia

tenant
arrendatario, inquilino, locatario, il propietario

term
plazo, término

testator
testador

third party
tercero

time-sharing
tiempo compartido

title
título

title insurance
seguro contra vicios en un título de propiedad

title search
investigación del título

topography
topografía

township
distrito municipal, sexmo

transfer
traspaso

trust
fideicomiso

trustee
fiduciario

trustee in bankruptcy
síndico

Truth in Lending Act (TIL)
Ley de Veracidad en los Préstamos

underimprovement
mejora insuficiente

unilateral contract
contrato unilateral

usury
usura

utility
utilidad

vacancy factor
porcentaje de vacancia

value
valor

value added
valor agregado

Veterans Affairs (VA) loan
Préstamo V.A.

waiver
reminsión de deuda

warehouse
bodega

waste
desperdicio

will
testamento

window sash
marco de ventana

witness
dar fe

yard
yarda

yield
rendimiento

zoning
zonificación

Spanish-English Key Terms

abono inicial
down payment

accesión
accession

acción reivindicatoria
ejectment

acre
acre

acreedor hipotecario
mortgagee

adjunción
adjunction

administración de inmuebles
property management

adquisición de hipoteca
assumption of mortgage

agua potable
potable water

albacea
executor

aljibe
cistern

alquiler
rent, let

ámbito de competencia
jurisdiction

amortización
amortization

análisis del mercado comparativo o competitivo
competitive market analysis (CMA)

apelación
appeal

apoderado
attorney-in-fact

arbitraje
arbitration

área
area

área de cultivo
farm area

arras
earnest money

arrendador
landlord

arrendamiento
lease

arrendamiento neto
net lease

arrendatario
tenant

arriendo
lease

asbesto
asbestos

asociación
association

asociación de propietarios de condominios
condominium owners' association

asociación en participación
joint venture

Asociación Gubernamental Hipotecaria Nacional
Government National Mortgage Association (GNMA)

Asociación Nacional Hipotecaria Federal
Federal National Mortgage Association (FNMA)

avalúo
appraisal

avulsión
avulsion

balcón
balcony

bancarrota
bankruptcy

base gravable
tax base

beneficiario
beneficiary

bienes inmuebles
real property

bienes raíces
real estate

bodega
warehouse

bono
bond

búsqueda en frío
cold canvass

cadena de título
chain of title

cálculo de costos
cost approach

calle sin salida
dead-end street

cambio
change

capitalización
capitalization

carga
load

carga total
floor load

carta de intención
letter of intent

carta de personería
power of attorney

casa abierta
open house

casero
landlord

caso fortuito
act of God

caveat emptor
caveat emptor

CC&Rs
CC&Rs

cerrada
dead end

certificado de título
certificate of title

certificado de valor razonable
certificate of reasonable value

certificar
certify

cheque
check

chimenea
chimney, fireplace

cierre
closing

cimbra
structure

cisterna
cistern

claraboya
skylight

cláusula de enajenación
alienation clause

cláusula resolutoria
cancellation clause

cliente
client

coacción
duress

código de ética
code of ethics

complejo
plant

condición observada
observed condition

condominio
condominium

conminación
injunction

contraoferta
counteroffer

contraparte
counterpart

contrato
contract

contrato de arrendamiento
lease

contrato de asociación en participación
joint venture

contrato de compraventa
contract of sale

contrato de garantía
security agreement

contrato de hipoteca
mortgage

contrato de opción
option

contrato de subarrendamiento
sublease

contrato por escritura
contract for deed

contrato de transacción
settlement

contrato unilateral
unilateral contract

contribución
contribution

convocatoria
summons

corporación
corporation

Corporación Federal Aseguradora de Depósitos
Federal Deposit Insurance Corporation (FDIC)

Corporación Federal de Préstamos Hipotecarios para Viviendas
Federal Home Loan Mortgage Corporation (FHLMC)

corredor
broker

corretaje
brokerage

costo de reposición
replacement cost

costo de reproducción
reproduction cost

costos indirectos
indirect costs

crédito
credit

curador
guardian

dar fe
witness

debe
debit

declaración de cierre
closing statement

decreto
decree

defectos ocultos
latent defects

demanda
demand

demografía
demography

demostración especial
open house

Departamento de la Vivienda y del Desarrollo Urbano
Department of Housing and Urban Development (HUD)

depósito
deposit

depósito en garantía
escrow

depreciación
depreciation

depreciación acumulada
accrued depreciation

derecho de primera opción
right of first refusal

derechos aéreos
air rights

desahucio
eviction

desalojo
eviction

desarrollador
developer

desperdicio
waste

desván, tapanco
loft

deudor
debtor

deudor hipotecario
mortgagor

día hábil
business day

día inhábil
holiday

discreción
nondisclosure

distrito municipal
township

documento
document

dominante
dominant estate (tenement)

drenaje
drainage

dueño
owner

dueño/inquilino
owner/occupent

edad
age

edificación complementaria
accessory building

elasticidad
elasticity

embargo
attachment

enajenación
alienation

endoso
endorsement

enganche
down payment

entrepaño de puertas y ventanas
muntin

entresuelo
mezzanine

escritura
deed

espacio abierto
open space

estado de pérdidas y ganancias
profit and loss statement

estructura
structure

estuco
stucco

estudio de costos
quantity survey

estudio de viabilidad
feasibility study

evicción
eviction

fachada
facade

fecha
date

fideicomisario
beneficiary

fideicomiso
trust

Fideicomiso de Inversiones en Bienes Raíes
Real Estate Investment Trust (REIT)

fiduciario
trustee

firma
signature

flujo de efectivo positivo
positive cash flow

fondo de amortización
sinking fund

fosa séptica
cesspool

fraccionamiento
subdivision

franquicia
franchise

fuerza mayor
act of God

fusión
merger

gablete
gable

galería
arcade

ganancia de capital
capital gain

gastos de operación
operating expenses

giro
draw

gravamen
lien

gravamen de tributación
tax lien

gravamen de constructor
mechanic's lien

heredero
heir

hipoteca
mortgage

hipoteca con pagos graduados
graduated-payment mortgage

hipoteca con participación
participation mortgage

hipoteca con tasa ajustable
adjustable rate mortgage (ARM)

hito
landmark

hotel
hotel

impuestos de ingreso
income tax

incapacidad
disability

indemnización
indemnification

informe de impacto ambiental
environmental impact statement

informe sobre la propiedad
property report

ingreso bruto
gross income

ingreso neto
net income

ingreso neto de operación
net operating income—NOI

inhábil
incompetent

inmatriculación
gap in title

inmueble
real property

inquilino
tenant

instrumento
instrument

interés
interest

interés compuesto
compound interest

intestado
intestate

inventario
inventory

investigación del título
title search

juicio
judgment

jurisdicción
jurisdiction

lanzamiento
eviction

legado
devise, subdivisor

legatario
legatee

letreros
signs

ley
law

Ley de Divulgación sobre las Hipotecas de Vivienda
Home Mortgage Disclosure Act

Ley de igualdad de oportunidades para obtener crédito
Equal Credit Opportunity Act (ECOA)

Ley de Igualdad de Vivienda
Fair Housing Act

ley de prescripción
statute of limitations

Ley de Reforma Recuperación y Ejeción de las Institutioner Financieras
Financial Institutions Reform, Recovery, and Enforcement Act (FIRREA)

Ley de Veracidad en los Préstamos
Truth-in-Lending Act (TIL)

leyes antimonopolios
antitrust laws

Ley Interestatal de Divulgación Completa en la Venta de Tierras
Interstate Land Sales Full Disclosure Act

Ley sobre los estadounidenses incapacitados
Americans with Disabilities Act

liberación
release

licencia
license

licitación
bid

limitaciones de construcción
building restrictions

limitaciones en la escritura
deed restrictions

liquidación
settlement

liquidez
liquidity

llamada en frío
cold call

locación
lease

locador
landlord

locatario
tenant

mandatario
attorney-in-fact

mantenimiento
maintenance

manzana
block

marco
casing

marco de ventana
window sash

martillador
auctioneer

mediación
mediation

medidas y limites
metes and bounds

mejora
improvement

mejora insuficiente
underimprovement

menor de edad
minor

mercado
market

mercado hipotecario primario
primary mortgage market

mercado hipotecario secundario
secondary mortgage market

método de asignación
allocation method

método de metros cuadrados
square foot method

mojón, mojonería
landmark

morada
dwelling

multiplicador de alquiler bruto
gross rent multiplier

multiplicador de ingreso bruto
gross income multiplier

muro de carga
bearing wall, structural wall

negligencia
negligence

nivel de referencia
datum

notificación
notice

novación
novation

nulo
null and void

obsolescencia
obsolescence

obsolescencia externa
external obsolescence

oferente
offeror

oferta
offer

oferta y demanda
supply and demand

Oficina Supervisora del Ahorro
Office of Thrift Supervision (OTS)

opción
option

ordenanzas
ordinances

orientación
orientation

pacto restrictivo
restrictive covenant

pagaré
promissory note

pago mayor
balloon payment

parcela
parcel

pared medianera
party wall

partición
partition

patente
patent

patrimonio neto
net worth

pendiente, declive
gradient

penthouse
penthouse

pérdida de capital
capital loss

permiso de edificación
building permit

permiso de ocupación
occupancy permit

permiso de uso condicionado
variance

persona
person

PITI
PITI

plano catastral
cadastral map

plan urbano maestro
master plan

plazo
term

pleno domino
fee simple

poderhabiente
proxy

porcentaje de vacancia
vacancy factor

posesión
possession

posesión por tolerancia
tenancy at sufferance

precio
price

precio demandado
asking price

predio dominante
dominant tenement

prescripción
prescription

prescripción adquisitiva
adverse possession

Préstamo V.A.
Veterans Affairs (VA) loan

prima
premium

prioridad
priority

progresión
progression

propiedad
property

propiedad comercial
commercial property

propiedad generadora de ingresos
income property

propiedad inmueble
real property

propiedad para uso especial
special purpose property

propietario
owner, tenant

prorratear
prorate

prórroga
extension

proyecto
project

punto de equilibrio
break-even point

punto de inicio
point of beginning (POB)

punto de referencia
benchmark

puntos porcentuales
points

quiebra
bankruptcy

quórum
quorum

radón
radon

REALTOR®
REALTOR®

rebaja
discount

recargo
surcharge

recibo
receipt

redlining
redlining

reglamento
regulation

reglamentos de construcción
building codes

reglamento Z
Regulation Z

regresión
regression

reminisión de deuda
waiver

rendimiento
yield

renta
rent

renta económica
economic rent

rescindir, revocar
rescind

residencia
residence

revestimiento exterior
siding

rompe cuadras
blockbusting

sección
section

seguro
insurance

seguro contra vicios en un título de propiedad
title insurance

seguro hipotecario
mortgage insurance

seguro hipotecario privado
private mortgage insurance (PMI)

servidumbre
easement

servidumbre por necesidad
easement by necessity

servidumbre por prescripción
easement by prescription

sexmo
township

síndico
trustee in bankruptcy

sistema alodial
allodial system

Sistema de la Reserva Federal
Federal Reserve System ("the Fed")

sobremejora
overimprovement

socio capitalista
silent partner

solicitud
petition

sótano
basement

subarrendamiento
sublease

subasta
auction

subdivisión
subdivision

subdivisor
developer

subrogación
subrogation

substancia peligrosa
hazardous substance

sucesión
descent

sucursal
branch office

tasación
assessment

tasa de capitalización
capitalization rate

tasa de ocupación
occupancy rate

tasador
appraiser

tasa global
overall rate

tasa interna de rendimiento
internal rate of return (IRR)

técnica de remanente de construcción
building residual technique

técnica de remanente de propiedad
property residual technique

tenedor
holder

tercero
third party

término
term

terreno
land

testador
testator

testaferro
straw man

testamento
will

tiempo compartido
time-sharing

título
title

topografía
topography

tragaluz
skylight

transacción
settlement

transacción donde se guarda distancia
arm's-length transaction

traspaso
conveyance, transfer

uso inconforme
nonconforming use

usura
usury

utilidad
utility

valor
security, value

valor agregado
value added

valor de mercado
market value

valor en libros
book value

valuador
appraiser

vecindario
neighborhood

vencimiento
maturity

venta exclusiva
exclusive listing

vida económica
economic life

violación de contrato
breach of contract

vivienda
dwelling

vivienda unifamiliar
single-family residence

yarda
yard

zonificación
zoning

Construction
Diagrams

Types of Houses

1st floor
Planta baja

Basement
Sótano

One-story house
Casa de una sola planta

Expansion attic
Desván expandido

1st floor
Planta baja

Basement
Sótano

One-and-a-half-story house
Casa de una planta y media

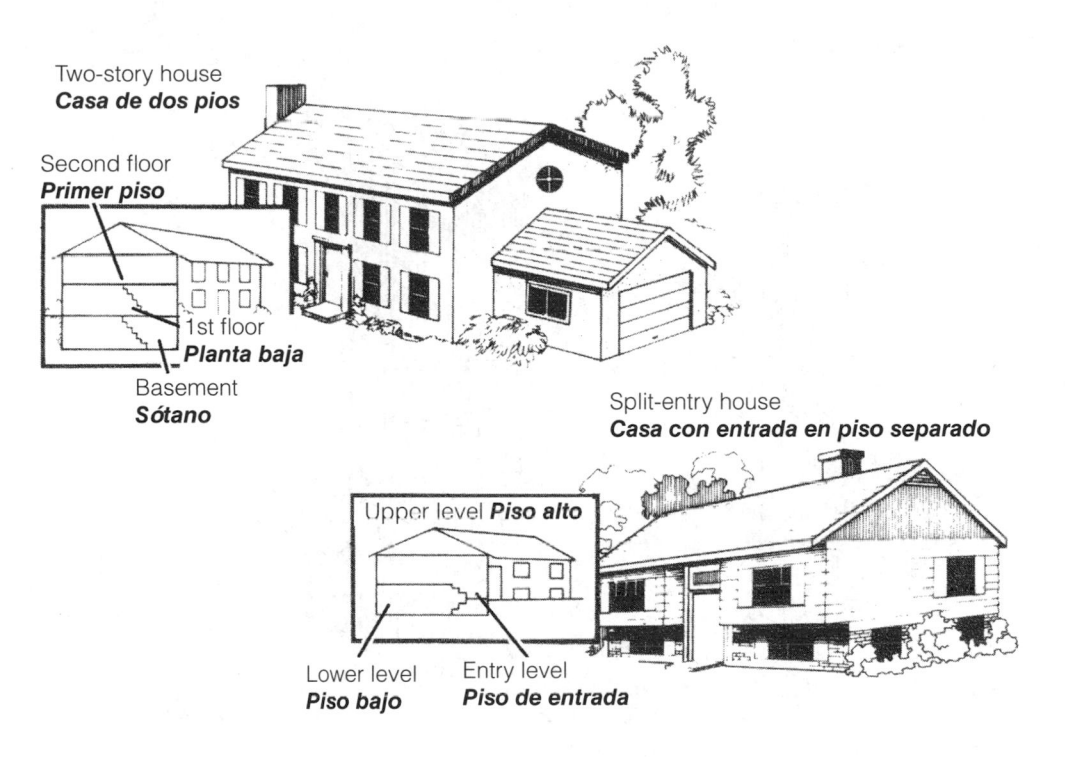

Two-story house
Casa de dos pios

Second floor
Primer piso

1st floor
Planta baja

Basement
Sótano

Split-entry house
Casa con entrada en piso separado

Upper level *Piso alto*

Lower level
Piso bajo

Entry level
Piso de entrada

Split-level house
Casa de pisos separados

Frame Construction Types

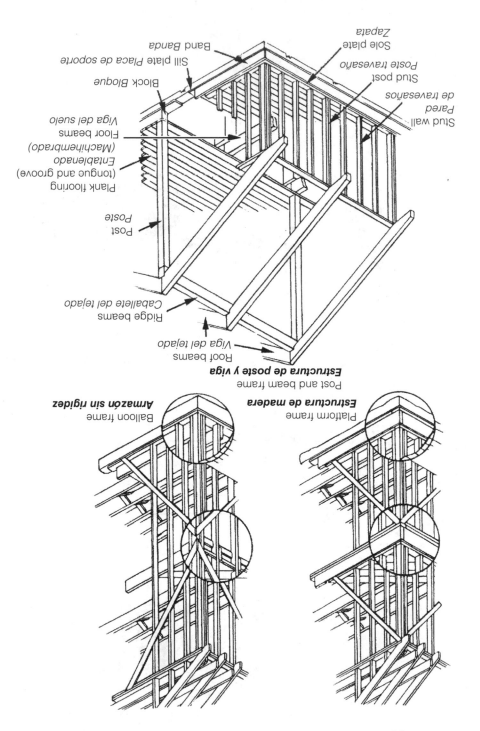

Post and beam frame
Estructura de poste y viga

Roof beams
Viga del tejado

Ridge beams
Caballete del tejado

Post
Poste

Plank flooring
(tongue and groove)
Entablado
(Machihembrado)

Floor beams
Viga del suelo

Block *Bloque*

Sill plate *Placa de soporte*

Band *Banda*

Sole plate
Zapata

Stud post
Poste travesaño

Stud wall
Pared
de travesaños

Platform frame
Estructura de madera

Balloon frame
Armazón sin rigidez

Roof Designs

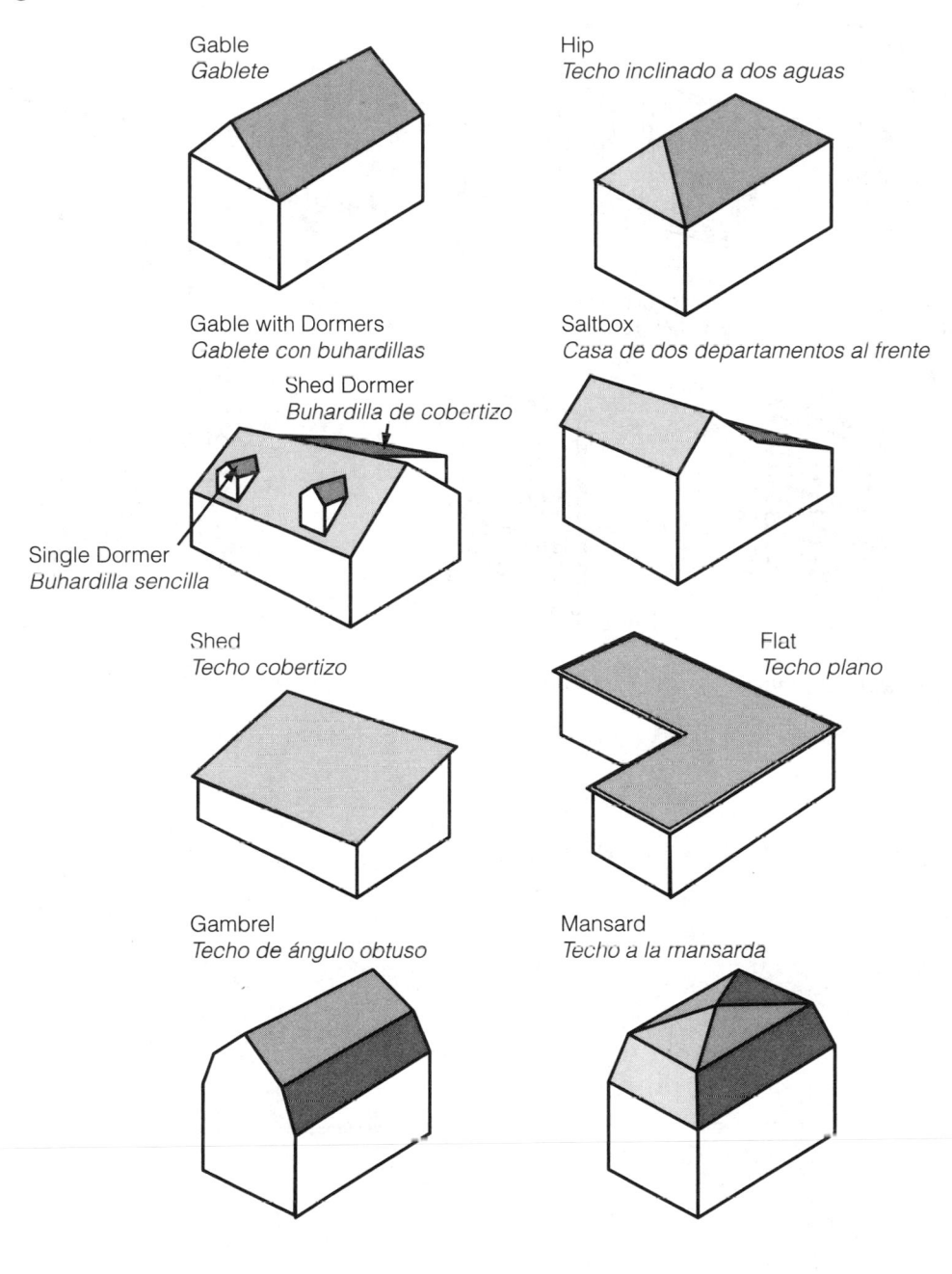

Gable
Gablete

Hip
Techo inclinado a dos aguas

Gable with Dormers
Gablete con buhardillas

Shed Dormer
Buhardilla de cobertizo

Single Dormer
Buhardilla sencilla

Saltbox
Casa de dos departamentos al frente

Shed
Techo cobertizo

Flat
Techo plano

Gambrel
Techo de ángulo obtuso

Mansard
Techo a la mansarda

Types of Windows

Fixed
Fija

Casement
Batiente

Horizontal Sliding
Deslizable horizontal

Double-hung
**Ventana
de contrapeso
doble**

Skylight
Tragaluz

Roof
Techo

Storm
Contraventana

Jalousie
Persiana de celosía

Types of Doors

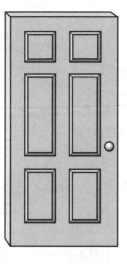

Panel
Panel

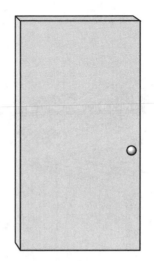

Flush
Puerta alineada

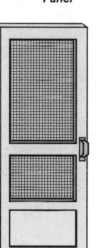

Screen door
Puerta de tela metálica

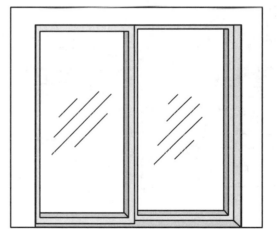

Sliding glass
Ventana deslizable de cristal

Construction of a Home

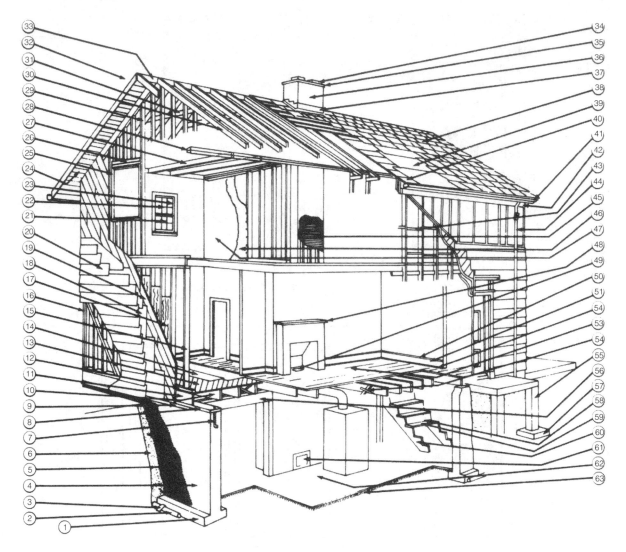

1. FOOTING
   Base de cimiento
2. FOUNDATION DRAIN TILE
   Tubo de drenaje de cimiento
3. CRUSHED WASHED STONE
   Piedra triturada y lavada
4. FOUNDATION WALL
   Muro de cimiento
5. DAMPPROOFING OR
   WEATHERPROOFING
   Revestimiento contra humedad,
   revestimiento contra la intemperie
6. BACKFILL
   Relleno
7. ANCHOR BOLT
   Bulón de anclaje
8. SILL PLATE
   Placa de soporte
9. TERMITE SHIELD
   Protector contra termitas
10. FLOOR JOIST
    Viga del suelo
11. BAND OR BOX BEAM
    Viga de banda o viga tubular
12. SOLE PLATE
    Zapata
13. SUBFLOORING
    Revestimiento bajo el suelo
14. BUILDING PAPER
    Papel de construcción
15. WALL STUD
    Travesaño de pared
16. CORNER STUDS
    Travesaños
17. INSULATION
    Aislamiento
18. HOUSE WRAP
    Envoltura de casa
19. WALL SHEATHING
    Revestimiento
20. SIDING
    Revestimiento exterior
21. MULLION
    Parteluz

22. MUNTIN
    Entrepaño de puertas y ventanas
23. WINDOW SASH
    Marco de ventana
24. EAVE (ROOF PROJECTION)
    Alero
25. WINDOW JAMB TRIM
    Cubierta de jamba de ventana
26. WINDOW HEADER
    Dintel
27. CEILING JOIST
    Viga de techo
28. TOP AND TIE PLATES
    Placas superiores y placas de tirantes
29. GABLE STUD
    Travesaño de gablete
30. RAFTERS
    Cabios
31. COLLAR TIES
    Tirantes de cuello
32. GABLE END OF ROOF
    Gablete del tejado
33. RIDGE BEAM
    Caballete del tejado
34. CHIMNEY FLUES
    Cañón humero
35. CHIMNEY CAP
    Sombrerete de chimenea
36. CHIMNEY
    Chimenea
37. CHIMNEY FLASHING
    Tapajuntas de chimenea
38. ROOFING SHINGLES
    Tablillas de tejado
39. ROOFING FELT/ICE AND WATER
    MEMBRANE
    Fieltro de tejado / membrana
    protectora de hielo y agua
40. ROOF SHEATHING
    Revestimiento
41. EAVE TROUGH OR GUTTER
    Canalón
42. FRIEZE BOARD
    Tabla de friso

43. FIRESTOP
    Viga retardadora de incendios
44. DOWNSPOUT
    Tubo para bajada de agua
45. LATHS
    Listones
46. PLASTERBOARD
    Panel de yeso
47. PLASTER FINISH
    Recubrimiento de yeso
48. MANTEL
    Repisa de chimenea
49. ASH DUMP
    Vertedero de cenizas
50. BASE TOP MOULDING
    Moldura de base
51. BASEBOARD
    Zócalo
52. SHOE MOULDING
    Moldura de zapata
53. FINISH MOULDING
    Moldura de terminación
54. CROSS BRIDGING
    Unión de puntales
55. PIER
    Pilar
56. GIRDER
    Viga
57. FOOTING
    Base de pilar
58. RISER
    Parte vertical de peldaño
59. TREAD
    Peldaño
60. STRINGER
    Zanca
61. CLEANOUT DOOR
    Puerta de limpieza
62. CONCRETE BASEMENT FLOOR
    Piso de cemento del sótano
63. CRUSHED WASHED STONE
    Piedra triturada y lavada

Notes